Contents

The Canadian population figures in this guide are based on the official 1996 Canadian census.

Addresses, telephone numbers, opening hours and prices given in this guide are accurate at the time of publication. We apologize for any inconvenience resulting from outdated information. Please send us your comments:

Michelin Travel Publications
Editorial Department, PO Box 19001, Greenville, SC 29602-9001

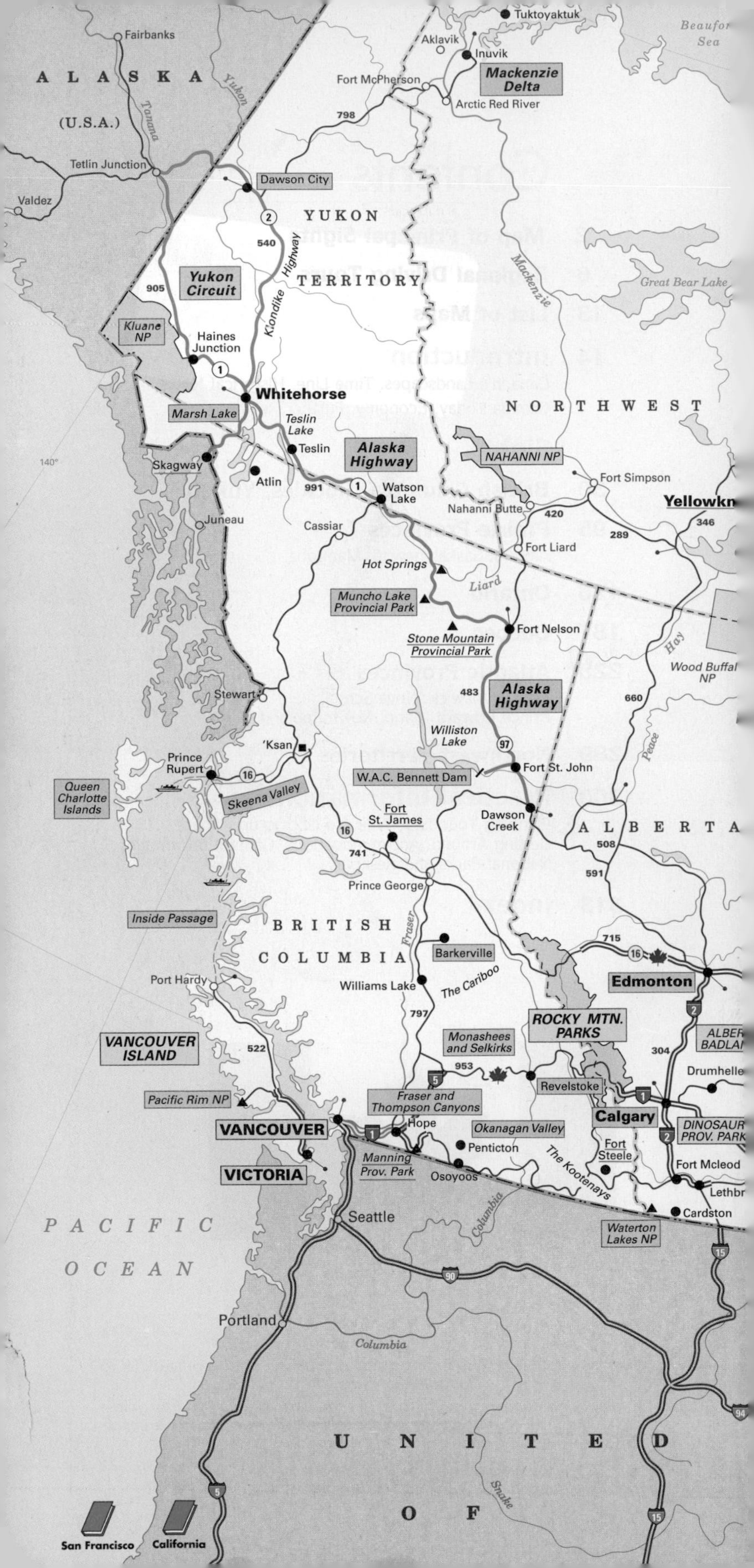

Tuktoyaktuk
Beaufort Sea
Aklavik
Inuvik
Mackenzie Delta
Fort McPherson
Arctic Red River
Fairbanks
ALASKA
(U.S.A.)
Yukon
Tanana
Tetlin Junction
Valdez
Dawson City
YUKON TERRITORY
Klondike Highway
Yukon Circuit
Kluane NP
Haines Junction
Whitehorse
Marsh Lake
Teslin Lake
Teslin
Alaska Highway
Skagway
Atlin
Watson Lake
Juneau
Cassiar
Hot Springs
Muncho Lake Provincial Park
Liard
Stone Mountain Provincial Park
Fort Nelson
NORTHWEST
Great Bear Lake
Mackenzie
NAHANNI NP
Fort Simpson
Nahanni Butte
Fort Liard
Yellowkn
Hay
Wood Buffal NP
Peace
Stewart
'Ksan
Williston Lake
W.A.C. Bennett Dam
Fort St. John
Prince Rupert
Skeena Valley
Queen Charlotte Islands
Dawson Creek
Fort St. James
Prince George
ALBERTA
Inside Passage
BRITISH COLUMBIA
Fraser
Barkerville
The Cariboo
Williams Lake
Port Hardy
Edmonton
ROCKY MTN. PARKS
VANCOUVER ISLAND
Monashees and Selkirks
Revelstoke
ALBER BADLA
Drumhelle
Pacific Rim NP
Fraser and Thompson Canyons
Hope
VANCOUVER
Okanagan Valley
Calgary
DINOSAUR PROV. PARK
Penticton
Fort Steele
Fort Mcleod
Lethbr
Manning Prov. Park
Osoyoos
The Kootenays
VICTORIA
Cardston
Waterton Lakes NP
Columbia
Seattle
PACIFIC OCEAN
Portland
Columbia
Snake
UNITED
OF
San Francisco
California
140°
798
540
905
991
420
289
346
483
660
741
508
591
715
797
522
953
304

Principal Sights

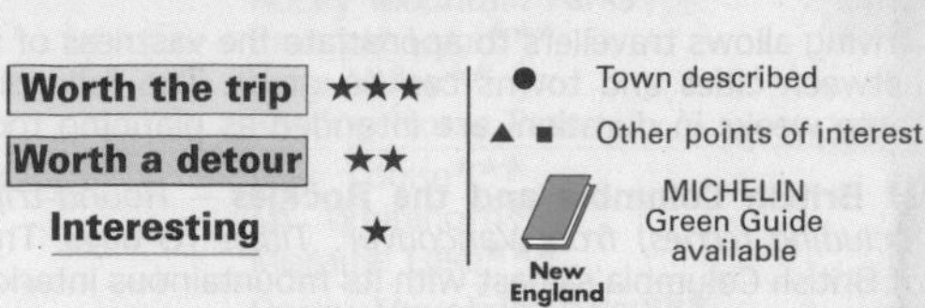

Place names in black type indicate the cities and sights described in this guide. *(See index)*

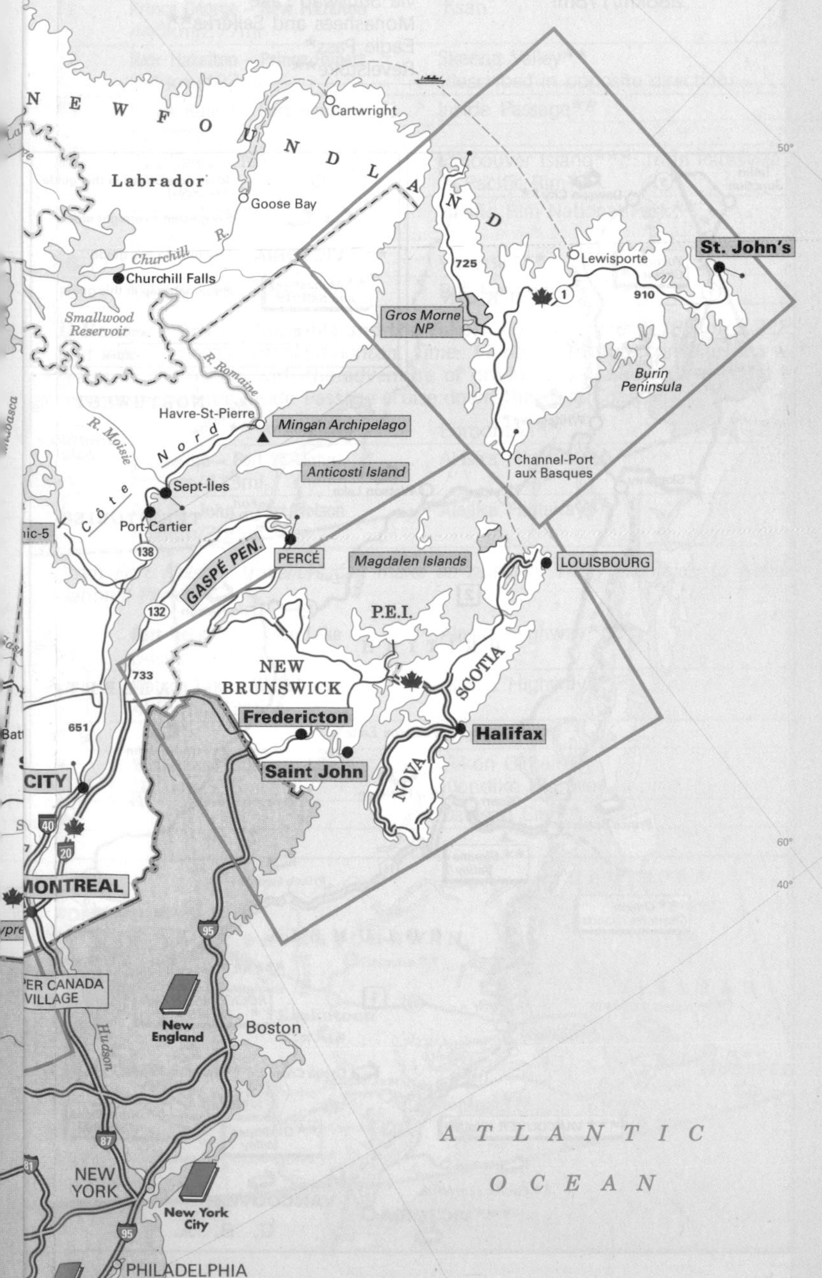

Distances between major cities

Seattle to **Vancouver**
272km/168mi
Vancouver to **Calgary**
953km/581mi
Calgary to **Edmonton**
304km/185mi
Calgary to **Regina**
744km/453mi
Saskatoon to **Regina**
251km/153mi
Regina to **Winnipeg**
573km/350mi
Winnipeg to **Sault Ste. Marie**
1395km/851mi
Sault Ste. Marie to **Toronto**
715km/436mi
Toronto to **Ottawa**
398km/242mi
Toronto to **Detroit**
378km/231mi
Ottawa to **Montreal**
185km/113mi
Montreal to **Quebec**
262km/159mi
Montreal to **New York**
635km/392mi
Quebec to **Fredericton**
521km/318mi
Fredericton to **Halifax**
480km/293mi

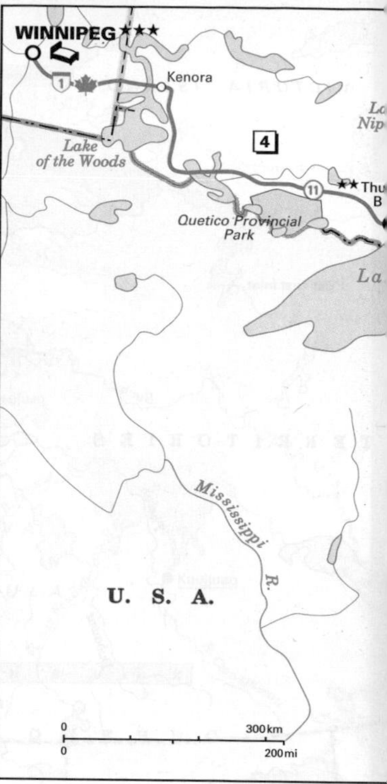

Days	Itinerary	Visits
10	**Dawson City – Haines Junction** 744km/462mi	Yukon Circuit★★ Top of the World Highway★★ Alaska Highway★ Kluane Lake★★
11	**Haines Junction – Whitehorse** 161km/100mi	Kluane National Park★★
12-13	**Whitehorse – Prince Rupert** 180km/112mi and ferry	Klondike Highway to Skagway★★ Skagway★ Inside Passage (US)

From Prince Rupert, travellers can take the ferry through the Inside Passage★ Seattle, arriving Day 15, or optional 3-day excursion to Queen Charlotte Islands★

Days	Itinerary	Visits
14-16	**Prince Rupert – Jasper** *(see Days 12, 11, 10 of Tour 1)*	
17	**Jasper – Edmonton** 361km/224mi	

3 Prairies – *Round-trip of 3,371km/2,095mi from Winnipeg. Time: 17 days.* tour enables visitors to discover some of the fascination of the Prairies: g vistas, wheat fields, ranches and cowboys. The oil-rich Alberta cities of Calgary Edmonton are visited as well as the interesting city of Winnipeg.

Days	Itinerary	Visits
1-2		Winnipeg★★★
3	**Winnipeg – Wasagaming** 265km/165mi	Riding Mountain National Park★★
4	**Wasagaming – Yorkton** 230km/143mi	Yorkton
5	**Yorkton – Saskatoon** 331km/205mi	Saskatoon★
6	176km/109mi	Excursion to Batoche★★
7	**Saskatoon – Lloydminster** 276km/171mi	The Battlefords★
8-9	**Lloydminster – Edmonton** 248km/154mi	Edmonton★★
10-11	**Edmonton – Calgary** 304km/185mi	Calgary★★
12	**Calgary – Elkwater** 432km/268mi	Alberta Badlands★★★

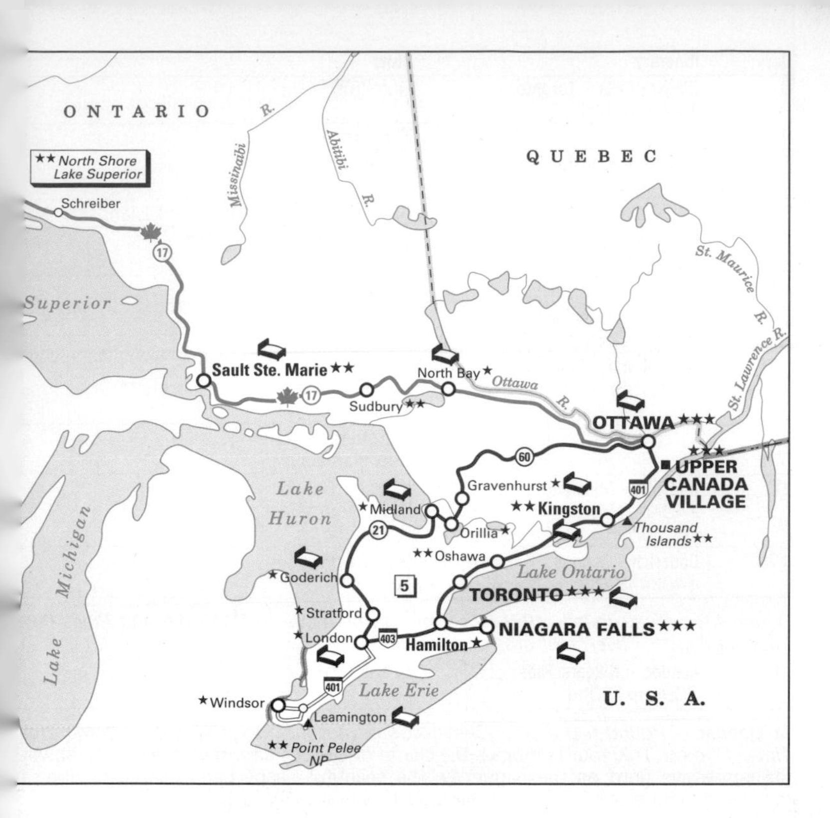

3	**Elkwater – Swift Current** 227km/141mi	Cypress Hills★★
4	**Swift Current – Regina** 243km/151mi	Moose Jaw★
5		Regina★★
6	**Regina – Brandon** 423km/263mi	Qu'Appelle Valley★
7	**Brandon – Winnipeg** 211km/131mi	Austin★

4 Northern Ontario – *Trip of 2,271km/1,411mi from Ottawa to Winnipeg. Time: 10 days.* On this tour visitors can experience the wild, untouched beauty of the Canadian Shield country with its rocks, trees and lovely lakes. The drive around Lake Superior is particularly attractive.

1-2		Ottawa★★★
3	**Ottawa – North Bay** 363km/226mi	North Bay★
4	**North Bay – Sault Ste Marie** 427km/265mi	Sudbury★★
5		Sault Ste. Marie★★
6	**Sault Ste. Marie – Thunder Bay** 705km/438mi	Lake Superior Drive★★ North Shore Lake Superior★★ (described in other direction)
7		Thunder Bay★★
8	**Thunder Bay – Kenora** 569km/353mi	Kakabeka Falls★★
9-10	**Kenora – Winnipeg** 207km/129mi	Winnipeg★★★

5 Southern Ontario – *Round-trip of 1,737km/1,079mi from Niagara Falls. Time: 18 days.* This tour combines the vibrant city of Toronto with the magnificent falls on the Niagara River, the highly cultivated southern Ontario, some Canadian Shield country and the nation's capital of Ottawa.

Days	Itinerary	Visits
1-2	60km/37mi	Niagara Falls★★★ Niagara Parkway (north)★★

Days	Itinerary	Visits
3	**Niagara Falls – Toronto** 147km/91mi	Hamilton★
4-7		Toronto★★★
8	**Toronto – Kingston** 269km/167mi	Oshawa★★
9		Kingston and the Thousand Islands★★
10	**Kingston – Ottawa** 201km/125mi	Upper Canada Village★★★
11-12		Ottawa★★★
13	**Ottawa – Gravenhurst** 406km/252mi	Gravenhurst★
14	**Gravenhurst – Midland** 56km/35mi	Orillia★ Ste.-Marie among the Hurons★★ Midland★
15		Penetanguishene★ Georgian Bay★★
16	**Midland – Goderich** 249km/155mi	Wasaga Beach★ Blue Mountains Goderich★
17	**Goderich – London** 140km/87mi	Stratford★ London★

Optional 2-day excursion, 482km/300mi, can be made to Windsor★ and Point Pelee National Park★★ ; overnight stop at Leamington.

18	**London – Niagara Falls** 209km/130mi	Brantford★

6 **Quebec** – *Round-trip of 2,359km/1,466ml (not including ferries) from Montreal. Time: 17 days.* This tour combines the charm of Quebec city, the ancient capital, with the impressive fjord on the Saguenay; the beautiful Gaspé peninsula culminating in the scenic wonder of Percé; and the modern vibrant city of Montreal.

1-3		Montreal★★★
4	**Montreal – Quebec City** 262km/159mi	Trois-Rivières★★
5-6		Quebec City★★★
7	**Quebec City – Île aux Coudres** 107km/67mi and ferry	Beaupré Coast★★ Charlevoix Coast★★★ Île aux Coudres★★
8	**Île aux Coudres – Tadoussac** 104km/65mi and ferry	Charlevoix Coast★★★ Tadoussac★★
9		Whale-Watching Cruise★★ or Cruise on the Saguenay Fjord★★★
10	**Tadoussac – Matane** 204km/127mi (ferry Les Escoumins – Trois-Pistoles)	Gaspé Peninsula★★★ Métis Gardens★★ Matane
11	**Matane – Percé** 369km/225mi	Forillon National Park★★ Gaspé★
12-13		Percé★★★

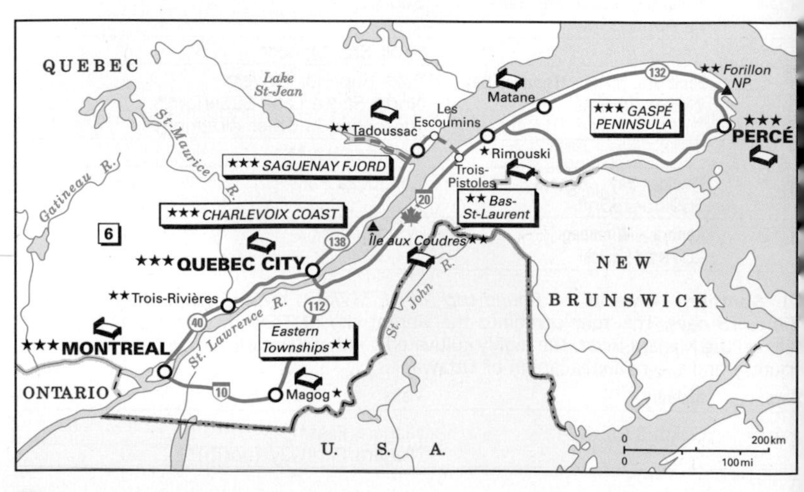

ays	Itinerary	Visits
4	**Percé – Rimouski** 466km/290mi	Gaspé Peninsula*** South Coast Rimouski*
5	**Rimouski – Quebec City** 312km/194mi	Bas-St.-Laurent** (described in opposite direction)
6	**Quebec City – Magog** 275km/171mi	Eastern Townships** Magog*
7	**Magog – Montreal** 210km/130mi	Richelieu Valley**

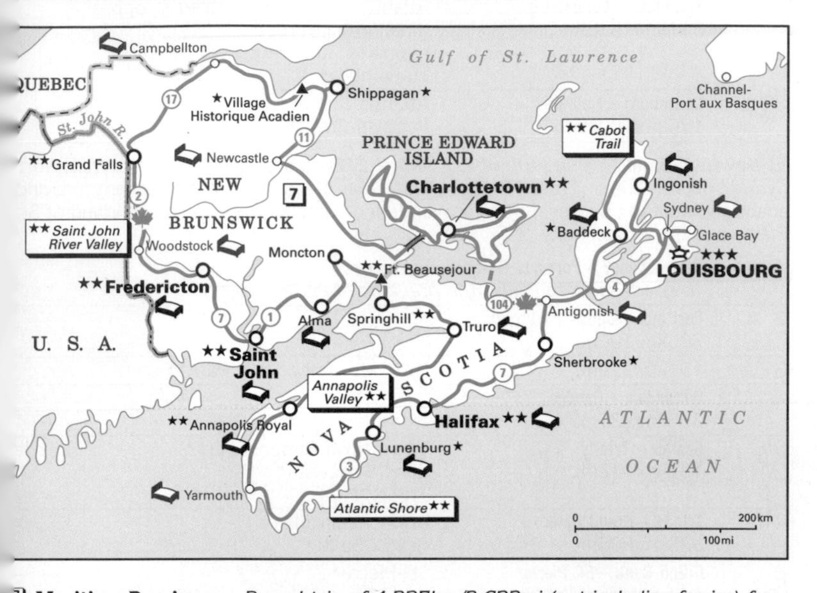

7 **Maritime Provinces** – *Round-trip of 4,235km/2,632mi (not including ferries) from Halifax. Time: 22 days.* This tour of the three Maritime provinces is an interesting blend of seascapes, rocky headlands, sandy beaches and the high tides of the Bay of Fundy with historical highlights such as the French fortress of Louisbourg, Halifax and its citadel, the Acadian country and the important port of Saint John.

Days	Itinerary	Visits
1-2		Halifax**
3	**Halifax – Antigonish** 261km/162mi	Sherbrooke*
4	**Antigonish – Sydney** 212km/132mi	Louisbourg Fortress***
5	**Sydney – Ingonish** 127km/79mi	Glace Bay (Miners' Museum**) Cabot Trail** (described in opposite direction) Ingonish
6	**Ingonish – Baddeck** 233km/145mi	Cabot Trail** Cape Breton Highlands National Park** Chéticamp Baddeck*
7	**Baddeck – Charlottetown** 263km/163mi and ferry	Prince Edward Island Charlottetown**
8-10	800km/500mi (maximum)	Prince Edward Island Scenic Drives
11	**Charlottetown – Newcastle** 259km/161mi and ferry	
12	**Newcastle – Campbellton** 301km/187mi	Shippagan* Village Historique Acadien*
13	**Campbellton – Woodstock** 311km/193mi	Saint John River Valley** (described in opposite direction) Grand Falls** Hartland*
14	**Woodstock – Fredericton** 101km/63mi	Kings Landing**
15	**Fredericton – Saint John** 109km/68mi	Fredericton**
16		Saint John**
17	**Saint John – Alma** 143km/89mi	Fundy National Park**

Days	Itinerary	Visits
18	**Alma – Truro** 254km/158mi	Hopewell Cape★★ Moncton Fort Beausejour★★ Springhill★★
19	**Truro – Annapolis Royal** 243km/151mi	Truro Annapolis Valley★★ (described in other direction)
20	**Annapolis Royal – Yarmouth** 131km/81mi	Annapolis Royal★★ Port Royal Habitation★★
21	**Yarmouth – Lunenburg** 311km/193mi	Atlantic Shore★★ (described in opposite) direction) Liverpool Ovens Natural Park★ Lunenburg★
22	**Lunenburg – Halifax** 176km/109mi	Atlantic Shore★★ Peggy's Cove★★

8 **Newfoundland** – *Round-trip of 2,073km/1,288mi (not including ferries) from Nort Sydney, Nova Scotia. Time: 12 days.* This tour of Canada's most easterly provinc enables visitors to discover the scenic wonders of Gros Morne, the French island of St. Pierre and the old port city of St. John's.

1	**North Sydney – Port aux Basques**	by ferry
	(it is advisable to spend the previous night in Sydney)	
2	**Port aux Basques – Wiltondale** 305km/190mi	
3	191km/119mi	Gros Morne National Park★★
4	**Wiltondale – Gander** 356km/221mi	
5-6	**Gander – Trinity** 182km/113mi	Terra Nova National Park★ Cape Bonavista★ Trinity★★
7	**Trinity – Grand Bank** 333km/206mi	Burin Peninsula Grand Bank
8	**Grand Bank – St.-Pierre** by ferry from Fortune	St.-Pierre★
9-10	**St.-Pierre – St. John's** 362km/224mi	St. John's★★
11	**St. John's – Cape Shore** 175km/109mi	Placentia (Castle Hill★) Cape St. Mary's★
12	**Cape Shore – North Sydney**	by ferry from Argentia

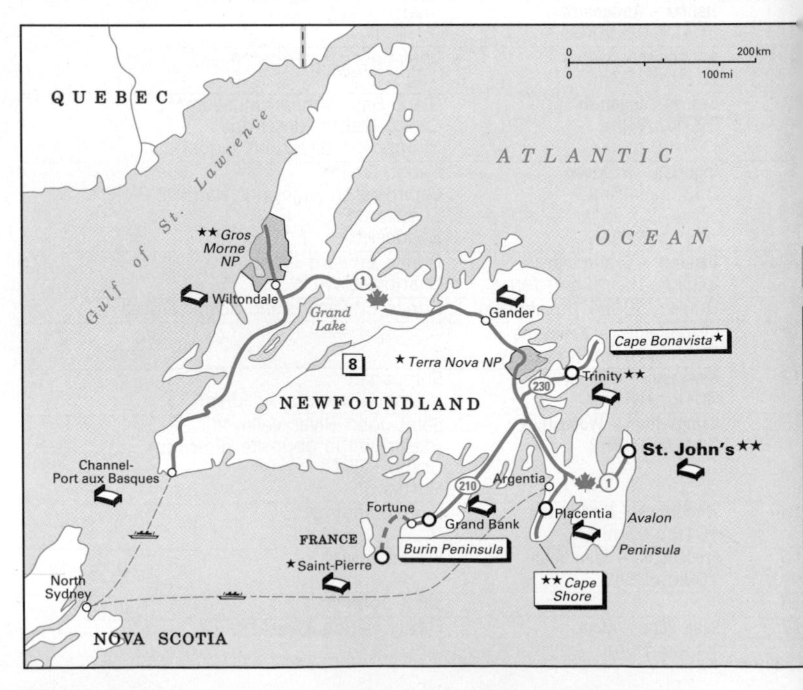

List of Maps

Mt Robson Provincial Park / © Dick Dietrich

Introduction to Canada

Canada's Landscapes

Covering nearly 10 million sq km/3.9 million sq mi, Canada is the second larges country in the world in terms of physical size. It is exceeded only by Russia, whos landmass totals some 17 million sq km/6.6 million sq mi. Having shores on thre oceans (Atlantic, Pacific and Arctic), Canada occupies most of the northern part o the North American continent. Yet its inhabitants, largely concentrated along th Canadian/US border, number just under 30 million—roughly the population of th state of California. The country is divided into ten provinces and two territories, soo to be three *(p 291)*.

Spanning six time zones *(p 309)*, the country stretches from latitude 41°47'N at **Pele Island** in Lake Erie (the same latitude as Rome, Italy) to 83°07'N at **Cape Columbia** o Ellesmere Island, a mere 800km/500mi from the North Pole. This north-south exter sion of about 4,600 km/2,900mi is countered only by its width. Canada covers mor than 5,500km/3,400mi from **Cape Spear** in Newfoundland (longitude 52°37'W) to th **Yukon/Alaska** border (141°W). One of the most remarkable features is the immense bit cut out of the coastline by **Hudson Bay**, named for famed British explorer Henry Hudson This enormous gulf or inland sea (637,000sq km/245,946sq mi) could be considere part of either the Atlantic or the Arctic Ocean. In common with the US, Canada share another noteworthy feature—the **Great Lakes**, which together form the largest body c fresh water in the world. Finally, the country is characterized by its extremely moun tainous western rim.

The Great Ice Ages – The physiographic regions described below have been exten sively modified in more recent geological times by the advance and retreat of glacia ice. Four times during the past million years, the North American climate has becom progressively colder. Snowfall became increasingly heavy in the north and was grad ually compressed into ice. This ice began to flow south, reaching its maximum exten at the Ohio and Missouri River Valleys in the US before retreating. At peak coverage 97 percent of Canada was submerged under ice up to 3km/2mi deep at the centr and 1.6km/1mi deep at the edges. Only the Cypress Hills and the Klondike region o the Yukon escaped this cover. The last Ice Age receded more than 10,000 years ago A sheet of ice of such thickness exerts a great deal of pressure on the earth below As the ice from each glacial advance retreated, hollows were scoured out of the lanc and filled with water, and mountain ranges were worn away and sculptured. Today about 2 percent of Canada is covered by glacial ice, mainly in the Arctic islands, bu glaciers are found in the western mountains (Columbia Icefield and St. Elias Mountains).

The Great Natural Regions

Physiographically, Canada has at its centre a massive upland known as the Canadiar Shield, which forms the geological platform for the whole country. This upland is partially surrounded by areas of lowland that in turn are rimmed by mountain ranges on three of Canada's four sides; to the south the country lies open to the US. Only in parts of the north do these mountain rims flatten out to form a coastal plain. Seven major physiographic regions can be distinguished.

Malak, Ottawa

Canadian Shield's Rocky Terrain

The Canadian Shield – This massive horseshoe-shaped region surrounding Hudson Bay encompasses nearly half of Canada's area. The terrain is formed of ancient, hard rocks of the **Precambrian** era (over 500 million years old) known for their great rigidity and strength. This strength and the region's shape are the origin of the name "Shield." The region is characterized by its innumerable lakes and rivers (Canada possesses as much as a quarter of the world's total supply of fresh water, largely concentrated in the Shield), by its rugged nature (a combination of

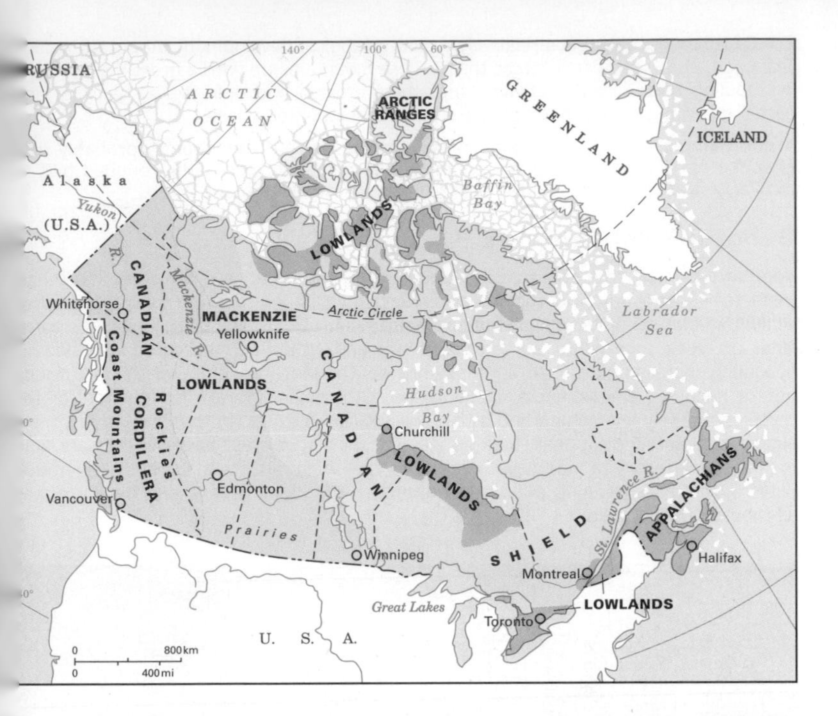

rock and bog that makes much of the area inaccessible) and by its lack of agricultural soil. However, the region is also the source of much of the country's extensive mineral, forest and hydro-electric wealth.

Great Lakes/St. Lawrence Lowlands – Despite their comparatively small size, these lowlands, which extend south into one of the great industrial and agricultural belts of the continent, are home to over 50 percent of the country's inhabitants. They were created in **Paleozoic** times (200-500 million years ago) when great stretches of the region were flooded by the sea for long periods. During this flooding thousands of feet of sedimentary rock accumulated on top of the Shield, providing fertile soil that has made the region important for agriculture today. This factor, combined with a favourable climate and proximity to the US, has made these lowlands Canada's richest and most industrialized area as well as its most populous.

Prairies and Mackenzie Lowlands – The geologic history of these lowlands is similar to those of the Great Lakes/St. Lawrence region. Material eroded from the Shield and the marginal mountains (in particular, the Rockies) was first deposited in shallow seas. Subsequently swept by glaciers, the flat plains in the south consist of fertile soils ideal for wheat and general farming. The Mackenzie Lowlands begin north of a low divide between the Saskatchewan and Athabasca Rivers, and support little agriculture because of their northerly latitude. In places where the Mackenzie Plain joins the Shield, there are large natural basins partially filled with water. Indeed, the dividing line between these two regions is marked by a series of great lakes—Winnipeg, Athabasca, Great Slave, Great Bear and others.

Hudson Bay and Arctic Archipelago Lowlands – The northern counterpart of the Great Lakes/St. Lawrence region, these lowlands are widely scattered portions of a partially drowned plain of Paleozoic rock that once covered the northern part of the Shield. They slope gently away from the latter with little relief. Owing to its northerly latitude, severe climate and frozen soil, this area supports little except a vegetation of moss and lichens.

Appalachian Mountains – About 200 million years ago, these mountains, which stretch from Alabama in the US to Newfoundland, were the first to be folded on the edges of the continent. Since then, extensive erosion by ice, rivers and sea has reduced them to mere stumps of their former heights. Today the region is a series of generally flat to rounded uplands, with few sharp peaks rising to no more than 1,280m/4,200ft. Prince Edward Island, and the Annapolis, Ristigouche and Saint John River Valleys are notable areas of plain where ancient glacial lakes have left fertile soil.

Canadian Cordillera – The Canadian Cordillera consists of five major parts (from east to west): the Rocky Mountains, the interior basins and plateaus, the Coast Mountains, the Inside Passage along the coast and finally, the outer system of islands. Covering the western quarter of the country, this great sweep of mountains is part of North America's long mountain systems known as the Western Cordillera.

The Canadian Cordillera is a relatively recent geological development. About 70 millic years ago, enormous earth forces thrust these mountains up with a great deal of faul ing, folding and volcanic activity. Since then, erosion and uplifting by glaciers, an partial drowning by sea have produced a deeply indented coast.

Arctic Ranges – These mountains in the extreme north of the country probably ros after the Appalachians. They consist of two fairly distinct parts: the rounded hills c the Parry Islands and the folded peaks of Ellesmere Island.

Geographical Features

Vegetation – The tree line crosses Canada in a rough diagonal from the Mackenz Delta to Hudson Bay and the Atlantic. North of this line lies the **tundra**, a land c lichens, miniature flowering plants and stunted shrubs. South of this line, the **bore forest** of black and white spruce, tamarack and other conifers gradually begins becoming increasingly dense as it extends south. More deciduous trees are foun until it becomes a **mixed forest**. But only in southern Ontario are the conifers of th north completely left behind and a true **deciduous forest** exists. In the Prairies, the tree almost completely disappear, making way for the flat former **grasslands** that are nov highly cultivated. The mountain region of the West also has its own vegetatio pattern, the trees thinning out as they approach the alpine tree line in the same wa as they do in the north.

Humpback Whale

Wildlife – Canada's varied landscape hosts several species of animals typical of regional fauna. Vast forests provide habitat for **white-tailed deer**, **black-tailed deer** and **mule deer**, while **wapiti**, also known as the American elk, populate mountainous terrain and prairieland. Largest of the deer family is a distinctively Canadian animal, the **moose**, inhabiting the forests of Newfoundland west to British Columbia as do **woodland caribou**, another member of the deer family. Also distinct is the Canada **lynx** previously located throughout the country, but now surviving in the northern mainland and in Newfoundland. Rare in Canada is the **wolverine** (of the weasel family), found in sparse populations in the western and northern part of the country. The **grizzly bear** and particularly the **black bear** *(illustration p 310)* are common denizens of Canada's coniferous and deciduous forests. Trapped nearly to extinction, **beavers** now thrive across Canada, occupying the streams and ponds of forested regions. Once common to forest, prairies and tundra, **wolves** reside primarily in the northern wilderness.
Populating Arctic coasts and islands are **polar bears** *(illustration p 107)* that feed on Canada's varied **seal** population, such as the grey, harp and hooded seals. Over 30 species of **whales** ply Canada's coastal waters, including the humpback and fin (off Newfoundland); the killer (or orca) and the grey (off British Columbia); and the beluga, blue, fin and minke (St. Lawrence estuary). The Arctic tundra supports **musk-oxen**, lemmings, white foxes and Arctic wolves as well as barren-ground caribou *(illustration p 312)*.
Wildlife of the prairies includes the **gopher**, **jackrabbit** and grouse in addition to **pronghorns** and **bison** (cattle family), known more commonly in North America as buffalo. Once numbering in the millions, bison were nearly extinct by 1885, hunted for their hides and meat. Wood Buffalo National Park protects a large population today.

Travel Alberta

Mountain Goats

Roaming the mountains of Western Canada are **mountain goats** and mountain sheep. Thinhorn or **Dall sheep** are found along Canada's Alaska Highway *(p 36)*, while **bighorn sheep** frequent British Columbia's southcentral ranges and the Canadian Rocky Mountains.

Canada's bird population ranges from waterfowl such as the Canada goose, Atlantic puffin and piping plover to the interior's peregrine falcon and rare whooping crane. The majestic **bald eagle** *(illustration p 88)* breeds in parts of northern and eastern Canada, but is confined largely to the coasts of north and central British Columbia. Although most species are migratory, over 400 species of birds have been documented as breeding in Canada.

Climate – Canada's climate is as varied and extreme as its geography. In a large area of the country, winter lasts longer than summer, yet the latter, when it comes, can be very hot. In the north, long hours of daylight cause prolific plant growth. The central provinces of Canada receive the most snow, far more than the Arctic, which in fact, receives the least precipitation of any region. One major factor influencing climate is proximity to large bodies of water: chiefly, the Pacific and Atlantic Oceans, Hudson Bay, and the Great Lakes. Such expanses tend to make winters warmer and summers cooler. Regions distant to them are inclined, therefore, to have much colder winters and hotter summers. But terrain is also a factor. In the West the high Coast Mountains shield the interior of British Columbia and the Yukon from the mild and moist Pacific air, making their climate more extreme than their location would indicate. The Rockies intensify this trend, leaving the Prairies vulnerable to both Arctic winds and hot southern breezes.

Each regional introduction has a summary of climatic conditions with average summer temperatures and precipitation.

Fall Foliage

Time Line

Pre-Colonial Period

c. 20,000-15,000BC First migration of Asiatic peoples to North American continent.
c. AD 1000 Norse reach Newfoundland.
1492 Christopher Columbus lands on San Salvador.
1497 **John Cabot** explores east coast of Canada.

New France

1534 **Jacques Cartier** claims Canada for France.
1565 St. Augustine, Florida, the oldest city in the US, is founded by Spaniards
1583 Sir Humphrey Gilbert claims Newfoundland for England.
1605 Samuel de **Champlain** establishes **Port Royal**.
1610 **Henry Hudson** enters Hudson Bay.
1620 Pilgrims found Plymouth, Massachusetts.
1670 **Hudson's Bay Company** is formed.
1713 Treaty of Utrecht is signed. France cedes Acadia to Britain.
1722 **Six Nations Iroquois Confederacy** is formed.
1730s-40s La Vérendrye family explores Canadian West.
1755 Acadians are deported from Nova Scotia.
1756-63 Seven Years' War.
1759 British defeat the French in Quebec City.
1763 **Treaty of Paris** is signed. France cedes New France to Britain.

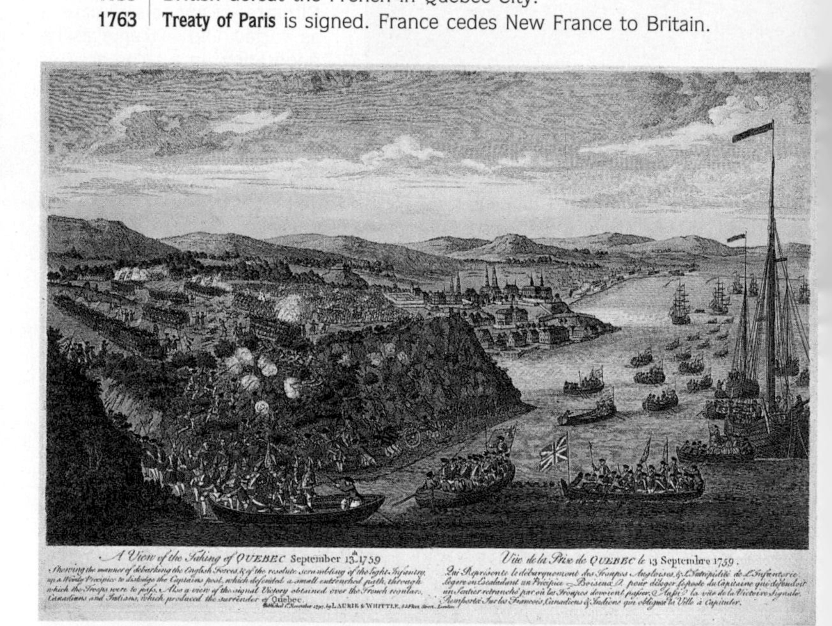

Battle of the Plains of Abraham

British Regime

1775 War of Independence begins in American colonies.
1778 James Cook explores coast of British Columbia.
1783 American colonies gain independence from Britain. Loyalists migrate to Canada.
1791 **Constitutional Act** creates Upper Canada (Ontario) and Lower Canada (Quebec).
1793 Alexander Mackenzie crosses British Columbia to the West Coast.
1812-14 War of 1812.
1837 Rebellions in Upper and Lower Canada.
1841 **Act of Union** creates the United Province of Canada.
1847 **Responsible government** system is implemented in Canada.
1848 California Gold Rush begins.
1858-61 British Columbia's gold rushes.
1861-65 American Civil War.

anadian Confederation

1867	British North America Act establishes Canadian Confederation.
1869-70	Riel Rebellion occurs in Red River Valley.
1870	Canadian Confederation buys Hudson's Bay Company land; Manitoba is created.
1872	**Dominion Lands Act** is passed.
1874	NWMP (Royal Canadian Mounted Police) is established.
1881-85	Canadian Pacific Railway is constructed.
1885	Northwest Rebellion occurs. Canada's **first national park** is created.
1896	Gold is discovered in the Klondike.
1914-18	World War I.
1931	**Statute of Westminster** grants Canada control of external affairs.
1939-45	World War II. Canada receives large numbers of European immigrants.
1942	Alaska Highway is completed.

ontemporary Canada

1959	**St. Lawrence Seaway** is opened.
1962	Trans-Canada Highway is completed.
1968	Québécois Party is founded.
1982	**Constitution Act** is passed. Quebec refuses to sign the new constitution.
1986	Nunavik is created.
1987	**Meech Lake Accord** calls for special status for Quebec.
1990	Manitoba and Newfoundland refuse to sign Meech Lake Accord. Quebec refuses to sign 1982 constitution. **Oka**, Quebec is site of armed conflict between Mohawks and Canadian government over native land claims.
1992	A national referendum to grant Quebec special status is defeated. Nunavut is established.
1993	Negotiation of **North American Free Trade Agreement** (NAFTA) among Canada, Mexico and the US.
1994	Approved by Canada, Mexico and the US, **NAFTA** takes effect Jan 1.
1995	Residents of Quebec vote by a narrow margin (50.6 percent to 49.4 percent) not to secede from the rest of Canada.
1996	Canada's last census of the century is conducted in May. The country's population stands at 28.8 million.
1998	Canada experiences its worst ice storm in the country's history. Some 3.5 million people in Quebec, Ontario and New Brunswick are without power.
1999	Self-administration for the new Territory of Nunavut officially begins.
2000	Newfoundland commemorates the landing of the Norse 1,000 years earlier. Canada celebrates the new millennium in festivals and events across the country.

Courtesy Royal Canadian Mounted Police

Royal Canadian Mounted Police

Historical Notes

The First North Americans – Man is not indigenous to North America. According recent archaeological findings, prehistoric tribes from the mountains of Mongolia ar the steppes of Siberia came to the continent some 15,000 to 20,000 years ago by land bridge that once existed over the **Bering Strait**. They gradually moved south acro the whole continent and into South America. Their descendants are the native India and Inuit peoples of Canada today, and they can be divided into six groups.

The **Northwest Coast tribes** constituted a highly developed civilization, well known for i totem poles and other carved objects. Principal tribal groups are the Bella Coola, Coa Salish, Haida, Kwakiutl, Nootka (along the West Coast), Tlingit and Tsimshian (i cluding the Gitksan). Also known as the Plateau culture (named after the Columbia Plateau region), the **Cordillera Indians** eked out an existence in the British Columb interior as hunters and fishermen. The Athapaskan, Salishan and Kutenai languag families represent this native culture. The **Plains Indians**—the Assiniboine, Blackfoo Cree, Gros Ventre and Sarcee tribes—were nomadic buffalo hunters who lived teepees and wore decorative clothing made of animal skins. The Beothuk, Cree, Den Montagnais and other **Sub-Arctic Indians** lived a nomadic existence hunting caribou ar other animals. The Algonquin and the Iroquoian peoples formed the **Eastern Woodlan** culture of bellicose farmers who lived in fortified villages, growing corn and squas Nomadic inhabitants of the most northerly regions, the **Inuit** traditionally lived in ic houses in winter, and in tents and sod houses during the summer. Using their high developed navigational skills, they hunted seals and whales off the coast and caribo and waterfowl in the interior.

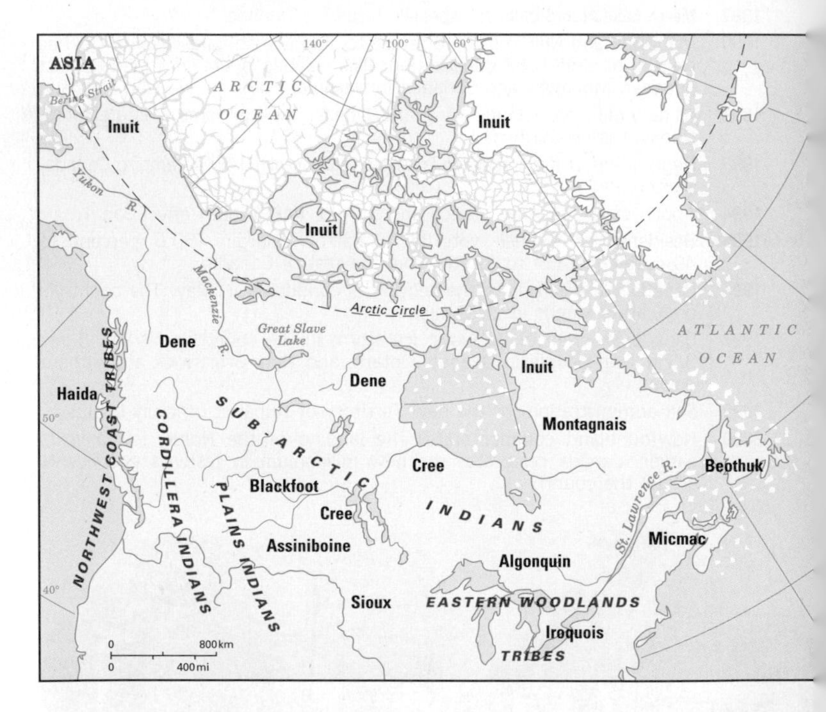

The Arrival of the Europeans – Long after the migrations of Asiatic peoples from the west, Europeans arrived on the shores of present-day Canada and proceeded to conquer the land and impose their own civilization. The Norse explored the coast of Labrador in the 10C and are believed to have founded the earliest known European settlement in North America around AD 1000 *(p 280)*. Basque and English fishermen knew of the rich resources of the Grand Banks as early as the 15C.

However, the first permanent settlements began in the 17C. Within seven years of each other (1603-10), Frenchman **Samuel de Champlain**, and Englishmen Henry Hudson and John Guy claimed the riches of the continent for their respective kings. Their claims led to nearly two centuries of war among the empires of France and England and the indigenous peoples for hegemony. The rivalry in North America revolved mainly around the lucrative fur trade. In 1713 the **Treaty of Utrecht** secured a temporary peace that lasted until the **Seven Years' War** (1756-63), in which France, Spain, Austria and Russia opposed Britain and Prussia. Before their final defeat by the British on the **Plains of Abraham** in 1759 *(p 188)*, the French not only established enduring settlements in the St. Lawrence Valley, but also explored half the continent, founding an empire known

Hudson's Bay Company Archives, Provincial Archives Manitoba

HBC Vancouver Store, Cordova Street (1887-1893)

s **New France**, which, at its greatest extent, stretched from Hudson Bay to New)rleans (Louisiana) and from Newfoundland nearly to the Rockies. This empire hrived on the fur trade. However, England's **Hudson's Bay Company (HBC)**, founded n 1670, gained control of all the lands draining into the great bay and exercised monopoly over that area, challenged only by Scottish merchants who established hemselves in Montreal after the British conquest of France and formed the **North Vest Company** in 1783.

'he Movement towards Confederation – In 1763, when the fall of New France was onfirmed by the **Treaty of Paris**, the population of the future confederation of Canada vas overwhelmingly French. A few settlements in Newfoundland and Halifax in Nova ;cotia were the only English-speaking exceptions. This imbalance was not to endure. 'he aftermath of the American Revolution brought thousands of **Loyalists** to the remaining British colonies (Nova Scotia, Prince Edward Island and Lower Canada, later named)uebec) and led to the creation of two more colonies—New Brunswick and Upper Canada (later Ontario).

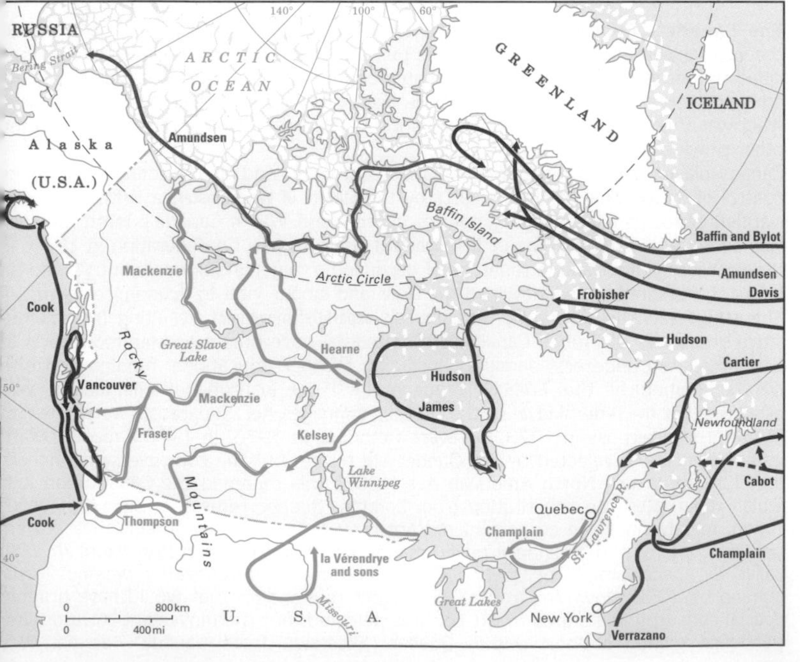

Lower Canada and Upper Canada were reunited by the British Parliament's **Act of Uni** in 1841. This law was prompted by a report by then–governor general Lord Durhar based upon his investigation of the 1837 rebellions in which Americans had partic pated. In addition to recommending union, the report proposed **responsible governmer** a system of majority party rule in the assembly (the British government did not fo mally implement this system until 1847), partly in the hope of reducing Americ influence.

Threats and incursions by Americans during the War of 1812, the Rebellions of 183 the American Civil War and the Fenian Raids of 1866-70 convinced the British gover ment that more settlers were needed if their colonies were to survive. The policy offering free land to potential settlers played a significant role in the development Canada during the 19C and early 20C.

Fear of American takeover encouraged the small groups of British colonists to uni for common defence. Their actions helped to propel the British Parliament into rat fying the **British North America Act** of 1867, which provided for **Canadian Confederation**. Th resulting new political entity, initially composed of four founding provinces—**Ontari** **Quebec**, **New Brunswick** and **Nova Scotia**—adopted a parliamentary system of governmer and separation of federal and provincial powers. Even as confederation was nego tiated, chief proponents John A. Macdonald and George-Étienne Cartier envisaged dominion stretching from coast to coast. Between the eastern provinces and the sma colony of British Columbia on the West Coast lay the immense, empty domain of th Hudson's Bay Company. Pressured by the British government, the company final agreed in 1868 to relinquish its lands to the new Confederation for a cash settlemer and rights to its posts and some land. As the new Dominion of Canada took posse sion, the Métis rebellion in the Red River Valley led to the creation of the fifth provinc **Manitoba**, in 1870. Meanwhile, **British Columbia** began negotiations to become the sixt province, prompted by fear of an American takeover, and **Prince Edward Island** joined it sister maritime provinces in Confederation in 1873. The Yukon Territory was create in 1898 and entered Confederation in the same year.

Construction of the Canadian Pacific Railway – To encourage British Columbia t join Confederation in 1871, the province was promised a transcontinental rail link After a few false starts, construction finally got underway in 1881. It was an immens and difficult project, the western mountain ranges alone posing a formidable barrie Building the line over the steep grades of **Kicking Horse Pass**, for example, was one c the great achievements of railroad engineering. **Rogers Pass** and **Fraser Canyon** were onl slightly lesser obstacles.

Serious problems beset the laying of track in the Canadian Shield country north o Lake Superior where, at one moment, tonnes of granite had to be blasted out and a the next, track lines would collapse into the muskeg. In the Prairies, however, a records for tracklaying were broken: in one day, a total of 10km/6mi were laid, record never surpassed by manual labour. This progress was achieved under th dynamic management of **William Van Horne**, who later became president of the Canadiar Pacific Railway Co. In only four years, the line was completed.

The Twentieth Century – Canada's purchase of land controlled by the HBC opene the way for settlement of the West; the building of the transcontinental rail line pro vided the means. Thousands of immigrants poured into the region, necessitating the creation of two new provinces in 1905—**Saskatchewan** and **Alberta**. Soon afterwards what was then much of the remaining Northwest Territories was redistributed to the other provinces.

Canada played a substantial role in both world wars, and finally achieved complet control of its external affairs in 1931 by the **Statute of Westminster**, a British law tha clarified Canada's parliamentary powers. After World War II Canada's tenth province was added when the citizens of **Newfoundland** voted to join Confederation in 1949. In the post-war years Canada found itself becoming a major industrial country, with ar influx of immigrants who provided the skills and labour vital to economic growth.

The 1960s saw the beginnings of Quebec's **separatist movement**, resulting from cumu- lative grievances of French Canadians. The federal government accelerated efforts to accommodate Quebecers' demands, including broader educational funding and offi- cial recognition of the French language. In 1969 institutional bilingualism was established at the federal level by the Official Languages Act. Separatists were defeated at the provincial polls in 1973, but were victorious in 1976. In 1980 a move toward independence was rejected by the Quebec electorate, but the controversy continued. In 1982 the British North American Act (1867) was renamed the Constitution Act, which repatriated the constitution from London. Quebec refused to sign the consti- tution, mainly since the agreement did not provide for transfer of legislative powers between federal and provincial governments. In 1987 the **Meech Lake Accord** *(p 189)* called for special status for Quebec. Federal and provincial ratification was not forth- coming by 1990, however. In 1992 a national referendum that would have granted special constitutional status to Quebec was defeated, but the movement toward inde- pendence gained support within Quebec. Secession from Canada was narrowly

:feated in the fall of 1995 by voters in the province by a margin of just over one ercent. In 1998 Canada's Supreme Court declared that, under constitutional law, uebec has no legal right of unilateral secession *(p 189)*.

nada's native population continues to press for autonomy and land settlements. The efeated 1992 referendum included a provision for self-governing powers for native habitants. Earlier that year, however, Canadians had voted in favour of dividing the orthwest Territories to form a self-administered Inuit homeland called **Nunavut** *(map p 3-4)* after a seven-year transitional period *(p 291)*. A goal of the **Assembly of First Nations** (AFN), representing some 500,000 Indians of the country's nearly one-million ative population, is constitutionally guaranteed rights of self-government.

ulticulturalism is nothing new to Canada, a nation of wide ethnic and racial diverty. It remains to be seen, however, if the current socio-political upheaval and esulting introspection will fracture national unity or restore it.

Canada Today

opulation – This immense country is inhabited by a relatively small number of people: 8.8 million in 1996, compared to over 260 million in the US. The United Kingdom's otal area of only 244,019sq km/94,216sq mi is home to some 57 million people. anada's inhabitants are largely concentrated in a band about 160km/100mi wide nmediately north of the Canadian/US border. The regional distribution is approximate- British Columbia, Rockies, Yukon 12 percent; the Prairie provinces 18 percent; ntario 37 percent; Quebec 25 percent; the Atlantic provinces 9 percent; Northwest erritories 0.2 percent. Although 62 percent of the population lives in Ontario and uebec, mainly between QUEBEC CITY and WINDSOR, Canada is strongly characterized by egional distinctions.

anguage and Culture – Canada is a land of immigrants. A population of 5 million 1900 grew to 12 million by the end of World War II and to almost 26 million in 988, thanks largely to immigration. Considered to be the **"founding" nations**, the British nd the French are the largest populations (37 and 32 percent respectively). To reflect his composition, Canada is officially bilingual. The largest concentration of French-peaking people is in Quebec, but Francophones are found in every province. The ederal government tries to provide services in both languages nationwide. There are ignificant numbers of Germans, Italians, Ukrainians, Dutch and Poles, especially in he Prairie provinces and, of native Indian and Inuit, resulting in an interesting mosaic f cultures across the country.

overnment – Canada is a **federal state** with ten provinces. Each province has its own lected legislature controlling regional affairs. The central government in **Ottawa**—the ederal capital—assumes responsibility for such matters as defence, foreign affairs, ransportation, trade, commerce, money and banking, and criminal law. The federal overnment is also directly responsible for administering Canada's two territories, the Yukon and the Northwest Territories (which is only one territory despite its name), and for overseeing the affairs of state of the country's Indian and Inuit peoples.

Though officially part of the Commonwealth, Canada functions in actuality as an independent nation. The Canadian head of State is the **British monarch**. Her authority is exercised by the **governor general**, who was at one time appointed by the monarch, but today is chosen by the elected respresentatives of the Canadian people. However, the governor general is little more than a figurehead as actual power lies in the hands of the Canadian **prime minister**, the leader of the majority party in Canadian **Parliament**. This latter institution consists of an elected legislature called the **House of Commons**, and an appointed **Senate**, members of which are chosen by the governing party. The prime minister rules through a cabinet drawn from the elected representatives (sometimes from members of the Senate also), and must submit his or her government for re-election after a maximum of five years, or if he or she is defeated in the House of Commons.

International Relations – After World War II Canada was catapulted to global leadership as a founding country in the United Nations and as a member of the North Atlantic Treaty Organization (NATO). The country retains diplomatic missions in over 80 countries and has earned respect as an international peacekeeper. In addition, Canada is a regular participant in international conferences, including the yearly economic summit of the seven major industrialized democracies, known as the G7. Canada, Mexico and the US ratified and are implementing the **North American Free Trade Agreement** (NAFTA), a pact designed to increase trade and investment among the three countries largely by eliminating tariffs and other barriers. Both NAFTA, which became effective in 1994, and an earlier free-trade agreement between Canada and the US have contributed to a sharp increase in Canadian exports in recent years.

Food and Drink – Food in Canada varies little from that in the US, but there are many regional specialities of interest. British Columbia is famous for its **seafood**, especially king crab and salmon. The country produces a variety of fruit, such as peaches,

cherries, grapes, and its own wine in the Okanagan Valley in British Columbia and the Eastern Townships of Quebec. In the Prairies the **beef** is excellent, along with fre lake fish in the north, wild rice (a great delicacy collected by certain Indian tribes berries of all types, and the heritage of many immigrant cultures—cabbage rolls, *pi rogis* (dumplings) and borscht, for example. Southern Ontario is the great fruit ar vegetable area of Canada and is also another wine-producing region.
Owing to its French heritage, Quebec has a fine culinary tradition. Many Frenc restaurants, especially in MONTREAL and QUEBEC CITY, serve traditional French-Canadia cuisine—pork dishes, meat pie *(tourtière)*, soups, and a generous quantity of map syrup. The Atlantic provinces are another great **seafood** region, especially oyster lobster, scallops, and mussels. In Newfoundland **screech**, a heady dark rum, or one c the country's fine **beers** is popular with meals—Canadians are great beer drinkers. Ne Brunswick is famous for **fiddleheads**, the new shoots of ferns available fresh in May ar June, and for **dulse**, an edible seaweed. **Moose meat** and fresh lake fish are available the Northwest Territories, as is **Arctic char**, a delicacy similar to trout and salmon taste.

"Few Englishmen are prepared to find it [Canada] what it is. Advancing quietly; old differences settling down, and being fast forgotten; public feeling and private enterprise alike in a sound and wholesome state; nothing of flush or fever in its system, but health and vigour throbbing in its steady pulse: it is full of hope and promise."

Charles Dickens, *American Notes*, 1842

Economy

The following is a very general account of economic activity in Canada. Additiona information can be found in the regional introductions. Statistics Canada (Ottawa Ontario) provides electronic publications for readers seeking detailed information (fee may apply): www.statcan.ca.

Canada's great strength lies in the wealth of its natural resources such as forests minerals, and energy fuels that contribute greatly to its economy. Mining and agriculture are part of the country's highly diversified economy, whereas energy is among the top-performing sectors, along with transportation and telecommunications Canada has become an important trading nation. Its largest single export market is the US. Since the signing of the North American Free Trade Agreement *(p 25)* Canada's exports to the US have grown rapidly.

Land of Forests – Forestry is of prime importance to Canada; trees in one form or another are among the country's most valuable assets. Over half the total land area is forested, and the forestry industry exists in every province. The industry is of great importance to British Columbia, which is best known for its sawn lumber, and to Quebec, a major producer of **newsprint**. Canada is the world's largest exporter of the latter commodity, supplying nearly a third of total world consumption.

Traditional Occupations – Despite Canada's tough climate and terrain, **agriculture** occupies an important position in the economy, making up 8 percent of the country's gross domestic product. Wheat has long been the leader in agricultural exports from the Prairie provinces, challenged in more recent years by canola, a new oilseed crop.
Beef cattle are also raised in the Prairie provinces, whereas dairy products, poultry and hogs are more important in British Columbia, Ontario and Quebec. Potatoes, which have been a mainstay of the Maritime provinces, are of growing significance in the prairie lands. Apples, grapes and several hardy small fruits are harvested in the southernmost areas of the country.
Fishing and **trapping** were for centuries Canada's primary industries and today, Canada is still a leading exporter of fish in the world. The Atlantic Coast supplies the vast majority of this resource, although 15 percent of the value is provided by the rich Pacific salmon fishery. Canada is one of the largest suppliers of animal pelts in the world.

Riches Beneath the Soil – Mining is an important activity in every region of Canada; it is the principal industry in the Northwest Territories and the Yukon. The country is a leading international producer of metals including nickel (Ontario, Manitoba), zinc (New Brunswick, Northwest Territories, Quebec, Ontario), molybdenum (British Columbia), uranium (Saskatchewan, Ontario), gold (Ontario, Quebec, British Columbia, Northwest Territories) and lead (New Brunswick, British Columbia, Northwest

Malak, Ottawa

Inspecting Grain in Saskatchewan

Territories). Leading nonmetals are potash (Saskatchewan, New Brunswick) and asbestos (Quebec). Iron ore is produced in the Labrador Trough (Quebec and Newfoundland) and in Ontario.

Alberta is the leading province for **fossil fuels**. Its oil and gas production are greater in dollar value than all of Ontario's mines. Alberta possesses immense reserves awaiting exploitation in its Athabasca oil sands, and shares substantial coal reserves with British Columbia. Although fossil fuel production is almost entirely restricted to Western Canada at present, recent offshore oil developments, including the Hibernia project *(p 274)* on the continental shelf off Newfoundland, could change this restriction in the future.

Manufacturing – Canada's manufacturing industry, traditionally based on resource-processing (forest products, minerals, food and beverages, for example), has largely shifted into secondary manufacturing. A significant petrochemical industry exists in Alberta, Manitoba, Ontario and Quebec. Automobile and auto parts manufacturing is based in Ontario and Quebec; electrical and electronics industries are strong in those same two provinces. British Columbia is becoming a centre for telecommunications, pharmaceuticals and biotechnology. In Atlantic Canada commercial medicine, environmental industries and information technologies (the latter most notably in New Brunswick) complement traditional industries.

Transportation – Because of Canada's size, transportation has always been of prime importrance. Until about 1850 waterways commanded the country's economic growth. Fishing and timber industries and the fur trade all depended on water transport. Since then, wheat farming, mining and pulp and paper industries have grown largely dependent on rail transport. Even in these industries, movement of goods by water is not insignificant. The network of locks and canals known as the **St. Lawrence Seaway** was opened in 1959, a massive joint engineering achievement between Canada and the US. This 3,790km/2,350mi waterway through the St. Lawrence River and the Great Lakes significantly boosted Canada's economy: in particular, the country became an exporter of iron ore after the seaway facilitated exploitation of Labrador and Quebec's huge deposits. The road network has expanded since World War II with the completion of the Trans–Canada Highway and the opening of the great northern roads—the Alaska and the Dempster Highways. Aviation plays an important role, especially in the North. Airplanes are sometimes the only means of supplying mineral exploration teams there and may, in the future, be used to remove exploited resources.

Hydro-electric Giant – The abundance and power of Canada's water sources off exceptional opportunities for generation of hydro-electricity. Almost two-thirds of t country's electricity comes from this source. Generating stations operate in every pro ince except Prince Edward Island, and Quebec's massive **James Bay Hydro-electric Proje** *(p 189)*, with a capacity of more than 12,000 megawatts, is one of the largest hydr electric engineering projects in the world. In Labrador a huge generating station located on the Churchill River. Other examples are in British Columbia on the Pea and Columbia Rivers, in Quebec on the Manicouagan and Outardes Rivers combine in both Ontario and Quebec on the St. Lawrence, in Saskatchewan on the Sou Saskatchewan, and in Manitoba on the Nelson.

The electricity produced powers industries involved in natural resource utilization suc as smelting businesses and pulp mills. Plentiful and inexpensive hydro-electricity h attracted other industries such as the aluminum industry to Canada (British Columb and Quebec). Canada's energy is transported via high-voltage power lines to souther Canada to heat Canadian homes. Canada's surplus electricity is exported to the US.

Daniel Johnson Dam at Manic-5

We welcome your assistance in the never-ending task of updating the texts and maps in this guide. Send us your comments and suggestions:

Michelin Travel Publications
Editorial Department
PO Box 19001
Greenville, South Carolina 29602-9001

Further Reading

Canada

A Concise History of Canadian Painting by Dennis Reid *(Oxford University Press, 1989)*

A Short History of Canada by Desmond Morton *(McClelland & Stewart, 1997)*

Canada: A Story of Challenge by J. M. S. Careless *(General Publishing Co. Ltd., 1991)*

Cycling Canada: Bicycle Touring Adventures in Canada by John M. Smith *(Bicycle Books Inc., 1995)*

British Columbia, Rockies, Yukon

The Canadian Rockies: A Pictorial Guide by Thomas Owen *(High Country Colour, Ltd. 1998)*

Looking at Indian Art of the Northwest Coast by Hilary Stewart *(Douglas & McIntyre, 1995)*

The National Dream and the Last Spike by Pierre Berton *(McClelland & Stewart, 1994)*

Native Sites in Western Canada by Pat Kramer *(Altitude Publishing Canada, Ltd. 1994)*

The Streets Were Paved with Gold by Stan Cohen *(Pictorial Histories Publishing Co., 1998)*

The Wild West by Bruce Patterson & Mary McGuire *(Altitude Publishing Canada, Ltd. 1993)*

Prairie Provinces

Blueberries & Polar Bears by Helen Webber and Marie Woolsey *(Centax Books, 1995)*

Forging the Prairie West by John Herd Thompson *(Oxford University Press, 1998)*

The People: A Historical Guide to the First Nations of Alberta, Saskatchewan and Manitoba by Donald Ward *(Fifth House Publishers, 1995)*

Who Has Seen the Wind? by W. O. Mitchell *(Bantam Books, 1989)*

Wilderness Man: The Strange Story of Grey Owl by Lovat Dickson *(General Publishing, 1991)*

Ontario

Ottawa by Jean E. Pigott *(Key Porter Books Ltd., 1990)*

Rideau Waterway by Robert Legget *(University of Toronto Press, 1986)*

Roughing it in the Bush by Susannah Moodie *(McClelland & Stewart, 1997)*

Toronto: No Mean City by Eric Arthur *(University of Toronto Press, 1994)*

Quebec

Discover Montréal: An Architectural and Historical Guide by Joshua Wolfe & Cécile Grenier *(Libre Expression, 1991)*

Maria Chapdelaine by Louis Hémon *(General Publishing, 1992)*

A Short History of Quebec (2nd ed.) by John A. Dickinson and Brian Young *(Copp Clark Pitman Ltd., 1993)*

Two Solitudes by Hugh Maclennan *(Fitzhenny & Whiteside Ltd., 1997)*

Atlantic Provinces

Anne of Green Gables by Lucy Maud Montgomery *(Dell, 1998)*

Coastal Nova Scotia Outdoor Adventure Guide by Joanne Light *(Nimbus Publishing, 1993)*

Nature Trails of Prince Edward Island by J. Dan McAskill and Kate MacQuarrie *(Ragweed Press, 1996)*

Rocks Adrift: The Geology of Gros Morne National Park edited by Michael Burzynski and Anne Marceau *(Canada Communications Group Publishing, 1991)*

Saint-Pierre and Miquelon by William Rannie *(W. F. Rannie, 1977)*

Northwest Territories

Company of Adventurers by Peter C. Newmann *(Penguin Books, 1987)*

People of the Deer by Farley Mowat *(Seal Books, 1993)*

Sculpture of the Inuit by George Swinton *(McClelland & Stewart, 1994)*

The Snow Walker by Farley Mowat *(Seal Books, 1995)*

British Columbia, Rockies, Yukon

Icefields Parkway/Travel Alberta

Known as the **Canadian Cordillera** *(p 17)*, this region consists of the province of British Columbia, part of the province of Alberta, and the Yukon Territory. Covering the extreme west, it stretches from the Pacific Ocean to the Rockies and from the Canadian/US border to the Beaufort Sea. The high snow-capped peaks, massive glaciers, rugged ranges, mighty rivers, wild streams and tranquil lakes of this land of beauty attract millions of tourists every year.

Geographical Notes

Mountainous Terrain – Contrary to the belief that all mountains between the Prairies and the Pacific Ocean are the Rockies, this famous mountain range is only one of many in the region. Starting in the west the **Coast Mountains** of British Columbia rise steeply out of the deeply indented and heavily forested Pacific Coast to over 3,000m/10,999ft. North of this chain in the Yukon are the high St. Elias Mountains, which peak with Mt. Logan at 5,959m/19,520ft, the highest point in Canada.
East of this coastal system lies an immense, elevated **plateau**. In the south, where it is nearly 300km/200mi wide, this plateau encompasses such diverse areas as the Cariboo ranch lands and the irrigated Okanagan fruit-growing belt. In the southeast the plateau ends at the **Columbia Mountains** where the Cariboo, Purcell, Monashee and Selkirk Ranges *(p 46)* are found. In the north the plateau changes to an area of rugged hills—the Skeena and Cassiar Ranges—before spreading out into the vast Yukon Plateau, a basin-like area of rolling uplands, encircled by high mountains and drained by the Yukon River and its tributaries.
It is east of this interior plateau, across the Columbia Mountains and the Rocky Mountain Trench, that the **Rockies** are reached. About 150km/94mi wide at most, the Canadian Rockies stretch from the 49th parallel to the Yukon/British Columbia boundary. Rugged, with numerous peaks over 3,000m/10,000ft, they are spotted with

aciers, especially in the area of the Columbia Icefield. In the east the Rockies' front nges rise abruptly above the foothills, giving the impression of a wall towering above e seemingly flat prairie lands of Alberta. At the Yukon/British Columbia boundary, e **Liard River**, a tributary of the Mackenzie River, carves a channel between the Rockies d the **Mackenzie Mountains**. North of the Mackenzies are the Richardson and British ountains, stretching almost to the Beaufort Sea.

imate – Tremendous variation marks the climate of this region, which extends from titude 49° to north of the Arctic Circle (66.3°), and has coasts on two oceans—the arm Pacific and the icy Arctic. Elevations range from sea level to nearly 6,100m/-),000ft.

ne climate of coastal British Columbia is influenced by the warm waters of the Pacific, e prevailing westerly winds and the high Coast Mountains. Winters are mild °–5°C/30°–40°F) and summers warm, though not hot (15°–24°C/ 60°–75°F). Rain- ll can be low in protected areas, but among the heaviest in the world in locations posed to the full blast of winds off the Pacific *(p 81)*. Similarly, cloud cover can be ht in protected places and heavy in exposed areas. East of the Coast Mountains, one counters a very different climatic regime with greater extremes of temperature and wer rainfall. Winters average –5°C/23°F and summers 22°C/72°F. Irrigation is needed the Okanagan Valley to allow cultivation of its famous fruits, whereas the Selkirk ountains have recorded the highest snowfall in Canada.

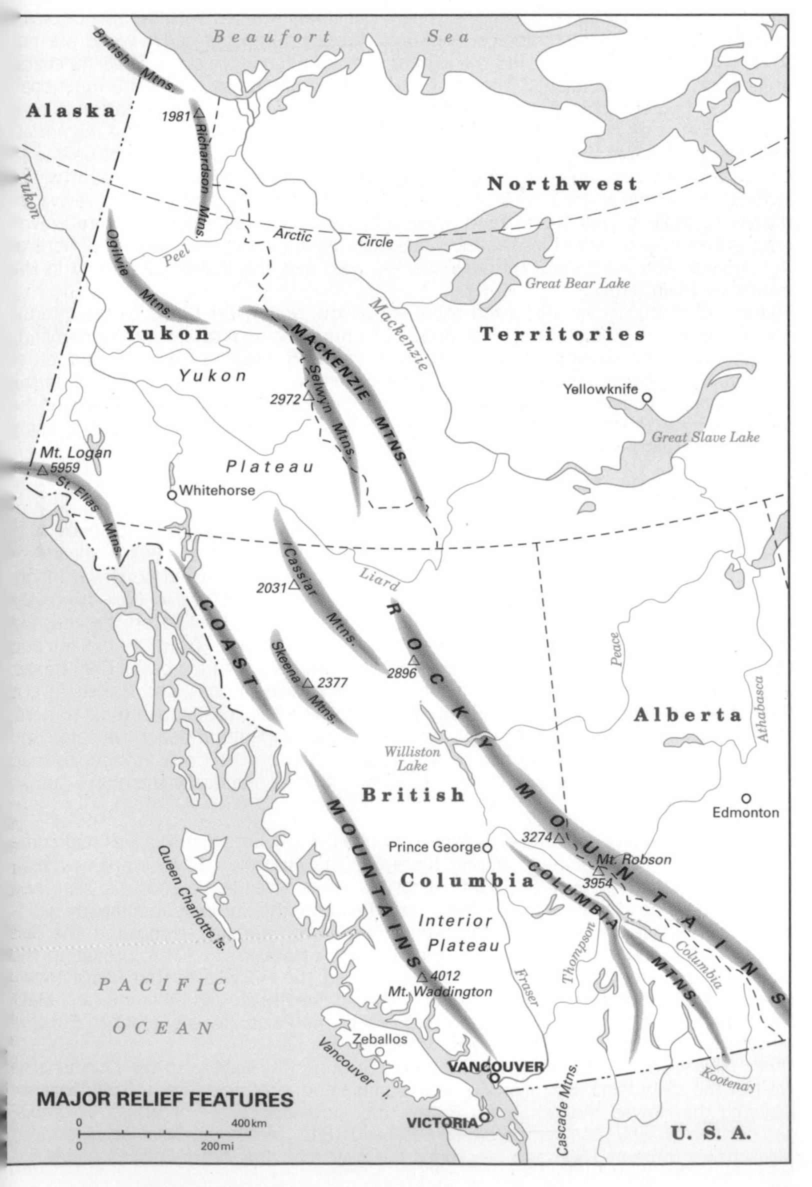

In the north the towering St. Elias Mountains cut the Yukon off from the moderati influences of the Pacific, but also from the high precipitation of the coast. Summe are pleasantly warm and dry (nearly 21°C/70°F and 230-436mm/9-17in of rain) wi long hours of daylight (an average of 20 hours) during which the sun shines a lar percentage of the time. Winters, however, are dark and cold, though temperatur vary widely (Dawson City –27°C/–16°F, Whitehorse –15°C/–5°F).

Historical Notes

The First Inhabitants – Native cultures of this region fall into three basic group the wealthy, artistic tribes of the Pacific Coast; the tribes of hunters and fisherme who inhabited the British Columbia interior (known as the Cordillera Indians); ar the Athapaskan-speaking tribes of the Yukon, whose lives were spent following th caribou in the same way as the Indians of the Northwest Territories. The civilizatic created by the **Northwest Coast tribes** is unlike any other in North America. Before th Europeans arrived, they enjoyed, in a country rich in resources, a high standard living—far above the subsistence living of tribes in other regions. Wood from giar **cedar trees** that proliferated along the coast, and **salmon** from the ocean were the bas of their livelihood.

Having leisure time to devote to art, they developed a creative expression unequalle on the continent north of Mexico. Tall tree trunks were chiselled with expressive form and raised as **totem poles** before the houses of the chiefs. Carved with designs of bird animals, humans and mythological creatures, these columns of cedar wood are nc solely works of art. Each carving is a sign or crest of a family or clan, similar to coats of-arms or heraldic emblems. Their purpose varied: sometimes they were functiona serving as house corner posts; sometimes decorative, serving as the entrance to house (a hole was made at the bottom of the pole); other times they were memoria to dead relatives, or actually part of the grave. They represent an art form unique t the Northwest Coast Indians. The golden age of carving was 1850 to 1900, after th introduction of metal tools by Europeans. In recent years there has been a revival o the art as Indians seek to re-create their traditions. The same designs were wove onto blankets, and carved into masks, chests, ornaments and jewellery. The more o the latter a man possessed, the wealthier he was, and the higher he ranked in th tribe's social structure.

The arrival of Europeans disrupted tribal life on the Northwest Coast, in the interio and in the Yukon. Indians were encouraged to hunt for furs to satisfy the demand of the European market. In exchange they received firearms, alcohol and othe imports, upon which many tribes became dependent, and their lifestyle altered. In th Yukon tribal life changed to a lesser degree because of the relative remoteness of th area. Along the Northwest Coast, perhaps because of the strength of the culture, man customs remain, however, and others are being revived ('Ksan *p 69*).

The Arrival of the Europeans – European discovery of the region occurred from two directions. Small ships explored the coast, while fur traders, seeking new sup-plies and transportation routes, approached the interior. Although **Francis Drake** may have sighted the coast of British Columbia during his around-the-world voyage o 1579, the area was not explored until the 18C. Spaniards journeyed northward from California, and Russians travelled southward from Alaska. Capt. **James Cook**, however made the first recorded landing during his voyage of 1778, sailing up the coast o British Columbia. Landing on VANCOUVER Island, he bought pelts from the Indians and sold them in China at great profit. News of this trade encouraged other Englishmer and Spaniards to visit the North Pacific. A clash was inevitable. The British forcec the Spaniards—who later retreated entirely—to declare the coasts open to all traders. To reinforce its claims, the British government sent an expedition under the command of Capt. **George Vancouver**, who had been a midshipman on the Cook voyage, to map the coast. Between 1792 and 1794 Vancouver mapped practically the entire British Columbia coast.

Fur-Trading Empire – The first European to glimpse the Canadian Rockies had come and gone with little fanfare. **Anthony Henday** of the Hudson's Bay Company (HBC) sighted the mountain wall in 1754, about 10 years after la Vérendrye's sons had viewed the range in Wyoming. Henday's report roused little interest at company head-quarters. **Alexander Mackenzie** of the rival North West Company completed the last section of the first crossing of the continent north of Mexico in 1793, predating the **Lewis and Clark** expedition by 12 years. He climbed the Rockies by the Peace River, reaching the Pacific after a hazardous traverse of the British Columbia interior. Mac-kenzie had sought a route for transporting furs to the Pacific for shipment to Europe, rather than the long canoe journey to Montreal.

Other "Nor'westers" sought alternative routes through the Rockies to the rich fur area west of the mountains. By following the Columbia and Kootenay Rivers, **David Thompson** explored the Howse and Athabasca Passes, the southeast corner of British Columbia, and northern Washington state between 1804 and 1811. Meanwhile **Simon Fraser** retraced Mackenzie's route in 1808 and descended the river that now bears Fraser's name.

hile Fraser and Thompson were establishing posts and encouraging trade with Indians the interior, an American fur-trading company created by **John Jacob Astor** founded a ɔst at the mouth of the Columbia, beginning the American challenge to British ownerıip of the Oregon territory. In 1846 the rivalry was settled when the HBC (which merged 1821 with its great competitor, the North West Company) was finally forced to accept e 49th parallel as the US frontier. The HBC moved its western headquarters from the ɔlumbia River area to **Vancouver Island**, which was declared a crown colony in 1849 with ctoria as its capital. The rest of British Columbia (known as New Caledonia) remained ıe exclusive domain of the company, as did the Yukon, where the firm established itself ter 1842. Thus, in 1858, British Columbia, the Rockies and the Yukon were predomiıntly a fur-trader's paradise—a state of affairs that was to change very quickly.

old – The discovery of gold in California in 1848 attracted countless people who ɔped to make a fortune. Nine years later the gold was gone, but prospectors did not ɔp looking. Many entered New Caledonia to search. In 1858 the news spread like ild fire—there was gold in the sandbars of the lower Fraser River. The small settleıent of **Victoria** (pop. 400) saw 20,000 people pass through en route to the gold fields. fraid the influx of Americans would lead to an American takeover (as had occurred in alifornia), the governor of the island colony, **James Douglas**, stepped in quickly to assert ritish sovereignty. The mainland was rapidly declared a British colony and named British olumbia, with Douglas as its first governor. Poor transportation routes made control f the new territory difficult. When rich gold strikes in the Cariboo brought even more eople, Douglas planned construction of a wagon road—the famous **Cariboo Road**, built etween 1862 and 1865, which helped ensure British control of the area.

onfederation and a Railway – The wealth from mining gold did not last long. The ıte 1860s saw economic disaster looming for the two western colonies (united in 1866; vhile in the east, the British colonies were discussing Confederation, which became a eality in 1867). US purchase of Alaska in 1867 again raised fears of an American akeover. Thus, negotiations concerning Hudson's Bay Company's domain were begun vith the new Canada, located 3,200km/2,000mi away, and completed in 1871.
British Columbia entered Confederation on the condition that, within 10 years, a ailway would be built to connect the province with the east. The birth pains of such massive project nearly led to British Columbia's withdrawal from Confederation; but he project, initiated in 1881, was completed within the remarkably short time of four ears. When the last spike was hammered in at Craigellachie in November 1885, and he transcontinental runs began the next year, the province was transformed. The ailway brought tourists, settlers and capital to the impoverished region, and encouaged the search for mineral wealth and the utilization of natural resources that have nade British Columbia what it is today.

'Ho for the Klondike" – When the Cariboo gold fields were exhausted, prospectors ıgain moved north. Gold was found in the Omineca and Cassiar Mountains. Then prosɔectors entered the Yukon, which was declared a district of the Northwest Territories n 1895 by the Canadian government, again because of fear of American encroachment. A detachment of the **Mounted Police** *(p 108)* was dispatched to maintain law and ɔrder—a timely move. The long-hoped-for big strike was made in 1896 on a small creek renamed "Bonanza," which drained into the Klondike River, a tributary of the Yukon. When news of the find became common knowledge, what has been described as "one of the world's greatest economic explosions" occurred. Thousands of men and women set off from all corners of the globe to reach the Klondike by a variety of means *(p 40)*, an event dubbed the Klondike Stampede. In eight years $100 million worth of gold was shipped out, providing an enormous stimulus for this western frontier.

The Region Today

British Columbia/Rockies – In this century, especially since World War II, the growth of British Columbia has been spectacular. Discovery of gold in the Klondike spurred the search for minerals all over the Cordillera region, leading to the development of THE KOOTENAYS as the principal mining area for the extraction of **lead**, **zinc** and **silver**. Copper and molybdenum are mined extensively in the province, especially in the Highland Valley near Kamloops. Sulphur, peat moss and gypsum are also found. The Crowsnest Pass area of the Kootenays is rich in **coal**, which is exported mainly to Japan. At Kitimat there is a huge aluminum smelter (the bauxite, the principal source of aluminum, is imported), and asbestos is mined at Cassiar.
An international mining centre, the Greater Vancouver area serves as headquarters for major producers, equipment manufacturers and laboratories. Natural gas and oil are found in the Peace River area and farther north near Fort Nelson. They are transported south by pipeline where the oil is refined at Kamloops. British Columbia exports today about 95 percent of its minerals; metals and coal are shipped primarily to Asia. About 50 percent of its oil and gas is exported, principally to the US.
Construction of the **Panama Canal**, opened in 1915, greatly stimulated exploitation and export of the province's minerals by providing a cheap means of transport to Europe. British Columbia's products were thereby competitive, worth exploiting. Roads and

PRACTICAL INFORMATION

Getting There

By Air – International and domestic flights to Vancouver International Airport *(15km/9mi south of downtown)* ☎604-276-6101 via Air Canada ☎604-688-5515, or 800-776-3000 (US) and Canadian Airlines International ☎800-426-7000 (Canada/US) and other major carriers. Affiliated airlines offer connections to Prince Rupert, Victoria, and to Whitehorse (Yukon Territory) as well as to more remote regions: Air BC ☎604-688-5515 and Canadian Regional Airlines ☎800-665-1177 (Canada) or 800-426-7000 (US). Taxi to downtown Vancouver *($20-25)*. Airport **shuttle** Vancouver Airporter ☎604-946-8866 *($10)*. Airport Limousine Service ☎604-273-1331. Major car rental agencies *(p 305)* at the airport.

By Bus and Train – Greyhound **bus** service to BC and the Yukon (Whitehorse via Edmonton or Vancouver): ☎604-482-8747 (in Vancouver). Greyhound, Maverick Coach Lines ☎604-662-8051 and other bus companies serve Vancouver Island *(consult the telephone directory)*. **VIA Rail** Canada operates the Skeena route from Vancouver to Prince Rupert, connects Victoria to Courtenay and links Vancouver to Toronto ☎800-561-8630 (in BC), or ☎800-561-3949 (US). **BC Rail** services Whistler and Prince George from Vancouver ☎604-631-3500.

By Boat – **BC Ferries** operates 25 different routes connecting 42 ports of call on the coastline and many of the islands. BC Ferries, 1112 Fort St., Victoria, BC, V8V 4V2 ☎250-386-3431. For ferries from the US to British Columbia *p 80.*

General Information

Accommodations and Visitor Information – The government tourist office produces annually updated guides on accommodations, camping, fishing, skiing and vacations. The *BC Travel Guide* suggests driving tours and gives general travel tips. All publications and a map are available free of charge from: **Tourism British Columbia**, Parliament Buildings, Victoria, BC, V8V 1X4 ☎800-663-6000 (Canada/US).
The *Vacation Guide to Canada's Yukon*, which is updated annually, provides details as to facilities and attractions, entertainment, adventure travel, outdoor activities and gives travel tips. This publication and a road map are available free of charge from **Tourism Yukon**, Box 2703, Whitehorse, YT, Y1A 2C6 ☎867-667-5340.

Road Regulations – *(Driver's license and insurance requirements p 304.)* BC and Alberta have good paved roads. In winter certain precautions are necessary, especially when crossing Rogers Pass. Unless otherwise posted, speed limits are: in British Columbia 80km/h (50mph) on provincial highways and 50km/h (30mph) in cities; in Alberta 100km/h (60mph) on provincial highways and 50km/h (30mph) in cities; in the Yukon 90km/h (55mph) on highways and 50km/h (30mph) in cities. For road conditions in British Columbia ☎604-299-9000 (then press 7623). For road conditions in the Yukon ☎867-667-8215. **Seat belt** use is mandatory. For listings of the **Canadian Automobile Assn. (CAA)**, consult the local telephone directory *(p 305)*.

Time Zones – Alberta and the BC Rockies region are on Mountain Standard Time. The rest of BC and the Yukon are on Pacific Standard Time. Daylight Saving Time is observed from the first Sunday in April to the last Sunday in October. The northeast corner of BC is on Mountain Standard Time year-round.

Taxes – In addition to the national 7% GST *(rebate information p 308)*, BC levies a 7% provincial sales tax, and an 8% accommodation tax (10% in some communities).

Liquor Laws – The legal drinking age is 19. Liquor is sold in government stores.

Provincial Holidays *(National Holidays p 308)*

BC Day	1st Monday in August
Discovery Day, Yukon	3rd Monday in August

Recreation

Outdoor Activities – The rivers, mountains and many parks of this vast and sparsely populated region offer the outdoor enthusiast a variety of recreational activities: hiking, horseback riding, fishing, river rafting, canoeing and kayaking. Some guest ranches include several days on a trail into backcountry wilderness in their program.

Many **fishing** lodges arrange fly-in packages to remote lakes that attract anglers from around the world. Licenses are required for both saltwater and freshwater fishing, and can be obtained locally. The many navigable waterways, especially in the Shuswap Lake district, offer a host of water sports as well as house-boating. Marine adventures and cruises that include nature observation are popular along the coastline.

Whistler, north of Vancouver, is a popular ski resort with first-class accommodations and **winter sports** facilities, including glacier skiing from June through October. The three ski resorts in the Rockies *(p 55)* offer a variety of winter activities. For information on recreation, contact Tourism British Columbia *(p 34)*.

Special Excursions – The **Rocky Mountaineer** journeys through some of the most spectacular mountain scenery in North America during a two-day trip from Vancouver to Jasper or Banff. The train travels in the daylight hours only; passengers spend the night in Kamloops. Eastbound, westbound and round-trip travel is possible *(departs from Vancouver May–Oct Tue,Thu & Sun 7am; one-way $485/person May & Oct or $585/person Jun–Sept, double occupancy; add-on to Calgary $60; cost of lodgings in Kamloops included; 2-7 day excursions in Dec also available; reservations required;* ✗ ♿ ◘*; Rocky Mountaineer Railtours, 1150 Station St., Suite 130, Vancouver, BC, V6A 2X7 www.rkymtnrail.com* ☎ *604-606-7245 or 800-665-7245, Canada/US).*

Principal Festivals

Feb	**Sourdough Rendezvous** *(p 88)*	*Whitehorse, YT*
May	**Swiftsure Yacht Race Weekend**	*Victoria, BC*
Jun–Jul	**Stampede** *(p 39)*	*Williams Lake, BC*
Jun–Aug	**Festival of the Arts**	*Banff, AB*
Jul	**Peach Festival**	*Penticton, BC*
Aug	**Loggers' Sports Day**	*Squamish, BC*
	Discovery Day *(p 41)*	*Dawson City, YT*
Aug–Sept	**Pacific National Exhibition**	*Vancouver, BC*
Sept	**Classic Boat Festival**	*Victoria, BC*
Sept–Oct	**Okanagan Wine Festival**	*Penticton, BC*

Travel Alberta

Skiing in Sunshine Village near Banff

railways were built to carry the minerals to smelters and ports. This transportatio network stimulated growth of the **forestry** industry. About a quarter of the marketab timber in North America is found in the province. In the moist climate of its coas trees grow to great size. Annual timber cut is about 74 million cu m/2.6 billion cu f making forestry British Columbia's prime industry.

Hydro-electricity has also boomed since World War II. Two vast projects—the W.A.C Bennett Dam with generating stations on the Peace River, and Mica Dam with station on the Columbia River—have capacities exceeding 2,000,000kW an 1,700,000kW respectively. Although British Columbia abounds with raw materials it supports a large manufacturing industry. The province is also known for its ric coastal **fishing industry**: salmon, halibut, herring, clams, oysters and crab abound Despite mountainous terrain and forest-covered slopes, **agriculture** thrives in som areas of the province. The lower Fraser Valley and Vancouver Island are largel devoted to dairy cattle and crops; the Okanagan is famous for its tree fruits an wine industry; the Kootenays are also known for fruit; the great interior platea called the Cariboo is cattle-raising country with large ranches, stampedes an rodeos; and the Peace River country east of the Rockies is British Columbia's chie grain-growing area.

Correspondingly, the **population** of British Columbia has increased from a little ove 50,000 at the turn of the century to 3,724,500 today. The great majority of thes inhabitants live in the southwest corner of the province, nearly half in the Vancouve metropolitan area.

The Yukon – This Territory's development has not been as spectacular as Britis Columbia's. The golden years of the Klondike Stampede were followed by years o economic stagnation, with the population falling from 27,219 in 1901 (even greater at the height of the stampede) to 4,157 in 1921. World War II saw the constructio of the Alaska Highway, which has led to increased exploitation of the Territory's mineral wealth. Zinc, lead, silver, cadmium, copper, tungsten and gold are mined and transported south by road through the Coast Mountains to Skagway. Today the 30,766 **population** exceeds the turn-of-the-century level. Well over half the residents live in the territorial capital of Whitehorse.

ALASKA HIGHWAY★★

British Columbia, Yukon, Alaska

Map of Principal Sights p 2

This great road to the North, and adventure, passes through a land of mountains and lakes of rare beauty, largely untouched by mankind except for a scattering of small communities. Beginning at Dawson Creek in British Columbia, the highway parallels the Rocky Mountains, enters the Yukon along the valley of the Liard, touches the Cassiar and the Coast Mountains of British Columbia, and follows the St. Elias Mountains to enter Alaska, finally terminating in Fairbanks.

Historical Notes – To link Alaska and the Yukon with the road system farther south, the highway was constructed in 1942 by joint agreement between Canada and the US. When the Japanese bombed **Pearl Harbor** in 1941, landed in the Aleutian Islands, and threatened sea routes to Alaska, Americans feared an imminent invasion of mainland Alaska. A land route between the US and Alaska was considered essential. Thus, in only nine months, 2,451km/1,523mi of highway were built by the US Army Corps of Engineers. Traversing muskeg swamps, bridging wide rivers, climbing or avoiding mountain ranges, the road has become a legend in the annals of road construction. Upgraded after World War II and opened to civilian traffic, the highway is of major economic importance as a means of transporting the region's mineral wealth and the tourists who travel its length.

FROM DAWSON CREEK TO FORT NELSON *483km/300mi*

The Alaska Highway begins at **Dawson Creek**, BC, in the region of the Peace River. The rural nature of the area is immediately striking: green and gold patches of wheat, barley and other crops, neatly laid out in grid patterns. The descent into the river valley is lengthy and somewhat winding. At **Taylor**, which sits on a vast natural gas and oil field, the river is crossed. Gas processing plants can be seen along the highway and oil pipelines run beneath fields of crops all the way to **Fort St. John**.

★★**W.A.C. Bennett Dam** – *Excursion: 1 day. 236km/146mi round-trip from Fort St. John via Hwy. 29. 11km/7mi north of Fort St. John, take Hwy. 29 to Hudson's Hope, then Dam Access Rd. Caution: steep, winding roads. Speed limits indicated* *for dangerous curves.* Except for the steep inclines of valley ascent and descent, this is a pleasant drive through lovely farmland with several breathtaking **views**★★ of the Peace River.

The road follows the river valley, climbing above it to permit exquisite **views**★ of the flat-topped hills and fertile fields. The little village of **Hudson's Hope** was the site of one of Simon Fraser's trading posts and the place where Alexander Mackenzie began his portage around the Peace River Canyon on his epic trek to the West Coast. From the village the winding dam access road ascends into the mountains with views of snow-capped peaks ahead.

Built between 1963 and 1967, the enormous earth-filled dam wedges the upper end of the canyon, creating a reservoir, **Williston Lake**. Measuring 362km/225mi in length, the lake encompasses part of the valleys of the Parsnip and Finlay Rivers, which meet in the Rocky Mountain Trench and flow out eastward as the Peace River. The dam itself (183m/600ft high and 2km/1.25mi across) was constructed of glacial moraine deposited during the last Ice Age, 7km/4mi away from the old valley of the Peace River. In the post-glacial period, the river cut a new channel, the aforementioned canyon. Material that blocked the river's course about 15,000 years ago was used to reblock it when the present dam was built.

At present the project generates over 2,416,000kW of electricity—23 percent of the total electrical requirements for the province of British Columbia.

★**G. M. Shrum Generating Station** – *Open late May–mid-Oct daily 9am–6pm. Rest of the year by appointment only.* ✗ ♿ ☎*250-783-5048.* The tour begins at the **visitor centre**, which houses several interactive exhibits on electricity, waterwheels, magnets and motors. A film *(10min)* on the history of the site and building of the dam follows. Then visitors descend by bus to the powerhouse, 152m/500ft underground and hewn out of solid rock *(visit by 1hr guided tour only, daily 9:30am–4:30pm).* At the manifold chamber, water surges from the turbines into the tailrace discharge tunnel. Explanatory diagrams are installed at each tour stop.

West Side Lookout – *3km/2mi across dam. Steep road.* This viewpoint affords good views of Williston Lake and the spillway. Part of the canyon of the Peace River is visible with the reservoir of the smaller Peace Canyon Dam downstream.

★**Peace Canyon Dam** – *8km/5mi south of Hudson's Hope, on Hwy. 29. Visitor centre open May–Labour Day daily 8am–4pm. Rest of the year Mon–Fri 8am–4pm.* ♿ ☎*250-783-9943.* Located 23km/14mi downstream, the Peace Canyon Dam reuses water from the larger W.A.C. Bennett Dam to generate additional electricity. The 200 tonne/220 ton turbine runners (or waterwheels) were manufactured in Russia and the generators in Japan. Visitors can view the powerhouse and the control room. The observation deck and walkway over the dam provide good **views**.

Practical Information

Driving the Highway – *(Driver's license and insurance requirements p 304.)* The Alaska Highway is either a paved or treated bituminous surface over most of its length. Travel on it is possible all months of the year. The period of thaw in spring can make driving conditions difficult some years, but highway advisories are broadcast promptly. Service stations able to perform repairs are situated at regular intervals; however, vehicles should be in good mechanical condition before starting out. The speed limit varies from 50km/h (30mph) to 100km/h (60mph); watch posted signs. Headlights should be kept on at all times. For the latest road conditions, ☎604-299-9000, then press 7623 (British Columbia); ☎867-667-8215 (Yukon); or contact the nearest tourist office *(pp 34-35).*

Distances are marked by kilometre posts and measured from Dawson Creek, BC. For example, Watson Lake is at km 1,017/mi 632. **Historical miles** are measurements originally used in the 1940s by lodgings along the route. Although inaccurate now, these readings are traditionally employed by businesses as indicators of their location.

Accommodations and Visitor Information – A most helpful annually updated publication is *The Milepost*, which describes natural and historical sights, eating establishments and overnight accommodations mile by mile. This book may be purchased from Vernon Publications, Inc., 3000 Northup Way, Suite 200, Bellevue, WA 98004 ☎800-726-4707 (Canada/US).

Many tourists stay in campgrounds provided by the governments of the Yukon and British Columbia. There are, however, motels and other accommodations.

After the junction with Highway 29, the Alaska Highway passes through flat an heavily wooded country that gradually becomes more mountainous. There is lovely **view★** of the Rockies at KM 314/mi 195, across the Minaker River Valley These views continue through heavy forest until the road reaches **Fort Nelson**, lumber centre and base for oil and gas exploration. The Liard Highway to Fo Simpson (Northwest Territories) via Fort Liard commences at this point, offerin access to spectacular Nahanni National Park Reserve *(p 296)*.

★★FROM FORT NELSON TO WHITEHORSE

991km/616mi (not including excursion)

After leaving Fort Nelson the highway turns west and offers many sweeping view of the mountains as the road traverses the end of the Rocky Mountains. Th country is very open and during the initial part of the drive, the mountains ar largely flat topped, more akin to the "mesa" mountains of the Southern Rockie in the US than to the pointed peaks of the Banff-Jasper area.

★**Stone Mountain Provincial Park** – *KM 627/mi 389. Open daily mid-May–Oct.* ⚠ *www.elp.gov.bc.ca/bcparks ☎250-787-3407.* A rocky and barren area resemblin a stone quarry, this park is named for a mountain to the north of the highway The mountains at this point are more rugged than previously. The highlight of th park is **Summit Lake★**, a lovely green-coloured stretch of water lying beside th highway.

After leaving the lake behind, the road passes through the rocky gorge of Mac donald Creek.

★★**Muncho Lake Provincial Park** – *KM 688/mi 427. Open daily mid-May–Oct.* ⚠ *www.elp.gov.bc.ca/bcparks ☎250-787-3407.* This park is one of the most beau tiful parts of the drive. At first the road follows the valley of the Toad River, a wide, rocky and rather desolate area softened only by the pale green colour of the river. The vista widens ahead, and more mountains come into view, many snow capped. Stone sheep can often be seen licking salt from the road bed. Reached after entering the park *(46km/29mi)*, **Muncho Lake★★** mirrors the surrounding folded mountains that rise over 2,000m/7,000ft. Its aquamarine colour is attri buted to copper oxide.

At KM 788/mi 490 the **Liard River** is first glimpsed. Rising in the Yukon, this wild and turbulent river flows south into British Columbia and finally north again into the Northwest Territories to join the Mackenzie River. Its valley marks the north ern limit of the Rocky Mountains. The highway follows the river for approximately 240km/150mi, providing some good views.

★**Liard River Hot Springs Park** – *KM 765/mi 478. Take side road on right to parking area; follow boardwalk. Open year-round. Changing rooms provided.* ⚠ *www.elp.gov.bc.ca/bcparks ☎250-787-3407.* This small park consists of large, hot sulphur pools (temperature averages 42°C/107°F) in natural surroundings, deep enough for swimming.

At KM 947/mi 588 the highway crosses the 60th parallel, entering the Yukon Ter ritory. The exit from British Columbia is not yet final, however, as the highway crosses and recrosses the boundary several times. Travellers along this road are rewarded with fine views of the **Cassiar Mountains**.

Watson Lake – *KM 1,016/mi 632.* This transportation and communications centre for southern Yukon is famous for its collection of **signposts** *(illustration p 300)*. In 1942 a homesick soldier, employed in the highway's construction, erected a sign with the name of his hometown and its direction. Tourists have kept up the tra dition. Today over 29,000 signs from all over the continent and abroad line the highway through town.

From the south the **Stewart-Cassiar Highway** (Route 37) joins the Alaska Highway at KM 1,044/mi 649. Winding 800km/500mi through western British Columbia, this road provides an alternative route to the Yukon. After this junction the Alaska Highway begins to cross the Cassiar Mountains, with pretty views of snow-capped peaks on both sides of the road.

At KM 1,162/mi 722 a rise of land is traversed that marks the divide between two great river systems, the Mackenzie and the Yukon, which empty into the Beaufort and Bering Seas respectively.

Teslin Lake – *KM 1,290/mi 802.* The name of this stretch of water means "long lake" in local Indian dialect. The highway crosses Nisutlin Bay and hugs the shore of this long narrow lake for about 48km/30mi. Frequently the mountains and lake are bordered by clusters of the Yukon's adopted emblem, the pinkish purple flower called **fireweed**, common throughout the Yukon and British Columbia. At the head of the lake, the road crosses the Teslin River by a high bridge, a remnant of the days when river steamers carried traffic in this area and needed clearance under bridges.

Teslin – *KM 1,294/mi 804.* This tiny town is the home of the **George Johnston Museum**, which contains native dress and artifacts *(open mid-May–Aug daily 9am–6pm; $2.50; ♿ ☎867-390-2550)*. Featured are the black-and-white **photographs** by Johnston (1884-1972) of his fellow Tlingit (KLING-it) Indians during the early 1900s.

★**Atlin** – *Excursion: 196km/122mi round-trip from Jake's Corner at KM 1,392/mi 865; take road south. This is a fairly isolated drive on unpaved road. Visitor centre (in the Atlin Museum, 3rd & Trainor Sts.) open mid-May–mid-Sept daily 10am–6pm. ☎250-651-7522.* An old gold-mining town, the small community of Atlin in British Columbia has a pretty **site**★ overlooking a beautiful lake of the same name, backed by majestic snow-covered peaks. From Warm Bay Road **Llewellyn Glacier** can be seen beyond Atlin Lake on a clear day.

★**Marsh Lake** – *KM 1,428/mi 887.* Surrounded by mountains, this beautiful blue-green lake is really an arm of the much larger **Tagish Lake** to the south, and therefore part of the Yukon River system. Because of its proximity to Whitehorse, the lake is not as deserted as others passed on the highway; many houses can be seen along its edge. The road follows the lake for about 16km/10mi, with several lovely viewpoints. At the end of the lake, the road then crosses the Yukon River at a dam.

At KM 1,445/mi 898 there is a good **view**★ from above of the steep, white cliffs and clear green water of the fabled **Yukon River**, which rises only 24km/15mi from the Pacific Ocean and meanders nearly 3,200km/2,000mi, crossing the Arctic Circle before it finally jettisons its waters into the Bering Sea.

★**Whitehorse** – *KM 1,474/mi 916. Description p 88.*

★★**From Whitehorse to Alaska Border (Alaska Highway)** – *491km/305mi. Description (in opposite direction) p 93.*

The CARIBOO★

British Columbia

Map of Principal Sights p 2

The Cariboo is the name given to the region in the valley of the Fraser River north of the Thompson River. Part of the central plateau of British Columbia, this region is a vast rolling plain of low arid hills, lakes and sagebrush, bounded to the east by the Cariboo Mountains—from which the area gets its name—and to the west, by the Coast Mountains.

Historical Notes

The Cariboo Gold Rush – Opened by fur traders, the Cariboo first reached prominence with the Gold Rush of 1861, which led to the building of the Cariboo Road. Gold was first found in this area in 1859 by prospectors who had made their way from California to the lower Fraser and then north, following the gold trail. By 1862 large quantities were being extracted from the upper part of Williams Creek when **Billy Barker**, a Cornish sailor who had jumped ship at Victoria to try his luck, hit pay dirt in its lower reaches. Within 48 hours he had extracted $1,000 worth of gold. The area boomed and towns such as Barkerville (named for Billy), Camerontown and Richfield sprang up.
Ten years after the first discovery, no more gold could be found, and the towns of the Cariboo were almost deserted. In Williams Creek alone more than $50 million worth of gold had been extracted. Barkerville was inhabited until 1958, when the provincial government transformed the site into a museum-town, carefully restoring it to its former splendour.

Cattle Country – Once the gold was gone, the miners left and farmers moved in. Today the main economic activity is cattle raising; some of the largest ranches in Canada are found in this region. The centre of the area is **Williams Lake**, which holds an annual stampede—considered the premier rodeo of the province—in the first week of July. Cowboys come from all over North America to vie for trophies. The largest stockyards of British Columbia are located in Williams Lake. A popular tourist area, the region is known for its sports fishing, game hunting, dude ranches and other traditional features of "Western" living, and for the restored Gold Rush town of **Barkerville**.

The Cariboo Road – To facilitate transportation to the boom towns of the gold discovery, the government of British Columbia (the province was created in 1858) decided to build a wagon road to Barkerville from the lower Fraser River near Yale, some 650km/403mi. Following the wild rocky canyon of the Fraser, the road, opened in 1864, was the remarkable engineering achievement of Royal Engineers from Britain, army engineers and private contractors. Over much of the route, solid rock had to be blasted. The old road has since been replaced by the Trans-Canada Highway, the Cariboo Highway (97) and Highway 26.

The **drive★** *(Hwy. 97 north, then Hwy. 26)* from Quesnel to Barkerville penetrates th Cariboo Mountains, passing **Cottonwood House** *(open May–Labour Day daily 8am–5pm rest of Sept 10am–4pm; $2; ✗♿ ☎250-992-3997)*, one of the few remaining roa houses on the old wagon road, and **Wells**, a mining community.

★★BARKERVILLE HISTORIC TOWN

90km/56mi east of Quesnel by Hwy. 26.

The old gold mining centre has a fine **site★** in the valley of Williams Creek, sur rounded by mountains. The restored buildings of Barkerville include the stores hotels, saloons and assay office of a mining community.

Visit – Kids *Open May–Sept daily 8am–8pm. Rest of the year daily dawn–dusk $5.50 ✗♿ ☎250-994-3332.* In the **visitor centre** the interesting video shows *(show regularly in summer)* and displays on the town, the Gold Rush and methods o mining are a good introduction. Note the rather unusually shaped **St. Saviour Anglican Church**, a structure of whipsawn timber and square nails. At the far end o the street is the Chinese section with its **Chinese Freemasons' Hall** (the Chinese fo lowed the other gold rushers north from California, but tended to stay within thei own community). **Billy Barker's claim** is marked, and the **Theatre Royal** stages typica Gold-Rush-era shows *(mid-May–Labour Day Sat–Thu 1pm & 4pm; additional show weekends 8pm; $8; reservations suggested; ✗♿ ☎250-994-3232). Visitors ca also pan for gold in the Eldorado Mine ($3.50).*

A dramatized sketch of **Judge Baillie Begbie** is performed *(mid-Jun–Sept daily 11am 2pm & 3pm)* in the Richfield Courthouse *(1.6km/1mi walk up Williams Creek)* Begbie was the famous Cariboo judge who enforced law and order in an unrul community.

DAWSON CITY★★

Yukon Territory

Population 1,287

Map of Principal Sights p 2

Tourist Office ☎867-993-5575

Set on a dramatic **site★** on the east bank of the wide Yukon at its confluence with the Klondike, this historic frontier town—the heart of the Gold Rush—is truly a delight. Remarkably like a Western movie set, the former destination of thousands of fortune seekers retains its unpaved streets, pedestrian boardwalks and false facades, which enhance the feeling of a bygone era.

Historical Notes

The Great Stampede – On August 16, 1896, **George Carmack** and his Indian brothers-in-law, Skookum Jim and Tagish Charlie, found gold on **Bonanza Creek**, a tiny stream emptying into the bigger **Klondike River**, itself a tributary of the mighty Yukon. When news of their find reached the outside world, an estimated 100,000 people left their homes as far away as Australia to begin the long, arduous trek to Dawson City, the town that sprang up at the mouth of the Klondike. Stories of their travels are legion. Many never made it; of those who did, few made a fortune.

The Routes of '98 – There were several routes to Dawson City during the Gold Rush. The longest, yet easiest, was by sea to the mouth of the Yukon and then by riverboat the 2,092km/1,300mi upstream to the city of gold. But this passage was only for the rich. A few people tried an overland course from Edmonton, Alberta, through almost impassable muskeg and bush, following more or less the present-day route of the Alaska Highway. The majority, however, sailed up the Pacific Coast via the Inside Passage to Skagway or Dyea, tiny way stations on the Alaska Panhandle, and trudged into the Yukon across the Coast Mountains.

Home of the Klondike – Soon after the discovery the whole area near Bonanza Creek was staked by prospectors. Instead of making a claim, a trader named **Joe Ladue** laid out a townsite on the level swampland at the mouth of the Klondike, amassing a fortune from his foresight. Lots were soon selling for as much as $5,000 a front foot on the main street. The heyday of Dawson was under way. Prices were skyhigh: eggs $1.00 each, nails $8.00 a pound; but everything was available, from the latest Paris fashions to the best wines and foods. At more saloons than one could visit in a night, drinks were normally paid for in gold dust.

Dawson had a unique feature: despite being the biggest and richest of all the mining boom towns, it was the most law-abiding. The North West Mounted Police maintained tight control. Everything was closed down on Sundays. No one carried a gun except the police. Offenders were given a "blue ticket" (i.e., run out of town).

E.A. Hegg/Yukon Archives

Dawson City (c.1898)

Decline and Revival – The heyday was short-lived. By 1904 the rich **placer** fields were exhausted: $100 million in gold had been shipped out. Complicated machinery was needed to exploit any gold that remained. People left; the glamour departed. The age of the giant dredges began, and Dawson became a company town.

Once the largest Canadian city (pop. 30,000) west of Winnipeg, Dawson City maintained its preeminence until World War II when Whitehorse—connected to the outside world by road (Alaska Highway), rail and air—took over, growing as Dawson shrank. In 1953 Whitehorse was made the capital of the Yukon. With this blow and the end of commercial gold mining in 1966, Dawson might have become a ghost town were it not for the tourist boom that is reviving the city. People still make a living mining the creeks, but little gold is found in comparison to the $22 million discovered in 1900.

The year-round population of just over 1,000 swells in summertime with the arrival of tourists and seasonal residents. Situated less than 300km/200mi south of the Arctic Circle on fertile soil untouched by the last Ice Age, Dawson enjoys hot summers with nearly 24 hours of daylight. Vegetables are cultivated in gardens, and flowers sprout through cracks along the streets. Many old buildings tell the story of a grandeur and wealth seen nowhere else so far north. Some sag sideways, however, because of permafrost. The Canadian government has embarked on a substantial restoration project that is returning the town to some of its former splendour.

Festivities – Two important dates for tourists in Dawson are: June 21 when the midnight sun barely dips down behind the Ogilvie Mountains, and the third weekend in August when the anniversary of **Discovery Day** is celebrated with a parade, raft races on the Klondike River and other activities.

Visiting Dawson City – Since Dawson's sights and tourist activities are numerous, it is best to first stop at the visitor centre *(Front & King Sts.; open mid-May–mid-Sept daily 8am–8pm; ♿ ☎867-993-5566)* for a schedule of events and guided tours as well as a map. Informative audiovisuals and displays are also in the centre. Sights that can be visited by guided tour only *(mid-Jun–mid-Aug daily 10:30am & 1pm; late May–early Jun & late Aug–early Sept daily 1pm; 1hr 30min; $5)* are indicated below by *"(guided tour)."* Historic buildings not open to the public usually have a window display [indicated (wd) below] depicting the structure's history.

★★DOWNTOWN *2 days*

Laid out in a grid pattern, this town lies in the shadow of the huge hill known as the Midnight Dome, easily visible from downtown. On its face is **Moosehide Slide**, a natural landslide—thought to be the result of an underground spring—which has been less of a threat to the community than floods and fires.

On **Front Street** (also called First Avenue) stands the **SS Keno**, a sternwheeler once used to transport silver, lead and zinc on the Stewart River from the mines in the Mayo district *(p 92)*. Built in Whitehorse in 1922, the steamer also made trips to Dawson. After its last voyage in 1960, it was permanently dry-docked there. Because damage was extensive, the flood of 1979 led to the building of a sand/gravel dike along the riverbank where the steamers once docked. Next to the *Keno* is the former **Canadian Imperial Bank of Commerce**, a stately building with a pressed-tin facade made to imitate stone. The plaque on the exterior refers to its famous teller Robert Service.

The former **British North American Bank** *(guided tour)*, with its handsome polishe wood teller enclosure, occupies the corner of Queen Street and 2nd Avenue. Th **assay office** contains a wide sampling of instruments used to weigh Klondike golc South on 2nd Avenue is **Ruby's Place** *(wd)*, one of several restored town building: At Princess Street and 3rd, the renovated **Harrington's Store** *(open Jun–Labour Da daily 11am–5pm)*, built in 1900, contains the comprehensive photo exhibi *Dawson As They Saw It*. Across the street is **Billy Bigg's** blacksmith shop *(wd)* an north on 3rd, note the **KTM Building** *(wd)*, which served as a warehouse for th Klondike Thawing Machine Co. in 1912.

Formerly a Carnegie Library, the Neoclassical **Masonic Temple** corners 4th and Queer while diagonally across the street is **Diamond Tooth Gertie's** Gambling Hall. Named fc a notorious female resident, this establishment boasts a legalized casino *(floc shows May–Sept nightly from 7pm; $5; ✗ ♿)*. Behind Gertie's is the colourful **Fir Hall**, which also contains city offices.

Back on 3rd Avenue are the **Dawson Daily News** (1898-1953) *(wd)*, and **Madame Trem blay's Store** *(wd)*, restored to its 1913 appearance. Opposite, a clapboard buildin with a squat tower houses the original 1900 **Post Office** *(open Jun–Labour Day dail noon–6pm)*, designed by Englishman **Thomas W. Fuller**, who served as Canada's chie architect for 15 years, influencing the country's federal architecture in particular He also designed the Government House and the Old Territorial Administratio Building *(below)*. Across King Street stands a replica of the **Palace Grand Theatre**★ *(guided tour)*, a distinctive pinewood structure with an elaborate false front. Buil in 1899 by "Arizona Charlie" Meadows, the original theatre offered everythin from opera to Wild West shows. Draped with Old Glory and Union Jacks, th colourful two-tiered, U-shaped interior seats audiences in rows of padded "kitcher chairs." *Gaslight Follies*, turn-of-the-century vaudeville and melodrama, plays nightly except Tuesdays *(May–Sept 8pm; $15-$17; ♿; for reservations ☎ 867-993-5575)*.

On Harper Street between 2nd and 3rd Avenues is a photographer's favourite: the delapidated **Old Guns and Ammunition Shop**, victim to permafrost action. One street over is aptly named Church Street, site of the clapboard **St. Paul's Anglican Church** built in 1902 with money collected from miners in the creeks.

Southward, double-porticoed **Government House**, where the Yukon's commissioner, or governor, lived in the early 1900s, overlooks Front Street. Designed by T.W. Fuller, the original residence had a more ornate exterior than the present structure, a replacement after a house fire in 1906. The house and grounds, once abundant with flowers, were the centre of Dawson's social life—host to afternoon teas, dinner receptions and summer garden parties. To the rear are the remains of **Fort Herchmer** *(grounds open to the public)*, a former North West Mounted Police barracks: married quarters, stables, jail and commanding officer's residence. The renovated St. Andrews **Presbyterian Manse** stands behind **St. Andrews Church**, at 4th Avenue.

ADDITIONAL SIGHTS

★ **Dawson City Museum** – *5th Ave. Open May–Sept daily 10am–6pm. Rest of the year by appointment. $4. ✗ ☎ 867-993-5291.* Dominating the upper section of 5th Avenue, the impressive Old Territorial Administration Building (1901, T.W. Fuller), in Neoclassical style, houses the museum. The South Gallery has exhibits and re-creations of Dawson's Gold Rush; the North Gallery features early-20C city life in Dawson City. Locomotives of the short-lived Klondike Mines Railway are on display in an outdoor shelter.

Robert Service Cabin – *8th Ave. at Hanson St.* Overlooking the town from the southeast is a small log cabin with moose antlers over the door—the residence from 1909 to 1912 of the "poet of the Yukon" (1874-1958). Here he wrote his only novel, *The Trail of '98* and his last Yukon verses, *Rhymes of a Rolling Stone*. Though he arrived in Dawson shortly after the Gold Rush, his poetry—*Songs of a Sourdough* in particular—vividly re-creates the atmosphere of the times. Outdoor **recitals** *(1hr)* of his poems are presented on the grounds *(Jun–Aug daily 9am–5pm; $6; ♿)*.

Jack London Interpretive Centre – *8th Ave. at Firth St.* The cabin of another writer who spent time in Dawson City during its heyday, American author **Jack London** (1876-1916), has been reconstructed on the property. His stories of the North, *Call of the Wild, White Fang* and *Burning Daylight* are among his best-known works. The adjacent centre *(open May–Sept daily 10am–6pm; $2; www.dawsoncity.com ☎ 867-993-5575)* houses a photo exhibit of London's life in the Klondike and of the mid-1960s search for his original cabin, found in the vicinity of Henderson Creek, some 73km/45mi south of Dawson City. There are also **readings** *(30min)* of his works *(twice daily)*.

EXCURSIONS

Midnight Dome – *9km/5mi by Dome Rd., a steep, winding road.* So named because of the midnight sun visible here on June 21, this mountain rises 884m/2,900ft behind the townsite. From the summit the **view**★★ is splendid, day or night. Below lies Dawson at the junction of the Yukon and Klondike Rivers—the Yukon weaving its way south to north, wide and muddy; the Klondike making a clear streak that is absorbed as it enters the Yukon. Even Bonanza Creek can be seen entering the Klondike. The devastation of the whole area caused by the dredges is evident. There are mountains in all directions; to the north, the Ogilvie Mountains are particularly impressive.

★★ **Bonanza Creek** – *4km/2.5mi by Klondike Hwy. from town to Bonanza Creek Rd. Unpaved road, maintained for 16km/10mi.* The road along Bonanza Creek winds through huge piles of **tailings**, or washed gravel refuse, left by the mining dredges. Large-scale mining activity still takes place here and throughout the Klondike today. The largest remnant of earlier mining equiment is **No. 4 dredge** *($5; tickets available from on-site visitor centre)* on Claim 17BD. (Claims of 152m/500ft were staked out and numbered in relation to the discovery claim: 17BD means 17 claims below, or downstream of, discovery; 7AD means 7 claims above discovery.) An enormous wooden-hulled, bucket-lined machine, the dredge consists of four basic parts *(shown in the exhibit panels)*: a barge for flotation; a series of steel buckets to excavate the gravel in front of the barge and to deliver it to the barge's housing; the housing itself where gravel was washed with water and the gold recovered; and a conveyor or stacker to disgorge barren gravel behind the barge, creating tailings.

Signs designate a claim provided by the Klondike Visitors Assn. for enterprising visitors who wish to **pan for gold** *(for details ☎867-993-5575).*

A simple plaque marks the place where the Klondike Stampede began: **Discovery Claim** itself *(14.5km/9mi from junction with Klondike Hwy.).* Farther on *(19km/12mi from junction)*, Eldorado Creek joins Bonanza. Some of the richest claims were located on Eldorado and the community at the junction, Grand Forks, was once a thriving place. Today nothing remains.

Bear Creek – *13km/8mi by Klondike Hwy. from town to Bear Creek Rd. Visit by guided tour (1hr) only, late May–early Sept daily 2pm & 3pm. $5. ☎867-993-7237.* Closed by the Yukon Consolidated Gold Co. in 1966, this sizeable compound was once a busy community of over 2,000 workers engaged in the maintenance of a fleet of dredges. The visit includes the cavernous machine shop and the orderly **gold room**, where each step in the refining process is clearly described. An archival film *(11min)* closes the tour.

FORT ST. JAMES★

British Columbia

Population 2,046

Map of Principal Sights p 2

In a lovely setting beside Stuart Lake, this town, 154km/96mi northwest of Prince George, is one of the oldest settlements in British Columbia. Simon Fraser founded a trading post here in 1806 that became the chief Hudson's Bay Company post in New Caledonia *(p 33)* after 1821. It remained in operation until 1971.

SIGHT

★ **Fort St. James National Historic Site** – *Beside lake in town. Open mid-May–Sept daily 9am–5pm. $4. ☎250-996-7191.* The park contains five restored Hudson's Bay Company buildings that date from 1884 to 1889. The **men's house**, trading store and officers' dwelling with their meticulously stored furnishings can be visited. Built off the ground, the **fish cache** with its displays of dried fish and pork and the dove-tailed log **general warehouse** with its fur store can also be seen. The visitor centre has displays on the fort's history.

■ Billy Miner, who gained notoriety as the robber of Canadian Pacific Railway's Transcontinental Express, took up residence in Canada in 1904. Known for his courtesy during a holdup, the American bandit is believed to have originated the command, "Hands up!"

FRASER and THOMPSON CANYONS★★

British Columbia

Map of Principal Sights p 2

Between the city of Vancouver and Shuswap Lake, the Trans-Canada Highway follow deep valleys, cut by two of the wildest rivers in the province, through the rocky Coa Mountains and the dry, hilly scrubland of central British Columbia.

Historical Notes – Alexander Mackenzie was the first European to see the Frase River. On his epic journey to the Pacific in 1793, he followed its northern course. Hi partner in the North West Company, Simon Fraser, descended and reascended th river's entire length in 1808, traversing on foot along rock ledges and down ladder slung over rockfaces by the Indians. Fraser gave the river his name and that of Davi Thompson, geographer and another North Westerner, to its major tributary.
Too wild for a fur-trading route, the Fraser was little used until gold was discovere at **Hill's Bar** near Yale in 1858. Much of the metal was found in the ensuing rush, bu the major strike occurred in the then-inaccessible Cariboo farther north. Above Yal the river was too turbulent for steamboat passage (a few boats were winched throug Hell's Gate, but a permanent water route was impossible). To solve the dilemma, th Cariboo Road was built, the section through the Fraser Canyon taking two years t construct.
The Fraser and Thompson Canyons were again selected in the 19C for another sub stantial transportation venture: the Canadian Pacific Railway. The 20C has seen thi once near-impassable passage become a major artery—now traversed by a seconc railway and the Trans-Canada Highway.

★★1 FRASER CANYON – From Hope to Lytton

109km/68mi (not including excursion). Map p 49.

★**Hope** – The mountains close in around this community as the valley narrows anc swings northwards. The wildness and unpredictability of the region were wel demonstrated by the **Hope Slide** of 1965. One January day an immense amount o rock from Johnson Peak *(21km/13mi east by Rte. 3)* slid into the valley, filling a lake and forcing its waters up the other side. Route 3 had to be rebuilt more thar 45m/148ft above its original level.

Manning Provincial Park – *Excursion: 52km/32mi round-trip from Hope by Rte. 3 east.* After entering **Manning Provincial Park**★ *(open year-round; hiking, horseback riding, bicycling, cross-country skiing; ⚠ ✗)*. Route 3 traverses an area called **Rhododendron Flats**, where these wild plants flower in profusion in mid-June and crosses **Allison Pass** (1,341m/4,400ft). This park is one of only two places in Canada where visitors can drive to extensive subalpine meadows *(Mt. Revelstoke p 47)*. In the **visitor centre** *(68km/42mi from Hope, just east of Manning Park Lodge; open Jun–Sept daily 8:30am–4:30pm; rest of the year Mon–Fri 8:30am–4pm; closed Dec 25; ♿ www.e/p.gov.b.ca/bcparks ☎250-840-8836)*, the three vegetation zones of the park are featured: the western slopes covered with the damp, dense growth of coastal British Columbia; the central area reflecting the transitional zone; and the eastern part with its dry and arid sagebrush country, so typical of the interior of the province.

After Hope, mountains close in abruptly and farmland is left behind. The river changes to a rushing torrent, and the road is often situated on high rocky ledges or lower, at river level.

★**Yale** – Surrounded by high and impressive cliffs, this tiny hamlet was once a town of 20,000. During the Gold Rush it was the terminus of river navigation and the beginning of the Cariboo Road.

Hill's Bar is located just to the south. To the north the most spectacular part of the **canyon**★★ begins. The cliffs are sheer, the valley narrow, tunnels are frequent, and the river below seethes along, around and over rocks. Just after Spuzzum the road crosses the river and continues on the east side.

★**Hell's Gate** – The canyon here is 180m/600ft deep, but the river, rushing past at 8m/25ft per second, is only 36m/120ft wide. The river was once wider, but during construction of the Canadian National Railway in 1914, a rockslide occurred, narrowing the gap. Thereafter, upstream passage was almost impossible for the salmon, their spawning grounds being the lakes and streams around Shuswap Lake. A sharp decline in the Pacific salmon fishing industry occurred until "fishways" were constructed between 1944 and 1946 to enable the salmon to bypass the turbulent water.
An **airtram** *(Apr–Oct daily 10am–4pm; $9.50; ✗ ♿ www.hellsgate.bc.ca ☎604-867-9277)* descends 150m/500ft to river level, where the canyon and the incredible speed of the water can be appreciated. There are displays on the salmon and the fishways as well as a film *(20min)*. The fishways are visible in the river, but because the water is murky, salmon are rarely seen except in September and October when the water's depth is lower.

Pacific Salmon

■ Every summer and autumn British Columbia's five salmon species—sockeye, pink, coho, chinook and chum—leave the ocean and swim far inland up the province's rivers and streams to spawn. In none are their numbers greater than in the Fraser River, where they travel as far as 48km/30mi a day. Soon after spawning, they die. Their offspring remain in fresh water for about two years before heading to the ocean, where they mature in two to five years. Then the epic return journey to their spawning grounds occurs.

After Hell's Gate the canyon becomes less dark and formidable, and there are more trees on its rocky slopes. From **Jackass Mountain** there is a fine **view★** of the canyon from high above the river, and at Cisco Creek two bridges can be seen as the railways switch sides.

Lytton – This community regularly registers the highest temperatures in Canada. Rather than the green pine trees of the lower Fraser Canyon, the vegetation is more the sagebrush of central British Columbia. At this point the clear blue waters of the Thompson River surge into the muddy brown Fraser, making a streak visible for a short distance downstream.

★★ 2 THOMPSON CANYON – From Lytton to Shuswap Lake

230km/143mi. Map p 49.

The Trans-Canada Highway and the two railways leave the valley of the Fraser and turn east along the Thompson, passing through a dry, treeless and steep-sided **canyon★★**. The road winds and weaves along, making sharp bends. Just before Spences Bridge, where the road crosses the river, the remains of a great landslide that occurred in 1905 can be seen.
Then the river **valley★** gradually widens into a semidesert area, where scrub vegetation and sagebrush predominate. Occasionally there is some cultivation of the terraces above the river, but only for irrigation. The remains of one such attempt can be seen 17km/11mi after Cache Creek at a place once called **Walhachin** ("abundance of the earth"). Between 1907 and 1914 a group of young British aristocrats built irrigation flumes to carry water to their fields, and for a while, the area flourished. World War I ended the experiment, as most of the men left to fight and were killed. Odd bits of flume and withered apple trees are all that remain.
Just before Savona the Thompson expands to form **Kamloops Lake**. From the Trans-Canada Highway there are some pleasant **views★** of this blue lake set in rocky arid hills. Again irrigation is bringing some of the land under cultivation. The highway bypasses the industrial city of **Kamloops** and follows the south branch of the Thompson to its headwaters in **Shuswap Lake.** Here the country changes from dry barrenness to verdant green with sparkling waters. Many salmon spawn in this region after their long swim up the turbulent Fraser and Thompson Rivers.

INSIDE PASSAGE★★

British Columbia

Map of Principal Sights p 2

This protected inland waterway, the result of past glaciation, cuts between the wildly indented northwest coast and the myriad islands that stretch from Puget Sound in Washington state to Skagway, Alaska—a total distance of 1,696km/1,060 statute mi. The portion of the route served by Canadian ferries extends from Port Hardy on the northern tip of Vancouver Island to Prince Rupert (507km/314mi), on the northwest coast of British Columbia, ushering visitors into a world of lush, tranquil beauty.

VISIT

Cruise – *Departs Port Hardy mid-May–mid-Oct every other day 7:30am, arrives Prince Rupert 10:30pm (odd-numbered days Jun, Jul & Sept; even-numbered days Aug). Weekly service rest of the year. Reservations required. One-way $318/car & driver plus $104 each adult passenger (summer rate). Check-in 1hr before sailing. ✕ ♿. BC Ferries, 1112 Fort St., Victoria, BC, V8V 4V2 ☎250-386-3431.* From Port Hardy the ferry crosses the open sea at Queen Charlotte Strait, then enters the sheltered waters of Fitz Hugh Sound. The remainder of this voyage through the narrow, spectacular Inside Passage offers close-up **views★★**, weather permitting, of islands to the west and the fjord-slashed coast of western British Columbia to the east. The low, mountainous terrain, densely forested in spruce and hemlock, drops steeply into the sea. Virtually uninhabited, the area retains only one sub stantial community, the town of Bella Bella, home to the native Heiltsuk. Severa abandoned cannery communities are passed during the cruise.

Eagles and sea birds, as well as such marine mammals as seals, dolphins, orca an humpback whales may be sighted during spring and fall migration. The highligh of the voyage comes near its northern end as the ferry enters the 40km/25mi **Gren ville Channel★★**. At its narrowest the channel measures only 549m/1,800ft across with a maximum depth of 377m/1,236ft.

The KOOTENAYS★

British Columbia

Map of Principal Sights p 2

A major tributary of the Columbia, the Kootenay River winds through the southeas corner of British Columbia—an area of mountains, beautiful lakes and lush valleys—giving the region its name. Rising in the Rockies, the Kootenay traverses its own national park, misses the headwaters of the Columbia by just over a kilometre at Cana Flats, flows south into the US, loops and returns to Canada to form Kootenay Lake and finally joins the Columbia at Castlegar.

At the south end of the lake, the valley around **Creston** is full of grainfields, orchards and other fruit-bearing plants. The **Crowsnest Pass** region has some of the largest soft-coal deposits in North America. Farther west, copper, lead, zinc and silver are minec and processed in the huge smelter at **Trail**.

Historical Notes – The first settlers came to the region in 1864 when gold nuggets were found in the valley of the Wild Horse River, a tributary of the Kootenay. At the junction of these rivers, a certain John Galbraith set up a ferry service, and the settlement that developed took the name Galbraith's Ferry. From New Westminister, the former capital of British Columbia, a road was pushed through the mountains to the site by a young English engineer, **Edgar Dewdney**. To this day the road (Route 3) bears his name. After the gold dwindled, settlers increasingly turned to farming and ranching. Land disputes with the Kootenay Indians resulted. A detachment of the North West Mounted Police was sent under the command of the famed Mountie **Sam Steele** (1849-1919). He restored peace and order to the settlement, which changed its name to Fort Steele to honour him and to mark the first posting of police west of the Rockies.

SIGHT

★**Fort Steele Heritage Town** – Kids *16km/10mi northeast of Cranbrook by Rte. 95. Open mid-May–mid-Oct daily 9:30am–dusk. Rest of the year daily dawn–dusk. $5.50. (summer) www.fortsteele.bc.ca ☎250-489-3351.* This former centre of a mining boom that brought prosperity to the Kootenays has a fine **site★** at the foot of the Rockies. The townsite has been re-created to represent a typical Kootenay community at the turn of the century.

The town of Fort Steele flourished in the early 1890s. Its death knell sounded when the railway over Crowsnest Pass bypassed the town, going instead to Cranbrook. In 1961 the provincial government began restoration of the practically deserted townsite. Today Fort Steele lives again.

Among the many restored buildings, the **museum**, set in an old hotel, is the most interesting, with excellent displays on the history of the region. The North West Mounted Police barracks can also be visited. Live entertainment is provided in the **Wildhorse Theatre** *(Jul–Aug Tue–Sun 2pm & 8pm; $8.50; ☎250-426-5682)*. An old steam locomotive offers rides *(20min; $4)* and there are stagecoach tours of the site. Overlooking the Kootenay River stands a large wooden waterwheel, once used to haul water out of the mines.

MONASHEES and SELKIRKS★★

British Columbia

Map p 48

Part of the Columbia Mountain System, the Monashee and Selkirk Ranges are located in southeastern British Columbia between the central plateau and the Rockies. Starting as rolling hills in the west, they soon develop sharp ridges, deep valleys and pyramid peaks—the results of heavy glaciation, especially in the Selkirks of Glacier National Park where several valley glaciers still exist. The Trans-Canada Highway crosses the two ranges by an often spectacular route through Eagle and Rogers Passes.

FROM SICAMOUS TO GOLDEN

Allow 6hrs. 219km/136mi by Trans-Canada Hwy.

★**Eagle Pass** – *71km/44mi from Sicamous to Revelstoke.* This pass through the Monashee Mountains (*Monashee* is a Gaelic word meaning "mountain of peace") was discovered by **Walter Moberly** in 1865. According to popular legend Moberly fired his gun at an eagle's nest and watched the birds fly away up a valley. Following them, he discovered the pass, henceforth known as Eagle Pass, which eventually became the chosen route for the Canadian Pacific Railway as well as the Trans-Canada Highway.

From the small town of **Sicamous**, set on the narrows between Shuswap and Mara Lakes, the Trans-Canada begins to climb the valley of the Eagle River. After 26km/16mi the highway reaches **Craigellachie**. On November 7, 1885, the last spike of the Canadian Pacific Railway, linking east and west, was driven here *(note the plaque erected beside the railway tracks off the road on the right). Craigellachie* is Gaelic and refers to the rallying point of the Grant clan in Scotland, a symbol well known to the Banffshire-born directors of the railway.

The highway rises more steeply and the valley narrows before the road reaches **Three Valley Gap**★ *(47km/29mi)*, occupying a lovely **site**★ beside Three Valley Lake, edged with sheer cliffs. Soon afterwards the road arrives at the top of the pass *(55km/34mi)*, and then begins a steep descent to the Columbia in the valley of Tonakwatla Creek.

★★**Revelstoke** – Set on the east bank of the Columbia River at its junction with the Illecillewaet, this small community has a picturesque **site**★ surrounded by mountains—the Selkirks to the east, the Monashees to the west. Named for **Lord Revelstoke**, head of the London banking firm of Barings, which financed completion of the Canadian Pacific Railway in 1885, the town has become a summer-winter sports centre because of its proximity to **Mt. Revelstoke National Park** *(hiking, fishing, skiing, cross-country skiing; open daily year-round; $4/day; http://fas.sfu.ca/parkscan ☎ 250-837-7500).*

Just to the north the **Revelstoke Dam** can be seen rising 175m/574ft above the Columbia River. A visitor centre *(4km/2.5mi north by Rte. 23; open mid-Jun–mid-Sept daily 8am–8pm; May–early Jun & late Sept–mid-Oct daily 9am–5pm; BC Hydro ♿ ☎ 250-837-6515)* features displays on its construction and a model of all Columbia River power projects.

★★**Mt. Revelstoke Summit Parkway** – *27km/16mi of gravel road, unsuitable for trailers. Begins on Trans-Can Hwy. 1.6km/1mi east of Revelstoke turnoff. 45min ascent.* This road ascends the southwest face of Mt. Revelstoke in a series of switchbacks. After 5.6km/3.5mi there is a **viewpoint**★ of the town of Revelstoke, spread out on the bank of the Columbia. The snowcapped twin peaks of Mt. Begbie dominate the Monashees, which backdrop the river. Just east of the town, the valley of Tonakwatla Creek is visible, cutting its way through the mountains.

At the summit the **view**★★ extends to the north. The Columbia's steep-walled valley and the glaciated mountains of the Clachnacudainn Range, with their jagged peaks and bare slopes, can be seen. A short distance from the parking area, a lookout tower has displays identifying the visible peaks. The vegetation has completely changed. Instead of the red cedars, hemlocks and spruce of the lower slopes, there are only stunted and wind-pruned firs. Paths at the summit descend into the **alpine meadows**, where multicoloured wild flowers abound in summer: Indian paintbrush (red), lupines (blue), arnica (yellow) and valerian (white).

★★**Rogers Pass** – *148km/92mi from Revelstoke to Golden.* After crossing the Rockies by Kicking Horse Pass, the Canadian Pacific Railway was supposed to follow the Columbia River loop *(map p 48)* because the Selkirks were considered an impenetrable barrier. In 1881 however, a determined surveyor, **Albert Rogers**, followed the Illecillewaet River into these same mountains and discovered the pass named for him. The railroad was routed this way, achieving a savings of 240km/150mi.

★★**From Rogers Pass to Golden** – *May be temporarily closed when avalanche control is underway. Winter travellers must follow instructions by park wardens.* The Trans-Canada Highway follows the high-walled valley of the Illecillewaet River into the Selkirks, and soon passes through snowsheds that provide winter

Provincial Archives of Alberta (B6011)

Snow Shed Construction (c.1903)

Avalanches – From the beginning, incredibly high snowfall in the Selkirks (annual average 940cm/370in) and avalanches were obstacles to construction through the pass. Since the steep slopes of the mountains had been worn smooth by previous slides, nothing blocked the path of new avalanches. Kilometres of snowsheds were constructed over the railway, but the yearly winter battle with the elements proved too costly for the Canadian Pacific. To avoid the most hazardous area, the Connaught Tunnel was built through Mt. Macdonald in 1916. For the next 40 years, the Rogers Pass section remained untouched.

In 1959 however, after surveys were conducted, the decision was made to extend the Trans-Canada Highway through the pass, using the original railway roadbed. The highway was completed in 1962 when the section through the pass, the most expensive and challenging segment, was finished. To double the track under Mt. Macdonald, a second railway tunnel, the longest in North America (over 14km/9mi), was opened in 1988.

An elaborate defence system is in place. Concrete snowsheds deflect slides over the road, while rubble barriers divert and break up dangerous falls. Rangers stationed high in the mountains monitor snow pile-up; a howitzer is fired to trigger avalanches before they become too large.

protection for the road. After 48km/30mi the highway enters **Glacier National Park** *(hiking, fishing, skiing, cross-country skiing; open daily year-round; $4/day; http://fas.sfu.ca/parkscan ☎ 250-837-7500)*. Ahead, the four pointed peaks of the **Sir Donald Range** are visible: *(left to right)* Avalanche Mountain, Eagle Peak, Uto Peak, and the great slanting slab of Mt. Sir Donald itself. To the north the steep pyramidal form of **Mt. Cheops** can be seen. To the south there are views of glaciers across the rocky and bounding Illecillewaet River.

The road swings around the Napoleon Spur of Mt. Cheops to reach the summit of the pass *(72km/45mi)*, where a double arch commemorates the completion of the highway in 1962. The **Rogers Pass Centre★** *(open May–Oct daily 8am–6pm; rest of the year daily 7am–5pm; $4; http://fas.sfu.ca/parkscan ☎ 250-837-7500)* has displays, models and films that explain the history of the pass and the annual battle against avalanches. The **view★** includes the slide-scarred peaks of **Mt. Tupper** and **The Hermit** to the north; the Asulkan Ridge and snowfields, including the Illecillewaet Glacier, to the south; and the peaks of the Sir Donald Range and Mt. Cheops.

The road begins its steep descent between the bare slopes of Mt. Tupper and The Hermit to the north and the looming form of **Mt. Macdonald**. Passing through a series of reinforced concrete snowsheds, it swings into the valley of the Beaver River, a tributary of the Columbia, which separates the spiky Selkirks from the more rounded Purcell Mountains. Then the road leaves the park, crosses the Columbia at the town of Donald and follows the river south to **Golden** in the Rocky Mountain Trench.

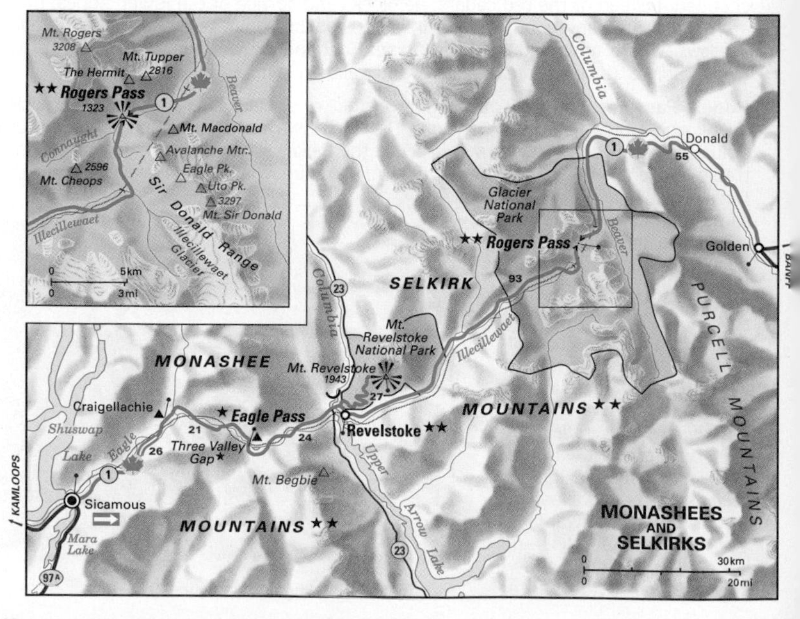

OKANAGAN VALLEY**

British Columbia

Map of Principal Sights p 2

An important fruit-growing and wine-making region, this valley in south central British Columbia consists of a large lake (Okanagan), several smaller lakes, and the river of the same name (south of the US border, it is spelled Okanogan). Combined with lots of sunshine, intensive use of lake water for irrigation has made apple, peach, plum, grape, cherry, apricot and pear growing possible in this area of low rainfall, arid hills and sagebrush. Beautiful lakes with sandy beaches have made the valley a popular resort.

FROM OSOYOOS TO VERNON

Allow 6hrs. 177km/110mi by Rte. 97. Map below.

* **Osoyoos** – This community lies on narrows in the middle of **Osoyoos Lake**. It is surrounded by arid hills and semidesert country where sagebrush, greasewood and cactus thrive, in sharp contrast to the green orchards on the lakeshore. **Anarchist Mountain** *(6km/4mi east by Rte. 3)* provides a fine **view**** of the area.

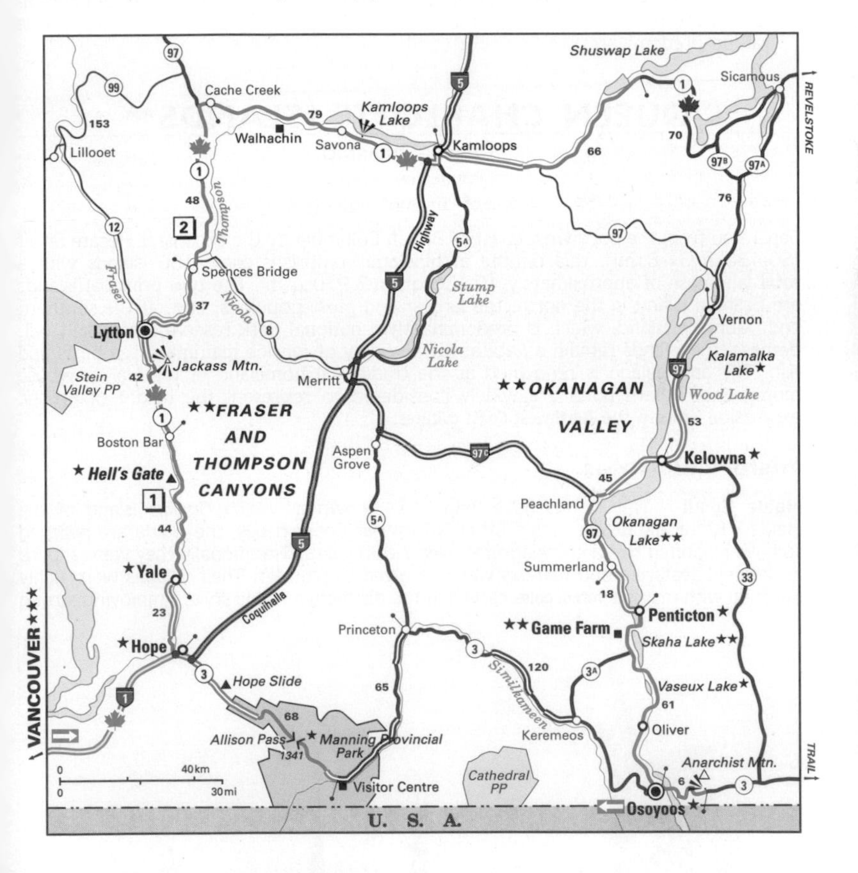

** **Route 97 to Penticton** – Through orchards and past fruit stands, Route 97 follows the Okanagan River to **Oliver**. As the road approaches **Vaseux Lake***, the scenery is impressive, with huge rocks and barren slopes. In contrast, the hills surrounding **Skaha Lake**** are sandy, covered with sagebrush and small trees. They offset the blue waters of this lovely lake.

** **Okanagan Game Farm** – Kids *8km/5mi south of Penticton. Open year-round daily 8am–dusk. $10.* ☎*250-497-5405.* Overlooking Skaha Lake, this pleasant zoo is set among the low, rolling hills and scrub vegetation typical of the area. A circular drive *(5km/3mi)* enables visitors to view the animals from all parts of the world.

* **Penticton** – A corruption of a Salish Indian word meaning "a place to live forever," Penticton has a pleasant **site*** on narrows between Okanagan Lake and Skaha Lake, surrounded by rolling hills. It is a tourist resort with attractive beaches and parks on both lakes. Beside Okanagan Lake lies the *SS Sicamous*, a stern-wheeler once used on the lake *(open Jun–Aug daily 9am–8pm; rest of the year Mon–Fri 9:30am–3:30pm; closed national holidays; $2; ☎250-4932-4055).*

★★ **Route 97 to Kelowna** – After leaving Penticton Route 97 borders **Okanagan Lake**★★ offering lovely views. Near Summerland steep, white cliffs stand beside the lake. The road then passes through terraces of orchards and vineyards supported by irrigation. Note the lovely contrast between the blue of the lake, the green orchards, and the semidesert sagebrush, rock and dry-soil hills.
The road follows the bend of the lake where, according to local Indian legend, the monster **Ogopogo** lives. Like his name, Ogopogo is supposed to look the same viewed from either end, but the descriptions of him are as varied as the people who claim to have spotted him. After Peachland the road climbs up above the lake, leaving it temporarily to pass through the orchards before Kelowna.

★ **Kelowna** – Route 97 crosses the narrows of Lake Okanagan to enter this town by a floating bridge, part of which can be raised to allow boats to pass. On this attractive **site**★ the town was founded by **Father Pandosy**, an Oblate priest who established a mission in 1859 and encouraged the settlers who followed him to cultivate the land. Today Kelowna is the marketing centre for the Okanagan Valley.

Route 97 to Vernon – After Kelowna the road skirts Wood Lake and winds along the eastern edge of **Kalamalka Lake**★, where the rolling hills, still rocky but greener than farther south, descend directly into the water. This change of terrain continues as the fruit-growing area is left behind. North of the town of Vernon cattle raising predominates.

QUEEN CHARLOTTE ISLANDS★★

British Columbia

Population 5,040

Map of Principal Sights p 2

Separated from the northwest coast of British Columbia by the expansive Hecate Strait (50-130km/31-81mi), this remote archipelago comprises some 150 islands with a total landmass of approximately 10,126sq km/3,910sq mi. The two principal islands are Graham Island in the north, the largest and most populous; and, at the southern end, Moresby Island, which is predominantly a national park reserve. Essentially wilderness, the islands remain a habitat for a variety of marine mammals, sea birds and fish. The archipelago is renowned as the traditional homeland of the Haida, whose monumental totem poles are widely considered to represent the height of artistic expression among the **Northwest Coast cultures**.

Historical Notes

Haida Gwaii – The islands have long been known as *Haida Gwaii*, "Island of the Haida." Ethnically distinct from other Northwest Coast tribes, the Haida are believed to have inhabited this archipelago for over 7,000 years. Traditionally they were superb craftsmen, seafarers and fearless warriors given to plunder. Their villages were richly adorned with massive **totem poles** carved in the distinctive Haida style. Employing strong

Canadian Museum of Civilization, photo 255

Haida Village, Skidegate (1878)

ovoid lines and animal motifs, the poles served different ceremonial and social purposes: house poles flanked doorways of clan longhouses; mortuary poles contained remains of important deceased villagers; memorial poles commemorated chiefs; heraldic poles recorded myths associated with a clan; and potlatch poles were raised during ceremonial feasts. The Haida were divided into two clans, Raven and Eagle, which were then subdivided into families. Kinship was traced matrilineally (through the mother's line).

European Contact – In 1774 Spanish navigator Juan Perez Hernandez was the first European to sight these islands while on an expedition north from California. In the 1780s and 90s, other Europeans sailed the Northwest Coast, bartering with natives for treasured sea otter pelts. George Dixon, a British trading captain, named the islands for **Queen Charlotte**, wife of King George III.

European contact introduced the Haida to iron tools that facilitated their wood carving. Larger, more elaborate totem poles were erected (some extant today) and more dugout canoes produced, allowing the Haida to trade and raid farther south. By the end of the 19C, however, Haida civilization was in decline: European diseases had decimated the population, and "pagan" potlatches and totem carving were halted as a result of missionary influence. By the early 20C most of the traditional villages were abandoned as the Haida relocated to Graham Island.

The Islands Today – Though located only 55km/34mi south of the Alaska Panhandle, the islands enjoy a temperate climate, thanks to the moderating effects of the warm Kuroshio Current. High annual rainfall and fertile soil support forests of Sitka spruce, hemlock and cedar. The southern third of the archipelago is a national park reserve that contains a World Heritage Site *(p 53)*. Year-round residents inhabit six communities on Graham Island and one on Moresby. Logging, fishing and tourism are major industries. A resurgence of Haida art and traditions, begun in the late 1950s, is evident today. Wood and argillite carvers, as well as silk-screen artists, are at work on Graham Island.

Practical Information

Getting There – **Air** service to Sandspit from Vancouver is provided daily by Canadian Regional Airlines ☎604-279-6611; to Masset daily from Prince Rupert by Harbour Air ☎250-627-1341. Car rentals (Budget Rent-a-Car) available at both airports ☎800-577-3228. Limousine service: Eagle Cab ☎250-559-4461. BC Ferries offers year-round **ferry** service between Prince Rupert and Skidegate *(late May–Sept 5-6 sailings/week, rest of the year 3 sailings/week; 8hrs; summer rates: $110/car & driver plus $23 each adult passenger; reservations required; for schedules & fares contact BC Ferries, 1112 Fort St., Victoria, BC, V8V 4V2 ☎250-386-3431)*. Another ferry service connects Skidegate to Alliford Bay *(departs year-round daily; 20min; $16/car & driver, $4.50 each adult passenger)*.

Accommodations and Visitor Information – A **guide** *($7.50)* about area history, attractions, parks, campsites and accommodations can be obtained from Observer Publishing Co., PO Box 205, Queen Charlotte, BC, V0T 1S0 ☎250-559-4680. B&Bs, full-service hotels, self-contained cottages and campgrounds offer a range of lodgings. For outfitters, kayaking tours and cruises contact Parks Canada, Box 37, Queen Charlotte, BC V0T 1S0 ☎250-559-8818 or Queen Charlotte Islands Chamber of Commerce, Box 448, Port Clements, BC, V0T 1S0.

GRAHAM ISLAND *Map p 52*

Largest of the Queen Charlottes, Graham Island is by far the most populated island. The majority of residents live in the small logging, fishing and administrative towns and Haida villages on the east side of the island. A continuation of the mainland's Yellowhead Highway, Highway 16 runs in a north–south direction along the east side of the island, between Queen Charlotte City and Masset.

Queen Charlotte City – This small town functions as the administrative heart of the islands. Catering to tourists from the mainland, many of whom arrive by ferry at nearby **Skidegate** (SKID-eh-get) **Landing**, the community centre consists of a line of hostelries, restaurants, gift shops and related services scattered along Skidegate Inlet.

★**Haida Gwaii Museum** – *1km/.6mi from ferry landing. Open Jun–Aug Mon–Fri 10am–5pm, weekends 1pm–5pm. Oct–Apr Mon & Wed–Fri 10am–noon & 1pm–5pm, Sat 1pm–5pm. May & Sept Mon–Fri 10am–noon & 1pm–5pm, Sat 1pm–5pm. $3. ♿ ☎250-559-4643.* Natural history exhibits and native artifacts, including argillite carvings and totem poles, are displayed in this museum.

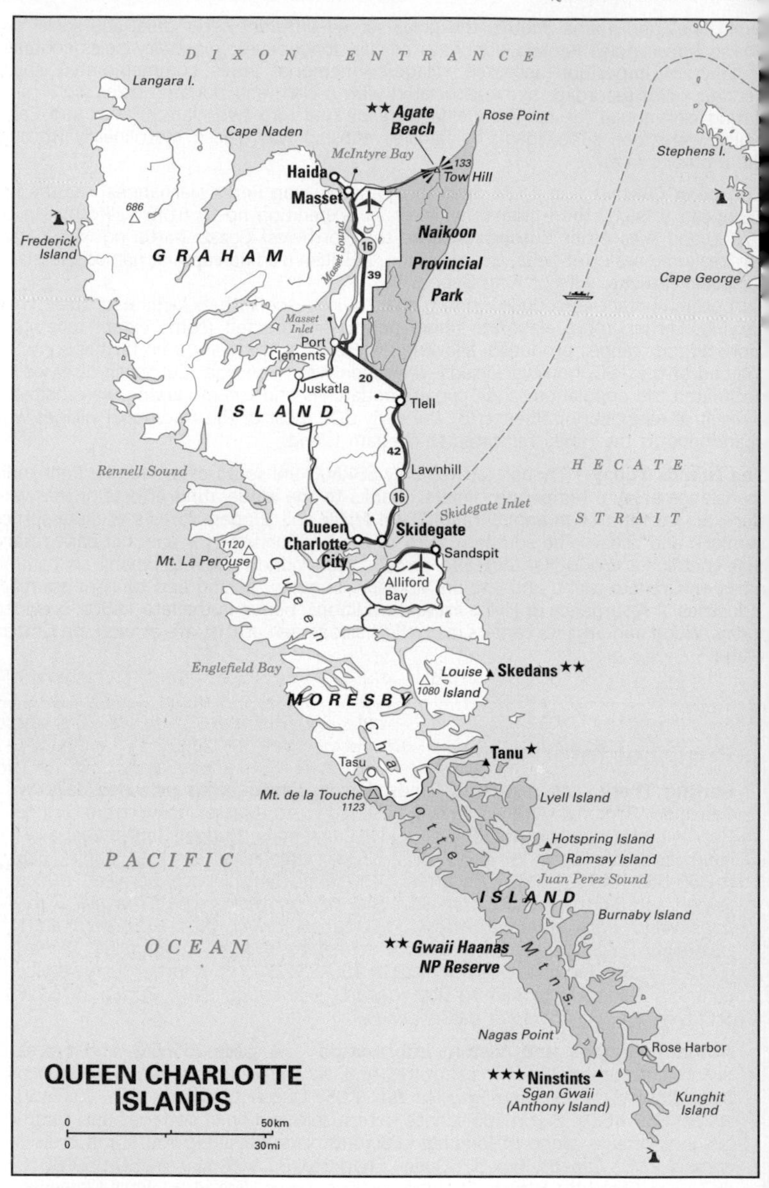

An adjacent shed *(open Mon–Fri 9am–4:30pm; Haida Gwaii Watchmen ☎ 250-559-8225)* houses the stunning **Loo Taas**, an ornate 15m/50ft hand-crafted dugout canoe produced in traditional Haida style for Expo '86 in Vancouver.
Nearby, a reproduction longhouse serves as the offices of the Haida Gwaii Watchmen.

Skidegate – *1.5 km/.9mi from ferry.* Facing Rooney Bay, this long-time Haida community, locally called "the Village," serves as a political and cultural centre of the present-day Haida Nation. The offices of the Skidegate Band Council are housed in an impressive reproduction of a cedar **longhouse**, painted with Haida motifs. Internationally known Haida artist **Bill Reid** created the elaborate frontal **totem pole★★**.

At the crossroads community of **Tlell**, the headquarters for Naikoon Provincial Park provides information on recreation and beach access *(open year-round daily 9am–4:30pm; ☎ 250-557-4390).*

Masset – Located on Masset Sound, near its entrance to the open waters of McIntyre Bay, this community is the islands' largest municipality, owing in part to the presence of the Canadian Forces station. The town attracts sports anglers and beachcombers interested in exploring the island's spectacular northern beaches.

★**Haida** – Adjacent to Masset, this town, also known as Old Massett, overlooks Masset Harbour. An important hub of Haida culture, the community boasts several totem poles erected in recent years. Note especially the one located in front of

St. John's Anglican Church by acclaimed Haida artist **Robert Davidson**. The works of Haida artists are sold in several village craftshops, including one whose exterior is painted with Haida designs and fronted by a finely carved totem pole by Davidson's brother, **Reg Davidson**.

Naikoon Provincial Park – *9km/6mi east of Masset. Unpaved, but well-maintained beach access road. Open year-round. Use fees in effect May–Sept. Park visitor centre in Tlell. Hiking, fishing, beachcombing.* ⚠. This 72,640ha/179,421 acre park encompasses the low-lying northeast corner of Graham Island, with broad beaches and dunes fronting both Hecate Strait (east) and Dixon Entrance (north). At **Agate Beach**★★ *(25km/15mi from Masset; public parking and beach access available at campground)*, beachcombers congregate to search for the elusive stones that give the beach its name. To the north is a parking area for **Tow Hill** *(26km/16mi)*, a forested basalt outcropping that rises 133m/436ft above the beach. An easy trail *(round-trip 1hr)* leads to the summit, affording **views**★ of the sweeping expanse of beach to the east and west. If weather permits, Alaska can be seen across the Dixon Entrance.

MORESBY ISLAND *Map p 52*

Rimmed with inlets, fjords and smaller islands, the second largest island in the archipelago forms the bulk of the Gwaii Haanas National Park Reserve. the southern three-fifths of Moresby is encompassed by the park. The island's only town, **Sandspit**, traditionally a logging community, has become an access point for kayakers and cruise passengers beginning a tour of the reserve.

Moresby Island has been periodically logged since the mid-20C. Beginning in the mid-1970s, a 10-year conflict between logging interests on the one hand, and Haida and environmentalists on the other, ultimately resulted in the creation of the park reserve. Scars of clear-cutting are still visible.

Forming the backbone of the island, the forested slopes of the Queen Charlotte Mountains (maximum elevation about 1,000m/3,300ft) often drop directly into the sea. Abundant rainfall has nourished impressive **rain forests**★★ of towering spruce and cedar, luxuriant ferns and mosses. Bald eagles are frequently sighted in this wilderness, as well as deer, otters and bears. Seals, sea lions, porpoises and orca whales can sometimes be seen. A variety of fish, including red snapper, salmon, halibut and cod, abound in island waters.

★★ **Gwaii Haanas National Park Reserve** – *Access by sea or air only. Touring with an outfitter is strongly recommended since waters can be hazardous and weather is subject to sudden changes. For a list of licensed operators of kayaking and diving tours and cruises contact Gwaii Haanas, Parks Canada, Box 37, Queen Charlotte, BC, V0T 1S0 ☎ 250-559-8818. Visitors are asked to register with Parks Canada.* Deserving its Haida appellation, this wild and verdant 1,400sq km/541sq mi "Island of Wonder" nurtures a variety of wildlife and shelters the remains of a number of Haida villages. In 1988 the reserve was created to protect these natural and historical treasures.

Though many villages have reverted to forest, at several sites totem poles still stand and the remains of longhouses are clearly discernible. At several important sites, **Haida Gwaii Watchmen**, in residence at base camps during the summer, serve as caretakers and share their culture with visitors. *Number of visitors limited at base camps at any one time. Reservations required. User fees in effect. Contact the park office ☎ 250-559-8818.*

Cruise – *The following describes an outfitter cruise along the east and south coast of Moresby Island with disembarkation at sites described. Note: not all outfitters stop at these sites.* Situated on the east coast of Louise Island *(outside the national park reserve)*, the remains of the village of **Skedans**★★ contain a few erect totem poles, the overgrown and decaying remains of toppled ones and the depressions of several longhouses. Located on the east coast of Tanu Island, the ancient site of **Tanu**★ also has the remains of fallen poles and longhouse depressions. Popular Hotspring Island offers three rock-lined natural **pools**★★ *(open for public bathing)* in a fine coastal setting.

Added to the World Heritage list in 1981, Sgan Gwaii (or Anthony Island) occupies a spectacular site at the edge of the Pacific. Believed to have been occupied for 1,500 years, celebrated **Ninstints**★★★ was one of the largest villages in the southern archipelago, with a population of 400. It faces a protected cove, and many of its totem poles have survived the effects of weathering. Today a score of poles are still upright, giving the visitor a rare taste of what Haida civilization was like in the 19C.

The Canadian population figures in this guide are based on the official 1996 Canadian census.

ROCKY MOUNTAIN PARKS★★★

Alberta, British Columbia

Map of Principal Sights p 2

Internationally renowned for its spectacular mountain scenery, this chain of four contiguous national parks is one of Canada's most popular natural attractions, beckoning some six million sightseers a year. These terrestial wonders, with their diverse topography, vegetation and wildlife, are the jewels of western Canada.
Modern parkways dissect the region's wide river valleys, and hiking trails crisscross the backcountry, allowing access to an awesomely rugged mountain world of soaring peaks, alpine lakes, waterfalls and glaciers.
The major parks in the Canadian Rockies are Banff, Jasper, Yoho and Kootenay National Parks and Mt. Robson Provincial Park. Situated next to each other in the southern part of the mountain range, they form one of the largest mountain parklands in the world, covering over 22,274sq km/8,600sq mi. The area contains other impressive provincial parks and reserves, notably **Mt. Assiniboine** *(between Banff and Kootenay; not accessible by road);* and the **Kananaskis Country**, a preserve 90km/56mi southeast of Banff that includes three provincial parks. Waterton Lakes National Park is situated apart from the other Rocky Mountain parks in the southwest corner of Alberta.

Geographical Notes

Canada's Rooftop – Frequently rising over 3,000m/10,000ft, the Canadian Rockies constitute the easternmost range of North America's **Western Cordillera** *(p 17)*. Beginning at the border with the US, the Canadian Rockies stretch roughly 1,550km/900mi through western Alberta and eastern British Columbia in a northwesterly direction. To the north these mountains are bounded by the broad plain of the Liard River; to the east by the Interior Plains; and to the west by the **Rocky Mountain Trench** *(map p 60)*, one of the longest continuous valleys in the world. The spine of the Rockies forms part of the **Continental Divide**.
Composed of sedimentary rock deposited by ancient seas some 1.5 billion years ago, the Rockies have a distinct layered appearance. They first began to uplift 120 to 70 million years ago because of the collision of tectonic plates. During the last Ice Age (75,000 to 11,000 years ago), glaciation carved the mountains into the terrain seen today: U-shaped valleys, glacially fed lakes, canyons, bowl-shaped cirques and hanging valleys with waterfalls and glaciers. Since the end of the Little Ice Age, or Cavell Advance, in 1870, the Rockies' glaciers have begun a significant retreat.

Fauna and Flora – Still largely wilderness, the Rockies are inhabited by a variety of animal and plant life. Even along roadways black bear, coyote, elk, moose, mule deer, mountain sheep, squirrels and chipmunks are often seen. More rarely, bighorn sheep and white-coated mountain goats may be sighted, and in more remote areas, grizzly bears and wolverines make an infrequent appearance.
Plant life varies greatly because of the drastic changes in elevation. Wildflowers are abundant throughout the vegetation zones. Their bloom follows the snowmelt up the mountainsides from late June through early August. Stands of Douglas fir, lodgepole pine, white spruce and quaking aspen often cover the valleys, gradually giving way to alpine fir, Lyall's larch and Engelmann spruce on the higher slopes. Just below the tree line lies a band of krummholz vegetation—trees dwarfed by the severe conditions. Above the tree line (normally 2,200m/7,200ft on south-facing slopes, lower on north-facing), only the low, ground-hugging vegetation of the alpine tundra survives: mosses, lichens, wildflowers and grasses.

Historical Notes

Archaeological evidence indicates early nomads traversed this region 10,000 years ago. The Indians living here were overwhelmed, prior to European contact, by the **Stoney tribe**, who moved into the Rockies in the early 1700s. During the mid- to late 18C, the European **fur trade** burgeoned in the Rockies, and by the mid-19C, mountaineers and explorers had arrived.
By 1885 the **Canadian Pacific Railway** (CPR) line had crossed the Rockies and reached the West Coast. Recognizing the mountains' tourist potential, the CPR company convinced the government to establish "preserves"—the origin of the current parks. During the late 18C and early 19C, the railway company built a series of fine mountain chalets and hotels, a number of which are still in operation. By the 1920s all four Rocky Mountain national parks had been established. In 1985 the combined four parks were designated a World Heritage Site.

★★★ 1 BANFF NATIONAL PARK *Allow 2 days. Map p 57.*

Canada's first and most famous national park, Banff encompasses impressive peaks, scenic river valleys and the popular resort towns of Banff and Lake Louise. This preserve lies at the southeastern end of the chain of mountain parks.
In the 1880s construction of the transcontinental railroad and discovery of natural hot springs on Sulphur Mountain elevated Banff to national prominence. The mineral springs were first noted by Sir James Hector in 1858, the first European to cross

PRACTICAL INFORMATION

Getting There

By Air – Flights daily on Canadian and US air carriers to Calgary International Airport (17km/11mi from downtown Calgary) ☎735-1246. Banff is 128km/79mi west of Calgary via Trans-Canada Highway and Jasper is 366km/227mi west of Edmonton via Hwy. 16. **Airport shuttle** from Calgary to the Banff/Lake Louise area: Brewster Tours ☎762-6767 *($36 and $41)* or Laidlaw Transportation ☎800-661-4946 (Canada/US) *($31)*. Car rentals (Avis, Hertz, Tilden and others) at Calgary Airport and in Banff.

By Bus and Train – Greyhound **bus** service from Calgary to Banff/Lake Louise area ☎265-9111. One-way fare $23.38. **VIA Rail** connects Jasper with Calgary, Edmonton and Vancouver ☎604-669-3050, or ☎800-561-3949 (US).

General Information

When to Go – The Rocky Mountain Parks are open year-round. The **summer season** is July to mid-September, peak season being July and August when daylight extends to 10pm. Visitors should be prepared for cold weather even in summer, since snowfall in August and September is not unusual. Throughout the **winter** most park roads are open. Parkways are regularly cleared, but snow tires are recommended from November to February.

Visitor Information – Each national park has a visitor centre, operated by Parks Canada, where schedules, pamphlets, maps and permits are available. Website addresses for the parks are:

www.worldweb.com/parkscanada-banff www.worldweb.com/parkscanada-kootenay

www.worldweb.com/parkscanada-jasper www.worldweb.com/parkscanada-yoho

A park pass *($8/day per vehicle, valid until noon the next day)* is required for entry to each national park (multiday and multipark passes available) and can be obtained from park visitor centres, entrance gates or campground kiosks. For information on Banff National Park, contact **Banff Visitor Centre**, 224 Banff Ave. in Banff ☎762-1550. At this location the Banff/Lake Louise Tourism Bureau ☎762-8421 provides information on area commercial facilities, services and activities. The **Lake Louise Visitor Centre**, next to Samson Mall ☎522-3833 provides information on Banff National Park and on Lake Louise area facilities and activities. A visitor guide to the area, *Where*, features activities, lodging, dining, shopping and maps.

Accommodations – The Canadian Rockies are known for their **backcountry lodges**, generally accessible only by hiking, skiing or helicopter. These wilderness hostelries, most of them family-operated, range from rustic cabins to comfortable alpine chalets with fine food. Primitive cabins that rent for $8-24/night per person can be reserved through the Alpine Club of Canada, PO Box 8040, Canmore, AB, T1W 2T8 ☎678-3200. Numerous commercial campgrounds are located adjacent to the national parks. For information and reservations for campgrounds within the national parks, contact the individual park. Hotels, resorts, motels, B&Bs, chalets and condominiums are available in the area. For information on lodging, contact the Banff/Lake Louise Tourism Bureau ☎762-8421.

Recreation

All four national parks offer **hiking, backpacking, bicycling, horseback riding, canoeing, fishing, swimming** (except Yoho) and **winter sports**. Banff and Jasper have facilities for **tennis** and **golf**; boat tours and canoe rental are also available; for details contact Parks Canada *(above)*.

The Banff Springs hotel boasts a 27-hole **golf** course. To reserve, contact the hotel ☎762-6801. Kananaskis Country Golf Course has two 18-hole courses; bookings should be made 60 days in advance ☎591-7272. Other area hotels offer golf. Outfitters specializing in **wilderness excursions** provide equipment, guides and transportation. Helicopter sightseeing excursions begin at $80. For more information contact the Banff/Lake Louise Tourism Bureau ☎762-8421.

The Banff/Lake Louise area offers **winter sports** from mid-November to mid-May including downhill skiing, heli-skiing, ice-skating, dogsledding and cross-country skiing. There are three ski resorts: Lake Louise (☎800-258-7669, Canada/US); Sunshine Village (☎800-661-1676, Canada/US); Banff Mt. Norquay (☎762-4421). Amenities include mountain lodges, daycare, ski rentals and professional ski schools. Access is offered with the purchase of a tri-area lift pass ($140/3 days). There is a free shuttle bus between hotels in Banff and all three ski resorts.
The site of the 1988 Olympic nordic events has 70km/43mi of trails for the intermediate and advanced skier. Facilities include ski rentals, lessons and a day lodge. Canmore Nordic Centre, Suite 100, 1988 Olympic Way, Canmore, AB, T1W 2T6 ☎678-2400.

Useful Numbers

	☎
RCMP (Police)	762-2226
Alberta Motor Assn. (CAA affiliate)	762-2711
Park Weather Forecasts	762-2088
Trail Conditions (summer); **Avalanche Hazard** (winter)	762-1460

Kicking Horse Pass, which became the rail route through the Rockies. In 1883 Siding 29 (sidings are switch tracks from the main track) was constructed near the hot springs. While prospecting for minerals, three rail workers discovered the springs and attempted to stake a claim. But the interests of the railroad magnates prevailed. Canadian Pacific president **George Stephen** felt the siding needed a romantic name, so he called it Banff after his native Banffshire, Scotland.
The 26sq km/10sq mi Banff Hot Springs Reserve was established in 1885 by the government around Cave and Basin Hot Springs. In 1887 bathhouses were installed and a rail station built. The federal reserve was expanded to 673sq km/260sq mi and renamed Rocky Mountain Parks Reserve. In 1888 the CPR opened what was then the world's largest hotel, the **Banff Springs Hotel**. Built at the confluence of the Bow and Spray Rivers, this renowned "chateau" remains the dominant landmark.
Banff gradually became a social gathering place for wealthy travellers, who arrived by train. Not until 1915, after a bitter fight, were automobiles admitted to the park, a factor that made the area more accessible to the general public. The reserve was renamed Banff National Park in 1930. One of Canada's major resort areas today, Banff draws an international crowd.

★★Banff Townsite and Area

At the southeast end of the park system, this well-known resort town on the Bow River sits at an elevation of 1,380m/4,534ft amid breathtaking mountains. Though bustling with visitors much of the year, the community maintains the charm of a small alpine town.

Lake Louise, Banff National Park

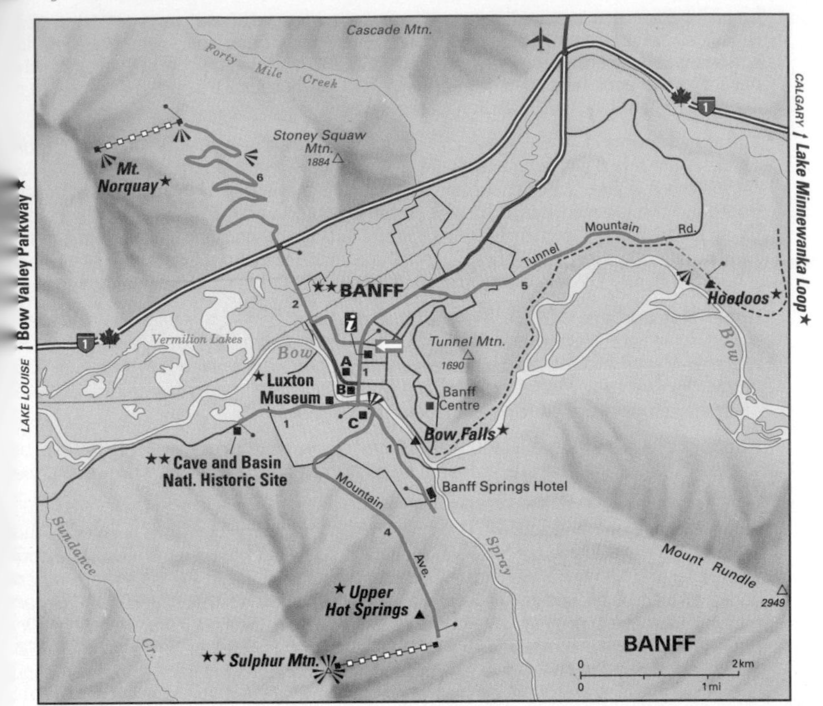

Tourists and residents alike celebrate artistic creations during the annual summer-long *(Jun–Aug)* **Banff Arts Festival**. A **visitor centre** *(224 Banff Ave.; open late Jun–Labour Day daily 8am–8pm; late May–mid-Jun & rest of Sept daily 8am–6pm; rest of the year daily 9am–5pm; closed Dec 25;* ♿ *www.wordweb.com/parkscanada-banff ☎ 403-762-1550)* operated by Parks Canada provides information on park activities. *Information on commercial facilities and services is available at the centre.*

★**Whyte Museum of the Canadian Rockies (A)** – *111 Bear St. Open mid-May–mid-Oct daily 10am–6pm. Rest of the year Tue–Sun 1pm–5pm. Closed national holidays. $4.* ♿ *www.whyte.org ☎ 403-762-2291.* Opened in 1968, this contemporary building houses a heritage gallery that traces the history of mountaineering and tourism in the Canadian Rockies, and art galleries featuring changing exhibits by regional and international artists. The museum sponsors tours of the on-site heritage homes.

★**Banff Park Museum (B)** – *93 Banff Ave. Open mid-Jun–mid-Sept daily 10am–6pm. Rest of the year daily 1pm–5pm. Closed Jan 1, Dec 25. $2.25. www.wordweb.com/parkscanada-banff ☎ 403-762-1558.* Constructed in the trestle-like "railway pagoda" style of the turn of the century, this historic museum maintains its 1905 appearance, both inside and out. Glass cases display a variety of minerals and taxidermied animals of the Rocky Mountains. Among the collections is a series of prints by renowned contemporary wildlife artist **Robert Bateman**.

★**Cascade Gardens (C)** – *At the south end of Banff Ave., across Bow River Bridge. Open daily year-round.* These terraced gardens, with their rock-lined pools and cascades, provide an excellent **view★** of **Cascade Mountain**, the 2,998m/9,836ft peak that towers above the north end of Banff Avenue. The stone Gothic Revival building at the centre of the grounds houses the park administration offices.

★**Buffalo Nations Luxton Museum** – Kids *1 Birch Ave., on the southeastern bank of the Bow River. Open mid-May–mid-Oct daily 9am–7pm. Rest of the year Tue–Sat 1pm–5pm. Closed Dec 25. $5.50.* ♿ *☎ 403-762-2388.* A replica of a log fur-trading fort, this museum displays native artifacts and life-size dioramas depicting aspects of Plains Indian life. Formerly owned by the Glenbow Museum of Calgary, the Luxton is now operated by the Buffalo Nations Cultural Society.

★**Bow Falls** – At the foot of the Banff Springs Hotel, the Bow River tumbles over a wide, low lip, just before its confluence with the Spray River.

★★**Cave and Basin National Historic Site** – *Open mid-Jun–mid-Sept daily 9am–6pm. Rest of the year Mon–Fri 11am–4pm, weekends 9:30am–5pm. $2.25.* ✗ ♿ *www.wordweb.com/parkscanada-banff ☎ 403-762-1566.* The Canadian park system began at this site. The arched stone building, restored to its 1914 appearance, surrounds an open-air swimming pool *(not open for swimming)* of hot springs water (average temperatures 30–35°C/86–95°F). The complex includes the natural cave pool fed by a hot spring, and a museum tracing the more than 100-year history of the Canadian parks system.

★★**Sulphur Mountain** – *3.5km/2.2mi from downtown. Access by gondola (8min ascent) Jan–Nov daily, hours vary. $14.* ✗ ♿ *www.banffgondola.com* ☎ *403-762-5438.* The 2,285m/ 7,500ft summit allows a 360° **panorama**★★★ of the Bow Valley, Banff and the turreted Banff Springs Hotel (east and north); the Spray Valley (southeast); Mt. Rundle and the more distant Fairholm Range and Lake Minnewanka (northeast); Mt. Norquay (north), and the Sundance Range (southwest). Bighorn sheep frequently browse along the trails here.

★**Upper Hot Springs** – Kids *3.5km/2.2mi from downtown. Open mid-May–mid-Sept daily 9am–11pm. Rest of the year Sun–Thu 10am–10pm, Fri–Sat 10am–11pm. $5 ($7 mid-May–mid-Sept).* ✗ ♿ *www.wordweb.com/parkscanada-banff* ☎ *403-762-1515.* Discovered a year after the Cave and Basin hot springs, the mineral waters (average temperature 38°C/100°F) now feed a large public pool.

★**Hoodoos** – These naturally sculpted pillars of cemented rock and gravel can be viewed from a scenic nature trail above Bow River *(1km/.6mi; trailhead off Tunnel Mountain Rd.).*

★**Lake Minnewanka Loop** – *Begins 4km/2.4mi from downtown.* Along this 16km/10mi drive, three lakes serve as natural water-sports playgrounds: Johnson; Two Jack; and Minnewanka, a dammed reservoir that is Banff Park's largest waterbody. Tour boats offer cruises down this lake to Devil's Gap *(depart mid-May–Labour Day daily 10:30am, 12:30pm, 3pm, 5pm & 7pm; mid-Sept–Oct daily 10:30am, 12:30pm, 3pm & 5pm; $26; Minnewanka Tours* ☎ *403-762-3473).* Included on the drive is **Bankhead**, an abandoned early-20C coal-mining operation. An interpretive park trail explains the history of the site.

★**Mt. Norquay** – *8km/5mi from downtown. Access by chair lift Dec–mid-Apr daily 9am–4pm (Fri 9pm). $35. Daily bus service from many Banff hotels.* ✗ ♿ *www.banffnorquay.com* ☎ *403-762-4421.* A well-graded switchback road climbs Stoney Squaw Mountain toward Mt. Norquay's chair lift, providing increasingly better **views** south and east over Bow Valley and of the townsite of Banff, back-dropped by **Mt. Rundle**, which is shaped like a tilted writing desk.

★Bow Valley Parkway to Lake Louise (Highway 1A)

48km/30mi. Begins 5.5km/3.5mi west of town. Map pp 60-61.

An alternative to the faster-paced Trans-Canada Highway, this scenic parkway was the original 1920s road connecting Banff and Lake Louise. Sightings of elk, deer, moose and coyote are not uncommon along the road. Curving through evergreen forests along the north bank of the Bow River, the route offers **views**★ of the Sawback Range to the northeast—in particular, crenellated Castle Mountain—and of the Great Divide peaks to the southwest. Frequent lookouts feature interpretation of regional geology, flora and fauna. At **Johnston Canyon**★★ *(17km/11mi)*, a paved, often cantilevered, pathway over the narrow limestone canyon leads to **lower falls**★★ *(about 1km/.6mi)* and **upper falls**★★ *(about 1.6km/1mi)*. The Inkpots, a collection of cold springs, are located beyond the upper falls *(6km/4mi).*

At Castle Junction, Highway 93 leads west from Bow Valley Parkway to Kootenay National Park.

★★★Lake Louise and Area *Map p 59*

Smaller and less congested than Banff, this townsite and its environs in the park's west-central section encompass massive, glaciated peaks and pristine lakes, most notably the legendary Lake Louise. Called "lake of little fishes" by the Stoney tribe, Lake Louise was first viewed by a nonnative in 1882. Taken there by a Stoney guide, **Tom Wilson**, a packer for railway survey crews, named the waterbody Emerald Lake because of its brilliant blue-green colour. Two years later the lake was renamed for Queen Victoria's daughter, Princess Louise Caroline Alberta. By 1890 a small guest chalet had been built on the shore. By the early 1900s a road had been built to the lake, a larger chalet constructed, and guests were flocking there. In 1925 the CPR completed the present hotel **Château Lake Louise**, which rises elegantly by the lake.

Lake Louise Village – A small resort crossroads with several shops, hotels and visitor facilities, the village is located just off the Trans-Canada Highway. A park **visitor centre** *(open late Jun–Labour Day daily 8am–8pm; late May–mid-Jun & rest* *of Sept daily 8am–6pm; rest of the year daily 9am–5pm; closed Dec 25;* ♿ *www.wordweb.com/parkscanada-banff* ☎ *403-522-3833)* features excellent **displays** on the natural history of the area, including the Burgess Shale, and provides information about drives, hikes and natural attractions.

★**Lake Louise** – *4km/2.5mi from village.* Set in a hanging valley backdropped by the majestic mountains of the Continental Divide, this beautiful glacier-fed lake, with the stately chateau near its shore, remains one of the most visited and photographed sites in the Canadian Rockies.

Visible at the far end, the **Victoria Glacier** once stretched to the site of the chateau. The 2km/1.2mi long, .5km/.3mi wide tarn (maximum depth 75m/246ft) was created when this glacier retreated, leaving enough morainal debris to serve as a dam. The chateau is actually built on the moraine. Fed by glacial meltwater draining off the surrounding peaks, the lake (maximum temperature 4°C/40°F) changes colour with light conditions and as the summer progresses. Known as glacial flour, fine powdery silt suspended in the water refracts the green rays of the spectrum and emits hues ranging from bluish-green to emerald.

The far end of the lake is dominated by **Mt. Victoria** (3,464m/11,362ft). To the left of Victoria stands the rocky face of **Fairview Mountain** (2,744m/9,000ft), and to the right of Victoria rises the distinctive rounded shape of **The Beehive**. A 3km/1.8mi trail circles the lake. Additional trails ascend into the backcountry. Two popular day hikes lead to teahouses: one at Lake Agnes *(3.5km/2.2mi from the lake)* and another at the Plain of Six Glaciers *(5.5km/3.3mi from the lake). Details on hikes available at the chateau and at park visitor centres.*

★★**Moraine Lake** – *13km/8mi from village.* Smaller and less visited than Lake Louise, Moraine Lake nonetheless occupies a splendid **site**★★ below the sheer walls of the Wenkchemna peaks.

Moraine Lake Road climbs above Bow Valley, offering an impressive **view**★★, first of one of the park's highest peaks—ice-capped **Mt. Temple** (3,543m/11,621ft)—and then of the glaciated **Wenkchemna** or **Ten Peaks**. A short walk leads up the rock pile damming the north end of the lake, providing the best **view**★ of the surroundings. The pile is believed to be the result of a rock slide from the adjacent pinnacle of rock called the Tower of Babel. Other trails lead around the lake and to nearby backcountry lakes and valleys.

★**Mt. Whitehorn** – *Access by gondola (15min ascent) Jul–Labour Day daily 8am–6pm. Jun & rest of Sept daily 8:30am–6pm. $10.* ✗ *www.skilouise.com* ☎ *403-522-3555.* From the top of the Friendly Giant gondola lift, a **panorama**★★ of Bow Valley is obtained, with the Wenkchemna peaks and Mt. Temple filling the horizon. To the west Lake Louise can be seen cupped below the Victoria Glacier.

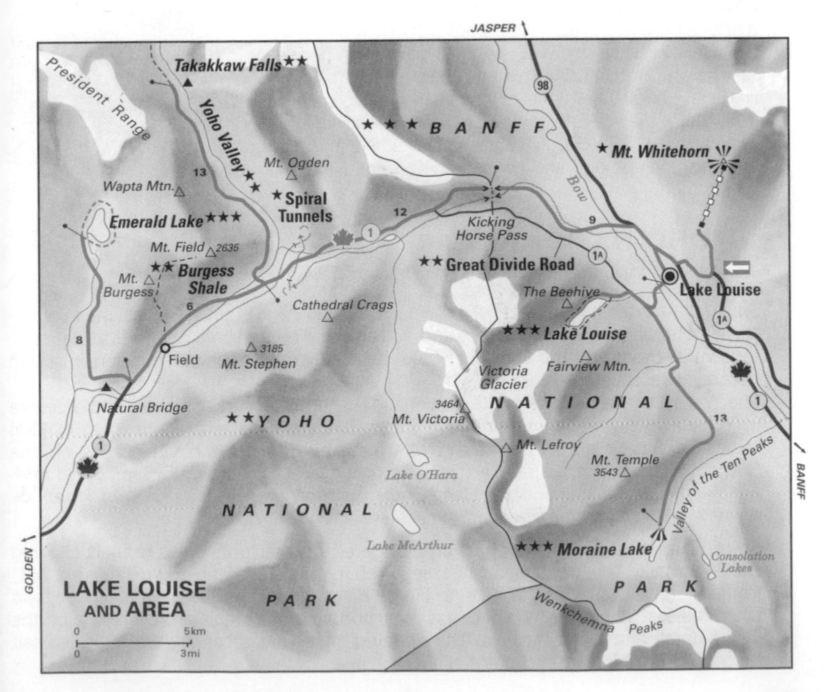

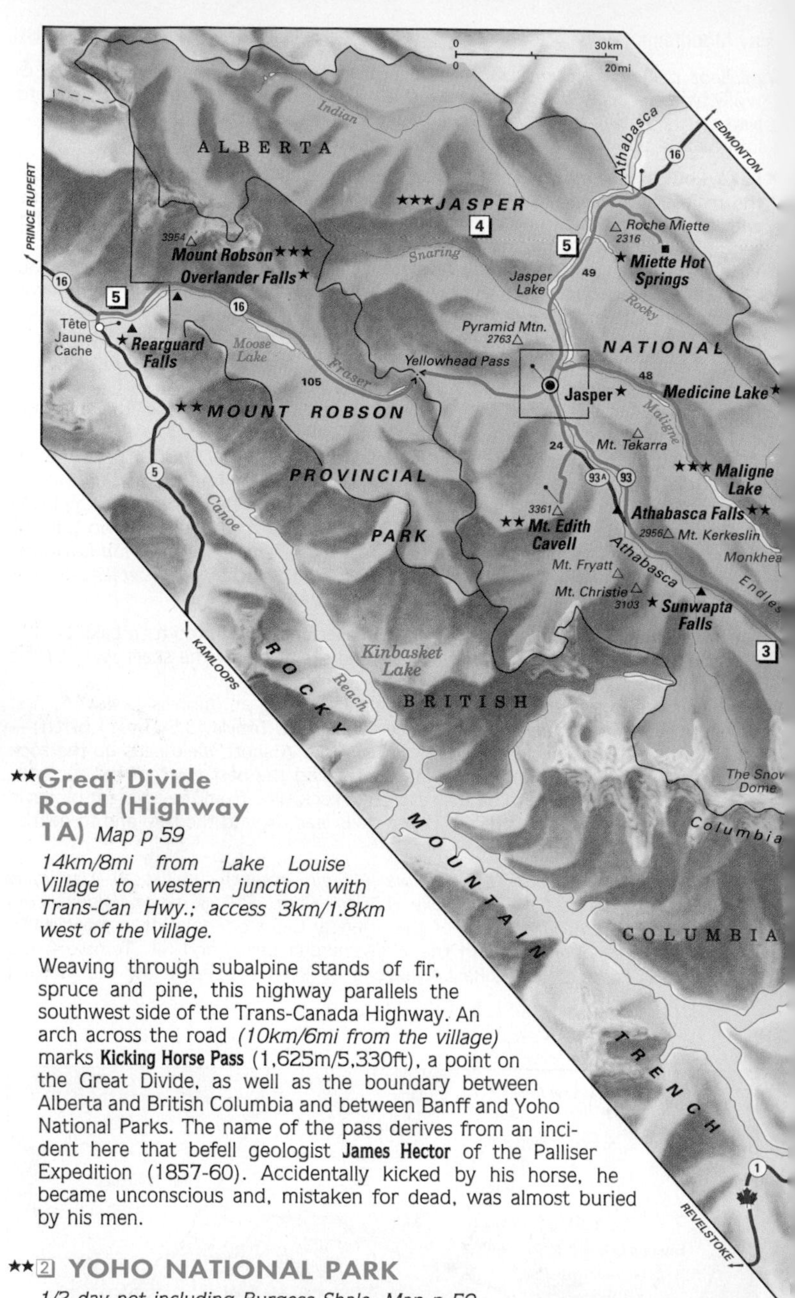

★★Great Divide Road (Highway 1A) *Map p 59*

14km/8mi from Lake Louise Village to western junction with Trans-Can Hwy.; access 3km/1.8km west of the village.

Weaving through subalpine stands of fir, spruce and pine, this highway parallels the southwest side of the Trans-Canada Highway. An arch across the road *(10km/6mi from the village)* marks **Kicking Horse Pass** (1,625m/5,330ft), a point on the Great Divide, as well as the boundary between Alberta and British Columbia and between Banff and Yoho National Parks. The name of the pass derives from an incident here that befell geologist **James Hector** of the Palliser Expedition (1857-60). Accidentally kicked by his horse, he became unconscious and, mistaken for dead, was almost buried by his men.

★★2 YOHO NATIONAL PARK

1/2 day not including Burgess Shale. Map p 59.

Smallest and most compact of the parks, Yoho (a native word meaning "awe") is a place of raging rivers and waterfalls. The preserve enjoys international renown as the site of the Burgess Shale, decidedly one of the most important fossil beds ever discovered.

The Trans-Canada Highway cuts diagonally through the park. Situated in the centre of Yoho in the valley of the roaring Kicking Horse River, the small town of **Field** serves as a park hub. The **visitor centre** features displays and videotapes on the Burgess Shale and other park attractions *(open late Jun–Aug daily 9am–7pm; mid-May–early Jun & Sept daily 9am–5pm; rest of the year daily 9am–4pm; ♿ www.worldweb.com/parkscanada-yoho ☎ 250-343-6783).*

★**Spiral Tunnels** – In the shape of an elongated figure eight, these tunnels allowed trains to make the treacherously steep, 4.5 percent descent down "the big hill" leading into the valley of the Kicking Horse River. A lookout about 9km/6mi beyond the northeast entrance to Yoho has interpretive signs tracing the history of the CPR's upper and lower tunnels. The opening of the lower tunnel in Mt. Ogden can be seen from this vantage point.

★**Yoho Valley** – *Access road of 13km/8mi with switchbacks; no trailers allowed.* Situated between Mt. Field and Mt. Ogden, lovely Yoho Valley is accessed by a climbing road that includes a lookout above the confluence of Yoho and Kicking Horse Rivers. Near the road's end Yoho Peak and Glacier can be seen straight ahead, with Takakkaw Falls to the right.

★★**Takakkaw Falls** – One of the highest waterfalls on the continent, this torrent of meltwalter from the Daly Glacier cascades in two stages for a combined total of 254m/833ft to join the Yoho River. A short paved walk leads to the base of the falls, which are visible from the road.

★★**Burgess Shale** – *Because of the fragile nature of the sites, the public can visit by guided hike only. 4km/2.5mi round-trip to Mt. Stephen's trilobite beds; 20km/12mi round-trip to Burgess Shale. Note: both are strenuous all-day hikes on steep trails. Jul-Sept, by reservation only. Space is very limited. Contact the Yoho-Burgess Shale Foundation in advance ☎250-343-6006 or 800-343-3006 (Canada/US). Instead of hiking, visitors may choose to view Burgess Shale exhibits at, for example, Field and Lake Louise visitor centres.* Located on **Mt. Field** (2,635m/8,6432ft), the Burgess Shale contains evidence of multicellular life found in the oceans 515 million years ago *(p 54)*. Because of its excellent fossil preservation, the Burgess Shale enjoys world renown among professional paleontologists and amateur enthusiasts and isconsidered the richest Cambrian site in the world.

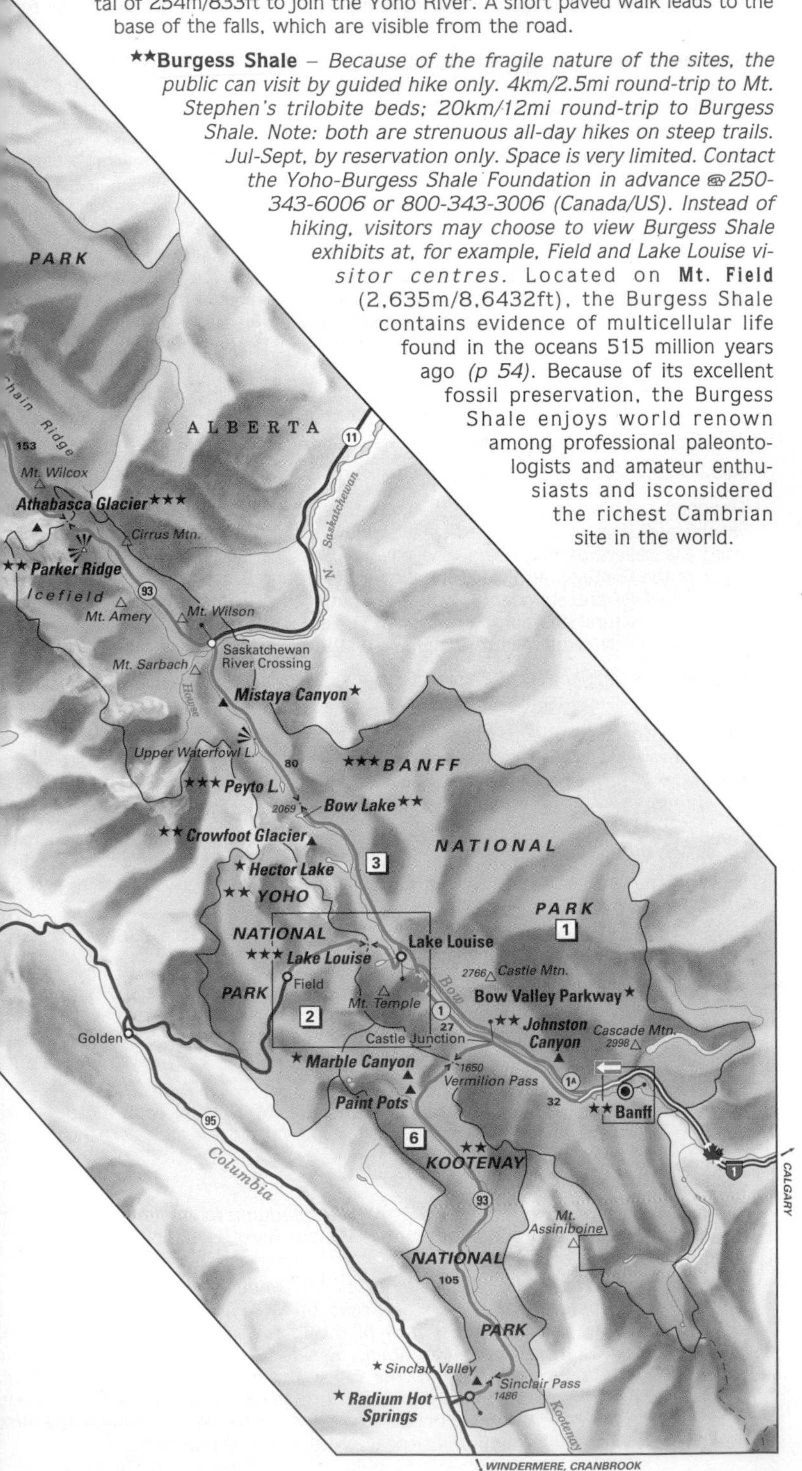

In 1886 an employee of the Canadian Pacific Railway discovered rich trilobite be on **Mt. Stephen** (3,185m/10,447ft). In 1909 American paleontologist **Charles Walc** found unique fossils of soft-bodied animals on loose pieces of shale on Mt. Fiel He later discovered a rich fossil-bearing shale layer higher up the slope and spe five summers quarrying this layer. The Royal Ontario Museum conducts ongoir research on the Burgess Shale.

The challenging trail to the Burgess Shale offers excellent **views★★** of Emerald La and the President Range, in particular. At the small, hillside quarry, visitors ca sometimes observe researchers excavating shale by hand and see recent fos finds.

★★★**Emerald Lake** – *Accessible via 8km/5mi road off Trans-Can Hwy. Refreshmen accommodations.* Aptly named by Tom Wilson in 1882, this beautiful lake lies the foot of the President Range. Glacial runoff from these mountains gives th water its striking green colour.

Shortly after leaving the highway, the road to the lake offers views, from a parkin area, of a **natural bridge** of limestone. Kicking Horse River has cut this passage fc its narrowed, turbulent course. The **site★** is lovely, with Mt. Stephen rising abov the river to the northeast and the mountains of the Van Horne Range visib downstream. The road ends at the lake. Situated at the southeastern end of th lake with Mt. Burgess rising behind it, Emerald Lake Lodge traces its beginning to a 1902 CPR chalet. Mt. Wapta lies to the northeast and the peaks of the Pre sident Range to the west. A pleasant **trail★** *(5km/3mi)* circles the lake. After th turnoff to Emerald Lake, the Trans-Canada Highway follows the scenic **lowe gorge★★** of the Kicking Horse River to its junction with the Columbia River an the town of Golden.

★★★ 3 ICEFIELDS PARKWAY

Allow 1 day. 233km/145mi (Trans-Can Hwy. junction to Jasper). Map pp 60-61

Designed expressly to dramatize the incredible landscape, this unequalled parkwa (Highway 93) runs below the highest mountains in the Canadian Rockies. Follo wing the valleys of five rivers, the road angles northwesterly along the easter flank of the Continental Divide, connecting Banff and Jasper Parks. Glaciers, lake and waterfalls are abundant along the route, as are interpretive lookouts tha explain the natural and human history of the area. From its southern terminus th parkway quickly climbs, with fine views of the Waputik Range.

★**Hector Lake** – *16km/10mi.* Named for James Hector *(p 60)*, the lake is set belov the Waputik Range (south), Mt. Hector (east) and Bow Peak (north).

★★**Crowfoot Glacier** – *33km/20mi.* After rounding Bow Peak the parkway reaches a viewpoint for this glacier spread across the lower rock plateaus of Crowfoot Mountain. Now in retreat, the glacier has lost some of the ice that made it resemble a crow's foot.

★★**Bow Lake** – *37km/23mi.* Directly by the road, this lovely lake is best seen from the lookout leading to historic, red-roofed Num-ti-jah Lodge, visible on the north shore of the lake. The Bow Glacier hangs above the lake between Portal and St. Nicholas Peaks.

Passing through a green meadowland of birch and willow, the parkway reaches Bow Summit (2,069m/6,786ft), the highest pass on the route.

★★★**Peyto Lake** – *40km/25mi to spur road; park in upper lot where short trail leads to a viewpoint.* The striking turquoise waters of this lake are fed by Peyto Glacier. Both lake and glacier are named for turn-of-the-century guide, Bill Peyto. **Mistaya Mountain** rises sheerly from the opposite side of the lake, with Peyto Peak on its left. The Mistaya River Valley stretches north beyond the lake.

The road descends to the valley and passes a series of lakes. At **Upper Waterfowl Lake** lookout *(56km/35mi)*, there is a fine **view★** of the formidable stone expanse of the Great Divide peaks, especially towering Howse Peak (3,290m/10,791ft) and pyramidal Mt. Chephren (3,307m/10,847ft).

★**Mistaya Canyon** – *72km/45mi to spur road for parking; follow trail into valley for 400m/.3mi.* This narrow gorge, cut by the Mistaya River, is notable for its smooth, sculpted limestone walls.

Continuing northward, the parkway passes Mt. Murchison (3,337m/10,945ft), which rises to the east, and the steep cliffs of Mt. Wilson (3,261m/10,696ft), looming above the road. Both are part of the **Castle Mountain Syncline**, a downfold stratum that runs from Castle Mountain, outside Banff, to Mt. Kerkeslin, near Jasper. After the road descends into the valley of the North Saskatchewan River, a lookout *(76km/47mi; trail through trees)* affords a **view** of the Howse River Valley. David Thompson travelled this corridor in 1807 on his way to set up the first trading post west of the mountains, near present-day Invermere.

Very quickly the parkway reaches its junction with Highway 11—the David Thompson Highway *(✗;services)*. The parkway then runs below the massive cliffs of Mt. Wilson (to the east), with views first of Survey Peak and Mt. Erasmus to the west and then the layer-cake facade of **Mt. Amery**.

At 105km/65mi the road hugs the base of Cirrus Mountain, the sheer cliffs of which are known as the **Weeping Wall** because streams cascade down them. Soon thereafter the parkway rounds what is called "the big bend" and climbs quickly above the valley where a lookout allows a spectacular **view**★★ of the North Saskatchewan Valley. A second, almost adjacent, lookout directly faces the filmy spray of **Bridal Veil Falls**.

★**Parker Ridge** – *118km/73mi.* This ridgetop affords a magnificent **view**★★★ of glaciated backcountry, particularly the **Saskatchewan Glacier**, one of the major outlet glaciers of the Columbia Icefield *(below)*. A switchback trail *(2.4km/1.5mi)* ascends through dwarf, subalpine forest and then through treeless tundra *(round-trip 1.5hrs)*, carpeted in summer with dwarf alpine flowers.

At 122km/76mi the parkway crosses Sunwapta Pass (2,035m/6,675ft) to enter Jasper National Park, with views ahead of Mt. Athabasca and other peaks surrounding the Columbia Icefield.

★★**Athabasca Glacier** – *127km/79mi.* This glacier is part of the vast **Columbia Icefield**, the largest subpolar icefield on the continent. The 325sq km/126sq mi Columbia lies along the Alberta/British Columbia boundary. The Athabasca and four other major outlet glaciers (Saskatchewan, Dome, Stutfield and Columbia), as well as smaller ones, flow off its eastern edge. Meltwater from these glaciers eventually feeds into three oceans: the Atlantic, Pacific and Arctic.

Situated along the high, remote tops of the Rockies at an altitude of over 3,000m/10,000ft, the icefield was apparently unknown until 1898, when a mountaineering expedition from Britain's Royal Geographical Society discovered and named it.

From the parking lot of the Columbia Icefield Chalet, a **view**★★★ encompasses the Athabasca, Kitchener and Dome Glaciers. Nearby, the Columbia Icefield Information Bureau serves as the southern **visitor centre** *(open mid-Jun–Labour Day daily 9am–6pm; rest of the year daily 9am–4pm; ♿ ☎403-852-7030) for Jasper National Park and functions as a small museum, with displays and an audio-visual presentation on glaciology.*

Across the parkway is Sunwapta Lake, fed by the Athabasca Glacier. From the parking area a short trail ascends to the toe of the glacier. In recent decades the glacier has retreated dramatically. The progress of its recession is marked on signposts along the parking lot's access road and the trail.

★★**SnoCoach Tours on the Glacier** – *Note: expect long waiting lines in Jul & Aug. Depart every 15min from Icefield Centre mid-Apr–mid-Oct daily 9am–5pm. Round-trip 1hr 30min. $25. ✗ ♿ Brewster Tours www.brewster.ca ☎403-762-6735.* These specially designed ultra-terrain vehicles travel a short distance onto the upper end of the Athabasca Glacier and allow passengers to get off to briefly experience the glacial surface.

★**Sunwapta Falls** – *176km/109mi; 400m/.3mi spur road to parking.* The Sunwapta River circles a small island, plunges over a cliff, makes a sharp turn around an ancient glacial moraine, and enters a deep limestone canyon.

Soon after the falls, the parkway enters the valley of the mighty **Athabasca River** and follows it to Jasper. This impressive valley is dominated on the west by the distinctive off-centre pyramidal shape of **Mt. Christie** (3,103m/10,180ft) and the three pinnacles of the Mt. Fryatt massif (3,361m/11,024ft). To the northwest the distant snow-capped summit of Mt. Edith Cavell *(below)* slowly assumes prominence, while **Mt. Kerkeslin** (2,956m/9,696ft), the final peak of the Castle Mountain Syncline, towers over the parkway to the east.

★★**Athabasca Falls** – *199km/123mi; turn left on Rte 93A for 400m/.3mi.* The silt-laden waters of the Athabasca River roar over a lip of quartzite and down a canyon smoothed by the force of the rushing waters. Backdropping the cataract, Mt. Kerkeslin, slightly reddish from quartzite, has the same layering as the rock by the falls.

As the parkway approaches Jasper townsite, the Whistlers can be seen to the west. Straight ahead rises Pyramid Mountain, and to the east, the pinnacled peak of **Mt. Tekarra**. At dusk elk are frequently spotted grazing alongside the parkway near the Wapiti Campground.

★★★ 4 JASPER NATIONAL PARK *Allow 2 days. Map p 64.*

The largest and northernmost of the four Rocky Mountain Parks, Jasper National Park covers 10,878sq km/4,200sq mi, most of which is remote wilderness. In addition to spectacular terrain, Jasper also offers frequent opportunities to view the varied wildlife.

★Jasper Townsite and Area

This pleasant town sits in the valley of the Athabasca River near its confluence with the Miette River. Small and very beautiful lakes—**Pyramid**, **Patricia**, **Annette**, **Edith** and **Beauvert**, site of the well-known **Jasper Park Lodge**—surround the townsite. The peaks of nearby mountains are visible on the horizon, most notably Mt. Edith Cavell to the south and rugged **Pyramid Mountain** (2,763m/9,063ft) to the north from the townsite. In the early 19C area Indians saw increased European presence as fur traders used the Athabasca River and Pass as a route through the Rockies. In 1801 Jasper Hawes, a clerk for the North West Company, established a supply depot on Brulé Lake, 35km/22mi north of the present townsite. The depot became known as "Jasper House," and ultimately gave the current townsite its name. In the 1860s the **Overlanders**, a party of 125 gold seekers, passed through the region on their way to the goldfields of the Cariboo Mountains *(p 39)*. Except for mountaineers and trappers, the area had few inhabitants until the early 20C.

In 1907 Jasper Forest Park, as it was then called, was created in anticipation of completion of the Grand Trunk Pacific Railway across the Yellowhead Pass. The townsite grew from a railroad construction camp set up in 1911. Situated at the junction of the Yellowhead Highway and the Icefields Parkway, Jasper is the focal point of activity for the park and contains a park **visitor centre** *(Connaught Dr. & Miette Ave.; open mid-Jun–Labour Day daily 8:30am–7pm; rest of the year daily 9am–5pm; closed Dec 25; ♿ ☎403-852-6176)*.

★★ **The Whistlers** – *Access by tramway (8min ascent) late May–Labour Day daily 8:30am–10pm. Early Apr–mid-May & rest of Sept–Oct daily 9:30am–4:30pm. $14.95. ✗ www.jaspertramway.com ☎403-852-3093.* The tramway ascends more than 900m/3,000ft to the terminal perched on the ridge of these 2,470m/8,102ft peaks named for the sound made by resident marmots. The **panorama**★★★ from this elevation includes the townsite, the lake-dotted Athabasca Valley and the Colin Range to the northeast, and Mt. Yellowhead and the Victoria Cross Ranges to the northwest. If visibility permits, the great white pyramid of Mt. Robson *(p 66)* can be spotted beyond them.

A trail climbs an additional 180m/600ft to the treeless ridgetop *(round-trip 1.5hrs)*, offering a **view** to the south of Mts. Edith Cavell and Kerkeslin.

★★ **Mt. Edith Cavell** – *24km/15mi from townsite. Access via Icefields Pky. to junction with 93A, then Mt. Edith Cavell Rd.* Known as the queen of the range, this massif (3,368m/11,047ft) was named for an English nurse executed by the Germans in World War I for assisting Allied prisoners of war.

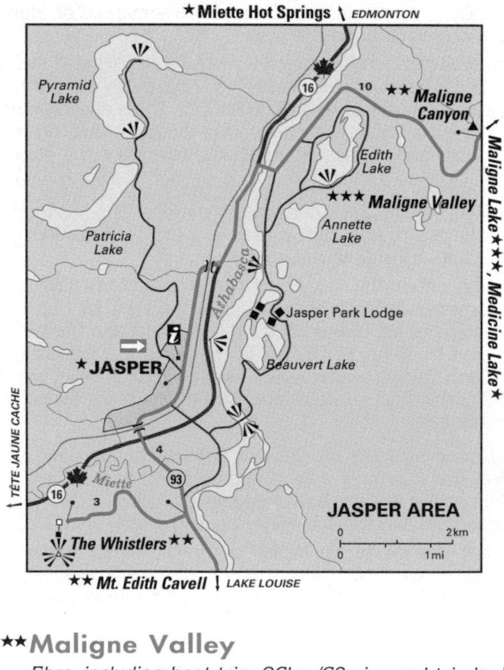

The narrow, twisting access road climbs steeply into the high country, paralleling the dramatic Astoria River Valley. By walking a short distance to **Cavell Lake** from the parking area for the Tonquin Valley Trail *(26km/17mi)*, visitors can obtain a good **view** of the mountain. The lake's bright-green waters feed from the fast receding, but lovely **Angel Glacier**, which is located on the mountain. At the end of the road *(2km/1.2mi drive)*, the trailhead is reached for the Path of the Glacier Trail *(round-trip 40min)*, which follows the toe of this ice river.

★★★Maligne Valley

5hrs, including boat trip. 96km/60mi round-trip by Hwy. 16 and Maligne Lake Rd. Maps p 60 and above.

This valley cradles a magnificent lake and canyon, both also named Maligne (Ma-LEEN), which can mean "malignant" or "injurious" in French. Despite its name, the valley is among the most beautiful in the Rockies.

© Dick Dietrich

Spirit Island, Maligne Lake

★★ **Maligne Canyon** – *7km/4mi from Rte. 93 junction.* The most spectacular of the Rocky Mountain gorges, this great slit carved in limestone reaches depths of 50m/164ft, while spanning widths of less than 3m/10ft in some places. A paved trail *(round-trip 30min)* follows the top of the canyon, descending with the drop of the Maligne River. Bridges crossing the canyon serve as viewpoints.

★ **Medicine Lake** – *22km/14mi.* The Colin Range to the north and the Maligne Range to the south hem in this lovely lake. From its highest levels during the snowmelt of early summer, the waterbody gradually shrinks as the season progresses, sometimes becoming only mud flats. Intriguingly the lake has no surface outlet, draining instead through sink holes in the limestone bedrock and resurfacing in the waters of the Maligne River. The road follows the edge of the lake for 8km/5mi with several advantageous viewpoints.

★★ **Maligne Lake** – *For boat rentals, hiking trips, white-water rafting contact Maligne Tours www.jaspertravel.com/malignelake ☎ 403-852-3370.* At 23km/14mi long, Maligne is the largest natural lake in the Rockies and one of the most spectacular. In 1875 surveyor Henry MacLeod was the first European to see the lake, naming it "Sore-foot." The lake and the peaks that rise from it were initially explored in detail in 1908 by an expedition led by Mary Schaffer, a middle-aged widow from Philadelphia who spent her summers in the Rockies.

The road ends at the northern shore of this glacial lake. As seen from the road, the twin peaks of **Mts. Unwin** (3,300m/10,824ft) and **Charlton** (3,260m/10,693ft) on the southwest side are most prominent. However these peaks and the others at the southern end can be appreciated only by boating down the lake.

★★ **Boat Trip** – *Departs from chalet at Maligne Lake May–early Oct daily 10am–3pm; additional departures mid-Jun–early Sept. Round-trip 1hr 30min. Commentary. $31. Maligne Tours www.jaspertravel.com/malignelake ☎ 403-852-3370.* As the boat proceeds down the lake, the water colour changes from green to deep turquoise because of the presence of suspended glacial silt. After passing Samson Narrows the boat stops so passengers can disembark near tiny **Spirit Island** to enjoy the **view**★★★ of the half-dozen glaciated peaks framing the south end of the lake.

★★ 5 THE YELLOWHEAD HIGHWAY *Map p 60*

Also designated Highway 16, this major thoroughfare runs east-west through Jasper and Mt. Robson Parks and continues westward to the Pacific at Prince Rupert. The highway was named for a fair-haired Iroquois fur trader known as Tête Jaune ("yellow head") who, in the 1820s, set up a cache in the small town now named in his honour.

★★ From Jasper to Miette Hot Springs *Allow 4hrs. 49km/31mi.*

Heading eastward from Jasper the highway enters, and then follows, the broad valley of the Athabasca River. The craggy pinnacles of the Colin Range are soon silhouetted against the eastern horizon.
For the remaining 40km/25mi, the highway offers breathtaking **views**★★★ of the braided course of the river and the peaks surrounding it. The road passes between **Talbot Lake** (east) and **Jasper Lake**, which is backdropped by the **De Smet Range**. At the

Disaster Point **animal lick★**, small pools on the east side of the road attract moun tain sheep and the less frequently sighted white-coated mountain goats. The clos proximity of the highway has led to animals being hit by cars; hence the point name. From approximately this location on, the drive holds fine views of **Roche Miet** (2,316m/7,599ft).

★**Miette Hot Springs** – *42km/26mi to junction with Miette Hot Springs R Open mid-May–mid-Jun daily 10:30am–9pm. Late Jun–Labour Day dai 8:30am–10:30pm. Rest of Sept–mid-Oct daily 10:30am–9pm. $5.* ♿ ☎ *403-866 3939.* A road winds 18km/11mi through a pleasant green gorge to the park's ho springs bathhouse. The springs are high in calcium and the hottest in the Cana dian Rockies (maximum temperature 54°C/129°F). The natural **setting★★** for th springs, with mountains hovering close by, makes this the most spectacular loca tion among all the mountain parks' bathhouses.

After this junction, the highway continues east another 7km/4mi to the east gat of Jasper National Park.

★From Jasper to Rearguard Falls *Allow 5hrs. 100km/62mi.*

West of Jasper, Highway 16 follows the narrowing valley of the Miette River. A **Yellowhead Pass**—the lowest pass on the Continental Divide, and also the boundar between British Columbia and Alberta—the road leaves Jasper National Par *(24km/15mi)* and enters Mt. Robson Provincial Park.

★★**Mt. Robson Provincial Park** – *East boundary at 24km/15mi. Open Apr–Oct dail 7am–11pm. Rest of the year Mon–Fri 8am–3:30pm.* ▲ X ♿ ☎ *250-566-4325* Encompassing magnificent mountain terrain, this 217,200ha/536,484 acre park is named for its greatest attraction: 3,954m/12,972ft **Mt. Robson★★★**, the highest peak in the Canadian Rockies.

After entering the park Route 16 picks up the course of the Fraser River, skirting Yellowhead Lake and larger Moose Lake. At **Overlander Falls★** *(88km/55mi; acces sible by trail, round-trip 30min)*, the blue-green Fraser River drops off a wide ledge, and then narrows as it enters a canyon. Just beyond the falls, the park **visitor centre**, backdropped by Mt. Robson, displays natural history exhibits on the area *(open Jul–Aug daily 8am–7pm; May–Jun & Sept daily 8am–5pm;* ♿ ☎ *250-566-4325)*.

★**Rearguard Falls** – *Allow 40min round-trip. 3.2km/2mi walk.* Part of a small pro- vincial park by the same name, these wide, low falls on the Fraser River are particularly noted as a place where chinook salmon can be seen leaping upstream during the August spawning season. The salmon have made a 1,200km/744mi journey inland, from the Fraser outlet on the Pacific to this point.

The crossroads town of Tête Jaune Cache is 5km/3mi farther west.

★★ 6 KOOTENAY NATIONAL PARK *Map p 61*

Kootenay National Park was formed in 1920 as a result of the federal govern- ment's completion of the Banff-Windermere Highway (Route 93)—which would provide an important commercial link between southwestern Alberta and the Columbia Valley—in exchange for land bordering the road. Extending 8km/5mi from both sides of the highway, the strip of land became Canada's tenth national park.

From Castle Junction to Radium Hot Springs

Allow 3hrs. 105km/65mi by Rte. 93.

This picturesque **route★★** through Kootenay National Park leaves the Trans-Canada Highway at Castle Junction and climbs steeply to the summit of **Vermilion Pass** (1,650m/5,412ft). The pass marks the Great Divide and coincides with the borders of Banff and Kootenay National Parks and the provincial boundaries between Alberta and British Columbia.

★**Marble Canyon** – *17km/11mi from junction.* The rushing waters of Tokumm Creek charge through this narrow limestone gorge on their way to meet the Vermilion River. The **visitor centre** *(open mid-May–late Sept daily 9am–6:30pm; early Apr–early May & early Oct–mid-Oct Fri–Sun & holidays 11am–6pm;* ♿ ☎ *250-347-9505, winter* ☎ *250-347-9615)* for the park's north entrance is located here. Interpre- tive signs explain the geology of white-dolomite outcroppings, a natural bridge and other features along a trail *(1.6km/1mi, round-trip 30min)* that leads through the canyon.

Paint Pots – *20km/12mi from junction; trail of 1.2km/.7mi.* Of historic interest, this area contains pools of ochre clay first used as body paint and dyes by Indians, and later mined by Europeans. The three cold **mineral springs★** near the end of the trail were considered places of spiritual power by native tribes.

The highway follows the Vermilion River to its confluence with the Kootenay. At 89km/55mi a lookout provides a sweeping **view★** of the wide, wooded **Kootenay Valley** and the **Mitchell Range** flanking its west side. After topping Sinclair Pass (1,486m/4,874ft), the road follows Sinclair Creek's tumbling descent through **Sinclair Valley★**, passing between the precipitous red cliffs called the **Iron Gates**, because of the iron oxides that give them their colour.

★Radium Hot Springs – Kids *103km/64mi.* The waters of Radium Hot Springs (average temperature 47°C/117°F) feed the swimming pools in the park complex *(open mid-May–mid-Oct daily 9am–11pm; rest of the year daily noon–9pm; $5.50;* ✗ ♿ *☎250-347-9485 or 800-767-1611).* The mineral content of the springs is generally lower than that of other springs developed in the Rockies.

Immediately after the hot springs, the highway passes through the rocky cleft of **Sinclair Canyon★** before reaching the park's southern entrance gate. A park **information centre** *(open late Jun–Labour Day daily 9am–7pm; late May–mid-Jun & early Sept–mid-Sept daily 9am–5pm; www.worldweb.com/parkscanada-kootenay ☎250-347-9505, winter ☎250-347-9615)* is located just inside the gate.

SKEENA VALLEY★★

British Columbia

Map of Principal Sights p 2

Cleaving the rugged Coast Mountains of northwest British Columbia, this verdant river valley holds the second largest river in the province. Rising in the Skeena Mountains of the interior, the 565km/350mi "river of mists" flows south to the town of New Hazelton, then southwest toward its confluence with Hecate Strait, following a massive channel cut by Ice Age glaciers. The valley is noted for its spectacular scenery and for the rich Tsimshian culture of the **Gitksan** tribe, which still inhabits the riverbanks.

Historical Notes

Ancestral Home – The Skeena River and its tributaries have been the territory of the Gitksan Indians for close to 10,000 years. Part of the native **Northwest Coast cultures** *(p 32)*, the Gitksan traditionally based their subsistence on salmon and berries, and western red cedar used to construct longhouses and to carve elaborate totem poles. Pole-raisings, as well as weddings, funerals and other important occasions, were accompanied by great feasts called **potlatches**.

European Contact – In the 19C European fur-trading posts, dominated by the Hudson's Bay Company, were established along the river. The area was further opened to European settlement in the 1880s with the coming of stern-wheelers to the Skeena. During the same period fishing and cannery operations, established near the mouth of the river, attracted Asians and more Europeans. In 1912 the Grand Trunk Pacific Railway was completed through the valley, an additional means of influx. Today the Yellowhead Highway follows the Skeena from east of Prince Rupert to New Hazelton.

Chilkat Blanket

from photo by Otto Nelson, Denver Art Museum

Native Decline and Renewal – The Gitksan Indians were greatly affected by the arrival of Europeans. Several factors combined to decimate the aboriginal culture of the Northwest: old patterns of hunting and gathering were curtailed in favour of supplying furs to the new immigrants; missionary zeal and European misapprehensions about the potlatch led to its ban between 1884 and 1951; totem poles were destroyed; and the introduction of diseases such as smallpox significantly reduced the native population. The Gitksan, however, maintained their system of clans and of matrilineal descent. In the 1970s a renaissance of native culture began. Today their language, Tsimshian, is taught in reserve schools, and traditional crafts such as wood- and stone-carving have been revived. The technique of silk-screening, introduced in the past few decades, has allowed artists to develop innovative approaches to classic designs.

PRINCE RUPERT

Served by BC Ferries (see Inside Passage p 45). Situated on Kaien Island near th mouth of the Skeena, this maritime city faces a scenic deep-water harbour dotte with islands. Canada's westernmost seaport, Prince Rupert was established in 190 when its site was chosen as the terminus of the Grand Trunk Pacific. Located jus south of the Alaska Panhandle, the town was expected to surpass VANCOUVER a Canada's major Pacific port. By 1922, however, Vancouver had secured that role Today with its ice-free harbour, the city is a fishing and fish-processing centre a well as a coal, grain, pulp and lumber port. It also serves as the major urban hu for northwest British Columbia. Known as the "City of Rainbows," Prince Ruper receives an annual rainfall of 2564mm/100in. Fine reproductions of Tsimshian an Haida *(p 50)* **totem poles★** are scattered throughout the city.

The **Cow Bay** area has a pleasant dockside atmosphere, with a few cafes and shops Removed to the Prince Rupert waterfront, the Grand Trunk Pacific Railway's sma **Kwinitsa Station★** serves as a railroad museum, which traces the history of railroad ing in this region through artifacts and old photographs *(open mid-May–Labou Day daily 9am–noon & 1pm–5pm; contribution requested; ☎250-624-3207 o 800-667-1994).*

★★ **Museum of Northern British Columbia** – *Open mid-May–Labour Day dail 9am–8pm (Sun 5pm). Rest of the year Mon–Sat 9am–5pm. Closed Jan 1, Dec 2 & 26. $5. ♿ ☎250-624-5637.* This museum displays selections from its holding of over 8,000 artifacts. Especially noteworthy is its fine collection of native Northwest basketry, argillite and wood carvings. At the carving shed visitors can watch craftsmen demonstrate their talents.

★★FROM PRINCE RUPERT TO 'KSAN

Allow 5hrs, including visits. 307km/184mi by Rte. 16.

★★ **North Pacific Cannery Village Museum** – *22km/14mi east of Prince* Rupert, southeast of Port Edward, 1889 Skeena Dr. Open May–Sept daily *9am–6pm. $6.* ✗ ♿ *☎250-628-3538.* In the late 19C this fish cannery was one of more than 220 on the British Columbia coast. Built in 1889 on an arm of the Skeena, the complex is the oldest surviving cannery village on the north coast. The picturesque village is still intact, as is the factory equipment, which has been out of operation since 1972. Fishing and canning methods are explained during guided tours. A historical drama about Prince Rupert is included on selected tours.

East of Port Edward the road meets the Skeena River, paralleling it through its magnificent valley. The entire route provides excellent views of the broad, turbulent river and of the cloud-shrouded, snow-capped Coast Mountains rising to 2,000m/6,000ft above. In the town of **Terrace**, the **Heritage Park**, a collection of eight old log buildings moved here from outlying areas, depicts pioneer life in the region. The river waters around the town and around nearby Kitimat to the south *(52km/31mi)* provide excellent sportfishing for trout and salmon. After Terrace, where the valley widens briefly, the road winds through the Hazelton Mountains. East of Terrace *(12km/ 7mi)* at the village of **Usk**, a small cable ferry breasts the treacherous waters of the Skeena.

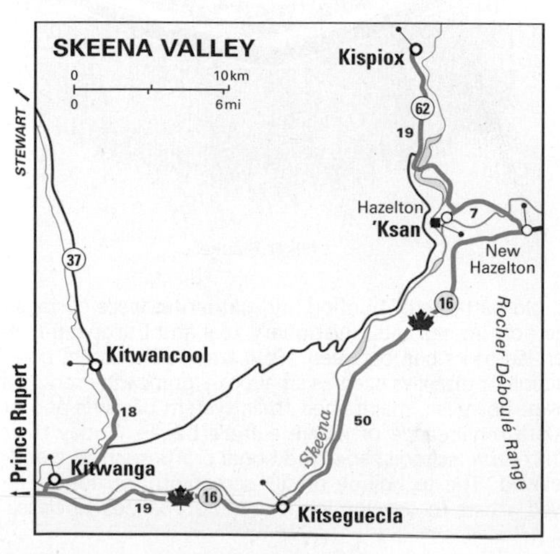

★★ **Tour of the Totems** – *Self-guided driving tour. Information about the native villages is available at the New Hazelton visitor centre on Rte. 16 (open Jul–Aug daily 9am–5pm; May–June Mon–Fri 9am–5pm; ♿ ☎250-842-6071).* Today the Gitksan still inhabit five ancient villages along the Skeena and its tributaries. Four of these villages have impressive stands of **totem poles★★★** that date from the late 19C. The weathered poles, devoid of paint, range in height from 5-9m/15-30ft.

Kitwanga – *Junction of Rte. 16 and Rte. 37 north, after crossing the Skeena River; then turn right on Bridge St.* Situated beside the Skeena River, a fine stand of about a dozen 19C totem poles graces a flat, grass-covered field against a backdrop of the impressive **Seven Sisters** Mountains (2,755m/9,039ft).

Kitwancool – *Rte. 37, 18km/11mi north of Kitwanga.* This village has the oldest existing stand of Gitksan totem poles, though several of its most venerable ones are now stored in a shed at the rear of the totem field for preservation. Active carving is still going on in this field.

Return to Rte. 16 and continue east.

Kitseguecla – *Rte. 16, 19km/12mi east of junction with Rte. 37.* The original totem poles in this village were destroyed by fire (1872) and by flood. New poles, however, now stand scattered throughout the village.

Continue east to New Hazelton and turn left on Rte. 62.

'Ksan – *Rte. 62, 7km/4mi northwest of New Hazelton. Grounds open year-round. Tour buildings open Jul–Aug daily 9am–6pm; mid-Apr–Jun & Sept daily 9am–5:30pm. $7 (grounds only $2). www.ksan-association.com ☎250-842-5544.* A complex of totem poles and longhouses re-created in the traditional style, this historical village museum provides an insight into the Gitksan culture. 'Ksan, the Gitksan name for the Skeena, is situated on the site of an ancient village near the confluence of the Skeena and Bulkley Rivers, with a magnificent view of Mt. Rocher Déboulé.

The village consists of seven major buildings: an exhibit hall featuring travelling displays and fine examples of Gitksan basketry, carving and weaving; a carving house and silkscreen workshop, where native artists from throughout the Northwest Coast work; a gift shop; and three longhouses where an extensive **native collection★★** of artifacts is used to explain the culture and lifestyle of these people. The acclaimed 'Ksan dancers perform in the summer *(last three Fri evenings of Jul & Aug; $7; ☎250-842-5544).*

Kispiox – *19km/12mi north of 'Ksan on Kispiox Valley Rd.* Situated near the confluence of the Skeena and Kispiox Rivers, this large village boasts a dozen impressive totems in a field by the waters of the Kispiox.

Canada's 7% Goods and Services Tax (GST), effective since January 1991, replaced the federal sales tax. The GST is a personal consumption tax levied, for example, on groceries, vehicles, accommodation, and health, dental, financial and educational services.
Non residents are entitled to a rebate. For information, see p 308.

VANCOUVER★★★

British Columbia
Metro Population 1,831,665
Map of Principal Sights p 2
Tourist Office ☎604-683-2000

Canada's third largest metropolis, this West Coast city has a magnificent **site★★★** on peninsula protruding into the Strait of Georgia. Situated between Burrard Inlet—th most southerly of a series of deep fjords cut into the coast of British Columbia—an the delta of the Fraser River, the city covers 113sq km/44sq mi of the peninsula' western end. A protected deep-sea port, accessibility to the Pacific Ocean, and a vir tually snow—free climate have contributed to Vancouver's prosperity and rapid growth The city is almost surrounded by mountains. To the north the Coast Mountains ris steeply, the most prominent peaks being **Hollyburn Mountain**, the twin summits of **Th Lions**, **Grouse Mountain** with its ski slopes and **Mt. Seymour** to the east. To the west acros the Strait of Georgia stand the mountains of Vancouver Island and to the southeas rises the Cascade Range, topped by the snow-clad peak of **Mt. Baker** in Washingto state. Despite heavy snowfall that provides superb skiing conditions in these moun tains, Vancouver itself rarely receives snow. Instead the city has a high rainfa compared with the rest of the country (1524mm/60in a year). Even in July an August, the sunniest months, a light rain and mist may shroud the mountains.

Historical Notes

Early History – The shores of the Strait of Georgia were the preserve of the Coas Salish Indians until 1791, when Spanish captain José Maria Narvaez was the first European to enter their waters. Surveying the coast for the British Navy, Capt. **George Vancouver** explored Burrard Inlet a year later. In 1808 Simon Fraser saw the area from the land side, at the end of his descent of the river bearing his name. Bypassed by the Fraser River gold rushers, the site aroused little interest until three Englishmen opened a brickworks in 1862 on land stretching over much of the present downtown. Having poured their life savings into what is today reputed to be the most densely populated square mile in Canada, they received the epithet "the three greenhorns." The 1860s saw the opening of sawmills on both sides of the inlet to process the area's rich timber. In 1867 John Deighton *(p 75)* opened a saloon for the mill workers. The community that developed around it became known as Gastown and was eventually named Granville in 1869, when a townsite was laid out by government surveyors.

The Coming of the Railway – The location of the terminus of the Canadian Pacific Railway was a long-standing controversy. When it was finally decided to route the railway down the Fraser Valley to Burrard Inlet, land prices skyrocketed at Port Moody, a tiny settlement at its head *(map p 79)*. The prices and lack of space there caused **William Van Horne** in 1884 to extend the line farther down the inlet to the site of Granville. Overnight a town was born. At its official incorporation in 1886, the city was baptized Vancouver, Van Horne's choice. Almost immediately thereafter fire destroyed the community, but by 1887 it had recovered sufficiently to welcome the first trans-Canadian passenger train.

Vancouver

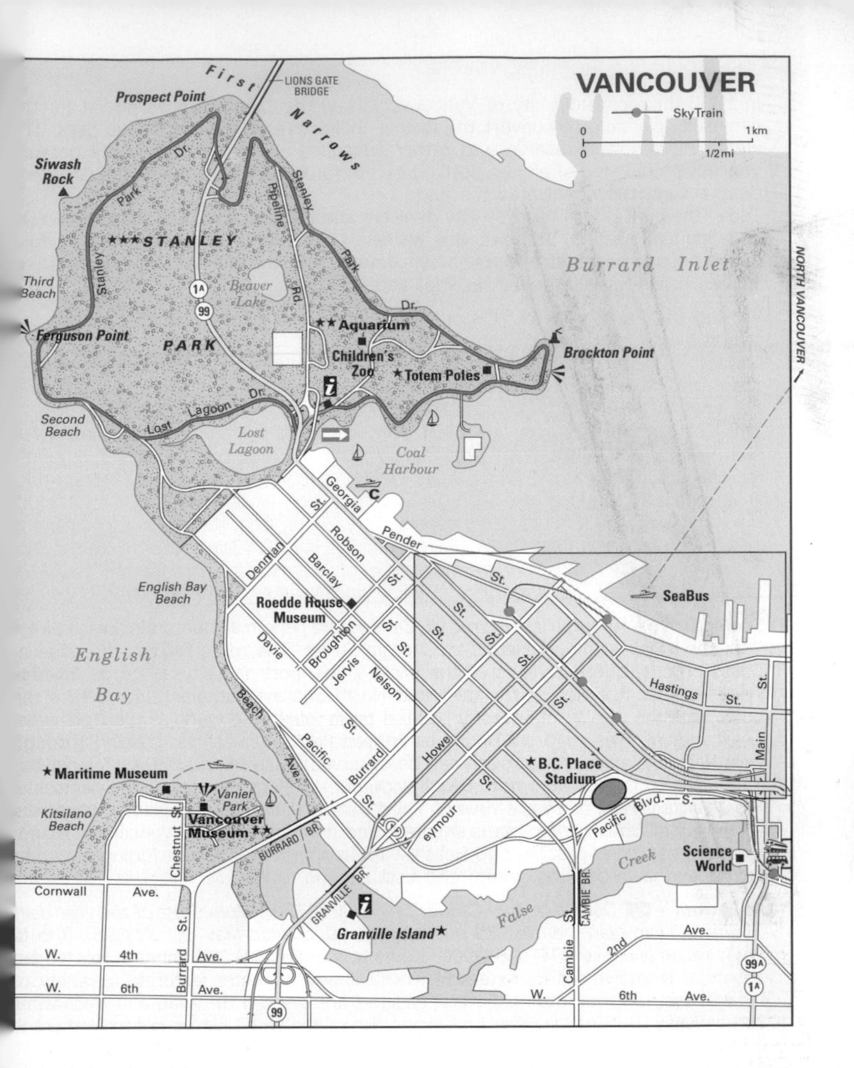

Vancouver Today – Vancouver has become the largest city in the province, with a metropolitan population of over 1.8 million; in Canada, only Toronto and Montreal have greater populations. The financial, commercial and industrial centre of British Columbia, Vancouver is also the province's major port—indeed, Canada's largest port. Bulk loads of grain and potash from the Prairies, and of lumber, logs, coal, sulphur and other minerals from interior British Columbia arrive by train and are exported chiefly to Japan and other countries bordering the Pacific Ocean. Vancouver is a centre for forestry and fishing as well. The city and its environs continue to be a popular tourist destination, particularly for cruise-ship passengers.

In 1986 Vancouver hosted the world exposition, **Expo '86**, as part of its centennial celebrations. The exposition site on the north and east shores of False Creek *(map above)* has been cleared for commercial and residential development.

In recent years Vancouver has added a variety of structures to its skyline, notably the turquoise-topped Cathedral Place, which mirrors its venerable neighbour, Chateau-styled **Hotel Vancouver** (1939); the swank 23-storey Waterfront Centre Hotel opposite Canada Place; the colosseum-shaped public library of controversial Library Square (Robson & Homer Streets) and, opposite it, the 1,800-seat Ford Centre for the Performing Arts. The glittering Price Waterhouse complex next door to Harbour Centre sports a domed atrium and garden. Overlooking False Creek, General Motors Place, a more intimate venue than its larger counterpart, BC Place Stadium, is home to Vancouver's ice hockey team, the *Canucks*.

★★★STANLEY PARK *Map above*

Vancouver's outstanding attraction, the 405ha/1000 acre park has a magnificent **site★★★** at the end of a peninsula that almost closes Burrard Inlet at **First Narrows.** Washed on three sides by the inlet waters, this densely forested expanse offers splendid views of the North Shore Mountains, the peaks of Vancouver Island, the city and the port.

In 1886 the month-old city of Vancouver asked the Canadian government for th
peninsula, planning to convert the former military reserve into a public park. Th
idea of a woodland reserve was rather advanced at the time, primarily becaus
Vancouver consisted of almost nothing except forest. Ottawa agreed, and Governo
General **Lord Stanley** dedicated the park.
Today the park is well used by city dwellers and tourists alike. Especially on week
ends joggers, skaters, amblers, dog-walkers (including professionals walking fou
to five dogs at once), stroller-pushers, camera-clickers and artists crowd the gree
spaces, beaches, recreational facilities and walkways.

Visiting the Park – The park is open daily year-round. To access the park by car
stay in the far right lane of Georgia St. and follow the overhead sign. Traffic withi
the park is routed counterclockwise one-way along the two-lane perimeter road *(se
scenic drive below)*, except for Pipeline Road near Beaver Lake. Coin-operated parkin
machines are located throughout the park for all spaces *($1/2hrs or $2/all day)*. Nume
rous walking trails crisscross the forested interior and a much-used 9km/5.5mi pave
path known as the "sea wall" rims the shoreline. Facilities include cricket grounds
tennis courts, shuffleboard, picnic areas, children's playgrounds, and a swimming poo
at Second Beach. Maps are available at information kiosk. ✗ ♿ ☎ 604-257-840
Horse-drawn carriage tours *(1hr)* depart every 20min from the parking lot near the
information booth on Park Drive *(Jul–Labour Day daily 9:40am–5:20pm; rest of Sep
& Apr–Jun daily 10am–5pm; mid-Mar–end of Mar & Oct daily 10am–4pm; $12
Stanley Park Horse-Drawn Tours Ltd. www.stanleyparktours.com ☎ 604-681-5115)*

Scenic Drive – *About 1hr. 10km/6mi.* Circling the park in a counterclockwise direc
tion, the drive begins and ends at Georgia Street. The route follows the edge o
Coal Harbour, offering views of the yacht clubs, port and city as far as **Brockton
Point**, with its fine **view** of the inlet and North Shore Mountains. Just before the
point note the display of brightly painted **totem poles★**, the work of the Northwest
Coast Indians. The road continues to **Prospect Point** where ships, passing through
First Narrows in and out of port, can be observed. Then the road turns inland, but
paths lead to the sea wall near **Siwash Rock**, cut off from the rest of the peninsula
From **Ferguson Point** there are **views** of Third Beach; Point Grey Peninsula, where the
University of British Columbia is situated; and the mountains on Vancouver Island
The road continues past Second Beach, various sports facilities (including a putting
course and lawn-bowling green) and Lost Lagoon.

★★ **Aquarium** – Kids *Open late Jun–Labour Day daily 9:30am–7pm. Rest of the year daily
10am–5:30pm (Jan 1 & Dec 25 noon–5pm). $9.95 (mid-May–Oct $11.95).* ✗ ♿ P
www.vanaqua.org ☎ 604-268-9900. Home to more than 8,000 animals, this lauded
aquarium is known for its extensive marine mammal centre featuring a variety of
whales, seals and sea otters. Several galleries are devoted to ocean and freshwater
fish native to British Columbia and exotic fish of the world. At its entrance there is
a bronze sculpture of a killer whale by acclaimed Haida sculptor Bill Reid.
The aquarium was first to publicly exhibit **killer whales** (also known as orcas), distinguished by their black and white colouring and dorsal fin. Performing regularly
for visitors in their 5 million litre/1.3 million gallon outdoor habitat, these large
mammals demonstrate their amazing power, grace and intelligence.
A special feature of the Arctic Canada section is the **beluga whales**, seen through
large viewing windows swimming underwater.
Indoors a highlight is the walk-in **Amazon Rain Forest** where crocodiles, anacondas,
turtles, lizards and two-toed sloths live in a steamy environment, complete with suitable vegetation and a multitude of brightly coloured birds. Adjacent to the rain forest,
tanks contain sharks, piranhas, electric and moray eels and other tropical creatures.

Near the aquarium is the **Children's Zoo and Miniature Railway** Kids *(open year-round
daily 11am–4pm, weather permitting; $2.30;* ♿ *☎ 604-257-8400)*.

★★DOWNTOWN *5hrs. Map p 74.*

Positioned along Granville Street the commercial centre is closed to all traffic except
buses for a six-block pedestrian thoroughfare known as **The Mall**. The major department stores and extensive underground shopping developments called the Pacific
and Vancouver Centres are located here. At the northern end is Granville Square,
a plaza with views of port activities at the wharves below. Steps lead to the attractively renovated rail station from which a passenger ferry service known as SeaBus
crosses Burrard Inlet, offering good **views** of the harbour and city.

★★ **Canada Place** – Designed by architect Eberhard Zeidler, this gleaming white structure resembles a flotilla of sailing ships at anchor in Burrard Inlet. Constructed as
the Canada Pavilion for Expo '86, the complex consists of a hotel, office tower and
convention centre. Exhibition halls are enclosed by the "sails" of fibreglass yarn
coated with teflon, tensioned to appear as though they are catching the ocean
winds. Along with cruise ships that moor at its sides, Canada Place has transformed
the waterfront.

PRACTICAL INFORMATION

Area Code: 604

Getting Around

By Public Transportation – Vancouver Regional Transit System operates an integrated network of rapid transit, ferries and buses. Hours of operation vary among the different services. **SkyTrain**, the city's rapid transit, services downtown, Burnaby, New Westminster and Surrey; *(daily 5:30–1am; every 2-5 min)*. **SeaBus**, passenger harbour ferries, operates between Vancouver and the North Shore *(Mon–Sat 6am–12:30am, Sun 8am–11pm; every 15-30min)*. Adult fare during off-peak hours is $1.50; weekdays before 6:30pm fares are based on zone boundaries. Fares are the same for all services; exact fare is required. FareSaver books of 10 tickets *($13.75)* and a DayPass *($6)* are available from ticket machines and outlets. Transfers are free for 90min of unlimited travel. **Bus** service connects SkyTrain and SeaBus at all stations. Buses operate 7 days/wk. A *Transit Guide* map *($1.50)* is sold at Ticketmaster outlets and convenience stores. For route information and schedules ☎521-0400.

By Car – Use of public transportation or walking is strongly encouraged within the city as roads are often congested and street parking may be difficult to find. Metered and garage parking available. Car rentals: Avis ☎606-2847; Hertz ☎688-2411; Tilden ☎685-6111.

By Taxi – Advance Cabs ☎876-5555; Black Top Cabs ☎731-1111; Yellow Cabs ☎681-1111.

General Information

Accommodations and Visitor Information – For **hotels/motels**, contact Tourism Vancouver ☎683-2000. Reservation services: Beachside B&B Registry ☎922-7773; AAA B&B Ltd. ☎872-0938; Best Canadian B&B Network ☎738-7207. Vancouver Tourist InfoCentre Plaza Level, 200 Burrard Street *(open mid-May–Sept daily 8am–6pm; rest of the year Mon–Fri 8:30am–5pm, Sat 9am–5pm)* or contact **Tourism Vancouver**, 200 Burrard Street, Vancouver, BC, V6C 3L6 www.tourism-vancouver.org ☎683-2000.

Local Press – Daily: *The Vancouver Sun* and *The Province.* Monthly guide *(free)* to entertainment, shopping and restaurants: *Where.*

Entertainment – Consult arts and entertainment supplements in local newspapers (Thursday edition) for schedule of cultural events and addresses of principal theatres and concert halls. Ticketmaster ☎280-4444 (major credit cards accepted).

Sports – BC Lions Football Club: home games at BC Place Stadium; season Jun–Nov; schedules ☎583-7747. Vancouver Canadians (baseball): home games at Nat Bailey Stadium; season Apr–Sept; schedules ☎872-5232. Vancouver Canucks (ice hockey): home games at General Motors Place; season Oct–Apr; schedules ☎899-7400. Vancouver Grizzlies (NBA basketball): home games at General Motors Place; season Oct–Apr; schedules ☎899-4667. Tickets for all events are sold through the venues or through Ticketmaster ☎280-4400 (major credit cards accepted).

Useful Numbers

	☎
Police	911 (emergency) or 717-3321
BC Rail (North Vancouver), *1311 W. 1st St.*	984-5246
VIA Rail, *1150 Station St.*	800-835-3037
BC Ferries (in province)	888-223-3779
Greyhound Lines of Canada (bus)	482-8747
Vancouver International Airport	276-6101
Canadian Automobile Assn., *999 W. Broadway*	268-5600
CAA Emergency Road Service (24hr)	293-2222
Shoppers Drug Mart (24hr pharmacy), *1125 Davie St.*	669-2424
Main Post Office, *349 W. Georgia St.*	662-5722
Road Conditions	660-9770
Weather (24hr)	664-9010

★**Harbour Centre Tower** – *Observation deck open May–mid-Oct daily 8:30am–10:30pm. Rest of the year daily 9am–9pm. $8 (valid for same date return visit at night).* ✂ ♿ *www.harbour-centre-tower.com ☎ 604-689-0421.* Visitors ascend this distinctive office building via exterior elevators to arrive at the circular observation deck (167m/553ft above ground) with its magnificent **panorama**★★★ of the city, mountains, ocean and Fraser River delta.

★★**Art Gallery** – *Open mid-May–mid-Oct Mon–Fri 10am–6pm (Thu 9pm), Sat 10am–5pm, Sun & holidays noon–5pm. Rest of the year Tue–Fri 10am–6pm (Thu 9pm), Sat 10am–5pm, Sun & holidays noon–5pm. Closed Jan 1 & Dec 25. $7.50 ($9.75 in summer).* ✂ ♿ P *www.vanartgallery.bc.ca ☎ 604-662-4719.* Designed in 1907 by Francis Rattenbury, the Neoclassical building served as the city courthouse for 70 years. It was tastefully converted by Arthur Erickson so that galleries open off the central rotunda with its glass-topped dome, through which natural light enters.

A highlight is the collection of paintings and drawings by British Columbian **Emily Carr** (1871-1945), one of Canada's best-known and original artists. Her portrayals of West Coast landscapes and Indian villages are striking, as evidenced in such famous works on display as *Big Raven* (c.1931) and *Scorned as Timber, Beloved of the Sky* (c.1936). There are also changing exhibitions of regional, national and international interest from the permanent collection.

★**Robson Square** – Stretching from Nelson Street almost to Georgia Street, this complex was also designed by Arthur Erickson. Opened in 1979, the square helped transform the downtown area and now houses the offices of the provincial court. A seven-storey **law court building** (**A**) with a spectacular slanted-glass roof complements a series of terraced gardens with waterfalls and plants on top of offices *(between Smithe and Robson)*. A plaza under Robson Street contains outdoor cafes, a skating rink and a conference centre.

★**BC Place Stadium** – *Guided tours (1hr 30min) available early-Jun–Labour Day Wed & Fri 11am & 1pm. $6.* ♿ P *www.bcplacestadium.com ☎ 604-669-2300.* Resembling an enormous quilted marshmallow, this stadium is the largest air-supported domed amphitheatre in the world. Designed by Phillips Barratt, it opened in 1983. Inflated by huge fans the teflon and fibreglass roof is secured by steel cables. Containing heating elements to melt winter snow, the roof is self-cleaning with the aid of area rainfall and translucent enough so that artificial lighting is rarely required. The stadium seats up to 60,000 with no interior supports. A glass-enclosed concourse on the upper level offers a city **panorama**.

★★**Chinatown** – *Pender St. between Carrall St. and Gore Ave.* This colourful quarter is the centre of Vancouver's large Chinese community. Many restaurants and shops sell oriental foods and wares. The neighborhood is particularly lively during the Chinese New Year.

★**Dr. Sun Yat-Sen Classical Chinese Garden** – *578 Carrall St. behind Chinese Cultural Centre on Pender St. Open May–mid-Jun daily 10am–6pm. Late Jun–mid-Sept daily 9:30am–7pm. Rest of the year daily 10am–4:30pm. Closed Jan 1 & Dec 25. $6.50.* ♿ *www.discovervancouver.com/sun ☎ 604-689-7133.* Modelled after classical gardens developed in the Chinese city of Suzhou during the Ming dynasty

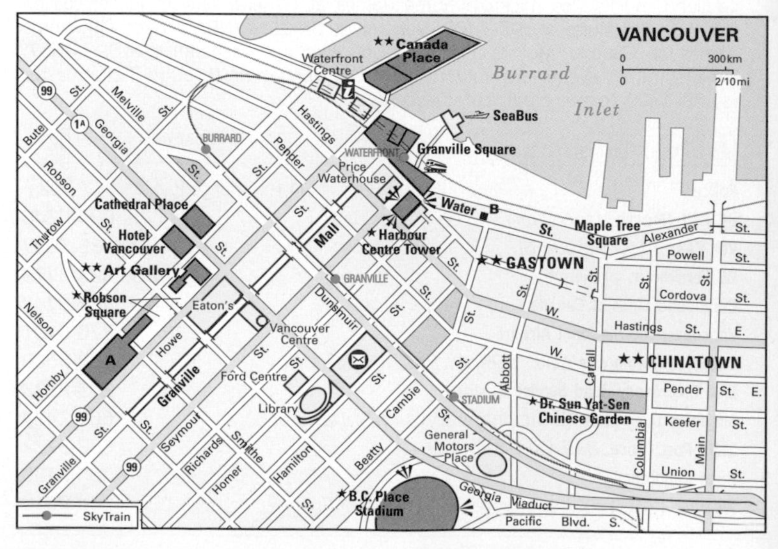

(14-17C), this garden is a small oasis of contemplative calm. Pine, bamboo and flowering plum trees grow amid limestone rocks, water, arched bridges and covered walkways.
Next door to the garden is the equally serene Dr. Sun Yat-Sen Park, graced by a large, placid pond.

★★ **Gastown** – This attractive area between Carrall and Richards Streets combines restored buildings of the late 19C with modern structures constructed to blend with their surroundings. Gastown has not always been chic. In the 1860s sawmill owners on Burrard Inlet had strict rules against consumption of alcohol on their premises. Thirsty mill employees had to walk 19km/12mi to New Westminster until an enterprising Englishman, John Deighton, arrived at the edge of mill property with a barrel of whisky. Nicknamed **Gassy Jack** because of his garrulousness, he enticed mill workers to build his saloon, rewarding them with whisky. Soon he had a lively trade and the resulting community took his name—Gassy's town or simply Gastown.
Over the years the character of the area has changed several times. Today its centre is **Maple Tree Square**, where a statue of Gassy Jack stands. **Water Street** is an attractive section with its gaslights and shops. On the corner of Cambie stands a **steam clock (B)** powered by a steam engine. The mechanism actually works by gravity and the clock "hoots" out the hour, half hour and quarter hour.

★ **Harbour Tour** (**C**) – *Map p 71. Departs from Coal Harbour Jun–Sept daily 11:30am, 12:45pm, 1pm & 2:15pm. Apr–May & Oct daily 2:30pm & 4pm. Round-trip 1hr 15min. Commentary. $19.* ✗ ♿ 🅿. *Harbour Cruises Ltd www.boatcruises.com ☎ 604-688-7246.* This boat trip by paddle-wheeler makes a pleasant excursion, enabling visitors to see Vancouver's busy port and offering fine views of the city and mountains.

Cathedral Place – The handsome glass and limestone high rise located opposite Hotel Vancouver is home to the **Canadian Craft Museum**, a showcase for international as well as Canadian crafts. Situated off the courtyard, the museum building houses furniture, textiles, jewellery and sculpture, displayed in changing exhibits in a large light-filled space on the ground floor. Note at the rear of the building the bevelled-glass doors (*Crystal Egress*, 1991), which are part of the collection *(open May–Labour Day Mon–Sat 10am–5pm, Sun & holidays noon–5pm; rest of the year Mon, Wed–Sat 10am–5pm (Thu 9pm), Sun & holidays noon–5pm; closed Jan 1, Dec 25 & Dec 26; $4;* ♿ 🅿 *☎ 604-687-8266).*

Roedde House Museum – *Map p 71. 1415 Barclay St. (at Broughton St.). Visit by guided tour (30min) only, year-round Tue–Fri 8:30am–5:30pm & 2nd, 3rd & 4th Sun of each month 2pm–4pm. $4 (Sun $5, includes tea).* ♿ 🅿 *☎ 604-684-7040.* This Queen Anne style house with a characteristic polygonal tower was built in 1893 for Vancouver bookbinder Gustav Roedde. Its design is attributed to Francis Rattenbury, architect of Victoria's famed Empress Hotel *(p 83)*. Furnished to the period, six rooms on the ground floor of the three-storey dwelling can be visited. On one side the house is bordered by a small Victorian garden with a gazebo and, on the other side, the intimate Barclay Heritage Square park.

SIGHTS OUTSIDE DOWNTOWN

★★★ **UBC Museum of Anthropology** – *Map p 78. Open mid-May–early Sept daily 10am–5pm (Tue 9pm). Rest of the year Tue–Sun 11am–5pm (Tue 9pm). Closed Dec 25–25. $6 (free Tue 5pm–9pm).* ✗ ♿ 🅿 *www.moa.ubc.ca ☎ 604-822-3825.* At the end of Point Grey Peninsula, the University of British Columbia has a large campus overlooking the Strait of Georgia and the mountains of Vancouver Island. Known for its site and for its research facilities in agriculture, forestry and oceanography, the university is also famous for its collection of Northwest Coast Indian art.
Opened in 1976 the **museum building**★★—the work of Arthur Erickson—is an architectural masterpiece. A glass and concrete structure, it admirably complements the site. Flanked by exhibits, a ramp leads down to the **Great Hall**★★. Glass walls rise 14m/45ft around the magnificent collection of Haida and Kwakwaka'wakw **totem poles** and other large wood carvings, many dating from mid-19C. The trees, sea, sky and mountains are visible through the glass walls, giving visitors the impression of seeing the poles in their original surroundings, not in a museum. The designs of the poles and Haida houses on the museum grounds were inspired by older carvings now decayed.
In contrast to the immense sculptures in the Great Hall, the carvings in the **Masterpiece Gallery** are tiny and intricate. Works in silver, gold, argillite, horn, bone, ivory, stone and wood bear the same designs in miniature as the monumental sculpture elsewhere.
One corner of the museum is devoted to **Raven and the First Men**★, a massive modern carving in yellow cedar by Bill Reid *(p 52)*, symbolic of birth. A huge raven stands on a clam shell that is being pushed open by a series of small figures. The remainder

of the building is predominantly "visible storage" galleries, where the museum's worldwide collections from ancient times to the present are on display, catalogued by region and civilization. There are also galleries for changing exhibits.

★★**Queen Elizabeth Park** – *Map p 78. West 33rd Ave. and Cambie St.* This beautiful park lies at the geographic centre and highest point (150m/500ft) of Vancouver. The road from the entrance climbs through an arboretum to the **Bloedel Floral Conservatory**★, a geodesic-domed structure of glass and aluminum *(open Apr–Sept Mon–Fri & holidays 9am–8pm, weekends 10am–9pm; rest of the year daily 10am–5pm; closed Dec 25; $3.30;* ✗ ♿ 🅿 ☎ *604-257-8584)*. On the grounds near the fountain stands Henry Moore's monumental sculpture *Knife Edge, Two Piece*. Inside the conservatory are examples of tropical and desert vegetation, enlivened by a number of colourful birds. In clear weather there are extraordinary **views**★★★ from the conservatory's plaza of the city and mountains by day and night, including the majestic snow-capped peak of Mt. Baker of the Cascades more than 110km/ 70mi away.
The other attraction of the park is the lovely **Sunken Gardens**★★. Paths weave among the flowers to a waterfall and a bridge, from which there are views of the gardens and city.

★★**Vancouver Museum** – *Map p 71. In Vanier Park. Open year-round Jul–Labour Day daily 10am–5pm. Rest of the year Tue–Sun 10am–5pm. Closed Dec 25. $8.* ♿ 🅿 *www.vanmuseum.bc.ca* ☎ *604-736-4431*. Through permanent and rotating exhibits, this museum specializes in the history and art of Vancouver and Canada's native cultures. It also has a fine collection of Asian art and artifacts. Representing the creature that traditionally guards the harbour in Indian legend, a huge stainless steel **crab**★—the work of sculptor George Norris—dominates the front entrance in an ornamental pool. From the parking area there is an excellent **view**★★ of the city and North Shore Mountains.
In the **Exploration and Settlement galleries**★, Vancouver's past is traced from the first arrival of Europeans. A Hudson's Bay Company trading store has been re-created, along with steerage quarters on an immigrant ship. The birth of Vancouver as a lumber village is shown with its growth after the arrival of the "iron horse." A series of room reconstructions of the 1910 era illustrates the city's rapid development.
Changing exhibits draw on the museum's rich collection of artifacts of the **Northwest Coast tribes**, which show an extraordinary artistic finesse. Tiny woven baskets of cedar and bear grass, argillite carvings, shaman regalia, canoe—size feast bowls, and masks with two faces—the first, an animal, opening to reveal the second, a human, reflecting the union between these two lifeforms—are examples of the variety of items in the collection.

To the left of the museum rises the distinctive conical dome of the **MacMillan Planetarium**, which has become a Vancouver landmark since its opening in 1968. The planetarium is part of the **Pacific Space Centre**★★ Kids, the adjoining multi-million dollar facility that houses a space station, flight simulator and other interactive exhibits *(open Jul–Aug daily 9am–5pm; rest of the year Tue–Sun 9am–5pm; closed Dec 25; $12;* ♿ 🅿 *http://pacific-space-centre.bc.ca* ☎ *604-738-7827)*. In the **Southam Observatory** visitors can look through the giant telescope at the sun, moon, planets and stars.

★**Maritime Museum** – Kids *Map p 71. In Vanier Park. Ferry to Granville Island departs from the museum wharf. Open Victoria Day–Labour Day daily 10am–5pm. Rest of the year Wed–Sat & holidays 10am–5pm, Sun noon–5pm. Closed Dec 25. $6.* 🅿 *www.vmm.bc.ca* ☎ *604-257-8300*. Ship models and artifacts illustrate the maritime history of Vancouver and British Columbia. The highlight of the collection is the **St. Roch**★★, a Royal Canadian Mounted Police patrol ship, which navigated the Northwest Passage in both directions.
After Roald Amundsen's completion of the passage *(p 291)*, various countries sought control of the Arctic. To assert sovereignty over the northland, the Canadian government decided to send a ship through the passage. Under Capt. Henry Larsen, the *St. Roch* left Vancouver in June 1940 and, after being frozen in several times, reached Halifax in October 1942. In 1944 the return trip of 13,510km/7,295 nautical mi in ice-strewn waters took only 86 days. Not only was the *St. Roch* the first ship to navigate the passage both ways, but the first to complete the east-west voyage in one season. The 32m/104ft wooden vessel has been completely restored, with authentic items in all the cabins and can be boarded.

★**Granville Island** – *Map p 71. Accessible by car from Granville Bridge & West 4th Ave. (follow signs to under the bridge), or by ferry from Vancouver Aquatic Centre on Beach Ave. or from Maritime Museum. Visitor centre, 1592 Johnson St., open year-round daily 9am–6pm.* ✗ ♿ www.granvilleisland.bc.ca ☎ *604-666-7535*. This one-time industrial area under Granville Bridge has been renovated to house art galleries and studios, boutiques, restaurants, theatres and a hotel, in addition to some surviving industry. Visitors can observe artists as they craft jewellery, textiles, ceramics, glass and other wares in the numerous warehouse-sized workshops. The Emily Carr Institute of Art and Design is a dominant structure here, populating the island with students. The island's highlight is the **public market**★ *(open mid-May–mid-Oct daily 9am–6pm; rest of the year Tue–Sun 9am–6pm; ✗ ♿ www.granvilleisland.bc.ca ☎ 604-689-8447)* where stalls of fresh produce vie with products of Vancouver's many ethnic groups.

★**VanDusen Botanical Garden (D)** – *Map p 78. On 37th Ave. at Oak St. Open year-round daily 10am–dusk. Closed Dec 25. $5.50. ✗ ♿ P www.hedgerows.com ☎ 604-878-9274.* This 22ha/55 acre garden offers fine displays of plants in geographic as well as botanical arrangements. In addition to a rose garden, a magnolia garden and a rhododendron walk, there are sections devoted to vegetation of the Southern Hemispheric, Mediterranean and Sino-Himalayan areas.

Science World – Kids *Map p 71. Quebec St. and Terminal Ave. Open Jul–Aug daily 10am–6pm. Rest of the year Mon-Fri 10am–5pm, weekends & holidays 10am–6pm. Closed Dec 25. $10.50. ✗ ♿ P www.scienceworld.bc.ca ☎ 604-268-6363.* Situated on the Expo '86 site overlooking False Creek, this stimulating centre, opened in 1989, features interactive exhibits such as a plasma ball that demonstrates the properties of an electric current, and a cyclone chamber that re-creates nature's forces. The complex includes an Omnimax theatre, where films are shown on a wrap-around, domed screen; the Music Machines Gallery, where visitors can operate a large synthesizer; and a children's problem-solving gallery.

★**Vanterm (E)** – *Map p 78. At north end of Clark Dr.; take overpass to visitor parking lot. Public viewing centre open year-round Mon–Fri 9am–4pm. P www.portvancouver.com ☎ 604-666-3226.* The enormous container-handling complex can be viewed from an observation lounge that overlooks the loading and unloading docks for ships, trucks and trains, against a backdrop of the North Shore Mountains.

★**The North Shore** – *Map p 78.* The mountains descend quite precipitously towards Burrard Inlet on its north side, cut not only by deep fjords such as Indian Arm and Howe Sound, but by steep valleys or canyons of several small rivers and creeks—Capilano, Lynn and Seymour being the best known. Houses on the north shore are, for the most part, expensive and often cling to mountain slopes that permit good views of the inlet and city.

★★**Cypress Provincial Park** – *12km/7mi from downtown by Lions Gate Bridge and Hwy. 1/Rte. 99. Open year-round (end of May–early Nov gates closed 11pm–7am). Hiking, picnicking, biking, skiing. ♿ P ☎ 604-924-2200. For trail maps contact BC Parks ☎ 604-924-2200.* This 3,000ha/7,400 acre expanse includes Hollyburn Ridge and Cypress Bowl, popular local ski areas. The access road leads through a forest of Douglas fir and western hemlock to Highview Lookout, which permits a breathtaking **view**★★★ of the Vancouver area. On clear days Mt. Baker adds its stunning snow-clad mass to the scene. At 1,300m/4,264ft above sea level, the ridgetops here abound with amabalis fir, mountain hemlock and yellow cypress, for which the park is named.

★**Capilano Canyon** – *9km/6mi from downtown by Lions Gate Bridge and Capilano Rd.* This deep canyon can be appreciated by visiting the narrow pedestrian **suspension bridge**★ (**F**) 70m/230ft above the Capilano River *(open May–Labour Day daily 8:30am–dusk; mid-Sept–Oct & late Mar–Apr daily 9am–dusk; rest of the year daily 9am–5pm; closed Dec 25; $9.95; ✗ P www.capbridge.com ☎ 604-985-7474).* Built in 1889 the bridge is 137m/450ft long and sways as visitors walk across it. On the opposite side is a pleasant glade of Douglas fir and western red cedar. The entrance side has been largely commercialized.

Farther along Capilano Road, **Capilano River Regional Park** offers pleasant walks and views of the canyon from below. At the northern end of the park *(access from Nancy Greene Way)* are Cleveland Dam and Capilano Lake, a reservoir for the city of Vancouver. Across the lake there is a **view**★ of the double peak of The Lions.

★**Grouse Mountain** – *13km/8mi from downtown by Lions Gate Bridge, Capilano Rd. and Nancy Greene Way. Tram operates year-round daily 9am–10pm. $16.95. ✗ ♿ P ☎ 604-984-0661.* The aerial tram rises to an elevation of 1,100m/3,700ft, offering, as it ascends, a splendid **view**★★ of the city, and from the summit, a panorama embracing, on clear days, Vancouver Island, the Fraser delta and Burrard Inlet.

★**Mt. Seymour Provincial Park** – *16km/10mi from downtown by Second Narrows Bridge; take the third exit (Mt. Seymour Parkway) and follow signs. Open year-round daily 8am–10pm. Hiking, horseback riding, mountain biking, skiing. ✗ (winter only) ♿ P. For trail maps contact park office ☎ 604-924-2200.* From the park entrance a road climbs steeply to Deep Cove Lookout *(8km/5mi)* from which there is a **view**★★ to the east. The village of Deep Cove, Indian Arm and Simon Fraser University in Burnaby are visible in clear weather. From just below the ski centre *(13km/8mi)*, there is a **view**★★ of the city and Vancouver Island on clear days. In the distance the peak of Mt. Baker in Washington state can usually be seen above the clouds.

★**Simon Fraser University** – *Map p 78. In Burnaby. Gaglardi Way. Guided tours (2hrs) available; 2-week advance reservations required. Closed Dec 25–Jan 1. ✗ ♿ P www.sfu.ca ☎ 604-291-3210.* Located within the traffic-laden suburb of

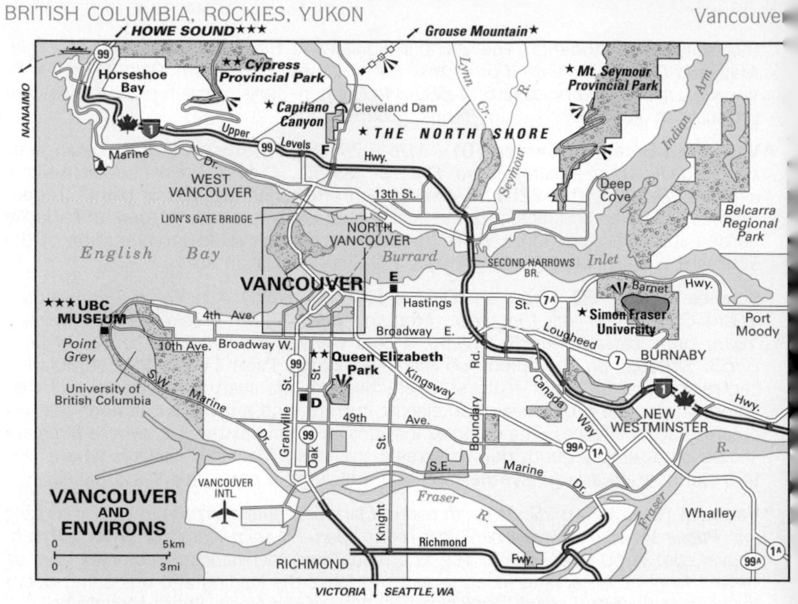

Burnaby, this architecturally famous, albeit controversial, university has a lovely isolated site on Burnaby Mountain, with **views** of the North Shore Mountains. The unique ensemble of interconnected buildings constructed along a tree-lined, partially covered pedestrian mall and around a large quadrangle with a pond was designed by Vancouver natives **Arthur Erickson** and **Geoffrey Massey**. The harmony of these somewhat harsh concrete structures derives from their design and construction as a unit. Erickson went on to design other interesting structures, among them the UBC Museum of Anthropology, Robson Square and the renovated Art Gallery, the Bank of Canada in Ottawa and Roy Thomson Hall in Toronto.
Since its opening in 1965, the university has gained a reputation as a progressive educational institution. It operates year-round on a trimester system, each term being independent so that students can study continuously or take only one or two terms a year.

EXCURSIONS *Map below*

★★★ **Howe Sound** – Extending some 48km/30mi into the Coast Mountains, this deep fjord provides some of the province's most dramatic coastal scenery. Howe Sound can be admired by train, boat or car.

A large steam engine that once pulled trains across Canada, the **Royal Hudson 2860**, makes regular trips to Squamish from the BC Rail Station in North Vancouver *(departs late May–mid-Sept Wed–Sun 9am; return by boat arriving Vancouver 4pm; round-trip 7hrs; commentary; reservations required; $72.95;* ✗ ♿ P *www.boatcruises.com ☎ 604-688-7246)*. The return trip is a spectacular voyage aboard the **MV Britannia**. The views of both sides of the fjord are excellent, as are those of Vancouver harbour, the point of disembarkation.

By car *(66km/41mi one-way, allow 3hrs)*, travellers follow Route 99, a road built through virtually sheer cliffs, providing incredible **views★★★** of the mountains and the blue-green waters of the sound between **Horseshoe Bay**, a picturesque ferry port *(best viewed from Route 99 on return trip)* for Vancouver Island transit, and Squamish. Travellers may wish to continue 50km/31mi north of Squamish to the popular ski resort of Whistler, BC *(below)*.

★★ **BC Museum of Mining** – *In Britannia Beach, 53km/33mi north of Vancouver. Open Jul–Aug daily 10am–4:30pm. Early May–Jun & Sept–mid-Oct Wed–Sun 10am–4:30pm. $9.50.* ✗ *☎ 604-896-2233.* Set in the Britannia mine, which was once the largest copper producer in the British Empire, this museum provides a fascinating introduction to mining. A video presentation *(20min)* traces the mine's history from discovery in 1888 to closure in 1974. Then follows a **guided tour** *(1hr 30min)* into one of the tunnels: visitors watch as mining equipment is demonstrated, and view the old gravity-fed mill. The mining house *(three levels)* has displays on mining in British Columbia, with particular emphasis on the Britannia mine.

★★ **Shannon Falls** – *60km/37mi.* These impressive falls cascade 335m/1,100ft over a cliff in pleasant surroundings.

As travellers approach the town of Squamish, the 700m/2,296ft granite monolith known as **Stawamus Chief** comes into view. Its sheer cliff face attracts rock-climbers from around the world.

Squamish – *66km/41mi.* This lumber centre occupies a fine site at the foot of snow-capped peaks, including Mt. Garibaldi (2,678m/8,786ft).

★★ **Whistler** – *117km/73mi north of Vancouver by Rte 99. Visitor centre in Whistler Conference Centre open year-round daily 9am–5pm (extended hours mid-Jun–mid-Sept & Dec–Feb). ☎ 604-932-2394.* This well-planned resort community with its three alpine hamlets (Whistler Village, Village North and Upper Village) is dominated by two massive peaks, **Blackcomb Mountain** (2,284m/7,494ft) and **Whistler Mountain** (2,182m/7,160ft), groomed for state-of-the-art skiing. Summer recreation is also plentiful: boating at nearby Alta Lake *(canoe rentals)*, fishing, horseback riding, tennis and golf. Hiking and biking trails abound *(map available from visitor centre or area hotels).*

Nearby **Garibaldi Provincial Park**, a hike-in only park, offers additional trails of varying difficulty as well as campsites *(open year-round; parking area accessible by unpaved road from Whistler Village; park map available from Whistler visitor centre or contact BC Parks ☎ 604-898-3678).*

★ **Fort Langley National Historic Site** – Kids *56km/35mi southeast of Vancouver by Trans-Can Hwy., Glover St. and Mavis Ave. or Rte. 7 and ferry. Open Mar–Oct daily 10am–5pm. $4. http://fas.sfu.ca/parkscan/fl ☎ 604-513-4777.* The fort was one of a network of trading posts established by the Hudson's Bay Company in British Columbia in the early 19C. Fur trading was the predominant occupation, though a large farm was operated, and salmon were caught and packaged for trade. Today the re-created buildings of the wooden-palisaded fort can be visited. The storehouse, the only structure original to the site, has a fine **collection**★ of furs and of the trading goods once exchanged for them. In the Big House, quarters of the resident Hudson's Bay Company officials can be seen. Costumed staff demonstrate smithery and barrelmaking in the reconstructed blacksmith's shop and cooperage.

★ **From Vancouver to Hope** – *Map p 49. 141km/88mi east of Vancouver by Trans-Can Hwy.* The Trans-Canada Highway heads east from Vancouver along the wide valley of the Lower Fraser River, flanked by the Cascade Mountains—notably the pyramidal peak of Mt. Baker to the south and the Coast Ranges to the north. Rich black soil, deposited over eons, supports dairy cattle, hay fields and market gardens. The small town of **Hope**★ serves as the gateway to the majestic Fraser and Thompson Canyons *(p 44).*

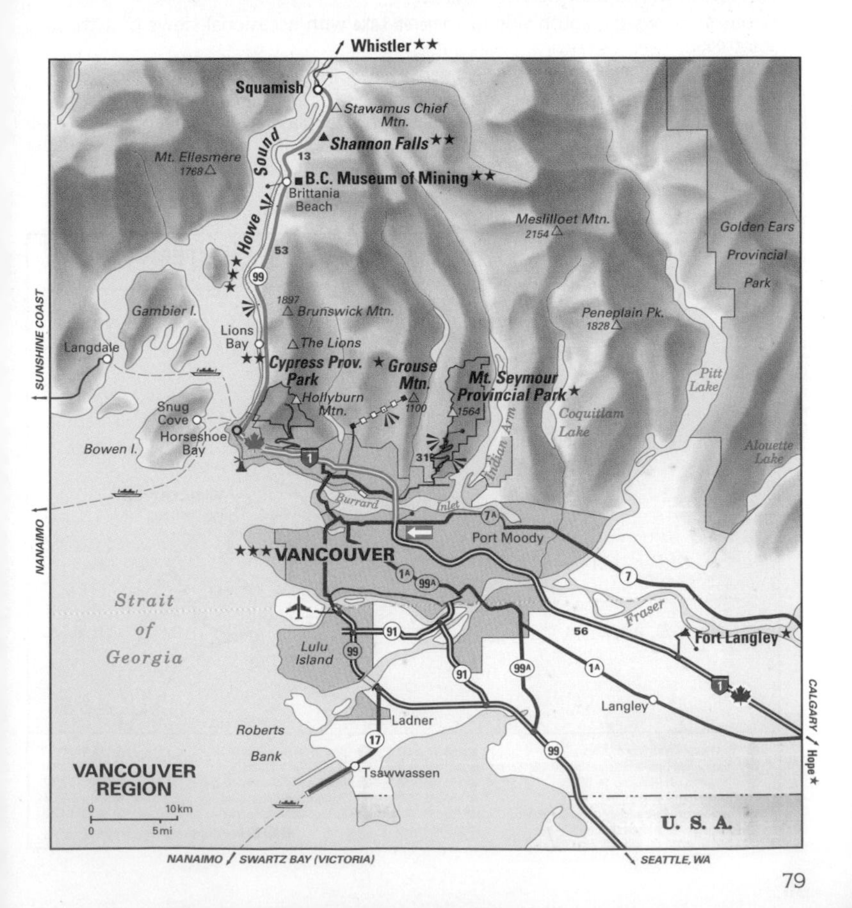

VANCOUVER ISLAND***

British Columbia

Map of Principal Sights p 2

Covering an area of more than 32,000sq km/12,000sq mi, Vancouver Island is the largest of the islands off the Pacific Coast of North America. Mountains rise over 2,100m/7,000ft to form the central core. The west coast is deeply indented by inlets or fjords that almost dissect the island. The east coast slopes gradually, with wide beaches in the south and mountains farther north.
The climate is temperate throughout the island, but rainfall varies greatly: Victoria in the southeast receives 680mm/27in annually, whereas **Zeballos** *(map below)* on the west coast receives 6480mm/255in. This high rainfall supports dense forest growth. Not surprisingly, the island's major industry is logging: sawmills and pulp mills dot the island. The population is concentrated mainly in the southeast corner around Victoria and along the shores of the Strait of Georgia.

Access – *Vancouver Island is served by 11 ferry services (map below).*

***Victoria** – *Description p 82.*

**FROM PARKSVILLE TO PACIFIC RIM

Allow 2hrs, 4.5hrs including visits. 154km/96mi by Rte. 4. Map below.

This winding route traverses the mountain backbone of the island through lovely scenery. Some parts are wild and untouched by mankind; other parts are the scene of great activity, particularly that of the logging industry.

***Englishman River Falls** – *from Parksville, take Rte. 4. After 5km/3mi, turn left and continue 8km/5mi.* This river tumbles over two sets of falls. The upper ones are narrow and deep, dropping into a gorge. A path bridges the river, following it to the lower falls *(round-trip 45min)* through a dense forest of tall trees, ferns and moss-covered rocks. The lower falls are twin jets dropping around a rock into a deep pool.

Route 4 leaves the plain behind and begins to enter the mountains.

Little Qualicum Falls** – *26km/16mi from Parksville; turn right to parking area.* The Little Qualicum River descends over two sets of falls connected by a gorge. The lower falls are small, but the walk to the upper falls *(round-trip 30min)* through forest is pleasant, providing views of the canyon. The **upper falls are on two levels, with a pool between them.

Route 4 follows the south side of **Cameron Lake** with occasional views of it through the trees.

****Cathedral Grove** – *35km/22mi from Parksville, part of MacMillan Provincial Park. Parking beside highway.* As the name suggests, Cathedral Grove contains some of the original tall trees of the island. Elsewhere Douglas firs have been cut for their wood, but fortunately this grove was preserved by the MacMillan Bloedel Paper Co. and donated to the province.

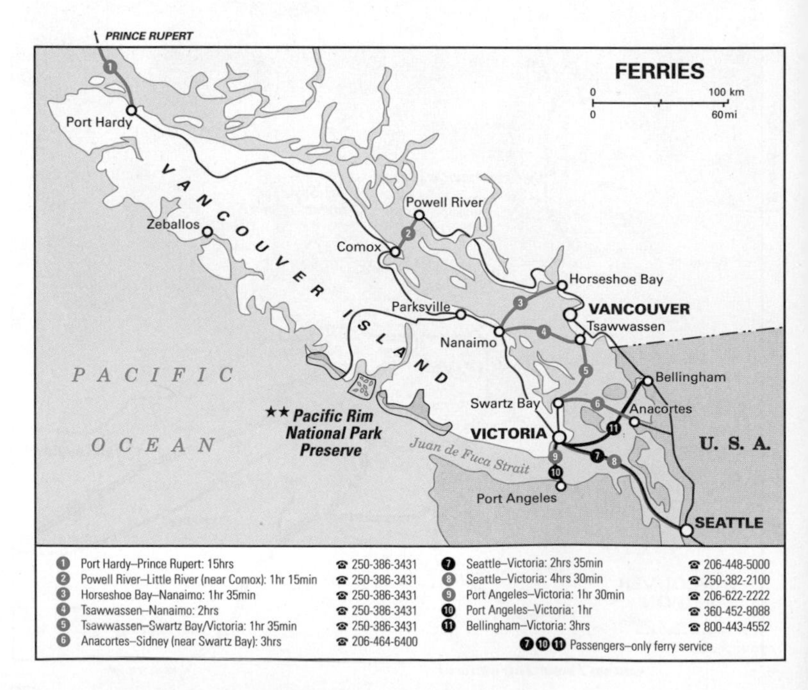

A walk *(45min)* under these giants is impressive, especially for those who have not seen the redwoods of California. Many of these firs rise to 60m/200ft or more. One is 3m/9.5ft in diameter and nearly 76m/250ft tall. The largest trees are 800 years old. Between them grow red cedar and hemlock trees.

Route 4 descends to the coast and bypasses **Port Alberni**, an important lumber centre that is situated at the head of Alberni Inlet. This arm of Barkley Sound reaches within 19km/12mi of the east coast of the island. The road then follows **Sproat Lake** with good views. Signs of logging activity are evident along the road, from cut areas to huge logging trucks. After leaving the lake Route 4 begins to climb Klitsa Mountain along the valley of the Taylor River.

After reaching the height of land, the road begins its winding descent to the Pacific along the Kennedy River, offering **views**★ of snow-capped peaks. The river widens into **Kennedy Lake**, the largest stretch of fresh water on the island. The road follows the lake, alternately rising above it and dipping to water level. Pacific Rim National Park Reserve is reached near the junction with the Tofino-to-Ucluelet road.

★★ PACIFIC RIM NATIONAL PARK RESERVE

Open year-round. Hiking, fishing, canoeing, sailing, swimming. Park visitor centre open mid-Mar–mid-Oct daily 10am–4pm (extended summer hours vary). $8/car day-use fee. ☎ 250-726-7721.

Situated on the rugged west coast of Vancouver Island, this reserve is a long, narrow strip of rocky islands and headlands, stretching intermittently for about 130km/80mi between Port Renfrew and Tofino. The park consists of the 77km/48mi **West Coast Trail** for backpackers between Port Renfrew and Bamfield *(each end is accessible by road; trail open May–Sept; reservations & quota system in effect; reservation & hiking fees; ☎ 800-663-6000, Canada/US)*, about 100 islands and rocky islets in Barkley Sound known as the **Broken Group Islands** *(cruise departs from Argyle St. dock in Alberni Jun–Sept Mon–Sat 8am; rest of the year Tue, Thu & Sat 8am; round-trip 9-11hrs; 1-2 week advance reservations required; $40-$45; Alberni Marine Transportation ☎ 250-723-8313)* and famous Long Beach.

★★ **Long Beach** – *Visitors can surf and swim. However the water is cold (10°C/50°F) and can be extremely dangerous due to changing tides and currents. For details contact the park visitor centre.* Pounded by the surf this 11km/7mi curve of sand and rock is backed by a dense rain forest and mountains rising to 1,200m/4,000ft. Offshore, sea lions bask on the rocks, and Pacific gray whales are often spotted. Numerous birds make the beach and forest their home, while many more visit seasonally.

The heavy rainfall and moderate temperatures of this coast have produced thick rain forests where Sitka spruce flourishes, and red cedar and hemlock grow. Breakers of the Pacific Ocean crash in, depositing huge drift logs over the beach one day and carrying them away the next. The power of these waves is immense; variation in sand level can be as great as 1.8m/6ft between winter and summer in one year. At low tide the beach is nearly 1km/.5mi wide, and tidal pools among the rocks brim with a variety of sea creatures.

There are several points of access to Long Beach. Paths weave through the high trees and mossy, fern-covered rain forest, offering views of the beach and ocean. From Combers Beach **sea lion rocks** can be seen offshore *(binoculars advisable)*.

★★ **Radar Hill** – *22km/14mi from Ucluelet junction. Take road to left, ascending 1.6km/1mi to viewpoint.* From this point above the forest, a splendid **panorama**★★ of the area is obtained *(telescope available)*. The mountains behind the park can be seen, as well as the wild and rocky coastline.

In 1972, the United Nations Educational, Scientific and Cultural Organization (UNESCO) established the World Heritage List of natural and cultural properties deemed of universal value. The following Canadian sites have been inscribed on the list:

Anthony Island (p 53)
Dinosaur Provincial Park (p 102)
Gros Morne National Park
Head-Smashed-In Buffalo Jump
Historic District of Quebec
Kluane National Park Reserve
L'Anse aux Meadows Natl. Historic Site
Nahanni National Park Reserve
Rocky Mountain Parks
Wood Buffalo National Park

VICTORIA★★★

British Columbia

Population 73,504

Map of Principal Sights p 2

Tourist Office ☎250-953-2033

Facing the **Juan de Fuca Strait** and the **Olympic** and **Cascade Mountains** in Washington state the capital of British Columbia occupies the southeast tip of Vancouver Island. Famous for its beautiful gardens, its elegance and gentility and its British traditions, the city contrasts with the rest of Vancouver Island, which is largely untamed forest and rugged mountains pounded by raging seas. Canada's "gentlest" city, with its annual rainfall of 680mm/27in and large amount of sunshine, is a popular tourist destination. Author Stephen Leacock *(p 48)* wrote of it, "If I had known of this place before I would have been born here."

Historical Notes – When it became clear that the location of their Pacific headquarters would be declared US territory, the Hudson's Bay Company built a trading post in 1843 on the site of present-day Victoria, naming the new post after the Queen of England. An important provisioning centre, the post grew in the 1850s and 60s during British Columbia's gold rushes *(p 33)*. In 1849 the settlement was made the capital of the crown colony of Vancouver Island. When the island was united with the mainland, Victoria became the capital of British Columbia (except between 1866 and 1868 when New Westminster was the capital). A centre of gracious living, the city avoided industrial development when the Canadian Pacific Railway was terminated at Vancouver (trains cross to the island by ferry), which grew into a major commercial centre. Other than the Canadian Forces' Pacific naval base in nearby **Esquimalt**, major employers for the Victoria area are the government and the tourism industry. The city's pleasant climate also has attracted a large retirement population.

★★DOWNTOWN *1 day. Map opposite*

The city centre is situated along Government Street, which is the main shopping area, and around the James Bay section of the harbour where ferries from Port Angeles and Seattle dock. Intriguing little squares and alleys such as **Bastion Square** and Trounce Alley house elegant shops, restaurants and sidewalk cafes. Just north, vibrant **Market Square**, a collection of older renovated buildings, has shops around courtyard gardens.

To the south, located off Belleville Street, is Heritage Court. The narrow columns and arches on the ground floor of this group of striking modern buildings add a distinct Islamic flavour. The complex houses the provincial archives and the Royal British Columbia Museum. At the front stands the **Netherlands Carillon Tower (A)**, an open-sided 27m/88ft tower containing 62 bells given to the province by Canadians of Dutch origin *(concerts Jul & Aug ☎250-387-1616)*.

★★★**Royal British Columbia Museum** – *Open year-round daily 9am–5pm. Closed Jan 1, Dec 25. $7 ($13.75 museum & IMAX). http://rbcm1.rcbm.gov.bc.ca ☎250-387-3701.* One of the top museums in the world, this eminent institution has focused on the natural and human history of the province for over 100 years. Built in 1968, the museum today welcomes more than 850,000 annual visitors.

A selection of First Nations totem poles is on display in the entrance hall. At the north end of the hall, an arcade called the **Glass House** contains a collection of totem poles from all over the province.

British Columbia's **natural history** is featured on the second floor. A series of spectacular **dioramas** of the coastal forest and seashore regions includes animal, bird and fish life. An unusual **Open Ocean** exhibit is based on William Beebe's deep-sea dive in 1930. Visitors follow his adventure through a succession of theatres, dioramas, observation platforms and models that portray life in the open seas *(30min; free timed ticket available from machine adjacent to exhibit)*.

The third floor is devoted to British Columbia's **human history**. Starting with the province today, visitors walk backwards through time. Highlights are the reconstruction of a turn-of-the-century street, complete with shops, hotel, movie house and station; vivid re-creations of a sawmill, fish-packing plant, farmyard and mine, illustrating the development of industry; and, in the section on European discovery of the province, a reconstruction of part of George Vancouver's ship, *The Discovery*.

The **Native History Gallery**★★ contains an extensive collection of Indian art, arranged in striking dioramas. These exhibits depict the way of life prior to the arrival of Europeans and the changes after contact, such as smallpox epidemics, land settlement disputes and the banning of potlatch ceremonies. Note especially the totem poles, the reconstructed **big house** and furnishings that once belonged to a Kwagulth chief and the re-created **pit house**.

★**Parliament Buildings** – On the south side of James Bay stands a long, squat stone building with a central dome, topped by a gilt statue of Capt. George Vancouver. Designed by **Francis Rattenbury** (1867-1935) and completed in 1898, "the buildings," as they are known, house the British Columbia legislature and government offices. Stationed in front of them is a bronze statue of Queen Victoria. A highly decorated arch beneath the dome marks the entrance *(open late May–Labour Day daily 9am–5pm, weekends visit by 30min guided tour only; rest of the year Mon–Fri 9am–5pm; closed national holidays; ♿ ☎250-387-3046)*. At dusk thousands of small lights outline the buildings' exterior, adding a romantic flair.

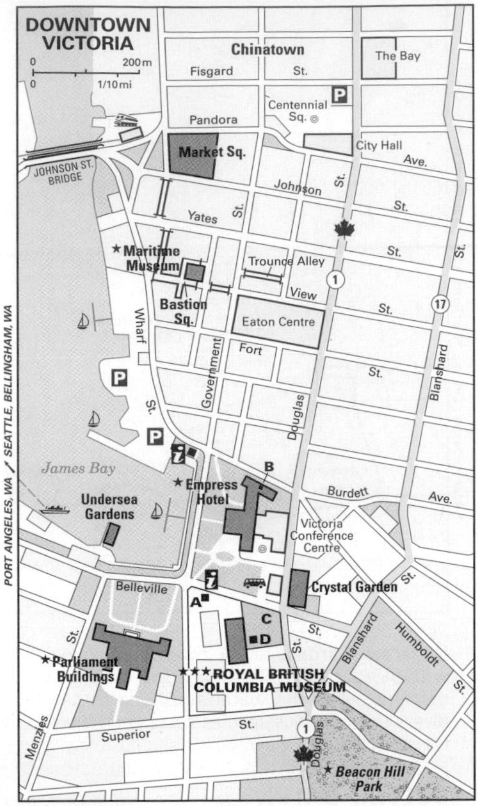

★**Empress Hotel** – Also designed by Francis Rattenbury, and built by the Canadian Pacific Railway in 1908, this enormous turreted, ivy-covered hotel is a city landmark. For many years "tea at the Empress," served in the **Palm Court**, was considered an essential part of gracious living. Still served at the hotel, tea is more a tourist attraction now than a facet of gracious living *(daily 12:30pm–5pm; $32; reservations required; no cutoffs or tank tops; ♿ ☎250-384-8111 or 800-644-6611)*. Be sure to see the clubby **Bengal Lounge** and the modern, airy Victoria Conference Centre with its outdoor fountain plaza.

Located within the hotel complex, on the Humboldt Street side, is **Miniature World (B)**, Kids featuring a host of small-size re-creations ranging from the Battle of Waterloo to the Canadian Pacific Railway *(open mid-Jun–mid-Sept daily 8:30am–9:30pm; rest of the year daily 9am–5pm; closed Dec 25; $8; ♿ ☎250-385-9731)*.

★**Thunderbird Park (C)** – *Open daily year-round. ♿ ☎250-953-2033.* This small park has a fine collection of original and replica totem poles and other Indian carvings. Many of the original works, on which these copies are based, were executed by Chief Mungo Martin, a famous carver. As each carving decays, it is copied and replaced *(carvers can sometimes be seen at work)*.

Next to Thunderbird Park stands a clapboard dwelling, **Helmcken House (D)**, the original core of which was built in 1852 for Dr. John Helmcken and his wife *(open May–Sept daily 10am–5pm; rest of the year daily 11am–4pm; closed early–mid-Jan & Dec 25, 26; $4; www.tbc.gov.bc.ca/culture/schoolnet/helmcken ☎250-361-0021)*. Physician to the Hudson's Bay Company at Fort Victoria, Helmcken expanded the house in 1856 and again in 1884 to accommodate his growing family of seven children. His medical equipment is on display along with various household possessions.

★**Maritime Museum of British Columbia** – *Open year-round daily 9:30am–4:30pm. Closed Dec 25. $5. ♿ www.mmbc.bc.ca ☎250-385-4222.* A lighthouse beacon stands in front of the law court building that houses this museum. Inside there are model ships, marine paraphernalia and displays on Northwest Coast explorers. Of special interest are the *Tilikum*, a converted Indian dugout canoe that sailed from Victoria to England in the early 1900s, and the *Trekka*, a 6m/20ft sailing boat built in Victoria that sailed around the world from 1955 to 1959, the smallest boat ever to undertake such a voyage.

Crystal Garden – *Open Jul–Aug daily 8:30am–8pm. Rest of the year daily 10am–4:30pm. $7. ✗♿ www.bcpcc.com/crystal ☎250-381-1277.* The immense glass house was once the location of orchestral concerts, art exhibits and a large underglass seawater swimming pool. Today it houses a tropical garden filled with exotic birds, monkeys and plants. Note the glassed-in emergence area in the walk-through butterfly room. Crystal Garden is also a pleasant place to have tea.

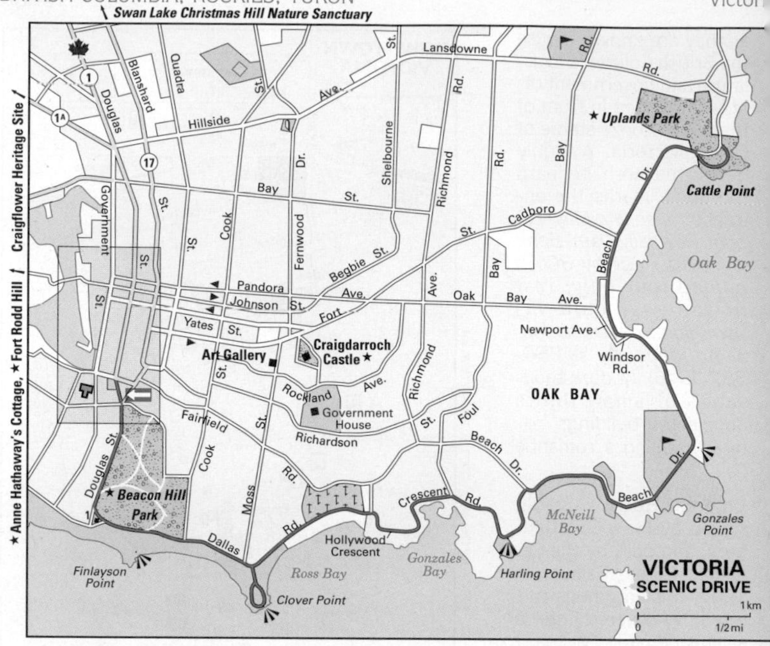

Undersea Gardens – Kids *Open year-round daily 10am–5pm. Closed Dec 25. $7. ☎250-382-5717.* Situated in the inner harbour, this structure enables visitors to descend below the water's surface to see fish in aquariums. During the shows divers bring various species such as wolf eels and octopuses close to the glass walls for spectators to view.

★★SCENIC DRIVE *Allow 1hr. 13km/8mi. Map above.*

Leave from Thunderbird Park and take Douglas St.

This beautiful drive enables visitors to appreciate Victoria's grand site on the Strait of Juan de Fuca and the lovely gardens of the city's residents.
Skirting the large, flower-filled **Beacon Hill Park★**, the road passes a plaque (**1**) marking the initial kilometer of the nearly 8,000km/5,000mi **Trans-Canada Highway**, which stretches to St. John's, Newfoundland.

Turn left on Dallas Rd.

From Finlayson and Clover Points, there are fine **views★★** of the Olympic Mountains.

Continue to Hollywood Crescent. Turn right on Ross St. (at Robertson St.); Ross becomes Crescent Rd. Bear left at King George Terrace and ascend the hill.

The drive enters the community of **Oak Bay**, a wealthy suburb with large houses, beautiful gardens, pretty views and a very English population. Harling Point provides a good **view** of the rocky coastline and the houses perched along the coast. Directly below on the right, Gonzales Bay is visible and the Trial Islands can be seen offshore to the left.

Take Beach Dr.

The drive continues around McNeill Bay with several more viewpoints. Bisected by the road, the Oak Bay golf course on Gonzales Point is one of the continent's most attractive courses with **views★★** of the sea *(weather permitting)*, the San Juan Islands and the snow-clad peaks of the Cascades, dominated by Mt. Baker.
The drive then passes through **Uplands Park★**, a pleasant section of Oak Bay with lovely homes and gardens. From **Cattle Point** there are views of the coast.

ADDITIONAL SIGHTS

★**Craigdarroch Castle** – *Map above. Open mid-Jun–Labour Day daily 9am–7pm. Rest of the year daily 10am–4:30pm. Closed Jan 1, Dec 25 & 26. $7.50.* P *☎250-592-5323.* Built by Robert Dunsmuir, a Scot who made a fortune from coal, the huge stone mansion has towers, turrets and a carved carriage entrance. This former centre of Victoria's society (one Dunsmuir son became premier of the province and later lieutenant-governor) once stood amid 11ha/27 acres of gardens. Today the house is gradually being restored to its 1880s grandeur. Note the wood-panelled hall and massive oak staircase. A large dance hall is found on the fourth floor, and from the top of the tower *(accessible from dance hall)*, there is a good view of Victoria.

Art Gallery of Greater Victoria – *Map above. 1040 Moss St. Open year-round Mon–Sat 10am–5pm (Thu 9pm), Sun 1pm–5pm. Closed national holidays. $6.* ♿ 🅿 *http://vvv.com/aggv ☎250-384-4101.* Housed in a Victorian mansion (1890), to which several modern additions have been made, the gallery is home to the works of **Emily Carr** *(p 74)*, whose paintings are on permanent display. Shown in regularly changing exhibits is the gallery's collection of Asian art, the highlight of which is the Shinto Shrine (1899-1900), constructed of copper, Keiyaki wood and sandstone, in the small Japanese outdoor garden.

Swan Lake Christmas Hill Nature Sanctuary – Kids *Map below. 3873 Swan Lake Rd. 8km/5mi north by Hwy. 17. Exit McKenzie Ave. Take first right onto Rainbow St. Follow the signs. Open year-round daily dawn–dusk. Visitor centre open year-round Mon–Fri 8:30am–4pm, weekends noon–4pm. Closed Jan 1, Dec 25 & 26.* ♿ 🅿 *www.swanlake.bc.ca ☎250-479-0211.* This peaceful 45ha/110 acre preserve includes wetlands, fields and forest. Nature House, which serves as a visitor centre, features thought-provoking displays geared toward children and a small resource library. The lily pad-filled lake provides refuge for waterfowl and nesting birds. A 2.5km/1.5mi trail *(30min)* up Christmas Hill traverses sections of residential streets, but the summit affords a **panorama★** of Victoria and environs, including Elk Lake to the north.

★**Fort Rodd Hill** – *Map below. 14km/9mi west by Rtes. 1, 1A and Ocean Blvd. Open Mar–Oct daily 10am–5:30pm. Rest of the year daily 9am–4:30pm. Closed Dec 25. $3.* 🅿 *☎250-478-5849.* Set in 18ha/44 acres of land at the southwest corner of Esquimalt's harbour, the fort contains the remains of three coastal artillery-gun batteries and displays on-shore defences. Built to protect the approaches to the naval base at Esquimalt, the batteries were in operation until 1956. From beside Fisgard Lighthouse, there are fine **views★** of Juan de Fuca Strait, the Olympic Mountains and the naval base.

★**Anne Hathaway's Cottage** – *Map below. In Esquimalt, 429 Lampson St., part of Olde England Inn complex. Visit by guided tour (45min) only, Jun–Sept daily 9am–7:15pm. Rest of the year daily 10am–4pm. Closed Dec 25. $7.50.* 🅿 *www.bctravel.com/oeinn.html ☎250-388-4353.* Covered with a thatched roof, this black and white half-timbered building is a replica of the Stratford (England) home of William Shakespeare's wife. Inside there are 10 rooms with period furniture. Note especially the wooden panelling on the ground floor. An attractive "old world" English garden fronts the cottage. Adjacent to the house is a lane of quaint shops housed in half-timbered buildings reflective of the architecture of 16C England.

Craigflower Heritage Site – *Hwy. 1A (Craigflower Rd.) at Admirals Rd. Open mid-Jun–Labour Day Wed–Sun noon–4pm. Rest of the year by appointment. $5.* 🅿 *☎250-383-4627.* This Georgian clapboard house (1856) was constructed by Kenneth McKenzie, bailiff for Puget Sound Agricultural Co., the first organization to develop the island for farming. One of the earliest buildings in Victoria, the house boasts a handsome studded-oak front door. Most of the manor is original and contains period furnishings. Visitors may play the piano in the parlour and don period attire in a child's bedroom upstairs. The kitchen pantry is often stocked with the harvest from two vegetable gardens maintained on the premises.

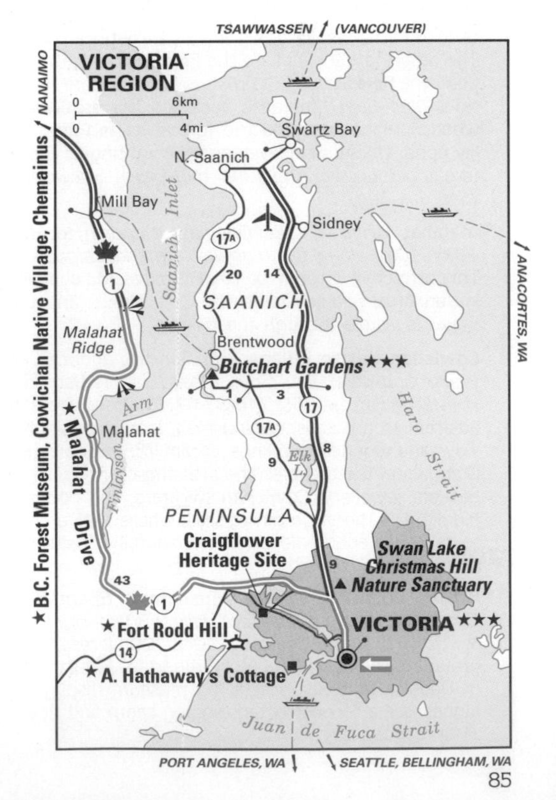

Sunken Garden, Butchart Gardens

EXCURSIONS

★★★ **Butchart Gardens** – *Map above. 21km/13mi north by Rte. 17 and Keating X Rd. or by 17A. Open year-round daily at 9am. Closing times vary. $15.50.* ✗ ♿ P *butchartgardens.bc.ca/butchart* ☎ *250-652-5256.* Expanded to approximately 20ha/50 acres, these internationally famous gardens were started in 1904 by Jennie Butchart to beautify the quarry pit resulting from her husband's cement business. Still operated by the family, the grounds are maintained by a small army of gardeners in summer.

The floral showpiece is the beautiful **Sunken Garden**★★★ with its green lawns, trees and exquisite flower arrangements that create a whirl of colour. The flowers change from season to season, but the effect is always striking. Set in a huge pit with ivy-covered sides, the garden is best viewed from above or from the rock island at its centre. Paths weave down into it through a rockery.

The other gardens include the **Ross Fountain** with changing water displays in a rocky pool; the **Rose Garden**★, its rose-covered arbors full of blooms overhead and on both sides *(Jun–Sept)*; the dark, secluded **Japanese Garden**★ with its lacquered bridges and wooden teahouses; and the formal **Italian Garden**★ with statues and a star-shaped lily pond. On summer evenings the lighting of the gardens provides an entirely different perspective *(mid-Jun–mid-Sept)*. Fireworks are also displayed in summer *(Sat, Jul–Aug)*.

★ **Malahat Drive** – *Take Douglas St. north to Hwy. 1 (Trans-Can Hwy.). About 16km/10mi along the highway a marker signals the beginning of Malahat Drive.* This attractive stretch of road crosses Malahat Ridge with good **views**★★ of Finlayson Arm, Saanich Inlet, the Gulf Islands and the mainland. On a clear day Mt. Baker is visible through the trees.

Cowichan Native Village – *In Duncan, about 60km/37mi north by Hwy. 1. Open year-round daily 9am–5pm. Closed Jan 1, Dec 25–26. $8.* ✗♿ *www.cowichannativevillage.com* ☎ *250-746-8119.* Enclosed by a high fence, the village, located adjacent to a busy shopping mall, is a surprisingly tranquil setting of paved walkways and wooden buildings. A film *(23min)* on the history of the Cowichan people is shown in the theatre. The arts and crafts gallery features exquisite masks, cedar baskets, jewellery, Cowichan sweaters, and books on Indian culture *(for sale)*. The highlight is the large **carving shed**, where native craftsmen apply traditional designs to tall red cedar poles, laid horizontally. Visitors are invited to try their carving skills.

★ **British Columbia Forest Museum** – *65km/40mi north by Hwy. 1, just after Duncan. Open daily Apr–Sept daily 9:30am–6pm. $8.* ♿ *www.bcforestmuseum.com* ☎ *250-715-1113.* Covering 40ha/100 acres, this museum provides some background to the province's most important industry. Visitors can walk through a forest of Douglas fir trees, visit a log museum displaying the evolution of logging techniques, see a reconstructed logging camp and ride the narrow-gauge steam railway *(May–Labour Day)*.

Chemainus – *78km/48mi north by Hwy. 1. Visitor center at 9796 Willow St. (open Jul–Aug daily 9am–5pm; rest of the year daily 9am–4pm; closed national holidays; http://tourism.chemainus.bc.ca 250-246-4701).* This small waterfront town has gained fame for over 30 murals painted on the exteriors of its buildings. Resident Karl Schutz promoted the idea to revitalize the community's economy when the closing of the local lumber mill was imminent in the early 1980s. The mill has since reopened, but the artwork is the driving force of Chemainus' present prosperity, attracting reputedly some 400,000 visitors annually. Scenes from the town's past celebrate people, buildings and events. Especially fine are *Native Heritage*, symbolizing the three tribes of the Coast Salish Nation and *Arrival of the "Reindeer" in Horseshoe Bay*, featuring a native woman in a colorful robe as she watches a ship entering the bay.

WATERTON LAKES NATIONAL PARK**

Alberta

Map of Principal Sights p 2

ituated in the province's southwest corner, this lovely preserve in the Canadian Rockies forms an International Peace Park with the larger Glacier National Park in Montana. Because its gently rolling hills (rarely over 1,200m/4,000ft) meet a vertical rock wall towering another 1,200m/4,000ft or more above the plains, the park has been described as the place "where the prairies meet the mountains."

The underlying sediment of these mountains, which once were part of an inland sea, was thrust up and sculptured by erosion and glaciation into sharp peaks, narrow ridges and interlocked U-shaped valleys. Among them, the three Waterton Lakes lie in a deep glacial trough. Formerly a Blackfoot Indian stronghold, the mountains of Waterton were first visited by Thomas Blakiston of the Palliser Expedition, who explored the area in 1858 and named the lakes for an 18C English naturalist, **Charles Waterton**. Oil was discovered a few decades later, but never proved profitable. The area was designated a national park in 1895.

VISIT

Open year-round. Hiking, horseback riding, fishing, boating, golf, winter sports. $4/day. www.worldweb.com/parkscanada-waterton 403-859-5133.

Waterton Townsite – Built on delta materials deposited by Cameron Creek, the town has a lovely **site**** near the point where Upper Lake narrows into the Bosporus Strait, which separates it from Middle Lake. Just south behind the townsite, the flat face of **Mt. Richards** can be distinguished. Beside it stands **Mt. Bertha**, marked by pale green streaks down the otherwise dark green surface. The streaks were caused by snowslides that swept trees down the mountainside. Across the lake rise **Vimy Peak** and **Vimy Ridge**. Upper Lake stretches south into Montana, separating the mountains of the Lewis and Clark Range, which tower steeply above it. In summer **tour boats** make trips down the lake to the US ranger station at the southern end *(depart from Waterton Marina Jul–Aug daily 9am–7pm; mid-May–Jun & Sept daily 10am–4pm; round-trip 2hrs 15min; commentary; $19; Waterton Shoreline Cruises 403-859-2362).* Behind the townsite, **Cameron Falls** can be seen dropping over a layered cliff.

****Cameron Lake** – *17km/11mi from townsite by Akamina Hwy.* Before reaching the lake the highway passes the site of the first oil well in western Canada. The lake itself is set immediately below the Continental Divide and, like Upper Waterton, it spans the international border. Dominating the view across the lake are, to the left, **Mt. Custer** and to the right, **Forum Peak**.

Red Rock Canyon** – *19km/12mi from townsite; turn left at Blakiston Creek.* The drive to this small canyon offers good **views of the surrounding mountains. A **nature trail** follows the narrow canyon *(2km/1.2mi)*, where characteristic colour is due to iron compounds in the rock that oxidized to form hematite.

Buffalo Paddock** – Kids *400m/.2mi from park entrance. Auto circuit 3km/2mi.* A small herd of buffalo occupies a large enclosure on a fine **site with Bellevue Mountain and Mt. Galway as a backdrop.

When driving the back roads of Canada, use caution, since these roads may be unpaved or have sharp curves and steep grades. Take special care during the spring thaw or after a rainfall, as unpaved roads will be muddy. Distances may be long between gas stations; begin with a full tank of gas.

WHITEHORSE★

Yukon Territory
Population 19,157
Map of Principal Sights p 2
Tourist Office ☎867-667-5340

Situated on flat land on the west side of a big bend in the Yukon River, Whitehors is the capital of the Yukon Territory and a regional service centre. Above it sharp clif rise to a plateau where the airport is located and across which the Alaska Highwa passes. On the river's east side, barren hills become mountains known as the Bi Salmon Range.

Historical Notes – The city owes its existence to the difficulty encountered by th Dawson City-bound Klondike Stampeders *(p 40)*, in negotiating Miles Canyon and th Whitehorse Rapids (now tamed by a hydro-electric plant) on the Yukon River. tramway was built to carry goods around these obstacles so that the boats could b piloted through with greater ease. The completion of the White Pass and Yukon Rout Railroad in 1900, from Skagway through the Coast Mountains, changed methods o transport in the area. The town soon bustled in summer with the transfer of passen gers and goods from railway to riverboat, and from railway to overland stage in winter The railway company's decision to end its line at Whitehorse (and not to continue t Dawson City) resulted in the birth of the city.

The presence of the railway and of a small airport were key factors when the deci sion to build the Alaska Highway was made in 1942. Whitehorse became a major bas for its construction, changing overnight at a time when Dawson City was declining ir importance. Reflecting this change, the territorial capital was moved here in 1953 Today the city is a centre for tourism as well as communications in the Yukon. Prouc of its part in the Klondike Stampede, the community stages a celebration ever February called the **Sourdough Rendezvous** when people dress in the costumes of 189 and race dog teams on the frozen Yukon River.

SIGHTS *1 day*

No longer a frontier town in appearance, Whitehorse retains, nevertheless, some historic structures, notably: the **old log church** on Elliott at Third, built in 1900; the **"skyscrapers"** on Lambert between Second and Third Avenues, built after World Wa II when there was a housing shortage, and still in use today; and the log **railway station** on First Avenue at Main. In contrast is the modern steel and aluminum Yukor government **Administration Building** on Second Avenue, opened in 1976. Its light and airy interior, finished in wood, features an acrylic resin mural that looks like stained glass. The Yukon Permanent Art Collection installed here features contemporary art as well as traditional native costumes and artifacts.

★**MacBride Museum** – *1st Ave. at Wood St. Open mid-May–Labour Day daily 10am–6pm. Rest of the year Thu–Sat noon–4pm. Closed national holidays. $4. ☎867-667-2709.* Situated in a log building (1967) built with a sod roof, this museum features Gold Rush memorabilia, Indian cultural objects and a splendid collection of old **photographs** of the men and women of the Yukon. A large number of preserved animals are displayed side by side, enabling the visitor to appreciate the relative size and characteristic markings of each, such as the differing antlers of moose, elk and caribou. Outside are relics of Yukon transport, examples of early machinery, Sam McGee's cabin and a government telegraph office c.1900.

© Lynn M. Stone

Bald Eagle

★★**SS Klondike** – *Second Ave. near Robert Campbell Bridge. Visit by guided tour (30min) only, mid-Jun–mid-Aug daily 9am–7:30pm. Mid-May–early Jun & late Aug–late Sept daily 9am–6pm. $3.50. ☎867-667-4511.* One of over 200 stern-wheelers that once plied the waters of the Yukon between Whitehorse and Dawson City, this well-restored 1937 craft is the only remaining steamboat open to the public in the Territory.

Carrying passengers, ore and supplies, the vessel required 32 cords of wood to fuel the 40-hour,

700km/436mi downstream trip to Dawson. The return trip against the current took 96 hours and burned 112 cords of wood. Visitors can see the huge boiler, engine room and cargo space; from the wheelhouse, envision the captain's vantage point; and view the galley and first-class passenger accommodation, including the observation room and dining area with its elegant table settings.

Cross the river via Robert Campbell Bridge and stop to see the **fish ladder** at **Whitehorse Dam**, built to enable the chinook salmon to circumnavigate the dam and reach their spawning grounds upriver *(usually occurs in August)*. Interpretive panels and windows for viewing the fish as they "climb" the ladder are provided. These salmon are near the end of the longest-known chinook migration in the world—3,200km/2,000mi. The dam is best viewed from the fishway's observation deck.

★★ **Miles Canyon** – *9km/6mi south of Whitehorse via Canyon Rd.* Following the edge of Schwatka Lake, **Canyon Road** passes the *MV Schwatka* dock *(below)* and climbs above the canyon *(sharp curves and steep grades)* where there is a good **view★** from the lookout. Near the parking lot above Miles Canyon, another fine **view★** is possible. The river can be crossed by a footbridge for other clifftop views.

For more than 1km/.75mi, the Yukon River passes through a narrow gorge of sheer columnar basalt walls, grayish red in colour. Created by the shrinkage of volcanic lava upon cooling, these walls rise straight up, 9-12m/30-40ft above the river. Here the Yukon still flows through rapidly, swirling around Devil's Whirlpool. But construction of the power dam downstream has very much lessened the speed and navigational hazards the stampeders experienced.

Canyon **cruises** afford good **views★** of the deep green waters of the Yukon and the steep canyon walls. The tremendous force of the river is better appreciated from the water level than from the viewpoints above. Interesting historical commentary is given *(MV Schwatka departs Jun–mid-Sept daily 2pm; round-trip 2hrs; commentary; reservations required; $18; ♿ Gray Line Yukon ☎ 867-668-3225). To access cruise boat landing, take South Access Rd. towards centre of Whitehorse, turn right onto unpaved road immediately past railroad tracks.*

Yukon Transportation Museum – *Alaska Hwy. near airport. Open mid-May–mid-Sept daily 10am–6pm. $3.50. ♿ ☎ 867-668-4792.* Exhibits include archival photos of Yukon aviation and a replica of the 1920s mail carrier plane, *Queen of the Yukon*.

★★ EXCURSION TO SKAGWAY *1 day. Map p 90.*

Note: Skagway is in Alaska. Canadian citizens need identification to enter the US. Other visitors need US visas, which are available from any US consulate, but not in Whitehorse.

An impressive trip in the Yukon is the traverse of the Coast Mountains to the Pacific tidewater at Skagway—terminus of the Klondike Highway—on the Alaska Panhandle. Tiny frontier towns, dramatic lake systems, barren flatlands, abandoned mines and coastal vistas season this outing with diversity, while summoning images of earlier sojourners struggling to reach the fields of gold.

Historical Notes – The majority of gold seekers en route to Dawson City sailed up the Pacific Coast to Skagway or Dyea *(below)* and trudged into the Yukon across the Coast Mountains. From Skagway the trail followed the **White Pass**, a narrow and slippery climb of 888m/2,914ft. More than 3,000 horses were forced along this route in 1897. Most died before reaching the summit. Their remains were quickly trampled underfoot by the mass of humanity behind them. "Dead Horse Trail," as it became known, was closed that same winter.

Stampeders who insisted on continuing turned to the more difficult **Chilkoot Pass**. Starting in Dyea, this route was 183m/600ft higher than the White Pass and much steeper—it climbed at an angle of 35° in places. Raw rock in summer, the pass became slick ice and snow in winter, and with temperatures of –50°C/–58°F, it was a nightmare to climb. Yet over the winter of 1897-98, some 22,000 people scaled it, not just once but 30 to 40 times! The North West Mounted Police at the Canadian border insisted that anyone entering Canada have a year's supply of food and equipment because of shortages in the Territory. To carry this "ton" of goods over the pass, stampeders had to make numerous trips. Thus the Chilkoot was a stream of climbing humanity for the entire winter.

Today a hiking trail is maintained over the Chilkoot Pass. The adventurous can relive the stampeder experience by hiking the legendary **Chilkoot Trail** *(53km/33mi)*, which starts at the abandoned site of Skagway's former rival, **Dyea** *(15km/9mi north of Skagway by dirt road)* and ends at Bennett Lake. The arduous 54km/33mi trek can take up to five days and requires proper equipment *(for trail information and maps, contact the National Park Service in Skagway ☎ 907-983-2921).*

★★ **Klondike Highway to Skagway** – *180km/112mi by Alaska Hwy. and Klondike Hwy. (Rte. 2). About 3hrs; US border open year-round daily 24hrs; Canada Customs in Fraser open Apr-Oct daily 24hrs; Nov–Mar daily 8am–midnight. ☎ 867-*

821-4111 (Canada Customs) or 907-983-2325 (US Customs). Adjoining the Alaska Highway south of Whitehorse, the Klondike Highway passes through forest and gradually enters the mountains, with views of snow-capped peaks ahead. At small, historic **Carcross**—where the final rail was laid for the White Pass and Yukon Route—the scenery changes dramatically as the road follows the shores of **Tagish Lake**, **Windy Arm** and **Tutshi** (TOO-shy*)* **Lake**. The sight is striking: imposing mountains rise straight out of the blue waters of the lakes. After leaving Tutshi Lake the road begins the traverse of the White Pass with another change in scenery. The pass is desolate, almost lunar—treeless flatlands with lichen-covered rocks. The steep descent to Skagway on the coast permits views of the **Taiya Inlet** of the Lynn Canal far below.

★**Skagway** – The wide Pacific lying at its door, the historic little community, known as the "Gateway to the Klondike," occupies a lovely **site**★ with snow-capped peaks as a backdrop. A port of call on the Inside Passage route *(p 45)*, this waterfront town, with its pervasive frontier flavour, attracts scores of visitors annually via road, rail and seaway.

Skagway was born with the Klondike Stampede. Until the first boatload of gold seekers docked in July of 1897, Capt. William Moore and his son were the only European settlers in the area, having arrived in 1888. Amid supplies, horses and equipment, tents and huts sprouted up everywhere. In three months the population swelled to roughly 20,000 and a grid pattern of streets sported saloons, casinos, dance halls and stores. Lawlessness was rife as the town became home to notorious characters such as **Soapy Smith**, a con artist *par excellence* who succeeded in divesting many greenhorn gold rushers of their money. In 1898 construction of the White Pass and Yukon Route Railroad *(below)* and a crackdown on crime helped stabilize the community.

Northern terminus of the southeast ferry system, the small but busy port has received regular calls since 1963. The Klondike Highway from Skagway to Carcross was laid in 1978, and the railway restored in 1988.

The Town – *2.5hrs. Skagway visitor centre at 335 5th Ave. (open May–Sept Mon–Fri 8am–6pm, weekends 9am–6pm; rest of the year Mon–Fri 8am–5pm; closed national holidays; ♿ www.skagway.org ☎907-983-2854)*. Designated a historic district by the US National Park Service, the area along **Broadway** from First to Seventh Avenues contains several turn-of-the-century wooden structures housing hotels, saloons and shops restored to evoke the days of the Gold Rush.

The former railroad depot, a handsome 1898 building, serves as the Park Service **visitor centre** *(open May–Aug daily 8am–6pm; rest of the year daily 8am–5pm; ♿ www.nps.klgo.gov ☎907-983-2921)* and departure point for walking tours conducted by park rangers. Particularly noteworthy is the **Arctic Brotherhood Hall** *(Broadway between 2nd & 3rd Aves.)* with its fanciful driftwood facade. This building houses Skagway's **museum**, which features artifacts and documents from the town's colourful past *(open May–Sept daily 9am–5pm; rest of the year hours vary, call ahead; $2; ♿ ☎907-983-2420)*.

★★**White Pass and Yukon Route Railroad** – *Departs from 2nd & Spring Sts. mid-May–late Sept daily 8:30am & 1pm (additional departure Tue & Wed 4:30pm). Round-trip 3hrs. Commentary. $78. (Through-service to Whitehorse available mid-May–mid-Sept; departs Skagway 12:40pm, transfer in Fraser, BC to motorcoach; arrives Whitehorse 5:30pm; $95 one way.) Reservations suggested. ♿ White Pass & Yukon Route www.whitepassrailroad.com ☎907-983-2217 or 800-343-7373.* Conceived in 1898 as an alternative to the treacherous ascent of the White Pass and Chilkoot Trails, this narrow-gauge railroad stands as a testimony to the inventiveness and determination of the stampeder spirit. The route, which originally linked Skagway to Whitehorse, functioned commercially from 1900 to 1982. Operating solely as a tourist attraction since 1988, the refurbished railroad cars climb, in a mere 32km/20mi, to an elevation of 873m/2,865ft, providing **views**★ of Skagway and the rugged peaks dominating the town. On-board commentary points out noteworthy features, such as waterfalls, bridges, and remnants of the White Pass Trail. After reaching the summit at White Pass, the train concludes its thrilling 45km/28mi run at the Canadian station in Fraser, BC.

Before planning your trip to Canada be sure to consult:
- *the Map of Principal Sights (pp 2-5);*
- *the regional driving tours (pp 6-12).*

YUKON CIRCUIT★★

Yukon Territory and Alaska

Map p 93

:overing a 483,450sq km/186,660sq mi triangle in Canada's northwest corner, the :gendary Yukon conjures up images of raging rivers, snow-capped mountains, eserted valleys, long winters, the midnight sun and gold. An adventure to one of the ·uly faraway places of the globe, this scenic journey rewards travellers willing to tra-erse a relatively isolated frontier to witness nature's grandeur and mankind's iversions. The majestic Yukon River, a silent, but ever-present companion, dominates alf the circuit.

listorical Notes

Vater Route to the Klondike – During the Gold Rush thousands of stampeders tra-elling from Skagway ended their winter trek through Chilkoot Pass *(p 89)* at **Bennett ake**, part of the lake system that forms the Yukon's headwaters. There, in the spring, hey constructed boats to complete the journey via the Yukon and its tributaries to)awson City, a distance of some 800km/500mi. Hazards on the voyage, such as Miles :anyon *(p 89)* and Five Finger Rapids *(p 92)*, seemed minor after the traverse of the reacherous pass, but were harrowing in their own right. Reputedly, in the first few lays of the mass exodus from Bennett Lake, 10 men drowned and 150 boats were vrecked in the rock-strewn rapids of Miles Canyon.

'oday thousands of people follow the route alongside the river, not to hunt for gold)ut to discover, as the Klondike Stampeders did, the beauty of that wild northland, ınd to experience what poet Robert Service called *The Spell of the Yukon:*

It's the great, big, broad land 'way up yonder,
It's the forests where silence has lease,
It's the beauty that thrills me with wonder,
It's the stillness that fills me with peace.

The Mighty Yukon – One of the longest rivers in North America, this giant of the ·emote North—its Loucheux Indian name *Yu-kun-ah* means "great river"—traverses 3,185km/1,975mi of rugged territory. Originating in Tagish Lake on the Yukon/British Columbia boundary, the river flows northward through the Yukon Territory and Alaska :o empty into the Bering Sea. The Teslin, Pelly, Stewart and White are its primary Canadian tributaries. Over the centuries this river's natural resources have sustained a native population, its wealth has lured fur traders and gold miners, its currents have transported scows and stern-wheelers, and today its awesome beauty beckons adven-turers from many countries.

VISIT *1 week (not including excursion to Skagway, Alaska).*

About 1,500km/930mi from Whitehorse via Klondike, Top of the World, Taylor and Alaska Hwys. Lengthy drive over stretches of gravel road; 4-wheel drive recommended. For road conditions, see p 37. In some sections, service facilities are few and infrequent. Prepare for emergencies with food, warm clothing and vehicle supplies. Be familiar with protection against weather and wild animals. The Milepost (p 37) is a useful reference for this trip.

★From Whitehorse to Dawson City

Allow 1 day. 540km/335mi by Klondike Hwy. (Rte. 2).

★**Whitehorse** – *1 day. Description p 88.*

The **Klondike Highway** skirts Lake Laberge *(barely visible from the road)*, through which the Yukon River runs. At the end of the unpaved access road to the campground, there is a lovely **view** of this lake and the mountains beyond. Passing through hilly and largely deserted country, the highway rejoins the river at **Carmacks** *(178km/110mi)*, named for the discoverer of Klondike gold. After 196km/122mi, just beyond a bend in the

Native Child with Fireweed

. Malak, Ottawa

Yukon, a series of small rock islands, varying in size, can be seen. These formation have divided the river into five fast-flowing channels, known as **Five Finger Rapids★** A hazard to navigation even today, these rapids caused problems during the stam pede; riverboats often had to be winched through the narrowest channel by cable From the lookout *(panel exhibit)*, a good view of the rapids is afforded.
In the vicinity of Minto, about 2km/1mi past Minto Resorts, an unpaved road lead to the riverside *(1.6km/1mi)*. Here, amid the ruins of earlier log structures, a sig marks the Overland Trail, a wagon road built in 1902 and the winter mail rout from WHITEHORSE to DAWSON CITY. The **view★** of the Yukon from the bank is grand Leaving the Yukon Valley the highway crosses the central plateau and bridges th Pelly and Stewart Rivers. At Pelly Crossing some descriptive **panels** tell the histor of the **Selkirk** people whose tradition it was to fish the area in spring, years prior t the coming of Europeans to the Yukon.

Note at Stewart Crossing Route 11 *(unpaved between Mayo and Keno)*, designa ted the **Silver Trail**, begins its 111km/69mi northeast traverse through the village o Mayo to Keno, a boomtown in the 1920s when mining of the area's vast silver de posits was in its heyday.
After Stewart Crossing the vast **Tintina Trench** runs parallel to the highway. From the designated lookout about 61km/38mi south of Dawson City, a good **view** o this valley can be obtained. Stretching through the Yukon and Alaska, the trench is another example of plate tectonics *(p 279)*.
There is a **viewpoint**, after 483km/300mi, of the valley of the Klondike River from above, with the Ogilvie Mountains to the northeast. The road then follows the Klon dike, but the river is not always visible because of the great mounds of tailings lef by mining dredges.
At 494km/307mi note that the **Dempster Highway** heads northward to Inuvik in the Mackenzie Delta across the Ogilvie and Richardson Mountains. Named for Corpora Dempster of the North West Mounted Police, who pioneered the route by dogsled at the turn of the century, it is the only road in North America that crosses the Arctic Circle *(open all year except spring breakup and fall freeze-up when the Pee and Mackenzie river ferries do not operate)*.
The Klondike Highway crosses the Klondike River after 538km/334mi and enters Dawson City. The word *Klondike* is a Han Indian adaptation for "hammer water," suggestive of the posts hammered into the riverbed to make salmon traps.

★★ **Dawson City** – *2 days. Description p 40.*

From Dawson City to Whitehorse

945km/586mi by Top of the World (Rte. 9), Taylor (US 5) (both highways closed in winter) and Alaska Hwys. Allow 2-3 days. Caution: Reduced speeds necessary, usually 40–64km/h/25–40mph on winding and often unpaved road. Drive with headlights on. Canada and US Customs offices at border crossing for Rtes. 9 & 5 open mid-May–mid-Sept daily 9am–9pm (8am–8pm Alaska time). Alaska Hwy. border open year-round daily 24hrs. ☎867-862-7230 (Canada Customs), 907-774-2252 (US Customs).

★★ **Top of the World Highway** – *108km/67mi to Alaska border; road closed in winter. Entry only when US Customs open (see above).* Route 9 is called Top of the World Highway because most of its length is above the tree line, allowing magnificent **views★★★** in all directions. It leaves Dawson by the ferry across the vast Yukon *(continuous 24hr service May–Oct)*. At this point the river's waters are no longer the sparkling green colour of Miles Canyon *(p 89)*, but a light gray blue, resulting from the earth brought in by major tributaries—the Pelly, the White and the Stewart. For about 5km/3mi, the road climbs to a **viewpoint** at a bend in the road providing a different perspective of the city and rivers from that seen from Midnight Dome. After 14km/9mi there is another **viewpoint** of the Ogilvie Mountains, the Yukon Valley and, visible to the north, the Tintina Trench. From then on the road follows the ridgetops for 90km/50mi, winding up and down for some distance. Ever-changing vistas of mountains and valleys greet travellers on this route.

The Route in Alaska – *306km/190mi. At Alaskan border, set watches back 1hr.* Route 9 joins the Taylor Highway (US 5) after 23km/14mi *(services available at Boundary, Alaska)* and heads south along the valley of the Fortymile River. Shortly before the great Klondike discovery, gold was found here. In the creeks along the highway, evidence of mining remains today. **Chicken**, Alaska, *(food and fuel)* offers local colour and frontier history. Wanting to name their camp "ptarmigan" for a local bird, miners settled on "chicken" instead, it is said, because they could spell it! The community was home to Ann Hobbs, who chronicled her life as Chicken's teacher in the book, *Tisha*. The old mining camp, including the author's home, can be visited *(contact the Chicken Creek Cafe, Airport Rd.)*. At **Tetlin Junction** take the Alaska Highway south to the Canadian border *(set watches forward 1hr)*.

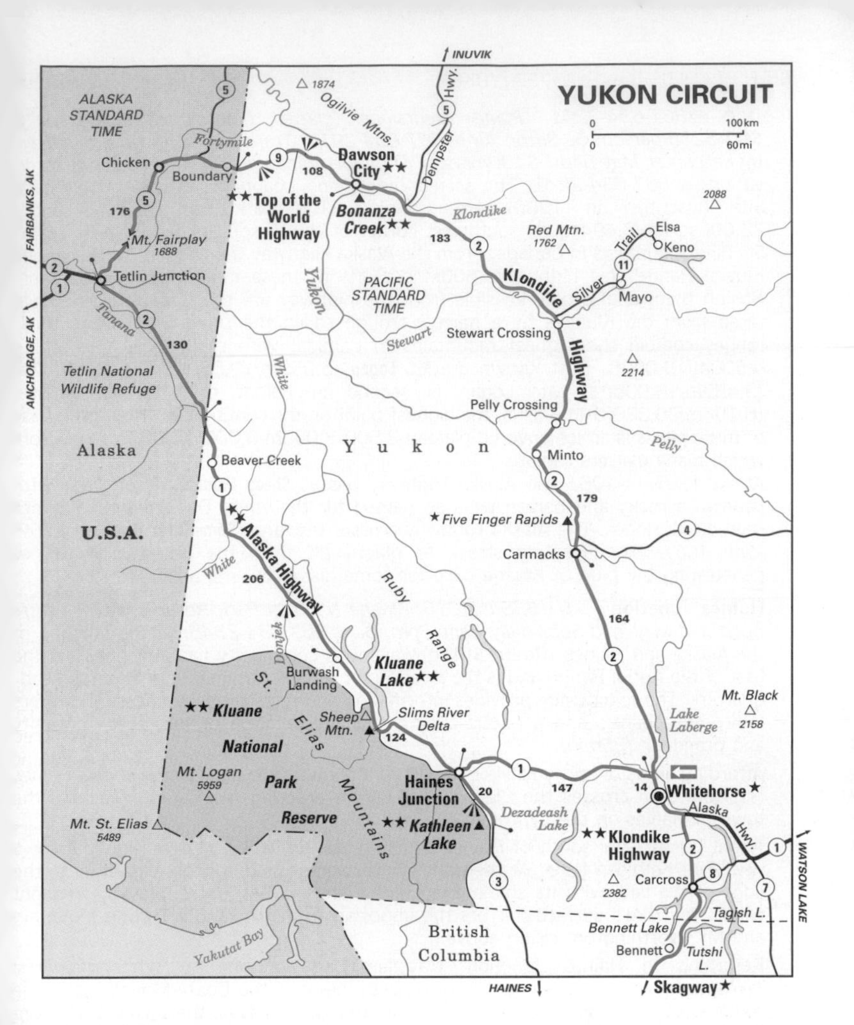

★★**Alaska Highway** – *491km/305mi from Alaska border to Whitehorse. Along the highway, posts indicate the distance from Dawson Creek, BC, where the highway begins. Kilometres/miles in this section are shown in descending order to conform with these post readings.* North of the Canadian/US border, in the vicinity of Northway, Alaska, is the **Tetlin National Wildlife Refuge**, a 384,620ha/950,000 acre preserve of boreal forest, wetlands, lakes and glacial rivers *(open daily year-round)*. At KM 1982/mi 1229, the US Fish and Wildlife Service visitor centre features exhibits of wildlife and flora indigenous to the Upper Tanana River Valley *(open Memorial Day–Labour Day daily 7:45am–4:15pm; ♿ ☎907-883-5312)*.

After crossing the Canadian/US border *(KM 1969/mi 1221)*, the highway *(caution: intermittent bumps)* passes through flat muskeg country and later bridges the White and then the Donjek Rivers, full of glacial silt. From the course of the latter *(KM 1810/ mi 1125)*, there is a **view** of the Icefield Ranges of the **St. Elias Mountains**.

★★**Kluane Lake** – Just before Burwash Landing *(KM 1759/mi 1093)*, the road approaches this vast lake, paralleling it for 64km/40mi and offering excellent **views**★★. The highest and largest lake in the Yukon, Kluane (kloo-ON-ee*)* is ringed by mountains and fed by glaciers, the factor in its incredibly beautiful colour. To the south and west lie the **Kluane Ranges**, to the north and east the **Ruby Range**. All of them are reflected in the icy blue waters of this lake, the surface of which can change from a rippling mirror to a heaving mass of waves in a very short period.

In Burwash Landing, the **Kluane Museum of Natural History** is housed in a six-sided log building. **Dioramas**★ of native wildlife line the building's interior while a reconstructed mountain occupies the center, covered with preserved birds and animals of varying sizes. There is also a large relief map of the mountain ranges of Kluane National Park *(open mid-May–mid-Sept daily 9am–9pm; $3.50; ♿ ☎867-841-5561)*.

★★**Kluane National Park Reserve** – *Park office in Haines Junction (below). Limited 4-wheel-drive vehicle access to park's interior (streams must be forded). Arrangements to visit interior must be made in advance with park authorities. Park open year-round. Hiking, rafting, fishing, cross-country skiing. Use fees in effect.*

867-634-7201. Plane excursions: glacier flights year-round daily $90–$235/person; Sifton Air 867-634-2916. Trans-North Air offers charter by helicopter May-Sept; $100/person (3 people minimum); for schedules & reservations 867-634-2242. The scenic variety and beauty of this World Heritag Site (inscribed in 1980) are stunning. The park occupies the entir 22,000sq km/8,494sq mi southwest corner of the Yukon, including most of th St. Elias Mountains in Canada. From the Alaska Highway the rugged, snow-cappe Kluane Ranges (as high as 2,500m/8,000ft) of these mountains can be seen Behind them and largely invisible from the highway are the **Icefield Ranges**. Separated from the Kluanes by a narrow trough called the Duke Depression, these ranges contain the highest mountains in Canada, with many peaks exceeding 4,500m/15,000ft. Best known are **Mt. Logan** (5,959m/19,550ft) and **Mt. St. Elia** (5,489m/18,008ft). Mt. Logan is second in height only to **Mt. McKinle** (6,194m/20,320ft) in Alaska, the highest point on the continent. Forming the bas of these peaks is an ice-covered plateau 2,500-3,000m/8,000-10,000ft high, from which many glaciers radiate.

At KM 1707/mi 1061 the Alaska Highway passes **Sheep Mountain** *(satellite visito centre)*, a rocky and barren peak so named for the white Dall sheep sometime seen on its slopes. The Alaska Highway crosses the large **Slims River Delta** *(KM 1707 2/mi 1061-58)*, its sandy streak of glacial silt from the Kaskawulsh Glacier penetrating the blue of Kluane Lake for some distance, until absorbed.

Haines Junction – *KM 1635/mi 1016. Kluane National Park Reserve visitor centre open mid-May–mid-Sept daily 8am–8pm. 867-634-2345.* At the junction of the Alaska and Haines (Route 3) Highways, this community has a fine **site★** at the foot of the Auriol Range and is the location for Kluane National Park Reserve headquarters. The **visitor centre** provides information and registration services, and offers interpretive panels and a poetic audio-visual presentation of the park's diversity and grandeur *(25min)*.

Affording views of lovely **Kathleen Lake★★** as it parallels the park to the south, Haines Highway then crosses the Chilkat Pass before entering Alaska and reaching the town of Haines on the Lynn Canal.

About 20km/12mi south of Haines Junction via Route 3, there is a lookout for a **view★★** of Kathleen Lake. At the park's only campground, visitors can drive to the edge of the lake with its shimmering blue waters. When untroubled by frequent winds, the lake's surface mirrors the imposing forms of King's Throne Mountain and Mt. Worthington, rising above.

Returning to Haines Junction, travellers can continue to Whitehorse (KM 1474/mi 916) on the Alaska Highway, with views of the Coast Mountains to the south most of the way. About 13km/8mi after the junction, there is a **view★** from the Alaska Highway *(weather permitting)* of two white pinnacles protruding above the Auriol and Kluane Ranges up the valley of the Dezadeash River: Mts. Hubbard and Kennedy of the Icefield Ranges.

For general information on admission, accommodations and activities in Canadian national parks, see p 309.

Prairie Provinces

Southey, Saskatchewan – Malak, Ottawa

Alberta, Saskatchewan and Manitoba, known collectively as the Prairie provinces, are often declared flat and monotonous by visitors who drive the long 1,500km/930mi journey from Ontario to Banff. But few who spend time exploring this vast region of nearly 1,963,000 sq km/758,000sq mi come away with this impression. There is something awe-inspiring about the wide open spaces, extensively cultivated, yet sparsely populated (just over 4.8 million people). Despite the seemingly endless plain, there are variations. Rivers have cut deep valleys into the soft soil, and in some of these, **badlands**—the eery lunar landscape of another age—can be seen.

The countryside is an ever-changing rainbow of colours. Green in the spring, the wheat turns gold before harvest. Flax has a small blue or white flower, rapeseed a yellow one. Tall colourfully painted **grain elevators**—the "cathedrals of the plains"—rise beside the railway tracks. Above extends an infinite blue sky, dotted with puffy white clouds, sometimes black as a storm approaches. Prairie sunsets are a sight not to be missed, and nighttime skies are so full of stars, it is rarely dark.

Yet among ample evidence of man's handiwork, wildlife survives. Wild ducks, geese and other birds are frequently seen on prairie **sloughs** (small ponds), and ground squirrels (gophers) are a common sight along the roadside.

The people of this land represent an amazing mélange of ethnic groups and cultures, each maintaining its identity, perhaps because of the distances between communities. From afar, villages with their onion-domed churches rise like mirages from the wheat fields.

Geographical Notes

Diverse Region – The idea that the word prairie is synonymous with endless fields stretching to the horizon is a recent phenomenon. The word is, in fact, of French origin and means "meadow." It was given to the large area of natural grassland that existed in the interior of the North American continent before the arrival of the Europeans. Characterized by its flatness and lack of trees, this grassland was an area where the buffalo, roaming in huge herds, were hunted by the various Plains Indians. Today little natural grasslan survives, and in Canada the term "Prairies" now applies to the whole of the three pro vinces, despite the fact that this immense region is geographically quite diverse.

Semiarid Southwest – The southernmost part of Alberta and Saskatchewan is a rela tively dry land of short grass. In 1857 a scientific expedition led by **John Palliser** commissioned by the British government to study the possibilities for settlement in the Prairies, decided that the southwestern corner would never be productive agri culturally. Palliser did not foresee the widespread use of irrigation, which has brought much of the region into cultivation today, nor did he fully realize the nutritional value of the native grasses, which today provide adequate pasture for cattle. This region especially the vicinity of Cypress Hills, rates second in importance to British Columbia's Cariboo for cattle raising in Canada.

Wheat-Growing Crescent – To the north of the arid lands lies a crescent-shaped region of fertile soil, graced with more abundant rainfall. Once, the grass grew shoulder high and few trees blocked the view of distant horizons over the flat plain. Today this is the wheat belt, the prairie of many people's imagination. Prim farm buildings dot the enor mous fields of thriving crops, contributing to a general air of prosperity.

Aspen Parkland – North of the wheat belt is another roughly crescent-shaped region where trees grow in good soil and mixed farming flourishes. This is a region of rolling parkland, a transitional zone between the prairie and the forest of the north. It is in this region that the majority of the inhabitants of the three provinces live.

Boreal Forest and Tundra – Nearly half the total area of the three provinces lies directly on the Precambrian rock of the Canadian Shield. This expanse is a pristine largely uninhabited land of lakes, trees and rocks. The few people who do call it home are involved either in the forestry industry or in mining. Along the shores of Hudson Bay in northern Manitoba, a small region of tundra thrives. Its treeless and forbidding winter landscape turns startlingly beautiful in summer.

Prairie "Steps" – Despite their reputation the Prairies are not actually flat. Apart from deep valleys cut by rivers, the Prairies rise gradually in three main levels or steps, from sea level at Hudson Bay to nearly 1,200m/4,000ft west of the Rockies. The first step ends with the **Manitoba Escarpment**, which rises to a maximum 831m/2,726ft. Encompassing the flattest lands, the second step ends with the **Missouri Coteau**, rising to a maximum 879m/2,883ft and visible from Moose Jaw. The third step borders the Rockies. The Prairies are broken by numerous ranges of small hills in the north, in addition to these steps, and by the Cypress Hills in the south.

Climate – The Prairies experience a climate of extremes that varies from year to year, making average conditions difficult to gauge. Winter is generally long and cold; summer is short and hot. Precipitation is low (380-500mm/15-20in a year), frequently arriving in the form of blizzards in winter and violent thunderstorms in summer, often after periods of drought. Sunshine is plentiful, especially in July, the driest and hottest month of the year (mean maximum for Calgary is 24°C/76°F, Regina 27°C/81°F, Winnipeg 27°C/80°F). In the southwest winter is alleviated by the chinook winds, which blow warm air from the Pacific through the Rockies. In a few hours temperatures can rise by as much as 28°C/82°F.

Historical Notes

Indians of the Plains – Once the only inhabitants of this region, the Assiniboine, Blackfoot, Cree, Gros Ventre and Sarcee Indians lived almost exclusively on buffalo. The animals were driven over cliffs or stampeded into pounds. Their meat was often dried and made into **pemmican**—a nutritious mixture of pounded meat, animal fat and sometimes saskatoon berries—which could be preserved for up to a year. Buffalo hides were used to make moccasins, leggings and tunics; the wool was left on to fashion robes for winter. Clothing was decorated with fringes and later, beads. Home was a **teepee**, a conical structure of poles (some almost 12m/40ft tall) covered with buffalo hides.
These nomadic tribes followed buffalo herds all summer, then dispersed in winter. Possessions were put on a **travois**, a structure of crossed poles pulled by a dog and later a horse (horses were in general use in the Canadian Plains by the mid-18C). In spring they reassembled to await the return of the buffalo and to celebrate the **sun dance** or medicine-lodge dance.
Existing rivalry and warfare among the tribes grew more lethal when fur traders began supplying guns. Since buffalo hunting was easier with guns, their use resulted in the gradual extinction of the great herds, which, in turn, destroyed the traditional life of the hunters. By the 1880s the herds were gone, and European settlers had arrived to cultivate and fence the once-open prairie. The Indians signed treaties and moved to reservations, but a sedentary life of farming did not come easily to the former nomadic hunters.

Fur Traders – The lucrative fur trade inspired the French to establish the first permanent settlements in mainland Canada in the 17C, and sent them farther into the continent in search of the elusive beaver. Eager to reduce the long journey by canoe between Ville-Marie (present-day Montreal) and Lake Superior, two traders, erre Radisson and **Sieur des Groseilliers**, proposed a quicker, cheaper way to transport furs Europe via Hudson Bay, the huge waterway discovered by Henry Hudson in 1610. his scheme met with little interest in France, but "Radish and Gooseberry," as they ecame known, found a warmer reception at the English court of Charles II. The ketch *onsuch* was equipped and sailed to Hudson Bay in 1668, returning with a rich load f furs. In 1670 Charles II granted a royal charter to the "Governor and Company of dventurers of England trading into Hudson's Bay." The **Hudson's Bay Company** (HBC), s it became known, held sole right to trade in the vast watershed that drains into the ay. Forts or factories were quickly established on its shores and trade thrived.

he first European to explore the interior of this large region was **Henry Kelsey**, who avelled across northern Manitoba and Saskatchewan in the early 1690s. Threatened y Kelsey's contacts with the Indians, the **Sieur de la Vérendrye** established the first French ading posts on the plains in 1730. While travelling through Alberta in 1754, **Anthony enday** of the HBC found the French so entrenched on the plains that he recommended he company abandon its policy of letting Indians bring their furs to the bay, and establish posts in the interior of the land. However, the fall of New France in 1759 *(p 188)* eemed to diminish the threat, and Henday's suggestion was not heeded.

itter rivalry developed among fur traders in the Prairies during the late 18C and the arly 19C. The Scots quickly established themselves in Montreal and founded the North Vest Company, soon a ferocious competitor of the HBC. Rival posts sprang up along the rairie rivers; every load of furs was grounds for contention. Competition finally ended n 1821 when the two companies merged; Hudson's Bay Company kept the upper hand.

he Métis and the Creation of Manitoba – A consequence of the fur trade was the reation of a new ethnic group, the Métis—offspring of Indian women and French *coureurs des bois* (and later of Scots and English traders). Though mainly French-speaking Roman Catholics, the Métis preserved the traditional lifestyle of their Indian forebears, unting buffalo and making pemmican to sell to fur traders. The first threat to their lifestyle came with the arrival of settlers along the Red River in 1812 *(p 120)*. Conflict ensued since farms and fences could not share the prairie with wandering herds of buffalo and their hunters. In 1870 the situation escalated when the new Dominion of Canada decided to take over the vast lands of the Hudson's Bay Company. The Métis saw their traditional ife disappearing with the arrival of more settlers and feared the loss of their language. When Dominion surveyors began marking out long narrow strips of Métis land into neat squares, these people turned to 25-year-old **Louis Riel**. Soon after his return from Montreal, where he had completed his religious training, Riel declared the surveys illegal, since sovereignty had not yet been established, and set up his own provisional government to ensure the recognition of Métis rights in the new government. Although supported by his own people, Riel gained no sympathy from English Métis and other settlers, particularly many Ontarians of Irish origin who had recently moved to the area in anticipation of the Canadian sovereignty. After foiling a plot to assassinate him, Riel executed a boisterous adventurer from Ontario, **Thomas Scott**, an act that he was long to regret. Nevertheless his plea on behalf of his people was heard. In July 1870 the new province of Manitoba was created. Land was set aside for the Métis, and both French and English settlers were given equal status. Riel was elected to Parliament several times, but was unable to take his seat in Ottawa because of anger in Ontario over Scott's death. Eventually Riel went into exile in the US, but resurfaced again 15 years later *(p 120)*.

A Human Mosaic – Once the Hudson's Bay Company had ceded its immense territory to the government, treaties had to be negotiated with the residents of the region. Though established by 1877 the treaties proved unsuccessful as the Northwest Rebellion of 1885 showed. Some means of enforcing law and order was also required. In 1873 the **North West Mounted Police** force was created. Thirdly, land had to be distributed. The **Dominion Lands Act** of 1872 allowed prospective homesteaders to register for a quarter section (65ha/160 acres). Title was given after three years if a homestead had been built and a certain amount of the land cultivated. Settlers also had an option on an additional quarter section. Finally, a means of reaching the region and transporting produce to market was required. To solve this problem, construction of the **Canadian Pacific Railway** was begun in 1881. By the year of its completion (1885), the population of the Prairies was about 150,000; by 1914 it had reached 1.5 million. The prospect of free land attracted inhabitants of an overcrowded Europe, especially those who lived in industrial cities, where factory hours were long and hard. The area also appealed to religious refugees who hoped to have the freedom to worship and live as they pleased. The Canadian government under **Sir Wilfrid Laurier** advertised all over the world: "Canada West—the last best west. Free homes for millions." Millions indeed came—from Ontario, the Maritimes (New Brunswick, Nova Scotia, Prince Edward Island), the US, Iceland, England, Scotland, Ireland, Germany, Austria, France, Scandinavia and Russia, especially the Ukraine. Mennonites, Hutterites and Doukhobors arrived from Russia, and Orthodox Christians from Eastern Europe. These immigrants were joined by Roman Catholics, Mormons, Jews and Protestants belonging to a variety of denominations. The provinces of **Alberta** and **Saskatchewan** were created in 1905. Since 1915 these peoples have been joined by those seeking refuge from political unrest in their homelands. They have made the Prairies a veritable mosaic of cultures. The **population** today stands at more than 4.8 million (Alberta 2,696,826; Manitoba 1,113,898; Saskatchewan 990,237).

PRACTICAL INFORMATION

Getting There

By Air – Major domestic and international airlines such as Air Canada ☎403-298-9200 and Canadian Airlines International ☎800-426-7000 (Canada/US) service Calgary, Edmonton, Regina, Saskatoon and Winnipeg. Regional carriers offer connections to cities within the Prairie provinces: Calm Air ☎204-778-6471; Canadian Regional Airlines ☎306-569-2307.

By Train – **VIA Rail** Canada has regularly scheduled transcontinental service to all three provinces. In Canada consult the telephone directory for nearest office; from the US ☎800-561-3949.

General Information

Accommodations and Visitor Information – The government tourist offices produce annually updated guides listing approved hotels, motels, B&B lodgings and cabins. Camping guides and discovery guides give detailed information on golf courses, outfitters, guest ranches and fishing camps. Winter vacation guides list ski areas, winter sports activities, hotels and ski lodges. These publications and maps are available free of charge from:

Travel Alberta, 10155 102nd St., Edmonton, AB, T5J 4G8 ☎403-427-4321 or 800-661-8888 (Canada/US).

Travel Manitoba, Tourism Division, 155 Carlton St. 7th floor, Dept. RA 6, Winnipeg, MB, R3C 3H8 ☎204-945-3777 or 800-665-0040 (Canada/US).

Tourism Saskatchewan, 500-1900 Albert St., Regina, SK, S4P 4L9 ☎306-787-2300 or 800-667-7191 (Canada/US).

Most major hotel chains have facilities in these provinces *(p 306)*. Independent hotels and B&B lodgings can be found along major routes. **Farm vacations** are offered in all three provinces, but Saskatchewan is especially popular. Alberta in particular boasts many **guest ranches** offering trail riding with overnight camping for the experienced or the novice rider, as well as families.

Road Regulations – *(Driver's license and insurance requirements p 304.)* All three provinces have good paved roads. Unless otherwise posted, speed limits on provincial highways are: Alberta 100km/h (60mph); Manitoba 90km/h (55mph); Saskatchewan 100km/h (60mph). Use of **seat belts** is compulsory. For listings of the **Canadian Automobile Assn. (CAA)**, consult the local telephone directory.

Time Zones – Alberta: Mountain Standard Time. Manitoba: Central Standard Time. Both observe Daylight Saving Time from the first Sunday in April to the last Sunday in October. Most of Saskatchewan is on Central Standard Time all year; it is the same as Alberta in summer, and as Manitoba in winter. Some border communities keep the same time as the neighbouring province all year.

Taxes – In addition to the national 7% GST *(rebate information p 308)*, Manitoba levies 7% and Saskatchewan 7% sales tax on all items. In Alberta there is a 5% hotel tax but no sales or restaurant tax. Manitoba offers a rebate of its provincial sales tax to nonresidents of Canada; contact Retail Sales Tax Office, 101-401 York Ave., Winnipeg, MB, R3C 0P8 ☎204-945-5603.

Liquor Laws – The legal drinking age is 18 in Manitoba and Alberta, 19 in Saskatchewan. In Manitoba and Saskatchewan, liquor and wine can be purchased only in government stores. In Alberta liquor can be bought in privately owned liquor shops, as well as in government stores. In isolated parts of the North where no government stores exist, grocery stores are licensed.

Provincial Holidays *(National Holidays p 308)*

Family Day *AB*	3rd Monday in February
Civic Holiday *MB, SK and AB*	1st Monday in August

Recreation

Outdoor Activities – The Prairies are especially prized by outdoor enthusiasts. **Water sports**—boating, sailing, canoeing, water skiing and swimming—are particularly popular because of the large number of lakes and river systems. Saskatchewan is famous for its **white-water rafting**, especially along the Churchill River.

The region is well endowed with national parks and provincial parks, offering hiking trails and campsites in summer and cross-country skiing, snowshoeing and snowmobiling in winter.

All three provinces offer good **fishing**, but northern Manitoba and Saskatchewan are particularly famous for their numerous fly-in lodges. Lac la Ronge in Saskatchewan is perhaps the best-known region for sport fishing. Fishermen and hunters must have a valid license, obtainable in most sporting goods stores. The *Anglers' Guide* and the *Hunting and Trapping Guide (available free from provincial tourist offices)* give valuable information such as hunting and fishing regulations, species and limits.

Special Excursions – The **Prairie Dog Central**, a turn-of-the-century steam train, makes weekly excursions from WINNIPEG northwest to Grosse Isle *(departs from St. James Station, 1661 Portage Ave., May–Sept Sun 11am & 3pm; round-trip 2hrs 30min; $13; Vintage Locomotive Society Inc. ☎ 204-832-5259)*.

Polar Bear watch excursions from Winnipeg are offered in CHURCHILL *(mid-Oct–mid-Nov; 6-9 days from $1,995; 6-9 months advance reservation suggested; Natural Habitat Wildlife Adventures ☎ 303-449-3711 or 800-543-8917, Canada/US)*.

To relive the days of the Wild West, join a **covered wagon trek** and travel through the wide expanses of Saskatchewan. Experienced scouts take visitors from May to September on excursions *(1-4 days)* that include campfire dinners. Contact Tourism Saskatchewan for details.

Principal Festivals

Feb	**Northern Manitoba Trappers' Festival**	*The Pas, MB*
	Festival du Voyageur *(p 123)*	*Saint-Boniface, MB*
	Winter Festival	*Prince Albert, SK*
Jun	**Manitoba Summer Fair**	*Brandon, MB*
	Western Canada Farm Progress Show	*Regina, SK*
	Red River Exhibition	*Winnipeg, MB*
Jul	**Folk Festival**	*Winnipeg, MB*
	Saskatoon Exhibition	*Saskatoon, SK*
	Manitoba Highland Gathering	*Selkirk, MB*
	Manitoba Threshermen's Reunion *(p 102)*	*Austin, MB*
	Calgary Exhibition and Stampede *(p 104)*	*Calgary, AB*
	Klondike Days *(p 110)*	*Edmonton, AB*
	Big Valley Jamboree	*Craven, SK*
Jul–Aug	**National Ukrainian Festival**	*Dauphin, MB*
	Pioneer Days	*Steinbach, MB*
	Buffalo Days	*Regina, SK*
Aug	**Whoop-up Days and Rodeo**	*Lethbridge, AB*
	Icelandic Festival	*Gimli, MB*
	Corn and Apple Festival	*Morden, MB*
	Folklorama *(p 121)*	*Winnipeg, MB*
	Folkfest	*Saskatoon, SK*
Nov–Dec	**Canadian Western Agribition**	*Regina, SK*

Economy

King Wheat – Between 1876 and 1915, the land where the fur trade once reigned supreme suddenly developed a wheat economy. The region where giant bluestem and needle grass thrived and prairie flowers bloomed in millions vanished under the plough. Several factors contributed to the striking changes. In 1842 David Fife, a Scottish farmer living in Ontario, developed a strain of wheat that later proved ideal for cultivation on the prairies. Called **Red Fife** for its rich colour, it was resistant to rust and thrived in the drought-ridden, short summer season. It is the ancestor of all the strains used today. Another factor was the building of the Canadian Pacific Railway, which brought settlers to cultivate the land and provided transport for their produce to market.

Wheat did not always flourish in this region of changeable and unpredictable climate. Drought and hardships in the 1930s caused many farmers to abandon the land. Today farmers depend less on wheat than in the past. Barley, oats, rye, flax, rapeseed, mustard, buckwheat, peas, sunflowers and potatoes are all widely cultivated; nevertheless 50 percent of the land annually seeded to field crops is devoted to wheat. More than 22 million tonnes/25 million tons of wheat are produced in the western provinces every year, about three-quarters of which is exported.

Cattle Country – Although grain is by far the major economic staple of the Prairies, ranch ing is firmly established as a secondary industry. Canadian ranching began in Britis Columbia and spread into southern Alberta and Saskatchewan after the Indian treaties o the 1870s. The dry, short-grass country turned out to be fine pasture for cattle, and th chinook winds made winter grazing possible as they melted the snow, exposing the grass Slowly, as ranchers discovered that cattle would not run off with buffalo or be kille by winter or Indians, the number of ranches increased. By the turn of the century cattle raising attained its present position as the second most important economic acti vity. To this day southern Alberta and Saskatchewan remain "cowboy country. Horseback riders among the herds are a common sight, and rodeos abound. The mos popular cowboy event is the Calgary Stampede.

Riches Below the Earth – One of the first minerals exploited in the Prairies was **coal** found in LETHBRIDGE, Alberta, in 1869. Later, coal was also mined near Estevan in Sas katchewan and at Canmore, Alberta. The giant **zinc**, **cadmium** and **copper** field at Flir Flon, Manitoba, was established in 1915. Today mining activity has spread across the border into Saskatchewan. Copper was discovered near Lynn Lake, Manitoba, and gold in the Lake Athabasca area of Saskatchewan.

In the 1880s Kootenay Brown found **oil** in the Waterton Lakes area of Alberta and sold it as machine grease. In 1914 oil was discovered in Turner Valley *(p 104)*, marking the beginning of Alberta's petroleum industry. The year 1947 saw the discovery of the Leduc oilfield *(p 109)* subsequently numerous other small fields underlying Alberta were exploited. Alberta accounts for the vast majority of Canada's oil and **natural gas** produc- tion. Alberta's reserves are supplemented by the **Athabasca oil sands** in the northern part of the province, said to be the largest known hydrocarbon accumulation in the world.

Uranium was found in the late 1940s in the Beaverlodge area of Saskatchewan, north of Lake Athabasca, and in the 1960s, the giant **nickel** field of Thompson, Manitoba, came into production. The first **potash** was mined in 1951 near Esterhazy in Saskatchewan. This province's potash reserves are estimated at more than 25 percent of the world's total supply and, at current rates of consumption, enough to supply world needs for 2,000 years. Just as oil and natural gas underlie Alberta, potash underlies Saskatchewan in a wide arc roughly corresponding to the aspen parkland zone *(p 96)*. Saskatchewan also has **sodium sulphate** and oil in the Lloydminster, Swift Current and Estevan areas.

ALBERTA BADLANDS***

Alberta

Map of Principal Sights p 2

The meltwaters of the last continental glacier eroded a deep valley across southern Alberta, which today is occupied by the Red Deer River. In so doing they exposed rocks formed during the Cretaceous period (64-140 million years ago) and created the Alberta Badlands, a striking panorama of steep bluffs and fluted gullies. The area was a subtropical lowland inhabited by huge reptilelike creatures known as dinosaurs. A number of these were fossilized and preserved to this day.

Historical Notes – Dinosaur bones have been found on all continents, but this valley in Alberta is one of the richest in deposits. The first fossils discovered in 1884, along with the bones and several hundred complete skeletons unearthed since then, are on display in many world museums, including the Royal Ontario Museum in Toronto and the Canadian Museum of Nature in Ottawa, Ontario.

The word dinosaur is derived from Greek, meaning "terrible lizard," a reference to the predatory habits and great size of some of these creatures. In fact there were many types: some were small and most were plant eaters, but the biggest weighed as much as 27 tonnes/30 tons and grew to 24m/80ft in length. The **duckbilled dinosaur** walked on its hind feet, which were webbed for swimming, and sported a snout resem- bling a duck's bill, thus its name. The **horned dinosaur** walked on four feet and had horns—usually one over each eye and one on the nose. The **armoured dinosaur** was equipped with a row of bony plates on its back and spikes on its tail as a form of protection. All of these were herbivorous, slow moving and prey to the ferocious **car- nivorous dinosaur** with its sharp claws and teeth, and muscular hind legs for running.

DINOSAUR TRAIL *2hrs. 51km/32mi circular drive.*

Connecting the sights of the Drumheller area, this loop on the plain above Red Deer River offers good views of the badlands.

★**Drumheller** – *Visitor Centre, 60 1st St. West. Open mid-May–Jun daily 9am–6pm (Fri 9pm). Jul–Labour Day daily 9am–9pm. Rest of the year Mon–Fri 8:30am–4:30pm. Closed national holidays.* ♿ ☎*403-823-8100.* This former coal- mining town, 138km/86mi northeast of Calgary, lies amid the badlands of the Red Deer River as does Dinosaur Provincial Park *(p 102)*. Drumheller is surrounded by a fertile wheat-growing plain, unbroken except by occasional oil pumps known as "donkey heads" because they bob up and down continuously. Upon the approach to the town, the extensively eroded valley, nearly 120m/400ft deep and about 1.6km/1mi wide, comes as something of a surprise.

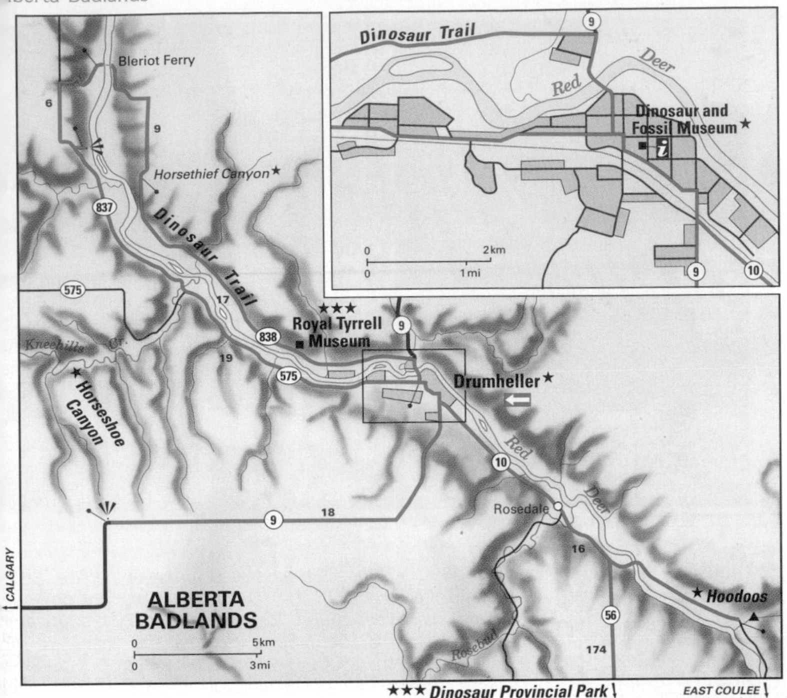

★**Dinosaur and Fossil Museum** – *335 1st St. East. Open Jul–Aug daily 10am–6pm. May–Jun & Sept–mid-Oct daily 10am–5pm. $2.50.* ♿ ☎ *403-823-2593.* Devoted to the region's geology, this museum features examples of dinosaur fossils. The most impressive is **Edmontosaurus**, a 9m/30ft long, 3.5m/11ft high duck-billed dinosaur with webbed feet and a strong tail for use when swimming.

★★★**Royal Tyrrell Museum of Palaeontology** – *6km/4mi northwest of Drumheller by Hwy. 838 (North Dinosaur Trail). Open mid-May–early Sept daily 9am–9pm. Labour Day–mid-Oct daily 10am–5pm. Rest of the year Tue–Sun 10am–5pm. $6.50.* ✂ ♿ *www.tyrrellmuseum.com* ☎ *403-823-7707.* This splendid museum, opened in 1985, is one of the largest in the world devoted to the study of life-forms from past geological periods. It has a fine setting in the badlands and blends well with its surroundings in a series of innovative structures designed by Douglas Craig of Calgary. The highlight is the enormous **Dinosaur Hall**, where the major types of dinosaurs formerly inhabiting this area are re-created, some with original fossils, others with modern casting materials. The huge *Tyrannosaurus rex, Albertosaurus*, the armoured *Stegosaurus* and some smaller birdlike dinosaurs can be seen. One part of the hall represents the bottom of the ancient Bearpaw Sea, which covered the western Canadian interior 70 million years ago. Here, mosasaurs—large marine reptiles up to 15m/50ft long—can be viewed.

In the **palaeoconservatory** visitors can admire a large collection of plants descended from those the dinosaurs would have known. Some have changed little in 140 million years.

The museum's main theme is a "celebration of life," featuring displays, films and slide shows on such topics as the creation of the universe, evolutionary theories, diverse environments, the age of the dinosaurs and the mystery of their disappearance, mammals (including species now extinct), the ice ages and the evolution of *Homo sapiens*.

After passing the museum, Dinosaur Trail provides a good view of the badlands from **Horse Thief Canyon**★, with its rounded, almost barren hills stretching to the river. The trail crosses the river by the **Bleriot cable ferry** and climbs to a fine **view**★ of the valley. The green pastures beside the river provide an interesting contrast to the cactus-strewn bluffs and gullies immediately below.

ADDITIONAL SIGHTS

★**Horseshoe Canyon** – *18km/11mi southwest of Drumheller by Rte. 9.* Paths leading through the hillocks to the river provide some of the best **views** of the badlands in the area.

★**Hoodoos** – *17km/10mi southeast of Drumheller by Rte. 10.* These strange rock formations, which look like giant mushrooms, illustrate the work of erosion in the valley. Soft rock has been worn away, leaving harder pieces behind.

Hoodoos

★★★ **Dinosaur Provincial Park** – *174km/108mi southeast of Drumheller by Rte. 56 & Trans-Can Hwy. east to Brooks. Take Hwy. 873 for 10km/6mi, then right on Hwy 544, and left on Hwy. 551. Open daily year-round. Visitor centre in Tyrrell Museum Field Station open mid-May–Aug daily 8:15am–9pm. Rest of the year Mon–Fri 8:15am–4:30pm. Closed national holidays. www.gov.ab.ca/~env/nrs/dinosaur ☎ 403-378-4342.* The park is set in the most spectacular part of the Red Deer River Valley and the richest fossil area. It is home to groves of rare cottonwood trees found along the riverside. In 1979 UNESCO recognized its importance by placing it on the World Heritage List.

Immediately upon entrance to the park, an excellent **viewpoint**★★★ overlooks nearly 3,000ha/7,000 acres of badlands cut by the Red Deer River. The road then descends to the valley.

A **circular drive**★ *(5km/3mi)* takes the visitor through this wild and desolate, almost lunar, landscape where little except sagebrush flourishes. At several points short walks can be taken to see dinosaur bones preserved where they were found. Explanatory panels offer details on the type of dinosaur and its size. Longer nature trails enable visitors to better appreciate this pristine terrain. Most of the park, however, is accessible only by a special **bus tour**★ *(departs from the Field Station mid-May–Aug daily; 1hr 30min; 1-day advance reservations required; $4.50; ☎ 403-378-4344)* or by conducted hikes *(contact visitor centre for details)*.

★★ **Tyrrell Museum Field Station** – *1.6km/1mi from park entrance. Open mid-May–Aug daily 8:15am–9pm. Rest of the year Mon–Fri 8:15am–4:30pm (phone for weekend hours). $2. www.eldnet.org/public/dinosaur/index.htm ☎ 403-378-4342.* Opened in 1987 this research satellite of the museum *(p 101)* is located within Dinosaur Provincial Park. The interpretation centre features habitat and fossil displays and an observation post, where visitors can watch staff prepare fossils.

AUSTIN★

Manitoba

Map of Principal Sights p 3

Set in the centre of a rich agricultural region, this community, 123km/76mi west of Winnipeg, is renowned for its collection of operating vintage farm machinery.

SIGHT

★ **Manitoba Agricultural Museum** – *On Hwy. 34, 3km/2mi south of Trans-Can Hwy. Open late May–early Oct daily 9am–5pm. Rest of the year, call for hours. $5. www.ag-museum.mb.ca ☎ 204-637-2354.* This museum has a splendid collection of "prairie giants"—steam tractors, threshing machines, and the cumbersome gasoline machines that replaced them in the early part of this century. Every year at the end of July, these machines are paraded and demonstrated in the Manitoba **Threshermen's Reunion and Stampede**. Drawing hundreds of visitors from all over the country, this festival features threshing, sheaf-tying and stooking contests, a stampede and steam engine races.

A **homesteaders' village** illustrates rural life at the end of the last century when the first giant steam engines were breaking the prairie sod and bringing it under cultivation. The village includes several log homes, a church and a school. The centennial building houses a large collection of pioneer artifacts.

The BATTLEFORDS★

Saskatchewan

Population 17,987

Map of Principal Sights p 3

Tourist Office ☎306-445-6226

urrounded by rolling country, the twin communities of **Battleford** and **North Battleford**, 38km/86mi northwest of SASKATOON, face each other across the valley of the North askatchewan River. North Battleford has a fine **site★** overlooking the river.

listorical Notes – Fur traders established posts on the Battleford (south) side of the iver in the 18C, but it was not until 1874 that the first settlers arrived. A North West lounted Police post was established in 1876, and the settlement was chosen as the ome of the government of the Northwest Territories. A bright future seemed assured. 'hen the Canadian Pacific Railway Co. decided to route its line through the southern lains, and in 1883 Battleford lost its status as capital when the government offices vere moved to Pile O'Bones Creek (later REGINA). To add insult to injury, the settle-nent of Battleford was looted and burned by Poundmaker Crees during the Northwest lebellion of 1885 while the fearful inhabitants took refuge in the police fort. The leath knell sounded in 1903 when the Canadian Northern Railway was built along he opposite side of the river, creating a new community, North Battleford, which jrew as Battleford shrank. Today North Battleford, served by the Yellowhead Highway is well as the railway, is a distribution centre of no small importance.

SIGHTS

★**Fort Battleford National Historic Site** – *Central Ave., Battleford. Open mid-May–mid-Oct daily 9am–6pm. $4.* ♿ *☎306-937-2621.* This North West Mounted Police post was the fifth established by the police in the Northwest Territories. Enlarged after the Northwest Rebellion, it was abandoned in 1924. Today restored, it provides insight into police life in the late 19C.

The **commanding officers' residence** suggests that police officers lived fairly comfortably. The **officers' quarters** house an office for the police. Just outside the palisade a former barracks has been converted into an **interpretation centre**, which provides a particularly good account of the 1885 rebellion.

★**Western Development Museum** – *On Hwy. 16 at junction with Rte. 40 in North Battleford. Open mid-May–early Sept daily 8:30am–6:30pm. $5.* ♿ *☎306-445-8033.* Devoted to agriculture, this branch of the Western Development Museum—one of four in the province (MOOSE JAW, SASKATOON, YORKTON)—displays a large collection of agricultural machinery and domestic artifacts used on farms in the 1920s.

Outside, an interesting **heritage farm and village** of 1925 is set out with homes and churches reflecting the diverse origins of the peoples who settled this province. Note the Ukrainian Orthodox Church with its onion dome, and the thatched *dacha* displaying the handicrafts and household fittings of a pioneer Ukrainian home. Also featured are a general store, a police post and a railway station complete with a train.

CALGARY★★

Alberta

Population 768,082

Map of Principal Sights p 2

Tourist Office ☎403-263-8510

Set in the foothills of the snow-capped peaks of the Canadian Rockies, this thriving city lies at the confluence of the Bow and Elbow Rivers, two mountain torrents of clear blue water. Covering the largest land area of any city in Canada (420sq km/162sq mi), Calgary was Canada's fastest-growing, most prosperous metropolis in the early 1980s, mainly because of Alberta's vast oil wealth and the city's own importance as a transportation centre. Blessed with a pleasant climate (moderate rainfall, low humidity, lots of sunshine and a moderately cold winter, tempered by warm chinook winds), this tourist mecca is known for its internationally famous stampede and remembered fondly by millions around the world as host of the 1988 Winter Olympic Games.

Historical Notes

Origins – In 1875 a North West Mounted Police post was built on this site and named Fort Calgary by Col. James Macleod *(p 113)*, commander of the police in the Northwest, for his home in Scotland. The name is derived from what is most likely a Gaelic word meaning "Bay Farm."

A small community grew up around the post, which quickly developed in the 1880s when the Canadian Pacific Railway Co. decided to route its railway south through Calgary and the Kicking Horse Pass, rather than through EDMONTON and the Yellow-

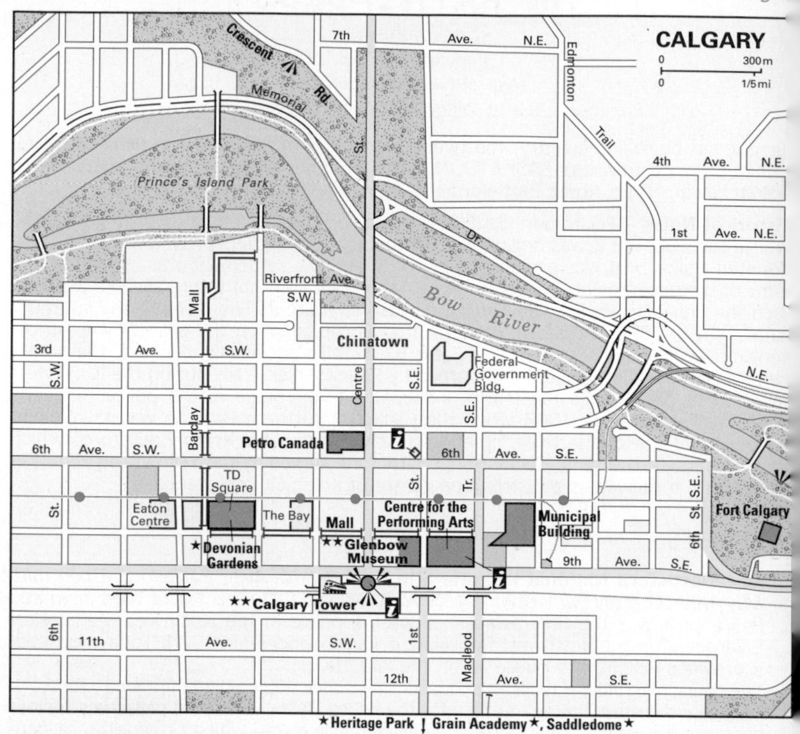

head Pass. This momentous decision resulted in a huge influx of settlers to the lush grazing lands of the region. The Dominion Lands Act *(p 97)* also encouraged the movement of cattle herds northward from the US. Canadians began to form their own herds in the area, and well-to-do Englishmen arrived from overseas to establish ranches.
Calgary rapidly became a marketing and meatpacking centre, gaining the nickname of Canada's Cowtown—a title it still has not relinquished, although cattle constitute a relatively minor part of its life today.

"Black Gold" – The discovery of oil in 1914 at Turner Valley, just southwest of Calgary, marked the birth of western Canada's petroleum industry. For about 30 years, this valley was the country's major oil producer. Then in 1947 a great discovery was made at Leduc *(p 109)*, and Calgary began a period of phenomenal growth. Although recent oil and gas discoveries have been closer to Edmonton, Calgary has predominated as the headquarters of the industry. According to recent statistics, Calgary is becoming one of the country's top financial centres, second only to Toronto in attracting corporate head offices.

"The Greatest Outdoor Show on Earth" – The **Calgary Stampede**, a grand 10-day event held in early July, attracts hundreds of thousands of spectators and competitors every year *(reservations recommended)*. The entire population dons western garb (boots, jeans and hats) and joins the festivities. There are flapjack breakfasts, street dances, and a huge parade in the city. Livestock shows and the famous **rodeo** and **chuckwagon races** are held in Stampede Park. Invented in Calgary the races recall the wagon races held by cowboys after a roundup. They are, without doubt, an exciting part of the stampede. *Details of all events can be obtained from the tourist office ☎ 800-661-1678 (Canada/US).*

DOWNTOWN *1/2 day.*

Calgary's downtown has undergone a phenomenal transformation since World War II and continues to develop. In more recent years the Calgary Tower, surrounded by a host of attractive glass-fronted high rises, has been overshadowed by the sloping-top, brown marble headquarters of **Petro-Canada**. A pedestrian **mall** stretches four blocks along 8th Avenue. At the western end lie the big bank blocks: the reflecting glass Royal Bank Centre, the Scotia Centre and the black towers of the Toronto Dominion (TD) Square, all connected to one another and to The Bay and Eaton's department stores by second-floor pedestrian bridges. More recently, CIBC Place adds a Postmodern look to the downtown core.

Toronto Dominion Square boasts a fine indoor greenhouse featuring tropical plants called the **Devonian Gardens★** *(4th floor, access from Eaton's or, outside store hours, via elevator from TD Square entrance on mall; open year-round daily 9am–9pm; ♿ 🅿 ☎ 403-268-5207).* East of the mall the tiered, blue-reflecting glass structure of Calgary's **Municipal Building** rises around a 12-storey atrium. Across 2nd Street Southeast stands the **Centre for the Performing Arts**, an attractive series of brick buildings.

★★ **Glenbow Museum** – *130 9th Ave. SE, in Convention Centre complex. Open Jun–mid-Oct daily 9am–5pm. Rest of the year Tue–Sun 9am–5pm. Closed Jan 1, Dec 25–26. $7 ($8 Jun–mid-Oct). ✂ ♿ www.glenbow.org ☎ 403-777-5506.* Administered by the Glenbow-Alberta Institute, this museum contains displays from an outstanding **Plains Indians collection★★**. Note in particular the fine beadwork.
European settlement in the province is traced through exhibits focusing on the fur trade, the North West Mounted Police, missionaries, the Canadian Pacific Railway, the arrival of the first farmers, ranching, the discovery of oil and Alberta life in the 1920s and 30s.
Displays on weapons and arms, tracing their development from Medieval times to recent years, are featured. In addition the museum mounts temporary exhibits of art and sculpture. A large acrylic and aluminum sculpture by James Houston, entitled **Aurora Borealis**, is the museum's focal point.

★★ **Calgary Tower** – *In Palliser Square, 101 9th Ave. SW. Observation deck open Jun–Sept daily 7:30am–11pm. Rest of the year Mon–Sat 8:00am–9pm, Sun 9am–9pm. Admission fee. ✂ ♿ 🅿 www.calgarytower.com ☎ 403-266-7171.* This 191m/626ft tower provides an excellent **view★★** of the city and its site. To the west the snow-capped peaks of the Rockies rise above the rolling, arid foothills on which the city is built. Immediately below the tower the maze of railway lines attests to the city's importance as a transportation centre.

ADDITIONAL SIGHTS

★★ **Crescent Road Viewpoint** – *Map p 104.* Standing above the Bow River and Prince's Island Park, this crescent offers a fine view of the downtown buildings and, on clear days, the snow-capped Rockies to the west.

Fort Calgary – *Map p 104. 750 9th Ave. SE. Open May–mid-Oct daily 9am–5pm. $5. ✂ ♿ 🅿 www.fortcalgary.ca ☎ 403-290-1875.* An **interpretation centre** on the site of the original North West Mounted Police post recounts the history of the city. The location of the post itself is indicated on the ground, and several rooms of Deane House, former home to the NWMP superintendent, can be visited *(today the house functions as a restaurant).* Paths afford **views** of the Bow River, and a pedestrian bridge allows access to St. George's Island and the zoo.

★★ **Zoo and Prehistoric Park** – Kids *1300 Zoo Rd. NE, on St. George's Island. Open Jun–Aug daily 9am–8:30pm. May & Sept daily 9am–6pm. Rest of the year daily 9am–4pm. $9.50. ✂ ♿ 🅿 (on St. George's Dr.) ☎ 403-232-9300.* Located on an island in the Bow River, this attractive zoo houses a wide variety of animals from all over the world and a tropical greenhouse filled with exotic plants, flowers, butterflies and birds. The **prehistoric park★★** re-creates western Canada as it might have looked in the age of the dinosaurs between 225 and 65 million years ago. Life-size reproductions of these giant creatures stand among mountains, volcanoes, hoodoos and swampland, along with the vegetation that might have existed in their day.

Malak, Ottawa

Saddledome, Calgary

★**Grain Academy** – *South of downtown by Macleod Trail, in Roundup Centre, Stampede Park, 17th Ave. and 2nd St. SE. Open Apr–Sept Mon–Fri 10am–4pm, Sat noon–4pm. Rest of the year Mon–Fri 10am–4pm. Closed holiday weekends.* ♿ 🅿 ☎ *403-263-4594.* This museum, Alberta's only grain interpretation centre, focuses on one of mankind's basic food sources. It presents a working model of a Prairie grain elevator, a model railway showing the movement of Prairie grain through the Rocky Mountains, and a film *(12min)* on the history of grain production in western Canada.

The museum is located in Stampede Park near the distinctive 20,240-seat Canadian Airlines **Saddledome**★ *(illustration p 105)* constructed in 1983. The flowing saddle design of the stadium's roof echoes Calgary's cowboy past *(visit by 1hr guided tour only, late May–late Aug Mon–Fri 11am & 2pm; for hours for rest of the year ☎ 403-777-1375; www.calgaryflames.com ☎ 403-777-2177).*

★**Heritage Park** – Kids *16km/10mi southwest of downtown. Take Macleod Trail SW to 1900 Heritage Dr. SW. Open mid-May–Labour Day daily 9am–5pm. Early Sept–mid-Oct & mid-Nov–mid-Dec weekends only 9am–5pm. $10 (not including rides).* ✗ 🅿 *www.heritagepark.org ☎ 403-259-1900.* Occupying a pleasant **site**★ in a recreation area overlooking Glenmore Reservoir, this park re-creates prairie life of a bygone era with a pioneer community and a reconstructed Hudson's Bay Company post. The turn-of-the-century town features a church, drugstore, bakery, general store, post office, newspaper office, pool hall, police post, houses and a station for a functioning steam train that gives tours of the site. Beside the tracks stands a working grain elevator, and on the outskirts of the town are farm buildings and a windmill. A replica of the *SS Moyie*, a stern-wheeler once used on Kootenay Lake, offers boat trips on the reservoir *(every 35min)* and memorable rides can be taken on the antique **midway**.

CARDSTON

Alberta

Population 3,417

Map of Principal Sights p 2

This small town, 25km/16mi north of the Montana (US) border, is an important Mormon centre. It was founded in 1887 by **Charles Ora Card**, a son-in-law of Brigham Young. Also known as the Church of Jesus Christ of the Latter Day Saints, the sect was established in 1830 by **Joseph Smith** at Fayette, New York. After his death most of his followers moved to Utah under the leadership of **Brigham Young**, establishing Salt Lake City in 1847.

SIGHTS

★★**Remington-Alberta Carriage Centre** – Kids *623 Main St. Open mid-May–Labour Day daily 9am–8pm. Rest of the year daily 9am–5pm.* ✗ ♿ ☎ *403-653-5139. Carriage rides seasonally (weather permitting).* This fascinating museum of transportation houses one of the most comprehensive collections of horse-drawn vehicles in North America. Over 200 restored wagons, carriages and sleighs are displayed in the main gallery, many within re-created scenes typical of the Western frontier such as a Prairie camp, a firehouse and a carriage factory. Highlights include a late-19C bull-wagon, a veteran from the Oregon Trail; a sheepwagon, the Great Plains version of a mobile home; and a Concord stagecoach. A film *(14min)* entitled *Wheels of Change* surveys the carriage industry, and in the **restoration shop** carriage overhaul can be observed. The well-stocked and orderly **tackroom** is also worth a peek.

Mormon Temple – *348 Third St. West. Temple not open to the public. Visitor centre open May–Sept daily 9am–9pm.* ♿ ☎ *403-653-1696.* This imposing white granite structure was completed in 1923 and is one of the few Mormon temples in Canada. The Mormon doctrine is based on the Bible, *The Book of Mormon* and Joseph Smith's writings. In Canada the church numbers about 135,000 and is largely concentrated in Alberta, Ontario and British Columbia.

CHURCHILL★★

Manitoba

Population 1,089

Map of Principal Sights p 3

On the shores of Hudson Bay, on the east side of the estuary of the wild and beautiful Churchill River, lies the little town of Churchill, Canada's most northerly deep-sea port. Situated north of the tree line, Churchill is bleak in winter, but during the summer months, a carpet of flowers covers the tundra, beluga whales abound in the blue waters of the bay, and myriad birds frequent the area. In autumn scavenging **polar bears**, a popular tourist attraction in and around the townsite, make their seasonal migration northward *(polar bear watch expeditions p 99)*. Because it experiences some of the world's most amazing spectacles of the Northern Lights, the town has attracted much scientific interest.

Churchill also boasts an interesting history. A fur-trading post was founded at the mouth of the river in 1685 by the Hudson's Bay Company. Named for the governor of the company, **John Churchill**, later Duke of Marlborough, it remained an important fur-gathering and export centre until this century when wheat took over. A railway was built in 1931, and a grain elevator and port facilities shortly thereafter. The Hudson Bay and Strait are navigable only three months a year *(Aug–Oct)*. During this period trains arrive constantly and ships of many nations visit the townsite to take on grain.

Access – *Regularly scheduled flights from Winnipeg. Also accessible from Winnipeg by VIA Rail (p 304).*

SIGHTS

Town Centre Complex – Opened in 1976 the centre combines recreational and health facilities, a library, high school and business offices under one roof. This low-lying complex with its **views** of the bay displays interesting art work.

★★**Eskimo Museum** – *Beside Roman Catholic Church. Open Jun–mid-Nov Mon 1pm–5pm, Tue–Sat 9am–noon & 1pm–5pm. Rest of the year Mon & Sat 1pm–4:30pm, Tue–Fri 10:30am–noon & 1pm–4:30pm. Closed Jan 1, Dec 25. Contribution requested. ☎204-675-2030.* This museum houses a fine collection of Inuit carvings in stone, ivory and bone. Collected over 50 years by the Oblate fathers, these carvings depict various aspects of life. Many refer to Inuit legends and others to the arrival of the first airplanes or snowmobiles in the North. A recorded commentary describes some of the works.

Steven Morello/Natural Habitat Adventures

Polar Bear

★**Prince of Wales Fort** – *Across Churchill River estuary from town. Access by helicopter or by boat depending on tides and weather conditions. Visit by guided tour (1hr) only, Jul–Aug daily. Contact visitor centre http://parkscanada.pch.gc.ca ☎204-675-8863.* Built by the Hudson's Bay Company to protect its fur trade, this large stone fortress took 40 years (1731-71) to complete. The long-standing threat from the French was eliminated after the defeat of New France on the Plains of Abraham in 1759. Subsequently a group of Montreal traders, who later founded the North West Company, challenged the Hudson's Bay Company's monopoly. In 1782 a French fleet attacked the fort, then under the command of the explorer Samuel Hearne. Not knowing that England and France were again at war, Hearne surrendered without a shot being fired. Most of his garrison was inland preventing the Montreal traders from taking all the furs. The French commander, Comte de La Pérouse, blew up parts of the walls and set fire to the fort. Returned to the British soon afterwards, the fort was never again used by the HBC, which preferred to establish outposts farther upstream.

Visit – The boat trip to the fort is an excellent means of viewing the beluga whales that inhabit the estuary of the Churchill River in July and August.
The **visitor centre** *(closed until May 1999 for renovation; otherwise open May–Nov daily 1pm–9pm; rest of the year daily 8am–4:30pm; closed national holidays; ☎204-675-8863)* offers videos, and a slide show on the **York Factory National Historic Site**, the remains of a major HBC trading post located 240km/149mi southeast of Churchill on Hudson Bay near the mouth of the Hayes River *(accessible only by canoe or charter plane; for information, contact the visitor centre)*. In the fort itself, note the massive stone walls nearly 12m/40ft thick at their base and 5m/17ft high, and 40 huge cannon.

CYPRESS HILLS★★

Alberta-Saskatchewan

Map of Principal Sights p 3

Straddling the Alberta/Saskatchewan boundary, 70km/43mi north of the state c Montana, the plains give way to rolling, forested hills cut by numerous coulees, valleys lakes and streams. These verdant hills rise prominently in the midst of otherwis unbroken, sunbaked, short-grass prairie. On their heights grow the tall, straight lodge pole pines favoured by Plains Indians for their teepees or lodges—thus the name. Th trees were probably mistaken by early French voyageurs for the jack pines *(cyprès)* of eastern Canada. Although no such trees are in the vicinity, a bad translation furthe compounded the error, and the name Cypress Hills was born.

Historical Notes

Oasis in the Desert – In 1859 John Palliser camped in these hills during his tour o the western domains for the British government *(p 96)*. "A perfect oasis in the desert we have travelled," was his brief description. Later, settlers found the hills ideally suited for **ranching** and today much land is devoted to cattle raising.
Not only is the scenic beauty of the hills a surprise, but they also present unique geographical features. The highest elevations in Canada between Labrador and the Rockies, they rise to nearly 1,500m/5,000ft. A 200sq km/80sq mi area of their heights was untouched by the last ice age, which covered the rest of this vast area with ice more than 1km/.6mi deep. The hills form a divide between two great watersheds: Hudson Bay and the Gulf of Mexico. Streams flow south to the Missouri-Mississippi system and north to the South Saskatchewan River, Lake Winnipeg and Hudson Bay. The flora and fauna of the hills offer a remarkable diversity. Wildflowers and songbirds normally associated only with the Rockies flourish here, cactus grows on the dry south-facing slopes and orchids thrive beside quiet ponds.

Cypress Hills Massacre – An event that occurred in these hills influenced the creation of that revered Canadian institution: the **Royal Canadian Mounted Police**. In the early 1870s several trading posts were established in the Cypress Hills by Americans from Montana. In exchange for furs, they illegally traded "fire water," an extremely potent and lethal brew. During the winter of 1872-73, Assiniboine Indians were camped close to two of these posts—Farwell's and Solomon's. They were joined by a party of Canadian and American wolf-hunters, whose entire stock of horses had been stolen by Cree raiders. Thinking the Assiniboines were the thieves, the "wolfers," fired up by a night's drinking, attacked the Indian camp, killing 36 people.
When news of this massacre reached Ottawa, Prime Minister Sir John A. Macdonald acted quickly. He created the **North West Mounted Police** (renamed the Royal Canadian Mounted Police in 1920) and dispatched them to the Northwest to stop such border incursions and end the illegal whisky trade. The perpetrators of the massacre were arrested but later acquitted for lack of evidence. However, the fact that white men had been arrested impressed the Indians with the impartiality of the new police force and helped establish its reputation.

Sitting Bull in Canada – In 1876 a force of Sioux warriors under their great chief, Sitting Bull, exterminated an American army detachment under Gen. **George Custer** on the Little Big Horn River in southern Montana. Fearing reprisals from the enraged Americans, Sitting Bull crossed into Canada with nearly 5,000 men. Inspector **James Walsh** of the North West Mounted Police was given the difficult task of trying to persuade the Sioux to return, in order to avoid war between the Sioux and their traditional enemies, the Cree and the Blackfoot, who inhabited the region. Riding into the sizeable Sioux encampment near Wood Mountain *(350km/217mi east of Fort Walsh)* with only four constables and two scouts, he informed Sitting Bull that he must obey Canadian law. Although this act of bravery won the respect of the chief, it was four years before Sitting Bull consented to returning to the US to live on a reservation.

SIGHTS

★★ **Cypress Hills Provincial Park** – *In Alberta, 65km/40mi southeast of Medicine Hat by Trans-Can Hwy. and Hwy. 41 south. Park office at Elkwater Lake. For road conditions check at park office ☎ 403-893-3777. Park open year-round. Visitor centre open Jul–mid-Aug daily 9am–9pm. Mid-May–Jun & late Aug–Labour Day daily 10am–6pm.* ⚠ ✂ ♿ *☎ 403-893-3833.* This park encompasses the highest part of the Cypress Hills. From Elkwater Lake an interesting drive *(40km/25mi)* leads past **Horseshoe Canyon** to **Head of the Mountain**, which affords pleasant views of coulees and hills as far as the Sweet Grass Hills and Bear Paw Mountains of Montana. The drive proceeds to Reesor Lake and the park boundary. This road crosses the provincial boundary and continues to Fort Walsh, approximately 18km/11mi south.

★**Fort Walsh** – *In Saskatchewan, 52km/32mi southwest of Maple Creek by Hwy. 271. Open mid-May–mid-Oct daily 9am–5:30pm. $6.* ♿ *306-662-3590.*
Reached from Cypress Hills Provincial Park or by a pleasant drive from Maple Creek, this North West Mounted Police post, named for its builder, Inspector James Walsh, was constructed close to the site of the Cypress Hills Massacre. From 1878 to 1882 it served as the force's headquarters.
At the **visitor centre** displays and films provide a good introduction. The fort can be reached by foot or by park bus service. The whitewashed log buildings include barracks, stables, a workshop and the commissioner's residence. At **Farwell's Trading Post**★ Kids *(2.5km/1.5mi south of the fort, access by park bus; visit by 45min guided tour only)*, visitors are shown around by costumed guides who depict historical figures of the trading post's past.

EDMONTON★★

Alberta
Population 616,306
Map of Principal Sights p 2
Tourist Office 403-496-8400

The capital of Alberta spans the deep valley of the North Saskatchewan River in the geographic midpoint of the province. This thriving metropolis is the heart of Canada's oil-refining and extraction industries. Located in a rich agricultural area, Edmonton is also a meat-processing and grain-handling centre as well as the major distribution hub for western Canada.

Historical Notes

From Fur Trade Post to Provincial Capital – By the end of the 18C, both the North West and Hudson's Bay Companies had erected fur-trading forts in the vicinity of present-day Edmonton. When the two merged in 1821, **Edmonton House** became the most important post in the West, serving not only Alberta but the territory west of the Rockies.
Settlement developed around the post, with goods arriving by York boat from York Factory *(p 107)* or overland from Winnipeg by Red River cart. The growing community suffered a relapse when the Canadian Pacific Railway Co. decided to build its line through Calgary, but recovered when other rail lines were built at the end of the century. People poured in, especially during the Klondike Stampede of 1896-99 en route to Dawson City, the beginning of Edmonton's development as a "gateway to the North." In 1905 the city became Alberta's capital; its strategic location between rich central farmland and northland resources was a major determinant.

Petroleum Centre – Edmonton might have remained a quiet administrative centre had it not been for **Leduc**, a small community located to the south. In February 1947 oil was found 1,771m/5,810ft below the ground, the first strike of what proved to be a 300-million-barrel bonanza. In 1948 the Redwater field was opened, followed

Travel Alberta

Oil Pump near Leduc

by other discoveries. The city is the major service and distribution centre for the vast Athabasca oil sands to the north. The majority of Canada's oil reserves lie in Alberta with the largest percentage of the province's producing oil wells concentrated in the Edmonton area.

Klondike Days – Every year in July Edmonton celebrates its role in the great **Klondike Stampede**. Bedecked in costumes of the Gay Nineties, inhabitants and visitors parade, eat flapjacks, dance in the streets, gamble at the casino, pan for gold at the Chilkoot Mine, compete in raft races on the river, and in general "whoop it up" for about 10 days.

DOWNTOWN *1/2 day. Map below.*

Edmonton's downtown is generally considered to be the vicinity of Sir Winston Churchill Square and Jasper Avenue. The square is surrounded by a collection of modern buildings including **City Hall**, the **Court House**, the Art Gallery *(below)*, the elegant glass and brick **Citadel Theatre** (**A**) with its three stages, the attractive **Stanley A. Milner Library** (**B**), and Edmonton Centre with its shops, restaurants and offices. Two blocks south, the steel and glass structure of Edmonton's **Conference Centre** rises opposite Canada Place, which houses offices of the federal government as well as a visitor centre for the city.

★**Art Gallery** – *2 Sir Winston Churchill Square. Open year-round Mon–Wed 10:30am–5pm, Thu–Fri 10:30am–8pm, weekends & holidays 11am–5pm. $3.* ♿ *www.eag.org* ☎ *403-422-6223.* Constructed in 1969 this modern building, with its open central stairway, presents regularly changing and permanent exhibits. The development of Canadian art is traced by a selection of works from the gallery's collections.

★**Muttart Conservatory** – *9626 - 96 A St. Open year-round Mon–Fri 9am–6pm, weekends 11am–6pm. Closed Dec 25. $4.25.* ✗ ♿ 🅿 ☎ *403-496-8755.* The four glass pyramids of this striking architectural ensemble provide a fine setting for displays of plants from three different climatic zones: tropical, temperate and arid. One pyramid is reserved as a showplace for changing displays of ornamental plants.

Behind the conservatory at riverside is the landing for the paddle-wheeler *Edmonton Queen*, which offers passengers a leisurely **cruise** on the North Saskatchewan River *(departs May–Oct daily noon, 3pm & 5pm; round-trip 1hr; reservations suggested; $7.95–$14.95; dinner & midnight cruises available;* ✗ 🅿 ☎ *403-424-2628).*

★**Legislature Building** – *Legislature Centre. Visit by guided tour (45min) only, May–Sept Mon–Fri 8:30am–5pm, weekends & holidays 9am–5pm. Rest of the year, phone for hours. Closed Jan 1 & Dec 25.* ✗ ♿ 🅿 *www.assembly.ab.ca*

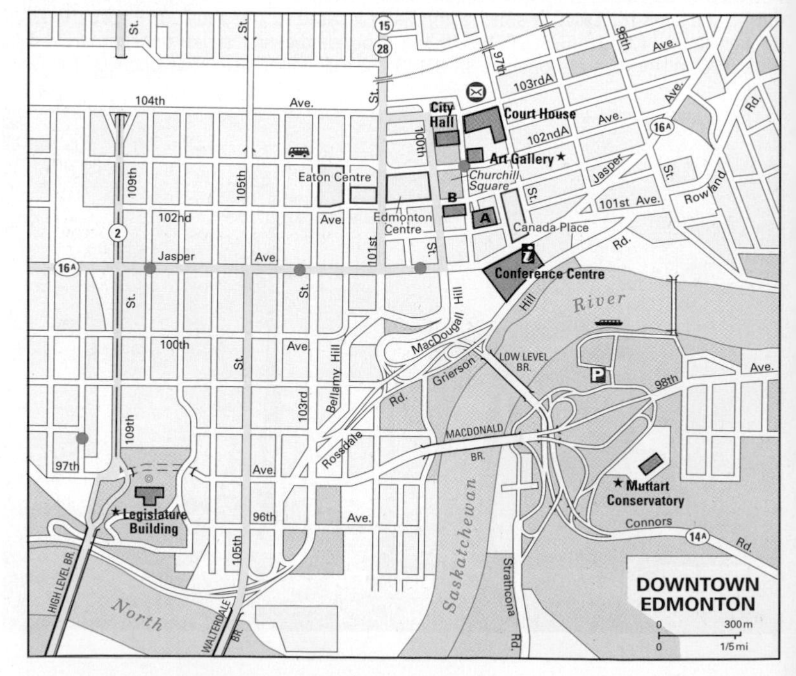

☎403-427-7362. Set in pleasant gardens overlooking the North Saskatchewan River, the yellow sandstone Alberta Legislature building (1912) occupies the original site of Fort Edmonton. The main entrance *(north side)* leads into an impressive hall from which a stairway ascends to the **legislative assembly**. The fifth floor of the dome presents an interesting display on Alberta history.

ADDITIONAL SIGHTS *Map p 112*

★★ **Fort Edmonton Park** – Kids *Open mid-May–Jun Mon–Fri 10am–4pm, weekends & holidays 10am–6pm. Jul & Aug daily 10am–6pm. Rest of the year phone for hours. $6.75. X P www.gov.edmonton.ab.ca/fort ☎403-496-8787.* Set in the ravine of the North Saskatchewan River, this park re-creates the history of European settlement in Edmonton. Board the vintage train *(free; continuous service)* to reach **Fort Edmonton**, the 1846 fur-trading post. Inside a high palisade, the buildings of the fort have been reconstructed. Dominant is the Big House, a four-storey residence with a third-floor balcony from which the chief factor, or governor of the fort, could survey his domain. Quarters of the other 130 inhabitants, such as clerks, artisans, labourers and servants, have been meticulously re-created. Also on view are trade and storage rooms, the forge, stable and boatshed, where York boats *(p 124)* are under construction (a completed one can be seen on the river), and the chapel built for Rev. **Robert Rundle**, the first missionary in Alberta, who spent the years 1840 to 1848 at Fort Edmonton.

Travel Alberta

Fort Edmonton Park

The **prerailway village** contains a reconstruction of Jasper Avenue in 1885, notable for its width and boardwalks. Along the avenue stand stores selling furs, jewellery, drugs, and hardware, as well as the North West Mounted Police post, the Dominion Land Office, and the offices of the local newspaper. One original building, the McDougall Church, erected downtown in 1873, was moved to this site. Built by Rev. **George McDougall**, it was the first Protestant church in Alberta. The village gradually becomes **1905 Street**, which shows Edmonton at a time of great growth. A street car *(free; continuous service)* runs down the middle of the road lined with a penny arcade, Masonic hall, two churches, a fire hall, civic centre and various other structures.

Eventually "1905 Street" becomes **1920 Street**, which is currently under development. Commercial concerns such as a brickyard and greenhouse complex can be visited along with a Ukrainian bookstore and the train station.

West Edmonton Mall – *170th to 178th Sts., 87th to 90th Aves.* Kids *Open year round Mon–Fri 10am–9pm, Sat 10am–6pm, Sun noon–6pm. Stores closed Jan 1, Easter Sunday & Dec 25. X ♿ P www.westedmontonmall.com ☎403-444-5200.* Covering over 483,000sq m/5.2 million sq ft, this huge shopping centre is reputedly the largest in the world. It encloses an amusement park, full-size ice rink, waterpark, hotel and some 800 stores and restaurants.

★★ **Provincial Museum** – *12845 102nd Ave. Open year-round daily 9am–5pm. Closed Dec 24–25. $6.50. X ♿ P www.pma.edmonton.ab.ca ☎403-453-9100.* A showcase of Alberta's culture and human and natural history, this complex occupies an attractive **site★** in a park overlooking the river beside the former residence of Alberta's lieutenant-governor.

On the ground floor are **dioramas★** of the wildlife of the four great natural regions of the province—prairie, parkland, forest and mountain. The **Gallery of Aboriginal Culture★★** details the life of the Plains Indians in western Canada. Displays encompass food, clothes (featuring exquisite beadwork), shelter, transportation, recreation and religion.

On the second floor, the **Natural History Gallery** features displays on Alberta's geology and mineral wealth. Giant mammals and dinosaurs are on view in the section on fossils. Educational displays on bird, mammal, floral and insect life complete the exhibit.

★**Edmonton Space & Science Centre** – Kids *11211 142nd St. Open Jun–Labour Day daily 10am–10pm. Rest of the year Tue–Sun 10am–10pm. Closed Dec 25. $7.* ✗ ♿ P *www.edmontonscience.com* ☎ *403-451-3344.* Resembling a large spaceship with its white steel cladding over a steel frame, the centre houses an IMAX theatre as well as a planetarium. Featured are exhibits on the planets, meteorites and space exploration. A variety of interactive displays and demonstrations help visitors understand the scientific world.

Housed separately, an **observatory** offers a close-up view of the stars and planets *(weather permitting; Jun–Sept daily 1pm–5pm & 8pm–midnight; rest of the year Fri 8pm–midnight, weekends & holidays 1pm–5pm & 8pm–midnight; closed Dec 25; ♿).*

EXCURSIONS

St. Albert – *19km/12mi north by Rte. 2.* In 1861 a Roman Catholic mission was founded here on the banks of the Sturgeon River by Father **Albert Lacombe** (1827-1916). The simple log structure that served as his **chapel** still stands today and is the oldest building in Alberta *(St. Vital Ave., open mid-May–Labour Day daily 10am–6pm; rest of the year by appointment; contribution requested;* ♿ P ☎ *403-459-2116).*

The crypt of the modern-day church contains Father Lacombe's tomb and that of Bishop **Vital Grandin** (1829-1902), whose adjoining residence can also be visited.

★**Elk Island National Park** – *On Hwy. 16, about 45km/28mi east. Open daily year-round. Hiking, canoeing, cross-country skiing, golfing.* ▲ ♿ ☎ *403-992-2950. Visitor centre open mid-May–mid-Oct daily, hours vary.* One of the smallest of Canada's national parks, the 194sq km/75sq mi Elk Island nevertheless abounds with wildlife, much of it visible to park visitors. Herds of wood bison stand or sit in the road in the early hours of the day; deer, beaver and coyote are routinely sighted. Elk, moose and pygmy shrews are other denizens of the park. At Tawayik Lake myriad waterfowl crowd the skies, and the rare trumpeter swan has occasionally been seen at Astotin Lake, located near the north gate. Over 100km/60mi of nature trails punctuate the park's wetlands, aspen forests and meadows. Visitors may even be treated to a glimpse of the Northern Lights.

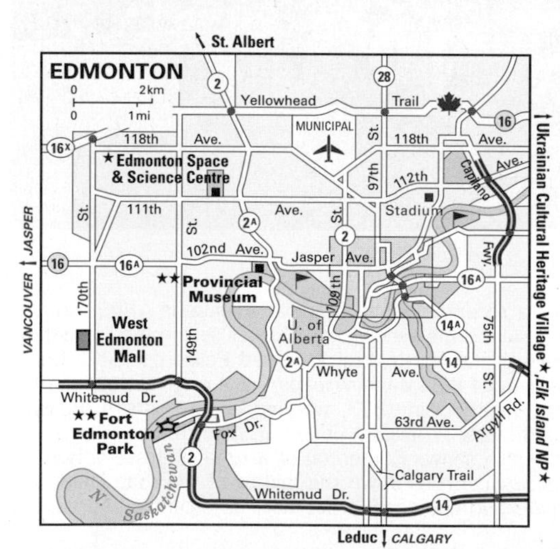

★**Ukrainian Cultural Heritage Village** – *On Hwy. 16, about 50km/30mi east. Open mid-May–Labour Day daily 10am–6pm. Mid-Sept–mid-Oct daily 10am–4pm. $6.50 ($3.25 mid-Sept–mid-Oct).* ✗ ♿ P *www.gov.ab.ca/~mcd/mhs/uchv/uchv.htm* ☎ *403-662-3640.* This well-reconstructed village traces Ukrainian settlement in Alberta since the 1890s. Displays in the visitor centre provide insight into the mass migration of Ukrainian people to the Canadian Prairies. Homestead development—from early sod-covered dugout to whitewashed dwelling—is explained in great detail by costumed interpreters. The village also includes a rural community and an early town, complete with a grain elevator, train station, provincial police post, domed churches and shops.

FORT MACLEOD★

Alberta

Population 3,034

Map of Principal Sights p 2

South of CALGARY (165km/102mi), this small town on the Oldman River was the site chosen for the first North West Mounted Police post in the West. In October 1874 a band of weary men arrived after a long and arduous trek from Manitoba. They had been quickly trained and dispatched to stop the illegal whisky trade and border incursions, such as the one leading to the Cypress Hills Massacre. Under the command of **Col. James Macleod**, they built permanent barracks on an island in the river.

Today Fort Macleod is a thriving agricultural community. Grain is grown with the aid of irrigation, and cattle are raised on the ranch land of nearby Porcupine Hills.

SIGHTS

★ **Fort Museum** – Kids *On Hwy. 3, one block from centre of town. Open Jul–Aug daily 9am–8:30pm. May–Jun & Sept–mid-Oct daily 9am–5pm. Rest of the year Mon–Fri 10am–4pm. Closed Dec 24–Feb. $4.50. ♿ www.discoveralberta.com/fortmuseum ☎ 403-553-4703.* This museum re-creates life in and around police posts during the early settlement of Alberta. Inside the wooden, palisaded walls stand a number of log structures. The **Kanouse House** with its sod roof is devoted to the early settlers of the region. The **Mounted Police Building** houses a model of the original fort and exhibits on the police. The Indian Artifacts Building contains a sizeable collection of native arts and crafts.

In summer students dressed in the police uniforms of 1878 (red jackets, black breeches, white pith helmets) perform a musical ride *(Jul–Aug daily, weather permitting).*

★★ **Head-Smashed-In Buffalo Jump** – *18km/11mi northwest by Hwy. 785 (Spring Point Rd.). Open mid-May–Labour Day daily 9am–7pm. Rest of the year daily 9am–5pm. Closed Jan 1, Easter Sunday, Dec 25. $6.50. ✂ ♿ www.head-smashedin.com ☎ 403-553-2731.* This buffalo jump has the most extensive deposits (9m/30ft deep) of any in North America. Its importance was recognized by UNESCO in 1981, when the site was inscribed on the World Heritage List.

For over 5,000 years, buffalo were driven to their deaths over this cliff. The buffalo provided most of the necessities of life for the Indians: meat, hides for clothing and shelter, and bone for scrapers and needles. A **visitor centre** contains excellent displays on three floors as well as films on buffalo-hunting cultures. Outside, paths lead to the top of the cliff, where visitors are afforded a spectacular **view**★★ of the region; at the bottom, visitors can follow another path to the area where the buffalo were skinned.

LETHBRIDGE★

Alberta

Population 63,053

Map of Principal Sights p 2

Tourist Office ☎ 403-320-1222

Located in southern Alberta, 216km/134mi southeast of CALGARY, this city overlooks a wide riverbed cut by the Oldman River. Constructed into the side of this riverbed are the striking buildings of the University of Lethbridge, and crossing it is the High Level Railway Bridge (about 1.5km/1mi long and 96m/314ft high).

Lethbridge was founded in 1870, after coal deposits were discovered in the valley. Today the city is the centre of a productive agricultural region. Widespread irrigation and the relatively mild winters moderated by the warm chinook winds *(p 96)* have made the cultivation of grain and vegetables, especially canola and sugar beet, very profitable. Livestock are also raised here.

SIGHTS

★ **Nikka Yuko Japanese Garden** – *In Henderson Lake Park on Mayor Magrath Dr. Open mid-Jun–Labour Day daily 9am–9pm. May & Sept–Oct daily hours vary. $4. ♿ ☎ 403-328-3511.* The city built this garden in 1967 as a symbol of Japanese-Canadian amity (*Nikka Yuko* means "Japan-Canada friendship"). It is a wonderfully serene place where visitors can gain an appreciation for traditional Japanese landscape architecture. When Canada declared war on Japan in 1941, about 22,000 Japanese-Canadians living on the west coast were placed in internment camps in central British Columbia and Alberta, although in many cases they were Canadian citizens. About 6,000 of these Japanese-Canadians were resettled in Lethbridge, where they chose to stay after the war.

Five types of formal landscapes are linked by meandering paths. At the centre lies a pavilion of Japanese cypress wood, laid out for a tea ceremony.

★**Fort Whoop-up** – *In Indian Battle Park by river, access from Hwy. 3. Open May–Sep Mon–Sat 10am–6pm, Sun noon–5pm. Rest of the year Mon–Fri 10am–4pm, Su. 1pm–4pm. $2.50. ✗ ♿ www.whoop-up.org/fort ☎403-329-0444.* In the dee riverbed of the Oldman River stands a replica of this once-notorious whisky tradin post. Founded by Americans from Fort Benton, Montana, the post attracted Indian from far and wide to trade buffalo skins, furs, and indeed almost anything, for a par ticularly lethal brew bearing little resemblance to whisky (ingredients included chewin tobacco, red peppers, Jamaican ginger and black molasses, as well as alcohol).
Such illegal liquor forts, of which Whoop-up was the most important, sprang u all over southern Alberta and Saskatchewan in the early 1870s. The Canadia government formed the North West Mounted Police to counter this America encroachment of Canadian territory and to stop a trade that was demoralizing th Indians. In 1874 the force arriving at the gates of Whoop-up found the premise vacated. The founding of Fort Macleod, and later Fort Calgary *(p 103)*, effectivel ended the illegal trade and brought law and order to the West.
The reconstructed fort flies not "the Stars and Stripes" (the American flag) but the trading flag of the original Fort Benton company. Below it, wooden buildings form a fortified enclosure. In the **visitor centre** a video presentation *(20min)* presents the history of the post in the context of the development of the Canadian West.

MOOSE JAW★

Saskatchewan
Population 32,973
Map of Principal Sights p 3

Rising out of the flat wheat lands of southern Saskatchewan, 71km/44mi due west of REGINA, is the province's third largest city. Reputedly named for a sharp turn in the river that resembles a protruding moose jaw, this industrial centre, with flour mills, grain elevator and stock yards, is an important railway junction for agricultural produce of the area. The city is also involved in the refining of Saskatchewan's oil.

SIGHT

★**Western Development Museum** – *At junction Trans-Can Hwy. and Hwy. 2. Open Apr–Dec daily 9am–6pm. Rest of the year Tue–Sun 9am–6pm. Closed Jan 1, Dec 25. $5. ♿ ☎306-693-5989.* One of four museums on Western development in the province (North Battleford, SASKATOON, YORKTON), this one is devoted to transportation in Saskatchewan. The water section has displays about the *Northcote*, a steamship used to take supplies up the South Saskatchewan River during the Northwest Rebellion, and on cable ferries, particularly that of the St.-Laurent *(p 119)*. The railway gallery features a Canadian Pacific locomotive, a reconstructed station and a 1934 Buick converted to run on rails and used as an inspection vehicle for 20 years. In addition there is an interesting collection of other automobiles. The air section presents several Canadian planes, including a 1927 Red Pheasant, and a gallery devoted to the British Commonwealth Air Training Plan.

PRINCE ALBERT NATIONAL PARK★

Saskatchewan
Map of Principal Sights p 3

Located in the geographic centre of Saskatchewan, this large park consisting of wooded hills dotted with lakes and streams constitutes a fine example of Canada's southern boreal plains, an area where the aspen forest of the south mixes with the true boreal wilderness. Isolated pockets of grassland near the southern boundary support prairie animals—coyotes, badgers and ground squirrels. The northern forests are home to wolves, moose, elk, bears, beaver, otter, mink and a small herd of woodland caribou. In the extreme north white pelicans nest on Lavallée Lake.

Grey Owl – Famous for his writings and lectures on the fate of the beaver and the vanishing wilderness, this man posed as an Indian, dressing in buckskins and wearing his long hair in braids. He travelled throughout North America and Europe with a conservation message, even lecturing to the British monarch, George VI, in 1937. Trying to reestablish beaver colonies, he worked for Canada's national park service, first in Riding Mountain National Park *(p 117)* and then in Prince Albert. At his death in 1938, he was exposed as an Englishman, **Archie Belaney**, who had taken the Indian name *Wa-sha-Quon-Asin* ("the Grey Owl") about 1920. Though discovered to be an impostor, Grey Owl remains one of Canada's finest nature writers and among the first to preach the importance of the wilderness. His most famous books are *Tales of an Empty Cabin*, *Pilgrims of the Wild* and *Sajo and Her Beaver People*.

Access – *80km/50mi north of Prince Albert by Hwys. 2 and 264.*

VISIT

Open year-round. Hiking, canoeing, swimming, horseback riding, golf, tennis, winter sports. $4/day. Map available at visitor centre (open mid-May–Labour Day daily 8am–10pm; rest of the year hours vary). ☎306-663-4522. Accommodations available in Waskesiu Lake.

The **nature centre** *(open late Jun–Labour Day daily 10am–6pm)* in Waskesiu (meaning "place of the elk") Lake provides an introduction to the park. The roads following both shores of Waskesiu Lake and **boat trips** on the lake in a paddle-wheeler afford pleasant views *(depart Jul–Aug daily 2pm, 4pm & 6pm; round-trip 1hr; $8; Neo-Watin Marine ☎306-663-5253)*. Hiking trails and canoe routes criss-cross the park. One interesting hike takes the visitor to the cabin and grave of Grey Owl *(19km/12mi)*.

The symbol indicates that campgrounds can be found on the premises of the sight described.

REGINA**

Saskatchewan
Population 180,400
Map of Principal Sights p 3
Tourist Office ☎306-789-5099

Set in an extensive, fertile, wheat-growing plain and located on the main line of the Canadian Pacific Railway and the Trans-Canada Highway, this provincial capital has long been an important agricultural centre. Regina is the headquarters for the Saskatchewan Wheatpool, one of the largest grain cooperatives in the world.

Historical Notes

Pile O' Bones – Few cities have been established in less congenial surroundings—treeless plains stretching to the horizon; a scanty water supply from a sluggish creek; soil of gumbo clay, muddy in wet weather, dusty in dry. Nevertheless in the early 1880s, the Canadian Pacific Railway Co. decided to build its line across the southern plains, leaving the existing capital of the vast Northwest Territories at Battleford high and dry. Determined to move the capital, the Dominion government, in collaboration with the railway company, chose a location where the future rail line would cross a creek long favoured by Indians and Métis for running buffalo into pounds to slaughter them. Testifying to their once great number, the remains of these animals had given this spot (as recorded by John Palliser, *p 96*) the Cree name, *Oskana*, translated as "pile o' bones." The choice was controversial, especially since the lieutenant-governor of the then Northwest Territories, Edgar Dewdney *(p 46)*, owned land at that place. In August 1882 when the first train arrived, Princess Louise, wife of Canada's governor general, rechristened it Regina ("Queen" in Latin) after her mother, Queen Victoria.

Historic Court Case – After the defeat of the Northwest Rebellion in 1885, the Métis leader, Louis Riel, was taken to Regina for trial. The court immediately became a centre of controversy. To Quebecers, Riel—a Catholic Métis who had studied for the priesthood in Montreal—was a patriot who had fought for the rights of his people. To Ontarians, he was a common rebel who had gone unpunished after murdering Thomas Scott during the Red River Rebellion. Defence counsel pleaded that Riel was insane: he had spent several years in asylums and had wished to set up a new Catholic state on the Saskatchewan River, with Bishop Bourget of Montreal as Pope. Riel himself rejected the plea and convinced the jury he was sane. But if sane, he was guilty: the verdict was death by hanging. Prime Minister Sir John A. Macdonald was inundated with petitions from both sides. The sentence was delayed while doctors studied Riel's mental health. The prime minister weighed the political consequences of hanging Riel and decided the sentence had to be carried out. Riel lost his life on November 16, 1885.
Every summer the MacKenzie Art Gallery *(below)* is the setting for a dramatic re-enactment of the **Trial of Louis Riel** based on actual court transcripts *(3475 Albert St.; Wed–Fri late Jul–late Aug 8pm; $10; tickets available at door or ☎306-584-8890)*.

Queen City of the Plains – Regina became the capital of Saskatchewan when that province was created in 1905. As immigrants poured in from all parts of the world, the city burgeoned. Their enterprising spirit helped overcome the physical shortcomings of the city's site. To solve the water problems, Wascana Creek was dammed, creating an artificial lake. Trees were planted and carefully nourished, defying the notion of a treeless wilderness.
Though the city's development in the 20C has been precarious, Regina has experienced steady growth since World War II. The downtown core has been revitalized, and imposing buildings constructed. Today, from 80km/50mi distant, Regina rises above the flat, treeless prairie like a mirage, its quiet grace testifying to its epithet, "Queen City of the Plains."

DOWNTOWN *1/2 day.*

★★**Royal Saskatchewan Museum** – *College Ave. and Albert St. Open May–Labou Day daily 9am–5:30pm. Rest of the year daily 9am–4:30pm. Closed Dec 25. Contri bution requested.* ♿ 🅿 ☎ *306-787-2815.* This long, low building of Tyndall stone housed one of the finest museums of natural history in Canada until a fire in 1990 destroyed the remarkable life sciences dioramas, highlight of the museum. Plans to re-create them are under way *(the Life Sciences Gallery is projected to reopen in the year 2000).* Exhibits in the Earth Sciences Gallery feature dinosaurs (including a robotic *Tyrannosaurus rex*) and woolly mammoths, volcanoes and glaciers from the province's geological beginnings to the appearance of mankind in Saskatchewan. The **First Nations Gallery** displays art and artifacts of the native cultures of the region. Especially noteworthy is the winter encampment, which features a bison-hide teepee.

★**Legislative Building** – *2405 Legislative Dr. Visit by guided tour (30min) only, mid-May–Labour Day daily 8am–9pm. Rest of the year daily 8am–5pm. Closed Jan 1, Good Friday, Dec 25.* ✗ ♿ 🅿 ☎ *306-787-5358.* Completed in 1912, this graceful building of Tyndall stone was built in the shape of a cross topped by a dome. It occupies a fine **site**★ overlooking gardens and Wascana Lake.
The guided tour visits the legislative chamber, legislative library, the rotunda, and art galleries named after the rivers of the province.

★**Wascana Centre** – *Open daily year-round. Picnicking, swimming, boating.* 🅿 ☎ *306-522-3661.* This 930ha/2,300 acre park, Regina's pride and joy, is reputedly the largest urban park in North America. Formal gardens of beautiful flowers and trees surround the western part of the artificial Wascana Lake. **Willow Island** is a picnic site accessible by ferry *(mid-May–Labour Day Mon–Fri noon–4pm; $2; reservations required).*

Also in the park, which can be toured by car, are the provincial legislative building and the **Diefenbaker Homestead**, a three-room pioneer dwelling *(open mid-May–Labour Day daily 9am–6pm;* ♿ 🅿 ☎ *306-522-3661),* home to John George Diefenbaker, prime minister of Canada from 1957 to 1963. This house was moved from its original site in Borden, Saskatchewan, where the Diefenbaker family homesteaded between 1905 and 1910.
East of Wascana Parkway the park is a bird sanctuary. Many species of waterfowl can be spotted, but by far the most common is the **Canada goose**. Some of these birds are year-round residents of the centre, benefiting from crops grown nearby. Visitors can also tour a waterfall display pond *(mid-May–Labour Day daily).*

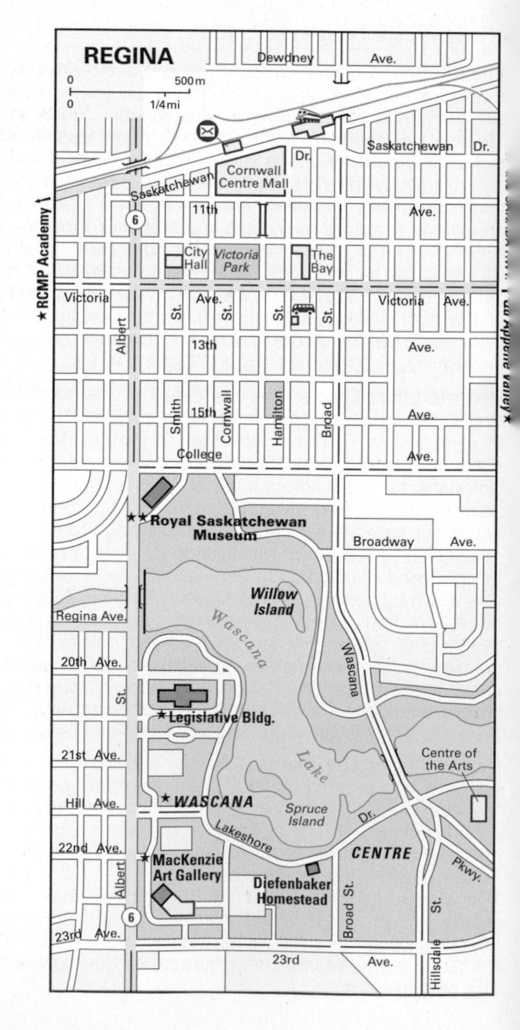

★**MacKenzie Art Gallery** – *3475 Albert St. Open year-round daily 11am–6pm (Wed & Thu 10pm). Closed Jan 1, Good Friday, Dec 25-26. Contribution requested.* ♿ 🅿 *www.uregina.ca/-macken/* ☎ *306-522-4242.* Occupying the western end of the T.C. Douglas Building in Wascana Centre, this expansive art gallery features seven viewing rooms devoted largely to the display of temporary and travelling exhibits. Consisting of more than 3,000 works, the permanent collection is showcased on a rotating basis with emphasis on Canadian historical and contemporary art, including Inuit prints and sculptures, First Nations pieces, and Saskatchewan folk art. The collection has grown from an original bequest in 1936 of 374 works by influential Regina lawyer Norman MacKenzie.

ADDITIONAL SIGHTS

★**Royal Canadian Mounted Police Training Academy** – *West of downtown by Dewdney Ave. Open Jun–mid-Sept daily 8am–6:45pm. Rest of the year daily 10am–4:45pm. Closed Dec 25. Guided tours (1hr) available. ♿ P ☎306-780-5838.* People who know nothing else about Canada have heard of the **Mounties**, the country's federal police force. Stories about them are legion, and many films have portrayed their ability to "always get their man." Created in 1873 as the **North West Mounted Police**, the force had to formulate as well as to preserve law and order in the Canadian West. Faced with problems such as the illegal sale of "fire water" to Canadian Indians by American traders, the police quickly established themselves as an effective force. They helped the various Indian tribes accept treaties and life on reservations, gave valuable aid to new settlers in the West, and enforced law and order during the Klondike Stampede.

In 1920 they were united with the Dominion Police as the **Royal Canadian Mounted Police**. Today they enforce federal laws across Canada and act as the provincial police in all provinces and territories except Ontario and Quebec. They are famous for their **musical ride**, a collection of early cavalry drills performed on horseback and culminating in a rousing "charge." *Sunset Retreat Ceremony Jul & Aug Tue 7pm.*

★**Museum** – *Same hours as the academy.* This museum illustrates the history of the Mounties and recalls such famous incidents as Sitting Bull's years in Canada *(p 108)*, the Northwest Rebellion, the Klondike Stampede and the voyage of the *St. Roch (p 76)*. Displays also explain the work of the force today.

EXCURSION

★**Qu'Appelle Valley** – *Map p 3.* From Lake Diefenbaker to the Manitoba border, the Qu'Appelle (kap-PELL) Valley cuts a deep swath across the otherwise flat prairie. It was carved out 12,000 years ago by meltwaters from a retreating glacier that left a wide valley with only a small stream at its midst, surrounded by low, round-topped hills. As visitors approach the Qu'Appelle from any direction, the prairie seems endless, and then suddenly the road drops and a 2km/1.2mi wide stretch of verdant green comes into view. As much as 120m/400ft deep in places, with several sparkling lakes, the valley presents a complete contrast to the surrounding plains. The name derives from Indian lore. According to legend a brave in his canoe heard his name called. *Qu'appelle?* ("who calls?" in French) he shouted, but only an echo answered him. On returning home he found his sweetheart lifeless—she had called his name moments before dying.

★**The Fishing Lakes** – *73km/45mi east of Regina by Trans-Can Hwy., northeast by Rte. 10; 1/2 day.* The best way to appreciate the Qu'Appelle Valley is to drive alongside the river where it forms the Fishing Lakes—Pasqua, Echo, Mission and Katepwa. North of Lake Echo there is a particularly attractive stretch of road on Route 56 leading to **Echo Valley Provincial Park**★ *(open year-round; visitor centre open mid-May–Labour Day, hours vary; ⛺ ☎306-332-3215).*

RIDING MOUNTAIN NATIONAL PARK★★

Manitoba

Map of Principal Sights p 3

Established in 1933 on the Manitoba plain, this lovely park is a rolling plateau of wooded slopes and lakes. Approached from the east and north, it rises 457m/1,500ft above the surrounding countryside (756m/2,480ft above sea level) and does indeed look like a mountain—or at least a hill.

Early fur traders named it "Riding" Mountain, the place where they exchanged canoes for horses to continue west. It is part of the **Manitoba Escarpment**, a jagged 1,600km/1,000mi ridge winding across North Dakota, Manitoba and Saskatchewan—a series of hills cut by many rivers, rather than a continuous ridge.

The park is also a crossroads where northern, western and eastern environments and habitats meet. High areas are covered with an evergreen forest of spruce, pine, fir and tamarack. Lower sections support a deciduous forest of hardwoods, shrubs, vines and ferns. In the west wildflowers thrive on meadows and grassland (July and August), forming some of the only true prairie left on the continent.

Access – *197km/122mi west of Winnipeg by Trans-Can Hwy., then 91km/56mi north of Brandon by Rte. 10.*

VISIT

Open year-round. Hiking, boating, fishing, horseback riding, tennis, golf, winte sports. Accommodations in Wasagaming. Map available at visitor centre $3.25/day. (for reservations 800-707-8480 Canada/US). 204-848 7275. The **visitor centre★★** *(open Jun–Aug daily 8am–11pm; May & Sept hours vary rest of the year weekends & holidays 10am–6pm; closed Dec 25)* in Wasagaming features excellent displays on the park's geological history, the different habitat therein and the native wildlife. Visitors can view films on related subjects.

Near Lake Audy *(47km/29mi from Wasagaming)*, a herd of buffalo roams a large enclosure *(accessible by Lake Audy Rd. off Rte. 10)*. From a viewpoint above the Audy plain, these animals can be seen in their true prairie environment. An exhibit explains how they nearly became extinct. Visitors can drive around the enclosure A good **view★** of the Manitoba Escarpment is obtained from an observation tower off Route 10 near the park's north gate.

SASKATOON★

Saskatchewan

Population 193,647

Map of Principal Sights p 3

Tourist Office 306-242-1206

Built on both sides of the South Saskatchewan River, this city, 259km/161mi northwest of REGINA, occupies a pleasant **site★** enhanced by wide, tree-lined streets as well as parkland beside the water (in particular, **Kiwanis Park** with its views of bridges and the University of Saskatchewan). The largest city in Saskatchewan, this manufacturing and distribution centre is set in a fertile wheat-growing area, amid the province's vast potash reserves. Surrounding prairie landscape is a little more rolling than around Regina, but is nonetheless dominated by the "heights" of **Mt. Blackstrap** (91m/300ft), an artificial ski hill rising south of the city *(40km/25mi)*.

Founded in 1883 by Methodists from Ontario, the city was to be the capital of a temperance colony. A leader of this venture, **John Lake**, selected the name *Saskatoon*, a small purplish berry native to the region. However the teetotallers' paradise did not attract many settlers and two decades later numbered only 113 souls. In 1908 the whole area quickly experienced a boom when colonists arrived by the new rail lines. German, Scandinavian, Ukrainian and British settlers transformed the city, and the early temperance ideals were laid to rest. Today the settlers are honoured once a year in July during **Pioneer Days**.

SIGHTS *1/2 day.*

★Mendel Art Gallery – *950 Spadina Crescent East. Open mid-May–Labour Day daily 9am–9pm. Rest of the year daily noon–9pm. Closed Dec 25. www.mendel.saskatoon.sk.ca 306-975-7610.* This attractive launched gallery

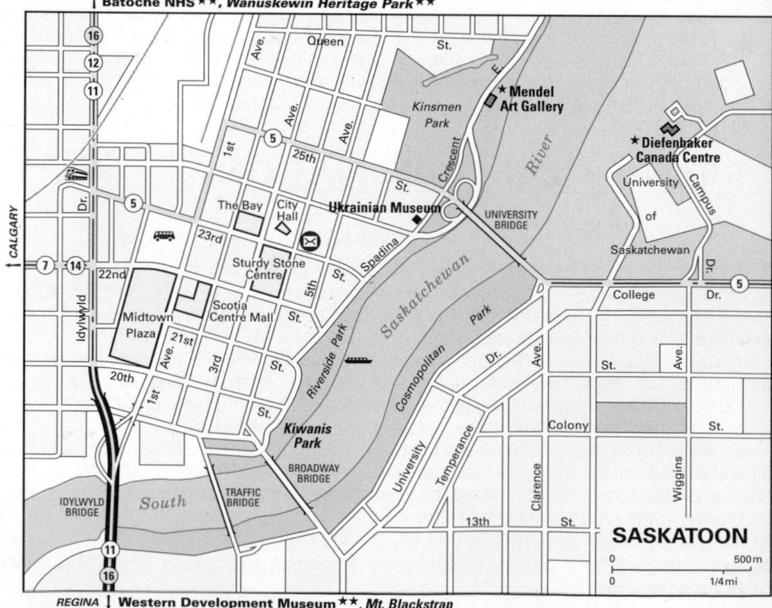

overlooking the river is named for **Fred Mendel**, a wealthy Saskatoon meatpacker of German origin who launched the idea of an art gallery and spent much of his time and money developing it.
The permanent collection includes works by the Group of Seven, Emily Carr and David Milne in the Canadian section, as well as Feininger, Chagall, Utrillo and Pissarro and other European painters. In addition, the gallery displays travelling exhibits. There is also a small, attractive conservatory of exotic flowers and plants.

Ukrainian Museum – *910 Spadina Crescent East. Open mid-May–Labour Day Mon–Sat 10am–5pm, Sun 1pm–5pm. Rest of the year Tue–Sat 10am–5pm, Sun 1pm–5pm. Closed national holidays. $2. ♿ P www.saskstar.sk.ca/umc ☎ 306-244-3800.* This museum presents displays of traditional costumes, tapestries, pioneer tools, wood-inlaid objects, and other handicrafts illustrating the heritage of the people who have played such a large role in the settlement of the Prairies.

Boat Trip – *Departs from Riverside Park (behind Delta Bessborough Hotel) May–Oct daily 10:30am–9pm every 1hr 30min. Round-trip 1hr. Commentary. $8. Shearwater Properties Ltd. ☎ 306-934-7642.* This cruise on the South Saskatchewan River is a pleasant way to discover the scenic beauty of the area and view the city from the waterside.

★ **Diefenbaker Canada Centre** – *On University of Saskatchewan campus, off Rte. 5. Open year-round Mon & Fri 9:30am–4:30pm, Tue–Thu 9:30am–8pm, Sun & holidays noon–5pm. ♿ P www.usask.ca/diefenbaker ☎ 306-966-8384.* Upon his death in 1979, the former Canadian prime minister left his papers to the university. They have been assembled to form a veritable shrine to this man, a legend in his own time. A lawyer by training, well known for his defence of the "little man," Diefenbaker entered politics and became a strong proponent of Western Canadian ideas in the Conservative Party. Elected party leader in 1956, he served as prime minister from 1957 to 1963, remaining influential in federal politics until his death. In addition to displays on his life and works, the centre features a replica of the office of the prime minister and the cabinet chamber as they existed in the Diefenbaker era.

★★ **Western Development Museum** – Kids *In Prairieland Exhibition Grounds, 8km/5mi south of downtown by Rte. 11/16. Open year-round daily 9am–5pm. $5. ✂ ♿ P www.sfn.saskatoon.sk.ca/arts/wdm ☎ 306-931-1910.* The grand attraction of the Saskatoon branch of this museum (other branches in North Battleford, Moose Jaw and Yorkton) is **Boomtown**, a faithful reconstruction of an entire street of 1910 vintage, complete with its Western Pioneer Bank, garage, stores, Chinese laundry, school, pool hall, theatre, hotel and railway station. The church, moved here in 1972, is the only original structure on the street. Several period automobiles and horse-drawn vehicles line the street. Separate halls house a large collection of automobiles and agricultural equipment, including steam tractors. The museum also features the Eaton collection of mechanized Christmas window displays *(seasonal)*.

★★ **Wanuskewin Heritage Park** – *3km/2mi north of downtown by Hwy. 11. Open late May–Labour Day daily 9am–9pm. Rest of the year Wed–Sun 9am–5pm. $6. ✂ ♿ P ☎ 306-931-6767.* A series of archaeological sites on the banks of the South Saskatchewan River forms the basis of this testament to the survival of the Plains Indians. Translated from Cree as "seeking peace of mind," *Wanuskewin* was a meeting place and hunting ground for these nomadic Indians for more than 6,000 years until their removal to reserves in the 1870s.
Several trails in the 120ha/290 acre park link the prehistoric sites, including a **buffalo jump** and the remains of a rare **medicine wheel**. Opened in 1992 a striking **visitor centre** features displays and demonstrations of native culture and allows observation of excavations and laboratory work.

EXCURSION

★★ **Batoche National Historic Site** – *88km/55mi northeast of Saskatoon by Rte. 11 to Rosthern, Rte. 312 east and Rte. 225 north. Open Jul–Aug daily 10am–6pm. Mid-May–Jun & Sept–mid-Oct daily 9am–5pm. $4. ✂ ♿ http://parkscanada.pch.gc.ca/parks/saskatchewan/batoche/batochee.htm ☎ 306-423-6227.* This quiet and beautiful **spot** on the banks of the South Saskatchewan River was the site of the final stand of the Métis in 1885. Today the site is a poignant tribute to the Métis.
Little remains of the village except the tiny **church** dedicated to St. Anthony of Padua, the **rectory** with its bullet holes and a cemetery of Métis graves, including Dumont's burial place. The buildings have been restored to the period and house historic artifacts.
The **visitor centre** offers a moving audio-visual presentation on the rebellion and displays on Métis history and culture.

The return trip to Saskatoon can be made by the St.-Laurent cable ferry *(10km/6mi north of Batoche)*, past the small community of Duck Lake on Route 11, where the rebellion had its beginnings.

The Northwest Rebellion

The seeds of the last armed conflict on Canadian soil were sown in Manitoba's Red River Valley early in the 19C when the Métis learned that land did not necessarily belong to those born and living on it. The uprising led to Louis Riel's provisional government of 1869, the formal creation of the province of Manitoba (1870) and the allocation of 567,000ha/1.4 million acres of land for Métis settlement *(p 97)*.

Unfortunately the Métis, left leaderless when Riel was banished for five years, were prey to speculators who bought their land for a fraction of its worth. Many moved northwest to the valley of the South Saskatchewan River, hoping to lead traditional lives of buffalo hunting and to avoid survey groups and European settlers. The buffalo were nearly extinct, however, and the march of "progress" continued. Again the Métis found they had no right to land they farmed. The Dominion government consistently ignored their petitions. In 1884 they sent for Louis Riel.

Riel hoped to repeat his earlier victory at Red River. He allied the Métis with Cree Indians who were also discontent with changes in their lifestyle. An unfortunate incident resulting in the deaths of some members of the North West Mounted Police at **Duck Lake** destroyed all hope of a peaceful solution. In eastern Canada there was outrage at the thought of police being killed by "lawless rebels," and a military force was quickly dispatched to the West under Maj-Gen. **Frederick Middleton**.

Restrained by Riel, the Métis—under their military leader, **Gabriel Dumont**, an experienced buffalo hunter—were unable to deter the advancing army by guerrilla tactics. Instead they made a stand at Batoche, which never could have succeeded against Middleton's overwhelming numbers. It was a heroic defence that lasted four days because of the strength of the Métis position. Afterwards Riel surrendered and was taken to Regina to stand trial for murder. He was found guilty and hanged *(p 115)*. Dumont fled to the US, though he was later pardoned for his part in the revolt and returned to Batoche. The struggle was not in vain, however, for in the wake of the rebellion, the Métis were offered the land title they had sought unsuccessfully for such a long time.

WINNIPEG★★★

Manitoba

Population 618,477

Map of Principal Sights p 3

Tourist Office ☎204-943-1970

Set on the banks of the Red and Assiniboine Rivers, the capital of Manitoba occupies the geographic heart of Canada and is often described as the place where "the West begins." Indeed, for over a century, it has been the traditional first stop for immigrants to the West. Not far to the east and north, the hilly and rocky tree-covered terrain of the Canadian Shield with its multitude of lakes gives way to the open fertile prairie with its endless horizons. This dramatic change clearly marks the division between east and west.

Named for the large and shallow lake to the north called *win-nipi* ("murky water") by the Cree, Winnipeg developed as the distribution and financial centre of the West. Although challenged by Vancouver and Alberta's cities in recent years, it retains a huge **commodity exchange** (the most important in Canada), vast stock and railway yards, a manufacturing industry and headquarters of the Hudson's Bay Company, so influential in the growth of the fur trade in the Prairies.

Historical Notes

The Red River Settlement – In the early 19C Thomas Douglas, Earl of Selkirk, obtained title from the Hudson's Bay Company to a large piece of land covering much of present-day southern Manitoba called **Assiniboia**. In 1811 he began resettling some of his poverty-stricken compatriots from the Scottish Highlands there in the Red River Valley. The success of this colony was slow in coming, mainly because of the Red River's tendency to flood, plagues of crop-eating grasshoppers and rivalry between the great fur-trading companies—the Hudson's Bay and the North West. The latter allied with the Métis, who had seen their traditional lifestyle gradually disrupted by settlers.

During the **Seven Oaks Massacre** of 1816, the Métis nearly succeeded in wiping out the colony: some 20 settlers were killed and the rest temporarily abandoned the settlement. Selkirk reestablished his colony, however, and it gradually grew in size as a commercial centre with brigades of Red River carts going to and from St. Paul,

Minnesota and steamboats chugging along the Red River. The settlement's connections below the border made annexation by the US seem likely, but the Northwest Rebellion and the creation of Manitoba in 1870 prevented it.

Winnipeg Today – The community's future was assured when the Canadian Pacific Railway Co. chose the site as a major maintenance and repair centre and built a rail line through town. Floods of immigrants poured in by train. Winnipeg (the name was adopted at the time of the rebellion) not only assumed an outfitting role, but became a distribution centre for the entire Northwest. In the 19C the population consisted of Scots, Irish, English, French, Métis and Indians. During the 20C Germans, Eastern Europeans and especially Ukrainians joined their ranks. Winnipeg's skyline, dotted with spires, towers and domes of Catholic, Protestant and Orthodox churches, reflects this diversity. Every August the city's varied cultural background is celebrated in **Folklorama**, a festival held in pavilions throughout Winnipeg. The Folk Festival held in July is also a popular event.
Winnipeg is rich in cultural institutions—the Manitoba Theatre Centre, the Symphony Orchestra, the Manitoba Opera Company and, most famous of all, the Royal Winnipeg Ballet.

DOWNTOWN *2 days. Map p 122*

The intersection of **Portage Avenue** and **Main Street** has traditionally been considered the centre of Winnipeg. In a bygone era it was said these principal thoroughfares were wide enough for 10 Red River carts to rush along side by side. Today this corner, long known as the windiest in Canada, is dominated by tall buildings, all connected underground by an attractive shopping area, **Winnipeg Square**. Extending for three blocks to the west, between Vaughan and Carlton Streets, is **Portage Place★**, a shopping and office complex with restaurants, three movie theatres and a giant-screen IMAX theatre.
Just south of the intersection at Portage and Main, in a small park below the Fort Garry Hotel, stands a stone gateway. It is all that remains of **Upper Fort Garry**, once the local headquarters of the Hudson's Bay Company. The present-day headquarters (**A**) rises a block away.
The **Forks**, 26ha/65 acres of riverfront property refurbished by the city, includes a **public market** housed within former stables, a National Historic Site, restaurants, shops, a children's museum and a waterside walkway *(boat rentals)*. Riverboat cruises on the Red River depart near the Provencher Bridge *(Gray Line ☎204-944-8000)*.
North of the intersection lies the **Exchange District**, which has some remarkable examples of early-20C architecture *(1hr 30min walking tours depart from Pantages Playhouse Jul–Aug Tue, Thu, Fri 11am & Wed, Sat, Sun 1:30pm; $5.50 ☎204-986-6927)*, and boutiques and restaurants around the **Old Market Square** *(King, Albert and Bannatyne Sts.)*. Close by is **Centennial Centre**, a complex enclosing a concert hall, theatre, museum and planetarium connected by terraced gardens. Just north is Winnipeg's **Chinatown**.

Another interesting quarter for shopping and dining is **Osborne Village**, south of the Assiniboine River between River and Stradbrook Avenues.

★★★ **Manitoba Museum of Man and Nature** – Kids *190 Rupert Ave., across from City Hall. Open Jun–Aug daily 10am–6pm. Rest of the year Tue–Fri 10am–4pm, weekends & holidays 10am–5pm. Closed Dec 25. $4.99. ♿ www.manitobamuseum.mb.ca ☎204-943-3139.* This excellent museum presents the history of human occupation in Manitoba by means of fascinating dioramas, displays and audiovisual presentations. It also portrays the great natural regions of the province.
On entering, the visitor is first struck by the magnificent diorama of a Métis rider, his spear poised, chasing several buffalo. The **Earth History Gallery** includes an explanation of the geological creation of Manitoba. The mural by Daphne Odjig portrays the creation of the world according to Odawa Indian tradition.
The **Arctic/Sub-Arctic Gallery** is devoted to the northernmost part of the province. At its entrance stands an **inukshuk** *(illustration p 294)*, a stone sculpture used as a navigational aid, campsite or hunting marker, or reminder of special occasions. Artifacts and photographs illustrate the dependence of the Inuit and Chipewyan Indians upon their environment; displays on Hudson Bay marine life and the phenomenon of the Northern Lights complete the exhibit.
In the **Boreal Forest Gallery** dioramas present the area's indigenous animals. One impressive "walk-through" diorama with a waterfall and cliffs depicts Cree Indians, one of whom is painting on a rock symbols that illustrate religious aspects of the hunt. Other displays feature life on the trapline and modern developments. A mural by Jackson Beardy depicts a world view of the Indians.
The highlight of the museum is the **Nonsuch★★★**, a replica of the ship that sailed from England to Hudson Bay in 1668 in search of furs. The successful enterprise led to the creation of the Hudson's Bay Company two years later *(p 97)*. Built for the company's tricentenary in 1970, the 15m/49ft ketch is anchored in a reconstructed 17C Thames River wharf. The wooden houses and the inn set around the harbour vividly re-create the scene.

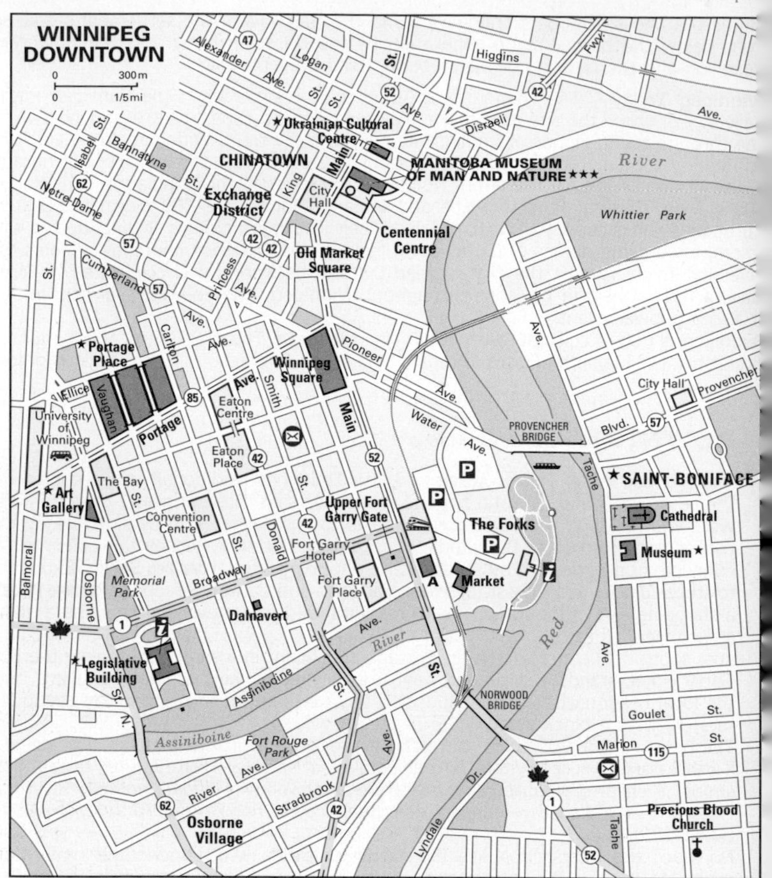

The **Grasslands Gallery** is devoted to the southern part of Manitoba. Insightful displays describe the Assiniboine Indians and first European settlers. There is an example of a **Red River cart**, the major means of pioneer transportation on the prairies; the axles never required greasing and the wheels were easily removed for river crossing. The gallery also has interesting displays on the diverse ethnic and religious groups of Manitoba's population.

The **Urban Gallery** captures a fall evening in Winnipeg in the 1920s. The wooden sidewalks, the railway station, shops, restaurant, rooming house, mission hall and theatre showing period movies have been frozen in time.

A **planetarium** *(daily shows on the hour; $3.99)* and an innovative science centre, **Touch the Universe**, exploring sensory perception, *(same hours as museum; $3.99)* are located on the lower level.

★**Ukrainian Cultural Centre** – *184 Alexander Ave. East. Open year-round Tue–Sat 10am–4pm, Sun 2–5pm. Closed national holidays. ☎204-942-0218.* A visit to this centre, one of the largest of its kind outside the Ukraine, forms an interesting introduction to the history and culture of Manitoba's second largest ethnic group, whose influence on the province is very marked.

The **museum** *(5th floor)* features exquisite examples of Ukrainian traditional embroidery, wood carving, ceramics and beautifully painted *pysanky* ("Easter eggs"). The centre also houses an art gallery, library and archives.

★**Art Gallery** – *300 Memorial Blvd. Open Jun–Aug daily 10am–5pm (Wed 9pm). Rest of the year Tue–Sun 11am–5pm (Wed 9pm). Closed Jan 1, Good Friday, Easter Sunday & Dec 25. $4. www.wag.mb.ca ☎204-786-6641.* Designed by Winnipeger Gustavo Da Roza, this unusual wedge-shaped structure contains a beautiful art gallery. Shown in a constantly changing series of exhibits, the permanent collection is large and varied. The gallery is best known for its **Inuit art**, a selection of which is always exhibited, and for the Lord and Lady Gort Collection of Gothic and Renaissance panel paintings *(displayed periodically)*.

★**Legislative Building** – *Broadway and Osborne St. North. Open mid-May–Aug daily 8am–7pm. Rest of the year Mon–Fri 8:30am–4:30pm. Closed Dec 25. www.gov.mb.ca/legtour/index.html ☎204-945-5813.* This harmonious Neoclassical building stands in an attractive park, close to the residence of

Manitoba's lieutenant-governor. Completed in 1919 the Tyndall stone building forms an "H" with a dome at its centre. Above the dome stands the **Golden Boy**, cast by Charles Gardet, a bronze gold-plated statue clutching a sheaf of wheat in one hand and holding a torch aloft in the other to symbolize Manitoba's glowing future. Above the main entrance *(north side)*, a pediment depicts Canada's motto "From Sea to Sea"; at the centre is Manitoba, the keystone province (symbolized by a woman seated on a throne), joining east and west.
The main entrance hall opens onto a stairway flanked by two **bronze buffalo**, the provincial emblem. The guided tour enables visitors to view the horseshoe-shaped legislative **assembly chamber** and two reception rooms.
The statues around the building and in the park represent important figures in Manitoba history. Across Assiniboine Avenue stands a striking modern **monument** to Louis Riel by Étienne Gaboury.

Dalnavert – *61 Carlton St. Visit by guided tour (1hr) only, Jun–Aug Tue–Thu & weekends 10am–6pm. Mar–May & Sept–Dec Tue–Thu & weekends noon–5pm. Jan–Feb weekends only noon–5pm. $4. P www.mhs.mb.ca ☎ 204-943-2835.* This large, brick Victorian house was built in 1895 by Sir Hugh John Macdonald, the only son of Sir John A. Macdonald, Canada's first prime minister. At the time of its construction, Dalnavert was equipped with numerous luxuries and state-of-the-art amenities, such as walk-in closets, electric lighting, indoor plumbing and central hot-water heating. Beautifully restored today, it reflects the life of this philanthropic politician (member of Parliament from 1891 to 1893, and premier of Manitoba from 1899 to 1900), who reserved part of his basement as a lodging for the homeless.

★**Saint-Boniface** – In 1818 Fathers Provencher and Dumoulin arrived from Quebec to establish a Roman Catholic mission on the banks of the Red River. They were followed by other French Canadians who created, with the largely French-speaking Métis, a lively community. Saint-Boniface was incorporated into the City of Winnipeg in 1972, but it retains its distinctive French character. Every February a **Festival du Voyageur** is held, celebrating the early fur traders with ethnic food, dancing and outdoor activities.

★**Museum** – *494 Ave. Taché. Open late May–Sept Mon–Fri 9am–5pm, Sat 10am–4pm, Sun & holidays 10am–8pm. Mid-Feb–mid-May & Oct Mon–Fri 9am–5pm, Sun & holidays noon–4pm. Rest of the year Mon–Fri 9am–5pm. Closed Dec 25–Jan 1. $2. ♿ P ☎ 204-237-4500.* This attractive frame structure of white oak was built for the Grey Nuns in 1846, making it the oldest building in Winnipeg. Inside are scenes portraying the work of this religious order and mementos of Saint-Boniface residents, in particular of Louis Riel.

Cathedral – Six churches have stood on this site since 1818. The fifth building was largely destroyed by fire in 1968, except for its white stone facade, which stands immediately in front of the new cathedral. Designed by Étienne Gaboury, the church features an attractive wooden interior. The **cemetery** contains the grave of Louis Riel.

Precious Blood Church – Also the work of Gaboury, this brick, shingle-roofed church is built in a shape that resembles an Indian teepee.

ADDITIONAL SIGHTS *Map p 124*

★**The Mint** – *Trans-Can Hwy. at Hwy. 59. Open May–Aug Mon–Fri 9am–5pm. Rest of the year by appointment. Closed national holidays. $2. ♿ P www.rcmint.ca ☎ 204-257-3359.* This branch of the Royal Canadian Mint is housed in a spectacular half-pyramid structure of rose-coloured reflecting glass. Inside, fountains and exotic plants surround a coin collection and displays on the history of coinage in Canada. The process of minting coins can be viewed.

Riel House – *330 River Rd., St. Vital. Visit by guided tour (30min) only, mid-May–Labour Day daily 10am–6pm. Contribution requested. ♿ P ☎ 204-257-1783.* The tiny wooden house was built in 1881 by the Riel family who occupied it until 1968. Although Louis Riel never actually lived in the house, his body lay in state there after his execution in November 1885. The residence has been meticulously restored to reflect the period immediately after his death. An interpretive display on the Riel family is presented outside.

Seven Oaks House – *115 Rupertsland Ave. East. Visit by guided tour (30min) only, late May–Labour Day daily 10am–5pm. $1. P ☎ 204-339-7429.* This nine-room log structure was completed in 1853 by John Inkster, a wealthy merchant. It is believed to be the oldest remaining habitable house in Manitoba. It lies in the parish of West Kildonan, part of the original Selkirk settlement, and near the site of the Seven Oaks Massacre of 1816. Inkster's store and post office, both furnished with period pieces, stand beside the house.

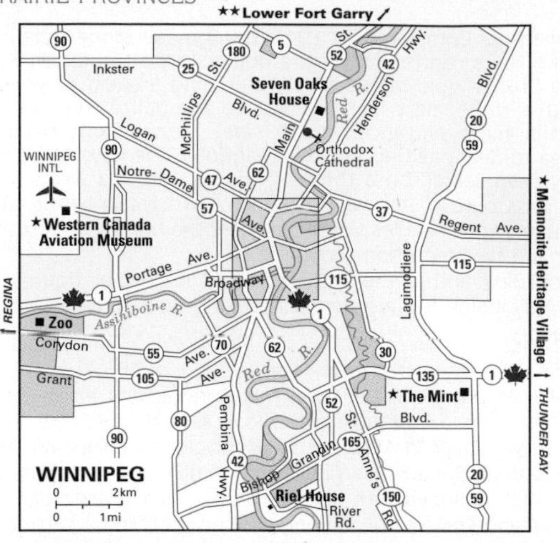

Zoo – Kids *In Assiniboine Park. Open year-round daily 10am. Closing hours vary. $3.* ♿ P ☎204-986-692 This large and pleasant zoo offers a **tropical house**, home to a variety of monkeys and birds who thrive among the exotic plants.

Not far from the zoo and within Assiniboine Park, is the **Leo Mol Sculpture Garden**, a delightful landscaped setting of trees, reflecting pools and flower plantings in which to showcase the Ukrainian sculptor's works.

★**Western Canada Aviation Museum** – Kids *At airport, Ellice and Ferry Rds. Open year-round Mon–Sat 10am–4pm, Sun 1pm–4pm. Closed national holidays. $3.* ♿ P *www.wcam.mb.c ☎204-786-5503.* Over 20 aircraft are on display, ranging from early bush planes to jets. Others can be seen in the process of restoration. A second-floor observation deck allows views of the airport runways.

EXCURSIONS

★★**Lower Fort Garry** – *32km/20mi north of Winnipeg by Hwys. 52 and 9.* This stone fort was built between 1830 and 1847 by the Hudson's Bay Company to replace district headquarters at Upper Fort Garry *(p 121)*, which was regularly subjected to flooding. An important company post until 1911, the fort received goods from the firm's warehouse at York Factory on Hudson Bay by means of **York boats**. These wooden-hulled boats were much larger and more unwieldy than canoes, but they could be sailed across lakes.

Visit – *Open mid-May–Labour Day daily 10am–6pm. $5.50.* ✗ ♿ P *☎204-785-6050.* The visit begins at the **visitor centre**, where an audio-visual presentation *(20min)* forms a good introduction. Restored to reflect life in its mid-19C heyday, the fort itself is surrounded by stone walls. At its centre stands a large and gracious stone dwelling with high chimneys, built to house the offices and residence of the governor. Nearby, the trading store and warehouse display a wide range of goods; note in particular the **furloft** with its splendid **collection**★ of furs. On the grounds a York boat and a Red River cart are on display.

★**Mennonite Heritage Village** – *In Steinbach, 61km/38mi southeast of Winnipeg by Trans-Can Hwy. and Hwy. 12.* This village presents the life of the first Mennonites who settled in Manitoba about 1874. Two groups of Mennonites exist in Canada: the Dutch-Germanic of Ontario and the Russian Mennonites of the West. Extreme pacifists who refuse to fight in any war, both are descended from the Protestant sect led by **Menno Simons**. Persecuted in 17C Europe, some fled to the US, some to Russia. Meeting persecution again, some of the Americans moved to Ontario and the Russians to Manitoba. The sect numbers approximately 100,000 in Canada—the majority live in Manitoba and Ontario.

Visit – *Open May–Sept Mon–Sat 10am–7pm, Sun noon–7pm. Rest of the year Mon–Fri 10am–4pm. $4.* ✗ ♿ P *☎204-326-9661.* Of particular interest is the farmhouse built in characteristic style with the kitchen and stove in the centre (to heat all rooms) and a barn on one end. Other buildings include a church, school and windmill. Within the visitor centre, a gallery displays pioneer artifacts and a map of the various Mennonite migrations. Located in the livery barn, the cafeteria serves Mennonite specialities.

Prairie Dog Central – *Steam train to Grosse Isle. Description p 99.*

Provincial abbreviations used in this guide, such as AB (Alberta), NS (Nova Scotia), PQ (Province of Quebec) and NT (Northwest Territories) are the official Canadian postal designations. A complete listing may be found on p 313.

YORKTON

Saskatchewan
Population 15,154
Map of Principal Sights p 3
Tourist Office ☎306-783-8707

nis city, 187km/116mi northeast of REGINA on the Yellowhead Highway, was first ettled by farmers from York County, Ontario. They were soon followed by a variety f other nationalities, especially Ukrainians. Today Yorkton is known as a manufactung centre for agricultural equipment and for its stockyards.

SIGHT

★**Western Development Museum** – *Hwy. 16 on west side of city. Open May–mid-Sept daily 9am–6pm. $5. ♿ www.wdmuseum.sa.ca ☎306-783-8361.* The Yorkton branch of this museum (other branches in North Battleford, MOOSE JAW and SASKATOON) is devoted to the various ethnic groups found in Saskatchewan, in particular in the Yorkton area. There are displays on the native inhabitants, and dioramas of Ukrainian, German, Scandinavian, English and American pioneer homes. In addition there is a collection of antique steam and gas traction engines and a display on Saskatchewan inventions.

A Sampling of Canada's Collections of Native Culture and Arts

Banff	Buffalo Nations Luxton Museum★ *(p 57)*
Calgary	Glenbow Museum★★ *(p 105)*
Churchill	Eskimo Museum★★ *(p 107)*
Edmonton	Provincial Museum★★ *(p 111)*
Fort Macleod	Head-Smashed-In Buffalo Jump★ *(p 113)*
Hull	Canadian Museum of Civilization★★★ *(p 200)*
'Ksan	Gitksan artifacts collection★★ *(p 69)*
Midland	Huron Indian Village★ *(p 135)*
Montreal	McCord Museum of Canadian History★★ *(p 209)*
Prince Rupert	Museum of Northern British Columbia★★ *(p 68)*
Queen Charlotte	Haida Gwaii Museum★ *(p 51)*
St. John's	Newfoundland Museum★ *(p 283)*
Toronto	Royal Ontario Museum★★★ *(p 179)*
Regina	Royal Saskatchewan Museum★★ *(p 116)*
Vancouver	UBC Museum of Anthropology★★★ *(p 75)* Vancouver Museum★★ *(p 76)*
Victoria	Royal British Columbia Museum★★★ *(p 82)*
Winnipeg	Manitoba Museum of Man and Nature★★★ *(p 121)* Art Gallery★ *(p 122)*
Yellowknife	Prince of Wales Northern Heritage Centre★★ *(p 298)*

Ontario

CN Tower, Toronto/CN Tower Limited

Canada's richest and most populous province (10,753,573 inhabitants), Ontario is the country's industrial, economic, political and cultural heartland. Stretching from the Great Lakes in the south to Hudson Bay in the north, the province encompasses a wide variety of scenery, the majority of its natural beauty spots being in or near water. Possessing nearly 200,000sq km/70,000sq mi of lakes, Ontario takes its name from the Iroquoian word meaning "shining waters."

Geographical Notes

A Land Shaped by Glaciers – When North America's last Ice Age receded about 10,000 years ago, it left the region that is now Ontario scarred and completely reshaped. Great holes gouged out of the earth had gradually filled with water and over much of the land, the geological core of the continent was revealed. The Precambrian rocks of this forested, lake-filled terrain known as the **Canadian Shield** are still exposed over a large part of the province today. Only in the north and in the extreme south are they covered with sedimentary deposits that allow a landscape other than one of rock, water and rock-clinging trees, so typical of the Shield.

The Great Lakes – These vast expanses of fresh water are one of the most extraordinary legacies of the glaciers. **Lake Superior**, the largest, deepest and coldest of the lakes, was created before the ice ages by a fault in the Shield. The other four (Lakes **Huron**, **Michigan**, **Erie** and **Ontario**) were formed by erosion of the original sediment over millions of years. With each advance and retreat of the glaciers, their basins were reshaped. At one time they drained south to the Gulf of Mexico. Today their waters flow northeast down the St. Lawrence to the Atlantic. All but Lake Michigan border Ontario, giving the province a freshwater shoreline of 3,800km/2,360mi, which greatly affects its climate.

The North – The large region north of an imaginary line from the Ottawa River to Georgian Bay via Lake Nipissing *(map p 128)* is referred to as "Northern Ontario." Sparsely populated except in areas of rich mineral deposits *(p 130)*, the land rarely rises above 460m/1500ft, other than a few higher rocky ridges near Lake Superior. Although a small number of farms exist in the clay belt between Lake Timiskaming and Cochrane, it is an unproductive region agriculturally. However, Northern Ontario does provide a large harvest of wood for the pulp and paper mills, and its many lakes have created a sportsman's paradise.

The South – The smaller region south of the Ottawa River–Georgian Bay dividing line is the most densely populated and industrialized part of Canada, especially the area at the western end of Lake Ontario, known as the **Golden Horseshoe**. Approximately a third of the region lies directly on the Canadian Shield. This section of the Shield cuts the rest of southern Ontario in two.

To the east lies a small agricultural triangle in the forks of the Ottawa and St. Lawrence Rivers. To the west are the fertile farmlands of the **Niagara Peninsula** and the region called "Southwestern Ontario". Once, hardwood forests of maple, beech, walnut, elm and ash trees grew here. Today agriculture dominates Canada's most southerly and climatically favourable region.

Climate – The climate varies widely in this province. Northern Ontario experiences long, bright but cold winters, and sunny summers with hot days and cool nights. In the south the winters are less severe because of the moderating influence of the Great Lakes. The summers are also longer than in the north but much more humid, again due to the Great Lakes.

Average daily temperatures

	January		July	
	low	high	low	high
Ottawa	–15°C/5°F	–6°C/21°F	15°C/59°F	26°C/79°F
Toronto	–7°C/18°F	–1°C/30°F	17°C/63°F	27°C/81°F
Thunder Bay	–21°C/-6°F	–8°C/16°F	11°C/52°F	23°C/75°F
Windsor	–9°C/16°F	–1°C/30°F	17°C/63°F	28°C/82°F

Evenly distributed throughout the year in most regions, the amount of precipitation varies over the province (660-1016mm/26-40in) and includes 200-250cm/80-100in of snow in the north. July rainfall is about 100mm/4in in Ottawa and 76mm/3in in Toronto and Thunder Bay. The number of frost-free days varies from 179 on the Point Pelee Peninsula in the south to 60 on the shores of Hudson Bay.

Historical Notes

Before the Europeans – Northern Ontario was inhabited by Indians of the sub-Arctic culture whose subsistence lifestyle in a meagre environment was similar to that of the tribes in the Northwest Territories. The south, on the other hand, was the realm of Indians of the Algonquian and Iroquoian language groups commonly known as the **Eastern Woodlands culture** *(map p 22)*. These tribes generally lived a fairly sedentary life in organized villages around which fields of beans, corn and squash were cultivated. No crop rotation was practised; every 10 or so years when the land was exhausted, the village was moved to a new site. Travelling by birchbark canoe in summer, and snowshoe and toboggan in winter, the men hunted and fished extensively, never staying away long from their palisaded villages.

Tribes lived in large rectangular huts made of a framework of poles covered with hides. These **longhouses** accommodated several families, each having their own fireplace and sleeping platform (some of the Algonquin tribes built circular, dome-shaped huts instead of longhouses). Minimal in summer, clothing consisted in winter of deerskin leggings, fur robes and moccasins.

Iroquoian society was matrilineal (descent was from the mother) and the women of these tribes wielded considerable power, selecting the male chiefs, for example. In contrast Algonquin society was patrilineal. Rich traditions of distinct religious and mythological beliefs and practices permeated both groups. To frighten away disease or other evils, the Iroquoian **False Face Society** performed dances in elaborate masks of wood and human hair.

Many of these tribes grew militant, owing in particular to their increasing dependency on European trade. Composed of five tribes (Mohawk, Onondaga, Seneca, Cayuga, Oneida), the **League of the Iroquois** warred repeatedly with the early French settlers, and defeated and dispersed the **Huron**, another Iroquoian group. Today little remains of the Eastern Woodlands Indians' former way of life.

Part of New France – The region that is now Ontario was crisscrossed by most of the 17C and 18C French explorers. First to visit was **Étienne Brûlé**, soon followed by **Champlain** himself, **Radisson** and **Groseilliers** in their search for a route to Hudson Bay,

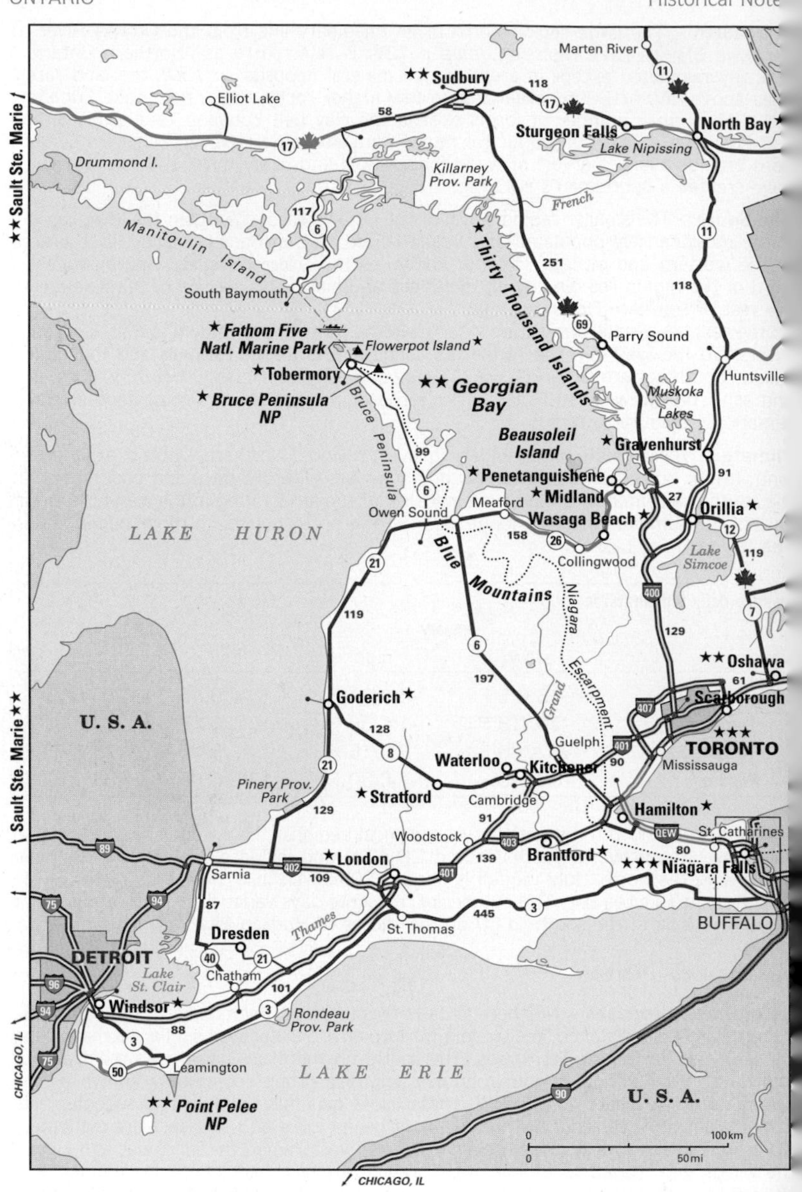

Marquette and Jolliet in their search for a river flowing west from Lake Superior, and **Sieur de La Salle** on his famous trip down the Mississippi. Fur trade was the main reason for exploration, and trading posts were set up all over the province. There were also two attempts at permanent settlement. In 1639 the **Jesuits** established a mission on the shores of Georgian Bay to convert the Huron to Christianity. Settlement lasted only until 1650 because of fierce attacks by the Iroquois who captured and martyred five of the Jesuit fathers. Then in the early 18C, farms were laid out on the shores of the Detroit River in Southwest Ontario. At the time of the fall of New France, about 400 people were living there.

At the same time, the **Hudson's Bay Company** was establishing itself in the province's northern section. In 1673 a post was founded at **Moosonee** on James Bay, which claims to be Ontario's oldest settlement. Despite these attempts at settlement, what is now Ontario was still very much the realm of Indians at the time of the American Revolution.

Arrival of the Loyalists – When the American colonies revolted against British rule in 1775, many people refused to join the rebels. Called Loyalists (or "Tories," to use the American term) primarily because of their loyalty to King George III, they may have numbered as many as 1.25 million—a third of the population. When the American Revolution ended, Loyalists found themselves very unpopular; most were forced to leave their homes and flee for their lives.

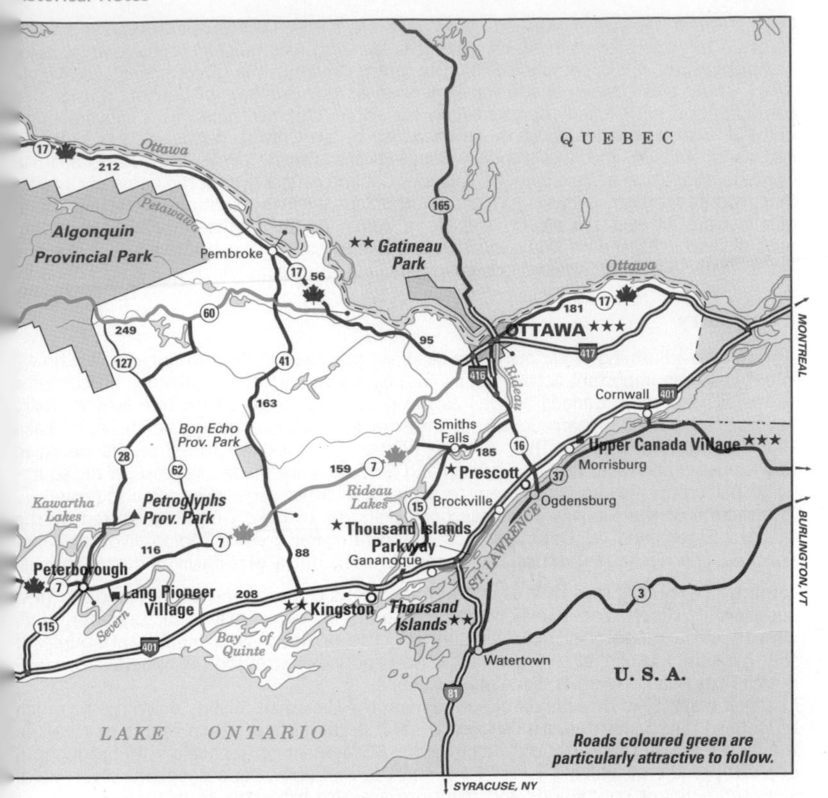

An estimated 80,000 Loyalists settled in Canada—in Nova Scotia, New Brunswick, Prince Edward Island, the Eastern Townships of Quebec, the St. Lawrence Valley and the Niagara Peninsula. They also fled to England and the West Indies, but Canada was popular because they were promised free land. Among the Loyalists in Ontario were Indians of the **Six Nations Iroquois Confederacy** (the Tuscarora joined the five-nation Iroquois league in 1722) who, under their great chief **Joseph Brant**, had fought for the British. The arrival of such a great number of people—one of the largest mass movements of the time—created, almost overnight, the province of Upper Canada (Lower Canada being present-day Quebec). In 1791 a separate administration was established in Niagara-on-the-Lake and later in Toronto. Although many more immigrants have settled in Ontario since that date, the influence of the descendants of these Loyalists is still strong in Ontario today.

Meanwhile, the waters and lakes of the province were alive with the brigades of fur traders of both Hudson's Bay and North West Companies. Indeed, the latter set up its great rendezvous point at Fort William on Lake Superior.

American Invasion – In 1812 the Americans, infuriated by British high-handedness on the open seas, declared war and invaded Canada, hoping to seize it quickly while the British were preoccupied fighting Napoleon in Europe. They were confident that the inhabitants would rush to join their standard. Instead they found the population of Upper Canada united in its dislike of the US, if not in its loyalty to Britain. The ensuing war was fought mainly in Upper Canada. Naval encounters occurred on the Great Lakes, during which Toronto was looted and burned. There was much fighting in the Niagara Peninsula where **Isaac Brock** and **Laura Secord** engraved their names in Canadian history; along the St.Lawrence, particularly at Crysler's Farm *(p 186)*; and in the province of Quebec at Chateauguay. Battles were often indecisive, but the Americans were kept out of Canada, and in Ontario at least, a sense of nationhood was born.

Toward Confederation – As a result of the war, the British government decided to encourage immigration to Upper Canada to bolster the population against further possible American attack. Free land was offered and, since economic distress in Britain was great, approximately 1.5 million people crossed the Atlantic from 1820 to 1840 to seek a better life in Ontario. Farms, villages and towns sprang up where previously there had been only bush. The face of the province was changed immeasurably.

These new settlers brought not only their industry but also their political ideas. Fresh from a struggle to promote electoral reform in England, they found Canada backward. Real political power lay not with the elected assembly but with the governor and a council dominated by several well-connected groups known as the **Family Compact**.

Opposition to this system was led by a fiery Scot, **William Lyon Mackenzie**, who eventuall resorted to armed revolt in 1837. While the uprising was quickly suppressed by colo nial authorities, it did persuade Britain to grant "responsible government" *(p 24)*. I 1841 Upper and Lower Canada were reunited as the Province of Canada in a kind o confederation with equal representation for each. This union led to a movement t unite all British colonies in North America, led by an Ontario politician, **John A. Macdo nald** and his Quebec colleague, **George-Étienne Cartier**. When union (Canadian Confederation) was achieved in 1867, Upper Canada officially took the name of Ontario Since Confederation, Ontario has grown enormously in population, attracting immi grants from all over the world. This large influx, added to the province's abundan natural resources and strategic location in relation to the rest of Canada and the US led to Ontario's rapid industrial development and its preeminence in modern Canada

Economy

Agriculture – Farming of various types has been practised in Ontario since earliest times and it is still an important activity today. The southern part of the province boasts some of the richest soil in Canada as well as the province's longest frost-free season. Dairy farming is the predominant activity in the southeast corner, along the shores of Lake Ontario and in the Upper Thames Valley. Other livestock are raised in the Georgian Bay–Upper Grand River region. Soybean and field corn are the staple crops of the southwest, but crops such as sweet corn, tomatoes and other vegetables are also grown.
The section of the Niagara Peninsula on the shores of Lake Ontario sheltered by the Niagara Escarpment is Ontario's most important **fruit-growing** region. Not only are peaches, cherries, strawberries and grapes grown, but a **wine-making** industry thrives.

Mining – No other province is as rich in minerals as Ontario, one of the world's largest suppliers of nickel, and a major producer of gold, silver, platinum, uranium, zinc, copper and a range of structural materials. The province is an important source of salt, gypsum and nepheline syenite. Ontario produces more nonfuel minerals for commercial use than any other Canadian province.
The vast majority of these minerals come from the Canadian Shield, which covers much of Ontario. The **Sudbury Igneous Complex** *(p 164)* is the largest single source of nickel in the world. Nickel from Sudbury accounts for 66 percent of Canada's total production, over 70 percent of which is exported to the US. Platinum, copper, cobalt, silver, gold, selenium, sulphur compounds and tellurium are also extracted from the ore.
In 1903 the great **silver** deposits of Cobalt were found during the building of a railway, followed by the discovery of **gold** in the Timmins-Kirkland Lake region. Gold was found at Red Lake to the west as well, and iron ore at Wawa, taken to SAULT STE. MARIE for smelting. During World War II, the iron ore deposits of Atikokan were developed, and a huge mining boom ensued in the wake of the war. In the 1950s the vast **Manitouwadge** field of copper, zinc and silver deposits was exploited, and the uranium of Elliot Lake was tapped for the first time. In the 1960s the Timmins-Kirkland Lake region was revived by zinc, copper, lead and iron finds to replace the exploited gold. Most notable was the Kidd Creek copper-zinc-silver discovery. Recent gold discoveries at Detour Lake and Hemlo continue to demonstrate the wealth of the Shield.
Not all of Ontario's minerals are found in the Shield, however. Southwestern Ontario has produced a small amount of oil and gas since 1859. **Salt** is mined extensively at GODERICH and WINDSOR, and gypsum and a range of structural materials are found in sizable quantities. Mining is an essential base of Ontario's economy, reflected by the number of mining interests listed on the Toronto Stock Exchange.

Forestry, Fishing, Furs and Hydro-Electricity – These four resources significantly affect Ontario's economy. The province is still largely covered with forest, despite serious depletion in the last century. Today pulp, paper and sawn lumber are the main products, and Ontario ranks third after British Columbia and Quebec in the value of production. The province leads the rest of Canada in the value of fish taken from inland waters, thanks to the Great Lakes. Fur production, the province's oldest industry, is still carried on both by trapping and fur farms. The development of hydro power has accompanied the province's overall economic growth in this century, especially since Ontario has little oil or gas and no coal. The harnessing of the Niagara River, the St. Lawrence and other waters was essential for industrial development. Today Ontario ranks third after Quebec and British Columbia in hydro-electric output.

Manufacturing – Over half of Canada's total output of finished goods comes from Ontario. The province's largest industry, manufacturing has made Ontario Canada's industrial heart. Motor vehicles and parts rank first in production value, but also important are the production of telecommunications systems, aerospace and defence electronics equipment, electrical machinery, primary and fabricated metals, rubber, chemical goods and food products as well as printing and publishing. Most of these industries are concentrated in the Greater Toronto Area and along the Highway 401 corridor from Windsor to KINGSTON, which, when combined, represent Canada's largest marketing area. Other important industrial regions include Sarnia (petrochemicals), Niagara (auto parts), Sault Ste. Marie (steel and paper) and Ottawa-Carleton (telecommunications, computers).

PRACTICAL INFORMATION

Getting There

By Air – Flights to Toronto's Pearson International Airport (25km/15mi west of downtown) ☎905-676-3506 are available via major domestic and international carriers. Air Canada ☎416-925-2311 or 800-776-3000 (US) and Canadian Airlines International ☎800-426-7000 (Canada/US) and their affiliates provide connections to regions throughout the province. Taxi to downtown *($30)*. Airport **shuttle**: Airport Express Aeroport ☎905-564-6333 *($12.50)*. Major car rental agencies at the airport *(p 305)*.

By Bus and Train – The major **bus** line is Greyhound ☎416-367-8747 (for local numbers consult the telephone directory). **VIA Rail** Canada links many cities within the province. In Canada consult the telephone directory for the nearest office; from the US ☎800-561-3949.

General Information

Accommodations and Visitor Information – The government tourist office produces annually updated regional guides that list accommodations, camping facilities, attractions and travel centres. The *Adventure Guide* and *Winter Guide* furnish recreational information for the province. All publications and a map are available free of charge from: **Ontario Travel**, Queen's Park, Toronto, ON, M7A 2E5 ☎416-314-0944 or 800-668-2746 (Canada/US). For information on campground vacancies, spring blossoms and fall colours, or skiing conditions ☎416-314-0998. For additional information, contact **Ontario Tourism**, 900 Bay St., 9th Floor, Toronto, ON M7A 2E1.

Road Regulations – *(Driver's license and insurance requirements p 304.)* The province has good paved roads. Speed limits, unless otherwise posted, are 100km/h (60mph) on freeways, 90km/h (55mph) on the Trans-Canada routes, and 80km/h (50mph) on most highways. The speed limit in cities and towns is 50km/h (30mph). **Seat belt** use is mandatory. For listings of the **Canadian Automobile Assn. (CAA)**, consult the local telephone directory.

Time Zones – Most of Ontario is on Eastern Standard Time. Daylight Saving Time is observed from the first Sunday in April to the last Sunday in October. In the western third of the province (west of longitude 90) Central Standard Time applies.

Taxes – In addition to the national 7% GST *(rebate information p 308)*, Ontario levies an 8% provincial sales tax, a 10% alcoholic beverages tax and a 5% accommodation tax. Non residents can request rebates of the provincial tax (a receipt must total $50 or more) from Retail Sales Tax, 5 Park Home Ave., Suite 200, North York, ON, M2N 6W8 ☎416-222-3226.

Liquor Laws – The legal drinking age is 19. Liquor is sold in government stores.

Provincial Holiday *(National Holidays p 308)*	
Civic Holiday	1st Monday in August

Recreation

Outdoor Activities – An abundance of lakes and waterways offers the outdoor enthusiast a wide variety of **water sports**. Scenic routes to explore by boat are the Rideau Canal and lakes from Ottawa to Kingston, and the Trent-Severn system from Trenton to Georgian Bay via the Kawartha Lakes and Lake Simcoe. **Canoeing** is one of the most popular outdoor activities ranging from lake and river to white-water canoeing.

Many outfitters offer an array of excursions that include transportation, lodging, equipment and the service of experienced guides. The best-known regions are: **Algonquin Provincial Park** (☎705-633-5572), which has 1,600km/1,000mi of canoe routes and **Quetico Provincial Park** (☎807-597-2735), through which the Boundary Waters Fur Trade Canoe Route passes with 43 portages along 523km/325mi. For additional information contact the Canadian Recreational Canoeing Assn., PO Box 398, 446 Main St. West, Merrickville, ON, K0G 1N0 ☎613-269-2910.

Hiking is a favoured activity during the summer. The famous Bruce Trail follows the Niagara Escarpment for 692km/430mi across the southern part of the province *(map p 128)*. Hikers pass through wilderness on the Coastal Trail along the shores of Lake Superior in **Pukaskwa National Park** (☎807-229-0801).

Ontario is a fisherman's paradise particularly in the north, where many fly-in lodges arrange **fishing** expeditions. Nonresidents must obtain a license available from local sporting good stores. For information on seasons, catch and possession limits contact the Ministry of Natural Resources, Information Centre, 900 Bay St., McDonald Block, Toronto, ON, M7A 2C1 ☎416-314-2000.

In winter cross-country skiing and snowmobiling are prevalent recreational activities. Thunder Bay, Blue Mountain, Burrie and Searchmont are among the province's popular alpine ski centres.

For more information on outdoor activities contact Ontario Travel *(above)*.

Special Excursions – Several **white-water rafting** excursions, led by experienced guides, are available on the Ottawa River *(May–Sept; round-trip 4-6hrs; from $85, including equipment & meals; accommodations extra; reservations required; Wilderness Tours, Box 89, Beachburg, ON, K0J 1C0 ☎613-646-2291)*.

A fascinating all-day train trip, the **Polar Bear Express**, takes the traveller across terrain of giant forests, bushland and muskeg through the Arctic watershed to Moosonee on Hudson Bay. Arriving at midday, visitors have ample time to tour Ontario's oldest English settlement, founded by the Hudson's Bay Co. in 1673 on Moose Factory Island *(departs from Cochrane late Jun–Labour Day Sat–Thu 8:30am; returns to Cochrane 10:05pm; commentary; reservations suggested; round-trip $46; ✗ ♿ 🅿; Ontario Northland www.ontc.on.ca ☎416-314-3750)*.

Luxury steamboat cruising, retracing routes of early explorers through inland waters, can be enjoyed aboard **MV Canadian Empress**. Cruises include shore visits to historic sites and to OTTAWA, MONTREAL, QUEBEC CITY and other cities. Trips of 5-7 days available *(depart from Kingston mid-May–late Oct; reservations required; ♿; for rates and schedules, contact St. Lawrence Cruise Lines, Inc., 253 Ontario St., Kingston, ON, K7L 2Z4 ☎613-549-8091.*

Principal Festivals

Feb	**Winterlude**	*Ottawa*
Mar	**Maple Syrup Festival**	*Elmira*
Apr–Oct	**Shaw Festival** *(p 147)*	*Niagara-on-the-Lake*
May	**Blossom Festival**	*Niagara Falls*
	Canadian Tulip Festival	*Ottawa*
May–Oct	**Stratford Festival** *(p 163)*	*Stratford*
Jun	**Metro International Caravan** *(p 168)*	*Toronto*
Jun–Jul	**International Freedom Festival** *(p 186)*	*Windsor*
Jul	**Great Rendezvous** *(p 165)*	*Thunder Bay*
	Molson Indy	*Toronto*
Jul–Aug	**Rockhound Gemboree**	*Bancroft*
	Glengarry Highland Games	*Maxville*
	Caribana *(p 168)*	*Toronto*
Aug	**Six Nations Native Pageant** *(p 133)*	*Brantford*
	Summerfolk	*Owen Sound*
Aug–Sept	**Canadian National Exhibition** *(p 168)*	*Toronto*
Sept	**Festival of Festivals**	*Toronto*
	Niagara Grape and Wine Festival	*St. Catharines*
Oct	**Oktoberfest** *(p 142)*	*Kitchener-Waterloo*
Nov	**Royal Agricultural Winter Fair**	*Toronto*
Nov–Jan	**Winter Festival of Lights**	*Niagara Falls*

Great Lakes/St. Lawrence Seaway System – Completed in 1959, this network of lakes, rivers, locks and canals extends 3,790km/2,350mi from the Atlantic Ocean to the western end of the Great Lakes. When combined, the St. Lawrence Seaway and the Great Lakes afford 15,325km/9,500mi of navigable waterways. Of the seaway's 15 locks between the St. Lawrence River and Lake Ontario, Canada operates and aintains 13, all of which are located within Ontario and Quebec; an additional lock . Sault Ste. Marie, closed for the past several years, reopened in 1998 for recrea- onal traffic.

heap water transportation on this system has been of unparalleled importance to the evelopment of Ontario. Iron ore, coal and grain are among the largest commodities iipped. Raw materials are transported to smelters and factories; finished products re moved to markets. Heaviest traffic is among the Upper Lakes; the four American cks at Sault Ste. Marie, though technically not part of the seaway, are some of the usiest in the entire system.

BRANTFORD★

Population 84,764
Map p 128
Tourist Office ☎519-751-9900

lamed for Six Nations chief Joseph Brant, this manufacturing city is also famous as he family home of Alexander Graham Bell.

listorical Notes

River Crossing – Brantford stands on what was once part of a grant of land in the alley of the Grand River given to the Six Nations Indians *(p 129)* in 1784 by the British overnment. Led by Chief Brant, these Indians fought on the British side in the American Revolution and, like other Loyalists at the end of the war, were forced to flee the US. To how his personal gratitude to his Indian subjects, George III provided money for the onstruction of a chapel *(below)*. European settlers purchased land from the Indians in 830, and the present city was founded, retaining the old name of the location—Brant's ord, because the chief had crossed the river there. The Indian reserve still exists to the outh, though much reduced in size. It is the scene every year of the **Six Nations Native Pageant** during which the Iroquois tribes commemorate their history and culture *(Aug)*.

Telephone City – In 1870 **Alexander Graham Bell** (1847-1922) moved with his parents o Ontario from Scotland. Soon afterwards he took a job as a teacher of the deaf in Boston, a profession he shared with his father. While trying to find a means of repro- ducing sounds visibly for his deaf pupils, he solved the problem by transmitting and receiving speech along an electrified wire. From this solution he developed the tele- phone, an idea he conceived in Brantford in 1874 while visiting his parents. He tested his invention in Boston the next year. The first "long distance" call was made from Brantford when Bell, in Paris, Ontario *(about 11km/7mi away)*, was able to hear his father's voice. The telephone's invention made Bell a fortune, enabling him to under- take research, in addition to his work for the deaf. Much of this research was carried out at his summer home in Baddeck, Nova Scotia *(p 258)*.

SIGHTS *3hrs*

★ **Bell Homestead National Historic Site** – *94 Tutela Heights Rd. From downtown, take Colborne St. West across Grand River, turn left on Mt. Pleasant St. and left again on Tutela Heights Rd. Open year-round Tue–Sun 9:30am–4:30pm. Closed Jan 1, Good Friday, Dec 25-26. $2.75. ✂ ♿ www.citybrantford.on.ca ☎519-756-6220.* This pleasant house with its covered veranda is furnished much as it would have been in Bell's day, with many original pieces. There is an interesting display on his life, inventions and research.

Next door stands a smaller clapboard structure moved to this spot from the centre of Brantford. Among other things it housed the first telephone business office in Canada. Inside there is an early telephone exchange and displays on the develop- ment of the telephone since Bell's day.

Woodland Cultural Centre – *184 Mohawk St. Open year-round Mon–Fri 8:30am–4pm, weekends & holidays 10am–5pm. Closed Dec 20–Jan 2. $4.10. ♿ www.woodland-centre.o.ca ☎519-759-2650.* This centre houses a **museum** that presents an interesting collection of native art and artifacts. The interior of a 19C longhouse and related displays depict the way of life of the Eastern Woodlands Indians, of which the Six Nations Indians are a part.

Nearby stands the the oldest Protestant church in Ontario, **Her Majesty's Chapel of the Mohawks** (it is of course "His" if the monarch is male), which was constructed with funds donated by the British Crown *(open Jul–mid-Oct daily 10am–6pm; rest of the year by appointment; ☎519-753-3813)*.

Canada's 7% Goods and Services Tax (GST), effective since January 1991, replaced the federal sales tax. The GST is a personal consumption tax levied, for example, on groceries, vehicles, accommodation, and health, dental, financial and educational services.
Nonresidents are entitled to a rebate. For information, see p 308.
Unless stated otherwise, all prices quoted in this guide are in Canadian dollars and do not always include GST tax.

DRESDEN

Population 2,589

Map p 128

The country around this small manufacturing centre was first settled by black slave who had escaped their masters in the US and fled to freedom in British North Americ One of these slaves was **Josiah Henson**, who arrived in Ontario with his family in 183 With the aid of donations from Britain, Henson purchased land in the Dresden are established a refuge for fugitives from slavery and founded a school to teach childre skills their parents had never learned. Unable to write, Henson dictated the story his life *(The Life of Josiah Henson–formerly a slave)*, which was subsequently pub lished. This manuscript so impressed **Harriet Beecher Stowe** that she met him and use him as the model for her influential novel, *Uncle Tom's Cabin.*

SIGHT

★**Uncle Tom's Cabin Historic Site** – *1.6km/1mile west off Hwy. 21. Open lat May–mid-Oct Tue–Sat 10am–4pm, Sun noon–4pm. Rest of Oct–Nov by appoin ment. $5. ♿ ☎519-683-2978.* This collection of wooden buildings include Henson's house (Uncle Tom's Cabin), a simple church of the same era as the on in which he preached and a fugitive slave's house. In the museum there are suc items as posters advertising slave sales, a ball and chain similar to those slave were forced to wear to prevent escape, slave whips, handcuffs and clubs. recorded commentary explains the exhibits and tells Henson's story. His grave i outside.

GEORGIAN BAY★★

Map p 128

Named for George IV of England, this immense bay is almost a lake in itself, cut of from the rest of Lake Huron by the Bruce Peninsula and Manitoulin Island. Most attrac tive sailing and boating country, it is a popular vacation spot; summer cottages line its shores and islands. More than a resort area, however, the region supports consi derable light industry. Owen Sound, Collingwood, Midland, Port McNicoll and Parry Sound are fair-size ports with grain elevators.

Geographical Notes – Immortalized by the Group of Seven painters, the eastern and northern shorelines are wild and rocky with numerous indentations and thousands of islands. Some of these islands are mere slabs of rock with perhaps a few windswept pines or other hardy plants maintaining a precarious hold. The western, and part of the southern, shores form a section of the **Niagara Escarpment** with one gently rolling slope and one steep escarpment. This ridge of limestone crosses Ontario from Niagara Falls, mounts the Bruce Peninsula, submerges and then resurfaces to form Manitoulin and other islands, and ends in Wisconsin. A complete contrast to these rocky shores, the coast along the western side of the Midland Peninsula has long sandy stretches, especially in the region of Wasaga Beach. Located in the southeast corner of the bay are 59 islands that form Georgian Bay Islands National Park, established in 1929.

Historical Notes – Étienne Brûlé, one of Champlain's men, visited Georgian Bay in 1610. Fur traders and Jesuits soon followed, arriving via the 1,300km/800mi canoe route from Quebec. Eager to convert Huron Indians to Christianity, the Jesuits built a mission post called Sainte-Marie near the present site of Midland in 1639. At this time the Huron were suffering frequent attacks from the Iroquois tribes to the south and, weakened as they were from the "white man's diseases," they were unable to resist the onslaught. Caught in the middle, several Jesuit fathers were killed after suffering incredible torture. The atrocities led to the abandonment of Sainte-Marie in 1649. After the Jesuits' return to Quebec, and the Huron's defeat, peace was restored until the early 19C when warfare erupted between the British and Americans over control of the Great Lakes. With peace, the present borders were established, and the region has seen no fighting since.

HISTORICAL SIGHTS

★**Midland** – This busy city on the bay is well known for its numerous historical and natural attractions.

★★**Sainte-Marie among the Hurons** – *5km/3mi east on Hwy. 12. Open mid-May–mid-Oct daily 10am–5pm. $9.75. ✂ ♿ www.saintemarieamongthehurons.on.ca ☎705-526-7838.* Consisting of 22 structures enclosed within a wooden palisade, the mission established by the Jesuits in 1639 and destroyed by them before their retreat in 1649, has been reconstructed.

An audio-visual presentation *(17min)* explains the mission's history and should be viewed before the rest of the visit. The chapel, forge, sawpit, carpentry shop, residences and native area are "peopled" by historical interpreters in 17C costume.

The mission is divided into separate sections for the Jesuits, the lay workers (called *donnes*) and the Huron. A rectangular, bark-covered longhouse and a hospital where the Jesuits tended the sick have been constructed in the native section. In the **museum★★** slide shows illustrate Sainte-Marie in the context of its times. Topics such as 17C Europe, New France, the Jesuits and the Huron are explained in excellent displays.

Beside Sainte-Marie is the **Wye Marsh Wildlife Centre** *(open mid-May–Labour Day daily 10am–6pm; rest of the year daily 10am–4pm; closed Dec (trails open); $5; ♿ www.bconnex.net/~bpm/wyemarsh.html ☎ 705-526-7809)* where nature trails, a boardwalk and an observation tower allow visitors to appreciate the life of a marsh. There are also slide and film shows, and a display hall.

★Martyrs' Shrine – *5km/3mi east of Midland on Hwy. 12 near Wildlife Centre. Open mid-May–mid-Oct daily 8:30am–9pm. $2. ✗ ♿ ☎ 705-526-3788.* This twin-spired stone church was built in 1926 as a memorial to the eight Jesuit martyrs of New France, who were declared saints in 1930. They were killed by the Iroquois between 1642 and 1649, the first five while they were missionaries at Sainte-Marie. On the front portico stand **statues** of Jean de Brébeuf and Gabriel Lalemant, the two Jesuits who were severely tortured before death. The church has a striking **interior** with wood panelling and a roof of sandalwood from British Columbia.

★Huron Indian Village – *In Little Lake Park on King St. Open Jul–Aug daily 9am–6pm. Rest of the year daily 9am–5pm. Closed Jan 1, Good Friday, Dec 25-26. $6. ♿ www.georgianbaytourism.on.ca ☎ 705-526-2844.* This village is a replica of a 16C Huron community. After viewing an introductory **film** *(15min)*, visitors pass through the wooden palisade to examine examples of the long, rectangular, bark-covered frame houses in which the Huron lived communally. Animal skins, plants and herbs are hanging to dry. The medicine man's house, a sweat bath, storage pits and a canoe-making site can also be visited.

Beside the village, in the park is the **Huronia Museum** *(same hours as village)*, which has an art gallery, a collection of Indian artifacts and pioneer displays.

★Penetanguishene – *12km/8mi west of Midland by Rtes. 12 and 93.* The southern entrance to this town, which has a large French-speaking community, is guarded by two angels symbolizing the harmony between the English and French cultures.

★Discovery Harbour – *93 Jury Dr. Open mid-May–Labour Day daily 10am–5pm. $5.50. ✗ ☎ 705-549-8064.* On a pleasant site above Penetang harbour stands this reconstruction of a British Naval dockyard and military garrison established here after the War of 1812.

An audio-visual presentation *(15min)* in the visitor centre presents the site's history. In the naval establishment, which existed from 1817 to 1834, costumed interpreters evoke the life of the commanding officer and his staff who worked in the naval storehouse and dockyard. At the wharf there are replicas of three 19C schooners. The military garrison was located here from 1828 to 1856. The original officers' quarters can be visited.

★Wasaga Beach – *Map p 128.* This popular resort is well known for its 14km/9mi stretch of white sand.

★Nancy Island Historic Site – *In Wasaga Beach Provincial Park, Mosley St. off Hwy. 92. Open mid-May–mid-Jun weekends only 10am–6pm. Late Jun–Labour Day daily 10am–6pm. Mid-Sept–mid-Oct Sat–Wed 10am–5pm. ♿ www2.georgian.net/~nancyisland ☎ 705-429-2728.* The museum stands on a small island near the mouth of the Nottawasaga River. The island was created by silt collecting around the hull of a sunken schooner, the **Nancy**. During the War of 1812, the vessel was requisitioned by British forces to act as a supply ship for their military bases. After the American victory at the naval battle of Lake Erie, this British ship—the only one left on the Upper Lakes—was tracked down and sunk by the Americans while hiding in this spot on the Nottawasaga.

In 1927 her hull was recovered from the silt and is now displayed in the museum building with explanations of its history, and that of the War of 1812.

NATURAL SIGHTS

★Thirty Thousand Islands – An excellent means of appreciating the natural beauty of Georgian Bay and its many islands is one of three boat cruises: from **Midland** town dock *(departs May–Oct daily 1:45pm, additional cruises late Jun–Sept; round-trip 2hrs 30min; commentary; reservations required; $14; ✗ ♿ PMCL Boat Cruises www.pmcl.on.ca/ ☎ 705-526-0161)*; from Penetanguishene town dock *(departs late Jun–early Sept daily 2pm, also 7pm Wed & Thu; less frequently in spring and fall; round-trip 3hrs; commentary; reservations suggested; $14; ✗ Argee Boat Cruises ☎ 705-549-7795)*; and from **Parry Sound** town dock *(departs Jun–mid-Oct daily 2pm; additional departure Jul & Aug 10am; round-trip 3hrs; commentary; reservations required; $17; ✗ ♿ 30,000 Island Cruise Lines Inc. ☎ 705-746-2311 or 800-506-2628, Canada/US).*

★**Tobermory** – This tiny village is located at the tip of the Bruce Peninsula wher the Niagara Escarpment becomes submerged and the waters of Georgian Bay mee those of Lake Huron. Tobermory provides hundreds of protected moorings aroun its double harbour known as Big Tub and Little Tub. The clear waters, underwate rock formations and number of old shipwrecks also attract divers.
The **MS Chi-Cheemaun** provides regular ferry service to Manitoulin Island *(departs lat Jun–Labour Day daily 7am, 11:20am, 3:40pm & 8pm; mid-May–mid-Jun & mic Sept–mid-Oct daily 8:50am & 1:30pm, additional departure Fri 6:10pm; one-wa 2hr; commentary; $24/car plus $11/adult; ✗ ♿ Ontario Northland Marine Service ☎ 800-265-3163, Canada/US).*

★**Bruce Peninsula National Park** – ☎ *Open daily year-round. Visitor centre o Little Tub Harbour open Jul–Aug daily 9am–9pm; call for spring and fall hours △♿ ☎ 519-596-2233.* Established in 1987 this national park is known for its trail along the spectacular Niagara Escarpment. There is a 242-site campground a Cyprus Lake, 15km/9mi south of Tobermory *(for reservations ☎ 519-596-2233)*

★**Fathom Five National Marine Park** – ☎ *Visitor centre on Little Tub Harbou open Jul–Aug daily 9am–9pm; call for spring and fall hours. ☎ 519-596-2233.* Thi "underwater" preserve, Canada's first national marine park, encompasse 19 islands and the treacherous waters off Tobermory. The remains of 19 know wrecks of sail and steam vessels from mid-19C to 20C can be viewed close u with scuba-diving or snorkeling equipment, or from above by **glass-bottomed boa** *(departs Jul–Aug daily 11am & 2:30pm; mid-May–Jun & Sept–mid-Oct daily 1pm round-trip 2hr 30min; drop-off at Flowerpot Island possible; commentary; $15.95 ✗ ♿ ▣ Blue Heron Co. www.blueheronco.com ☎ 519-596-2999; also contac Seaview III ☎ 519-596-2950 or True North II ☎ 519-596-2600 for rates & departure times).*
Tiny **Flowerpot Island**★, the best known of the park islands, was at one time completely covered by the waters of Lake Huron. Caves high up on the cliffs and two rock pillars, known as the **flowerpots**, are evidence of the ancient water levels. These grey pillars have a dolomite base that has been eroded. They stand 7m/23ft and 11m/35ft high and can be closely approached by boat or on foot from the island. The tour boats circle the island, affording good views of the flowerpots.

Beausoleil Island – *Part of the Georgian Bay Islands National Park. Access by private boat or water taxi only from Honey Harbour (about 40km/25mi northeast of Midland via Rte. 12, Hwy. 69 and Rte. 5). Open daily year-round. $3/day use fee (late May–mid-Oct). △. Information & maps available at park office in Honey Harbour www.parkscanada.pch.gc.ca ☎ 705-756-2415.* There are walking trails, a picnic area and a visitor centre *(open late Jun–Labour Day daily 1pm–5pm; ♿)* on this island.

The Blue Mountains – *56km/35mi from Wasaga Beach to Meaford by Rte. 26.* This drive is pretty, with the waters of Georgian Bay on one side of the road and the Blue Mountains, the highest part of the Niagara Escarpment, on the other.

GODERICH★

Population 7,553
Map p 128

Built on a bluff above the point where the Maitland River joins **Lake Huron**, this town was founded in 1828 as the terminus of the Huron Road, a right-of-way built in the early 19C to encourage settlement. The town has wide, tree-lined streets that radiate like the spokes of a wheel from central, octagonal **Court House Square**. Goderich has a sizeable harbour and several industries, including rock-salt mining.

SIGHTS

Huron County Museum – *110 North St. Open May–Labour Day Mon–Sat 10am–4:30pm, Sun 1pm–4:30pm. Rest of the year Sun–Fri 10am–4:30pm. Closed Jan 1, Easter Monday, Dec 25-26. $4. ♿ www.odyssey.on.ca/~hcm-chin ☎ 519-524-2686.* All aspects of the region's history are depicted in this museum. Outside stands a stump puller used by pioneer farmers in clearing their land.

Huron Historic Gaol – *181 Victoria St. North. Open May–Labour Day daily 10am–4:30pm. Mar–early May & mid-Sept–Oct phone for hours ☎ 519-524-6971. $4. www.odyssey.on.ca/~hcm-chin ☎ 519-524-2686.* This unusual 150-year-old octagonal stone structure housed the county jail (*gaol* is British spelling) until 1972. The governor's house, which was constructed in 1901, can also be visited.

"The Americans are our best friends whether we like it or not."
Robert Thompson, in the House of Commons, 1960s

GRAVENHURST★

Population 10,030
Map p 128

his attractive town with its tree-lined streets, elegant houses, and opera house (now performing arts centre) on the main street lies at the southern end of the **Muskoka akes**, Ontario's most popular vacation region. Lake Joseph, Lake Rosseau and Lake luskoka itself, on which Gravenhurst stands, are picturesque bodies of water with ndented shorelines and numerous islands.

listorical Notes – Gravenhurst is the birthplace of Norman Bethune, surgeon, nventor, advocate of socialized medicine and a national hero in China. Born in Graenhurst in 1890, the son of a Presbyterian minister, Bethune studied in Toronto. He hen practised in Detroit, where he contracted tuberculosis. Confined to a sanitorium n Saranac Lake, he learned of a little-known method of treating tuberculosis by colapsing a lung and insisted that this operation be performed on him. The operation vas successful. Between 1928 and 1936, he worked as a chest surgeon in MONTREAL ut, disillusioned with the lack of interest in socialized medicine in Canada, he departed or Spain to fight on the Republican side in the civil war. There Bethune set up the irst mobile blood-transfusion unit to treat soldiers where they fell. In 1938 he went o China and worked alongside the Chinese Communists fighting the Japanese. The urgeon organized a medical service for the Chinese army, but died of blood poisoning late in 1939. Fame in his own country stemmed from Bethune's status as a hero o the Chinese.

SIGHTS

★**Bethune Memorial House National Historic Site** – *235 John St. Visit by guided tour (1hr) only, late May–late Oct daily 10am–5pm. Rest of the year Mon–Fri 10am–5pm. Closed national holidays in winter. $2.25. ♿ ☎ 705-687-4261.* The doctor's birthplace contains several rooms restored to their 1890s appearance, and an excellent **interpretive display** in three languages (English, French and Chinese) on his life and importance. A visitor centre offers an orientation video *(15min)*.

Steamship cruises – *Depart early Jun–mid-Oct daily. Round-trip 1hr 15min to 8hrs. Commentary. Reservations required. $9.95-$51.50. ✗ ♿ Muskoka Lakes Navigation www.segwun.com ☎ 705-687-6667.* Visitors can board the **RMS Segwun** at Gravenhurst's wharf to appreciate the beauty of the lakes and see some of the summer homes along their shores.

HAMILTON★

Population 322,352
Map p 128
Tourist Office ☎ 905-546-2666

The city of Hamilton lies at the extreme western end of Lake Ontario. This city has a fine landlocked harbour bounded on the lake side by a sandbar. A canal has been cut through the bar to enable ships of the seaway to reach port with their loads of iron ore for Hamilton's huge steel mills. The sandbar is crossed by Burlington Skyway, part of the **Queen Elizabeth Way (QEW)**, which connects Toronto with Niagara Falls. Hamilton is set on the Niagara Escarpment, which swings around the end of Lake Ontario at this point, rising steeply to 76m/250ft in the city. Known locally as "the mountain," it provides pleasant parks and views.

SIGHTS *Map p 138*

★**City Centre** – Hamilton has a modern downtown area *(along Main St. between Bay and James Sts.)* with many attractive buildings, in particular City Hall; the Education Centre; the Art Gallery; and Hamilton Place, a cultural centre with two theatres. A few blocks west is **Hess Village**★ *(junction Hess and George Sts.)*, a collection of attractive older homes now containing fashionable boutiques, restaurants and cafes.

Also in the vicinity is the **farmers' market** *(York Blvd.; open year-round Tue & Thu 7am–6pm, Fri 9am–6pm, Sat 6am–6pm; closed Good Friday, Dec 25-26; ♿ ☎ 905-546-2096)*, one of Ontario's largest indoor markets selling the produce of the Niagara Peninsula, Canada's chief fruit-growing region.

★**Art Gallery** – *Open year-round Wed–Sat 10am–5pm (Thu 9pm), Sun 1pm–5pm. Closed national holidays. $4. ♿ www.culturenet.ca/agh ☎ 905-527-6610.* This distinctive concrete structure stands across a plaza from City Hall. Its attractive interior is open and airy with wooden ceilings. Changing exhibits from its extensive permanent collection are displayed, as well as visiting shows.

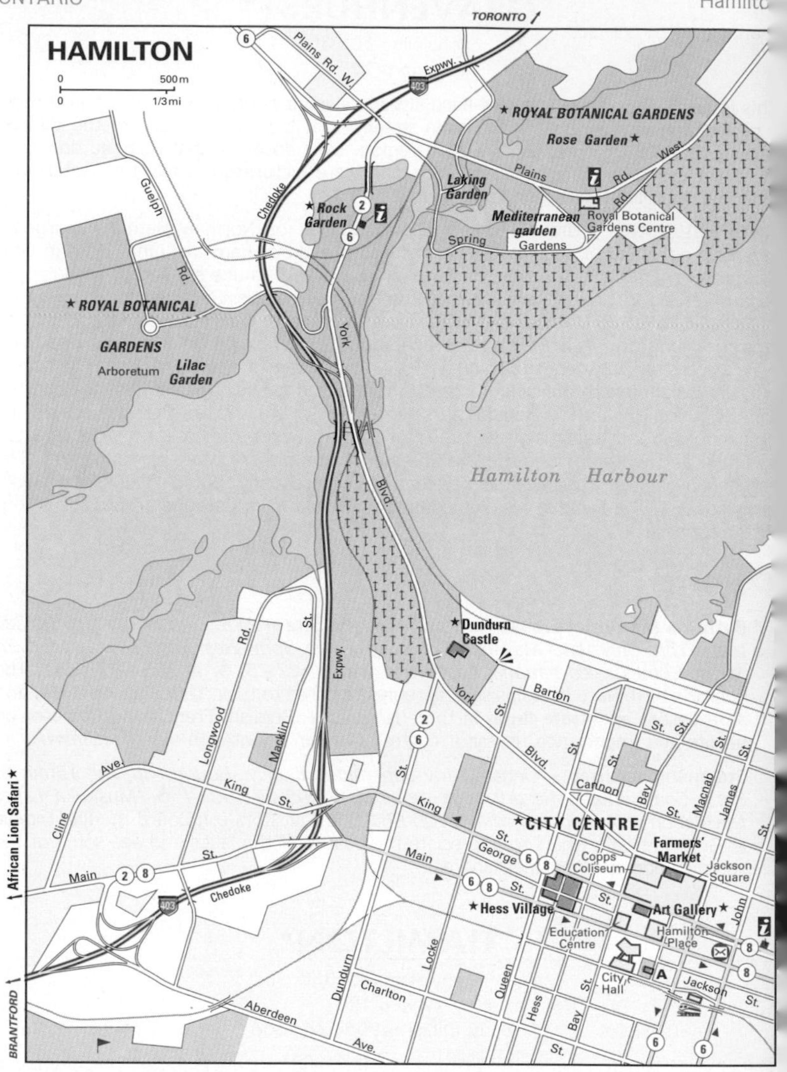

Whitehern (A) – *Visit by guided tour (1hr) only, mid-Jun–Labour Day Tues–Sun 11am–4pm. Rest of the year Tue–Sun 1pm–4pm. Closed Jan 1 & Dec 25-26. $3.50. www.city.hamilton.on.ca/cultureandrecreation ☎ 905-546-2018.* In small but pleasant gardens surrounded by Hamilton's city centre, this Georgian house was the residence of three generations of the McQuesten family until 1968. It reflects the life of a prosperous Ontario family between the years 1840 and 1960. The McQuestens, who arrived in Hamilton in the early 19C, were pioneers in the heavy industry that became Hamilton's lifeblood. Involved in public life, they inspired such projects as the Royal Botanical Gardens and the Niagara Parkway. The house contains the original furnishings.

★ **Dundurn Castle** – *Visit by guided tour (1hr) only, Jun–Aug daily 10am–4:30pm. Rest of the year Tue–Sun noon–4pm. Closed Jan 1 & Dec 25. $6. ☎ 905-546-2872.* This grand stone house with its Neoclassical portico entry stands on a hill overlooking Hamilton Bay. A showplace of 19C privilege, it illustrates the wealth and power of the Family Compact *(p 129)*.

The residence was completed in 1835 by Sir Allan Napier MacNab—soldier, lawyer, politician and member of the Family Compact. In 1838 he was knighted by Queen Victoria for fighting against Mackenzie. From 1854 to 1856 MacNab served as prime minister of the Province of Canada.

The interior is elaborately furnished, though the contents are not original. Of particular interest is the basement, the domain of the army of servants needed to run a house of this magnitude in the mid-19C. (MacNab actually died in debt, however.) The house is situated in Dundurn Park, which commands a good **view** of the bay and the city. A small military museum is situated in the grounds.

★**Royal Botanical Gardens** – *Open May–Oct daily 9:30am–dusk. Rest of the year daily 9:30am–6pm. Closed Dec 25. $7. www.rbg.ca ☎905-527-1158.* These gardens occupy 1,000ha/2,700 acres of land at the western tip of Lake Ontario. Much of this area is natural parkland with walking trails. Several featured gardens are worth visiting *(car required)*.
At the Royal Botanical Gardens Centre, the **Mediterranean garden** can be visited. This conservatory houses vegetation from the five regions of the world that have this climate (the Mediterranean Rim, Southern Africa, Australia, California and Chile). Across the road the **rose garden**★ features magnificent displays *(Jun–Oct)*. Nearby, the **Laking garden** abounds in irises and peonies *(May–Jun)*, and herbaceous perennials *(May–Oct)*. Farther afield, the **rock garden**★ is a whirl of colour in summer, with its flowering plants and shrubs set amid water and rocks. In the arboretum *(return along York Blvd. and turn right)*, the **lilac garden** is especially lovely *(late May–early Jun)*.

★**Museum of Steam and Technology** – *900 Woodward Ave., just south of Queen Elizabeth Way (QEW). Visit by guided tour (1hr 30min) only, Jun–Labour Day Tue–Sun 11am–4pm; rest of the year Tue–Sun noon–4pm. Closed Jan 1 & Dec 25. $3.50. www.city.hamilton.on.ca/cultureandrecreation ☎905-546-4797.* Hamilton's former water-pumping station, completed in 1859, now provides a rare example of 19C steam technology. Architecturally interesting with its arches and cast-iron Doric columns, the engine house contains two Gartshore steam-powered beam engines of 1859 in full working order. They once pumped as much as 5 million gallons of water a day, until they were replaced in 1910. The old boiler house has displays on the use of steam power and a working model of the beam engines.

EXCURSION

★**African Lion Safari** – Kids *32km/20mi northwest by Hwy. 8, right on Rte. 52N after Rockton and left on Safari Rd. Open late Apr–late Oct Mon–Fri 10am–4pm, weekends 10am–5pm. $16.95. www.lionsafari.com ☎519-623-2620.* Visitors drive their own cars *(safari tram available at additional cost)* through various enclosures of African and North American free-roaming animals. One enclosure called the monkey jungle contains about 70 African baboons that will climb over your car and steal any removeable part they can.

KINGSTON and the THOUSAND ISLANDS★★

Map p 129

The city of Kingston lies on the north shore of Lake Ontario, at the point where the St. Lawrence River leaves the lake in a channel full of islands.

★★KINGSTON

Tourist Office ☎613-548-4415

This one-time capital of the Province of Canada owes its political and economic development to its location at the junction of Lake Ontario and the St. Lawrence River. One of the main shipbuilding centres on the Great Lakes in the 19C, the former colonial stronghold is home to several military colleges.

Historical Notes – On the site of the present city in 1673, a French fur-trading post, called Cataraqui and Fort Frontenac at various times in its history, was established. Abandoned when New France fell, the area was later resettled by Loyalists, who called their community Kingston. The settlement soon became an important British naval base and dockyard, and a fort was built to protect it during the War of 1812. After the war Kingston's importance increased with the building of the Rideau Canal and of a stone fortress, Fort Henry. Having served as capital of the Province of Canada from 1841 to 1843, Kingston lost that honour, but remained a vital military centre. Today the **Royal Military College** (Fort Frederick), the Canadian Army Staff College and the National Defence College are evidence of the military's continuing presence. Kingston is a pleasant city, with tree-lined streets, parks, and public buildings constructed of local limestone. Among these is the handsome **City Hall**★ in Confederation Park on the harbour, built as a potential home for parliament; the **Court House**★ with a small dome similar to that of City Hall; the **Cathedral of St. George**, which is reminiscent of Christopher Wren's London churches; the **Grant Hall** building of Queen's University; and some of the buildings of the Royal Military College.

Sights *1/2 day*

★**Marine Museum of the Great Lakes** – *Open May–Oct daily 10am–5pm. Rest of the year Mon–Fri 10am–4pm. Closed Jan 1 & Dec 25. $3.95. www.MarMus.ca ☎613-542-2261.* Set in old shipbuilding works beside Lake Ontario, this museum has displays on sail and steam vessels that have plied the Great Lakes. An interesting shipbuilders' gallery explains various construction methods, and a special section is devoted to Kingston's shipbuilding days. There are audio-visual presentations and changing exhibits on various aspects of marine life.

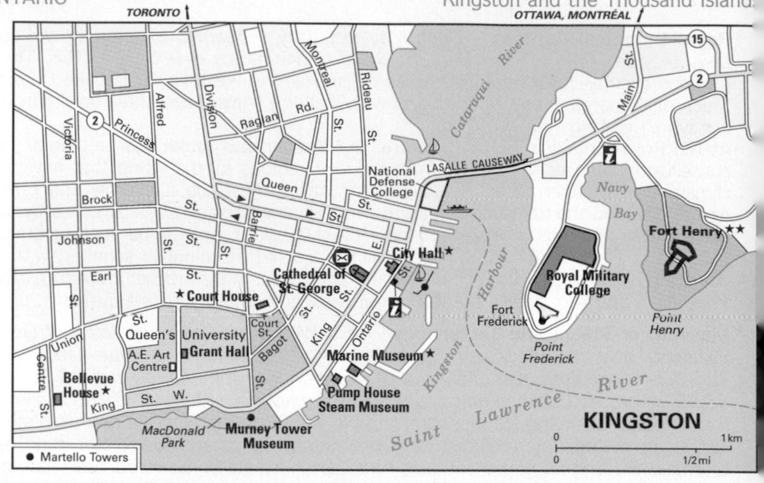

Pump House Steam Museum – *Open Jun–Labour Day daily 10am–5pm. $3.95. www.Mar.Mus.ca ☎613-546-2261.* Kingston's 1849 pumping station has been restored to pay tribute to Canada's steam age. Among the many machines and scale models are two enormous steam pumps once used in the pump house, restored as they were in 1897.

Murney Tower Museum – *Open mid-May–Labour Day daily 10am–5pm. $2. ☎613-544-9925.* This squat stone tower in a pleasant park beside the lake is one of Kingston's Martello towers, a National Historic Site. It is in good repair with fine stonework and vaulting. Inside, living quarters of the garrison have been re-created, and the gun platform with its 15kg/32lb cannon on a circular traverse can be seen.

★**Bellevue House** – *Open Jun–Labour Day daily 9am–6pm. Apr–May & mid-Sept–Oct daily 10am–5pm. $2.75. //parkscanada.pch.gc.ca/parks/ontario/bellevuehouse.htm ☎613-545-8666.* Variously named the "Pekoe pagoda" and "Tea Caddy Castle," this somewhat exotic Italian-styled villa contrasts sharply with Kingston's more traditional stone buildings. When completed (c.1840), it caused quite a sensation and, for a short time (1848 to 1849), served as the residence of Canada's first prime minister.

A Scot by birth, **Sir John A. Macdonald** (1815-91) spent much of his youth in Kingston, and opened his first law office in the city in 1835. He went on to enter provincial politics, becoming one of the chief architects of Canadian Confederation in 1867. During his terms in office (1867-73, 1878-91), the building of the Canadian Pacific Railway was the realization of one of his dreams. The house is furnished to reflect Macdonald's time of residence. In the visitor centre there are exhibits and an introductory film *(8min)*.

★★**Fort Henry** – *Open mid-May–late Sept daily 10am–5pm. Rest of the year by appointment. $9. ☎613-542-7388.* Completed in 1837 this large, exceedingly strong stone fortress is set on a peninsula above Lake Ontario. Its main defences face inland, expressly to guard the land approach to the naval dockyard at Point Frederick. The water approaches were covered by Martello towers built later. Having never been attacked, the fort eventually fell into decay. Restored in 1938, it is now best known for the **Fort Henry Guard**, a troop of specially trained students who re-create the life of the 19C British soldier, guide visitors around the restored quarters and storerooms, and perform military manoeuvres. In particular, the **commandant's parade** should not be missed *(daily)*.

★★THE THOUSAND ISLANDS

Tourist Office ☎315-482-2520

As it leaves Lake Ontario, the St. Lawrence River is littered, for an 80km/50mi stretch, with about 1,000 islands (the exact number varies from 995 to 1,010, depending upon how many boulders are counted as islands!). Among the oldest and most popular vacation areas in northeastern North America, the islands with their sparkling waters and pink granite rocks attract Americans and Canadians.

All of the islands are of Precambrian rock, the remnants of the **Frontenac Axis**, which links the Canadian Shield with the Adirondacks of New York state. The islands are large and lushly forested, small with a few ragged pine trees, or barren—mere boulders of rock worn smooth by retreating glaciers. The international border passes among them, leaving the greater number on the Canadian side.

Visit *Allow 1/2 day*

★★ **Boat Trip** – *Departs from Crawford Wharf in Kingston May–Oct daily; round-trip 3hrs; commentary; reservations suggested; $18;* ✗ ♿ *Kingston 1000 Islands Cruises www.1000islandcruises.on.ca ☎ 613-549-5544. Also cruises from Gananoque (28km/17mi northeast of Kingston by Rte. 2) depart from customs dock late Jun–late Sept daily; round-trip 3hrs; commentary; $16;* ✗ *Gananoque Boat Lines www.ganboatline.com ☎ 613-382-2144. Cruises from Ivy Lea (10km/6mi north of Gananoque by Hwy. 648) depart daily mid-May–mid-Nov; round-trip 1hr 30min; commentary; $11;* ♿ *Gananoque Boat Lines www.ganboatline.com ☎ 613-659-2293. From Rockport (7km/4mi northeast of Ivy Lea by Hwy. 648) cruises depart May–Oct daily 9am–5pm; round-trip 1hr; commentary; reservations suggested; $11.25;* ♿ 🅿 *Rockport Boat Line www.rockportcruises.com ☎ 613-659-3402.* This relaxing cruise through the maze of islands affords views of trees, rock and water interspersed at times with summer homes. These dwellings range from small shacks on rocky islets to the palaces of Millionaire's Row on Wellesley Island. The huge ships of the St. Lawrence Seaway, which follows the American coast, can be seen alongside private cruisers, yachts and canoes. A stop can be made at Heart Island to visit **Boldt Castle**, built by a German immigrant at great cost, but never finished *(in US, non-Americans must have identification to land).*

★ **Thousand Islands Parkway** – *Map p 129. Begins 3km/1.8mi east of Gananoque at Interchange 648 (Hwy. 401); 37km/23mi to Interchange 685 (Hwy. 401), south of Brockville.* This scenic drive follows the shore of the St. Lawrence, offering many good views. The **Skydeck** *(open Jun–Labour Day daily 8:30am–8:30pm; mid-Apr–May & mid-Sept–mid-Oct daily 8:30am–6pm; $6.95;* ✗ ♿ *☎ 613-659-2335)* on Hill Island provides a fine **view**★ of the islands and surrounding area *(take bridge to island, toll $2; do not enter US).*

At Mallorytown Landing the headquarters of the **St. Lawrence Islands National Park** can be visited *(open daily mid-May–mid-Oct; for use fees, contact the park office;* ♿ *http://parkscanada.pch.gc.ca ☎ 613-923-5261).* Beside the visitor centre, a hut encloses the remains of the wreck of an early-19C gun boat.

Malak, Ottawa

The Thousands Islands

For a listing of selected French terms used in this guide, see p 227.

KITCHENER–WATERLOO

Population 256,369
Map p 128
Tourist Office ☎519-748-0800

Attractive, orderly and clean, these twin industrial cities in Southern Ontario reflect their German heritage. The skills and industriousness of their immigrant founders created a diverse economy still evident today.

Historical Notes – At the beginning of the 19C, the first settlers here were Pennsylvania Dutch or **Mennonites**, a Protestant sect persecuted in Europe for its religious ideas and pacifism (members refused to serve in any army). Many emigrated to Pennsylvania in the 17C, but during the American Revolution, their pacifism again got them into trouble. Many moved with the Loyalists to Ontario, where they were granted land in the Kitchener area. Strict Mennonites live a simple, frugal life as farmers. They use no modern machinery, cars or telephones. They can sometimes be seen in the country to the north and west of Kitchener–Waterloo, driving along in horse-drawn buggies that display a fluorescent triangle on the back as a modern-day safety precaution. The men wear black suits and wide hats, the women ankle-length black dresses and small bonnets *(see also p 124)*.

Other German-speaking people came to this area in the 19C, and the German influence remains strong. Every fall there is a nine-day **Oktoberfest** featuring German food and drink, oompah-pah bands and dancing. At the **farmers' market** *(entrance Market Sq. at Frederick & Duke Sts.; St. Jacobs Market: year-round Thu & Sat 7am–3pm, also Tue in summer; Kitchener Market: year-round Sat 6am–2pm)*, German specialties are for sale. On Queen Street stands the **Centre in the Square**, which comprises a concert hall, studio theatre and art gallery.

SIGHTS

Woodside National Historic Site – *528 Wellington St. North, Kitchener. Open mid-May–mid-Dec daily 10am–5pm. Closed Remembrance Day. $2.50. //parkscanada.pch.gc.ca/parks/woodside.htm ☎519-571-5684.* This low-lying brick Victorian house stands in an attractive park. Built in 1853 it was for some years the boyhood home of **William Lyon Mackenzie King**, prime minister of Canada 1921-26, 1926-30, 1935-48. The house has been restored to reflect the period of King's residence in the 1890s. In a theatre located in the basement, an audio-visual presentation *(14min)* provides an introduction, and there is an excellent **display** on King's life and association with Woodside. The influence of his grandfather, the rebel leader William Lyon Mackenzie, is of particular note.

Joseph Schneider Haus – *466 Queen St. South, Kitchener. Open mid-Jun–Labour Day Mon–Sat 10am–5pm, Sun 1pm–5pm. Mid-Feb–early Jun & mid-Sept–mid-Dec Wed–Sat 10am–5pm, Sun 1pm–5pm. $2.25. www.region.waterloo.on.ca/jsh ☎519-742-7752.* This Georgian frame house was built about 1820 by Kitchener's founder, Joseph Schneider. It is restored and furnished to the period of the mid-1850s. Special events and seasonal activities reflect the family's Mennonite roots.

Doon Heritage Crossroads – Kids *About 3km/2mi from Hwy. 401; Exit 275; turn north. Open May–Aug daily 10am–4:30pm. Sept–Dec Mon–Fri 10am–4:30pm. $5.50. ♿ www.region.waterloo.on.ca/doon ☎519-748-1914.* Many authentic buildings have been removed to this site to depict a small rural Waterloo village c.1914. The visitor centre's orientation video *(8min)* incorporates vintage photographs from the sight's archival collection. Throughout the village costumed interpreters demonstrate daily activities typical of rural life. The two-storey frame house at the **Peter Martin Farm**, originally constructed c.1820, has been restored to its 1914 appearance and permits an overview of Mennonite family life.

LONDON★

Population 325,646
Map p 128
Tourist Office ☎519-661-5000

This major industrial centre serves Ontario's rich agricultural south. London is also the location of the University of Western Ontario.

In 1792 **John Graves Simcoe**, lieutenant-governor of Upper Canada (now Ontario), chose the present site of London as his capital. He considered the existing administrative centre, Niagara-on-the-Lake, too close to the American border. Simcoe named the site for the British capital and called the river on which it stood the Thames. However, approval of the choice of capital from higher authorities was never forthcoming, and York (TORONTO) received the honour instead. Today London is a pleasant city of tree-lined streets and attractive houses.

SIGHTS

★**Regional Art and Historical Museum** – *421 Ridout St. North. Open year-round Tue–Sun noon–5pm. Closed Dec 25. Contribution requested. ✗ ♿ ☎519-672-4580.* Set in a park overlooking the river Thames, this spectacular museum is remarkable chiefly for its architecture. Designed by Toronto architect Raymond Moriyama, and opened in 1980, the structure of concrete barrel vaults covered by aluminum and baked enamel is unusual. Each vault contains skylights—Moriyama's answer to the problem of providing indirect natural lighting without damaging the art. The result is a series of airy and spacious galleries where changing exhibits are displayed. Selections from the permanent Canadian collection of 18C and 19C works are usually on view. The historical museum features exhibits on the city's past.

★**Eldon House** – *481 Ridout St. North. Open year-round Tue–Sun noon–5pm. Closed Dec 25. $3 (contribution only Tue & Sun). ☎519-672-4580.* Just north of a series of restored Georgian houses stands this large and elegant frame residence, completely surrounded by a veranda. Constructed in 1834 by John Harris, a retired Royal Navy captain, London's oldest house was for many years a centre of social and cultural activities in 19C Southern Ontario. Its furnishings reflect a refined way of life at a time when most pioneer settlers were living in log cabins. Owned by four generations of the Harris family, the house was donated to the City of London. The library and drawing room are particularly noteworthy.

EXCURSIONS

Fanshawe Pioneer Village – Kids *In Fanshawe Park, 15km/9mi northeast. Open May–mid-Dec Wed–Sun 10am–4:30pm. $5. ✗ www.pioneer.wwdc.com ☎519-457-1296.* This reconstructed 19C community is part of a large park beside Fanshawe Lake, a reservoir constructed to control flooding by the river Thames. The village contains several houses and shops, the Lochaber Presbyterian Church with a Gaelic bible, a fire hall, and an Orange Lodge—the social centre of the community. A Protestant fraternity founded in Ireland in 1795 and named for William III (of Orange), the **Orange Order** had considerable influence in the foundation of Ontario. Costumed guides lend life to the village.

Ska-Nah-Doht Iroquoian Village – *In Longwoods Road Conservation Area, 32km/20mi southwest by Hwy. 2. Open Jul–Labour Day Mon–Fri 9am–4:30pm, weekends & holidays 10am–5pm. Rest of the year Mon–Fri 9am–4:30pm. $2.75. ♿ www.lowerthames-conservation.on.ca ☎519-264-2420.* This village is a re-creation of the type inhabited by Iroquois in Ontario 800 to 1,000 years ago. These Indians cultivated the land, trapped animals and fished.

The village is surrounded by a stake palisade with a complicated entrance to make it easy to defend. Inside, daily life is depicted through displays and artifacts such as three longhouses where the families lived, a primitive sauna called a sweat lodge, drying racks for smoking meat, stretching racks for hides, storage pits and a fish trap. In the fields outside the palisade, corn, squash and tobacco crops are grown. The park visitor centre nearby features audio-visual programs and displays.

NIAGARA FALLS★★★

Map p 128

Tourist Office ☎905-356-6061

Roughly halfway along its course from Lake Erie to Lake Ontario, the Niagara Rive suddenly changes its level by plunging over an immense cliff, creating one of earth' great natural wonders. These famous falls are the most visited in the world, attrac ting more than 12 million people a year.

In the 19C Niagara was a hucksters' paradise where every conceivable ruse wa employed to separate tourists from their money. The Province of Ontario and the Stat of New York stepped in, buying all the land on both sides of the river adjacent to th falls. Today beautiful parks full of flowers line the riverbank. Hucksterism still exist in the city of Niagara Falls, but visitors can enjoy the natural dignity of the falls withou being bothered.

Geographical Notes

Two Cataracts – There are, in fact, two sets of falls separated by tiny Goat Islanc which stands at their brink. The **American Falls** (so-called because they are on the U. side of the river) are 300m/1,000ft wide and more than 50m/160ft high. The Cana dian or **Horseshoe Falls** (named for their shape) are nearly 800m/2,600ft wide, abou the same height, and contain 90 percent of the water allowed to flow down the river It is the latter falls that people think of as Niagara.

Diverting the Waters – The river's water volume varies by hour and season. By mean of canals, major power developments divert up to 75 percent of the water above th falls to generating stations downstream. Flow of water over the falls is reduced a night when additional electricity is needed to illuminate them. In winter so much wate is diverted that the falls partially freeze—a spectacular sight. Standing on the brin of the falls, watching the mighty rush of water, visitors should consider today's wate diversion and try to imagine the cataract's appearance in 1678 when **Louis Hennepi** was the first European to view them. Hennepin heard such a mighty noise on Lak Ontario that he followed the river upstream to discover its source.

Erosion of the Falls – In geological terms the falls are not old. At the end of the las Ice Age, the waters of Lake Erie created an exit channel for themselves to old Lak Iroquois. The edge of the ancient lake was the present-day Niagara Escarpment, ove which this new river plunged to the lake. The water's force immediately began t erode the underlying soft shale, causing the harder limestone to break off. A gorg was eventually created.

Today the waters of Lake Iroquois have receded to the present level of Lake Ontaric and the Niagara River has cut a gorge some 11km/7mi back from the edge of th escarpment at Queenston to the present position of the falls *(map p 147)*. In anothe 25,000 years or so, unless mankind intervenes, the gorge will extend back to Lak Erie, and the falls as we know them will practically cease to exist.

Niagara Falls

SIGHTS

Operated by Niagara Parks Commission, the People Mover stops at more than 20 attractions along Niagara Parkway from the falls to Queenston Heights Park. Shuttle buses run every 20min mid-Jun–early Sept daily 9am–11pm. Apr–early Jun & mid-Sept–mid-Oct daily 10am–6pm (Sat 10pm). Onboard commentary. Tickets obtainable at main terminal, 7369 Niagara Parkway (southwest of the falls), or from People Mover booths along the parkway; $4.50 (unlimited boarding throughout the day). Parking available at main terminal $13/car; People Mover tickets are included in the parking fee.

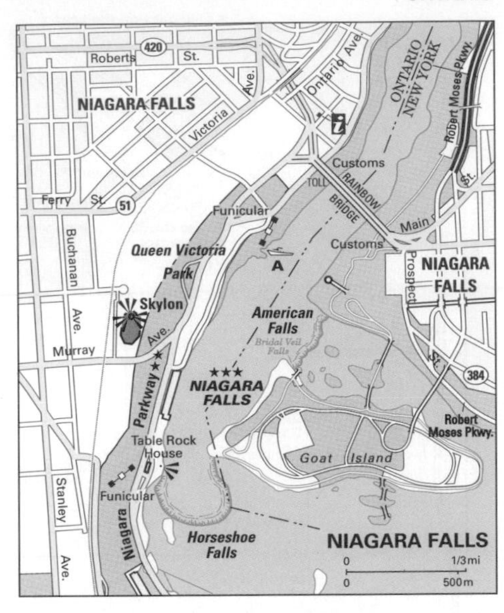

★★★The Falls

The falls can be viewed from the riverbank level, from the water level at the bottom of the cataract and from the summit of various towers constructed especially for viewing purposes.

★★★The Walk from Rainbow Bridge to Table Rock – *About 1.6km/1mi.* From Rainbow Bridge visitors can wander along the bank beside the river, passing **Queen Victoria Park** and its beautiful flowers *(especially lovely in April when daffodils are in bloom)*. The American Falls are in view, and it is possible to stand on the brink of Horseshoe Falls at Table Rock. Watching the water cascade over the edge is an impressive experience. In Table Rock House, elevators descend to enable visitors to walk along **tunnels★** to see this immense curtain of falling water *(open Jun–Aug daily 9am–9pm; rest of the year daily 9am–5pm; closed Dec 25; $6; ♿ www.niagaraparks.com ☎877-642-7275, Canada/US)*.

★★★Maid of the Mist (A) – *Access from River Rd. Elevator & boat ride (weather permitting). Departs from Maid of the Mist Plaza Apr–May 21 & mid-Sept–late Oct Mon–Fri 10am–5pm, weekends 10am–6pm. Hours vary rest of May–Labour Day (phone ahead). Round-trip 30min. Commentary. $10.65. ♿ Maid of the Mist Steamboat Co. Ltd. www.maidofthemist.com ☎905-358-0311.* This boat trip is exciting, memorable and wet *(visitors are equipped with raincoats and hoods)*. After passing the American Falls, the boat goes to the foot of the horseshoe cataract, the best spot to appreciate the mighty force of the water.

★★★The View from Above – Three towers in Niagara Falls provide a spectacular elevated **view★★★** of the cataract. The best view is from the **Skylon** *(Robinson St.; open Jun–Labour Day daily 8am–midnight; rest of the year daily 10am–11pm; $7.95 ✕ ♿ ☎905-356-2651)*, which looks like a miniature CN Tower *(p 169)* and is ascended by exterior elevators known as yellow bugs.

Additional Sights *Maps p 146 and p 147*

Niagara Parkway (north)★★ follows the river to its junction with Lake Ontario. Maintained by the Niagara Parks Commission, the parkway has good viewpoints and attractive gardens. From the falls the parkway passes under Rainbow Bridge, through a pleasant residential area and past the Whirlpool Bridge.

★★Great Gorge Adventure – *Open mid-Jun–Labour Day daily 9am–8pm. Late Apr–early Jun & mid-Sept–late Oct daily 9am–5pm. $5. www.niagaraparks.com ☎877-642-7275 (Canada/US).* An elevator descends to the bottom of the gorge. It is here that visitors can see some of the world's most hazardous water thundering, broiling and rising into huge **rapids★★**.

★★The Whirlpool – A colourful Spanish aerocar *(weather permitting, operates Jun–Labour Day daily 9am–9pm; Mar–May & mid-Sept–Oct daily 10am–5pm; $5.25; ✕ 🅿 www.niagaraparks.com ☎877-642-7275, Canada/US)* crosses the gorge high above the river, with excellent **views★★** of the water as it swirls around the whirlpool and the rocky gorge. After another 1.5km/1mi, visitors reach the far side of the whirlpool. Thompson's Point scenic look provides a fine **view★**.

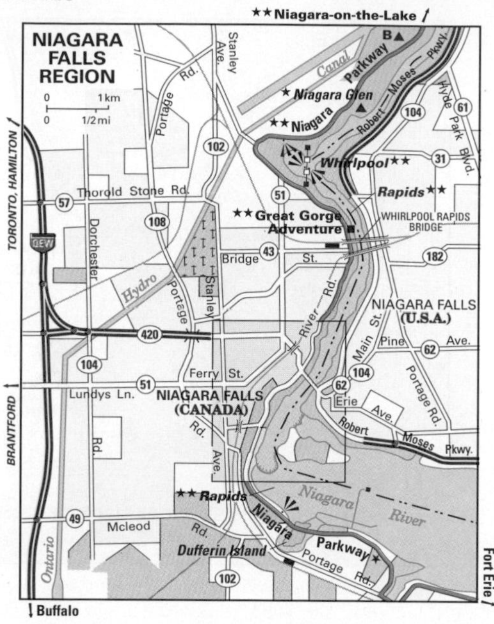

★**Niagara Glen** – There is a view of the river from above. Trails lead to the water's edge *(15min to descend, 30min to ascend)*.

★**Niagara Parks Botanical Gardens** (**B**) – *Open year-round daily 9am–dusk.* *www.niagaraparks.com ☎877-642-7275 (Canada/US).* Beautiful plantings of flowers, shrubs and trees are maintained by students of the Niagara Parks Commission School of Horticulture, which offers a three-year course. The **rose garden**★ is particularly lovely in early June. A recent addition to the gardens is the 1,022sq m/11,000sq ft **butterfly conservatory**, which shelters some 2,000 butterflies in climate-controlled comfort *(open late Jun–early Sept daily 9am–9pm; rest of the year daily 9am–5pm; closed Dec 25; $7.50)*.

The industrial sector of Niagara is reached about 1.6km/1mi from the botanical gardens. Across the river on the US side, the immense **Robert Moses Generating Station** can be seen.

Farther on, still on the Canadian side, the **Sir Adam Beck Generating Station** is visible. These two large stations use water diverted from the river above the falls to generate electricity.

Just after the power stations, be sure to note the large **floral clock**.

★**Queenston Heights** – *Open daily year-round.* These heights are part of the Niagara Escarpment and were once the location of Niagara Falls. Today they have been made into a pleasant park that provides good views of the river. At the centre of the park stands a monument to **Gen. Sir Isaac Brock**, the Canadian military hero of the War of 1812. The heights were captured by the Americans during the war. Brock was killed while leading the charge to recapture them. The heights were recaptured, and now Brock's statue overlooks them from the top of his monument.

EXCURSIONS *Map p 147*

From Queenston to Niagara-on-the-Lake

3hrs with visits. 12km/7mi.

★**Queenston** – This village at the foot of the escarpment has attractive houses and gardens.

Laura Secord Homestead – *Partition St. Visit by guided tour (20min) only, mid-May–Jun daily 9am–4pm. Jul–Labour Day daily 10am–5pm. $1.75 ☎905-262-4851.* In 1813 Laura Secord set out from her home in enemy-held Queenston and walked 30km/19mi through the bush to warn the British of a surprise attack planned by the Americans. Forewarned, the British won a great victory at the subsequent Battle of Beaver Dams. Her rather plain house has been beautifully restored by the candy company named after this Canadian heroine. An interpretive display about Secord's life stands outside.

As visitors continue along the parkway, they can look back to see the statue of General Brock *(above)* at the summit of the escarpment. For the remainder of the drive to Niagara-on-the-Lake, there are several parks with picnic tables, and occasional fine views of the river. In summer, stalls selling the produce of the Niagara Peninsula line the route.

★★**Niagara-on-the-Lake** – *12km/7mi.* Situated at the north end of the Niagara River where it joins Lake Ontario, this town resembles a picturesque English village. Settled by Loyalists, it was the first capital of Upper Canada. Burned to the ground by the Americans in 1813, it was rebuilt soon afterwards, and seems to have remained unchanged. The town is filled with tree-lined streets and gracious 19C houses with lovely gardens. Pleasant shops, restaurants, teahouses, hotels and the

Niagara Apothecary, an 1866 pharmacy *(open May–Labour Day daily noon–6pm; ♿ ☎905-468-3845)* line a wide, main thoroughfare, **Queen Street★**, with a clock tower at its centre. Niagara-on-the-Lake is also a cultural centre, home to the **Shaw Festival**, a season of theatre devoted to the works of the Irish playwright, **George Bernard Shaw** (1856-1950).

The main theatre, a brick structure with a beautiful wood interior, stands at the junction of Queen's Parade and Wellington Street. There are two other theatres in the town. *For details regarding performances (Apr–Oct Tue–Sun), contact the Box Office, PO Box 774, Niagara-on-the-Lake, ON, L0S 1J0 ☎905-468-2172 or 800-267-4759 (Canada/US).*

★**Fort George** – *On River Rd. near the theatre. Open Apr–Oct daily 10am–5pm. Rest of the year by appointment. $6. ♿ ☎905-468-6614.* Built by the British in the 1790s, this fort played a key role in the War of 1812, being alternately captured by the Americans and recaptured by the British. Restored in the 1930s, it has grassy earthworks and a wooden palisade enclosing officers' quarters, a forge, powder magazine, guard house and three blockhouse barracks of 25cm/10in thick timbers housing military displays. Costumed staff demonstrate activities of the period.

★★Welland Canal

From Niagara-on-the-Lake, take Niagara Stone Rd. (Rte. 55) to its end; turn left on the south service road, right on Coon Rd. to Glendale Ave.; turn right and cross the canal as above.

From Niagara Falls, take Queen Elizabeth Way (QEW) to St. Catharines; exit at Glendale Ave. interchange, follow Glendale Ave. and cross the canal by the lift bridge; turn right or left on canal service road (Government Rd.).

The early explorers and fur traders portaged their canoes around the falls and rapids on the Niagara River, but navigation of any larger watercraft between Lakes Ontario and Erie was impossible until canals and locks were built in the 19C. The present canal, which is part of the St. Lawrence Seaway system, is 45km/28mi long, crossing the Niagara Peninsula between St. Catharines and Port Colborne. The canal's eight locks raise ships a total of 99m/326ft—the difference in the level between the two lakes.

★★**The Drive along the Canal** – *About 14km/9mi from Lake Ontario to Thorold on Government Rd.* There are fine views of the huge ships on the seaway negotiating seven of the eight locks of this section. Just north of the lift bridge at Lock 3, the visitor centre *(open mid-May–Labour Day daily 9am–9pm; rest of the year daily 9am–5pm; closed Jan 1, Dec 24–25; ✗ ♿ ☎905-984-8880 or 800-305-5134)* includes a convenient **viewing platform★** of the seaway. The times ships pass through the lock are posted and are fairly continuous *(it takes about half an hour for a ship to negotiate a lock)*. Locks 4, 5 and 6 in Thorold raise ships over the Niagara Escarpment. They are twin-flight locks having two parallel sets of locks, so that one ship can be elevated as another comes down.

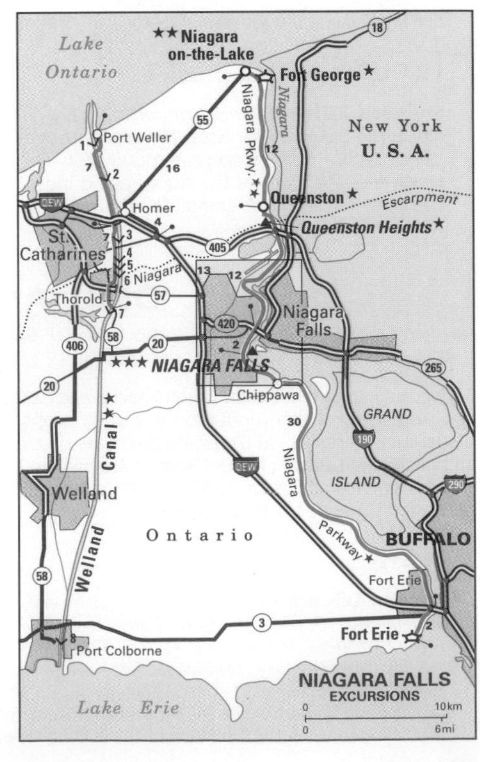

From the Falls to Fort Erie

1hr. 32km/20mi.

Rushing along at 48km/h (30mph), Niagara River is impressive, revealing its **rapids★★** as it prepares to plunge over the cliff. **Niagara Parkway (south)★** crosses to **Dufferin Island**,

where a pleasant park *(open year-round daily dawn–dusk)* has hiking trails, stream and a swimming area. The parkway passes the large international control dam and gates that divert water along canals to the generating stations downstream. In complete contrast to its lower stretch, the river slowly becomes a broad, quietly flowing stream. There are some pleasant views of the US shore and Grand Island.
At the city of **Fort Erie**, the Peace Bridge crosses the river to the large American city of **Buffalo**. There are good **views★** of the Buffalo skyline.

Historic Fort Erie – *Open mid-May–early Sept daily 10am–6pm. Rest of Sept daily 10am–4pm. $5. ✗ www.niagaraparks.com ☎877-642-7275 (Canada/US).* A reconstruction of the third fort built on this site, the star-shaped stone stronghold is set at the mouth of Lake Erie. The first two forts were destroyed by storm and flood, the third by the Americans in 1814. Visitors enter by a drawbridge and can tour reconstructed officers' quarters, barracks, a guard house and powder magazine. Students in early-19C uniforms perform manoeuvres and serve as guides.

NORTH BAY★

Population 54,332
Map p 128
Tourist Office ☎705-472-8480

This resort centre on the shores of **Lake Nipissing** was located on the old canoe route to the West. The La Vase portage connected the waters of Trout Lake and the Ottawa and Mattawa Rivers with Lake Nipissing, the French River and Georgian Bay. Today these waters are used solely for recreational purposes. From the government dock on Main Street, there are **cruises** across Lake Nipissing and down the attractive French River, with several stops *(depart from Government Dock, Memorial Dr., early Jun–Labour Day; round-trip 1hr 30min–5hrs; commentary; reservations required; $8–20; ✗ ♿; for schedules & reservations, contact the City of North Bay ☎ 705-474-0400 or 705-494-8167)*.
North Bay is also the centre of a rich fur-trapping industry. Four times a year *(Dec, Feb, Apr, Jun)* beaver, marten, muskrat and other furs are auctioned at Fur Harvesters Auction, Inc., which ranks among the largest in the world *(1867 Bond St.; for information www.trillium.net/fha ☎ 705-495-4688)*.

SIGHT

Quints' Museum – *Beside tourist office on Hwy. 11/17. Open Jul–Aug daily 9am–7pm. Mid-May–Jun & Sept–mid-Oct daily 9am–5pm. $2.75. ☎ 705-472-8480.* On May 28, 1934 the **Dionne quintuplets** were born in this house. These five little girls quickly became the world's sweethearts. The museum displays "quint" memorabilia.

EXCURSION *Map p 128*

Sturgeon Falls – *37km/23mi west by Hwy. 17.* Just southwest of this community is the **Sturgeon River House Museum** *(museum closed for renovation until summer 1999; nature trails open year-round Mon–Fri 10am–4pm; $3; ☎ 705-753-4716)*, which tells the story of the fur-trapping industry. Exhibits include a Hudson's Bay Company trading post complete with equipment, pelts that can be touched and a wide range of traps.

ORILLIA★

Population 27,846
Map p 128

Set on the narrows between Lakes Simcoe and Couchiching, this small industrial centre and resort town has a reputation out of all proportion to its size. Orilla served as the model for "Mariposa" in *Sunshine Sketches of a Little Town* by famed humourist and author **Stephen Leacock** (1869-1944). Possibly the best known of Canada's literati, this political-science professor at McGill University spent his summers here, finding inspiration for some of his finest works.

SIGHT

★**Stephen Leacock Museum** – *In Old Brewery Bay off Hwy. 12 Bypass. Open mid-Jun–Labour Day daily 10am–7pm. Rest of the year daily 10am–5pm. $7. ✗ www.transdata.ca/~leacock ☎ 705-329-1908.* Set amid pleasant grounds overlooking Brewery Bay, this attractive house was designed and built by Leacock in 1928. The nonsensical, uproarious humour of this man, who stated he would rather have written *Alice in Wonderland* than the whole of the *Encyclopaedia Britannica*, pervades the house and the tour guides.

OSHAWA★★

Population 134,364
Map p 128
Tourist Office ☎905-728-1683

'his industrial city on the north shore of Lake Ontario is one of the main centres of :anada's automobile industry. Its name has long been synonymous with industrialist ınd philanthropist **Robert S. McLaughlin** (1871-1972).

SIGHTS *3hrs*

★★**Parkwood Estate** – *270 Simcoe St. North, 2.5km/1.5mi north of Hwy. 401. Mansion: visit by guided tour (1hr) only, Jun–Labour Day Tue–Sun 10:30am–4pm. Rest of the year Tue–Sun 1:30pm–4pm. $6. ✗ (summer only) ☎905-433-4311.* This gracious, imposing residence was built by McLaughlin in 1917. Bequeathed by him to Oshawa General Hospital, the house is open to the public, maintained by the hospital as it was at his death.

Apprenticed in his father's carriage works, McLaughlin converted the manufacturing business into a motor company, and used an American engine in his famous **McLaughlin Buick**. In 1918 he sold the company to the General Motors Corp. of the US, but remained chairman of the Canadian division, whose main plant is in Oshawa.

A visit to Parkwood provides insight into the lifestyle of the immensely wealthy McLaughlin family. Beautifully and tastefully appointed, the house contains priceless antiques from all over the world. Every room has furnishings of the finest woods and fabrics representing the work of skilled craftsmen.

This gem of a house is set in some of the most beautiful **gardens** in the eastern half of Canada. Containing mature trees, manicured lawns and shrubbery, formal gardens, statuary and fountains, they are a delight to wander in. A visit is further enhanced by a stop at the pleasant **teahouse** *(light lunches, afternoon tea, Jun–Aug)* set beside a long pool with fountains.

★**Canadian Automotive Museum** – *99 Simcoe St. South, about 1.5km/1mi north of Hwy. 401. Open year-round Mon–Fri 9am–5pm, weekends 10am–6pm. Closed Dec 25. $5. ☎905-576-1222.* The history of the automobile industry in Canada is explained by means of photographs, illustrations, models, and of course, by actual vehicles. Primarily from the 1898-1930 period, about 70 automobiles, in mint condition, are on display. Noteworthy among them are the 1903 Redpath Messenger built in Toronto—the only remaining example of its type, the 1912 McLaughlin Buick, and the 1923 Rauch and Lang electric car.

Robert McLaughlin Gallery – *Civic Centre next to city hall. Open year-round Tue–Fri 10am–5pm (Thu 9pm), weekends noon–4pm. ✗ ♿ www.rmg.on.ca ☎905-576-3000.* Originally built in 1969, the expanded gallery designed by Arthur Erickson displays the works of the **Painters Eleven**, a group of artists who united in the 1950s to exhibit abstract art in Toronto. Changing exhibits feature contemporary Canadian art.

Cullen Gardens – Kids *In Whitby, 5km/3mi north of Hwy. 401 by Hwy. 12 and Taunton Rd. Open Jul–Aug daily 9am–9pm. Mid-Apr–Jun & Sept–mid-Nov daily 10am; closing hours vary (phone ahead). $10. ✗ www.cullengardens.com ☎905-668-6606.* These attractive gardens combine flower beds, a rose garden, topiary, ponds and a stream with miniature reproductions of historic houses from all over Ontario.

The symbol ✗ indicates that eating facilities can be found on the premises of the sight.

OTTAWA★★★

Population 323,340
Map p 129
Tourist Office ☎613-237-5158 or 613-239-5000

Defying the stereotypical image of a capital city, this seat of national government lack the imposing architecture, sweeping vistas and vast monuments of other world capitals. The city's attraction is its charm, captured in such scenes as joggers following the Rideau Canal in summer, briefcase-clutching civil servants skating to work on the frozen canal waters in winter, Sunday bicycle brigades rounding a corner, or rows o colourful tulips adorning the many parks and green expanses.

The city sits on the south bank of the **Ottawa River** at the point where it meets the **Ridea River** from the south and the **Gatineau River** from the north. The capital is due west o MONTREAL, about 160km/100mi upstream from the confluence of the Ottawa and ST LAWRENCE RIVERS. The Ottawa River marks the boundary between the provinces o Ontario and Quebec, but the National Capital Region spans the river, encompassing a large area in both provinces that includes the cities of OTTAWA and HULL.

Historical Notes

The First Settler – Although the region was known to the Outaouais Indians and visited by French explorers, there was no settlement in the Ottawa area until 1800. The first settler was **Philemon Wright**, an American who harnessed the **Chaudière Falls** to power grist-mills and sawmills on the Hull side of the river. He cut wood and floated the first raft of squared timber to Quebec in 1806, beginning what was to become a vast industry.

Changing of the Guard, Parliament Buildings

The Rideau Canal – The War of 1812 exposed the dangers of the St. Lawrence as a communications and supply route from MONTREAL for the military in Upper Canada. Ships were vulnerable to perilous rapids and gunfire from the US. After the war the **Duke of Wellington** sent men to Canada to look for a safer passage. The route selected followed the Ottawa, Rideau and Cataraqui Rivers and a series of lakes to reach the Royal Navy base at KINGSTON on Lake Ontario. Construction of the canals and locks necessary to make the route navigable was entrusted to **Lt.-Col. John By** of the Royal Engineers in 1826. The lieutenant-colonel established his base at the present site of Ottawa. Soon a thriving settlement developed known as Bytown. By 1832 the canal system was completed, but its cost was so great that By returned to England unemployed and penniless.

Lumbertown – The completion of canal construction did not signal the end of Bytown's boom. By the mid-1830s the community had become the centre of Ottawa Valley's squared-timber industry. Using the power of Chaudière Falls, as Philemon Wright had, residents built sawmills on the Bytown side of the Ottawa River. Splendid stands of red and white pine fell victim to the new industry. Over the century the industry concentrated more on exporting lumber to the US and less on floating timber to Quebec for export to England. Having never been used militarily, the Rideau Canal blossomed briefly as a means of transporting the lumber south. Bytown became a rowdy centre for lumberjacks and rivermen skilled at negotiating the rapids (so skilled that the British government recruited them to negotiate the hazardous cataracts of the Nile in order to relieve Gen. Charles George Gordon at Khartoum in 1884).

Westminster within the Wilderness – The 1850s saw great rivalry among Montreal, Toronto, Kingston and Quebec, over which should be selected as the capital of the new united Canada. Contention was so intense that the government asked **Queen Victoria** to decide the issue. She chose Bytown, which had hastily changed its name to Ottawa as a more suitable appellation for a capital. The choice did not please everyone: "the nearest lumber village to the north pole" wrote Torontonian **Goldwin Smith**. But the American press discovered Ottawa's advantage—it eluded capture by the most courageous of invaders, because they would become lost in the woods trying to find it! Despite such quips, the parliament buildings were begun in 1859 and completed enough by 1867 to be used by representatives of the new Confederation, of which Ottawa was accepted as the capital—this time without demur.

Malak, Ottawa

Ottawa Today – A city of parks, pleasant driveways and bicycle paths, Ottawa is also a city of flowers, especially in May when thousands of tulips bloom—a gift from the Dutch whose queen spent the war years in Ottawa. It is a city that has capitalized on the the cause of its founding—the **Rideau Canal**. Flanked by tree-lined drives, this waterway is a recreational haven: canoeing, boating, jogging, strolling, biking in summer, and skating and cross-country skiing in winter when little "chalets," set on the ice, offer food and skate rentals. The canal can be followed its entire 200km/125mi length to Lake Ontario through picturesque countryside with lovely lakes. Ottawa boasts other driveways that follow the Ottawa and Rideau Rivers *(p 158)*.

Although still a centre for forestry and for the rich agriculture to the south, Ottawa is chiefly a seat of government. Not here do "temples of finance" rule the skyline as in

Toronto and Montreal. Instead, high rises contain government departments and ministries, the most dominant being government-owned **Place du Portage** across the river in Hull.

Finally, Ottawa is a cultural centre, with a fine selection of museums and music, dance and drama at the **National Arts Centre**. The city is particularly lively in February during the winter festival titled **Winterlude**, in May for the **Canadian Tulip Festival**, and from late June to early July when **Canada Day** is celebrated in style on Parliament Hill.

**PARLIAMENT HILL AND AREA

Parliament Hill, with its three Gothic style parliament buildings, dominates the northern side of **Confederation Square**, a triangular-shaped "island" that serves as the centrepiece for several of the capital's historic and cultural institutions. In the middle of the square stands the towering granite archway of the **National War Memorial** (**1**), which was dedicated in 1939 by King George VI. Neighbouring "the Hill," as it is familiarly known, is **Château Laurier**, a distinguished hotel recognizable by its turrets and steeply pitched copper roofs. The government conference centre stands opposite and, bordering the southern tip of Confederation Square, is the National Arts Centre.

The Hill was purchased in 1859 from the British military, which used it for barracks during the building of the canal. Construction began immediately on the parliament buildings. **East Block**, with its whimsical windowed tower that looks like a face, and **West Block**, both designed by Strent and Laver, were completed in 1865. The **Parliamentary Library**, begun in 1859 and designed by Thomas Fuller and Chilion Jones, was not finished until 1877. **Centre Block**, originally designed by Fuller and Jones, was reworked in 1863 by Fuller and Charles Baillairgé, and officially opened in 1866. In 1916 a disastrous fire destroyed the middle building, which was rebuilt in 1920. The **Peace Tower** at its centre was added in 1927 as a monument to Canadians killed since Confederation. Today Centre Block contains the Houses of Parliament—the Commons and the Senate. West and East Blocks contain the offices of senators and members of Parliament. Once, these buildings were sufficient to house not only Parliament, but the entire civil service.

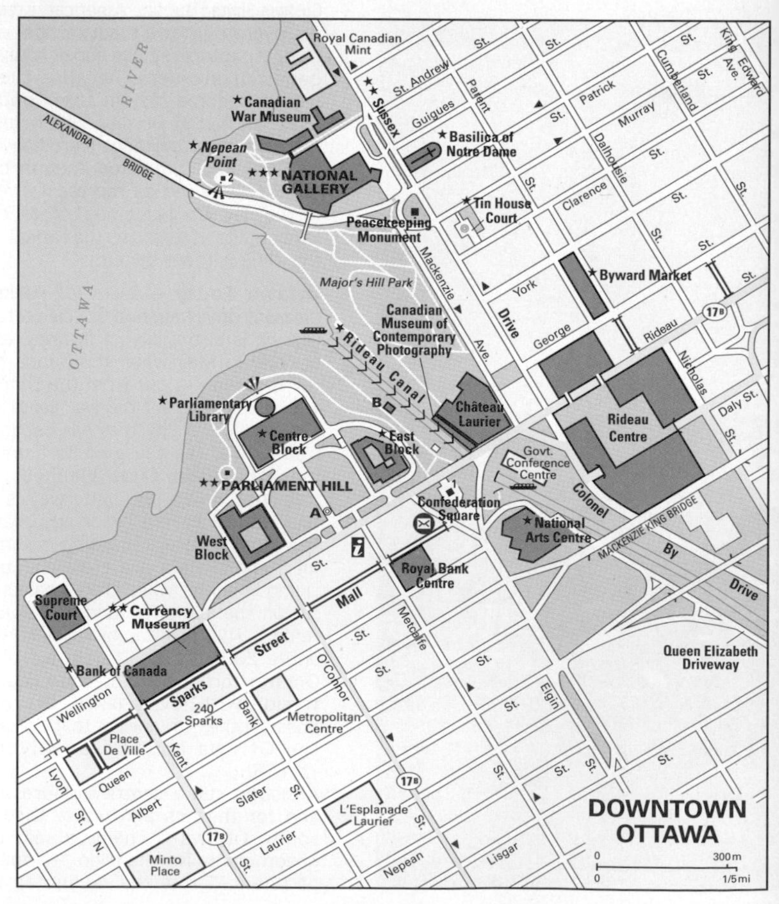

Visiting Parliament Hill – No public parking is permitted on the Hill. Pay lots are available in the downtown area south of Wellington Street; metered parking is also provided there.
Since Parliament Hill's tourist activities are numerous during peak season *(mid-May to Labour Day)*, it is advisable to stop first at the large white tent **(Info-tent)** located between Centre Block and West Block for a schedule of the day's events. Information can also be obtained from the National Capital Commission's **visitor centre** at the corner of Wellington and Metcalfe Streets *(open mid-May–Labour Day daily 8:30am–9pm; rest of the year daily 9am–5pm; closed Jan 1, Dec 25–26; ☎ 613-239-5000)*.
Parliament Hill is "guarded" by the Mounties—members of the Royal Canadian Mounted Police, attired in their famous ceremonial uniforms of stetsons, red tunics, riding breeches, boots and spurs *(summer only)*. Regiments of Foot Guards wearing bearskin caps, scarlet tunics and blue trousers are also stationed on the Hill in summer. A **Changing of the Guard**★★ is performed in summer *(Jul–Aug 10am)*, resembling the ceremony held outside Buckingham Palace and a seasonal **sound and light** show *(45min)* presents Canada's history *(nightly mid-May–early Sept; different hours for English & French productions; in case of rain show may be cancelled; ♿ ☎ 613-239-5000)*.

Sights *1 day*

Approached from Wellington Street, Parliament "Hill" seems to belie its name. Canada's Parliament actually stands on a bluff overlooking the Ottawa River and must be viewed from that angle to appreciate its designation.

★★**Ottawa River Boat Trip** – *Departs from Ottawa locks mid-May–mid-Oct daily 11am–7:30pm; cruise departs from Hull dock 30min earlier. Round-trip 1hr 30min. Commentary. $12. ✗ ♿ Paul's Boat Lines ☎ 613-225-6781.* This is an excellent trip, especially at dusk, affording close-up views of Parliament Hill, the Rideau Falls and the houses along Sussex Drive overlooking the river, in particular the prime minister's residence. The sheer size and force of the Ottawa River are impressive.

★**Centre Block** – *Visit by guided tour (20min–1hr) only, year-round daily; phone for hours. Closed Jan 1, Jul 1 & Dec 24-25. ♿ ☎ 613-996-0896.* Tours enable visitors to enter the House of Commons, the Senate, a committee room and the **Parliamentary Library**★, the only part of the original structure to escape the 1916 fire. The wood-panelled library is modelled on the reading room of the British Museum. Separately, the Peace Tower can be ascended for a fine **view**★ of the sprawling capital. Parliamentary proceedings are open to the public if the House is in session. Each session begins with the **Speaker's Parade** through the Hall of Honour to the Commons.

★**East Block** – *The interior can be visited by guided tour only; phone for hours. Closed Jan 1, Jul 1 & Dec 24-25. ♿ ☎ 613-996-0896.* The interior of this mid-19C building has been restored to its 1872 appearance. Some of the offices have been authentically furnished to represent their occupants at the time: Prime Minister Sir John A. Macdonald; his Quebec colleague and fellow Father of Confederation, Sir George-Étienne Cartier; the governor general, Lord Dufferin; and the Privy Council.

The Grounds – In front of the parliament buildings is a low-lying fountain called the **Centennial Flame** (**A**) because of the natural gas always burning at its centre. Symbolizing the first 100 years of Confederation, it was lit at midnight on New Year's Eve, 1966. Around the flame the 12 shields of Canada's provinces and territories are displayed, with the date they entered Confederation.
The walk around Centre Block is pleasant, affording **views**★ of the river and of Hull *(p 200)*, which has rapidly changed from an industrial city to a federal government annex containing large office complexes. A notable collection of statues graces this walk, many of which are the work of well-known Quebec sculptor **Louis-Philippe Hébert** (1850-1917). Most commemorate Canadian prime ministers, with the exception of the Queen Victoria and Queen Elizabeth II statues.
At the back of Centre Block, the attractive exterior of the polygonal library looks like the chapter house of a Gothic cathedral.

★**Rideau Canal** – *Heritage Canal.* From Wellington Street visitors can descend into the small gorge where the Rideau Canal begins. Eight **locks**★ raise boats from the Ottawa River to the top of the cliff. There is also a **boat trip** on the canal *(departs from conference centre mid-May–mid-Oct daily from 10am–8:30pm; round-trip 1hr 15min; commentary; $12; ♿ Paul's Boat Lines ☎ 613-225-6781)*.
Beside the locks stands the **Old Commissariat Building** (**B**), completed by Colonel By in 1827 as a military supply depot and treasury. The historic edifice now houses the **Bytown Museum** *(open mid-May–mid-Oct Mon–Sat 10am–5pm, Sun 1pm–5pm; Apr–early May & late Oct–Nov Mon–Fri 10am–5pm; Dec–Mar by appointment; $2.50; ☎ 613-234-4570)* and a display on the canal builders.

Ontario Ministry of Tourism & Recreation

Rideau Canal

Above the canal, and next t Château Laurier, is the **Cana dian Museum of Contempora Photography**, an affiliate of th National Gallery *(p 155)*, which features changing ex hibits of works by Canadia photographers *(ope May–Aug Fri–Tue 11am 5pm, Wed 4pm–8pm, Th 11am–8pm; rest of the yea Wed–Sun 11am–5pm, Th til 8pm; closed Good Frida & Dec 25;* ♿ *http:/ cmcp.gallery.ca* ☎ *613-990 8257)*. South of Wellingto and facing the canal, th handsome **National Art Centre★** consists of interrela ted concrete structures Opened in 1969 the comple *(visit by 45min guided tou only, year-round Mon–Fr 8am–9pm, Sat 10am–6pm Sun & holidays noon–5pm* ✗ ♿ 🅿 *www.nac-cna.c* ☎ *613-947-7000)* contains theatres and a charming cafe with an outdoor terrace *(summer only)* located be side the waterway. Across the canal stands the **Rideau Centre**, a hotel, conventior and popular shopping com plex.

★**Byward Market** – *Open May–Oct daily 6am–6pm. Rest of the year Mon–Fr 8am–5pm, Sat 7am–4pm, Sun 8am–4pm. Closed Jan 1 & Dec 25.* ✗ *https/ city.ottawa.on.ca* ☎ *613-244-4410.* Stretching over several blocks, this colourfu market *(indoors in winter)* has existed since 1846. From spring to fall there are stalls of flowers, fruit and vegetables. Year-round, people are also attracted to the neighbouring shops, cafes and restaurants.

★**Tin House Court** – In this pleasant square with its stone houses and fountain, a strange object can be seen hanging on the wall of a building. It is the facade of a house built by Honore Foisy, a tinsmith. Foisy spent his time decorating the front of his home with sheet metal, making it look like wood or stone. When his house was destroyed, the facade was moved here to preserve this example of tinsmithing.

★**Basilica of Notre Dame** – *Open year-round Mon–Sat 7am–6pm, Sun 8am–6pm.* ♿ ☎ *613-241-7496.* This church with its twin spires is a Roman Catholic cathedral built between 1841 and the 1880s. Note the gold-leaf statue of the Madonna and Child between the steeples. To the right of the basilica, there is a statue of Joseph-Eugene Guigues, the first bishop of Ottawa, who was responsible for the cathedral's completion.
The very fine **woodwork★** of the interior was carved in mahogany by Philippe Parizeau. Around the sanctuary there are niches that contain statues of the prophets, patriarchs and apostles crafted in wood by Louis-Philippe Hébert, though they have been painted to look like stone.

Peacekeeping Monument – Across the street, and adjacent to the basilica, is a prominent memorial to Canadians who have served as international peacekeepers. Entitled *The Reconciliation*, the monument, which was dedicated in 1992, features two male and one female bronze figures in military dress. They look toward a grove, the symbol of peace, their backs to the detritus of war lying between converging granite walls.

★**Nepean Point** – Situated high above the river beside Alexandra Bridge, this point offers a splendid **view★★** of Parliament Hill, Hull and the Gatineau Hills across the river. The statue is of **Samuel de Champlain** (**2**), who sailed up the Ottawa River in 1613 and 1615.

Sparks Street Mall – South of Parliament Hill stretches this pleasant pedestrian mall with trees, seating and cafe tables between the shops. Note the **Royal Bank Centre**, and, at the opposite end of the mall, the attractive **Bank of Canada★** designed by Arthur Erickson and opened in 1980. Set within a 12-storey court, this

Neoclassical building is now flanked by two 12-storey towers of solar-tinted glass and oxidized copper. In the court are trees, shrubs, a pool and the Currency Museum *(p 156)*. Outside the east tower in a small park stands a bronze sculpture by Sorel Etrog entitled *Flight* (1966).

Supreme Court – *Visit by guided tour (30min) only, May–Aug Mon–Fri 9am–5pm, weekends & holidays 9am–noon & 1pm–5pm. Rest of the year Mon–Fri 9am–5pm. Reservations required.* ♿ *www.scc-csc.gc.ca* ☎ *613-995-5361.* Created in 1875, but not "supreme" until 1949 (when appeals to England's Judicial Committee of the Privy Council were abolished), Canada's Supreme Court occupies a building with green roofs overlooking the Ottawa River. The court itself consists of nine judges, five of whom constitute a quorum. Visitors can listen to the legal arguments if the court is in session, and visit two other court rooms.

★★THE MUSEUMS

As befitting a capital city, Ottawa has a number of fine museums, many of which are national museums and hence are large in size and comprehensive in scope. Several are concentrated within walking distance of one another within the city core. Others, such as the Aviation Museum and the Agriculture Museum, are on the outskirts of the city proper.

★★ **National Gallery of Canada** – *Map p 157. 380 Sussex Dr. Open May–Sept daily 10am–6pm (Thu 8pm). Rest of the year Wed–Sun 10am–5pm. Closed Jan 1, Good Friday & Dec 25.* ✗ ♿ 🅿 *//national.gallery.ca* ☎ *613-990-1985.* This magnificent glass, granite and concrete building (1988, Moshe Safdie), capped by prismatic glass "turrets" rises on the banks of the Ottawa River across from the Victorian Gothic parliament buildings. Its bold beauty, light and airy exhibit spaces and tranquil interior courtyards provide a unique setting for the remarkable national collections.

Canadian Art – *Second floor.* This collection is displayed in a series of galleries arranged to trace the development of Canadian art. Both the **garden court** with its colourful plantings and the restful **water court** add grace and beauty to the transition from gallery to gallery. In the centre is the reconstructed **chapel** of the Convent of Our Lady of the Sacred Heart (1888) with its decorative fan-vaulted ceiling, cast-iron columns and carved woodwork. Other highlights include the Croscup Room murals, painted in Nova Scotia in the mid-19C; early Quebec religious art, including Paul Jourdain's gilt tabernacle and Plamondon's *Portrait of Sister Saint-Alphonse*; the works of Paul Kane and Cornelius Krieghoff; Lucius O'Brien's *Sunrise on the Saguenay*; a series of paintings by Tom Thomson and the Group of Seven (notably Thomson's *The Jack Pine*, Jackson's *The Red Maple*, Harris' *North Shore, Lake Superior* and the Group of Seven murals from the MacCallum-Jackman cottage on Georgian Bay). Emily Carr and David Milne are represented along with Marc-Aurèle Fortin, Jean-Paul Lemieux, Alfred Pellan *(On the Beach)*, Goodridge Roberts, Guido Molinari and Claude Tousignant. Contemporary works by Paul-Émile Borduas, Harold Town, Jack Shadbolt, Michael Snow and Yves Gaucher are also featured.

Galleries devoted to Inuit art *(accessed from second-floor level)* feature contemporary sculpture, prints and drawings.

Malak, Ottawa

National Gallery of Canada and Parliament Buildings

European and American Art – *Third floor.* In addition to its Canadian art, the Nationa Gallery owns an impressive and comprehensive collection of European art. Amon the highlights are Simone Martini's *St. Catherine of Alexandria*, Lucas Cranach th Elder's *Venus*, Bernard van Orley's *Virgin and Child*, Rembrandt's *The Toilet c Esther*, El Greco's *St. Francis and Brother Leo Meditating on Death*, Bernini's fin bust of *Pope Urban VIII* and Benjamin West's *Death of General Wolfe* (the origina of this much-reproduced painting). Impressionists are well represented, as are suc 20C masters as Fernand Léger *(The Mechanic)*, Picasso and Gustav Klimt.

Sculpture on view in the Asian Galleries spans the third century AD to the present

The National Gallery's extensive collection of contemporary art is exhibited on bot floors.

★★★ **Canadian Museum of Civilization (Quebec)** – *Description p 200.*

★★★ **National Aviation Museum** – *Map p 159. Rockcliffe Airport. Open May–Labou Day daily 9am–5pm (Thu 9pm). Rest of the year Tue–Sun 10am–5pm (Thu 9pm) Closed Dec 25. $5.* X ♿ P *www.aviation.nmstc.ca* ☎ *613-993-2010.* This enormous triangular-shaped, high-tech building recalls the three-sided pattern of the numerous airfields built across the country during World War II, when Canada was known as the "Aerodrome for Democracy." Opened in 1988 the museum is devotec to the history of aviation from pioneer days to the present, with special emphasis on Canadian contributions.

A selection of old aviation films and videos accompanies the exhibits, presenting an interesting glimpse of the past. There is a replica of the *Silver Dart*, the first aircraft to fly in Canada *(p 258)*. There are fighters and bombers used in both world wars: a Spad 7, a Sopwith Snipe, Hawker Hurricane, Supermarine Spitfire and a Lancaster Bomber. The beginnings of modern passenger service can be traced to the Boeing 247, the Lockheed 10A and the Douglas DC-3, examples of which are on view. Early "bush" float planes illustrate the importance of aviation in opening up Canada's vast northland. The **RCAF Hall of Tribute**, a memorial room adjacent to the entrance lobby, honours men and women of the Royal Canadian Air Force.

★★ **Canadian Museum of Nature** – Kids *Map p 157. Open May–Labour Day daily 9:30am–5pm (Thu 8pm). Rest of Sept–mid-Oct daily 10am–5pm (Thu 8pm). Rest of the year Tue–Sun 10am–5pm (Thu 8pm). Closed Dec 25. $5. ($2.50 Thu ti 5pm; free 5pm–8pm).* X ♿ P *www.nature.ca* ☎ *613-566-4700.* In 1989 the museum took over the entire building at McLeod and Metcalfe Streets, which it formerly shared with the Canadian Museum of Civilization. The earth's geological history and the origin of life are the predominant topics of this comprehensive museum.

Interesting exhibits on the creation of oceans and continents, particularly North America, and an outstanding display on **dinosaurs**★★ with several complete reconstructions of skeletons, await visitors.

An interesting **Birds in Canada** gallery features lifelike dioramas from all regions of the country. Note in particular the Canada geese, complete with sound effects. Also noteworthy are films and **dioramas**★★ of Canadian mammals, such as the musk ox of the Northwest Territories, the pronghorn antelope of Saskatchewan, British Columbia's grizzly bear and the moose of New Brunswick.

Other galleries explore animal life in a more general way with displays on such topics as animal geography, animal behaviour and relationships with mankind. Finally, there is a large conservatory called the **Hall of Plant Life**.

★★ **Currency Museum** – *Map p 152. In Bank of Canada complex, 245 Sparks St. Open May–Labour Day Mon–Sat 10:30am–5pm, Sun 1pm–5pm. Rest of the year Tue–Sat 10:30am–5pm, Sun 1pm–5pm. Closed national holidays. $2.* ♿ *www.bank-banque-canada.ca* ☎ *613-782-8914.* This museum presents the history of money from early China, Greece, Rome, Byzantium, Medieval and Renaissance Europe to its introduction and use in North America. The development of Canadian money is highlighted, with examples of wampum, the card money of New France, Hudson's Bay Company tokens, the first banknotes and decimal currency. The Bank of Canada's emergence is also depicted.

★★ **National Museum of Science and Technology** – Kids *Map p 159. 1867 St. Laurent Blvd. Open May–Labour Day daily 9am–6pm (Fri 9pm). Rest of the year Tue–Sun daily 9am–5pm. Closed Dec 25. $6.* X ♿ P *www.science-tech.nmstc.ca* ☎ *613-991-3044.* The flashing beacon of the old Cape North (Nova Scotia) lighthouse marks the museum's location. Visitors can tour the lighthouse *(visit by 30min guided tour only, Jun–Labour Day daily 1pm)* and see outdoor exhibits such as an Atlas rocket and a steam locomotive.

Displays inside concentrate on transportation. The hall of **steam locomotives** is impressive because of the sheer size of the vehicles. Exhibits on early automobiles (1900-30) in Canada and ship models are also featured. Other sections of the museum are devoted to such themes as the development of printing, communications, computers, physics, astronomy and the exploration of space.

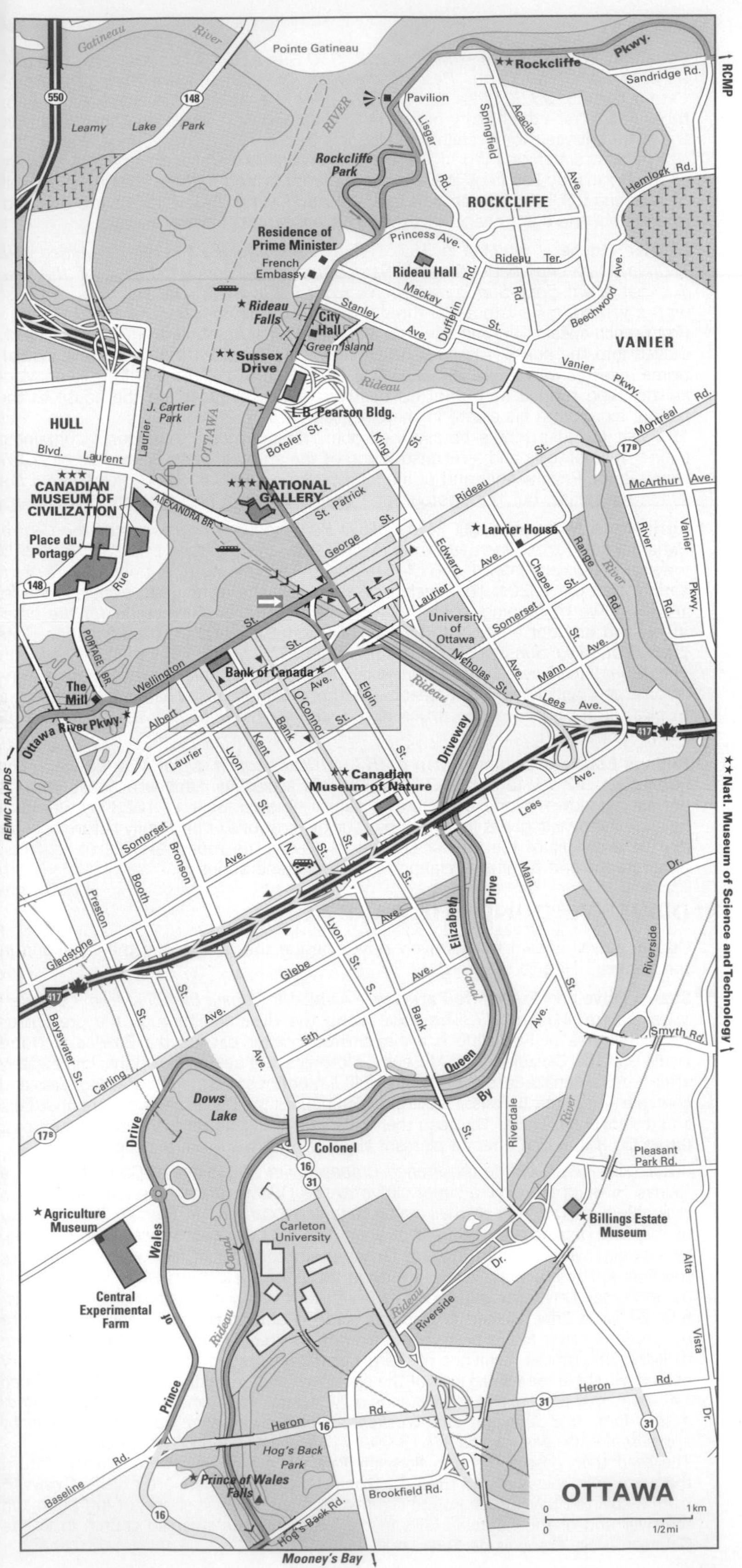
OTTAWA
Pointe Gatineau
Gatineau River
Leamy Lake Park
Rockcliffe Park
Pavilion
Rockcliffe Pkwy.
Sandridge Rd.
RCMP
ROCKCLIFFE
Residence of Prime Minister
French Embassy
Rideau Hall
Rideau Falls
City Hall
Green Island
Sussex Drive
VANIER
HULL
J. Cartier Park
L.B. Pearson Bldg.
NATIONAL GALLERY
CANADIAN MUSEUM OF CIVILIZATION
Place du Portage
Laurier House
University of Ottawa
Bank of Canada
The Mill
Ottawa River Pkwy.
REMIC RAPIDS
Canadian Museum of Nature
Natl. Museum of Science and Technology
Dows Lake
Agriculture Museum
Central Experimental Farm
Carleton University
Billings Estate Museum
Hog's Back Park
Prince of Wales Falls
Mooney's Bay
Colonel By Drive
Queen Elizabeth Driveway
Prince of Wales Drive
1 km
1/2 mi

★**Canadian War Museum** – *Map p 152. 330 Sussex Dr. Open May–mid-Oct dai 9:30am–5pm (Thu 8pm). Rest of the year Tue–Sun 9:30am–5pm (Thu 8pm) Closed Dec 25. $3.50 (free Sun 9:30am–noon).* ♿ ☎ *819-776-8600.* Exhibits o three floors trace the history of war in Canada and wars involving Canadians, fro the strife between the French and Iroquois in the 17C to the Korean War. A life size reconstruction of a World War I trench complete with sound effects, a diorama of the Normandy Landings in 1944, and a large armoured Mercedes Benz capabl of reaching 170km/105mph and used by Adolf Hitler in the 1930s are featured In addition, there are changing exhibitions on various military themes.

★**Laurier House** – *Map p 157. 335 Laurier Ave. East. Visit by guided tou (30min) only, Apr–Sept Tue–Sat 9am–5pm, Sun 2pm–5pm. Rest of the yea Tue–Sat 10am–5pm, Sun 2pm–5pm.* ♿ ☎ *613-992-8142.* This yellow brick hous with a veranda pays tribute to three Canadian prime ministers. In 1897 Canada's first French-speaking prime minister, **Sir Wilfrid Laurier**, in office from 1896 to 1911 moved into the house. After his death Lady Laurier willed the house to Canadiar prime minister **William Lyon Mackenzie King**, grandson of the rebel William Lyon Mac-kenzie. King resided here until his death in 1950, bequeathing the house to the nation, along with his estate in the Gatineau Hills *(p 201)*.
The visit includes King's library, bedroom, dining room, two rooms containing Laurier memorabilia and a reconstruction of the study of **Lester Bowles Pearson**, 1957 Nobel Peace Prize winner and prime minister from 1963 to 1968. Pearson did not live in the house, but the photographs and cartoons in his study are fascinating.

★**Agriculture Museum** – Kids *Map p 157. Building 88, on grounds of the Centra Experimental Farm. Open year-round daily 9am–5pm. Closed Dec 25. $3.* ✗ ♿ P *www.agriculture.nmstc.ca* ☎ *613-991-3044.* This museum is housed in a barn dating from the 1920s. The machinery displayed, the techniques, even the smells, are evocative of farming in times past. The museum's dairy cattle *(in the basement)* and draught horses can be seen. Seasonally, visitors can take wagon rides *(Jun–Sept, Wed–Sun $2.50)* on the premises.
The 425ha/1,050 acre **Central Experimental Farm** is the headquarters of Canada's Agriculture and Agri-Food Department. On the grounds are ornamental gardens, a tropical greenhouse and an arboretum *(open year-round daily dawn–dusk;* ♿ P ☎ *613-759-1994)*.

★**Billings Estate Museum** – *Map p 157. 2100 Cabot St. Open May–Oct Sun–Thu noon–5pm. $2.50.* P ☎ *613-247-4830.* This attractive clapboard house with its dormer windows is one of Ottawa's oldest houses. Built in 1828 by Braddish Billings, the dwelling was inhabited by four generations of his family before becoming the property of the City of Ottawa in 1975. The rooms are full of artifacts, photographs and furniture relating to all four generations.

★★ DRIVES AROUND THE CAPITAL

Ottawa is well known for its lovely drives beside the river, along the canal and in the Gatineau Hills to the north.

★★**Sussex Drive and Rockcliffe Parkway** – *Allow 1hr 30min. 8km/5mi from Confederation Square. Map p 157.* This drive along the river and through the prestigious residential area of Rockcliffe is a pleasant one. After passing the Basilica of Notre Dame and the Canadian War Museum, motorists will see on the right, immediately after the Macdonald-Cartier Bridge to Hull, a modern structure of darkened glass and concrete—the **Lester B. Pearson Building**, which houses the Department of Foreign Affairs and International Trade. The road then crosses the Rideau River to Green Island past **Ottawa City Hall**, which offers a pleasant **view**★ of the river from the top floor.

★**Rideau Falls** – *Park beside the French Embassy.* On both sides of Green Island, the Rideau River drops over a sheer cliff into the Ottawa River. The falls are said to resemble a curtain, hence their name meaning "curtain" in French. The intensity of the flow depends on the time of year. The falls are best viewed in the spring, or in winter when they are frozen. To see the second set of falls, visitors can cross the first set by a bridge. There are good views of the Ottawa River and Hull.
Along Sussex Drive, the entrance to the official residence of Canadian prime ministers, **24 Sussex Drive**, is seen on the left. Hidden among the trees, the stone house overlooks the river and is best viewed from the water. Around the corner is the gate to **Rideau Hall**, official residence of the governor general *(p 25)*, guarded by military personnel. There are **walking tours** of the residence and grounds *(visit by 45min guided tour only, mid-May–mid-Jun weekends only, 10am–4pm; late Jun–Labour Day daily 10am–4pm; mid-Sept–late Oct weekends only, noon–4pm; rest of the year by appointment;* ♿ *www.gg.ca* ☎ *613-998-7113 or 800-465-6890, Canada/US)*.
The road then passes through **Rockcliffe Park** via a one-way route. On the return there are good views of the river. Farther on, however, there are excellent **views**★★ from a covered pavilion of Pointe Gatineau on the Quebec shore, of log booms in the river and of the Gatineau Hills in the distance. The steepled church in Pointe Gatineau is St. François de Sales, built in 1886.

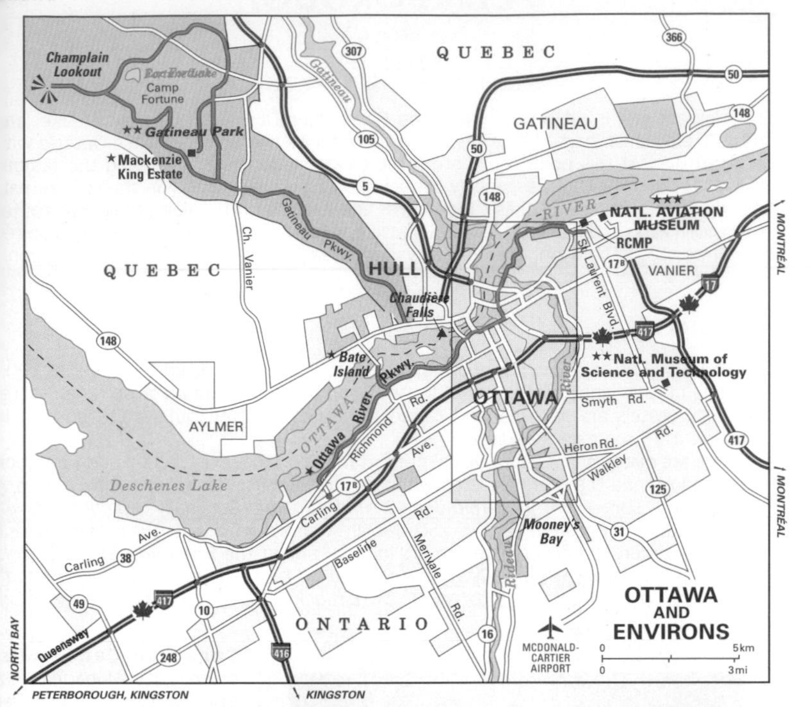

Rockcliffe is an area of large stone houses, tree-lined streets and lovely gardens, occupied by senior civil servants and members of the diplomatic corps. The drive ends at **RCMP Rockcliffe**, where members of the famous **musical ride** and their horses are trained. When the troop is not on tour, the horses can be seen in training *(May–Aug Mon–Fri 8:30am–3:30pm; rest of the year Mon–Fri 8:30am–3pm; ♿ www.rcmp-grc.gc.ca ☎ 613-993-3751)*.

★**Rideau Canal Driveways** – *Allow 1hr for both. Each drive is about 8km/5mi from Confederation Square. Map p 157.* These drives are especially picturesque in tulip time *(May)*. In all seasons the canal is a centre for sports.

The **Queen Elizabeth Driveway** follows the canal's west bank; the **Colonel By Drive** parallels the east bank. The University of Ottawa is soon passed on the left. Later on, Carleton University will also be seen. At **Dows Lake** where the canal widens out, there are fine tulip displays in May and paddle boats can be rented. At this point the two driveways diverge, the Colonel By continuing along the canal, the Queen Elizabeth entering the Central Experimental Farm. From Colonel By Drive, there are views of Prince of Wales Falls and the Rideau Canal locks before the drive ends at Hog's Back Road.

★**Prince of Wales Falls** – *Free parking in Hog's Back Park.* After leaving Mooney's Bay, the Rideau River drops over these falls and rushes through a small gorge. The result of a geological fault that exposed underlying formations and strata, the falls are particularly impressive in the spring thaw. The dam was built by Colonel By in 1829.

Mooney's Bay marks the end of the canal section of the Rideau Canal, after which the river is navigable. The bay, with its beach and picnic grounds *(access from Riverside Dr.)*, is one of Ottawa's main recreational areas.

★**Ottawa River Parkway** – *Allow 1hr. 11km/7mi from Confederation Square. Maps above and p 157.* Wellington Street passes the parliament buildings, the Bank of Canada and the Supreme Court, and becomes the parkway just south of Portage Bridge to Hull. Almost immediately, there are signs on the right to the **Mill**. Built in 1842 this old stone structure was once a sawmill and gristmill, standing near a log flume—a means by which timber could be floated downstream without being battered by the Chaudière Falls. The drive beside the Ottawa River is lovely, offering several lookout points for the Remic Rapids. The best view of these rapids is from **Bate Island**★ *(take Champlain Bridge to Hull and exit for island)*. The parkway continues, affording other good viewpoints.

★★**Gatineau Park (Quebec)** – *Allow 3hrs. Circular drive of 55km/34mi from Confederation Square. Cross Portage Bridge to Hull, turn left on Rte. 148 for just over 2km/1.2mi, then turn right on the Gatineau Parkway. Map above. Description p 201.*

PETERBOROUGH

Population 69,535
Map p 129
Tourist Office ☎705-742-2201

This pleasant city is set on the Otonabee River where it widens into Little Lake, an on the Trent Canal, part of the Trent-Severn Waterway, which links Lake Ontario wit Georgian Bay. At this point there are three locks on the canal, including the famou lift lock *(below)*. Boating, especially canoeing, is a popular activity in the region, par ticularly on the Kawartha Lakes to the north and, farther north, along the canoe route in **Algonquin Park** *(map p 129)*, the impressive wilderness famous for having inspire the painter Tom Thomson. The Peterborough area is also known for its petroglyph Indian relics.

SIGHTS

★**Lift Lock** – *In operation mid-May–mid-Oct.* This hydraulic lift lock built in 190 is one of only eight in the world. In two chambers mounted on large rams, recre ational vessels are lowered and raised 20m/65ft. Visitors can watch the lock i action from the park beside it.

There are displays and audio-visual presentations on the construction and operatio of the lock and the Trent-Severn Waterway in the **visitor centre** *(open late Jun–earl Aug daily 9am–6pm; Apr–mid-Jun & mid-Aug–mid-Oct daily 10am–5pm; $ contribution requested; ☎705-750-4950)*. Visitors who lack their own marin transportation can experience the lift lock by taking the **boat cruise** *(departs fron Holiday Inn downtown; mid-May–mid-Oct daily 11am & 1:30pm; 2hrs; $15; com mentary; reservations suggested; ♿ Liftlock Cruises www.liftlockcruise.con ☎705-742-9912)*.

Ontario Ministry of Tourism & Recreation

Canoeing

★**Canadian Canoe Museum** – *910 Monaghan Rd. Open late May–Labour Day daily 10am–4pm. Rest of the year Mon–Fri 10am–4pm, weekends 1pm–4pm. Closed Dec 25. Contribution requested. ♿ www.canoemuseum.net ☎705-748-9153.* A former factory houses this fascinating array of more than 600 canoes, kayaks and rowing craft of all types and construction. The fledgling museum incorporates the Kanawa International Collection of watercraft, which was formerly on view in Haliburton Highlands, Ontario. Examples of boats of the various native cultures include West Coast dugouts, Inuit kayaks, a Kutenal canoe from central British Columbia and a Mandan Bull boat used by the Prairie Indians to cross rivers. Several finely crafted canoes made by immigrant artisans are displayed, along with paddles, models and related artifacts.

EXCURSIONS *Map p 129*

Lang Pioneer Village – Kids *16km/10mi southeast of Peterborough by Rte. 7 and Country Rd. 34. Open mid-May–Labour Day Sun–Fri noon–5pm, Sat 1pm–4pm. Mid-Sept–early Oct call for hours. $6. ☎705-295-6694.* Set on 10ha/25 acres in a delightful rural setting, this 19C village contains reconstructed buildings and an original gristmill (1846), still in working order. The log cabin of David Fife *(p 99)*, famed for his hardy strain of wheat, has been moved here from its nearby place of construction. Costumed staff demonstrate daily chores and trades.

Petroglyphs Provincial Park – *55km/34mi northeast of Peterborough via Hwy. 28. Open mid-May–mid-Oct daily 10am–5pm. $7.50/car. ♿ www.ontarioparks.com ☎705-877-2552.* The largest concentration of petroglyphs anywhere in Canada is protected in this park, located near Stony Lake. About 900 carvings of between 500-1,000 years of age can be seen.

For general information on admission, accommodation and activities in Canadian national parks, consult the blue pages at the end of the book.

POINT PELEE NATIONAL PARK★★

Map p 128

ituated on a pointed peninsula extending into **Lake Erie**, this park is one of the few ›laces where the true deciduous forest of eastern North America still exists. Well ‹nown to ornithologists across the continent, the southernmost tip of the Canadian nainland possesses a unique plant and animal life, owing largely to its latitude of 42°N, he same as that of Rome.

The peninsula took its shape 10,000 years ago when wind and lake currents deposited sand on a ridge of glacial till under the waters of Lake Erie. Today the ridge is covered vith as much as 60m/200ft of sand. The sand bar continues under the waters of the ake for some distance, creating a hazard for shipping. The sandspit is itself mantled vith a lush forest of deciduous trees (there are few evergreens). White sassafras flourishes alongside hop trees, sumac, black walnut, sycamore, shagbark hickory, ıackberry and red cedar. Beneath them, many species of plants thrive, including the prickly pear cactus with its yellow flower.

An Ornithologist's Paradise – For most people **birds** are Point Pelee's major attraction. Its location at the convergence of two major flyways, its extension into Lake Erie and its lack of cultivation have combined to foster large bird populations. Spring and fall migrations can be spectacular—as many as 100 species have been sighted in one day. Over 300 species have been recorded in the park, approximately 100 of them remaining to nest. September is the month of the southern migration for the **monarch butterfly**. Visitors can see trees covered with these beautiful insects.

Access – *About 10km/6mi from Leamington. Follow the signs.*

VISIT *Allow 1/2 day*

Open early Apr–mid-Apr & late May–late Oct daily 6am–9:30pm. Late Apr–mid-May daily 5am–9:30pm. Rest of the year daily 7am–7:30pm. Hiking, fishing, canoeing, bicycling (bicycle & canoe rental), swimming, ski trails, skating. $3.25/day. www.parkscanada.pch.gc.ca/parks/ontario/pointpelee/pointpeleef.htm ☎519-322-2365. For recorded information on migration, weather conditions, events ☎519-322-2371. Excellent flora and fauna displays await discovery in the **visitor centre★★** together with an interesting account of the peninsula's creation *(7km/4mi south of park entrance; open year-round daily 10am, May 8am; closing hours vary)*. Films and a wide-screen slide presentation about the park *(20min)* are shown regularly. Be sure to view the day's recording in the visitor log of sighted species and buy a copy of *Checklist of Birds ($0.25)* to keep track of birds you see. From the visitor centre the Woodland Nature Trail *(2.75km/1.7mi)* begins *(trail guide $2)*.

Transit to the tip of the peninsula departs from the visitor centre *(every 20min, Apr–Nov)*. At the tip visitors can observe birds across the lake beginning their southern migration in the fall. From the peninsula's tip, paths lead in both directions along the park's 19km/11mi fine sandy beaches *(swimming prohibited at the tip; swimming beaches accessible from picnic areas)*.

An 1840s house and barn are focal points of the DeLaurier Trail *(1km/.6mi)*, along which panels and artifacts provide a brief history of the area's settlement.

Marshland between the sand bars can be toured by a **boardwalk★** *(1km/.6mi)*, where two lookout towers provide good **panoramas★** of the marsh. Resident muskrats, turtles and fish as well as birds can be seen.

PRESCOTT★

Population 4,480

Map p 129

This small industrial town on the St. Lawrence is the only deep-water port between MONTREAL and KINGSTON. Originally settled by Loyalists, the community was the chosen location for a fort to protect ships from American attack during the War of 1812. It was also the site of the **Battle of the Windmill** in 1838 when rebel supporters of William Lyon Mackenzie and their American sympathizers were dislodged, only with difficulty, from a windmill on the riverbank.

Today an international bridge spans the river near the town, one of 13 bridges linking Ontario with the US.

SIGHT

★**Fort Wellington** – *On Hwy. 2, just east of town. Open mid-May–Sept daily 10am–5pm. $3. http://parkscanada.pch.gc.ca/ontario/fortwellington ☎613-925-2896.* Built by the British, this small earthen fort includes officers' quarters and a three-storey stone **blockhouse**, restored to reflect its 1840s appearance. Costumed interpreters can be seen on the grounds, including those attired in British regimental uniforms of the period.

East of the fort *(1.5km/1mi)*, between Highway 2 and the river, stands the **windmill** of battle fame. It features displays on the battle and offers a pleasant **view** of the river *(picnic tables)*.

SAULT STE. MARIE★★

Population 80,054
Map of Principal Sights p 4
Tourist Office ☎705-949-7152

Connected to Michigan's city of the same name by road and railway bridges, this Ontario city is an industrial centre with huge steelworks and a pulp mill. The "Soo," as it is commonly called, lies on the north side of **St. Mary's River**, the international boundary and waterway that connects Lakes Superior and Huron, forming an important link in the Great Lakes/St. Lawrence Seaway system *(p 132)*. The rapids in the river between the two cities were a gathering place from earliest times when Ojibwa Indians came to catch whitefish here. Étienne Brûlé visited the rapids in 1622, as did many of the great explorers of New France: Nicolet, Radisson, Groseilliers, Marquette, Jolliet, La Salle, the La Vérendrye family and others. In 1668 Père Marquette established a mission beside them, calling it Sainte Marie du Sault (*sault* means "falls" in French). Gateway to the wild and uninhabited **Algoma** wilderness, Sault Ste. Marie today is also the headquarters of the Firebirds, the province's aerial firefighters who control the spread of forest fires by such methods as waterbombing.

SIGHTS

★**The Soo Locks** – *Visitor centre, 1 Canal Dr., open mid-May–mid-Oct daily; tours available afternoons & evenings; rest of the year by appointment. ☎705-941-6205.* To bypass the rapids, the **North West Company** completed the first lock and canal in 1798 (destroyed during the War of 1812). Since then, locks of increasing size have been constructed and today, the enormous ships of the Great Lakes are able to bypass the rapids by four parallel locks on the American side of the river. These locks are one of the busiest sections of the entire seaway system, handling in excess of 8,000 lockages per year and an average of more than 73 million tonnes/80 million tons of cargo annually.

In July, 1998, a newly constructed lock was opened within the existing Canadian lock, which had been closed for a number of years; the new lock handles recreational craft only.

At the base of Huron Street, there is a reconstruction of the **first lock** (**A**). The vast lock system in the river can be appreciated by taking a **boat trip** that passes through one of the large American locks *(departs from Roberta Bondar Park Jun–mid-Oct daily 10am–6pm; round-trip 2hrs; commentary; $17; ✕ ♿ Lock Tours www.soonet.ca/locktour ☎705-253-9850).*

★**City Hall** – At the base of Brock Street, Sault Ste. Marie has a pleasant riverfront area dominated by its attractive City Hall, built of copper-coloured reflecting glass. Nearby stands the permanently berthed **MS Norgoma** (**B**), the last overnight passenger ship used on the Great Lakes *(docked next to Roberta Bondar Pavilion; open mid-Jun–mid-Sept daily 10am–8pm; $2.50; ☎705-256-7447).* On board the ship is a museum of Great Lakes history.

★**Ermatinger/Clergue Heritage Site** – *Open Jun–Sept daily 10am–5pm. Apr–May & Oct–Nov Mon–Fri 10am–5pm. Rest of the year by appointment. $2. ♿ ☎705-759-5443.* This attractive Georgian stone house was built in 1814 by Charles Oakes Ermatinger, a partner in the North West Company, and his Ojibway wife Charlotte. It has been restored to reflect the period when it stood almost alone in the region and received many eminent visitors.

Among the guests was **Paul Kane** (1810-71), who made several long canoe trips across Canada, sketching and making notes about the Indians of the Great Lakes, Plains and Pacific Coast regions. On his return to Toronto, he wrote *Wanderings of an Artist among the Indians of North America*, which was published in 1859.

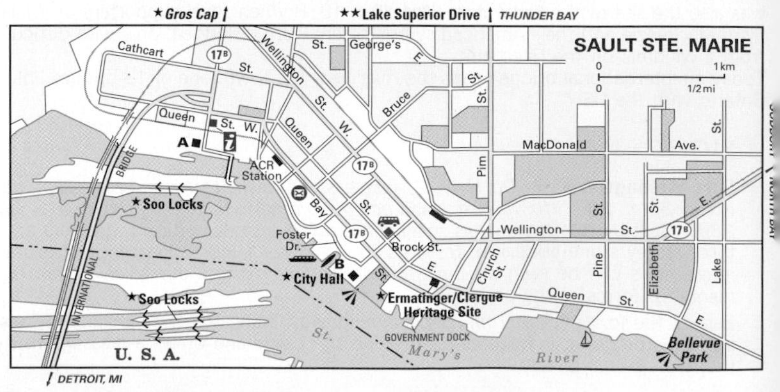

On the second floor there are interesting displays on the history of Sault Ste. Marie and of the Ermatinger family.

Bellevue Park – From this park on the river, there are fine **views★** of the ships using the locks and of the bridge to the US.

EXCURSIONS

★**Gros Cap** – *26km/16mi west by Hwy. 550.* From this headland there is a good **view★** of Lake Superior and the beginning of the St. Mary's River.

Train Trip to Agawa Canyon – *183km/114mi. Departs from Bay St. depot Jun–mid-Oct daily 8am. Round-trip 9hrs. $62 ($52 summer). Jan–mid-Mar weekends only 8am. Round-trip 8hrs. Commentary. Reservations required. ✗ ♿ Algoma Central Railway Inc. www.wclx.com ☎705-946-7300 or 800-242-9287 (Canada/US).* The train traverses some of the Algoma wilderness north of Sault Ste. Marie. At a stopover in Agawa Canyon *(2hrs, except in winter)*, travellers can climb to a lookout for a fine **view★** of the canyon and the Agawa River. The trip is especially popular in late September for viewing the autumn colours.

★★**Lake Superior Drive** – *Map p 4. 230km/143mi by Trans-Can Hwy. (Rte. 17) to Wawa.* This drive is ruggedly beautiful. The road cuts through some of the oldest rock formations in the world, the Canadian Shield. After Batchawana Bay the wild shore of Lake Superior is followed for a lengthy stretch, with views of headlands, coves, islands, rocks and high granite bluffs pounded by the waters of this, the deepest of the Great Lakes. The drive is especially fine around **Alona Bay★** *(viewpoint after 108km/67mi)* and **Agawa Bay★** *(viewpoint after 151km/94mi)*. Lookouts have been built beside the road.

For 84km/52mi the road passes through **Lake Superior Provincial Park** *(swimming, hiking; boat rental; open daily late May–late Oct; $7.50/car; ♿ www.ontarioparks.com ☎705-856-2284)*, a wilderness area of forested hills and cliffs rising straight out of the lake. The park is known for its Indian **pictographs**—primitive rock paintings often commemorating great events or relating to nature. After 153km/95mi a side road leads to a parking lot from which a rugged trail *(10min)* descends to the lake. A series of pictographs possibly several hundred years old can be found on **Agawa Rock★**, a sheer rock face rising out of the water. The **view★** of the lake is excellent.

STRATFORD★

Population 28,987
Map p 128
Tourist Office ☎519-273-3352

This community is home to the annual **Shakespeare Festival**, a major theatrical event of the English-speaking world that attracts people from all over North America. Though the focus is still Shakespearean, the festival offers a wide variety of drama and music.

The festival is said to have had its beginnings in 1830 when one William Sargint called his establishment on the Huron Road to Goderich the Shakespeare Inn. The community that grew up around the hostelry adopted the name of the birthplace of the famous English dramatist and named the river the Avon. In 1952 local journalist **Tom Patterson** dreamed of creating a festival to celebrate the works of the town's namesake. From modest beginnings in a tent a year later, the festival has grown to its present seven-month season *(May–Nov)* in three theatres, drawing a yearly audience of nearly 500,000. *For performance schedule & reservations contact the Box Office, Stratford Festival, PO Box 520, Stratford, ON, N5A 6V2. www.stratford-festival.on.ca ☎519-273-1600 or 800-567-1600 (Canada/US).*

VISIT *2hrs (not including performances)*

Festival Theatre – Reflecting the tent of its origin, this building resembling a circus "big top" contains an *apron* or thrust stage, surrounded by audience seating on three sides. This modern development of the Elizabethan stage used in Shakespeare's day was revolutionary in the 1950s (but much copied since) because no elaborate scenery could be used and no member of the audience was more than 20m/65ft from the stage.

The theatre is set at the edge of a pleasant park that stretches down to the river, dammed at this point to form **Victoria Lake**, the home of many swans. Before evening performances in the summer, the beautifully manicured lawns and the small island in the lake are covered with picnicking theatre-goers. At intermission the elegantly attired crowd wanders among the formal flower beds and over the lawns surrounding the theatre.

SUDBURY★★

Population 92,059
Map p 128
Tourist Office ☎800-465-6655 or 705-522-0104

Located on the largest single source of nickel in the world, Sudbury is the biggest and most important mining centre in Canada. Sudbury is also a principal centre of francophone culture in Ontario; about a quarter of the population of the region is **Franco-Ontarian. Laurentian University**, which serves the northeastern part of the province, is bilingual.

Historical Notes – The nickel-bearing rock strata are part of the **Sudbury Igneous Complex**, an approximately 60km/37mi long and 27km/17mi wide geological formation created by a meteorite impact or volcanic eruption millions of years ago. Geological opinion is divided on the issue. Whatever its origins, the area's wealth (platinum, copper, cobalt, silver and gold, in addition to nickel) was discovered in 1883 during the construction of the Canadian Pacific Railway. A blacksmith named **Thomas Flanagan** noticed a rust-coloured patch of rock while working with a crew in a recently blasted area just west of the present city.
Today the discovery is commemorated by a plaque *(on Hwy. 144 near the Murray Mine)*, and Sudbury claims the world's largest integrated nickel mining, smelting and refining complex. The **Super Stack**, an enormous smoke stack rising 380m/1,250ft above the surrounding countryside, tops the complex. In addition to its industrial importance, the Sudbury region is typical Canadian Shield country of beautiful lakes, rocks and trees. A number of lakes are encompassed within city limits, including **Lake Ramsey**, which has enough yellow pickerel (walleye) to supply local fishermen, and beaches just a short walk from the civic centre.

SIGHTS *1/2 day*

★★★**Science North** – *About 1.5km/1mi south of Trans-Can Hwy. From Hwy. 69 bypass, take Paris St. to Ramsey Lake Rd.* Perched on a rock outcropping on the shores of Lake Ramsey, this dramatic science centre was designed by Raymond Moriyama in association with local architects. A hexagonal exhibit building resembling a snowflake (to represent the glacial action that shaped Northern Ontario) is set over a cavern blasted out of the rock (to represent the probable creation of Sudbury Basin by a meteor). Exhibits emphasize first-hand experience with science and northern technology in a vivid way.

Visit – Kids *Open May–Sept daily 9am–5pm. Rest of the year daily 10am–4pm. Closed Jan 1, Dec 24–25. $9.95. ✗ ♿ http://sciencenorth.on.ca ☎705-522-3701 or 800-461-4898 (Canada only).* Visitors enter a small reception building (also hexagonal in shape) and proceed to the centre proper via a **rock tunnel**. Raw rock is exposed as it is in the impressive **rock cavern** (9m/30ft high by 30m/100ft in diameter), where a 3-D film and laser show highlights geological history. Visitors then ascend to the exhibit floors via a spiral ramp that zigzags over the **Creighton Fault**, a geological fracture within the Canadian Shield, active over 2 billion years ago, that left a groove 4m/13ft deep at this point. Hanging over the fault is a 23m/72ft fin whale skeleton, weighing 1800kg/4,000lb, recovered from Anticosti Island. The glass walls of the ramp offer views of Lake Ramsey. Museum staff are on hand in the fitness centre, for example, where visitors can be tested for correct body weight, or in the Alex Baumann Human Performance Lab, where visitors can discover their fitness level. The small creatures area houses such insects as a walking-stick or the museum's pet porcupine, who grows his furry coat in summer when the building is air-conditioned and loses it in winter when his home is heated. State-of-the-art monitoring equipment can be viewed in the weather station, and science shows are presented regularly in the Discovery Theatre.

From the dock **boat tours** of the lake can be taken *(depart May–Aug daily; round-trip 1hr; commentary; $9.95; ✗ ♿ Cortina Cruise ☎705-522-3701).*

★★**Big Nickel Mine** – *On Big Nickel Mine Dr., 5km/3mi west of Science North by Regent and Lorne Sts. Open May–mid-Oct daily 9am–5pm. $9.95. ♿ ☎705-522-3701.* Operated by Science North, this mine is one of a few authentic hard-rock mines open to the public in Ontario. Visitors descend 21m/70ft by a miners' cage to the underground "drifts" or tunnels where the mining process (drilling, blasting and other procedures) is explained and demonstrated. There is even a simulated blasting sequence.
Near the mine stands the **Big Nickel**, a replica of the 1951 Canadian commemorative five-cent piece. Long a Sudbury landmark, the replica is 9m/30ft high and 0.6m/2ft thick.

The Kids symbol indicates areas of special interest to children.

THUNDER BAY★★

Population 113,662
Map of Principal Sights p 4
Tourist Office ☎807-625-2149

Situated almost in the centre of Canada on the shores of Lake Superior, the city of Thunder Bay is an important port and the Canadian western extremity of the Great Lakes/St. Lawrence Seaway system. Its rail lines and roads transport a wide range of commodities—wheat from the Prairies being the most important—to docks for transfer to the huge ships of the seaway.

Historical Notes – This exchange of goods and transportation is not the result of the St. Lawrence Seaway's construction. For many years the area was the linchpin of the fur trade. Every summer brigades of canoes left the widespread posts of the North West Company in the northwest to transport a year's collection of furs to a trading post called Fort William. There these "wintering" partners (so named because they spent the winter in the wilds) met the Montreal partners who had made the long canoe trek through the Great Lakes with the trading goods their counterparts would need for the next year. Lasting about six weeks the "**rendezvous**" was a time of wild celebration, as well as serious discussion of trading policy and strategy against the rival Hudson's Bay Company, who took their furs to market by way of the great bay. When the two fur-trading companies merged in 1821, Fort William lost its position as the place of the great rendezvous, but remained a fur-trading post until late in the century. In 1970 the communities of **Fort William** and **Port Arthur** were amalgamated to create the city of Thunder Bay. The fort has been re-created as it was at its peak, and every year the rendezvous is re-enacted *(Jul)*.
The port's nine enormous grain terminals dominate the city skyline. Prairie grain arriving by rail is cleaned and stored in these terminals for transfer to the ships of the Greak Lakes fleet. Port facilities also include two terminals for coal, potash and other dry-bulk commodities, a malting plant, a bagging facility for specialty grains and a general cargo facility noted for its ship/rail heavy lift transfers.

SIGHTS

★**The Waterfront** – To appreciate the impressive port, and the sheer size of the grain **terminals** and ships, view them from **Marina Park** *(end of Red River Rd.; open daily year-round)*. The largest of these ships is 222m/728ft by 23m/75ft, capable of carrying up to a million bushels of grain—the yield of 20,650ha/51,000 acres of land. The breakwater protecting the harbour from the storms of Lake Superior can also be seen. Waves can reach 12m/40ft in height in autumn. In summer the lake is calmer, and sailboat races are held weekly within and outside of the breakwater.

★**Viewpoints** – Thunder Bay is surrounded by the hills of the Canadian Shield. The city is hemmed in across the bay by a long peninsula that rears its head at the end to form a cape that is called **Sleeping Giant** because its resembles the prone figure of a man.

★**Mt. McKay** – *At end of Mountain Rd. on Indian reserve.* This prominent flat-topped peak is the highest (488m/1,600ft) of the Norwester Chain. From a ledge 180m/600ft high, there is a fine **view** on clear days of the city, port and Sleeping Giant guarding the entrance to the harbour.

★**Hillcrest Park** – *High St. between John St. Rd. and Red River Rd.* Located on a cliff above Port Arthur, this park provides a good **view** of the port, elevators, ore dock and, in the distance, Sleeping Giant and the islands that close the harbour mouth.

★★**Old Fort William** – Kids *16km/10mi south by Broadway Ave. Map below. Open mid-May–mid-Oct daily 10am–5pm. $10. ✗ ♿ www.oldfortwilliam.on.ca ☎807-473-2344.* Located on the Kaministikwia River, part of the trade route to the northwest, the fort of the great rendezvous has been superbly reconstructed. From the visitor centre, visitors can walk through the woods to the palisaded fort, which is almost a town. Inside the palisade, there is a large square of dovetailed log buildings, two of which are raised above the ground on stilts (the river still floods). Some 42 structures represent all aspects of early-19C fur-trade society. Costumed guides help re-create fort life. The North West Company partners can be seen discussing business in the council house; the warehouses are full of furs and trading goods; and birchbark canoes, tinware and barrels are being crafted by hand. Other highlights at the fort include a farm, apothecary, Indian encampments, living quarters and a jail.

EXCURSIONS *Map p 166*

★★**Kakabeka Falls** – *29km/18mi west by Trans-Can Hwy. (Rte. 17). Provincial park open year-round. Park open to vehicles mid-May–mid-Oct daily 8am–11pm. $7-$9/car. ⛺ ♿ www.ontarioparks.com ☎807-473-9231.* The Kaministikwia River plunges 39m/128ft over a cliff around a pinnacle of rock into a narrow gorge.

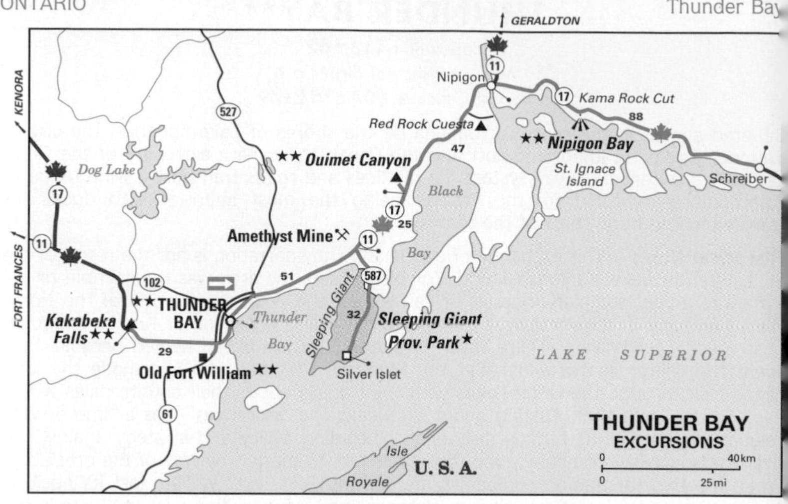

A bridge crosses the river to enable visitors to view the falls from both sides. These falls were the first obstacle negotiated by the fur traders of the North West Company when leaving Fort William on their return trip to the northwest.

★★ **North Shore Lake Superior** – *211km/131mi to Schreiber by Trans-Can Hwy.* This route passes several interesting features northeast of Thunder Bay.

Terry Fox Monument and Scenic Lookout – *1km/.6mi east of Hodder Ave.* The fine bronze monument commemorates the heroic efforts of Terry Fox to raise money to fight cancer. Deprived of his right leg by the disease at age 18, he undertook a cross-Canada run in 1980, starting in Newfoundland. Two months later, he was forced to abandon his run close to this spot because of recurring cancer from which he died in 1981. The monument overlooks Lake Superior.

★ **Sleeping Giant Provincial Park** – *After 51km/32mi, take Rte. 587. Open daily May–Oct. Jan–Mar cross-country ski trails accessible. $8/car.* ▲ ♿ ☎ *807-977-2526.* Occupying most of the peninsula that has the Sleeping Giant at its end, this pleasant park features trails, high cliffs, fine **views**★ of Lake Superior and the remains of the village of Silver Islet. This community was formed in 1868 when a rich silver vein was discovered on the tiny islet offshore. The vertical vein yielded $300 million worth of ore before the shaft flooded at a depth of 400m/1,300ft.

Amethyst Mine – *After 56km/35mi, take East Loon Rd. for 8km/5mi. Open Jul–early Sept daily 10am–7pm. Mid-May–Jun & mid-Sept–mid-Oct daily 10am–5pm. $3.* ♿ ☎ *807-622-6908.* Amethyst is found in many places along the north shore of Lake Superior. This open-pit mine is a rock hound's delight as pieces of the purple quartz can be collected *(charge of $1/lb.)*, or polished stones purchased.

★★ **Ouimet Canyon** – *After 76km/47mi, take road for 12km/8mi. Open May–Oct daily dawn–dusk.* ☎ *807-977-2526.* This incredible canyon is quite a startling find in the country north of Lake Superior. Gashed out of the surface of the Canadian Shield during the last Ice Age, possibly along an existing fault line, the canyon is 100m/330ft deep, 150m/500ft across and more than 1.6km/1mi long. It is rocky and barren except for a few Arctic flowers that grow on its floor; the cold, sunless environment will support little else.

Just after the Red Rock turnoff on the Trans-Canada Highway, a cliff of layered limestone coloured red by hematite can be seen. Called the **Red Rock Cuesta**, this unusual geological formation is nearly 210m/690ft high and about 3km/2mi long.

★★ **Nipigon Bay** – *88km/55mi from Nipigon to Schreiber.* After crossing the Nipigon River, the Trans-Canada Highway runs along the shore of this bay, offering **views**★★ of rocky islands covered with conifers and rocks worn smooth by the action of Lake Superior.

The **view**★★ of Kama Bay through the Kama Rock Cut *(27km/17mi from Nipigon)* is particularly fine. The rock itself indicates the type of problems involved in the construction of this highway in 1960, the same encountered in the building of the Canadian Pacific Railway.

Sights described in this guide are rated:

★★★ *Worth the trip*
★★ *Worth a detour*
★ *Interesting*

TORONTO★★★

Population 2,385,421
Map of Principal Sights p 4
Tourist Office ☎416-203-2500

Dynamic, cosmopolitan, stimulating, Toronto is the heartbeat of Canada. Having surpassed MONTREAL in size in 1977, the country's largest metropolis ranks among the most populous in North America. Toronto is the hub of the **Golden Horseshoe**, the 60km/100mi wide arc stretching from OSHAWA to HAMILTON where at least a quarter of Canada's manufacturing is based.

Sprawling over 600sq km/372sq mi in the southeast leg of the province, the metropolis is set on the broad north shore of **Lake Ontario**. Its fine harbour is almost landlocked by a chain of offshore islands *(p 171)* that provide the city with its major parkland. Flat beside the lake, the land rises noticeably about 5km/3mi inland at the old shoreline of prehistoric Lake Iroquois. The plain is intersected by a number of small rivers that have created a network of ravines. On the westside Toronto is bordered by the **Humber River** *(map p 183)* and to the east, the **Don River**. In the recent past the ravines and river valleys have been used largely for parks.

A forward-looking metropolis protective of its past, Toronto has restored its architectural treasures and preserved its history. Waves of immigrants have repeatedly integrated with the population, enhancing the city's cultural legacy. Toronto's size, heritage and diversity have much to offer: world-class exhibits, colourful neighbourhoods, lively markets, historic mansions, a vibrant harbourfront, wide-ranging cultural events and cuisine, and multiple recreational activities.

Historical Notes

"Toronto Passage" – In their search for food and trade, native inhabitants of the area had long used the rivers as a transportation system. Prior to 1600 the **Huron** and **Petun** peoples abandoned their north shorelands to the warring **Iroquois Confederacy**. The Iroquois occupied the vacated territory to strengthen their fur trade, only to be evicted themselves by French traders, to whom this "Toronto Passage" of trails and canoe routes between Lakes Huron and Ontario was well known.

The French Regime – The site of Toronto was important to the burgeoning fur trade. As early as 1615 it was visited by **Étienne Brûlé**, one of Champlain's men who travelled widely in Ontario. Years later French traders under royal command met native and English traders at a bartering post on the banks of the Humber River in the vicinity of what is now Toronto, a Huron word for "meeting place." Attempting to curb competition, the French began construction in 1720 of several forts around mammoth Lake Ontario. The remains of **Fort Rouillé** have been found in Toronto's Exhibition Grounds. To prevent British use, the French destroyed the fort in 1759 during the Seven Years' War, the war that signalled the end of French presence in the area.

Muddy York – The site was first ignored by the new British rulers, but in 1787, **Sir Guy Carleton**, the governor of British North America, made arrangements to buy land equivalent in size to present-day metropolitan Toronto from the **Mississaugas**, who had occupied it after the Iroquois. Loyalists fleeing the US had also settled along the lake; their demands for English law eventually led to the formation of Upper Canada (now Ontario) in 1791. Col. **John Graves Simcoe**, lieutenant-governor of the new territory, decided upon Toronto, despite its swamps, as the site for a temporary capital *(p 142)*, because of its fine harbour and distance from the American border. (The existing capital, Niagara-on-the-Lake, was considered too close to the enemy.) Baptized **York** after the victorious soldier-son of George III, the new outpost grew slowly, despite such grandiose projects as the building of **Yonge Street**. By the outbreak of the War of 1812, the unpaved streets of this swamp town gave the village the unfortunate sobriquet "Muddy York."

In April 1813 the town was jolted by an American fleet that captured and set fire to the Legislature and other imposing buildings. In retaliation for this assault and the burning of Niagara-on-the-Lake, the British attacked and set fire to part of Washington, DC, the capital of the US, in 1814.

The Family Compact – After 1814 York grew as waves of immigrants from Britain came to Ontario in the wake of the Napoleonic Wars. A small group of wealthy, privileged men with strong British ties dominated the government of York—and the whole of Upper Canada. By appointing officials only from their ranks, they guarded their exclusive elite. New arrivals began to challenge the power of what was called "the Family Compact." An outspoken Scot named **William Lyon Mackenzie** (1795-1861) attacked the group in his newspaper, *The Colonial Advocate*. In 1828 he was elected to the legislative assembly, becoming leader of the radical wing of the Reform Party. Expelled by the compact, he was reelected and reexpelled five times. However, in 1835, he was elected the first mayor of the City of Toronto, newly incorporated in 1834 (the city's original name had fallen from favour as its namesake, the Duke of York, continued to lose in battle). Mackenzie then reassumed his seat in the legislature. The assembly was dissolved in 1836 by Gov. **Sir Francis Bond Head**, and subsequent elections brought the defeat of the Reform Party.

The Rebellions of 1837 – Gaining no satisfaction from the British Parliament, Mackenzie turned to armed rebellion in December 1837. When Toronto's garrison was away in Lower Canada, he gathered supporters at **Montgomery's Tavern** (which stood near the present intersection of Yonge Street and Eglinton Avenue) and marched towards the city. Loyal citizens hurriedly formed a defence, but quickly dispersed after a skirmish with Mackenzie's men. Unknown to them, Mackenzie's forces had also retreated. Reinforcements arrived under Col. Allan MacNab the following day, the revolt collapsed, and Mackenzie fled to the US. Although two of Mackenzie's men were publicly hanged, the revolt was effective in that British Parliament ultimately granted "responsible government" to the Canadian colonies. The united Province of Canada was created *(p 24)*, and Mackenzie was permitted to return in 1849.

Montreal was the site of another armed rebellion, also in 1837, against British rule *(p 203)*. Although it was crushed, the insurgence subsequently resulted in representative government for Quebec.

Toronto the Good – The revolt bred among Torontonians an enduring hatred of violence and a resulting support for government. By the end of the 19C, Toronto's reputation was one of Anglo-Saxon rectitude. As a major manufacturing centre, the city had become immensely wealthy. Prosperous financiers, industrialists and merchants were united in their desire to preserve Sunday as a day of rest and church-going, and in their belief that intemperance was a fundamental social problem. Toronto was nicknamed "the Good" but considered dull.

Toronto Today: The Urban Miracle – As late as 1941 Toronto was 80 percent Anglo-Saxon, but since World War II, this once-homogeneous city has opened its doors to immigrants from around the world. Today Italians, Germans, Ukrainians, Dutch, Poles, Scandinavians, Portuguese, East Indians, Chinese, West Indians and other nationalities have made their home here, giving Toronto a stimulating mix of indigenous and imported cultures. **Kensington Market** *(Kensington Ave., east of Spadina and north of Dundas)*, several adjacent streets containing outdoor and indoor vendors, is the realm of the Portuguese and East Indian communities *(best time to visit is Mon-Sat mornings)*. One of the largest Chinese districts in North America, **Chinatown** *(Dundas St. from Elizabeth to Spadina)* is also vibrant with street vendors, notably exotic-produce merchants. The Italian districts *(College St. and St. Clair Ave., west of Bathurst)* evoke the mother country. **Greektown** *(Danforth Ave. between Coxwell and Broadview; ● Chester)* offers numerous cafes, specialty shops and fruit markets featuring Greek food. Particularly active between Spadina and John Streets, **Queen Street West** has become a colourful area of trendy bistros, unusual bookstores and young designer boutiques.

The last 30 years have seen the Toronto skyline transformed. Shining glass-fronted skyscrapers and "spacescraper" CN Tower overshadow the once-dominant **Royal York Hotel** and old **Bank of Commerce**. Rapid development has been highly controversial, however. Citizen-action groups formed to halt destruction of residential areas for proposed freeways and high rises. The city was the first in North America to adopt a tiered system of metropolitan government to solve problems caused by 19C municipal boundaries.

Toronto's port has suffered since the opening of the St. Lawrence Seaway when the era of containerization began. Cargo unloaded at ports such as HALIFAX and ST. JOHN'S on the East Coast is containerized, and shipped inland via rail, bypassing Toronto's waterways.

At the beginning of 1998 Toronto became a megacity when the six municipalities that comprise Greater Toronto—Etobicoke, North York, Scarborough, York, Toronto and East York—were amalgamated. With a total population of nearly 4.5 million, the new Metropolitan Toronto now ranks among the continent's largest cities.

Cultural and Sports Centre – The centre of English-language culture in Canada, Toronto boasts the Toronto Symphony and the Mendelssohn Choir at Roy Thomson Hall, concerts at Massey Hall, the National Ballet of Canada, the Toronto Dance Theatre, Harbourfront Centre's Premiere Dance Theatre, and the Canadian Opera Company at the Hummingbird Centre. The St. Lawrence Centre for the Arts, the Royal Alexandra, and the Elgin and Winter Garden Theatre Centre stage traditional and popular drama. Every fall the city hosts a world film festival, and summer brings a variety of outdoor entertainment. Several annual events draw visitors: the **Canadian National Exhibition** *(at the Exhibition Grounds late-Aug–Labour Day)*, reputedly the world's largest exhibition, now primarily of consumer goods; the **Metro International Caravan**, a festival of ethnic cultures *(mid-Jun, pavilions throughout the city, special buses)*; the **International Dragon Boat Festival**, a Chinese celebration *(Jun)*, and **Caribana**, a West Indies festival of steel bands and floating nightclubs on the lake *(mid-Jul–early Aug)*. Spectator sports are plentiful: Toronto Blue Jays baseball, Maple Leaf ice hockey games, an annual harbour regatta *(Jul 1)*, horse shows *(particularly the Royal Agricultural Winter Fair)*, soccer and auto racing. A new sports arena, the Air Canada Centre, is under construction at the south end of Bay Street, and, upon completion, will host the Toronto Raptors basketball team and the Maple Leafs hockey team *(first games in the new arena are scheduled for mid-Feb, 1999). For details contact the Metropolitan Toronto Convention & Visitors Assn. ☎ 416-203-2600 or 800-363-1990.*

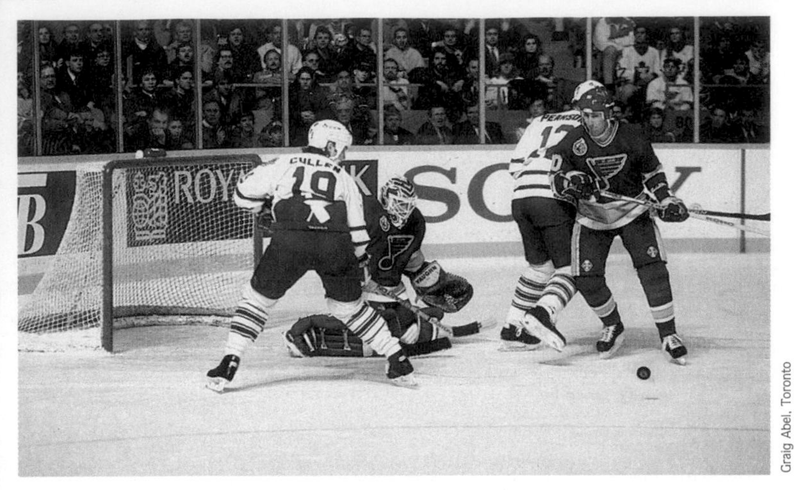

Graig Abel, Toronto

Maple Leaf Ice Hockey Game

★★THE WATERFRONT *2 days. Maps pp 172 and 175.*

Built largely on land reclaimed in the mid-19C to mid-20C for the city's growing port installations, the area south of Front Street contains Toronto's foremost landmarks and its largest lakefront revitalization.

Crucial to the city's founding, the waterfront experienced growth and eventual decline of its maritime functions, now transferred to the commercial port east of Yonge Street. Lake shipping waned in the 1960s, and recession subsequently idled the harbourfront. Although scarred by the remains of defunct industries, the area underwent gradual revitalization beginning in the early 1970s. Over the following 20 years, land north of the expressway was selected as the site of two major building projects—the CN Tower and SkyDome.

Several quays were overhauled to house colourful shops, galleries, performance arenas, restaurants and sailing schools. Completion of an outdoor stage known as Molson Place in 1992 and a 105,000sq ft expansion to the **convention centre** southeast of the CN Tower in 1997 confirm the area's growing popularity. Most recent construction includes the Air Canada Centre at the foot of Bay Street, south of Union Station. This new sports arena will host the Toronto Raptors basketball team and the Maple Leaf hockey games.

The grounds of both CN Tower and SkyDome can be reached on foot from Union Station by way of **Skywalk**, *a large glass-enclosed walkway containing eateries and souvenir shops.*

★★★**CN Tower** – *Illustration p 126. Entrance at Front and John Sts.* ● *Union, then via Skywalk. Open May–Sept daily 8am–10pm. Rest of the year daily 9am–10pm. $15.* ✗ ♿ *www.cntower.ca* ☎ *416-868-6937.* The city's most prominent landmark, this concrete, rocketlike structure reaches 180 storeys (over 553m/1,815ft in height). Constructed at a cost of $63 million, the tower is the tallest freestanding structure in the world and a popular Toronto tourist attraction (1.8 million visitors a year).

Beginning in 1972, the tower was built over a four-year period by federally owned Canadian National (formerly Canadian National Railways) to provide telecommunications services. Topped by a powerful antenna, the tower serves FM radio and television stations *(telecommunications facilities not open to the public)* whose transmitters line the mast.

In only 58 seconds visitors are "beamed up" 346m/1,136ft (nearly the height of the Empire State Building) in one of six exterior glass-front elevators to **Skypod**, a circular steel "turban" seven storeys high. From its observation decks, **views**★★ of the city and suburbs, the lake and shoreline are superb *(illuminated panels identify buildings and parks)*, providing a vivid aerial orientation to Toronto. One floor down, intrepid visitors can stand or sit on the **glass floor**, a small section of thick glass panels that permit an impressive view 342m/1,122ft straight down to the ground below.

Not for the faint-hearted is an ascent 33 storeys higher to the smaller observation gallery named **Space Deck**, a flying saucer-shaped, windowed ring 447m/1,465ft above the ground, reached via an elevator inside the tower. The sweeping **views**★★★ of the cityscape and Lake Ontario are spectacular. The feeling of height is reinforced by planes from nearby Toronto Island Airport flying below. If visibility is good, NIAGARA FALLS and Buffalo, 120km/75mi away, can be seen.

PRACTICAL INFORMATION

Area Code 416

Getting Around

By Public Transportation – The Toronto Transit Commission (TTC) operates an extensive public transit system of buses, streetcars and subway. Hours of operation: Mon–Sat 6am–1am, Sun 9am–1am. Adult fare $2 one-way for unlimited travel with no stopovers. Day Pass $6.50. Tokens 10 for $16. Exact fare required. Free transfers between buses & streetcars. System maps & timetables available free of charge. For route information www.city.toronto.on.ca ☎393-INFO.

By Car – Use of public transportation or walking is strongly encouraged within the city as streets are often congested and street parking may be difficult to find. Toronto has a strictly enforced tow-away policy. Motorists should park in designated **parking** areas; public, off-street parking facilities are located throughout the city. For parking fee information & free map ☎393-7275. Car rentals: Avis ☎777-AVIS; Hertz ☎620-9620; Tilden ☎922-2000.

By Taxi – Co-op ☎504-2667; Diamond ☎366-6868; Metro Cab ☎504-5757.

By Trolley – Connections ☎675-6656 or 675-9710.

General Information

Accommodations and Visitor Information – For **hotels/motels** contact Tourism Toronto ☎203-2500 or 800-363-1990 (Canada/US). For listing of major chains *(p 306)*. Reservation services: Utell International ☎800-448-8355 (Canada/US); Abodes of Choice B&B Assn. of Toronto ☎537-7629; B&B Homes of Toronto ☎363-6362; Downtown Toronto Assn. of B&B Guest Homes ☎368-1420. The visitor centre is located at Metropolitan Toronto Convention & Visitors Assn., 207 Queen's Quay West, Toronto, ON, M5J 1A7 *(open year-round Mon–Fri 8:30am–5:30pm)*.

Local Press – Daily: the *Toronto Star*, the *Toronto Sun*, the *Globe and Mail*. Monthly guides (free) to entertainment, shopping, and restaurants: *Where, Now*.

Entertainment – Consult arts and entertainment supplements in local newspapers (Thursday edition) for schedule of cultural events and addresses of principal theatres and concert halls. Ticketmaster ☎870-8000 for concerts or 872-1111 for theatre & arts (major credit cards accepted). T.O. Tix ☎536-6463 for half-price, same-day tickets for theatrical, dance and musical events; must be purchased in person at Eaton Centre, Yonge St. (major credit cards accepted).

Sports – Toronto Blue Jays (baseball):season Apr–Oct at SkyDome ☎341-1111. Toronto Maple Leafs (ice hockey): season Oct–Apr at Maple Leaf Gardens until mid-Feb, then Air Canada Centre ☎977-1641 (schedules) ☎872-5000 (Ticketmaster). Toronto Argonauts (football): season mid-Jun–Nov at SkyDome ☎341-5151 (schedules), ☎872-5000 (Ticketmaster). Toronto Raptors (basketball): season Nov–Apr at SkyDome until mid-Feb, then Air Canada Centre ☎366-3865.

Useful Numbers

	☎
Police	911 (emergency) or 808-2222
Union Station (VIA Rail), *Front & Bay Sts.*	366-8411
Bus terminal, *610 Bay St.*	393-7911
Toronto (Pearson) International Airport	905-676-3506
Canadian Automobile Assn., *461 Young St.*	221-4300
CAA Emergency Road Service (24hr)	222-5222
Shoppers Drug Mart (24hr pharmacy) *various locations*	493-1220
Post Office Station A, *25 The Esplanade*	979-8822
Road Conditions	235-1110
Weather (24hr)	661-0123

★★**SkyDome** – ● *Union, then via Skywalk.* *www.skydome.com ☎416-341-3663. For tours ☎416-341-2770.* Dominating railway land next to CN Tower—one of the few central locations big enough to hold it—this huge, domed sports/entertainment complex is home to American League Baseball's *Toronto Blue Jays*. The multipurpose stadium hosts rock concerts, conventions and trade shows as well as sports. Designed by architect Roderick Robbie and engineer Michael Allen, SkyDome was built (1989) by a private consortium in partnership with local and provincial governments for over $570 million.

Projecting from the Front Street facade 5m/16ft above street level, Michael Snow's collection of 14 painted-fiberglass sculptures *(The Audience)* towers over arriving visitors. SkyDome boasts a 3ha/8 acre **retractable roof**, a 348-room hotel overlooking the playing field, a 150-seat cinema, several restaurants and underground parking for 575 vehicles. In the open-air mode, the four roof panels are stacked over the north end of the field. In 20 minutes the panels can be closed by pushing a button to activate a computer-controlled operation. Tall enough to accommodate a 31-storey building, the roof is 205m/674ft at its widest and rises to a height of 91m/299ft at its centre. The arena's flexible field (basketball, football, tennis, track or baseball configurations) and seating can be arranged for a crowd of 53,000 or an audience of 10,000.

★★ **Harbourfront Centre** – *Access from York, Spadina and Bathurst Sts.; ● Union or Spadina, transfer to bus 77B or LRT York Quay. Visitor centre at York Quay Centre open Apr–Oct Mon–Sat 10am–11pm, Sun 10am–6pm. Nov–Dec & Feb–Mar Wed–Sat 10am–8pm, Sun 10am–6pm. ♿ www.harbourfront.on.ca ☎ 416-973-3000.* Initiated in 1976, this colourful 40ha/100 acre development has transformed Toronto's previously neglected lakeshore into an attractive mix of marinas, outdoor cafes, antiques and crafts markets, modern hotels, sleek condominiums and pleasant miniparks. A focal point of the city's cultural life, especially in summer, Harbourfront is also the scene of year-round recreational, educational and commercial activities, commonplace in the renovated warehouses as well as outdoors. The granddaddy of the waterfront warehouses, **Queen's Quay Terminal** (1927), with its imposing clock tower and rectangular solidity, was completely overhauled, perforated from top to bottom with wide bottle-green windows, and opened in 1983. Designed by Eberhard Zeidler, the refurbished terminal accommodates airy offices, plush living spaces, fashionable boutiques and eateries, the 450-seat Premiere Dance Theatre and, on the fifth floor, the Metro Toronto Convention and Visitors Assn. Nearby, **York Quay Centre** houses an art gallery, a craft studio and summer theatre. Fronting the **Power Plant** (**A**), now a contemporary art gallery *(open year-round Tue–Sun noon–6pm; closed Jan 1 & Dec 25; $4; www.culturenet.ca/powerplant ☎ 416-973-4949)*, the multipurpose **du Maurier Theatre Centre** (**B**), with its glass-faceted foyer, evolved from a former 1920s icehouse. **Molson Place** (**C**), an open-air 1,750-seat concert facility, occupies the southwest corner of the quay. Sailing schools, nautical stores and restaurants are located at **Pier 4**, and the Marine Division of the Metro Police is based at John Quay.

★★ **Toronto Islands** – *Ferries depart from Queen's Quay to three points: Centre Island, Ward's Island and Hanlan's Point (in winter to Ward's Island only) Apr–Oct daily every 15min 6:35am–11:30pm (11:45pm weekends). Rest of the year daily every 15min 6:35am–11:30pm. $4 round-trip. ♿ 🅿 www.city.toronto.on.ca ☎ 416-392-8195.* A popular retreat from the bustle of nearby downtown, these islands function as Toronto's principal public parkland. Formed from the erosion of Scarborough Bluffs *(p 183)*, this narrow landmass was a peninsula until 1853, when a violent storm severed it from the mainland, creating the present string of islands. Extending 6km/3.7mi from end to end, the islands are graced with expansive lawns, age-old shade trees, sandy beaches, marinas and spectacular **views**★★ of downtown Toronto. Attractions on **Centre Island** include restaurants, cafes, a beach *(on the Lake Ontario side)* and a delightful theme/amusement park for youngsters *(open mid-May–Labour Day; ☎ 416-203-0405)*. On foot or by bike *(motor vehicles prohibited on the islands)*, visitors can explore the adjacent islands, particularly **Algonquin** and **Ward's Islands**, whose quaint roads lined with small, privately owned cottages lend a decidedly rural charm. Near the small airport located on the islands' western end is Hanlan's Point, renowned for its **views** of the city *(a trackless train operates continuously between Centre Island and Hanlan's Point)*.

For visitors pressed for time, the hour-long **harbour cruise** offers a waterside perspective of the harbourfront and the islands. The return trip provides fine **views** of downtown *(departs from Pier 6, Queen's Quay West, York St. Jun–Aug daily 10am–9pm every 30min; Apr–May & Sept–Oct daily 10am–5pm every hour; round-trip 1hr; commentary; $15.75; 🅿 Toronto Harbour Tours www.we-know-toronto.com ☎ 416-869-1372)*.

★ **Fort York** – *Access by Bathurst streetcar or by car: from Lakeshore Blvd. take Strachan just before Princes' Gate entrance to Exhibition Grounds, then right on Fleet St. and left on Garrison Rd. (under Gardiner Expressway). Open May–Sept daily 10am–5pm. Rest of the year Tue–Fri 10am–4pm, weekends 10am–5pm. $5. 🅿 www.torontohistory.on.ca ☎ 416-392-6907.* In stark contrast to the backdrop of Toronto's towering skyline stand the dwarfed remains of this historic garrison. Once strategically positioned on the lake's edge, Fort York was the primary guardian of Toronto's harbour.

Constructed in 1793, the post was fortified 18 years later when Anglo-American relations soured. Devastated in 1813 during American capture, the fort was rebuilt by the British. As US threats subsided, its military importance diminished.

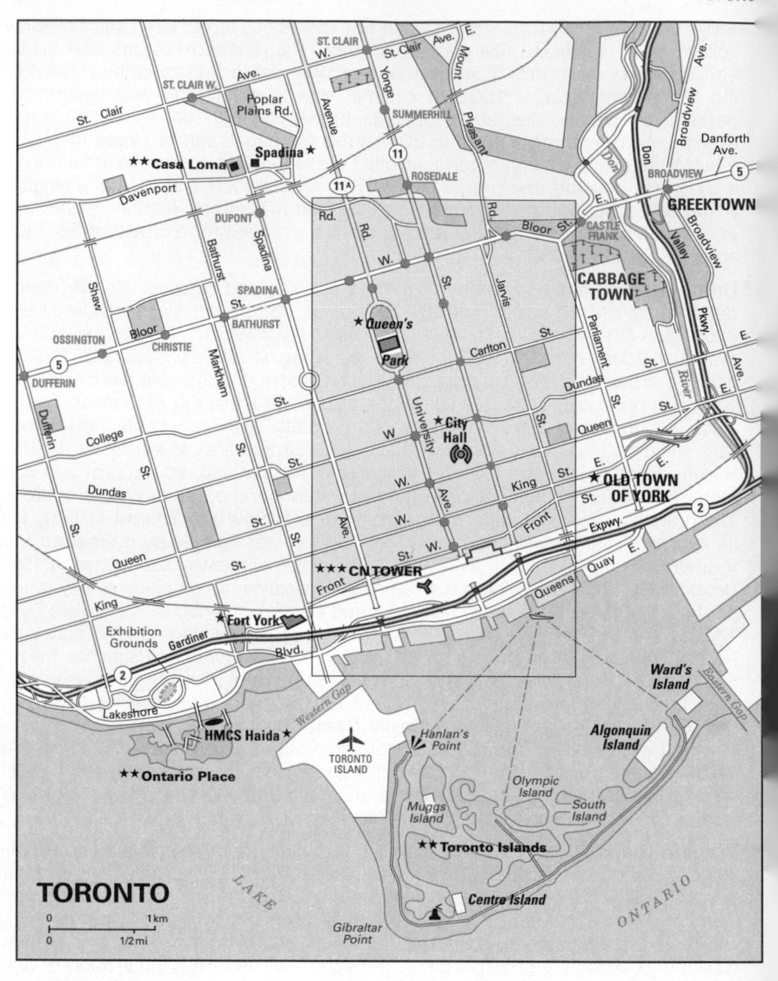

A new fort was constructed to the west after 1841. Renovated for the city's centennial in 1934, this popular tourist attraction celebrated its 200th birthday in 1993.

The wooden blockhouses, powder magazines and barracks, completed in 1815, have been faithfully restored. The **officers' barracks** is furnished to show the lifestyle of senior officers of the period. Canada's military history is revisited in the junior officers' barracks, the only 20C building. Other exhibits include York in 1816 and an illuminated map of Toronto's changing lakeshore. Costumed staff conduct tours and perform demonstrations and, in summer, stage military manoeuvres *(Jul–Aug)*.

★★ **Ontario Place** – Kids *955 Lakeshore Blvd. West, access from Exhibition Grounds. Open Jun–Aug daily 10am–dusk. Mid-to-end May & Sept weekends only 10am–dusk. (Cinesphere open year-round.) $9.95.* ✗ P *www.ontarioplace.com ☎416-314-9900.* Like a space-age lunar base, this innovative, modular-piece leisure complex emerges from an extraordinary setting of lagoons, marinas and man-made islands on the lakefront bordering the Exhibition Grounds. The park's emphasis is on entertainment and leisure activities.

Metallic and fabric structures glorify the geometric shapes of modern technology, a trademark of architect **Eberhard Zeidler** (b.1926). The metal "pods" suspended above the lake enclose children's play areas and a theatre in which 3D films are shown. Resembling a giant golf ball, **Cinesphere** features IMAX films on a screen six storeys high. The **amphitheatre** is a 16,000-seat outdoor performance space used to stage a variety of musical productions. In the **waterplay area**, a series of wading pools full of water jets and games is a popular attraction.

At the large marina, Canadian **HMCS Haida**★, veteran of World War II and the Korean War, can be boarded *(open mid-May–Labour Day daily 10am–7pm; early Sept–mid-Oct weekends only 11am–5pm; $3.95; www3.sympatico.ca/hrc/haida ☎416-314-9755)*.

★OLD TOWN OF YORK *2hrs. Map p 172.*

In 1793 Lieutenant-Governor Simcoe approved a surveyor's gridiron plan for York—10 city blocks bordered by present-day Front, George, Adelaide and Berkeley Streets. By 1813 Jarvis Street marked the west boundary. The block between Front and King Streets served as a public market.

Although not original to Simcoe's town, some remaining historic structures date from the first half of the 19C, including an active marketplace, the **South St. Lawrence Market** *(91-95 Front St. East at Jarvis St., ● King; open year-round Tue–Thu 8am–6pm, Fri 8am–7pm, Sat 5am–5pm; ✗ ♿ www.stlawrencemarket.com ☎416-392-7219)*, a cavernous brick building sheltering a two-storey food hall. Especially lively on Saturday mornings when early-bird shoppers converge on countless fruit stands, bakeries, meat counters and delicatessens, the market encases the surviving portion of the **Second City Hall** (1845-99). The former second-floor council chamber houses the **Market Gallery** of the City of Toronto Archives, which presents rotating exhibits of historical documents and artifacts *(open year-round Wed–Fri 10am–4pm, Sat 9am–4pm, Sun noon–4pm; closed national holidays; ♿ www.city.toronto.on.ca ☎416-392-7604).*

To the west, along Front Street, stands a handsome row of brick and stone 19C commercial buildings.

Directly across the street is **North St. Lawrence Market**, a bustling farmers' market *(open year-round Sat 5am–5pm; ✗ ♿ www.stlawrencemarket.com ☎416-392-7219)* housed in a smaller building, where farm-fresh or prepared food is available. From the entrance there is a good view, to the west, of Toronto's **flatiron building**, the Gooderham (1892) on Wellington Street, against a backdrop of the towers of BCE Place *(p 174.*

Adjoining the market via a charming pedestrian mall is the Neoclassical **St. Lawrence Hall** *(King and Jarvis Sts.)*, distinguished by its domed cupola. Former site of the city's market and social gatherings, this renovated mid-19C building houses various commercial enterprises.

Malak, Ottawa

Flatiron Building

Opposite St. Lawrence Hall is lovely St. James Park, complete with bandstand. A seasonal delight, especially at tulip time, this small manicured expanse offers res and refreshment to passersby.

Farther east is Toronto's **First Post Office★** *(260 Adelaide St. East; open year round Mon–Fri 9am–4pm, weekends 10am–4pm; closed national holidays;* ♿ *www.websights.com/tfpo ☎416-865-1833)*, formerly York's fourth post office opened in 1833. Re-created to the period, it operates again, with replicas of the original boxes and a reading room, complete with fireplace, where residents once read their mail. Costumed staff demonstrate quill-and-ink letter-writing.

★★DOWNTOWN *2 days. Map p 175.*

Containing the city's formidable financial core, Toronto's downtown exudes a sense of momentum and prosperity, exemplified in its soaring skyscrapers and early-20C halls of commerce. Site of the country's leading banks, legal, insurance and brokerage firms, and the Toronto Stock Exchange, the area of King and Bay Streets constitutes Canada's "Wall Street."

By the 1840s growing commerce fostered creation of several banks. Warehouses and offices followed within the next 10 to 20 years. At the time of Confederation *(p 24)*, 11 financial institutions had head offices in Toronto, and another 9 had branches. The desire to appear forward-looking led to successive replacement of these mid-19C stalwarts with newer-style buildings.

The skyscrapers are connected by an **underground city** of shops, eateries, banks and concourses—a welcome haven in inclement weather. Reputed to be the largest in the world, this subterranean complex extends eight blocks from Union Station and the Royal York Hotel to City Hall, Eaton Centre and on up to Dundas Street. The PATH network of walkways, clearly marked, covers10km/6mi.

One of the best-known and longest roads (1,896km/1,178mi) in Canada is **Yonge Street**, the city's east-west dividing line. Built by Simcoe in 1795 as a military route, this thoroughfare sports fancy boutiques, colourful flower stands, trendy restaurants, inviting bookstores and classy antique shops.

★★Financial District ● *King or St. Andrew*

A stunning ebony-coloured ensemble covering an entire city block, the **Toronto-Dominion Centre★★** was the first component of the current financial district. A fine example of International Style, the spartan black-glass towers, known locally as the T-D Centre, reflect the design of eminent 20C architect Mies van der Rohe, consultant for the project. Begun in 1964 the headquarters of the Toronto Dominion Bank consisted originally of three structures; today the towers number five. Fronting Bay Street, the Ernst & Young tower (1992) incorporates the former Art Deco Stock Exchange Building (1937) within its base. On view throughout the centre are works by contemporary artists, predominantly Canadian.

The downtown abounds in other skyscrapers by noted architects, among them, the adjacent **Royal Bank Plaza★** (**D**) designed by Boris Zerafa. Completed in 1976 the 41-storey and 26-storey gold, reflecting-glass towers are linked by a 40m/130ft high glass-walled banking hall, entry point to the underground city. A suspended sculpture of 8,000 aluminum tubes, the work of renowned Venezuelan artist Jesus Rafael Soto, dominates the interior of the hall.

The tiered, aqua-glass towers of **BCE Place**, designed by Spanish architect Santiago Calatrava, abut a lower central building bisected into matching office wings by an elaborate arched, aluminum **atrium★**. The southernmost tower is topped by a square telecommunications "cross." A 1990s newcomer to the financial district, the complex is the headquarters of Bell Canada Enterprises, and home of the **Hockey Hall of Fame★** (**E**), Kids where the Stanley Cup is generally on display in the stately, domed lobby (1886) of the former Bank of Montreal building, which has been preserved and encased within BCE Place *(take the escalator to lower level; open mid-Jun–Labour Day Mon–Sat 9:30am–6pm, Sun 10am–6pm; rest of the year Mon–Fri 10am–5pm, Sat 9:30am–6pm, Sun 10:30am–5pm; closed Jan 1 & Dec 25; $10;* ♿ P *www.hhof.com ☎416-360-7765)*.

Four buildings (1931 to 1972) form **Commerce Court**, an office complex surrounding an outdoor courtyard of trees, benches and a central fountain. The dominant 57-storey stainless-steel tower, head office of the Canadian Imperial Bank of Commerce, was designed by famed architect I.M. Pei.

Opposite Commerce Court, the ruby-coloured **Scotia Plaza** (1988) by Boris Zerafa is a striking addition to Toronto's skyline. At street level an "erector-set" canopy marks the entrance to the slender 68-storey building, distinguished by a V-shaped wedge in its summit.

First Canadian Place consists of a 72-storey white tower (1975) housing the Bank of Montreal and the 36-storey tower (1983) containing the **Toronto Stock Exchange** (**F**) *(open year-round Mon–Fri 9am–4:30pm; closed national holidays* ✗ ♿ P *www.tse.com ☎416-947-4676)*. Richly coloured wall hangings adorn the

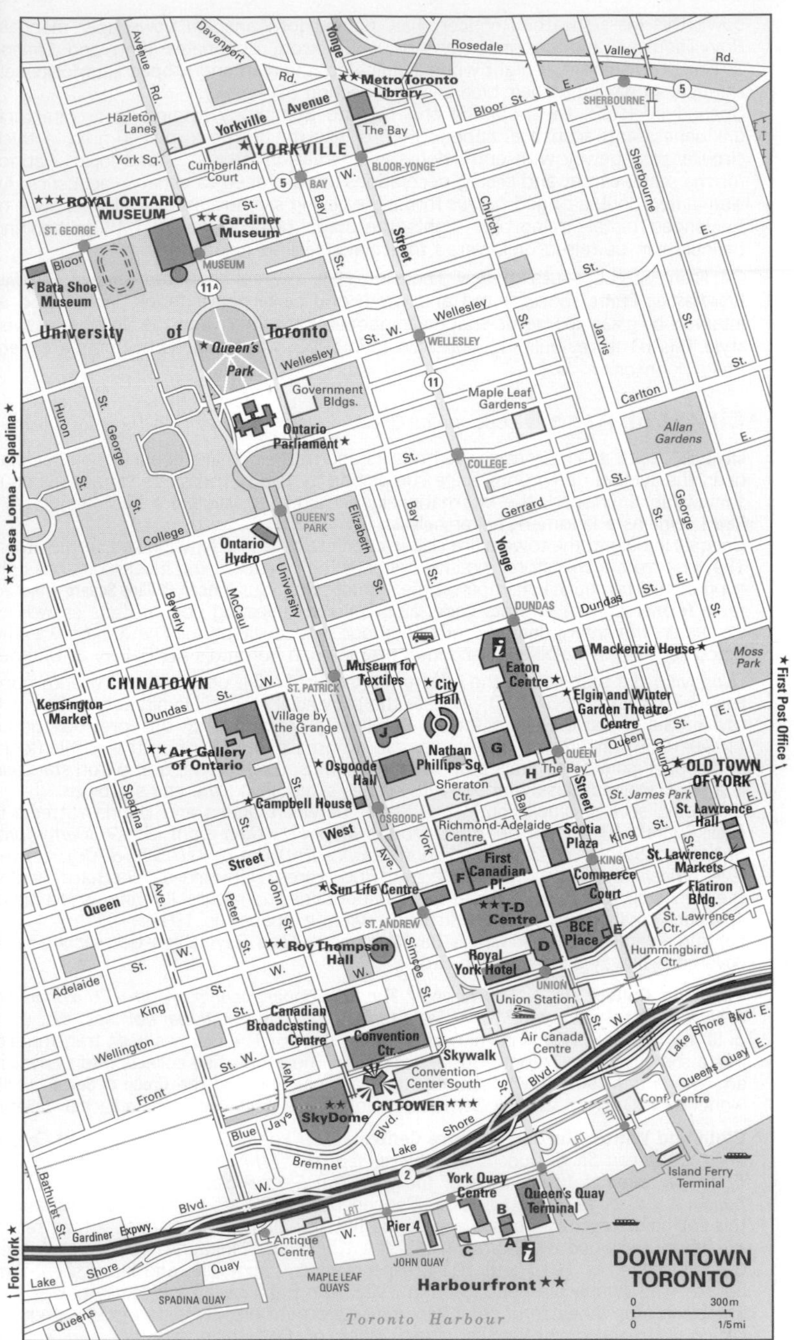

white-marbled lobby at the King Street entrance. Connecting the towers is a three-level plaza with elegant shops and an attractive water wall. Under Adelaide Street, the PATH walkway leads to a grouping of shops known as the Lanes and another called the Plaza Shops, which extend to Sheraton Centre.

Designed by Boris Zerafa, the multifaceted glass towers of **Sun Life Centre★** (1984) frame the east and west sides of University Avenue at King Street. Near the entrance to the 28-storey east tower, an outdoor sculpture by Sorel Etrog suggests a massive wheel-based tool.

★★Roy Thomson Hall – *60 Simcoe St. ● St. Andrew. Visit by guided tour (45min) only, Jul–Aug Mon–Sat. Rest of the year daily. $3. Reservations required.* ♿ P *www.roythomson.com ☎416-593-4822 ext 363.* Resembling a large inverted

bowl, this glass-sheathed concert hall, named for Canadian newspaper magnate Roy Thomson and designed by Arthur Erickson, dominates King and Simcoe Streets. Transparent at night when illuminated, the diamond-shaped exterior panels shimmer in daylight, their blue cast a reflection of the sky.
Opened in 1982, the home of the Toronto Symphony retains its architectural uniqueness and acoustical superiority. To insulate the performance area, a thick circular passageway with entry doors at intervals creates a "sound lock." Fabrics for the seats, carpet and ceiling decorations are designed to enhance acoustics. An illuminated double-ringed *oculus* forms the ceiling's centrepiece, while a shower of suspended metal "raindrops" lights the stage below. Woven, tubular hanging banners can be raised or lowered to achieve desired resonance.

On Front Street, south of Roy Thomson Hall, the concrete box-shaped **Canadian Broadcasting Centre** sports a red and white grid-patterned exterior, interrupted at intervals by glass geometric-shaped components. Illustrative of the Deconstructivist style, this 10-storey building, constructed in 1992, was designed by noted architect Philip Johnson.

★City Hall Area ● *Osgoode or Queen*

City Hall★, with its crescent-shaped towers and mushroomlike council chamber, has been the symbol of Toronto since completion in 1965. Today, its former glamour somewhat diminished, the internationally acclaimed masterpiece by Finland's **Viljo Revell** remains a landmark nevertheless.
Unequal in height, the towers are clad in concrete on one side, windows on the other. They rise from a two-storey podium, as does the "stem" of the mushroom, the only support for the council chamber at the summit. Spacious **Nathan Phillips Square** (named for a former mayor) with its wide, arch-covered reflecting pool attracts crowds of ice skaters in winter. Henry Moore's outdoor bronze sculpture, *The Archer*, was the precursor for the sizeable collection of his pieces in Toronto's Art Gallery of Ontario.

Occupying the east side of the square, **Old City Hall★** (**G**), designed by Toronto-born **Edward J. Lennox** (1855-1933), houses the provincial courts. Dominated by its clock tower, the massive Richardsonian Romanesque exterior of this previous home (1899-1965) of the city fathers conceals an ornate interior of patterned-tile floors and copper-painted capitals atop marble columns. Backing the grand iron staircase is a large stained-glass window with scenes symbolizing the city's growth.
Extending several blocks on Yonge Street between Queen and Dundas Streets is **Eaton Centre★** *(● Queen; open year-round Mon–Fri 10am–9pm, Sat 9:30am–6pm, Sun noon–5pm; ✗ ♿ P www.torontoeatoncentre.com ☎416-598-8700)*, a five-level office/shopping complex with over 300 stores. Designed by Eberhard Zeidler the megastructure, with its trees, plants, fountains and natural lighting, was a novel approach to shopping-mall construction when it opened in 1977.
Longtime retailer, the Hudson's Bay Company ("The Bay"), can be reached by a covered walkway across Queen Street.

Thomson Gallery (**H**) – *9th floor of The Bay department store at 176 Yonge St. ● Queen. Open year-round Mon–Sat 11am–5pm. Closed national holidays. $2.50. ✗ ♿ P ☎416-861-4571.* A portion of the ninth floor of The Bay has been transformed into a showplace for Toronto businessman Ken Thomson's fine collection of Canadian art. The larger **20C gallery★** features important paintings by the **Group of Seven**, while works by 19C artists such as Cornelius Krieghoff are displayed in the adjacent gallery.

★**Elgin and Winter Garden Theatre Centre** – *189 Yonge St., opposite Eaton Centre north of Queen St. ● Queen. Visit by guided tour (1hr 30min) only, Jul–Aug Thu 5pm & weekends 11am. Rest of the year Thu 5pm & Sat 11am. Closed national holidays. $4. ♿ ☎416-314-2901.* Reopened in 1989 after extensive restoration, this splendid structure houses one of the few remaining double-decker theatres in the world. Designed by Thomas Lamb, the 1,500-seat Elgin and 1,000-seat Winter Garden opened in 1913 and 1914 respectively as vaudeville, and later, silent-film houses. The Winter Garden closed in 1928; the Elgin became a movie palace.
The plush amphitheatre of the Elgin, with its ornate box seats and gold-patterned ceiling, is reached through a gilded lobby of Corinthian pilasters and arched mirrors. A seven-storey marble staircase leads to the fanciful Winter Garden, with its unique ceiling of hanging beech boughs. Original *olios* ("hand-painted scenic drops") are on display.

★**Mackenzie House** – *82 Bond St. ● Dundas. Visit by guided tour (1hr) only, May–Sept Tue–Sun noon–5pm. Rest of the year Tue–Fri noon–4pm, weekends noon–5pm. Closed holidays. $3.50. www.torontohistory.on.ca ☎416-392-6915.* This 19C brick row house, with its four chimneys and single dormer, was the last home of William Lyon Mackenzie. Friends purchased the house in 1859 for the publisher-turned-politician, who resided there until his death.
Rooms on the three floors have been restored to the 1850 period. In the kitchen visitors can sample baked goods based on 19C recipes and baked in the cast-iron oven. In the modern annex at the rear, a small display chronicles Mackenzie's life and times, and a replica of his **print shop** includes a hand-operated flatbed press on which his newspapers were printed *(demonstrations)*.

★**Osgoode Hall** – *130 Queen St. West. ● Osgoode. Quiet is necessary, since courts may be in session. Open year-round Mon–Fri 9am–5pm. Guided tours Jul–Aug Mon–Fri 1:15pm. www.lsuc.on.ca ☎ 416-947-3300.* Home of the Supreme Court of Ontario and the Law Society of Upper Canada, this stately Neoclassical edifice graces expansive lawns west of Nathan Phillips Square. Erected in 1867 allegedly to keep cows out, an ornate cast-iron fence isolates the judicial bastion from the bustle of the city. Begun in 1829 the hall consisted of only the east wing. Damaged by troops quartered there after Mackenzie's rebellion, the building was upgraded in 1844. The central pavilion and west wing were added, and the facade and interior were altered. Until as late as 1991, sporadic changes continued.

Enclosed by a rectangular stained-glass roof, the two-tiered, arched interior courtyard induces admiration, as does the magnificent **Great Library**—said to be "perhaps the noblest room in Canada." Supported by rows of Corinthian columns, a 12m/40ft vaulted ceiling, richly adorned with intricate plaster work, crowns its interior.

North of Osgoode Hall stands the Metro Toronto **Court House** (**J**), with its circular rotunda and walkway to Nathan Phillips Square.

★**Campbell House** – *University Ave. at Queen St. ● Osgoode. Visit by guided tour (30min) only, mid-May–mid-Oct Mon–Fri 9:30am–4:30pm, weekends noon–4:30pm. Rest of the year Mon–Fri 9:30am–4:30pm. Closed Jan 1, Dec 25-26. $3.50. www.advsoc.on.ca/campbell ☎ 416-597-0227.* Once belonging to **Sir William Campbell** (1758-1834), Chief Justice of Upper Canada from 1825 to 1829, the Georgian brick mansion was moved to this site in 1972 from its location in historic York. As it had been in the old town, the house is only a short walk from the city's courthouse. The restored rooms contain some fine period pieces and surviving portraits of the Campbell family. On the second floor, a model of York of 1825 can be seen. The property once belonged to the Canada Life Assurance Co., whose headquarters rises just behind Campbell House. A prominent landmark, the building is distinguished at night by its tower, the lights of which indicate the barometer reading.

★★**Art Gallery of Ontario** – *317 Dundas St. West. ● St. Patrick. Open mid-May–mid-Oct Tue–Fri noon–9pm, weekends 10am-5:30pm. Rest of the year Wed–Fri noon–9pm, weekends 10am–5:30pm. $5 contribution requested. ✗ ♿ www.ago.net ☎ 416-979-6648.* Occupying nearly a city block, this low-rise, brick and concrete building with its distinctive metal tower retains the world's largest public collection of works by renowned British sculptor **Henry Moore** (1898-1986). The permanent collection ranges from 15C European paintings to international contemporary art, and includes Canadian art from the 18C to the present. Tastefully incorporated into the complex is a historic 19C mansion, the Grange—original home of the Art Gallery of Ontario (AGO).

Established in 1900 as the Art Museum of Toronto, the gallery was permanently housed in the Grange by 1911. Adjacent quarters were constructed in 1918 and enlarged twice in less than 50 years. As its scope expanded, the publicly supported institution underwent name changes. Modified in 1919, the Art Gallery of Toronto adopted its provincial status in 1966. After visiting Toronto to see his work in situ at the new City Hall, Moore announced, in 1968, his momentous gift to the gallery of over 150 of his works. He returned in 1974 to officially open the new sculpture centre named in his honour. Extensively renovated with additions in 1977, and again, beginning 12 years later, the AGO now possesses a permanent collection of over 16,000 pieces. The new and renovated galleries, opened in 1993, increased exhibit space by 50 percent.

★★**Henry Moore Sculpture Centre** – The centre owns over 1,000 of Moore's works, including 689 prints, 139 original plasters and bronzes and 74 drawings. Many were donated by the artist when he learned that the AGO intended to devote a gallery to him. Occupying a spacious room on the upper level, the centre was designed by the artist to use natural light from the glass-panelled roof. More than 20 massive forms—all plaster casts or original plasters for some of Moore's famous bronzes—electrify this spartan space. At night, the effect of artificial lighting, with its interplay of shadows on these sculpted shapes, is stunning. Selected smaller bronzes and miniature maquettes are on display in the entryway.

★★**The Permanent Collection** – *Selections change regularly; not all of these works may be on display at one time.* Housed in galleries around Walker Court, the **European Collection** *(ground level)* covers the Old Masters, Impressionism and early-20C movements. Highlights include works by Peter Brueghel the Younger, Rembrandt, Franz Hals, Renoir, Degas, Monet, Sisley, Gauguin, Matisse, Picasso, Bonnard, Chagall and Dufy. Displayed in several galleries, the **Canadian Collection** *(upper level)* features 18C to contemporary works. Early Quebec artists are represented along with Cornelius Krieghoff, Tom Thomson *(The West Wind)* and the Group of Seven, Emily Carr, David Milne and Paul Peel, to name a few.

Contemporary **Inuit art** on exhibit *(upper level)* dates from 1948 to the present. Carved in ivory, whalebone, gray stone or mottled greenstone, the sculpture (mostly miniatures) depicts native animals or Inuit people. Large fabric hangings of embroidery and felt, as well as prints (stonecuts and stencil on paper) complete the collection. Contemporary art and 20C art are displayed in galleries on both levels.

Henry Moore Sculpture, Art Gallery of Ontario

★**The Grange** – *Entrance through Art Gallery.* This Georgian brick mansion (c.1817) once stood on a 41ha/100 acre site reaching from Queen to Bloor Streets. Socio-political life in Upper Canada during Family Compact days revolved around the residence of the Boulton family, Loyalists from New England who became leaders in the oligarchy. Lawyer and politician **Henry John Boulton** (1790-1870) was largely responsible for four of the five expulsions of William Lyon Mackenzie from the legislature. In 1875 the Grange became the home of a well-known scholar, **Goldwin Smith**, Regius Professor of History at Oxford, who made it a centre of intellectual pursuits and progressive ideas. After Smith's death in 1911, his widow bequeathed the house to the Art Gallery of Toronto.
Restored to its mid-19C appearance in 1973, the mansion is meticulously furnished to give the aura of Family Compact days. Although few pieces are original to the home, much of the furniture is from the Georgian and Regency periods. All three floors are open to visitors. Of special interest is the beautiful, curved staircase in the entry hall. The basement contains kitchens typical of a 19C gentleman's house. The residence faces lovely Grange Park, from which visitors can appreciate the mansion's gracious facade. The present entrance portico is a stone version of the original wooden one.

Museum for Textiles – *55 Centre Ave. ● St. Patrick. Open year-round Tue–Fri 11am–5pm (Wed 8pm), weekends noon–5pm. Closed national holidays. $5.* ♿ 🅿 *www.museumfortextiles.on.ca ☎ 416-599-5515.* Occupying two floors of a high-rise hotel/condominium complex, the only Canadian museum devoted exclusively to the study, collection and display of textiles features traditional and contemporary works from around the world. The permanent collection of 7,000 pieces is presented alongside loaned works, on a rotating basis, in a series of temporary exhibits.

★QUEEN'S PARK *2hrs. Map p 175.*

Based on E.J. Lennox's landscape scheme of 1876, this oval-shaped park in the heart of Toronto is the setting for Ontario's Parliament and nearby government buildings. To the west and east sprawls the **University of Toronto**, Canada's largest institute of higher education, perhaps best known for its medical school where, in 1921, **Frederick Banting** and **Charles Best** succeeded in isolating insulin. To the south, the curved, mirrored, multistoried headquarters of **Ontario Hydro** (1975, Kenneth R. Cooper) rises above the surroundings. Inside, energy radiated by artificial lighting, equipment and people is stored in basement thermal reservoirs to be recirculated throughout the building, which has no furnace or heating plant.

★**Ontario Parliament** – *● Queen's Park. Open May–Labour Day Mon–Fri 9am–5pm, weekends 9am–4pm. Rest of the year Mon–Fri 9am–5pm. Closed national holidays.* ✂ ♿ *www.ontla.on.ca ☎ 416-325-7500.* Dominating the south end of the park, the imposing sandstone **Legislative Building** typifies the solidity and mass of Richardsonian Romanesque architecture. Also called the Parliament Buildings, this seat of provincial government opened in 1893 after a controversial six-year, million-dollar construction. The focus of the dispute, American-based architect **Richard Waite** (1846-1911), had awarded himself the project after serving as a judge in a fizzled design competition.

The ponderous exterior belies the interior's elegant beauty, particularly the white-marbled **west wing**, rebuilt after a fire in 1909, and the stately **legislative chamber** with its rich mahogany and sycamore. On view is the 200-year-old mace *(ground floor)*, a ceremonial gold "club" mandatory at House proceedings. Taken by the Americans during their 1813 assault on York, it was returned years later by President F.D. Roosevelt.

★★**Gardiner Museum of Ceramic Art** – *111 Queen's Park, across from the Royal Ontario Museum. Open year-round Tue–Sat 10am–5pm (Tue 8pm), Sun 11am–5pm. Closed Jan 1 & Dec 25. $5. ♿ www.gardinermuseum.on.ca ☎416-586-8080.* Located in a modern granite building, this museum, the project of collectors George and Helen Gardiner, features pottery and porcelain from a variety of countries and cultures.

The Pottery Gallery *(ground floor)* showcases **pre-Columbian** works from Mexico, and Central and South America dating from 2000 BC to about AD 1500—primarily figurines, vessels and bowls of Olmec, Toltec, Aztec and other cultures. The orange Mayan pottery and *plumbate* (fired with silica glaze) vases are especially noteworthy. Made in Italy in the 15C and 16C, **Italian maiolica** is colourful tin-glazed earthenware. Blues, greens and bright yellows dominate the exhibited pieces, mostly large plates with intricate designs and religious scenes. Tin-glazed earthenware made in England in the 17C became known as **delftware**, probably because of its similiarity to wares from the Dutch town of Delft. Note the chargers or large plates with an English monarch painted on each.

A gallery for temporary exhibits is also housed on the ground floor.

The Porcelain Gallery *(2nd floor)* features **18C porcelains** of Du Paquier, Sèvres (characterized by bright yellows), the great English companies—Worcester, Derby, Chelsea—and others. Highlights are the Meissenware pieces, in particular, the large tea service (c.1745) in a fitted leather travel case, and the *commedia dell' arte* figures *(in the centre of the gallery)* crafted throughout Europe after this 16C form of improvised theatre spread from Italy. There is also an assemblage of tiny, exquisite scent bottles (1715-65) made primarily in England and in Germany.

★★★ROYAL ONTARIO MUSEUM *Map p 175. ● Museum.*

Renowned for extensive research, this enormous museum, commonly referred to as the ROM, is housed in an H-shaped, five-floor building at Avenue Road and Bloor Street. Maintaining over 20 departments in art, archaeology and the natural sciences, the museum, known especially for its East Asian holdings, possesses a remarkable collection of six-million-plus artifacts and artworks from around the world.

In the early 1900s Toronto banker Sir Byron E. Walker campaigned to start a public museum. United in effort was archaeologist **Charles Trick Currelly**, whose world travels provided the first treasures for a collection. In 1912 the Ontario Legislature passed the ROM Act, and in 1914 the museum first opened as part of the University of Toronto. Independent by 1968, the ROM became a separate body under the provincial government. Officially reopened in 1982 after an ambitious four-year, $55 million expansion, the ROM remains one of the country's leading museums, attracting visitors and scholars worldwide.

Visit *Allow 1/2 day*

Open year-round Mon–Sat 10am–6pm (Tue 8pm), Sun 11am–6pm. Closed Jan 1 & Dec 25. $10. ✗ ♿ www.rom.on.ca ☎416-586-8000. The ROM continues to open new galleries; some sections may be temporarily closed. The museum's floor plan, available at the information desk in the entrance rotunda, is especially useful.

Ground Floor – The grand entrance **rotunda** is vaulted, with an exquisite domed **ceiling** of golden mosaic *tessarae*—tiny squares of imported Venetian glass. The marble in the floor, with its radiant sun pattern, was extracted from an Ontario quarry. Before entering the galleries, note the two **totem poles** in the stairwells. Crafted of red cedar by the Nisgaas and Haida peoples of British Columbia in the second half of the 19C, the poles are so tall that their upper sections can be viewed from the second and third floors. The taller pole, 25m/81ft in height, depicts the family history of the chief who owned it.

In the Samuel Hall Currelly Gallery, which houses a museum restaurant, small centrepiece exhibits offer an excellent overview of the ROM's research activities, illustrating through photos, documents, artifacts and equipment, the scientific process of artifact collecting.

The outstanding exhibit on this floor is the **Chinese collection**★★★, one of the largest and most important of its kind outside China. Spanning nearly 6,000 years, the exhibits range from the Shang dynasty 1523 BC (the Chinese Bronze Age) to the overthrow of the Qing or Manchu dynasty (1644-1911) and the setting up of the Republic in 1912. Artifacts were gathered mainly by **George**

Crofts, a fur merchant who lived in Tientsin and, after his death in 1925, **William C. White**, Anglican Bishop of Honan. Assisted by Dr. Currelly, these men procured Chinese works of art when such pieces were little known to the Western world. Later in 1960, the museum acquired the coveted treasures of **Dr. James Menzies**, a missionary-scholar who lived in China for many years.

The collection is noted for its clay **tomb figures**, small replicas of people and animals buried with the dead as their "servants," and dating from the 3C AD. The star attraction, however, is the **Ming Tomb**, the only complete example in the Western world. Within the archways, larger-than-life statues of animals and humans guard the "spirit way" to the tumulus, or mound, that marked the position of the subterranean chamber containing the coffin. This tomb is reportedly the burial place of Zu Dashou, a 17C general who served the last Ming emperors and lived into the Qing period.

A series of interconnected galleries is devoted to **Later Imperial China** (10-19C). Traditional room settings, a life-size Chinese courtyard and a moon gate re-create the life of the gentry during the Ming (1368-1644) and Qing dynasties. Ceramics pieces, including the ROM's famous Ming porcelain, are also on display.

Remarkable for its ink and colour clay wall paintings, the **Bishop White Gallery** simulates the interior of a Northern Chinese temple. Flanked by two Daoist frescoes from Shanxi province with a probable date of 1325, the largest painting —"The Paradise of Maitreya"—is Buddhist, c.1298. Life-size polychromed and gilded statues of *bodhisattvas* (those enlightened, compassionate individuals destined for Buddha status) of 12-14C stand in the centre.

Gems and minerals, some very large in size, can be seen off the Southwest Atrium. The S.R. Perren Gem and Gold Room houses exquisite collections of smaller gems and jewellery.

Second Floor – Kids Natural history exhibits occupy this floor, the highlight of which are the magnificent, reassembled **dinosaurs** in authentic settings. Many of these skeletons come from upper cretaceous rocks exposed in the badlands of the Red Deer River Valley in central Alberta, one of the richest collecting sites in the world. The glass atrium of the **Bird Gallery** is filled with Canadian geese, turkeys, owls, ducks, and an assortment of smaller birds, preserved in flight. A somewhat eery, sensory, sound and light experience is a walk through the **Bat Cave**, a lifelike reconstruction of the St. Clair Cave in Jamaica, complete with hundreds of handmade bats.

Third Floor – Interlinked galleries present a fascinating look at civilization around the Mediterranean basin in Egypt, the Classical World and the Near East. Opened in 1992 the **Ancient Egypt★** exhibit depicts **daily life** via tools, utensils, jewellery and miniature figures. The section on **religion** includes coffins, animal mummies and canopic jars, the remarkably preserved **Antjau mummy** and the upright **mummy case** of a female musician. A chronological survey from predynastic times to the Ptolemaic period is featured on the **history wall.** The **Punt wall reliefs★**, sculptural casts from the temple of Queen Hatshepsut (1503-1482 BC), illustrate her trade mission along the Nile. The exhibit on **Nubia**—a region south of the Sahara in present-day Lower Egypt and Northern Sudan whose early cultures date to 4500 BC—features pottery, glassware, arms and jewellery from 2000 BC to the 19C.

Classic forms of marble sculpture, gold coins, decorated amphora and a model of the Acropolis are displayed in the **Greeks and Etruscans Gallery** (1100-100 BC) while the **Islamic** section reproduces a life-size Middle East house and bazaar. The small exhibit devoted to **Byzantium** (AD 330-1453) includes a display of gold bracelets, rings and other gold jewellery dating from AD 500-700.

Ming Tomb

The **Samuel European Galleries★** are devoted to decorative arts from Medieval times to the present. Note the elaborately carved coconut cups with their ornate silver mounts from the **Lee Collection**, exquisite Medieval and Renaissance wares of gold and silver. In the **Arms and Armour** gallery, armaments from Medieval chain mail to modern-day weaponry can be examined. Judaica, metalwork (1300 to the present), glass, and ceramics are given separate sections. **Costume and Textiles** is a well-organized exhibit featuring Victorian women's clothing. **Culture and Context** presents partial-room reconstructions, such as a Victorian parlour (1860-85). Art objects and furnishings from Medieval times to the 20C are displayed in the South Wing, which was opened in 1994.

Lower Level – In the **Ontario Archaeology Gallery**, human-scale dioramas capture the life of the early Algonquin and Iroquoian peoples. Reproductions of limestone petroglyphs and a large mural of red-ochre rock paintings can also be seen.
The **Sigmund Samuel Canadiana Gallery** presents paintings and decorative arts from the late 17C to the early 20C, reflecting, for the most part, Canada's French and British cultural heritage. Note in particular the panelled room from the Bélanger House c.1820.

The **Discovery Centre** Kids *(2nd level below; same hours as museum, except closed weekdays 10am–noon when school is in session)* is a "hands-on" room where visitors *(5 years and older)* can examine a dinosaur bone, inspect a Ming vase or don a Medieval helmet, among other activities.

ADDITIONAL SIGHTS *Maps pp 172 and 175*

★**Bata Shoe Museum** – *327 Bloor St. ● St. George. Open year-round Tue–Sat 10am–5pm (Thu 8pm), Sun noon–5pm. Call for holiday hours. $6 (free first Tue of month). ♿ ☎416-979-7799.* Housed in a five-storey building designed by renowned architect **Raymond Moriyama** to resemble a shoebox, this unique museum draws on its 10,000 piece collection to illustrate a 4,500-year history of mankind's footwear. Shoes in the permanent exhibit range from 3,550-year-old Theban funerary slippers and 1,500-year-old Anasazi sandals to singer Elton John's platform shoes. Changing exhibits are shown on two floors.

★**Yorkville** – ● *Bay.* Once the hangout of drug addicts and dropouts, Yorkville today represents all that is chic in Toronto—and a remarkable transformation. Between Yonge Street and Avenue Road, **Yorkville Avenue** presents charming Victorian houses converted to expensive boutiques or trendy cafes sporting the latest architectural facades.
In York Square at the corner of Avenue Road and Yorkville Avenue, shops surround an interior brick courtyard where summer dining is *al fresco*. Behind the square, on University Avenue, lies posh Hazelton Lanes *(open during business hours)*, a labyrinthian shopping/office/condominium complex designed by Boris Zerafa (1978). On the other side of Yorkville Avenue, Cumberland Court is a rambling enclosure of old and new shops, eateries and offices, with a passageway to Cumberland Street.

★★**Metro Toronto Library** – *789 Yonge St. ● Bloor-Yonge. Open May–mid-Oct Mon–Thu 10am–8pm, Fri–Sat 10am–5pm. Rest of the year Mon–Thu 10am–8pm, Fri–Sat 10am–5pm, Sun 1:30pm–5pm. ✂ ♿ www.mtrl.toronto.on.ca ☎416-393-7131.* An architectural gem designed by Raymond Moriyama, this massive brick and glass building contains Canada's most extensive public library. The five-storey structure, completed for $30 million in 1977, contains nearly 1.5 million volumes.
Rising from a wide, light-filled centre, the tiered balconies are bordered by solid undulating balustrades. Special baffles in the ceiling reduce sound to a minimum. The gallery on the main floor regularly showcases materials, often rare, from the library's collections.
In a cozy corner on the fifth floor is a tiny room *(access from 4th floor)* brimming with the **Arthur Conan Doyle Collection**—famed Sherlock Holmes stories, Sherlockian criticism, Doyle's autobiography, historical novels, poetry and other writings. Worn Victorian furnishings complement mementos of the great detective's presence, felt chiefly in his pipes, a slipper and the inevitable deerstalker on the hat rack *(Sat 2pm–4pm & by appointment)*.

★★**Casa Loma** – *2hrs (including gardens). 1 Austin Terrace. ● Dupont, then climb steps. Open year-round daily 9:30am–4pm. Closed Jan 1 & Dec 25. $9. ✂ P ☎416-923-1171.* This enormous sandstone castle, completed in 1914, was the lavish 98-room residence of prominent industrialist **Sir Henry Pellatt**. Maintained since 1937 by the Kiwanis Club, the Medieval mansion is a popular tourist attraction.
Casa Loma's creator amassed a fortune from hydro-electric exploitation of Niagara Falls. Edward J. Lennox combined sketches of castles Pellatt drew as a youth during world travels to design a home to the owner's liking. Three years and $3.5 million later, the interior was still not finished; nevertheless, in 1914 the Pellatts moved in, staying less than 10 years. High upkeep plus a reversal in Sir Henry's enterprises led to his losing Casa Loma to the City of Toronto for back taxes.
The "house on the hill," as its Spanish name translates, stands on the crest of Davenport Ridge—the edge of glacial Lake Iroquois, which existed after the last Ice Age. Seven storeys in height, the castle boasts two towers—one open-aired, the other

enclosed—which offer good views of the city; secret passageways; and a 244m/800ft underground tunnel to the magnificent **carriage house** and stables. The palatial residence includes 21 fireplaces, a **great hall** (22m/70ft ceiling), a marble-floor **conservatory**, an oak-panelled drawing room, and a **library** for 10,000 books. Especially well-appointed are the **Round Room★** with its exquisite Louis XV tapestry furnishings, the **Windsor Room** and **Lady Pellatt's suite**. Awash in conveniences uncommon to pre–World War I homes, the estate features an unfinished indoor swimming pool, 52 telephones, an elevator, a pipe organ and concealed steam pipes.

★**Spadina** – *285 Spadina Rd. ● Dupont, then climb steps. Visit by guided tour (1hr) only. May–Nov Tue–Sun noon–5pm. Dec & Apr weekends only, noon–4pm. Jan–Mar Tue–Sun noon–4pm. Closed Jan 1, Good Friday, Dec 25. $5. ♿ www.torontohistory.on.ca ☎416-392-6910.* Built on a former 32ha/80 acre hillside estate outside mid-19C Toronto, Spadina overlooks its remaining 2.5ha/6 acre grounds amid a fashionable residential district. The 50-room brick mansion was home to businessman **James Austin** and his heirs, who adapted the structure to prevailing architectural styles and family size.

In 1866 Austin acquired the estate, replacing the existing 1836 dwelling with a new Georgian-style house. His successful grocery store business had enabled him to become a major shareholder in, and eventually head of (1874-97), the Consumers' Gas Co. He later founded Dominion Bank, incorporated 1869, serving as its first president. Austin's son added the spacious billiard room in 1898, and in 1907, added the terraces and porte-cochere. The third floor, with its hipped roof and pedimented dormers, was built in 1912.

Reflecting the grandeur of Victorian and Edwardian styles, the spacious **drawing room** with its matching striped seating, and the airy wicker-furnished **palm room** show the comforts the Austin family expected.

METRO SIGHTS *Map p 183*

★★★**Ontario Science Centre** – Kids *1/2 day. 770 Don Mills Rd., 11km/7mi from downtown (22km/14mi by car via Don Valley Pkwy. to Eglinton Ave.). ● Eglinton and then no. 34 Eglinton East bus (to Don Mills Rd. stop). Open Jul–Aug daily 10am–8pm. Rest of the year daily 10am–5pm. Closed Dec 25. $10. ✗ ♿ P www.osc.on.ca ☎416-696-3127. Demonstrations and Omnimax films daily. For times and locations, check notice board at the bottom of escalator, level C.* Cascading down Don River ravine, this sizeable complex takes full advantage of its natural site. Raymond Moriyama designed a series of concrete and glass buildings on different levels connected by enclosed escalators. Opened in 1969 this popular attraction consists largely of interactive exhibits on science and technology.

Visitors learn, for example, by pushing buttons, rotating cranks, pedalling bicycles and turning wheels. Chemistry, printing, electricity and laser demonstrations, to name a few, provide another means of education.

The five levels are designated by letters, levels C, D and E being the exhibit/activity floors. Level C's **Earth/Food** section has a 5m/15ft high stack of grocery-filled shopping carts to illustrate "Food for a Year," while **Space** includes a rocket chair, hydroponics, supergravity and other exhibits. Highlights of level D are the **Living Earth** exhibit, where visitors explore a limestone cave and experience a rain forest; the **Hall of Transportation** with its ascending model hot-air balloon, CA-3 powerboat and old-fashioned bicycles; the **Science Arcade** with humourous electricity demonstrations; and **Communications**, where visitors can participate in papermaking. The **Hall of Technology** features, among other displays, life-size and model cantilever bridges for observing the effects of strain, and most recently, an "Information Highway" exhibit where visitors can access the Internet.

★★★**Metro Toronto Zoo** – Kids *1/2 day. 35km/22mi from downtown. ● Kennedy, transfer to bus 86A. Open Jan–mid-Mar & late Oct–Dec daily 9:30am–4:30pm. Late Mar–mid-May & mid-Sept–mid-Oct daily 9am–6pm. Late May–early Sept daily 9am–7:30pm. Closed Dec 25. $12. ✗ ♿ P www.torontozoo.com ☎416-392-5900. A useful site map is available at the entrance gate. In summer begin your visit by boarding the narrated shuttle, the zoomobile (daily mid-May–Labour Day; $2.50), which provides an excellent overview of principal attractions. Disembark at the Serengeti station and continue the visit on foot.* Opened in 1974 this world-class zoological park features a remarkable variety of wildlife on 287ha/710 acres of tableland and forest. The 5,000 animals are divided into six "zoogeographic" regions: Africa, Australasia, Eurasia, the Americas, Indo-Malaya and Canada. Among the 550 species represented are numerous endangered or rare animals such as the Siberian tiger, the snow leopard, the Malayan tapir, the pygmy hippopotamus and the Indian rhinoceros. Designed by Raymond Moriyama, harmoniously integrated glass and wood pavilions provide shelter for animals unadapted to Canada's climate. The popular **Africa Pavilion**, abundant with tropical vegetation and exotic birds, is home to lowland gorillas, mandrills and other primates. Nearby resides Canada's largest herd of African elephants. The smaller Indo-Malayan and the Americas pavilions should not be overlooked. The **Edge of Night** exhibit *(in the Australasia Pavilion)* provides a journey into a nocturnal world inhabited by seldom-seen species like the Tasmanian devil.

★★ **Black Creek Pioneer Village** – Kids *2.5hrs. In North York, 29km/18mi northwest of downtown. 1000 Murray Ross Parkway. ● Yonge and Finch, transfer to Steeles bus 60. Open May–Jun Mon–Fri 9:30am–4:30pm, weekends 10am–5pm. Jul–Sept daily 10am–5pm. Oct–Dec 9:30am–4pm, weekends 10am–4:30pm. $9.* ✗ P *☎ 416-736-1733. Site plan is distributed at the entrance.* This 12ha/30 acre re-created farming community evokes the traditions and architecture of Ontario's rural past. Opened in 1960 the village comprises 40 buildings, including 5 from the original farm established between 1816 and 1832 by Pennsylvania-German settlers, and a collection of 19C structures moved to the site.

Upon exiting the modern structure housing the **orientation centre**, visitors enter mid-19C Ontario. Set among abundant greenery and dirt roads flanked by wooden sidewalks and split-rail fences, the ensemble exudes a bygone-era charm, marred only by the din of the nearby freeway and the sight of neighbouring high rises above the trees. The restored buildings are appointed with furnishings characteristic of the 1860s. Highlights include: the tinsmith shop; the **Stong farm**; the Half Way House, a spacious white inn with a two-tiered veranda; **Roblin's Mill**, a handsome four-storey stone, water-powered gristmill; and the printing office, complete with a working flatbed press. Costumed guides demonstrate traditional 19C crafts and trades.

Scarborough – This sprawling urban centre with its sizeable Asian population has seen rapid growth in the last 10 years. Named by Lieutenant-Governor Simcoe's wife, who kept a diary of their life in early York, it is known for picturesque cliffs along Lake Ontario, which reminded her of the town in Yorkshire, England.

★ **Scarborough Civic Centre** – *35km/ 22mi from downtown Toronto. 150 Borough Dr., south of Hwy. 401 at McCowan Rd. Open year-round daily 8:30am–10pm. Closed Dec 25. Guided tours available.* ✗ ♿ P *www.city.toronto.on.ca ☎ 416-396-7216.* One of the area's first civic showplaces, the gleaming white concrete and glass complex, designed by Raymond Moriyama, was opened in 1973 by Queen Elizabeth II.

The interior is airy, filled with natural light from a central open shaft rising five storeys. Plant-bedecked balconies curve around in tiers that contain the office space. The council chamber is underground—the architect's solution to the necessity of constructing a large room without sacrificing structural lines.

Separating the centre from an adjacent shopping plaza is Albert Campbell Square. This outdoor space accommodates concerts and other activities in summer, and ice-skating in winter.

★ **Scarborough Bluffs** – Easily Toronto's most dramatic geographical feature, these buff-coloured cliffs, sprouting fingerlike hoodoos *(illustration p 102)*, protrude into Lake Ontario for about 16km/10mi along its shoreline. The focus of much interest from scientists around the world, the bluffs contain layers of fossil-rich sand and clay—a unique geological record in North America of the final stages of the great Ice Age. The **Scarborough Bluffs Park** *(from Kingston Rd. South, turn left on Midland Ave., then immediate left onto Kelsonia and right onto Scarborough Crescent; open daily year-round)* offers good **views**★ of the high sand structures branching out from the cliffs, the vast lake and Bluffers Park below.

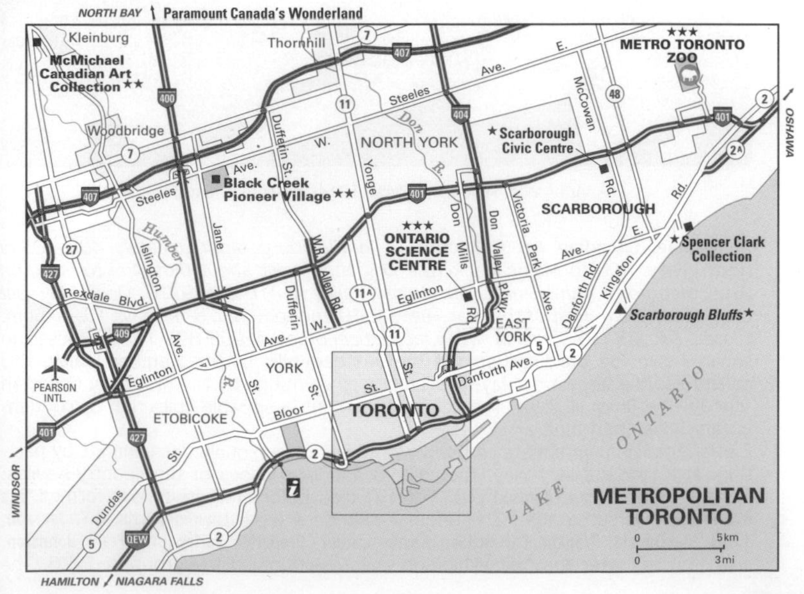

Bluffers Park – *Return to Kingston Rd. and travel east to Brimley Rd.; turn right and follow to the end. Open daily year-round.* The road descends the cliffs, emerging onto an artificial peninsula that has been constructed to protect the bluffs. This is a pleasant park on the lake with a marina.

★ **Spencer Clark Collection of Historic Architecture** – *On grounds of Guild Inn, 201 Guildwood Parkway off Kingston Rd. Open daily year-round.* ✗ ♿ 🅿 ☎ *416-261-3331.* This unusual sculpture park contains architectural features from about 60 demolished Toronto buildings. The collection was the idea of Rosa and Spencer Clark, who founded a haven for artists called "The Guild of All Arts" on this site in 1932. Among the most striking artifacts on view are the Corinthian columns and capitals of the Bank of Toronto (demolished 1966), which have been assembled to form a Greek theatre, and the white marble facade of the Imperial Bank of Canada (demolished 1972). Modern sculpture works, many by Guild members, adorn the grounds.

EXCURSIONS *Map p 183*

Paramount Canada's Wonderland – Kids *In Vaughan, 30km/19mi north by Hwy. 400 and Rutherford Rd. 9580 Jane St. GO TRANSIT from* ● *Yorkdale or York Mills* ☎ *416-869-3200. Open Jun–Labour Day daily 10am (closing times vary). May & mid-Sept–mid-Oct weekends only 10am (closing times vary). Rest of the year Mon–Fri 9am–5pm. $37.95.* ✗ ♿ 🅿 *www. canadas-wonderland.com* ☎ *905-832-7000.* This theme park opened in 1981 and features areas such as International Street, Medieval Faire, Grande World Exposition of 1890 and Hanna Barbera Land. Visitors can climb a man-made mountain, enjoy the outdoor wave pool and experience a variety of rides and shows.

Afternoon, Algonquin Park (1914) by Tom Thomson

★★ **McMichael Canadian Art Collection** – *In Kleinburg, approximately 40km/25mi north. Hwy. 400 to Major Mackenzie Dr., then west about 6km/4mi to Islington Ave., then north 1km/.6mi. Connections Trolley* ☎ *416-675-9710. Open May–Oct daily 10am–5pm. Rest of the year Tue–Sat 10am–4pm, Sun & holidays 10am–5pm. Closed Dec 25. $7.* ✗ ♿ 🅿 *www.mcmichael.on.ca* ☎ *905-893-1121.* Housed in square-hewn log buildings among the wooded hills of the Humber Valley, this gallery has the largest display in existence of paintings by the first truly Canadian school—the **Group of Seven**. The centre also owns a sizeable collection of contemporary Indian and Inuit art.

Eight Canadian painters are credited with forging a uniquely Canadian art by painting, in a revolutionary way, the colours and landscapes of the country's wilds. Though pioneer **Tom Thomson** (1877-1917) died before the group was formed, his influence was substantial. The original members were **Lawren Harris**, **A.Y. Jackson**, **J.E.H. MacDonald**, **Franklin Carmichael**, **Arthur Lismer**, **Frederick Varley** and **Frank Johnston**. Johnston left after the first exhibition; **A.J. Casson** joined the group in 1926. The group officially disbanded in 1932, but some members formed the Canadian Group of Painters, which had much the same aims. In 1952 **Robert and Signe McMichael** bought land in rural Kleinburg, decorating their home with Group of Seven paintings. In 1965 they donated their famed collection and property to the province of Ontario. Subsequent gifts by such individuals as R.S. McLaughlin have enlarged the collection.

The ground level is devoted largely to the group's precursor, Tom Thomson; to A.Y. Jackson, "grand old man of Canadian art"; and to Lawren Harris, the "soul" of the group and a prime leader in Canadian art for decades. Examples by artists influenced by the seven, notably **Clarence Gagnon**, **Emily Carr**, and **David Milne**, are also displayed. On exhibit upstairs are fine works of contemporary Indian artists such as **Clifford Maracle**, **Norval Morrisseau**, **Daphne Odjig** and **Arthur Shilling**. There are excellent samples of **Inuit Art** as well, principally stone carvings and lithographs.

★★ **Niagara Falls** – *1 day trip. 130km/81mi.* *Description p 144.*

★★ **Parkwood Estate** – *1/2 day trip. 61km/38mi.* *Description p 149.*

★ **Royal Botanical Gardens** – *1/2 day trip. 70km/44mi.* *Description p 139.*

UPPER CANADA VILLAGE★★★

Map p 129

Reflecting 1860s community life in Ontario, this 27ha/66 acre living museum is without equal in Canada, and is one of the finest restoration projects in North America. Lying in an area settled by Loyalists after the American Revolution, the village was created when plans were made to flood a large part of the St. Lawrence River Valley during the construction of the St. Lawrence Seaway and the control dam at Cornwall. Some of the older homes and buildings were moved to this site to preserve them.

Access – *11km/7mi east of Morrisburg off Country Rd. 2 (exit Hwy. 401 at Upper Canada Rd.; take Country Rd. 2 east) in Crysler Farm Battlefield Park.*

VISIT *Allow 1/2 day*

Kids *Open mid-May–mid-Oct daily 9:30am–5pm. Horse-drawn transportation (free) on premises. $12.75 ✗ ♿ www. parks.on.ca ☎613-543-3704 or 800-437-2233.*

The first impression upon entering the village is one of bustling activity. Visitors are transported at once to the 19C. Suitably attired "inhabitants" walk the streets or travel about by stagecoach or other 19C conveyance. They perform a variety of activities: cheese and bread making, quilting, cabinetmaking, printing and tinsmithing, in addition to farm chores. The progress in the life of the first settlers from pioneer shanties to substantial dwellings of brick and stone is excellently illustrated. Note in particular the elegant refinement of the **Robertson House**, the solid prosperity of the **farm**, and the evident wealth and luxury of **Crysler Hall** with its Greek Revival architecture. There are churches and schools, a village store, doctor's surgery and a tavern. An 1860s-style meal can be eaten at **Willard's Hotel.**

Malak, Ottawa

Quilting at Upper Canada Village

The **sawmill**, **woollen mill** (where woollen cloth was and is once again being produced) and flour mill operate on water power, and show the gradual trend toward industrialization evident in Ontario by 1867. Regular demonstrations are given for visitors. The flour mill has an 1865 steam engine.

Battlefield Monument – *Beside Upper Canada Village in the park.* This monument commemorates the Battle of Crysler Farm in 1813, when a small force of British and Canadian troops routed a much larger American force. It stands beside the St Lawrence River with a fine **view** over the site of the farm now flooded by the seaway.

WINDSOR★

Population 197,694
Map p 128
Tourist Office ☎519-255-6530

The city of Windsor lies on the south side of the **Detroit River** opposite the American city of that name. A suspension bridge and tunnel connect both cities. Like Detroit, this industrial centre is a major automobile manufacturer and a port on the Great Lakes/St. Lawrence Seaway system.

Historical Notes – The Windsor/Detroit area was first settled by the French in the early 18C. In 1701 **Antoine de la Mothe Cadillac** built a post on the north side of the Detroit River that became the headquarters of the French fur trade in the Great Lakes/Mississippi River area. It was captured by the British in 1760. After the American Revolution, the fort and town were handed over to the Americans, and the Detroit River became the international border, except for a brief period during the War of 1812. The town of Sandwich developed on the Canadian side, but it was later engulfed by Windsor, founded in the early 1830s. In 1838 there were several invasions across the river by the American supporters of William Lyon Mackenzie, but since that time, relations between the two cities have been very cordial.
Every year an **International Freedom Festival** is celebrated *(Jun–Jul)* to include the national holidays of both countries: July 1st and 4th. Today Windsor is one of Canada's busiest points of entry.

SIGHTS

★**Dieppe Gardens** – The outstanding attraction of this park, which stretches several blocks along the river west of the main thoroughfare *(Ouellette Ave.)*, is its **view**★★ of the Detroit skyline across the water. It is also a good vantage point from which to watch the huge ships of the seaway.

★**Art Gallery of Windsor** – *In Devonshire Mall, 3100 Howard Ave. Open year-round Tue–Fri 10am–7pm, Sat 10am–5pm, Sun noon–5pm. Closed national holidays. Contribution requested. ♿ www.mnsi.net/agw ☎519-969-4494.* Featured on two levels are changing exhibits from the gallery's permanent collection of over 2,500 works of Canadian art dating from 1750 to the present, including paintings from the Group of Seven.

EXCURSIONS

★**Fort Malden** – *In Amherstburg, 25km/15mi south via Rtes. 2 and 18. Open May–Oct daily 10am–5pm. Rest of the year Sun–Fri 1pm–5pm. Closed national holidays. $2.50. ♿ //parkscanada.pch.gc.ca ☎519-736-5416.* This fort, built by the British at the end of the 18C when they had abandoned Detroit to the Americans, occupies a fine **site**★ overlooking the seaway. Some ramparts remain, now grass-covered, and a barracks has been restored to its 1819 state. In the **visitor centre** a video *(6min)* explains the fort's role in the War of 1812 and the Rebellions of 1837. In the **interpretation centre** military displays include an example of Mackenzie's rebel flag.

Route 50 – *31km/19mi from Malden Centre to Kingsville.* This quiet road runs through long stretches of the flat farmland that borders Lake Erie, offering occasional vistas of the lake. It affords opportunities to view marshland birds and the colourful market gardens that grow a variety of fruit and vegetables.

Jack Miner's Bird Sanctuary – *In Kingsville, 2km/1.5mi north of town centre via Rte. 29 (Division Rd.); then left on Road 3 West. Open year-round Mon–Sat 9am–5pm. www.jackminer.com ☎519-733-4034.* Founded by conservationist **Jack Miner** (1865-1944), this sanctuary, one of the earliest in Canada, is a well-known stopping place for wildfowl on their seasonal migration. The best time to visit is late October and November when an estimated 40,000 geese and ducks land to feed. A small museum on the premises houses Miner memorabilia.

★★**Point Pelee National Park** – *65km/40mi by Rtes. 3 and 33. Description p 161.*

Suggestions for further reading are given on p 29.

L'Anse Saint-Jean – Malak, Ottawa

Encompassing an area of 1,540,680sq km/594,860sq mi, or one-sixth of Canada's total landmass, this vast province is first and foremost the bastion of French-Canadian culture. More than 80 percent of its population of 7.1 million is francophone, the survivors of an empire founded in the early 17C, which once covered half the continent. Very proud of this long tradition, the **Québécois** have maintained their own culture and lifestyle, creating a unique society in a North American milieu. About nine percent of the province's population claims British origin and is concentrated largely on Montreal Island. About one percent claims native ancestry, primarily Indians as well as Métis and Inuit, who live in small settlements in the Great North. The remainder of Quebec's population hails from a wide variety of ethnic origins.

Geographical Notes

Regional Landscapes – Stretching almost 2,000km/1,240mi from the US border to Hudson Strait, Quebec is Canada's largest province. The extreme north is a forbidding land of treeless tundra underlain with permanently frozen ground that gradually turns to forest farther south. This forest covers most of the province, leaving only a sliver of arable land near the St. Lawrence River. The majority of Quebec's population is concentrated in the St. Lawrence Valley.

Three main physiographic regions can be distinguished in Quebec. The northern tundra and vast forested area lie on the **Canadian Shield** *(map p 17)*, a rocky expanse consisting of extensive plateaus interrupted by a few mountain massifs. In Quebec the Shield rises to heights of 1,166m/3,824ft at Mt. Raoul Blanchard in the Charlevoix region, but otherwise presents a flat and monotonous surface, strewn with lakes. The extreme south of the province and the GASPÉ PENINSULA, on the other hand, are part of the **Appalachian Mountains**. These chains reach heights of 972m/3,188ft in the EASTERN TOWNSHIPS and 1,288m/4,227ft in the GASPÉ PENINSULA, and provide large sections of arable land, especially in the south. Lodged between these two regions, the **St. Lawrence Lowland** a triangular wedge graced with fertile soils and a moderate climate, support most c the province's agricultural production. Stretching some 1,197km/742mi in length, th **St. Lawrence River** issues from Lake Ontario and flows in a northeasterly direction alon Ontario and through Quebec to the wide Gulf of St. Lawrence and into the Atlant Ocean. Combined with the Great Lakes, this lengthy waterway reaches nearl 3,800km/2,400mi into the interior of the continent. Glacial recession created it riverbed some 10,000 years ago. Principal tributaries of the St. Lawrence are th Ottawa, Saguenay, Manicouagan, St. Maurice and Richelieu Rivers.

Climate – Quebec experiences a wide range of temperatures because of its location Although bright and sunny, the winters can be bitterly cold, especially in the north Snowfall can accumulate up to 150cm/5ft in much of the central interior. Followin a short spring season, the southern regions of the province are suddenly plunged int summer, when hot weather and extremely humid conditions predominate. Summ departs slowly, and fall arrives with its beautiful colours. Sometimes, after all the leave have dropped in late October or early November, summer returns briefly for a las fling. This "Indian summer" is another characteristic of Quebec's climate.

January temperatures in MONTREAL average –9°C/16°F, with an average of 254cm/8ft c snowfall for the entire winter season. Located farther north, Sept-Îles registers –10°C/14° with 422cm/14ft of snow—the heaviest recorded snowfall in eastern Canada.

In July Montreal registers maximum means of 26°C/79°F, QUEBEC CITY 25°C/77°F an Sept-Îles 20°C/68°F. Temperatures in excess of 32°C/90°F are not uncommon however, in the southern regions, and humidity frequently exceeds 80 percent. Tota annual precipitation in the south varies from 750–1000mm/30–40in and is fairl evenly distributed throughout the year.

Historical Notes

Birth of New France – Before the arrival of Europeans, Quebec's territory was inhab- ited by Indians of the Eastern Woodlands culture, including Algonquins and Montagnais During the 15C, Basque fishermen came to fish off the coast. A century later, during the era of European explorers, French navigator **Jacques Cartier** (1491-1557) set ou across the Atlantic Ocean in search of riches and a route to the Orient. He landed or the GASPÉ PENINSULA in 1534 and claimed this new land for the King of France, Fran- çois I. Although Cartier returned to the New World in 1535 and 1542, France did no establish a firm presence on the continent until 1608, when **Samuel de Champlain** left Por Royal in Acadia *(p 252)*, ascended the St. Lawrence, and founded Quebec City.

Soon after establishing his "Habitation" *(p 215)*, Champlain and his young colony suf- fered repeated attacks by Indians of the Iroquois nations. The **Iroquois Wars** continue until 1701, when the Montreal Peace Treaty established a temporary truce. The wars, combined with France's lack of interest in the colony, kept settlement to a minimum. The administration of New France consisted of an appointed governor responsible for conducting the colony's military and external affairs, and an intendant in charge of administrative and economic functions. The young colony was organized according to the feudal system that existed in France until the Revolution in 1789. A *seigneurie* or piece of land was granted to a **seigneur** or landowner who swore loyalty to the king. He in turn granted parts of his land to tenant farmers who paid him various dues. To provide as many people as possible with access to the river, the major means of trans- port, the land was divided into *rangs*—long thin strips that started at the river bank.

A Vast Empire – During the mid-17C the *coureurs des bois* (fur traders) and mission- aries from New France explored wide areas of the continent. Champlain himself discovered the lake named after him, as well as the Ottawa River, Georgian Bay, Lake Simcoe and Lake Ontario. His followers, Étienne Brûlé, Jean Nicolet and Nicolas Perrot, reached Lake Superior. In the 1650s Pierre Radisson and the Sieur des Groseilliers travelled through the Great Lakes and north perhaps as far as Hudson Bay. They planned a quicker trade route to Europe via the bay that would avoid the long canoe/portage route back to Montreal. When France showed no interest in this scheme, Radisson and Groseillers turned to the British who eventually founded the Hudson's Bay Company.

The greatest explorers of them all were the **La Vérendrye family**. Pierre Gaultier de Varennes, Sieur de la Vérendrye, explored much of Manitoba and Saskatchewan between 1731 and 1738, setting up a series of trading posts. His sons François and Louis-Joseph explored even farther west, reaching the foot of the Rockies in present- day Montana in 1742, the first Europeans to behold this mountain range.

Anglo-French Wars – Part of a broader struggle in Europe and elsewhere, the conflict between France and England in North America centred on the profitable fur trade. Repeated assaults by the British led to the capture of Quebec City in 1629. The French regained control of the city three years later. The Treaty of Utrecht ushered in a period of peace that lasted until the Seven Years' War *(p 22)*. On September 13, 1759, British Gen. **James Wolfe** (1728-59) defeated French Gen. **Louis-Joseph de Montcalm** (1712-59) on the **Plains of Abraham** in Quebec City, signaling the end of the French colony. After Montreal's surrender in September 1760, France capitulated. The colony was ceded to England in 1763 by the Treaty of Paris.

A British Colony – Faced with a Roman Catholic, French-speaking population, the new governor, **Sir Guy Carleton**, decided to recognize the rights of the Roman Catholic church, the seigneurial system and French civil law as a basis for government. These rights were enshrined in the **Quebec Act** of 1774.

uring the American Revolution, the inhabitants of the 13 colonies tried unsuccessfully) persuade the French Canadians to join them. After the Revolution many Loyalists noved to the EASTERN TOWNSHIPS. In order to satisfy their demands for representation, ne British government divided the colony into Upper and Lower Canada in 1791. Both olonies were granted elected assemblies, but their powers were strictly limited. Frus-ration over these limitations led to the **Rebellions of 1837** *(p 168)* in both colonies. The sue was further inflamed in Quebec because the governor and his council were British nd the assembly French. Led by **Louis-Joseph Papineau** (1786-1871), the **Patriots** peti-oned for the right of self-government. Rejection of their demands by the British overnment ultimately resulted in fighting that left 325 soldiers and rebels dead. The atriots were defeated, but full representative government was eventually granted.
s a result of the Durham Report *(p 24)*, the Act of Union joined both colonies. lthough the union was to usher in a period of political liberalism, frequent crises led he British Parliament to ratify the British North America Act in 1867, establishing **anadian Confederation**. Facing a progressive loss of rights, Quebec entered an era of ationalism that advocated greater autonomy for the province.

Sovereign State? – During the 1960s, a climate of social, economic and political change, abelled the "Quiet Revolution," emerged in Quebec. Provincial powers grew and an ncreased nationalist ideology continued to dominate the political landscape. Spearheaded y the leader of the Parti québécois (1968), **René Lévesque** (1922-87), the issue of Quebec overeignty became a hotly debated topic. In May 1980, however, Lévesque's party lost referendum on Quebec sovereignty when 60 percent of Quebecers voted against eparation. Two years later, still under Lévesque's leadership, Quebec refused to sign the anadian Constitution *(p 24)*. When the Liberal government of Robert Bourassa took ower in 1985, negotiations with the other Canadian provinces resumed. The **Meech Lake ccord** (April 30, 1987), which provided a special status for Quebec as a "distinct society," ad to be ratified by the federal government and all ten provinces before June 23, 1990. he provinces failed to reach a consensus, and Quebec was left debating sovereignty, or dherence to the Canadian Constitution. In October 1992, a national referendum on, among other issues, Quebec's status as a distinct society was voted down by a majority of Canadians. However, in a provincial referendum in 1995, Quebec sovereignty was only arrowly defeated (50.6 percent of Quebecers voted "no"). In August, 1998, Canada's upreme Court declared that, under constitutional law, Quebec has no legal right to ecede unilaterally. The historic ruling mandated that Quebec negotiate possible secession vith the other Canadian provinces. The emotionally charged issue of the province's rela-ionship to the rest of the country will likely dominate the political scene for some time.

Economy

Although over 65 percent of the gross domestic product stems from manufacturing and services, Quebec's economy relies on the province's abundant natural resources and on traditional activities such as fishing, trapping and agriculture.
Since the opening of the **St. Lawrence Seaway** in 1959, the economy of Quebec has been closely tied to that of the US. Over 50 percent of the province's manufactured goods are exported, 80 percent of which are bound for the US.

Forest, Mines and Water Resources – Covering more than 1,550,000sq km/ 600,000sq mi, the province's extensive forest has been exploited for centuries. Quebec is the Canadian leader in production of **pulp and paper**, manufacturing about one-third of the country's total output, and about 15 percent of the world's supply of **newsprint**. The province supports some 60 processing mills located along the St. Lawrence, Ottawa, St. Maurice and Saguenay Rivers and in the EASTERN TOWNSHIPS.
Mining is concentrated in several regions lying on the Canadian Shield whose age-old rocks are a great source of mineral wealth. The Abitibi and Témiscamingue regions (Noranda, Matagami, Chibougamau) contain large deposits of **copper** as well as gold, silver, zinc, lead and nickel in smaller quantities. Copper is also found at Murdochville in the Gaspé Peninsula. Quebec is the world's largest exporter of asbestos, a fibrous silicate mineral found mainly in the Eastern Townships region *(p 196)*.
The province's industrialization has been closely linked to its abundant **hydro-electric resources**. The St. Lawrence, St. Maurice and Saguenay Rivers generate large amounts of electricity mainly for industrial use. The Manic-Outardes *(p 195)* project, located on the north shore of the St. Lawrence, produces in excess of 6,800 megawatts (1 megawatt=1 million watts). The enormous project on the La Grande River, which runs into James Bay, has a capacity of more than 15 million kilowatts.
The low-cost energy generated from hydro-electric plants has spurred the province's electro-metallurgic industries. With smelters located at Beauharnois and Bécancour on the St. Lawrence, Shawinigan on the St. Maurice and Arvida on the Saguenay River, Quebec has become a major producer of **aluminum**.

Agriculture, Fishing and Trapping – These regionally based activities still form the traditional supports of the province's economy. Agriculture predominates in the southern regions of Quebec, in particular the island of Montreal, St. Lawrence Valley and Lake Saint-Jean area, which produce fruit, vegetables, beef and dairy products in sufficient quantities to supply the province's population. The major fishing centres are located on the Gaspé Peninsula, Magdalen Islands and Côte-Nord. Although trapping is no longer as important as it was during the settlement of the province, it is still practised in the northern areas.

PRACTICAL INFORMATION

Getting There

By Air – International and domestic flights arrive at Montreal's Dorval airport (22km/14mi west of downtown) ☎514-633-3105 and Quebec City's Jean-Lesage airport ☎418-640-2600. Montreal's Mirabel airport (55km/34mi north of downtown) ☎514-476-3010 is used for charter and cargo flights. Air Canada ☎514-393-3333 or 800-776-3000 (US). Canadian Airlines International ☎800-426-7000 (Canada/US) and other affiliated carriers offer connections to many cities within Quebec. Major car rental agencies *(p 305)* are located at the airports.

By Bus and Train – Intercity **bus** service and connections throughout the Montreal-Quebec City-Gaspésie corridor are offered by **Autocars Orléans Express Inc.** ☎514-395-4000. **Amtrak** links Montreal and the US with daily connections from Washington DC via New York City. For information in the US ☎800-872-7245. **VIA Rail** train service is extensive within the province; ☎514-989-2626 (Canada); 800-561-3949 (US).

By Boat – The province has an extensive **ferry** boat system; for schedules contact Tourisme Québec *(below)*.

General Information

Accommodations and Visitor Information – The official government tourist office publishes annual summer and winter vacation brochures as well as regional guides that include points of interest, driving tours, hotels, activities, camping, etc. These publications as well as road maps can be obtained free of charge from: **Tourisme Québec**, CP 979, Montreal, PQ, H3C 2W3 www.tourisme.gouv.qc.ca ☎514-873-2015 or 800-363-7777 (Canada/US). Major hotel chains can be found in urban areas. Small hotels and Bed & Breakfast lodgings offer quality accommodations at moderate prices throughout the province. **Farm holidays** may be especially appealing to families. For the guide *Gîtes du Passant au Québec ($21)*, listing facilities throughout the province, contact Fédération des Agricotours du Québec ☎514-252-3138.

Language – The official language of Quebec is French, spoken by 82% of the population. The second language is English. Quebeckers in urban areas tend to be bilingual. Tourist information is generally available in both languages. Telephone operators are bilingual. Road signs are in French.

Road Regulations – *(Driver's license and insurance requirements p 304.)* Quebec has a network of highways *(autoroutes)* and well-maintained secondary roads. Road signs are in French only. The speed limit on highways, unless otherwise posted, is 100km/h (60mph), on secondary roads 90km/h (55mph), and 50km/h (30mph) within city limits. Turning right on red is prohibited. **Seat belt** use is mandatory. **Canadian Automobile Assn. (CAA)**, Montreal ☎514-861-7111.

Time Zones – Quebec is on Eastern Standard Time, except the Magdalen Islands, which are on Atlantic Standard Time (one hour ahead of the rest of Quebec). Daylight Saving Time is observed from the first Sunday in April to the last Sunday in October.

Taxes – In addition to the national 7% GST *(rebate information p 308)*, Quebec levies a provincial sales tax of 7.5% for all goods and services. Nonresidents can request rebates of the provincial tax from Revenue Canada, Visitor Rebate Program *(address p 308)* ☎800-668-4748 (Canada), 902-432-5608 (outside Canada).

Liquor Laws – The legal drinking age is 18. The sale of wine and liquor is regulated by the provincial government and sold in "Société des Alcools" stores. In Montreal and Quebec City, wine and liquor are also sold at *Maisons des Vins.* Beer and wine are also sold in grocery stores.

Provincial Holiday *(National Holidays p 308)*

Saint-Jean-Baptiste Day	June 24

Recreation

Outdoor Activities – Parks Canada operates three **national parks** in Quebec, which offer year-round activities such as hiking, backpacking, nature programs, biking, sailing, canoeing, fishing, camping and winter sports. For trail maps and brochures ☎418-648-4177, or in Quebec ☎800-463-6769; for camping reservations ☎902-426-3436, or in Quebec ☎800-213-7275.
A guide entitled *Découvrez votre vraie nature* (available free in English) gives in-park accommodations, boat or ski equipment rentals, hunting and fishing information and other details for **provincial parks** and **nature reserves** and is obtainable free of charge from the Ministère de l'environnement et de la faune ☎418-521-3935 or 800-561-1616 (Canada).

Canoeing is practised on most of the rivers except those used for logging. **Kayaking** is popular in the northern regions of Saguenay and NUNAVIK, where camps have been set up. Ranch vacations that include **horseback riding** are prevalent in the EASTERN TOWNSHIPS, Gaspé Peninsula and Bas-Saint-Laurent regions. For further information on all outdoor activities contact Regroupement Loisir Québec ☎514-252-3000.
Major ski areas offering alpine and cross-country **skiing** are the Laurentians (Mt. Tremblant ☎819-425-8711), the Eastern Townships (Mt. Orford ☎819-843-6548) and the Quebec City region (Mt. Ste-Anne ☎418-827-4561). Abundant snowfall extends the ski season to mid-April, although some northern locations have good snow conditions through mid-May. **Snowmobiling** is a popular outdoor activity. A network of well-marked trails crisscrosses the countryside interspersed with heated cabins and other accommodations. A registration card is required to operate a snowmobile: contact the Fédératon des Clubs de Motoneigistes in Montreal ☎514-252-3076. For a free copy of the *Trans-Quebec Snowmobile Trail Network Map*, contact Tourisme Québec *(p 190)*.
Many regions in Quebec are known for excellent **hunting** and **fishing**. Outfitters' lodges, easily reached by land or air, offer packages that include accommodations, transport to remote locations, equipment rental, permits and game registration. Above the 52nd parallel, nonresidents are required to hire the services of an outfitter. For regulations and seasons contact the Ministère de l'environnement et de la faune ☎418-521-3935 or 800-561-1616 (Canada). An annual publication on outfitters' lodges is available at tourist information kiosks or from Fédération des pourvoyeurs du Québec ☎418-877-5191. The rivers of the Gaspé Peninsula and ANTICOSTI ISLAND are well known for salmon fishing; central Quebec is known for its variety of fish species.

Special Excursions – Organized nature tours for canoeing, rafting, horseback riding, biking or hiking in the Montreal/Ottawa region are offered through New World River Expeditions ☎819-242-7238. Activities such as rock climbing, dogsledding, canoeing and kayaking can be arrranged through CÉPAL ☎418-547-5728. For information on additional adventure travel, contact Tourisme Québec *(p 190)*. Seal-watch excursions off MAGDALEN ISLANDS depart from HALIFAX, Nova Scotia *(p 235)*.

Principal Festivals

Feb	**Quebec Winter Carnival**	*Quebec City*
	Carnaval-Souvenir	*Chicoutimi*
	Winter Festival	*Hull*
Mar	**Maple Sugar Festival**	*Saint-Georges*
Jun	**Grand Prix Player's**	*Montreal*
Jul	**International Jazz Festival**	*Montreal*
	World Folklore Festival	*Drummondville*
	International Summer Festival	*Quebec City*
	International Swim Marathon	*Péribonka*
Jul-Aug	**Blueberry Festival**	*Mistassini*
	Festival Orford	*Magog*
Aug	**Hot Air Balloon Festival**	*Saint-Jean-sur-Richelieu*
	Montreal World Film Festival	*Montreal*

For in-depth information on the the sights found in the province of Quebec, consult the Michelin Green Guide to Quebec, which highlights over 1,150 points of interest throughout the French-speaking province.

In addition, insightful essays trace Quebec's history, geography and artistic heritage, while detailed city and regional maps accompany various walking and driving tours.

ANTICOSTI ISLAND★★

Map of Principal Sights p 5

Stretching more than 222km/138mi in length and 56km/35mi at its widest point Anticosti Island is mantled with coniferous forests and crisscrossed by more than 10 rivers teeming with Atlantic salmon and trout. Well known by deer hunters for th abundance of game, the island is also a pleasant vacation spot for nature lovers. French industrialist **Henri Menier**, who purchased Anticosti for the sum of $125,000 i 1895, transformed the island into his private paradise, constructing a sumptuou hunting lodge (destroyed by fire in 1953) and importing animals, in particular, white tailed deer. In 1926 the island was sold for $6.5 million to the Anticosti Corporation The Quebec government acquired Anticosti in 1974, and the majority of the island i now part of a reserve (4,575sq km/1,766sq mi).

Access – *Air service available through Inter-Canadian ☎418-962-8321 or Aviatio Québec Labrador ☎418-962-7901. Boat service available through Relais Nordik Inc. from Rimouski ☎418-723-8787, Sept-Îles ☎418-968-4707 and Havre-Saint-Pierr ☎418-538-3533. A 4-wheel drive vehicle is indispensable on the island.*

VISIT *Allow minimum 2 days*

A tour of the island from **Port-Menier**, the island's only remaining permanen settlement, leads past such scenic wonders as Kalimazoo Falls and La Patate Cavern, **Vauréal Falls and Canyon★★**, with a 70m/230ft waterfall, and **Tour Bay★★** renowned for its spectacular limestone cliffs that plummet dramatically into the sea. Located to the west of Port-Menier, Baie-Sainte-Claire provides an ideal setting for observing **white-tailed deer**, sometimes seen in herds of up to 100.

BAS-SAINT-LAURENT★★

Map below

Situated on the south shore of the St. Lawrence River, between QUEBEC CITY and the GASPÉ PENINSULA, this region is characterized by fertile plains, plateaus and, to the north, the foothills of the Appalachians. The peaceful, rural landscapes along the shore are divided into long, narrow strips of farmland, perpendicular to the river. To the north, the Laurentian Mountains plunge into the St. Lawrence, creating picturesque scenery.

Route 132 passes through the principal communities of this region, affording superb views of the St. Lawrence and of various islands dotting the river.

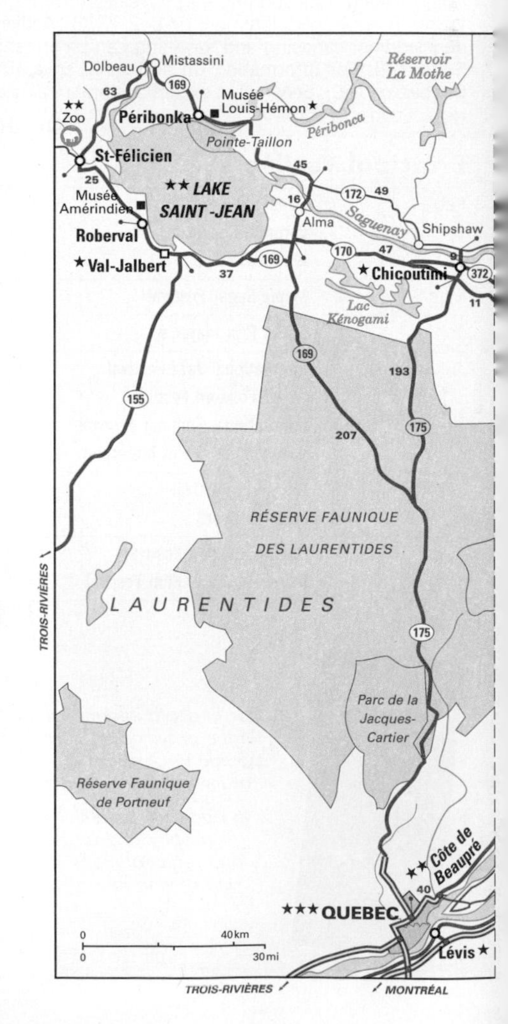

SIGHTS

★**Lévis** – *250km/155mi east of Montreal by Rte. 20 or Rte. 132. A ferry connects Lévis to Quebec City.* Located on the south shore of the St. Lawrence, opposite Quebec City, this important business centre is noted for its port and its wood-related industries. The city is also the birthplace and headquarters of the Desjardins cooperative savings and loan company *(Caisse populaire Desjardins)*. Founded in 1900 by journalist Alphonse Desjardins (1854-1920), this people's bank sought to bring economic independence to French Canadians.

At the corner of Avenue Mont-Marie and Rue Guenette, the white clapboard **Alphonse-Desjardins House★** (Maison Alphonse-Desjardins) presents a video *(15min)* and displays of artifacts *(open year-round Mon–Fri 10am–noon & 1pm–4:30pm, weekends noon–5pm; closed Jan 1 & Dec 25; ♿ P ☎418-835-2090).*

★**Fort No. 1 National Historic Site** (Lieu historique national Fort-Numéro-Un-de-la-Pointe-de-Lévy) – *Open mid-May–mid-Jun Mon–Fri & Sun 9am–4pm. Late Jun–Aug daily 10am–5pm. Sept–late Oct Mon–Sat by appointment, Sun noon–4pm. $2.75. ♿ P ☎418-835-5182.* Forming an irregular pentagon, the fort (1865-72) stands atop Pointe-Lévis, the highest point on the south shore of the St. Lawrence. It is the sole vestige of three such forts built to protect Quebec City from possible American attack after the threat of the American Civil War, and from the Fenian Raids. The fort is composed of a series of massive earthen ramparts with a tall embankment protecting the casemates, ditches and vaulted tunnels leading to the *caponiers*—stone and brick structures armed with small cannon.

★**National Historic Site of Grosse-Île (Lieu historique national de Grosse-Île)** – *Open May–Oct daily 8:30am–4:30pm. ☎418-563-4009. Several companies offer ferries to Grosse Île departing from Berthier-sur-Mer & Montmagny May–Oct. One-way 30min. Commentary. Reservations required. Visit & ferry $26–$45. ✕ P Further information: Office du tourisme de la Côte-du-Sud ☎418-248-9196.* The ever-increasing number of European immigrants to Canada prompted the government to establish, in 1832, a quarantine station on Grosse Île, one of 21 islands making up the Île aux Grues archipelago. In the station's first year of operation, some 50,000 immigrants were examined in an effort to limit the spread of cholera into Canada. The western part of the island was known as the Hotel Sector. The Village Sector in the island's centre housed employees of the station and their families. To the east the Hospital Sector included 21 hospitals of which one is still standing. In 1990 Parks Canada opened the site to the public.

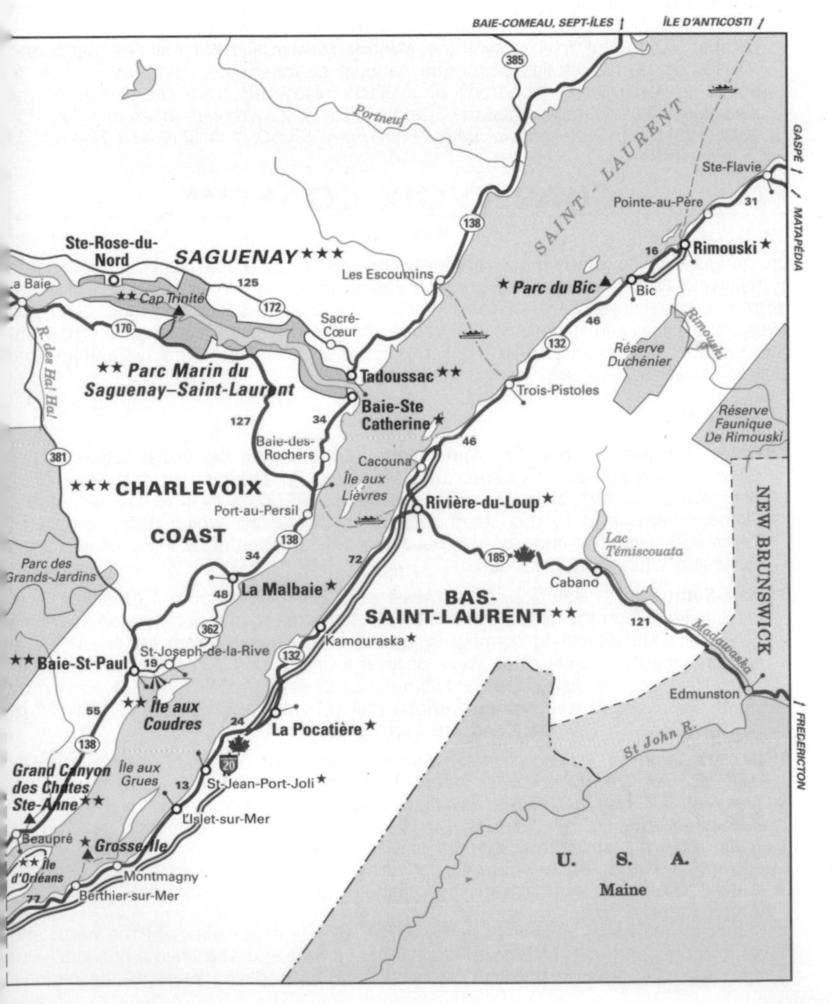

Route 132 continues through **L'Islet-sur-Mer**, a small maritime community known a the birthplace of famed Arctic explorer, Capt. Joseph-Elzéar Bernier (1852-1934 and through **Saint-Jean-Port-Joli**★, the craft and wood-carving capital of Quebec.

★**La Pocatière** – *60km/37mi from Montmagny.* Situated on a terrace above th coastal plain, this community is a leading centre for agricultural research. The **Fra çois Pilote Museum**★ (Musée François-Pilote) illustrates rural life in the province a the turn of the century *(open May–Sept Mon–Sat 9am–noon & 1pm–5pn Sun 1pm–5pm; rest of the year Mon–Fri 9am–noon & 1pm–5pm, Sun 1pm–5pn $4; P ☎418-856-3145).* Route 132 passes across a wide flood plain, affordin expansive views of the Laurentian Mountains across the St. Lawrence. Perpend cular to the shoreline, eel traps extend into the river. From the pleasant communit of **Kamouraska**★, lines of stakes can be seen in the tidal flats. These traps divert fis and eels into enclosures where they can be netted.

★**Rivière-du-Loup** – *72km/45mi from La Pocatière.* Situated halfway betwee Quebec City and Gapsé Peninsula, this town has developed into a commercial an resort centre. A walk through the downtown leads past several buildings c interest, including the imposing Gothic Revival **St. Patrick's Church and Presbytery**, sur rounded by verandas, and the **Viatorian Clerics' Residence**. North of downtown, th Loup River drops over the cliff terrace in 38m/125ft high falls. Steps lead to lookout providing an expansive view of the town and river.

★**Bic Park (Parc du Bic)** – *81km/50mi from Rivière-du-Loup.* This 33sq km/13sq m provincial conservation park, created in 1984, boasts a variety of flora, includin both deciduous and boreal forests. The small town of **Bic** is known for its specta cular **setting**★★ on the shores of the St. Lawrence.

★**Rimouski** – *25km/16mi from Bic Park.* Built along the banks of the St. Lawrence this industrial city has developed in a semicircular pattern around the mouth c the Rimouski River and is now considered a major metropolis of eastern Quebec Among sights of interest, note the **Lamontagne House**★ (Maison Lamontagne), on of the few remaining examples of masonry half-timbering in North America *(ope mid-May–mid-Oct daily 9am–6pm; $3; P ☎418-722-4038).*

Located 10km/6mi from town, the **Maritime Museum and Pointe-au-Père Lighthouse**★ (Musée de la mer et lieu historique national du phare de Pointe-au-Père) a Pointe-au-Père display hundreds of artifacts recovered from the wreck of the *Empress of Ireland*, nicknamed the "Titanic of the St. Lawrence" *(open mid-Jun–Au daily 9am–6pm; Sept–mid-Oct daily 10am–5pm; $5.50; ✗ ♿ P ☎418-724-6214)*

CHARLEVOIX COAST★★★

Map p 193

One of Quebec's loveliest, most varied regions, this rugged coast is best appreciated by following Routes 138 and 362, which weave up and down, affording magnificent clifftop or water-level views of forested hills, the pristine shore and mountains that sweep down into the mighty St. Lawrence. Named for Jesuit historian Pierre-François-Xavier de Charlevoix (1682-1781), this resort spot has long attracted and inspired painters, poets and writers.

SIGHTS

★★**Grand Canyon of the St. Anne Falls (Grand Canyon des Chutes Sainte-Anne)** – *52km/32mi northeast of Quebec City. Open Jun 24–Labour Day daily 9am–6pm. May–Jun 23 & early Sept–Oct daily 9am–5pm. $6.50. ✗ ♿ P ☎418-827-4057.* Pleasant paths lead to this steep and narrow waterfall, which drops a total of 74m/243ft over the edge of the Canadian Shield, creating a mass of shattered rocks and whirlpools at its base.

★★**Baie-Saint-Paul** – *95km/59mi northeast of Quebec City.* Route 138 offers spectacular **views**★★ on the descent to this celebrated artist haunt. Surrounded by rolling green hills, the charming community boasts more than a dozen art galleries and an **arts centre** that displays the work of local artists *(open Jun 24–early Sept daily 9am–7pm; rest of the year daily 10am–5pm; P ☎418-435-3681).* Departing by Route 362, visitors will find an overlook that provides another splendid **view**★★ of the town, the St. Lawrence and the south shore.

★★**Île aux Coudres** – *Ferry service: departs from Saint-Joseph-de-la-Rive Apr–Oct daily 7:30am–11:30pm every hour. Rest of the year daily 7:30am–7:30pm (Jan–Feb 8:30pm) every 2hrs. 15min. ♿ Société des traversiers du Québec ☎418-438-2743.* Named by Jacques Cartier in 1535 for its abundant hazel trees *(coudriers)*, this enchanting island, home to farmers, boat builders and fishermen, occupies a spectacular offshore **site** linked by ferry to the mainland. Each year, the island's inhabitants demonstrate their canoeing skills on the icy river at the Quebec Winter Carnival *(p 191)*.

A tour of the island *(21km/13mi)* by car or bicycle offers views of the north and south shores of the St. Lawrence. Remnants of a past age—beached schooners—dot the coast. The **Schooner Museum**★ (Musée Les voitures d'eau) presents the region's maritime history *(open mid-Jun–mid-Sept daily 9am–6pm; late May–mid-Jun & mid-Sept–mid-Oct weekends 9:30am–5pm; $4; ✗mid-Jun–mid-Sept ♿ P ☎418-438-2991)*. The **Île-aux-Coudres Mills★** (Moulins de l'Isle-aux-Coudres), both dating from the 19C, provide a rare opportunity to compare the mechanisms of a windmill and a water mill *(open Jun 24–early Sept daily 9am–7pm; late May–Jun 23 & mid-Sept–mid-Oct daily 10am–5pm; $2.50; P ☎418-438-2184)*. At La Baleine the **Maison Leclerc**, a simple stone dwelling, is among the oldest homes on the island.

★La Malbaie – *26km/16mi northeast of Île aux Coudres.* Occupying a beautiful **site★**, this resort community was named "Malle Baye" (bad bay) by Samuel de Champlain in 1608, when he discovered his anchored ships had run aground. After the British defeated the French, Scottish soldiers renamed it Murray Bay in honour of the colony's chief administrator. The picturesque **Manoir Richelieu** *(in Pointe-au-Pic)* is a grand reminder of the resort hotels that sprung up during the 19C.

★Baie-Sainte-Catherine – *74km/46mi northeast of La Malbaie.* Located at the mouth of the Saguenay River, this small community was settled in the 1820s. **Whale-watching cruises★★** have become a popular attraction, just as in Tadoussac across the fjord. Overlooking the mouth of the Saguenay in the **Saguenay-St. Lawrence Marine Park**, a lookout tower provides occasional glimpses of the large mammals frolicking in the water below *(park visitor centre open mid-Jun–Labour Day daily 9am–6pm; early Sept–mid-Oct Fri–Sun 9am–5pm; ♿ P ☎418-237-4383)*.

CÔTE-NORD★

Map of Principal Sights p 5

The Côte-Nord, or North Shore of the St. Lawrence River extends from the mouth of the Saguenay River north to the Labrador border. This geographic entity is divided into three regions: the southernmost stretching from Tadoussac to Sept-Îles; the central North Shore from Sept-Îles to Havre-Saint-Pierre; and the northernmost region *(accessible only by boat or plane)*, encompassing the vast expanse of taiga and the villages between Havre-Saint-Pierre and Blanc-Sablon.
Long known as an untamed wilderness of forests with occasional fishing villages, Côte-Nord underwent gradual industrialization with the development of **pulp mills** in the 1920s and 30s and later, the discovery of rich **iron-ore** deposits. In the 1960s the region's enormous hydro-electric potential was harnessed, prompting another surge of economic growth. A drive along Route 138 leads through desolate stretches of pristine, rocky landscape, occasionally interrupted by developing towns and hydro-electric plants.

SIGHTS

Manic-Outardes Complex – *Manic-5 is located 210km/130mi north of Baie-Comeau (422km/262mi northeast of Quebec City) on Rte. 389.* Begun in 1959 the harnessing of the Manicouagan and Outardes Rivers took 20 years to complete. Today the seven plants strung along both rivers have a combined capacity of 6,821 megawatts (1megawatt=1,000,000 watts). The first power plant of the complex to produce electricity was **Manic-2★** *(visit by 1hr 30min guided tour only, mid-Jun–Labour Day daily at 9am, 11am, 1pm & 3pm; ♿ P ☎418-294-3923)*. The spectacular **Daniel Johnson Dam★★** of **Manic-5★★** is the largest arch-and-buttress dam in the world, measuring 214m/702ft in height and 1,314m/4,307ft in length *(visit by 1hr 30min guided tour only, mid-Jun–Labour Day daily at 9am, 11am, 1:30pm & 3:30pm; ♿ P ☎418-294-3923)*. Named for a former premier of Quebec, it was completed in 1968. During construction two semicircular lakes were united, creating the distinctive doughnut-shaped reservoir with a diameter of 65km/40mi.
On the Manic-5 tour, guides explain how electricity is produced and transmitted to consumers. A bus takes visitors to the base of the massive arches and then across the dam where good views of the reservoir and surrounding landscape are permitted.

★Sept-Îles – *640km/397mi northeast of Quebec City by Rte. 138.* Occupying a superb **site★★** in a circular bay on the St. Lawrence, this dynamic city constitutes the administrative centre of the Côte-Nord. Sept-Îles' deep-water port enables ocean-bound vessels to transship coal and iron ore throughout the year. Stroll along the old wharf to enjoy views of the magnificent bays and the seven islands for which the city is named.
The reconstructed **Old Trading Post** (Le Vieux-Poste) pays tribute to the region's first inhabitants, the Montagnais *(open late Jun–mid-Aug daily 9am–5pm; $3.25; ♿ P ☎418-968-2070)*. Offshore, the **Sept-Îles Regional Park★** (Parc régional de l'Archipel des Sept-Îles) offers a good introduction to the history and natural beauty of the Côte-Nord.

The community of **Havre-Saint-Pierre** marks the end of Route 138. The ferries for Anticosti Island and the **Mingan Archipelago★★**, a national park reserve, depart from the wharf. The string of approximately 40 islands is renowned for its spectacular rock formations and unique flora and fauna. Havre-Saint-Pierre is also the departure point for the boat trip *(3 days)* to Blanc-Sablon, situated 1.5km/1mi from the Labrador border. *For more information, consult the Michelin Green Guide to Quebec.*

EASTERN TOWNSHIPS★★

Map below

A region of lush rolling hills named for its location east of MONTREAL, "the Townships as they are generally called, occupy the southwest corner of the province along the US border. This area of deep valleys, tree-covered hills rising nearly 1,000m/3,280ft, and beautiful, sparkling lakes such as Brome, Memphrémagog, Magog and Massawipi, is a popular retreat for Montrealers, offering a variety of recreational activities.

The northeastern section, in particular the towns of **Asbestos** and **Thetford Mines**, is known for its asbestos production. Directly north of Asbestos lies the Bois-Francs (hard woods) area, named for the predominant maple tree. To the east, drained by the Chaudière River, the flat fertile farmland referred to as the **Beauce**★ contains the greatest concentration of maple groves in Quebec. In spring, sugaring-off parties are a popular pastime. After the American Revolution, land parcels along the border were granted to Loyalists fleeing the US. The towns and villages these first settlers established reflect their New England heritage. After 1850 increasing numbers of French-speaking people moved into the region, and today its population is predominantly francophone.

SIGHTS

★**Sherbrooke** – *150km/93mi east of Montreal by Rtes. 10 and 112.* Straddling the confluence of the Saint-François and Magog Rivers, this industrial centre is the principal city of the townships. The **Museum of Fine Arts** (Musée des Beaux-Arts) exhibits a fine collection of Quebec art, focusing on the Eastern Townships *(open Jun 24–early Sept Tue–Sun 11am–5pm, Wed 9pm; rest of the year Tue–Sun 1pm–5pm, Wed 9pm; closed Dec 24–26 & Dec 31–Jan 2; $2.50; ✗ ♿ P ☎819-821-2115).* Standing atop the Marquette Plateau, the imposing Gothic Revival **cathedral**★ was designed in 1958 by Louis-Napoléon Audet, who also designed the basilica at Sainte-Anne-de-Beaupré. From this vantage point the **view**★ encompasses the entire city.

★**Magog** – *124km/74mi east of Montreal by Rte. 10.* This popular resort community enjoys a splendid **setting**★ on the shores of Lake Memphrémagog, which stretches over 50km/31mi, crossing the border into Vermont. **Scenic cruises**★ on this long and narrow lake afford splendid views of the snow-capped peaks of Mt. Orford, Sugar Loaf and Owl's Head *(depart from Quai Fédéral Jun 24–Labour Day daily 10am–6pm, mid-May–Jun 23 & early Sept–mid-Oct weekends noon–2pm; depending on destination, round-trip 1hr 45min, $12, reservations suggested; or 7hrs, $45, reservations required; commentary; ✗ ♿ P Croisières Memphrémagog Inc. ☎819-843-8068).*

★**Saint-Benoît-du-Lac Abbey** (Abbaye de Saint-Benoît-du-Lac) – *20km/12mi south of Magog by Rte. 112 west; follow signs. Open year-round daily 8am–11am & 1pm–5pm. ♿ P ☎819-843-4080.* The pleasant drive to this Benedictine monastery offers lovely glimpses of the sparkling lake waters. Distinguished by its impressive bell tower, the complex was designed by Dom Paul Bellot (1876-1944), who is buried in the cemetery. The monks are famous for their Gregorian chant and for the cheese (L'Ermite and Mont-Saint-Benoît) they produce and sell on the premises.

★**Mount Orford Park** – *116km/72mi east of Montreal by Rte. 10 (Exit 115) and Rte. 141. Park open daily year-round. Le Cerisier Interpretation Centre open year-round daily 8:30am–4:30pm. $3.50. ⛺ (mid-May–mid-Oct) ✗ ♿ P ☎819-843-9855.* Created in 1938 this provincial park is dominated by Mt. Orford (881m/2,890ft), a well-known ski centre. Follow a short path around the

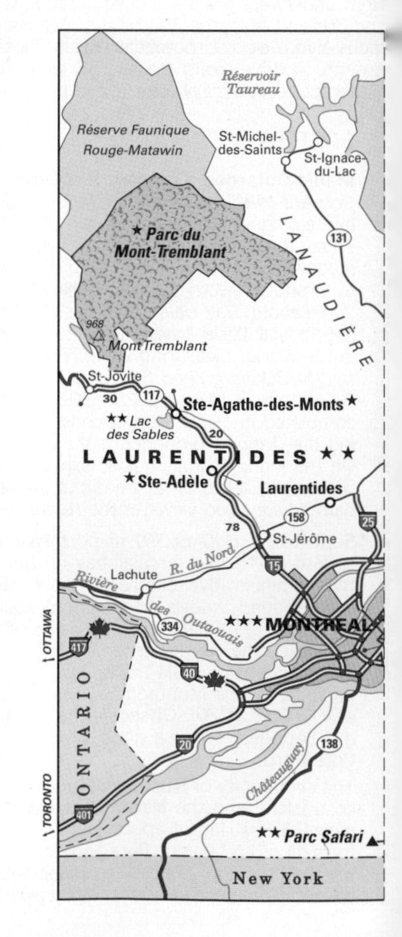

television tower at the summit for a sweeping **panorama**★★ north to the St. Lawrence Valley, west to the Monteregian Hills, south to Lake Memphrémagog and east to the Appalachians.

Orford Arts Centre (Centre d'Arts Orford) – *Open Jul–Aug Mon & Sun 9am–9pm, Tue–Fri 9am–5pm. Apr–Jun & Sept–Nov Mon–Fri 9am–5pm. ☎819-843-3981.* Founded in 1951 the centre is renowned for its annual summer music festival (Festival Orford). The great concert hall was formerly the Man and Music Pavilion of Montreal's Expo '67.

Compton – *172km/107mi east of Montreal by Rtes. 10, 143 and 147.* This quiet village is the birthplace of **Louis-Stephen Saint-Laurent** (1882-1973), Canada's 12th prime minister. An ardent Canadian nationalist, Saint-Laurent fought to establish a distinct Canadian identity during his years in office (1948-57).

★**Louis-S.-St.-Laurent National Historic Site** (Lieu historique national Louis-S.-St-Laurent) – *Rue Principale. Open mid-May–mid-Oct daily 10am–5pm. $3. ☎819-835-5448.* The simple clapboard house, full of mementos of the Saint-Laurent family, has been restored to represent various periods of the prime minister's life. The adjoining general store, originally run by Saint-Laurent's father, is stocked with replicas of goods sold here at the turn of the century. A **multimedia biography** *(20min)* presents the highlights of Saint-Laurent's life and career.

Granby – *80km/50mi southeast of Montreal by Rte. 10 (Exit 68) and Rtes. 139 and 112.* Set on the banks of the Yamaska River, this small industrial centre was settled by Loyalists in the early 19C. Today it is especially known for its **zoo**★ Kids one of the largest in Canada, featuring over 1,000 animals, including 225 species of mammals and birds *(Blvd. Bouchard; open mid-May–Labour Day daily 10am–5pm; Labour Day–mid-Oct weekends 10am–5pm; $15; ☎514-372-9113).* Of particular interest is the reptile house, with over 350 reptiles displayed in a near-natural environment.

Valcourt – *130km/81mi east of Montreal by Rte. 10 (Exit 90) and Rtes. 243 and 222.* Long a small agricultural community, Valcourt is today the centre of a thriving **snowmobile** industry, begun by one of its residents. Joseph-Armand Bombardier

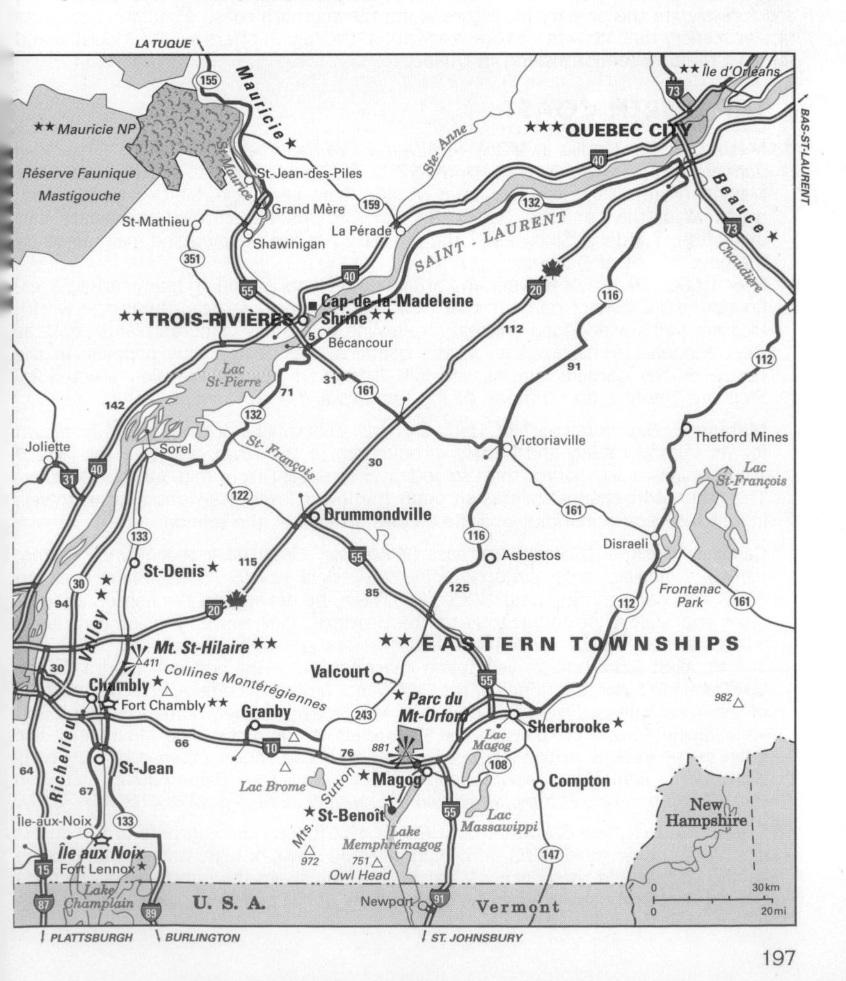

(1907-64) first developed a drive-wheel and track mechanism to power vehicle over snow in 1937. In 1959 he introduced the **Ski-Doo**, which went on to transform life in the north. Today J.-A. Bombardier Industries develops and sell snowmobiles all over the world.

★**J.-Armand Bombardier Museum** (Musée J.-Armand Bombardier) – Kids *1001 Ave J.-A Bombardier. Open Jun 24–Aug daily 10am–5:30pm. May–Jun 23 & Sept–mid-Oc daily 10am–5pm. Rest of the year Tue–Sun 10am–5pm. Closed Jan 1–2 Dec 24–26 & 31. $5. ♿ P ☎514-532-5300.* Divided into three sections, this fascinating museum highlights the life and work of Valcourt's native son. One section illustrates the Ski-Doo's assembly and usage; another section re-creates the garage where Bombardier worked as a mechanic and inventor.

Drummondville – *110km/68mi east of Montreal by Rte. 20 (Exit 177).* Founded as a military outpost after the War of 1812, this community is today an important industrial centre for the garment industry.

★**Québécois Village of Olden Times** (Village québécois d'antan) – Kids *Rue Montplaisir, Exit 181 off Rte. 20. Open Jun 1–23 daily 9:30am–5pm. Jun 24–Labour Day daily 10am–6pm. Rest of Sept weekends only 10am–6pm. $10. ✕ P ☎819-478-1441.* About 30 authentic buildings (church, school, tavern, forge, farm and homes) were relocated to this pleasant site to re-create life in the region during the 19C. Costumed interpreters explain the daily life of the former occupants.

GASPÉ PENINSULA★★★

Map of Principal Sights p 5

This peninsula extends along the southern shore of the St. Lawrence, advancing into the gulf of the same name. The interior is largely an impenetrable wilderness of mountains and forest, dominated by a continuation of the Appalachians—the mountains known as the **Chic-Chocs**, which rise to their highest peak at **Mt. Jacques Cartier** (1,288m/4,227ft). Tiny fishing villages dot the wild and rocky northern coast of the peninsula, culminating in the breathtaking beauty of Forillon and Percé. Agriculture and forestry are the primary industries along the southern coast. In addition to spectacular scenery that attracts visitors year-round, the region offers excellent cuisine and some of the best salmon fishing in Quebec.

THE NORTH COAST

★★**Métis Gardens** (**Jardins de Métis**) – *350km/217mi southeast of Quebec City. Open Jun–mid-Oct daily 8:30am–6:30pm. $7. ✕ ♿ P ☎418-775-2221.* In 1918 Elsie Meighen Reford inherited this tract of land from her uncle, Sir George Stephen, president of the Canadian Pacific Railway Co. She transformed the estate into magnificent gardens. Since 1961 the property has been owned and maintained by the government of Quebec.

Over 1,000 varieties of flowers and ornamental plants, including many rare species, flourish in six distinct gardens that rank among the most beautiful in the world. Pleasant paths wind along a stream, revealing beautifully coloured plants, such as lilies, rhododendrons, azaleas, Asiatic gentians and Tibetan blue poppies. In the centre of the gardens stands the **Villa Reford**, an elegant mansion erected by Stephen. The first floor houses dining facilities and a craft shop.

Matane – *55km/34mi east of Métis Gardens.* This small industrial centre is known for its salmon fishing and shrimp production. In the town centre, a **fish ladder**★ *(passe migratoire)* enables the fish to travel upstream from mid-June to October. The 44m/144ft channel passes through the lower level of an observation tower, in which several port holes provide a close-up look at the salmon.

★**Gaspésie Park** – *103km/64mi east of Matane. Open daily year-round. Hiking, fishing, canoeing, cross-country skiing. ▲ ✕ ♿ P ☎418-763-3301.* Created in 1937, this park encompasses 800sq km/309sq mi devoted to the conservation of plant and animal life indigenous to the province. It is the only place in Quebec where caribou, moose and white-tailed deer are known to co-exist.

The **Mt. Albert Sector** reflects vegetation characteristic of the northern tundra. In the **Lake Cascapédia Sector**, the ridges of the Chic-Chocs Mountains offer spectacular **views**★★ of the Appalachians. From the summit of Mt. Jacques Cartier, home to caribou and arctic-alpine flora, an expansive **view**★★ extends to the McGerrigle Mountains. The **nature centre** presents exhibits, films, lectures and slide shows *(open early Jun–early Sept daily 8am–8pm; early Sept–mid-Oct Mon–Thu 8am–4:30pm, Fri–Sun 8am–7:30pm; hiking & camping equipment rental & sales; ✕ ♿ P ☎418-763-7811).*

★★**Scenic Route** – Past Gaspésie Park, Route 132 follows the contours of the coastline, up and over rocky cliffs, affording splendid views of hills, valleys, picturesque fishing villages and the ocean. Of particular interest are the impressive shale cliffs around **Mont-Saint-Pierre** and the expansive views of the gulf from the bustling fishing village of **Rivière-au-Renard**.

★**Forillon National Park** – *217km/135mi east of Gaspésie Park. Open daily year-round. $3.50. ☎418-368-5505.* Located on the eastern tip of the peninsula, this 245sq km/95sq mi park includes limestone cliffs towering over the sea; mountains of spruce, fir, poplar and cedar; wildflower meadows; and sandy beaches tucked away in hidden coves. The visitor centre features displays and films on the park, as well as saltwater aquariums *(open Jun–Aug daily 9am–6pm; Sept–mid-Oct daily 9am–4pm; ☎418-368-5505)*. A road leads to **Cape Bon Ami**, providing magnificent **views**★★ of the sea and the limestone cliffs. At **Cape Gaspé**★, a pleasant walk affords **views**★ of the Bay of Gaspé and Île Bonaventure. Nearby in the former fishing village of **Grande-Grave**★, several historic buildings have been restored.

★**Gaspé** – *42km/26mi south of Forillon National Park.* Occupying a pleasant site at the point where the York River empties into the Bay of Gaspé, this city is now the administrative and commercial centre of the peninsula. The **Museum of the Gaspé Peninsula**★ (Musée de la Gaspésie) *(open Jun 24–Labour Day daily 8:30am–8:30pm; mid-May–Jun 23 & early Sept–Oct Mon–Fri 8:30am–5pm, weekends 1pm–5pm; rest of the year Tue–Fri 9am–5pm, weekends 1pm–5pm; $4; ☎418-368-1534)*, dedicated to the preservation of Gaspesian culture and heritage, highlights historical events such as Jacques Cartier's discovery of the peninsula in 1534, the Micmac Indian population and regional geography. Completed in 1969 the **Cathedral of Christ the King**★ (Cathédrale du Christ-Roi) is distinguished by its unusual lines and a cedar exterior that blends harmoniously with the environment.

THE SOUTH COAST

★★**Percé** – *76km/47mi south of Gaspé.* This bustling town was named for the massive offshore rock pierced *(percé)* by the sea. The landscape, a culmination of all the scenic beauty of the peninsula, is marked by reddish-gold limestone and shale rock, pushed and folded into a wonderful variety of cliffs, bays and hills. A tiny fishing village until the advent of tourism at the turn of the century, Percé now boasts some of the finest restaurants and tourist facilities on the peninsula.

★★**Percé Rock** (Rocher Percé) – Once attached to the mainland, this mammoth rock wall is 438m/1,437ft long and 88m/289ft high. At one time the limestone block may have had up to four archways. One of them crumbled in 1845, leaving a detached slab called the Obelisk. Today only a 30m/94ft arch remains. The sculptured limestone rock is connected to **Mont Joli**★★ by a sand bar, accessible at low tide.

★★**The Coast** – The shoreline along Route 132 offers spectacular **views**★★ of the area. Just before entering Percé, a path leads up to **Cape Barré**, which affords a commanding view to the west of the the cliffs known as Trois-Sœurs ("Three Sisters"). South of Percé a promontory at **Côte Surprise** offers another superb view of the rock and the village.

B. Terry/REFLEXION

View of Percé Rock from Mt. Sainte-Anne

Rising 320m/1,050ft above Percé, **Mt. Sainte-Anne** features extraordinary red-rock fo mations. Lookouts stationed along the way to the summit *(2hr trail)* provic increasingly expansive **views★★★** of Percé Rock, the village and the surrounding are Following the top of the sheer cliff on the west side of Mt. Sainte-Anne, another tra provides views of the **Great Crevasse★**, a deep fissure in the red conglomerate rock.

★**Île Bonaventure and Percé Rock Park** (Parc de l'Île-Bonaventure-et-du-Rocher-Percé) *Open early Jun–Jun 24 daily 8:15am–4pm. Jun 25–Aug daily 8:15am–5pm Sept–mid-Oct daily 8:15am–4pm.* ✗ ♿ P *☎ 418-782-2240.* In summer this flat topped island is home to North America's largest **gannet** colony, with some 60,00 birds. These large, white sea birds *(illustration p 234)* nest in the crevices, crack and ledges of the cliffs lining the island. A pleasant **boat trip** leads past Percé Roc and then around the island, affording superb views *(departs from Percé wharf mic Jun–mid-Sept daily 8am–5pm; May–mid-Jun & mid-Sept–mid-Oct daily 9am–4pm round-trip 1hr 15min; commentary; reservations required; $11;* ♿ P *Les Batelier de Percé Inc. ☎ 418-782-2974).* In summer passengers can disembark on th island for a closer look at the birds and walk along the nature trails.

Bonaventure – *131km/81mi southwest of Percé.* Founded in 1760 by Acadia settlers, this village is known for its salmon river and for its **Quebec Acadian Museur** (Musée acadien du Québec), which illustrates the influence of these people o Quebec's culture *(open Jun 24–Labour Day daily 9am–8pm; rest of the yea Mon–Fri 9am–5pm, weekends 1pm–5pm; $3.50;* ✗ ♿ P *☎ 418-534-4000).*

Carleton – *63km/39mi west of Bonaventure.* Nestled between the mountains an the sea, this community was founded by Acadians in the late 18C and has sinc become a choice summer resort. Carleton is dominated by **Mt. Saint-Joseph**, risin to 558m/1,830ft. From the summit, near a small stone shrine, the **panorama★★** encompasses Chaleur Bay from Bonaventure to the Miguasha Peninsula, an extends south to New Brunswick.

★**Miguasha Park** – *24km/15mi west of Carleton. Open Jun–Aug daily 9am–6pm Sept–mid-Oct daily 9am–5pm.* ✗ ♿ P *☎ 418-794-2475.* This national conserva tion park lies on an escarpment jutting out into Chaleur Bay, which contains fossil embedded in sedimentary rock since the Devonian Period (400 million years ago) Visitors are introduced to the world of fossils through exhibits at the interpreta tion centre, demonstrations in the laboratory and on-site observation of the cliff.

Battle of the Ristigouche National Historic Site (Lieu historique national Bataille-de-la Ris tigouche) – *44km/27mi from Miguasha Park. Open Jun–mid-Oct daily 9am–5pm Mar–May & mid-Oct–Nov by appointment only. $5.* ♿ P *☎ 418-788-5676.* France's last attempt to save its North American colony from British domination during the Seven Years' War was thwarted in the estuary of the Ristigouche River in 1760. A **visitor centre** features exhibits and an animated film *(15min)* on the battle and displays the hull and anchor of the French warship *Le Machault*, which sank nearby.

HULL★

Population 62,339

Map of Principal Sights p 4

Facing OTTAWA across the wide waters of the Ottawa River, this bustling community was founded in 1800. Though Hull remains an important lumber, pulp and paper centre, today it functions primarily as an annex to Canada's federal capital. The down-town area has witnessed a great deal of change, including the construction of two large federal government complexes and creation of a new campus for the University of Quebec.

SIGHTS *1 day*

★★★**Canadian Museum of Civilization (Musée canadien des Civilisations)** – *Map p 157. 100 Rue Laurier. Open Jul–Labour Day daily 9am–6pm (Thu–Fri 9pm). May–Jun & early Sept–mid-Oct daily 9am–6pm (Thu 9pm). Rest of the year Tue–Sun 9am–5pm (Thu 9pm). $5 (free Sun 9am–noon).* ✗ ♿ P*($8) 819-776-7000.* Inaugurated in 1989 this sizeable museum is dedicated to the history of Canada and to the art and traditions of native cultures and ethnic groups. The sweeping curves of the two large buildings designed by Douglas Cardinal evoke the emergence of the North American continent and its subsequent molding by wind, water and glaciers. The **Canadian Shield Wing** houses administrative offices and conservation laboratories, while the **Glacier Wing** provides 16,500sq m/33,792sq ft of exhibit halls. In the **grand hall** six cultural regions of the Canadian Pacific Coast are illustrated through the wooden homes of village chieftains and majestic totem poles, rising to the ceiling. In the **Canada Hall** artifacts and reconstructed buildings re-create 1,000 years of Canadian heritage. The delightful **children's museum** Kids encourages young people to explore the world, from a Mexican village to a Pakistani street. A costume room, puppet theatre, games section and art studio complete the exhibit.

Malak, Ottawa

Canadian Museum of Civilization (Ottawa in the Background)

In the **CINÉPLUS Theatre** *(tickets available at main entrance; for films & screening times ☎ 819-776-7010)*, a 6-storey IMAX screen and an OMNIMAX dome provide unparalleled viewing opportunities for 295 spectators.

★★ **Gatineau Park** – *Map p 159. Open daily year-round. Parkways closed from first snowfall until early May. Visitor centre open mid-May–Labour Day daily 9am–6pm; rest of the year Mon–Fri 9:30am–4:30pm, weekends 9am–5pm. $6/car.* ☎ *819-827-2020.* Covering 356sq km/137sq mi, this enchanting place lies nestled between the valleys of the Ottawa and Gatineau Rivers. Formerly Algonquin and Iroquois territory, the land was designated a park in the 1930s with the assistance of **William Lyon Mackenzie King**, tenth prime minister of Canada. Today the park encloses several federal government buildings. A scenic parkway winding its way through dense hardwood forests leads to **Champlain Lookout**, which offers a magnificent **panorama**★★ of the Ottawa Valley.

★ **Mackenzie King Estate** (Domaine Mackenzie-King) – *Open mid-May–mid-Oct Mon–Fri 11am–5pm, weekends 10am–6pm.* ☎ *819-827-2020.* King willed his estate to Canada in 1950. His primary residence, **Moorside**, features exhibits as well as an audio-visual presentation *(15min)*, and houses a delightful tea room.

LAURENTIANS★★

Map p 196

Stretching along the north shore of the St. Lawrence, this range of low, rounded mountains rises to an altitude of 968m/3,175ft at **Mt. Tremblant**. Part of the Canadian Shield, the Laurentians (*Laurentides* in French), formed more than a billion years ago in the Precambrian era, are among the oldest mountains in the world.

The area north of MONTREAL between Saint-Jérôme and Mt. Tremblant is especially noted for its string of resort towns that offer an attractive blend of recreational activities and fine cuisine. In winter alpine skiers have a choice of over 100 ski lifts and tows, while cross-country enthusiasts can explore a variety of lengthy trails. In summer water sports prevail on the innumerable lakes, and the surrounding hills cater to hikers, horseback riders and golfers. In the towns several renowned summer theatres open their doors to visitors.

Weaving through forest-clad hills, the drive along Route 117 from Saint-Jérôme to Saint-Jovite is particularly splendid in fall, when the mountains display a dazzling array of colours.

SIGHTS

★ **Sainte-Adèle** – *68km/42mi north of Montreal by Rte. 15 and Rte. 117.* This resort community nestled around a small lake is popular with artists and writers. The **Séraphin Village Museum**★ (Musée village de Séraphin) Kids comprises some 20 buildings re-creating the life of the first settlers in the area *(4km/2.5mi north of town; open late Jun–Labour Day daily 10am–6pm; mid-May–mid-Jun &rest of Sept weekends 10am–6pm; $9;* ☎ *514-229-4777)*. Inspired by Claude Henri Grignon's 1933 work, *The Woman and the Miser*, several structures illustrate episodes in the life of Séraphin Poudrier, the novel's protagonist.

★**Sainte-Agathe-des-Monts** – *18km/11mi north of Sainte-Adèle by Rte. 117.* Set on the shores of the H-shaped **Sables Lake**★★, this lively town is the capital of the Laurentians region. A **scenic cruise** is recommended to discover the magnificent lake and the sumptuous homes lining its shores *(departs from dock at foot of Rue Principale mid-May–late Oct daily 10:30am, 11:30am, 1:30pm, 2:30pm & 3:30pm; additional departures late Jun–Labour Day; round-trip 50min; commentary; $11 ♿ 🅿 Les Croisières Alouette ☎819-326-3656).*

★**Mt. Tremblant Park** – *About 140km/87mi north of Montreal. Park open daily late Jun–mid-Oct. Apr–mid-Jun & late Oct–mid-Dec daily 7am–10pm. Late Dec–Mar daily 8am–4pm. Sections of the park's roads are closed during winter. ⛺ ✕ ♿ 🅿 819-424-2954 (Saint-Donat visitor centre) ☎514-883-1291 (Saint-Côme visitor centre), ☎819-688-2281 (Lac-Monroe visitor centre).* Dominating the long, narrow Lake Tremblant, Quebec's oldest provincial park abounds in lakes, waterfalls and hiking trails. This recreational wonderland is also home to rich and diverse fauna and a multitude of birds.

Laurentides – *62km/38mi north of Montreal by Rte. 15, then east on Rte. 158.* This small industrial town is known as the birthplace of **Sir Wilfrid Laurier** (1841-1919), the first French-Canadian prime minister of Canada (1896-1911). The **National Historic Site** (Lieu historique national de Sir-Wilfrid-Laurier), a simple brick structure, stands on the place of Laurier's presumed birthplace *(visit by 1hr guided tour only, mid-May–Jun Mon–Fri 9am–5pm; Jul–Aug Wed–Sun 10am–6pm; $2.50; ♿ 🅿 ☎514-439-3702).* Next to it, a visitor centre exhibits displays on the influential role Laurier played in Canadian politics.

MAGDALEN ISLANDS★★

Population 13,802
Map of Principal Sights p 5
Tourist Office ☎418-986-2245

Located in the middle of the Gulf of St. Lawrence, this isolated, windswept outpost consists of eight islands and numerous islets connected by sandspits that form a hook-shaped mass about 72km/45mi long. The archipelago's most striking features are the spectacular rock formations, cut into the stone by the pounding sea. Contrasting with the red sandstone, expansive white beaches stretch to the blue sea.
Though discovered in 1534 by Jacques Cartier, the islands were not permanently inhabited until 1755, when they became a refuge for **Acadians** deported from Nova Scotia—the ancestors of many of the present population known as *Madelinots*.
Supplemented by agriculture, logging and a growing tourism industry, fishing remains the primary economic activity of the archipelago. Today the islands offer a wealth of outdoor recreation, from sightseeing to swimming and hiking.

Access – *Ferry from Souris–Cap-aux-Meules (5hrs): daily service (except Mon) Apr 1–Jun & Sept–Oct from Cap-aux-Meules (8am) and from Souris (2pm). Daily service (except Tue) Jul–Aug from Cap-aux-Meules (8am) and from Souris (2pm). Limited service Nov–Jan. One-way $34.50/person, additional $65.75/car. Reservations required. ✕ ♿ 🅿 CTMA Traversier Ltd. Cap-aux-Meules ☎418-986-3278 or Souris ☎902-687-2181. Additional information ☎418-986-6600. Flights between Montreal and l'Île du Havre aux Maisons on Inter-Canadian ☎514-631-9802 and Air Alliance ☎514-422-2282. For information on guided tours, scenic cruises, restaurants and accommodations, contact the tourist office in Cap-aux-Meules ☎418-986-2245.*

SIGHTS

★★**Cap aux Meules Island** – The largest of the islands is also the archipelago's administrative and commercial centre. Cap-aux-Meules' highest point, **Butte du Vent**, affords extensive **views**★★ of the entire chain of islands. The western coast features some of the most dramatic **rock formations**★★ on the Magdalen Islands. The sea has carved the red sandstone into deep crevasses and defiant promontories, creating a spectacular landscape of crumbled arches and solitary columns of stone.

★**Havre Aubert Island** – Marked by gentle, rolling hills, this southernmost island is the centre of the archipelago's cultural life. At the **Maritime Museum**★ (Musée de la Mer) displays of boats and navigational instruments aquaint visitors with the maritime history and culture of the Magdalen Islands *(open Jun 24–late Aug Mon–Fri 9am–6pm, weekends 10am–6pm; rest of the year Mon–Fri 9am–noon & 1pm–5pm, weekends 1pm–5pm; $3.50; ♿ 🅿 ☎418-937-5711).* The historic site of **La Grave**★ encompasses some 15 buildings, including stores, ironworks, *chaufauds* (sheds where cod was dried) and warehouses.

★**Havre aux Maisons Island** – This elongated island has retained its rural charm and features some of the best examples of local domestic architecture, including the **baraque**, a small building designed to shelter hay. At **Dune du Sud**★ a fine beach and elaborate rock formations attract visitors.

On **Grande Entrée Island**★, coastal hiking trails afford spectacular **views**★★★ of jagged cliffs and jutting promontories, tidal pools and vast beaches, twisted trees and colourful wildflowers. **Grande Échouerie Beach**★★ to the northeast is lovely.

MONTREAL★★★

Metro Population 1,775,846
Map of Principal Sights p 5
Tourist Office ☎514-873-2015

Canada's second largest metropolis after Toronto is located on a large island wedged into the mighty St. Lawrence River, some 1,000 miles from the Atlantic. Owing in part to its key geographical position, this cosmopolitan city has emerged as a leading industrial, commercial and financial centre.

Home to the world's largest francophone population outside Paris, Montreal presents a unique combination of Old World cultures and North American modernity. A sizeable English-speaking community is particularly prominent in the business sector. The city offers visitors a wealth of cultural attractions and a diversity of urban settings, each with its distinctive ambience—from the charming cobblestone streets of Old Montreal to the landmark skyscrapers dominating the downtown cityscape.

Historical Notes

Early Exploration – While searching for riches and a route to the Orient in 1535, Jacques Cartier landed on the island of Montreal and visited the Mohawk village of **Hochelaga**. After founding Quebec City, Samuel de Champlain sailed upriver and set foot on the nearby island of St. Helen *(p 213)* in 1611. However, European settlement of the area did not occur until the arrival, in 1642, of Paul de Chomedey, **Sieur de Maisonneuve** (1612-76), who is considered the founder of Montreal.

Under the French Regime – Early in the 17C, two superiors of the Sulpician order in France decided to found a mission on the island of Montreal, as part of an effort to revive Roman Catholicism in the aftermath of the Protestant Reformation. They chose Maisonneuve to sail across the Atlantic with some 40 companions and establish the mission of **Ville-Marie** (City of Mary).

Amid continued fighting between Iroquois inhabitants and the French settlers, Ville-Marie slowly developed into a commercial centre and was renamed Montreal in the early 18C. Seeking profit, the French set off across the Great Lakes to trap fur-bearing animals. The furs were highly prized in Europe, where they were transformed into luxurious apparel, and the trade boomed. By the time of the surrender of Montreal in 1760 *(p 188)*, the city had become a well-established, thriving community. After the British victory, most of the French nobility returned to France. A large number of Scots, attracted to the fur trade, and an influx of Loyalists from the US swelled the anglophone population.

From Rebellion to Confederation – The fur trade reached its heyday in the late 18C and early 19C, bringing great prosperity to Montreal. Two partnerships, the **North West Company** (based in Montreal) and the **Hudson's Bay Company**, established trading posts all over northern Canada and monopolized the market. By the time the companies merged in 1821, however, Montreal's dominance in the trade was in decline. Montreal was the centre of one of the **Rebellions of 1837**, a political uprising against British rule, which, in Lower Canada, contested the power held by the Crown-appointed governor and his council. Led by Louis-Joseph Papineau, George-Étienne Cartier and other French Canadians, the **Patriots** engaged in several armed revolts against British troops. Although the insurgents were defeated, the British government subsequently decided to grant Quebec a representative government.

By the time of Confederation in 1867, Montreal stood at the forefront of railway development and claimed the world's largest grain port. Financial institutions sprouting along Rue Saint-Jacques promoted growth of the city and country and contributed to Montreal's dominance in Canada's financial sector until the 1970s.

Montreal Today – Following a period of slow growth after the Great Depression, Montreal experienced a revival in the 1950s and 60s, manifested in restoration projects throughout the city. Montreal has emerged as an international centre of commerce and culture. In addition to hosting such events as the 1967 World Fair (Expo '67), the 1976 Olympic Games and the 1980 International Floralies, the city features annual international festivals in jazz, film and comedy, attracting thousands of visitors. Internationally acclaimed artists regularly perform at Montreal's premier cultural complex, **Place des Arts★★**, home to the Montreal Symphony Orchestra, the Grands Ballets Canadiens and the Montreal Opera.

The city remains a major centre of francophone culture. Its numerous cafes and restaurants, especially along Saint-Denis and Crescent Streets, reflect Montrealers' *joie de vivre*. Visitors to this vibrant city will also enjoy the variety of shops and boutiques. In 1992 Montreal celebrated the 350th anniversary of its foundation.

In Montreal, the Sun Rises in the South – The St. Lawrence River generally flows in a west-to-east direction, and its banks are referred to as the north and south shores. At Montreal, however, the river takes a sudden turn northward. The streets parallel to the river are called east-west streets, although they actually run north-south, and the perpendicular streets are designated north-south, although they extend east-west.

PRACTICAL INFORMATION

Area Code 514

Note: At presstime, a new area code, **450**, was being introduced in the current 514 region of Quebec to address an increased demand for telecommunications services. The new area code is effective for Laval, the North and South Shores, the Laurentians and Richelieu.

Getting Around

By Public Transportation – Local metro and bus service are provided by Société de Transport de la Communauté Urbaine de Montréal (STCUM) ☎288-6287. The system generally operates from 5:30am–1:30am *(lines 1, 2 & 4)* or 11pm *(line 5)*. Each metro line is designated by a number and a colour. Metro tickets (which may also be used on buses) are available at metro stations and may be purchased individually *($1.85)*, or in a book *(carnet)* of six *($8)*. Tourist passes *(cartes touristiques)* are also available *($5/day or $12/3 days)*. Lost and found ☎280-4637.

By Car – Rental agencies include Avis ☎866-7906; Budget ☎866-7675; Hertz ☎842-8537; National-Tilden ☎878-2771.

By Taxi – La Salle ☎277-2552; Diamond ☎273-6331; Champlain ☎273-2435.

General Information

Accommodations and Visitor Information – Reservation services: Hospitality Canada ☎393-1528; Montreal Reservations Centre ☎284-2277. Infotourist Office: 1001 Rue du Square-Dorchester, ● Peel *(open mid-Jun–Labour Day daily 8:30am–7:30pm; rest of the year daily 9am–6pm; ☎873-2015)*. For a listing of major hotel chains *p 306*.

Local Press – English *The Gazette*. French *Le journal de Montréal, Le devoir, La presse* (daily).

Entertainment – For current schedules and for addresses of principal theatres and concert halls, consult the free tourist publications *Mirror* and *Hour* (English), *Le guide Montréal* (bilingual) and *Voir* (French) or the arts and entertainment supplements in local newspapers (weekend editions). Tickets may be purchased from Admission ☎790-1245, Teletron ☎790-1111 and Voyages Astral Inc. ☎866-1001 (most major credit cards accepted).

Sports – Montreal Canadians (National Hockey League): season from Oct–Apr at the Molson Centre (● Bonaventure) ☎932-2582. Montreal Expos (National Baseball League): season from Apr–Sept at Olympic Stadium (● Viau) ☎846-3976.

Useful Numbers

	☎
Police–Ambulance–Fire	911
Tourisme Québec	873-2015
Central Station (VIA Rail), *895 Rue de la Gauchetière Ouest*	989-2626
Orléans Express or Vermont Transit (Bus terminal), *505 Blvd. de Maisonneuve Est*	842-2281
Dorval International Airport	633-3105
Canadian Automobile Assn., *1180 Drummond St.*	861-7575
Jean Coutu Drugstore (extended hours)	527-8827
Post Office, *1025 Rue Saint-Jacques Ouest*	846-5390
Road Conditions	873-4121
Weather (24hr)	283-4006

★★★OLD MONTREAL (Vieux-Montréal)

1 day. Map p 207. ● Place d'Armes.

Bounded by the Old Port, Saint-Jacques, Berri and McGill Streets, Montreal's historic core was originally enclosed within imposing stone walls erected in the early 1700s. During the 19C the settlement expanded and Montrealers moved outside the fortifications. Warehouses and commercial buildings gradually replaced stone dwellings and gardens, and the area fell into decline. Interest in Old Montreal was revived in the 1960s: the surviving 18C homes were renovated, warehouses were transformed into apartment buildings, and restaurants and shops opened. Today

Old Montreal is a pleasant area that caters mainly to tourists. Amphibious buses **(Amphibus)** tour part of Old Montreal *(map p 207)* before embarking on a cruise around Cité du Havre *(depart from the corner of Blvd. Saint-Laurent & Rue de la Commune May–Jun 23 daily 10am–10pm every 2hrs; Jun 24–Aug daily 10am–midnight every hour; Sept–Oct daily 10am–8pm every 2hrs; round-trip 1hr; commentary; reservations required; $18;* 🅿 Amphibus Inc. ☎514-849-5181).

★**Place d'Armes** – Designed in the 17C by the Sulpician Dollier de Casson, this square long served as military drill grounds. A **monument**★ (**1**) (Louis-Philippe Hébert) in the centre honours the founder of Montreal, Sieur de Maisonneuve, who, according to legend, killed the local Indian chief on this site during a 1644 battle. The west side of this charming green space is dominated by the **Bank of Montreal**★ (1847), one of the city's finest examples of the Neoclassical style.

Extending south, **Rue Saint-Jacques**★, the financial heart of Canada until the 1970s, is lined with elegant 19C and 20C edifices. Note in particular the Canadian Imperial Bank of Commerce *(no. 265)*, with its facade of fluted Corinthian columns, and the **Royal Bank of Canada**★ *(no. 360)*, whose tower is a distinct feature of the city's skyline.

★★**Notre Dame Basilica** – *Open Jun 24–Aug daily 7am–8pm. Rest of the year daily 7am–6pm.* ♿ *☎514-842-2925.* This twin-towered church rises on the south side of the Place d'Armes. Completed in 1829 under the supervision of James O'Donnell, the Gothic Revival basilica is especially renowned for its magnificent **interior**. The opulent decor, designed by Victor Bourgeau, features sculptures, wainscoting and giltwork typical of provincial religious architecture. The main nave, lined on both sides by deep-set double galleries, measures 68m/223ft long, 21m/69ft wide and 25m/82ft high. As visitors enter, eyes are drawn to the ensemble of white oak statues, part of the imposing **reredos** that stands out against the background's soft blue hues. The massive black walnut **pulpit**★ is the work of Louis-Philippe Hébert. Behind the choir the Sacred Heart Chapel is dominated by an impressive **bronze reredos** representing mankind's difficult journey to heaven.

The **Old Sulpician Seminary**★, the oldest structure in the city, stands beside the basilica. Note the facade **clock**, installed in 1701, believed to be the oldest public timepiece in North America.

★★**Place Jacques-Cartier** – *Scheduled for transition to pedestrian-only street in 1998.* Lined with outdoor cafes and flower parterres, this charming cobblestone square is lively all summer, especially in the evenings, when street musicians and acrobats entertain the crowds. Created in 1847 the square was named for the famous explorer who, according to tradition, docked his ship here in 1535. Marking the north end of the plaza, a **statue** (**2**) of Horatio Nelson (1809) commemorates the British general's victory at Trafalgar. Montreal's **City Hall**★ (Hôtel de Ville), an imposing Second Empire building, stands across Rue Notre-Dame *(visit by 1hr guided tour only, year-round Mon–Fri 8:30am–4:30pm; closed national holidays;* ♿ *☎514-872-3355)*. Charles de Gaulle delivered his famous "Vive le Québec libre" speech in 1967 from the balcony overlooking the main entrance. The southern end of the square leads to **Rue Saint-Paul**★★, a charming street lined with lovely 19C buildings, and several warehouses transformed into shops and artists' studios. Along with Rue Notre-Dame, this narrow street is one of the oldest in Montreal.

★**Old Port (Vieux-Port)** – Stretching along the St. Lawrence River, at the foot of Place Jacques-Cartier, the former port has been transformed into a pleasant waterfront park with bike and walking paths, a skating rink, exhibition spaces, a flea market and an IMAX cinema *($12.50; ☎514-496-4629)*. Stroll along the wide boardwalk or take a **harbour cruise**★ to enjoy scenic **views**★ of the city and the majestic river *(departs from Quai de l'Horloge & Quai Jacques Cartier May–Oct daily noon, 2:30pm & 4:30pm; round-trip 2hrs; commentary; reservations required; from $19.95; dancing & dinner cruises also available;* ✗ ♿ 🅿*($9) Croisières AML ☎514-842-3871)*.

★★**Jet Boat Trips on the Lachine Rapids** (Expéditions dans les rapides de Lachine) – *Depart from Quai de l'Horloge May–Aug daily 10am–6pm. Sept–mid-Oct 10am–4pm. Round-trip 1hr 15min. Commentary. Reservations suggested. $48.* ♿ 🅿*($7) Lachine Rapids Tours/Saute-Moutons ☎514-284-9607.* On this wet and exciting voyage, passengers are whisked upriver in specially designed vessels that mount and descend the ferocious Lachine Rapids. The **views**★★ of Montreal and the surrounding areas are spectacular.

★**Château Ramezay** – *280 Rue Notre Dame Est. Open Jun–Sept daily 10am–6pm. Rest of the year daily 10am–4:30pm. Closed Jan 1–2 & Dec 25–26. $5.* ♿ *☎514-861-3708.* Situated across from City Hall, this squat, fieldstone residence (1705) is a lovely example of early-18C domestic architecture. Constructed for Claude de Ramezay, 11th governor of Montreal during the French Regime, the building has undergone several renovations, yet remains relatively unchanged in appearance. It was acquired by the British government to serve as the official gubernatorial residence until 1849.

Restored and transformed into a **museum** in 1895, the interior presents Montreal' economic, political and social history. The highlight is the exquisite, hand-carve mahogany **panelling** produced in 1725 in Nantes, France.

★**Sir George-Étienne Cartier National Historic Site** – *458 Rue Notre-Dame Open Jun–Aug daily 10am–5pm. Apr–May & Sept–late Dec Wed–Sun 10am–5pm $3.25.* ☎*514-283-2282.* This limestone, mansard-roofed structure, com posed of two adjoining houses, was the home of **George-Étienne Cartier** (1814-73) one of the Fathers of Confederation. Displays trace his life and career as a lawyer businessman and politician. Refurbished in the Victorian style, period rooms illus trate the lifestyle of 19C middle-class society.

★**Rue Bonsecours** – This attractive street leading from Rue Notre-Dame to Rue Saint Paul offers a charming perspective of the little Notre-Dame-de-Bon-Secours Chape *(below)*. At no. 440 stands the **Papineau House** (Maison Papineau), a large grey edific topped by a steeply pitched roof that is pierced by two rows of dormer windows During an 1831 reconstruction, the original stone walls were covered in wood sculpted and painted to resemble limestone. The building was home to six genera tions of the Papineau family, including Louis-Joseph, leader of the Patriots during the 1837 Rebellions. The fieldstone walls, firebreaks, corner consoles, tall chimneys and pitched gables of the **Calvet House**★ (Maison du Calvet) (1798), located at the corner of Rue Saint-Paul, are characteristic of a traditional 18C urban residence.

★**Chapel of Our Lady of Perpetual Help** (Chapelle Notre-Dame-de-Bon-Secours) – *400 Ru Saint-Paul Est.* This small church, topped by a copper steeple, stands on the site of a wooden edifice commissioned by Marguerite Bourgeoys in 1657 and destroyed by fire in 1754. Facing the St. Lawrence, a 9m/30ft statue of the Virgin Mary

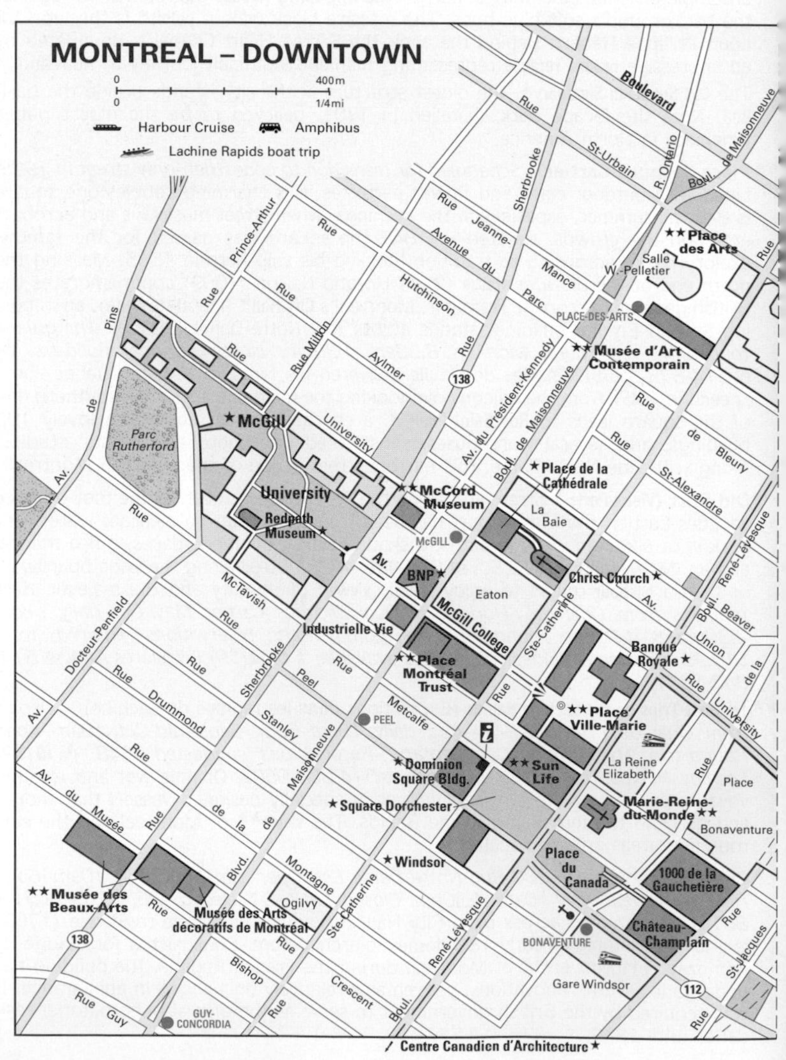

crowns the rear of the church. Climb the observatory, accessible from the tower, to enjoy a **panorama**★ of the river, Old Montreal and the Old Port. An archaeological site is scheduled to open here *(late 1998)* as a result of findings from excavation work under the chapel.

Located in the basement, the **Marguerite Bourgeoys Museum** *(open May–Oct Tue–Sun 10am–4:30pm; mid-Mar–Apr & Nov–mid-Jan Tue–Sun 11am–3pm; $5;* ♿ ☎*514-282-8670)* features a collection of dolls that re-creates the life of Bourgeoys (1620-1700), who came to Montreal with Maisonneuve in 1653 to found the Congregation of Our Lady. Bourgeoys was canonized in 1982.

Near the church, on Rue Saint-Paul, stands the **Bonsecours Market**★ (Marché Bonsecours) *(open year-round, hours vary;* ✂ ♿ 🅿 ☎*514-872-7730)*, a large Neoclassical stone structure crowned by a lofty dome. It served as the city hall from 1852 to 1878, housing municipal offices thereafter and today is leased for office space, temporary exhibits and other purposes.

★**Place d'Youville** – Located south of Place d'Armes, this pleasant square is surrounded by grand edifices. Housed in a brick structure reflecting the Dutch baroque architectural style, the **Montreal History Centre**★ (Centre d'histoire de Montréal) presents the city's rich past through interactive displays, artifacts, animated mannequins and a 10min slide show *(open May–Aug daily 10am–5pm; Sept–early Dec Tue–Sun 10am–5pm; $4.50;* ♿ 🅿 ☎*514-872-3207)*. To the east of the square stand the **Youville Stables** (Écuries), an ensemble of grey stone structures (1828) enclosing a lovely garden courtyard. Located in a former warehouse, the **Marc-Aurèle Fortin Museum**★ *(118 Rue Saint-Pierre; open year-round Tue–Sun 11am–5pm; closed late Dec–Jan & Good Friday; $4;* ♿ ☎*514-845-6108)* exhibits the works of this 20C Québécois artist. His subjects include regional flora and fauna and

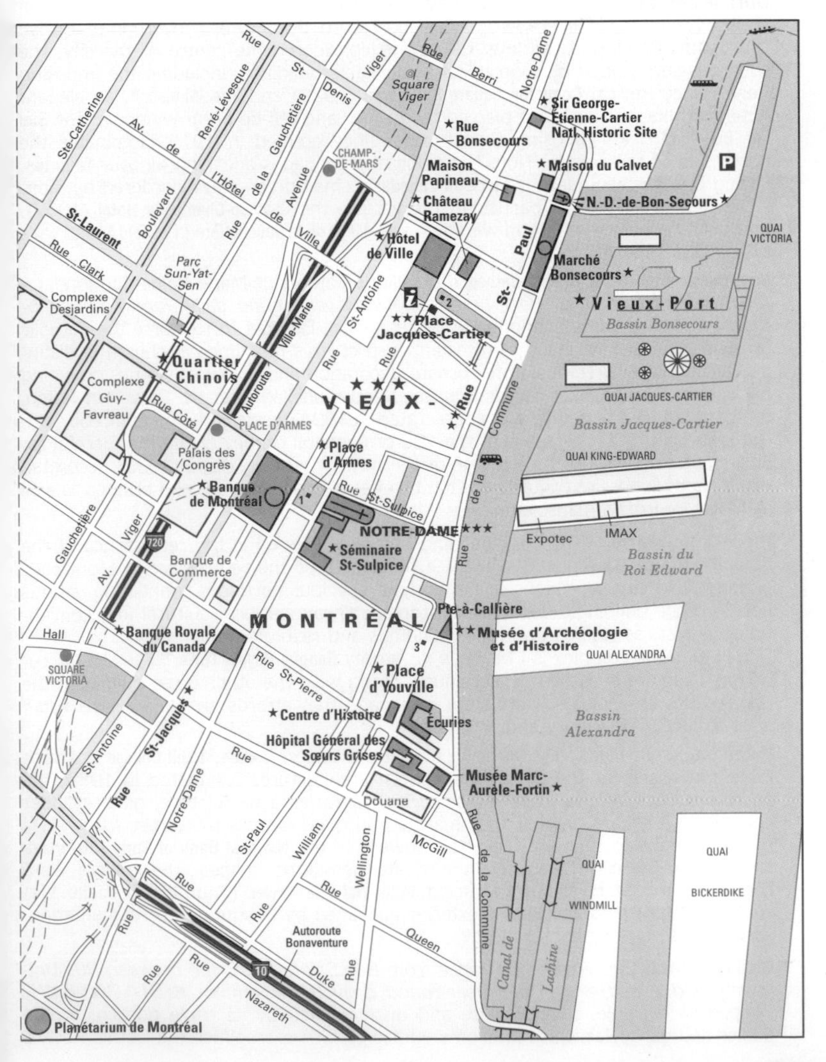

St. Lawrence River landscapes. Spanning the block between Saint-Pierre and Normand Streets, the **Grey Nuns Convent** (Hôpital général des Soeurs Grises) was erected in 1694 and extended in 1753 by Marie d'Youville, founder of the Grey Nuns order.

Callière Point (Pointe-à-Callière) – Maisonneuve established the settlement of Ville-Marie on this small triangle of land. A 10m/33ft **obelisk** (**3**) commemorates the occasion of his landing in May 1642. Opened in 1992, the **Montreal Museum of Archaeology and History★★** (Musée d'Archéologie et d'Histoire de Montréal), composed of a modern building, an archaeological crypt and an 1838 Neoclassical edifice (the Old Customs House, 1838) presents Montreal's fascinating history through permanent and temporary exhibits and a multimedia presentation *(open Jul–Aug Tue–Fri 10am–6pm, weekends 11am–6pm; rest of the year Tue–Fri 10am–5pm, weekends 11am–5pm; $8;* ✗ ♿ ☎*514-872-9150)*. Located under Place Royale, the crypt displays vestiges recovered during archaeological excavations.

★★DOWNTOWN *1 day. Map pp 206-207.* ● Rue Peel.

Bordered by Rue Saint-Jacques to the east, Rue Sherbrooke to the west, and Saint-Denis and Atwater Streets to the north and south, the city's commercial and cultural heart lies to the west of Old Montreal. The downtown developed into a prosperous and bustling quarter during the late 18C and 19C, and today features some of Montreal's most famous buildings and institutions. A walk along Sherbrooke, one of the most prestigious arteries in the city, reveals a lively retail sector alongside choice residences. Rue Sainte-Catherine is home to major department stores (Ogilvy, La Baie, Eaton Centre) and commercial centres, while Avenue McGill College is lined with the city's landmark 20C skyscrapers.

★**Dorchester Square** – Formerly known as Dominion Square, this pleasant green space was renamed in 1988 in honour of Lord Dorchester, governor of British North America during the late 18C. Long considered the centre of the city, the square is surrounded by a group of remarkable buildings, including the imposing Renaissance Revival **Dominion Square Building★** (1929) and **The Windsor★**, an elegant hotel, with its mansard roof pierced by dormer and œil-de-bœuf windows. The **Sun Life Building★★**, an imposing Beaux-Arts edifice erected in 1913, dominates the north side of the square. Note the colossal colonnades adorning all four facades. Facing Dorchester Square is **Place du Canada**, a small green plaza bordered by more recent constructions. Of particular interest are the **Château-Champlain Hotel** (1967), marked by convex, half-moon windows and **1000 de la Gauchetière** (1992), Montreal's tallest skyscraper.

★★**Mary Queen of the World Basilica-Cathedral** (Basilique-Cathédrale Marie-Reine-du-Monde) – *Main entrance on Blvd. René-Lévesque. Open year-round daily 7am–7:30pm.* ♿ ☎*514-866-1661.* Commissioned by Msgr. Ignace Bourget to reinforce the Catholic presence in a predominantly Protestant district, this monumental church is distinguished by large Greek columns, ornate decoration and a row of statues crowning the cornice. Designed by Victor Bourgeau and modelled after St. Peter's in Rome, the Baroque Revival edifice was consecrated in 1894. Inside is the magnificent gold-leaf **baldachin** (1900), a replica of the 16C ornamental canopy created by Bernini for St. Peter's Basilica. On the left side of the nave, a **mortuary chapel** (1933) decorated with beautiful mosaics contains the tombs of several archbishops and bishops as well as Msgr. Bourget's mausoleum.

★★**Place Ville-Marie** – This four-building complex ushered in the renaissance of the downtown area. Completed in the 1960s, it became the centrepiece of Montreal's underground city, an extensive network of spacious corridors connecting various hotels, office buildings, department stores, railway stations, cultural and conventions centres, as well as boutiques, cinemas and restaurants.
Dominating the complex is I.M. Pei's 42-storey **Banque Royale Tower★** (1962), a cruciform structure sheathed in aluminum. Along with the other three buildings, the Banque Royale encloses a concrete esplanade that affords an unparalleled **vista★** west to McGill University and Mt. Royal.

Extending from Place Ville-Marie to McGill University, **Avenue McGill College** is a veritable showplace for the city's Postmodern architecture. Completed in 1989, the enormous **Place Montréal Trust★★** *(no. 1500)* features a pastel blue, glass cylinder encased in a square base of rose marble and glass. Across the street *(no. 1981)* rise the sprawling, metallic-blue twin towers of the **National Bank of Paris (BNP)/Laurentian Bank Towers★**. Designed in intricate geometric shapes, the towers were completed in 1981. The granite-clad **Industrial Life Tower** (Tour l'Industrielle Vie) *(no. 2000)* presents an elegant exterior enlivened by Postmodern ornamentation, such as the huge fanlight window.

★**Christ Church Cathedral** – *Entrance from Rue Sainte-Catherine between Rue University and Ave. Union. Open year-round daily 8am–5pm.* ♿ ☎*514-288-6421.* Topped by a single, slender spire and distinguished by its triple portico, ornate gables and gargoyles, this handsome edifice (1859) exemplifies the Gothic Revival style. The ivy-covered church preserves a graceful interior, embellished by stained-glass windows and a beautifully carved stone **reredos**. The capitals of the arcaded nave are decorated with leaves representing trees indigenous to Canada.

Rising behind the church is a prominent landmark, the **Place de la Cathédrale★**, formerly the Coopérants Building. Designed to be viewed in tandem with the church, the copper-coloured edifice features colonnades, pointed entrances, arched windows and a pitched roof.

★★ **McCord Museum of Canadian History (Musée McCord d'Histoire canadienne)** – *690 Rue Sherbrooke Ouest. Open year-round Tue–Fri 10am–6pm, weekends 10am–5pm (& Mon 10am–5pm Jul–Aug). $7. ☎514-398-7100.* One of Canada's foremost historical museums, the McCord was founded in 1921 and underwent extensive renovation in 1991. Holdings provide a fascinating insight into Canadian history, from the era of Indian settlement to the present day. In addition to more than 100,000 artifacts, the museum houses an outstanding compilation of over 750,000 photos that chronicle Canadian life in the 19C and 20C.

★ **McGill University** – *End of Ave. McGill College.* Set on the slopes of Mt. Royal, Canada's oldest university (1821) has witnessed much growth over the years and today claims an enrollment of some 30,000 students. The buildings gracing the 32ha/79 acre campus reflect a variety of architectural styles. Located on the campus and housed in a large structure designed in the style of an antique temple, the **Redpath Museum of Natural History★** (Musée d'histoire naturelle Redpath) displays vertebrate and invertebrate fossils, minerals, zoological artifacts, African art objects and Egyptian antiquities *(open Jun 24–Labour Day Mon–Thu 9am–5pm, Sun 1pm–5pm; rest of the year Mon–Fri 9am–5pm, Sun 1pm–5pm; closed national holidays; P ☎514-398-4086).*

Avenue McGill and McGill University

★★ **Montreal Museum of Fine Arts (Musée des Beaux-Arts de Montréal)** – *1380 Rue Sherbrooke Ouest. Open year-round Tue–Sun 11am–6pm (Wed 9pm). Closed Jan 1 & Dec 25. $10 (permanent collection, free). ☎514-285-1600.* Ranked among Canada's finest museums, this 135-year-old institution boasts a permanent collection of over 25,000 objects ranging from Old Masters to contemporary Canadian art. The Beaux-Arts main edifice, known as the North Pavilion (1912), presents Canadian art on its three floors, while the South Pavilion (1991) displays masterpieces from all over the world. The buildings are linked by a series of underground galleries that exhibit Ancient, Asiatic and African art as well as **Islamic art**. Created by renowned architect **Moshe Safdie**, the new annex showcases travelling exhibits in five large vaulted galleries.

The North Pavilion's collection of **Canadian art**, ranging from the 18C to 1960, features paintings, sculpture and decorative arts. Of note are works by Paul Kane, Cornelius Krieghoff, J.W. Morrice, Suzor-Côté, the Group of Seven and modern artists Paul-Émile Borduas and Jean-Paul Riopelle. Of particular interest on the ground floor is the native American collection, including Inuit art. A fine collection of **prints and drawings**, including several by Albrecht Dürer, is found on this level. The fourth floor of the South Pavilion is devoted to **European art** spanning the Middle Ages to the 19C, including works by Mantegna, Memling, El Greco, Rembrandt Canaletto and Gainsborough. Displayed on the third level and the second underground level, the museum's rich collection of **20C Art** is represented by works of Picasso, Alexander Calder, Sam Francis, Betty Goodwin and others.

★**Montreal Museum of Decorative Arts (Musée des Arts décoratifs de Montréal)** – *2200 Rue Crescent. Open year-round Tue–Sun 11am–6pm. $4.* ✗ ♿ ☎*514-284-1252* Formerly located at Château Dufresne, the international design collections of this museum were moved in 1997 to exhibit space next to the Museum of Fine Arts: a passageway connects the two museums. Ceramics, sculptures, textiles and other works trace major trends in decorative arts from Art Nouveau to Postmoderism.

★**Canadian Centre for Architecture (Centre canadien d'Architecture)** – *1920 Rue Baile. Open Jun–Sept Tue–Sun 11am–6pm (Thu 9pm). Rest of the year Wed–Fri 11am–6pm (Thu 8pm) & weekends 11am–5pm. $5.* ♿ 🅿 ☎*514-939-7026.* Designed by Peter Rose and Phyllis Lambert, the CCA (1989) is both an acclaimed museum and research facility and an original example of Postmodern architecture. Forming the core of the horseshoe-shaped building is **Shaughnessy House**, a Second Empire mansion built in 1874.

The main building's interior is embellished with limestone, black granite, maple panelling and aluminum fittings. Seven galleries display temporary exhibits on architectural themes. Also open to the public are the Shaughnessy House reception rooms and the delightful **conservatory** and **tea room**, which have been restored to their 19C splendour.

Across Boulevard René-Lévesque is an **architectural garden** by Melvin Charney, featuring an array of sculptures illustrating architectural elements such as pediments and columns.

★★**Montreal Contemporary Art Museum (Musée d'art contemporarin de Montréal)** – *185 Rue Sainte-Catherine Ouest. Open year-round Tue–Sun 11am–6pm (Wed 9pm). $6.* ✗ ♿ 🅿*($6)* ☎*514-847-6212.* Housed in the most recent addition to the Place des Arts complex, this museum presents selections from the permanent collection of over 5,000 works of art, 60 percent of which is Quebec art. Emphasis is placed on post-1940 artists such as Paul-Émile Borduas, Alfred Pellan and Jean-Paul Riopelle. The rotating exhibits are supplemented by selections of contemporary art from all over the world.

Montreal Planetarium (Planétarium de Montréal) – *1000 Rue Saint-Jacques.* ● Bonaventure. Open late Jun–Labour Day daily 12:45pm–5pm & 7pm–8:30pm. Rest of the year Tue–Wed 9am–5pm, Thu–Fri 9am–5pm & 7:30pm–8:30pm, weekends 10:30am–5pm & 7:30pm–8:30pm. Call for show times. $6. ♿ 🅿 ☎*514-872-4530.* Superb multimedia shows *(50min)* are shown in the planetarium's 385-seat theatre. Temporary and permanent exhibits offer an introduction to the universe and showcase recent astronomical events.

★★MT. ROYAL AND SURROUNDINGS *1/2 day*

Known to Montrealers as "the Mountain," Mt. Royal has become one of the city's most popular leisure spots. Rising abruptly from the otherwise flat plain, the 233m/764ft mountain forms part of the Monteregian Hills, a series of eight peaks located between the St. Lawrence and the Appalachians. The peaks are actually igneous plugs of magma that solidified before reaching the surface. To the west of Mt. Royal lies the former anglophone enclave of **Westmount**, one of the city's choicest residential areas. Gracing the hill's eastern flank is the town of **Outremont**, home to Montreal's francophone bourgeoisie.

★★**Mt. Royal Park (Parc du Mont-Royal)** – *Drive up Voie Camillien-Houde or Chemin Remembrance to the parking areas or climb on foot (20min) from Rue Peel at Ave. des Pins.* ● *Mont-Royal. Open year-round daily 6am–midnight.* ✗ ♿ 🅿 ☎*514-844-4928.* Opened to the public in 1876, the city's premier urban park was designed by American landscape architect **Frederick Law Olmsted**, creator of New York City's Central Park. Along with various plants and animals, the park has a lake, two lookout points, a chalet/visitor centre, an illuminated cross and numerous winding paths. In summer the park is lively with joggers; in winter horse-drawn sleds plow the snowy paths.

Viewpoints – The terrace fronting the **Chalet Lookout** (**A**) (Belvédère du Chalet) *(7min walk from parking area)* affords a splendid **view**★★★ of the bustling downtown. Looming on the horizon, the Monteregian Hills dot the southern St. Lawrence shore. The walk around the summit leads to the **cross** (**B**), a 36.6m/120ft metal structure, illuminated at night, that commemorates a wooden cross placed here by Maisonneuve. From the popular **Camillien Houde Lookout** (Belvédère Camillien-Houde) *(accessible by vehicle on the Voie Camillien-Houde)*, the superb **view**★★ of eastern Montreal is dominated by the Olympic Stadium *(p 212)*.

★★**St. Joseph's Oratory (Oratoire Saint-Joseph)** – *Entrance on Chemin Queen Mary. ● Côte-des-Neiges. Open May–Sept daily 6:30am–9:30pm. Rest of the year daily 6:30am–9pm.* ✗ ♿ 🅿 ☎*514-733-8211*. Dominating the northern section of Montreal, this famed Roman Catholic shrine, set on the slope of Mt. Royal, is distinguished by its colossal dimensions and an octagonal, copper-clad dome.

A small chapel dedicated to the healing powers of St. Joseph was erected on this site in 1904 by Alfred Bessette, known as Brother André. Crowds of afflicted people came to pray with the friar. Leaving the chapel cured, they spread the lay brother's reputation as a healer. By the early 20C, a basilica was planned to receive the increasing number of visitors. Constructed under the supervision of the Benedictine monk and architect, **Dom Paul Bellot**, the monument was completed in 1967. Today over a million pilgrims visit the shrine annually.

In the immense, austere **interior**, note the carved bronze grilles executed by Roger Prévost, and the oak statues of the apostles and stone altar chiselled by Henri Charlier. From the wide terrace an excellent **view** of northern Montreal and the Laurentian Mountains can be obtained. Also contained within the edifice are a votive chapel, a 56-bell carillon and the **Brother André Museum** (Musée du Frère André), which displays a collection of photographs and mementos tracing the friar's life *(same hours as the oratory)*. The **original chapel** (chapelle du Frère André) and Brother André's room are open to the public. Completed in 1960 the **Stations of the Cross**★ are located in a pleasant hillside garden.

Boulevard Saint-Laurent – This bustling thoroughfare has traditionally divided the city into its predominantly francophone eastern section and the anglophone west. Today the boulevard attracts a diverse crowd to its shops, cafes, restaurants and "in" boutiques. Established in 1672 the artery long formed Montreal's principal passageway, hence its nickname "the Main." For centuries the Main has welcomed immigrants. During the 19C Chinese settled in the southern section, giving rise to a lively **Chinatown**★ (Quartier chinois) *(at Rue de la Gauchetière)*. Jewish merchants arrived in the 1880s and moved into the northern section. Greeks moved to the area during the early 20C. More recent arrivals include Slavs, Portuguese and Latin Americans.

Hospitallers Museum (Musée des Hospitalières de l'Hôtel-Dieu de Montréal) – *201 Ave. des Pins Ouest, entrance at Rue Saint-Urbain and Ave. du Parc. Open mid-Jun–mid-Oct Tue–Fri 10am–5pm, weekends 1pm–5pm. Rest of the year Wed–Sun 1pm–5pm. Closed Good Friday, Easter Monday & Dec 25–Jan 1. $5.* ♿ ☎*514-849-2919*. Housed in a former chaplain's residence (1925), this museum traces the history of the Hospitallers of St. Joseph (a religious order devoted to caring for the sick) and their presence in Montreal through documents, medical instruments and sacred art selected from the museum's permanent collection of over 7,000 artifacts. The viewing of temporary exhibits and a video *(15min, French only)* about the order's world role complete the visit.

★★★OLYMPIC PARK AREA *1 day*

This vast recreational area is situated in the eastern part of Montreal, which was known in the past as the city of **Maisonneuve**. Created by wealthy francophone businessmen, the prosperous community launched a program of development during the late 19C, erecting grandiose mansions such as the Château Dufresne along its wide boulevards. The exorbitant cost drove Maisonneuve into bankruptcy, and the city was annexed to Montreal in 1918. Today, dominated by the striking silhouette of the Olympic Park, the area is home to Montreal's Botanical Garden and the 204ha/504 acre **Maisonneuve Park**.

★★**Olympic Park** – ● *Viau, or by car (entrance to the parking lot from 3200 Rue Viau). Information desk and ticket office at base of tower. Free shuttle service among the park, the Botanical Garden and the Biodome.* Constructed to accommodate the 1976 Olympic Games, this gigantic sports complex has become the symbol of Montreal's East End. The park includes a stadium and tower, a sports centre with six swimming pools, and a velodrome, which now houses the Biodôme *(below)*, a living museum of natural sciences. The **Olympic Village**—two striking 19-storey towers designed to lodge 11,000 athletes during the Games—now contains a residential and commercial complex.

Begun in 1973, the project soon encountered a series of technical difficulties, delaying construction of the stadium's roof and tower until 1987. Tremendously expensive ($1.2 billion), the complex became the city's most controversial public project. However, it has made a valiant effort to remain lucrative and has welcomed over 40 million visitors since 1976.

Olympic Park

Stadium – *Visit by guided tour (30min) only, year-round daily 11am & 2pm. Closed early Jan–early Feb. $5.25. ✗ ♿ 🅿 ($10) ☎514-252-8687. The visit of the park installations does not include ascent to the top of the tower.* Conceived by French architect Roger Taillibert, this immense concrete structure consists of 34 cantilevered ribs crowned by a structural ring and dominated by the world's tallest inclined tower. The building was originally designed to be covered by a retractable roof that could be hoisted into a niche at the summit of the tower by means of 26 cables and 46 winches anchored at the tower's base. Made of Kevlar—an ultra-thin synthetic fiber with the strength of steel—the roof has nevertheless been subject to deterioration. *(Plans are under way to permanently cover the structure by immobilising the roof.)* With a seating capacity of 55,147, the stadium hosts sporting events, rock concerts, opera and conventions. Hovering at a 45° angle above the stadium, the 175m/574ft **tower** can be ascended by a funicular elevator *(open mid-Jun–Labour Day Mon noon–9pm, Tue–Thu 10am–9pm, Fri–Sun 10am–11pm; Mar–mid-Jun & early Sept–Oct Mon noon–6pm, Tue–Sun 10am–6pm; rest of the year hours vary; closed early Jan–early Feb. $7.25. ✗ ♿ 🅿 ☎514-252-8687).* From the observation deck, the **panorama**★★★ extends as far as 80km/50mi, weather permitting. Large skylights and windows afford breathtaking views of the stadium, downtown Montreal, the Laurentian Mountains and the Monteregian Hills. Located below the deck, an interactive interpretation centre presents exhibits on various aspects of the park.

★**Biodôme** – Kids *Open late Jun–Labour Day daily 9am–7pm. Rest of the year daily 9am–5pm. $9.50. ✗ ♿ 🅿 ☎514-868-3000. Shuttle service (free) between the Biodome and the Botanical Garden.* Opened in 1992, this innovative museum occupies a **building**★ that was constructed as an Olympic cycling venue—the velodrome; its appearance resembles a cyclist's helmet. Re-created habitats, complete with climatic regulators, support plants and animals indigenous to four ecosystems: a tropical forest, the Laurentian forest, the St. Lawrence Marine and the polar region.

★★**Montreal Botanical Garden** (**A**) – Kids *4101 Rue Sherbrooke Est.* ● *Pie-IX. Open May–Oct daily 9am–7pm. Rest of the year daily 9am–5pm. $9. ✗ ♿ 🅿 ($7) ☎514-872-1400. An overview of the garden can be obtained by taking the narrated train ride (30min). Shuttle service (free) between the Biodome and the Botanical Garden.* Founded in 1931 this 75ha/185 acre botanical garden ranks among the world's finest horticultural facilities. Over 21,000 international plant species are exhibited in 10 greenhouses and 30 outdoor gardens. *(Certain areas of the garden were badly damaged by ice storms in January 1998.)*

The **reception centre** (1995) leads to an introduction greenhouse for a preview of the plant kingdom. The **conservatories**★ (serres d'exposition) present a wide range of tropical and semitropical plants alongside begonia, cacti and succulent plants. The

Chinese Greenhouse, called the "Jardin céleste," displays the superb **Wu Collection** of *penjing*, or "landscape in a pot." Opened in 1991 the **Chinese Garden★** (Jardin de Chine) is a replica of a typical Ming Dynasty (14-17C) garden from southern China, with pavilions, a rock mountain and waterfall. The combination of mountains and water is thought to provoke contemplation. The 2.5ha/6.2 acre **Japanese Garden** (Jardin japonais), designed in the traditional Oriental style, creates a peaceful atmosphere. The **Japanese pavilion** houses exhibit spaces, a tea library, Zen garden, a tea garden and a collection of **bonsais** *(on view seasonally)*.

Other sections not to be missed include the **Rose Garden**, with over 10,000 specimens, the **Marsh and Bog Garden**, a re-created monastic garden, an Alpine garden, and an enclosure of toxic plants. Covering more than half of the total area, the **Arboretum** features over 10,000 tree specimens.

Near the Rose Garden, the **Montreal Insectarium★**, built in the shape of a giant bug, offers a wide selection of preserved and living insects from all over the world.

★**Château Dufresne** – *Entrance on Blvd. Pie IX. ● Pie IX. Currently closed to the public.* Completed in 1918, this sumptuous Beaux-Arts mansion, commissioned by Marius and Oscar Dufresne, evokes the lifestyle of Montreal's moneyed class in the 1920s and 30s.

A total of 44 period rooms present a variety of styles, blending Gothic, Renaissance, Elizabethan and Louis XV and XVI influences. Among the highlights are the beautiful mahogany panelling in the sitting room, the Moorish-style smoking room and the Hepplewhite furnishings in the dining room.

OTHER AREAS OF INTEREST *1/2 day*

★**St. Helen's Island** – *Access by car on Jacques-Cartier or Concorde Bridge; ● Île Sainte-Hélène.* Located east of Montreal, this small island, discovered by Samuel de Champlain in 1611, was named for his wife, Hélène Boulé. Transformed into a pleasant park, it has become a popular weekend spot.

Old Fort (Vieux-Fort) – *Open mid-May–Aug daily 10am–6pm. Rest of the year Mon & Wed–Sun 10am–5pm.* ✗ P ☎*514-861-6701.* After purchasing the island in 1818, the British government erected a citadel, now known as Old Fort, on this strategic point. The shaded woods and clearings are interspersed with fortress remnants.

Located in the Old Fort today is the **David M. Stewart Museum★**, which presents the history of European settlement in Quebec through displays on the early discoverers and first settlers, their explorations across the continent, the British Conquest, and the effects of the American Revolution, the War of 1812 and the Patriots' Rebellion. Be sure to see the model of the city of Montreal as it appeared in 1760. Note also the wonderful collection of maps and globes, ship models, kitchen ustensils, weapons, navigational instruments and archival documents.

The island became federal government property after Confederation, and in the early 20C, it was annexed by the city. In 1967, along with Notre Dame Island, St. Helen's hosted the 1967 World Fair (Expo '67). Constructed to house the US pavilion, the **Biosphère★** Kids, a geodesic dome designed by Buckminster Fuller, now contains Canada's first eco-watch centre *(open Jun 24–Labour Day daily 10am–6pm; rest of the year Tue–Sun 10am–5pm; closed Dec 25–26 & Jan 1; $6.50;* ✗ ♿ P ☎*514-283-5000).* Hands-on exhibits and a multimedia presentation *(10min)* highlight the importance of water and the fragility of our natural environment.

La Ronde Kids, Montreal's major amusement park, occupies a pleasant site on the north end of the island *(open mid-May–early Jun weekends 10am–9pm; mid-Jun–late Jun Mon–Fri 10am–9pm, weekends 10am–11pm; late Jun–early Sept Mon–Thu & Sun 11am–11pm, Fri–Sat 11am–midnight; $23;* ✗ ♿ P ☎*514-872-4537).*

The road skirting the island's western edge provides **views★** of Old Montreal, the port installations, and the **Cité du Havre** peninsula, which links the city to St. Helen's Island via the Concorde Bridge. **Habitat★** (Moshe Safdie), a futuristic, modular apartment complex built for Expo '67, dominates the peninsula.

★**Notre Dame Island (Île Notre-Dame)** – *Access by car on Concordia Bridge or by free bus service from St. Helen's Island metro station.* This artificial island, created in 1959 and enlarged in 1967, contains a Formula 1 race track, a pleasant lake and beach, and a superb **floral garden** designed for the International Floralies of 1980 *(open daily mid-May–late Oct; closed during the Grand Prix;* ✗ ♿ P ☎*514-872-4537).* The Expo '67 French pavilion, formerly known as the Palais de la Civilisation, houses the **Montreal Casino**.

★★**Cosmodôme** – *Located in Laval, 12km/7mi northwest of Montreal, at 2150 Autoroute des Laurentides (Chomedey). From Montreal, take Rte. 15 (Exit 9) and follow signs. Space Science Centre open late Jun–Aug daily 10am–6pm. Rest of the year Tue–Sun 10am–6pm. Closed Jan 1 & Dec 25. $8.75.* ✗ ♿ P

☎*514-978-3600.* The Cosmodôme opened in 1994 with a mission to "promote the study and practice of space science and technology." A replica of an Ariane rocket stands in front of the ultramodern complex. In the **Space Science Centre**, interactive exhibits, replicas and models, mural panels and videos introduce visitors to the history and exploration of space. Don't miss the space rock donated by the National Aeronautics and Space Administration. **Space Camp Canada** offers space-oriented educational activities for children and adults *(some programs necessitate overnight stays)*. Workshops, training programs and mission simulations initiate campers into the life and work of real astronauts.

Sault-au-Récollet – *Located 12km/7mi north of Montreal by Sherbrooke Est (Rte. 138), Cartier and Rachel Sts. and Ave. Papineau. Gouin Blvd. is a one-way street east.* Set on rapids beside the Prairies River, Sault-au-Récollet is best known for its **Church of the Visitation of the Blessed Virgin Mary★** (Église de la Visitation-de-la-Bienheureuse-Vierge-Marie), the oldest religious structure on the island. The large nave and absence of lateral chapels illustrate the style of Récollet churches, which were popular in New France during the French Regime. The edifice boasts an elaborate **interior★★** fashioned by Louis-Amable Quévillon and his followers. Of particular interest are the turquoise and gold vault, adorned with diamond-shaped barrels; the sculpted decor in the chancel; and the magnificent **pulpit★**, one of the most beautiful pieces of liturgical furniture in Quebec.

NUNAVIK★★

Map of Principal Sights p 4

Officially recognized in 1988, after creation in 1986 by referendum, as the homeland of Quebec's **Inuit** population, the province's northernmost region offers the adventurous visitor a unique travel experience. Nunavik's spectacular expanses of rugged and pristine land, encompassing some 505,000sq km/194,980sq mi, appeal to travellers eager to explore one of the world's few remaining frontiers.

Located on the **Ungava Peninsula**, this vast territory also encompasses numerous offshore islands and part of the James Bay region to the west. A multitude of lakes and waterways drain east into Ungava Bay, or west into Hudson Bay. The lack of vegetation is characteristic of regions with harsh climates. In fact, most of the peninsula is under permafrost, reaching 275m/902ft in depth in Nunavik's northernmost areas.

The region's first inhabitants were hunters from Asia who crossed the Bering Strait some 9,000 years ago. Travelling in small family groups, the Inuit ancestors caught marine mammals along the coast and ventured inland to hunt musk ox, caribou and waterfowl. The arrival of Europeans in the 17C dramatically transformed the traditional nomadic lifestyle and led to the creation of permanent settlements.

Today the majority of the Inuit population inhabits 14 coastal villages and has access to schooling and professional training. Living in modern, prefabricated housing equipped with modern amenities, the Inuit have nevertheless maintained their traditional values and heritage.

Deception River, Salluit Region

Practical Information

Getting There – The 14 villages lining Nunavik's eastern and western shores are accessible by airplane only. Contact Canadian Airlines and its affiliates (☎514-847-2211), First Air (☎613-738-0200), Air Inuit (☎613-738-0200) or Air Creebec (☎819-825-8355) for schedules & flight information.

Accommodations and Visitor Information – It is best to contact an official tourism agency for Nunavik for exact information about the availability of accommodations and about different packages offered by adventure outfitters. Organizations that visitors may find helpful: **Nunavik Tourism Association**, C.P. 218, Kuujjuaq, Québec J0M 1C0 ☎819-964-2876; **Tourisme Québec Far North** ☎418-643-6820.

VISIT

The largest among the 14 villages, **Kuujjuaq**★ is the seat of regional government offices. Located to the west, **Inukjuak**, serves as headquarters for the Avataq Cultural Institute, a nonprofit organization devoted to the preservation and development of the Inuit heritage in Nunavik. The northeasternmost villages of **Kangiqsujuaq** and **Salluit** are especially remarkable for their spectacular **sites**★★, surrounded by rugged mountains and jagged cliffs. Located on the western shore, **Povungnituk** has gained recognition as a centre for Inuit sculpture. The village's **museum**★ features a collection of Inuit tools, objects and crafts. Situated just north of James Bay, **Kuujjuarapik** is home to a sizeable number of Cree Indians and to most of Nunavik's nonnative population.

QUEBEC CITY★★★

Metro Population 504,605
Map of Principal Sights p 5
Tourist Office ☎418-651-2882

Built atop the Cape Diamant promontory jutting into the St. Lawrence River, Quebec's capital has delighted visitors for centuries. Throughout the years the city has retained its Old World charm, evident in the multitude of historic and religious monuments, fortifications and narrow cobblestone alleys. The distinctive French flavour is enhanced by fine restaurants, outdoor cafes and a lively nightlife. In 1985 the city became the first urban centre in North America to be inscribed on UNESCO's World Heritage List.

Historical Notes

Birthplace of New France – Long before Jacques Cartier's arrival in 1535, Indian hunters and fishermen inhabited the area of the village of Stadacona. Following a fruitless search for precious stones, Cartier soon abandoned the site, and interest in the area declined. Attempting to establish a fur-trading post, Samuel de Champlain set foot here in 1608 and constructed a rudimentary wooden fortress, known as the **Habitation**. The first settlers arrived in Quebec during the 17C. Primarily craftsmen and merchants attracted to the profitable fur trade, they erected houses in the Lower Town, which became the centre of commercial activity. Seeking protection offered by the fortifications, numerous religious institutions and colonial administration settled in the Upper Town.

18C and 19C – Quebec City's location atop the 98m/321ft high Cape Diamant promontory provided the colony with a naturally fortified area. Despite this strategic military location, the French city was repeatedly attacked—first by the Iroquois, then by the British. The escalating hostility between the small French colony and Britain culminated in the Battle of the Plains of Abraham *(p 221)*, which precipitated the British Conquest of 1759.
Following the Treaty of Paris in 1763, Quebec City became capital of the new British dominion, and quickly assumed a dominant position. Owing mainly to its busy port activities, the city maintained a competitive position with Montreal until the mid-19C. As the population shifted westward, Quebec City gradually lost its position as centre of production and trade in New France.

Quebec City Today – Since the turn of this century, most jobs have been related to public administration, defence and the service sector. The growth of the provincial government in the past 25 years has provided the capital city with renewed vitality. Throughout its turbulent history, the city has remained a bastion of French culture in North America. Although the anglophone community accounted for more than half the population in 1861, Quebec City claimed less than 2 percent British residents in 1996, a factor that contributes to the city's distinctly francophone character. The main metropolitan event is the famous winter **Carnival** in February, which attracts thousands of visitors.

★★★THE OLD CITY *Map p 218*

The oldest part of the city is divided into Upper Town, set atop the massive Cap Diamant, and Lower Town, nestled between the rocky cliff and the St. Lawrence It is best to visit the Old City on foot, in order to absorb the distinct character c the narrow, winding streets.

★★★Upper Town (Haute-Ville) *1/2 day*

The site of Samuel de Champlain's Fort Saint-Louis (1620), Upper Town was no developed until a group of wealthy merchants decided to increase settlement i the colony. Although a few houses appeared toward the end of the 17C, the are retained its administrative and religious vocation for over two centuries.
The handful of seigneurs and religious institutions who had established themselve on Cape Diamant, seeking protection from the military, refused to divide their lan plots. It was only during the 19C that elegant residential neighbourhoods evolve along the Rues Saint-Louis, Sainte-Ursule and d'Auteuil, and Avenues Sainte-Geneviève and Saint-Denis. Today Upper Town still functions as the city's administrativ centre.

★★★**Place d'Armes and Vicinity** – Bordered by prestigious buildings and restaurants this pleasant square, once used for military drills and parades, forms the heart o Old Quebec, attracting throngs of visitors. It is dominated by the city's most prominent landmark, the **Château Frontenac**★★. A massive structure erected in 1893 in th Chateau style, this renowned hotel stands on the site of the former governor's residence. Next to the chateau the Governors' Garden features the **Wolfe-Montcalm Monument** (**1**) (1827), a joint memorial to the two enemies who died in combat and whose meeting resulted in the creation of the Canadian nation.
Located behind the chateau, **Dufferin Terrace**★★★, a wide wooden boardwalk, is perched 671m/2,200ft above the majestic St. Lawrence, offering breathtaking **views**★★ of Lower Town and the river. A **monument** (**2**) to Samuel de Champlain, founder of New France, marks the northern end of the terrace. At the southern end, a flight of steps ascends to the **Governors' Walk**★★ (Promenade des Gouverneurs) *(closed in winter)*, a spectacular boardwalk, precariously suspended along the steep cliff that leads from the terrace to National Battlefields Park *(p 221)*.
In the narrow **Rue du Trésor**, a quaint pedestrian street off Place d'Armes, artists exhibit sketches and engravings of typical city scenes.

★**Fort Museum (Musée du Fort)** (**M**[1]) – Kids *10 Rue Sainte-Anne. Visit by guided tour (30min) only, Apr–Jun daily 10am–5pm. Jul–mid-Sept daily 10am–8pm. Late Sept–Oct daily 10am–5pm. Rest of the year hours vary. $6.25. ☎ 418-692-1759.* Housed in a castle-like structure, this museum features a sound and light presentation *(30min)* that traces the city's military and civil history.

★**Old Post Office (Ancien bureau de poste)** (**A**) – *3 Rue Buade. Open year-round Mon–Fri 8am–3:45pm. Closed national holidays.* ♿ *☎ 418-694-6103.* Erected in 1873, this large edifice presents an imposing facade adorned with Beaux-Arts embellishments. Inside, Parks Canada presents exhibits on the development of the country's historical and natural sites.

Château Frontenac and Lower Town

★**Basilica-Cathedral of Our Lady of Quebec (Basilique-cathédrale Notre-Dame-de Québec) (B)** – *Open May–mid-Oct daily 7:30am–2:30pm. Rest of the year daily 7:30am–4:30pm. ♿ P ($10) ☎418-694-0665.* Originally consecrated in 1674, the cathedral was destroyed during the fighting between French and British forces in 1759. The church was reconstructed between 1768 and 1771 by Quebec's most prominent architects, the Baillairgé family. Jean Baillairgé rebuilt the south belfry with its two openwork drums surmounted by domes. François Baillairgé was responsible for the interior and designed the plans for the magnificent baldachin. His son, Thomas, designed the monumental Neoclassical facade in 1843. Although the structure was destroyed by fire in 1922, it was rebuilt to reflect its original appearance. Of note in the interior are the stained-glass windows, the baldachin and the Casavant organ.

The majestic **Quebec City Hall** (Hôtel de ville de Québec) dominates the Place de l'hôtel de ville across from the basilica. In the square stands a **monument** (**3**) to Elzéar Alexandre Taschereau, the first Canadian cardinal.

Located north of the basilica, Quebec City's **Latin Quarter**★ is the oldest residential district in Upper Town. Narrow, crisscrossing streets add to the charm of the quarter, today inhabited mainly by students.

★★**Quebec Seminary (Séminaire de Québec)** – *2 Côte de la Fabrique. Guided tours available in summer. $3 (includes admission to the Museum of French America); ♿ P ($11/day) ☎418-692-2843.* Founded in 1663 by Msgr. François de Laval to train priests for the colony, this institute of higher learning is the oldest in Canada. In 1852 the seminary was granted a university, Université Laval, which grew within the seminary walls until the Sainte-Foy campus opened in 1950.

The seminary comprises three sections arranged around an inner court. Note the sundial on the facade of the **Procure Wing**, completed in 1681. The highlights of the guided tour include the **Msgr. Olivier Briand Chapel**★, noteworthy for the fine wood panelling adorning its walls, and the **Congregational Chapel**, featuring a statue of the Virgin Mary crafted by Thomas Baillairgé.

Operated since 1995 as part of the Museum of Civilization *(p 219)*, the **Museum of French America**★ (Musée de l'Amérique Française) (**M²**) presents France's historic, cultural and social heritage in North America *(9 Rue de l'Université; open Jun 24–Labour Day daily 10am–5:30pm; rest of the year Tue–Sun 10am–5pm; closed Dec 25; $3; ♿ P ☎418-692-2843).* The vast collections include some 195,000 rare books and journals. On display in the **François Ranvoyzé Pavilion**★ (occupying the former outer chapel) is one of the most important collections of **relics**★ outside St. Peter's in Rome.

★**Augustine Monastery (Monastère de l'Hôtel-Dieu de Québec)** – *32 Rue Charlevoix.* Founded by Augustinian Nuns in the 1640s, this monastery is best known for its hospital, the Hôtel-Dieu, which still operates today. The **church**★ *(same hours as museum, below)*, designed by Pierre Émond in 1800, features a Neoclassical facade adorned with a sculpted Ionic portal. Highlights of the interior, crafted by Thomas Baillairgé, include the high-altar **tabernacle**, the retable and the basket-handle wooden vault.

Opened in 1958, the **Augustine Museum**★ (**M³**) presents a collection of objects and artworks tracing the Augustinian Nuns' history and heritage *(open year-round Tue–Sat 9:30am noon & 1:30pm–5pm, Sun 1:30pm–5pm; closed national holidays; ♿ ☎418-692-2492).* The museum includes one of the foremost collections of **paintings**★ dating back to the time of New France.

Rue Saint-Louis – This charming, bustling street is home to a variety of restaurants and boutiques. It also features some of the city's oldest architectural gems. The **Maillou House**★ (**C**) (Maison Maillou) (1736), located next the Château Frontenac, now houses the Quebec City Chamber of Commerce. The offices of the Consulate General of France occupy the adjacent house, the **Kent House** (**D**) (Maison Kent), dating from the 1830s. Standing at the corner of Rue Desjardins, the **Jacquet House**★ (**E**) (Maison Jacquet) was built in 1674. Reputedly the oldest house in Quebec City, it is occupied today by a restaurant specializing in traditional Quebec cuisine.

★★**Ursuline Monastery (Monastère des Ursulines)** – *Rue Donnacona.* Founded in 1639 by Madame de la Peltrie and Marie Guyart (Mère Marie-de-l'Incarnation), the monastery is the oldest educational institution for young women in North America and is still in operation today. The **chapel** (1902) is particularly remarkable for its **interior decoration**★★ *(open May–Oct Tue–Sat 10am–11:30am & 1:30pm–4:30pm, Sun 1:30pm–4:30pm; ☎418-694-0413).* Most of the ornaments were crafted between 1726 and 1736 under the supervision of Pierre-Noël Levasseur. Of particular interest are the wood sculptures of St. Augustine, St. Ursula and St. Joseph, the nuns' choir surmounted by a wooden vault, and the collection of paintings.

The **Ursuline Museum**★★ (**M⁴**) (Musée des Ursulines) occupies the former site of the house belonging to Madame de la Peltrie, the order's benefactress, in the 17C *(12 Rue Donnacona; open May–Aug Tue–Sat 10am–noon & 1pm–5pm, Sun 12:30pm–5pm; rest of the year Tue–Sun 1pm–4:30pm; $3; ☎418-694-0694).*

Reflecting the occupations of the Ursuline Nuns, the collection features documents furnishings, paintings, sculptures and numerous **embroideries★** of rare beauty. The museum also contains altar frontals and ecclesiastic vestments of the 17C and 18C

★**Price Building** – *65 Rue Sainte-Anne.* This 16-storey Art Deco edifice, Quebec City's first skyscraper, was built in 1930 to accommodate the head office of Price Brothers, famed for introducing the pulp and paper industry to the Saguenay region. Its copper roof blends well with the surrounding buildings.

★**Holy Trinity Anglican Cathedral (Cathédrale anglicane de la Sainte-Trinité) (F)** – *31 Rue des Jardins.* Modelled after London's Church of St. Martin in the Fields, this edifice (1804) was the first Anglican cathedral built outside the British Isles. King George III provided the funding and sent English oak from the royal forests of Windsor for the pews. In summer, the courtyard is a gathering place for artists.

★★★Lower Town (Basse-Ville) *1/2 day*

From Dufferin Terrace, take the steep Frontenac stairway to Lower Town. Follow Côte de la Montagne down the hill to the Casse-Cou stairway on the right descending to Rue du Petit-Champlain. A funicular (cable car) also connects Dufferin Terrace to the Lower Town (in service Jun–mid-Oct daily 8am–midnight; rest of the year daily 7:30am–11:30pm; $1.25; ☎418-692-1132).

This narrow stretch of land dominated by Upper Town was the site of Champlain's "Habitation" *(p 215)*. The first settlers arrived here in the late 17C and established shops and residences around the fort and the market square, now known as Place Royale. As commerce, shipbuilding and port activities increased, residents filled in parts of the shores, constructed numerous wharves and created new streets. By the

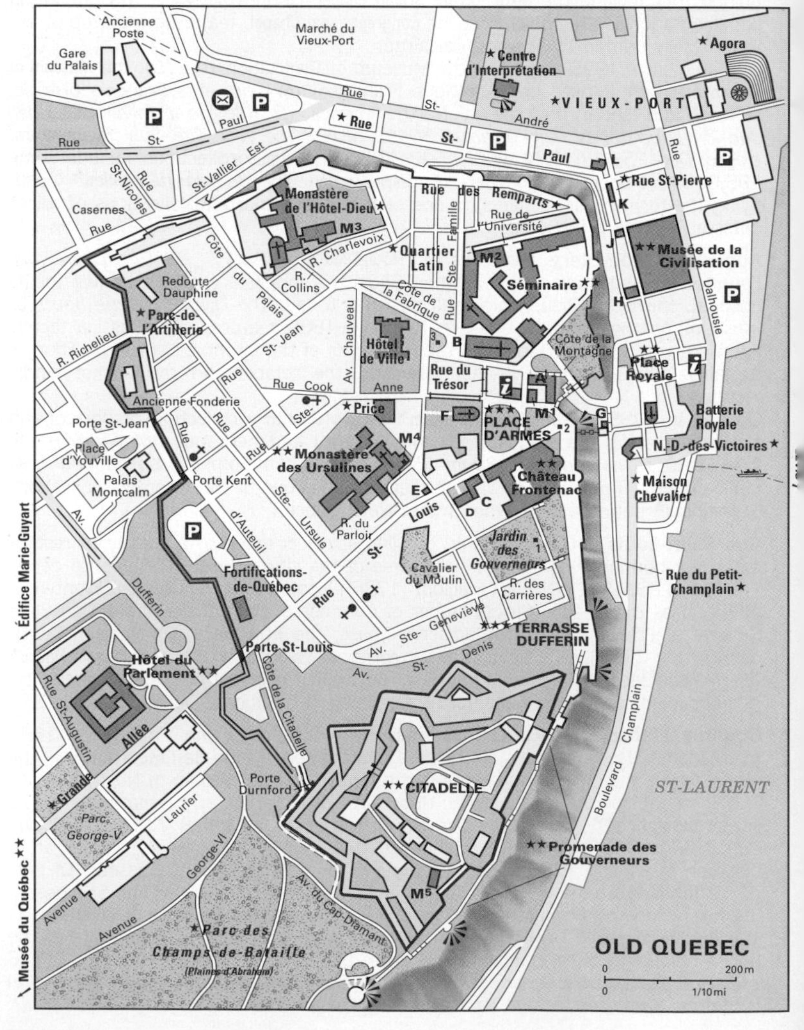

19C the area of Lower Town, the city's commercial centre, had doubled in size. As port activities declined in the 1860s, the neighbourhood lost its appeal and fell into decay. In 1970 the Quebec government began restoring the area.

Today restaurants, cafes and boutiques abound in the historic quarter of Place Royale. Lined with boutiques and art galleries, the pedestrian **Rue du Petit-Champlain**★ reflects the quarter's 18C appearance. Facing the Place de Paris, a **visitor centre** offers guided tours of the area *(215 Rue du Marché-Finlay; open early May–late Sept daily 10am–6pm; rest of the year by appointment; ☎418-643-6631).*

★**Chevalier House (Maison Chevalier)** – *Corner of Rue du Marché-Champlain and Blvd. Champlain. Open Jun 24–Labour Day daily 10am–6pm. Early May–Jun 23 & mid-Sept–late Oct Tue–Sun 10am–6pm. Rest of the year weekends 10am–5pm.* ✗ P *($10) ☎418-643-2158.* This imposing stone structure, topped by a red roof and high chimneys, is composed of three separate buildings. The west wing was built in 1752 for a wealthy merchant, Jean-Baptiste Chevalier. Restored in 1956, the house now serves as part of the Museum of Civilization *(below)* and features exhibits on traditional Quebec architecture and furniture.

Royal Battery (Batterie Royale) – *At the end of Rue Sous-le-Fort and Rue Saint-Pierre. Open daily year-round.* ♿ *☎418-643-6631.* Constructed in 1691 this thick, four-sided earthen rampart formed part of the fortifications of the city. It was destroyed during French-British fighting in 1759 and gradually buried. Archaeologists excavating the area unearthed it in 1972. It has been reconstructed and replicas of 18C cannon are positioned in the 11 embrasures.

★**Economuseum of Glass (Économusée du Verre) (G)** – *58 Rue Sous-le-Fort at Rue du Petit-Champlain. Visit by guided tour only, Nov–mid-Jun; $3; reservations required. Studio open Jun–Oct Wed–Sun 10am–4:30pm; rest of the year Mon–Fri 10am–4:30pm. Closed national holidays. ☎418-694-0445.* Examples of richly coloured glass are on view in the studio. Here glass blowers can be seen at work and visitors can ask them questions about the process. On the second floor, galleries display glassware from different countries and panels recount the history of glassmaking.

★★**Place Royale** – Today the heart of Lower Town, this charming cobblestone square was the hub of the city's economic activity until the mid-19C, when the port, and subsequently the area, fell into decline. Bordered by typical 18C stone houses, topped by steep roofs and chimneys, the square features a bronze bust of King Louis XIV as its centrepiece.

★**Church of Our Lady of the Victories** (Église Notre-Dame-des-Victoires) – *Place Royale. Open May–mid-Oct Mon–Sat 9am–5:30pm, Sun 1pm–5:30pm. Rest of the year Mon–Sat 9am–4pm, Sun 1pm–4pm. ☎418-692-1650.* Completed in 1723, this stone edifice topped by a single spire stands on the site of Champlain's "Habitation" *(p 215)*. It was named in thanksgiving for two successful occasions when Quebec City resisted the sieges of the British. Inside, the magnificent **retable** represents the fortified city.

★★**Museum of Civilization (Musée de la Civilisation)** – *85 Rue Dalhousie. Open Jun 24–Aug daily 10am–7pm. Rest of the year Tue–Sun 10am–5pm. $7.* ✗ ♿ P *☎418-643-2158.* Designed by Moshe Safdie, this acclaimed museum is housed in two stark, angular buildings crowned by copper roofs and a glass campanile. A monumental staircase links the buildings and leads to a terrace overlooking an inner court and the **Estèbe House** (Maison Estèbe), a 1752 stone structure, which was integrated into the museum. Inside the spacious entrance hall, note *La Débâcle* (Astri Reusch), a massive sculpture representing ice breaking up in spring.

The museum presents permanent and temporary thematic exhibits focusing on such topics as thought, language, natural resources, the human body and society. Among the permanent exhibits, **Objects of Civilization** highlights Quebec furnishings, tools and costumes. Covering over four centuries of Quebec history and culture, the **Memories** exhibit takes visitors on a thought-provoking journey through the past. Displayed artifacts illustrate a people's struggle to create a new life in a new land. The **Barque** is one of several 18C flat-bottomed boats uncovered during archaeological excavations on Place Royale.

★**Rue Saint-Pierre** – During the 19C this busy thoroughfare emerged as the city's principal financial district. Among the noteworthy commercial buildings still lining the street are the **National Bank (H)** *(no. 71)*; the former **Molson Bank (J)** *(no. 105)*, now occupied by the Post Office; and the **Imperial Bank of Canada (K)** *(nos. 113-115)*. Dominating the corner of Rues Saint-Paul and Saint-Pierre, the **Canadian Bank of Commerce (L)** exemplifies the Beaux-Arts style.

The charming **Rue Saint-Paul**★ is renowned for its antique shops and art galleries.

★**Old Port (Vieux-Port)** – Located on the Louise Basin, the port played a major role in the development of Canada until the late 19C, when it fell into disrepair. Created by the federal government in the 1980s, the **Agora**★ complex includes an amphitheatre, a wide boardwalk on the river and a marina. The Old Port of Quebec

interpretation centre★ is devoted to the port city's prominence during the 19C *(10 Rue Saint-André; open early May–Aug daily 10am–5pm; Sept–late Oct dai noon–4pm; rest of the year by appointment; $2.75; ♿ P ☎418-648-3300)*. Exh bits on logging and shipbuilding and films on the port confirm the importance c these industries to Quebec's economy. The glassed-in terrace on the top floc serves as a fine **viewpoint** for Lower Town and the modern port.

★★FORTIFICATIONS *1/2 day. Map p 218.*

Much of the charm of Quebec City stems from the fact that it is the only walled in city in Canada. Although fortification projects were undertaken during the Frenc Regime, most of the existing walls, batteries and the citadel were erected by th British after the Conquest, and never used. **Lord Dufferin**, governor general of Canad between 1872 and 1878, initiated a beautification project that included refurbish ing the fortified enceinte, rebuilding the gates to the city and clearing the ramparts

★★**Citadel** – *Entrance at end of Côte de la Citadelle. Visit by guided tour (1hr) only Apr–mid-May daily 10am–4pm. Late May–mid-Jun 9am–5pm. Late Jun–Labou Day 9am–6pm. Rest of Sept 9am–4pm. Oct 10am–3pm. $5. ♿ P ☎418-694 2815. Some areas of the citadel are off-limits, as it is still a military base for th Royal 22e Régiment.* Erected between 1820 and 1832, this massive fortress enclosing 16ha/40 acres, is typical of star-shaped fortifications. Advanced works or outworks, were devised to protect entrances and ramparts from enemy fire while sloping earthworks forced the enemy to be exposed to cannon fire from the garrison. The enceinte was composed of bastions, linked together by curtain (straight walls) that protected the ditches. The guided tour leads past the renovatec powder magazine, the old prison, and the governor general's residence to the Princ of Wales bastion. Occupying the old powder magazine, the **Museum of the Roya 22e Régiment** (**M**[5]) contains a collection of military objects dating from the 17C tc the present.

Quebec Fortifications National Historic Site (Lieu historique national des Fortifications-de-Québec) – *100 Rue Saint-Louis. Open mid-Apr–mid-May Wed–Sun 10am–5pm Late May–early Nov daily 10am–5pm. $2.50. ♿ ☎418-648-7016.* The **interpretation centre** presents the history of Quebec via the evolution of its defence systems Near the centre *(to the right of the St. Louis Gate)*, lies the **powder magazine** (poudrière), built in 1810 on the Esplanade, a vast field used for military exercises between 1779 and 1783.
Visitors can stroll south along the ramparts over the **St. Louis Gate** (Porte Saint-Louis), and the Kent and St. John (Saint-Jean) Gates to Artillery Park. The fortifications afford panoramas of the city and surrounding areas.

★**Artillery Park National Historic Site (Lieu historique national du Parc-de-l'Artillerie)** – *The main entrance at 2 Rue d'Auteuil is located near St. John gate. Visitor centre open Apr–Oct daily 10am–5pm; rest of the year noon–4pm; closed mid-Dec–mid-Jan; $3; ♿ ☎418-648-4205.* This huge site that includes barracks, a redoubt and an old foundry commemorates three centuries of military, social and industrial life in Quebec City. Designed by Chaussegros de Léry in 1750, the barracks, housed in a structure 160m/525ft in length, contained armouries, stock rooms, a guard room and six prison cells. The redoubt (1748) is remarkable for its massive stone buttresses added to the original building after 1763. Inside, exhibits feature costumes, paintings and artifacts that offer insight into a soldier's life in the 18C and 19C. Housed in the **old foundry**, the visitor center contains a **scale model**★★ of Quebec City, produced between 1806 and 1808 by British engineers, that presents a stunning picture of the city as it appeared at the beginning of the 19C.

★**Rue des Remparts** – Until approximately 1875, this street was a mere path that ran alongside the ramparts, connecting the various bastions and batteries. Today a pleasant stroll down the street allows visitors to recapture the atmosphere of the old fortified city.

OUTSIDE THE WALLS *1/2 day*

★**Grande Allée** – Departing from the St. Louis Gate and extending southward of Old Quebec, this wide avenue is to the city what the Champs-Élysées is to Paris. Lined with innumerable restaurants, bars, outdoor cafes, boutiques and offices, the bustling thoroughfare provides an elegant setting for the city's nightlife.

★★**Parliament Building (Hôtel du Parlement)** – *Visit by guided tour (30min) only, Jun 24–Labour Day Mon–Fri 9am–4:30pm, weekends 10am–4:30pm. Rest of the year Mon–Fri 9am–4:30pm. ✂ ♿ P ☎418-643-7239.* Overlooking the old city, this majestic edifice is the finest example of Second Empire architecture in Quebec City. Note the imposing **facade**, which presents a historic tableau wherein bronze figures commemorate the great names of Quebec history.

Inside, a grand staircase leads to the parliamentary chambers, which are accessed through finely chiselled doors. The Chamber of the National Assembly is used by Quebec's National Assembly, while the Chamber of the Legislative Assembly accommodates meetings of parliamentary committees and official receptions.

★ **National Battlefields Park (Parc des Champs-de-Bataille)** – *Map p 218. Open year-round daily 6am–1am.* ✗ ♿ 🅿 *($3/hr)* ☎ *418-648-4071.* Stretching 107ha/250 acres along a cliff overlooking the St. Lawrence, this park memorializes battles fought between the British and the French. A large section of the park occupies the former **Plains of Abraham**, where the French and British armies fought a major battle (1759) that eventually sealed the fate of the French colony. Both commanding generals, Wolfe and Montcalm, were mortally wounded during the short but decisive event. Located in the Quebec Museum *(below)*, the **interpretation centre** for the park presents the history of the Plains of Abraham *(open May–Labour Day daily 10am–5:30pm; rest of the year Tue–Sun 11am–5:30pm; $2;* ✗ ♿ 🅿 *($1/hr)* ☎ *418-648-5641).*

★★ **Quebec Museum** (Musée du Québec) – *In National Battlefields Park. Entrance located between the two main buildings, on ground level. Open Jun–Aug daily 10am–6pm (Wed 10pm). Rest of the year Tue–Sun 11am–6pm (Wed 9pm). Closed Jan 1 & Dec 25–26. $5.75.* ✗ ♿ 🅿 *($2.50/hr)* ☎ *418-643-2150.* This remarkable three-building complex provides an overview of Quebec art from the 18C to the present. Temporary and permanent exhibits drawn from a collection of over 22,000 works of art are organized throughout the modern Main Hall, the Beaux-Arts Gérard Morisset Pavilion and the Renaissance Revival Baillairgé Pavilion. Highlights include canvases by Charles Alexander Smith and Antoine Plamondon, sculptures by Alfred Laliberté and François Ranvoyzé's silver work.

Marie Guyart Building (Édifice Marie-Guyart) – *1037 Rue de la Chevrotière. Open year-round Mon–Fri 10am–4pm, weekends 1pm–5pm. Closed mid-Dec–mid-Jan.* ♿ ☎ *418-644-9841.* The Anima G observatory occupying the 31st floor of this administrative building provides a splendid **view★★** of Old Quebec, the citadel and fortifications as well as the surrounding areas.

★ **Cartier-Brébeuf National Historic Site** – *75 Rue de l'Espinay, 3km/2mi from St. John Gate by Côte d'Abraham, Rue de la Couronne, Drouin Bridge and 1re Ave. Open Apr–early May by appointment. Mid-May–mid-Sept daily 10am–5pm. Late Sept–mid-Oct daily 1pm–5pm. Rest of the year by appointment. $2.75.* ♿ 🅿 ☎ *418-648-4038.* This park commemorates Jacques Cartier, who wintered on this spot in 1535-36, and Jean de Brébeuf, a Jesuit missionary. The **interpretation centre** features insightful displays that recall Cartier's second voyage to New France and his meetings with the Iroquois, as well as the Jesuit's first mission, established in 1626.
The highlight of the visit is a replica of **La Grande Hermine★**, the largest of Cartier's three vessels. Measuring less than 24m/80ft in length, the two-masted ship carried up to 60 men across the Atlantic.

EXCURSIONS

★★ **Beaupré Coast (Côte de Beaupré)** – *Map p 192.* Bordering the St. Lawrence, this narrow stretch of land extends from Quebec City to Cape Tourmente. Its name is attributed to an exclamation made by Cartier, who, noting the lush green meadowland, said *ÒQuel beau pré!"* ("What a fine meadow!"). A pleasant drive along Route 360 leads through a string of charming communities dating from the French Regime.

★★ **Montmorency Falls Park** (Parc de la Chute-Montmorency) – *10km/6mi east of Quebec City. Open year-round daily 8:30am–11pm.* ♿ 🅿 *($7)* ☎ *418-663-2877.* Before emptying into the St. Lawrence, the Montmorency River cascades over a cliff in spectacular falls 83m/272ft high (30m/98ft higher than Niagara Falls). In winter, the spray creates a great cone of ice that sometimes exceeds 30m/98ft in height. Elegant **Montmorency Manor** (1780) houses a restaurant and a **visitor centre**, which presents the area's heritage *(open May–Oct daily 9am-11pm; rest of the year Thu–Sat 9am–11pm, Sun–Wed 9am–4pm;* ✗ ♿ 🅿 ☎ *418-663-3330).* From the **upper lookout**, visitors can fully appreciate the height and force of the falls. The **lower lookout** affords the opportunity to approach the base of the falls *(rain gear is advised).* An **aerial tram** returns visitors to the upper level *(late Apr–mid-Jun daily 8:30am–7pm; late Jun–early Aug daily 8:30am–11pm; mid-Aug–early Sept daily 8:30am–9pm; mid-Sept–late Oct 8:30am–7pm; rest of the year hours vary; round-trip $7).*

★★ **Sainte-Anne-de-Beaupré Shrine** – *In Sainte-Anne-de-Beaupré, 35km/22mi east of Quebec City. Basilica open mid-Jun–mid-Sept daily 6:30am–9:30pm. Rest of the year daily 6:45am–5pm.* ♿ 🅿 ☎ *418-827-3781.* Named for the patron saint of Quebec, this Roman Catholic shrine is visited by over a million and a half people yearly. An imposing, medieval-style basilica, consecrated in 1934, dominates the site. Divided into five naves separated by huge columns, the interior is lit by 200 **stained-glass windows**. Note also the glimmering **mosaics** adorning the barrel vault

above the main nave. On the shrine's grounds are the memorial chapel and th
Chapel of the Scala Sancta (Chapelle du Saint Escalier). Life-size representatior
of the Stations of the Cross (Chemin de la Croix) dot the hillside.

★★**St. Joachim Church** (Église Saint-Joachim) – *In Saint-Joachim, 40km/25mi northea. of Quebec City. Open mid-May–mid-Oct Mon–Fri 10am–4pm, Sat 10am–5pm, Su 9am–4pm. ☎ 418-827-4020.* The small church (1779) is best known for its magn ficent **interior**★★, fashioned between 1815 and 1825 by François and Thoma Baillairgé. Of particular interest are the panelling, enhanced by gilded bas-relief and the main altar, surrounded by majestic columns and freestanding sculpture of the Evangelists.

★★**Île d'Orléans** – *10km/6mi northeast of Quebec City. Map p 193.* This almonc shaped island wedged in the St. Lawrence was named Isle of Bacchus by Jacque Cartier in 1535, and renamed in 1536 to honour the son of King François I, th Duke of Orléans.

Route 368 runs along the 67km/41mi circumference, passing through six com munities, each with its distinct flavour. Driving along the road, the visitor wi discover splendid scenery and magnificent **views**★★ of the St. Lawrence shore line.

The village of **Saint-Laurent**★, traditionally the island's maritime centre, still claim the island's only marina. In **Saint-Jean**★, the **Mauvide-Genest Manor**★, built in 1734 is considered the finest example of rural architecture under the French Regim *(visit by 30 min guided tour only, mid-Jun–early Sept daily 10am–5pm ever half-hour; mid-Sept–mid-Oct Tue–Sun 11am–5pm; $4; ✗ ♿ 🅿 ☎ 418-829 2630).* The manor now houses a restaurant and a museum featuring traditiona Quebec furniture. The community of Sainte-Famille is best known for its tris teepled **church**★★ (1748), dating from the French Regime. In the Neoclassica interior, note the sculpted vault by Louis-David Bazile, student of Quévillon, an the tabernacle crafted by the Levasseur family. This elaborate edifice contrast with the **old church**★ in Saint-Pierre, remodelled in the 1830s by Thoma Baillairgé.

RICHELIEU VALLEY★★

Map p 197

Some 130km/81mi long, the majestic Richelieu River flows north from its sourc in Lake Champlain (New York) to join the St. Lawrence at Sorel. Samuel de Champ lain discovered the waterway in 1609, named later for **Cardinal Richelieu**, chief ministe of Louis XIII. The river served as an invasion route and was heavily fortified durin the French Regime. The forts at Chambly, Saint-Jean-sur-Richelieu, Lennox anc Lacolle were built initially to protect Montreal against attacks by Iroquois, and late by British and American troops. The valley also played an important role in the Rebellions of 1837, which resulted in several uprisings in Saint-Denis, Saint-Charles and Saint-Eustache. To facilitate transportation between the US and Quebec, an extensive canal system was built along the Richelieu in the mid-19C. The regior remains one of the richest agricultural areas in the province. A popular weekenc retreat for Montrealers, the valley attracts thousands of travellers and tourists every summer.

SIGHTS

★**Chambly** – *30km/19mi from Montreal by Rte. 10.* A residential suburb of Montreal, this community enjoys a beautiful site on the Richelieu. A pleasant walk along the river leads past the canal and Fort Chambly to **Rue Richelieu**★, lined with sumptuous 19C residences.

★★**Fort Chambly National Historic Site** (Lieu historique national du Fort-Chambly) – *Open Jun–Labour Day daily 10am–6pm. Mid-Sept–Oct Mon 1pm–5pm, Tue–Sun 10am–5pm. $3.50. ♿ 🅿 ☎ 514-658-1585.* Located in a magnificent park on the Chambly Basin, this fort is the only remaining fortified complex in Quebec dating back to the French Regime. Erected between 1709 and 1711, the stone structure replaced an earlier wooden edifice constructed in 1665 by Jacques de Chambly. The fort is laid out in a square with bastions at each corner. An **interpretation centre** features displays and dioramas on the history of the fort and a description of the restoration project. Located near the fort, the **Guard House** (Corps de Garde) (1814) exemplifies the Palladian style adopted by the military throughout the British colonies. Inside, displays illustrate the period of British occupation of the city (1760-1851). Built in 1820, the small fieldstone **St. Stephen's Church** served as the garrison's place of worship.

★★Mt. Saint-Hilaire Nature Centre (Centre de la nature du mont Saint-Hilaire) – *23km/14mi north of Chambly. Open year-round daily 8am–1hr before dusk. $4.* ✗ ♿ 🅿 *☎514-467-1755.* Rising abruptly above the valley, Mt. Saint-Hilaire (411m/1,348ft) is the most imposing of the Monteregian Hills. Several trails criss-cross the lush forests covering the mountain, and lead to the summit, which affords sweeping **views★★** of the Richelieu Valley.

★Saint-Denis-sur-Richelieu – *33km/20mi north of nature centre.* This agricultural community was the site of a Patriot victory in 1837. At the **Patriots' National House★** displays and an audio-visual presentation *(23min)* explain *(in French only)* the background of the uprising and highlight the events leading to the Patriots' fight for freedom and democracy. *Open Jun–Aug Tue–Sun 11am–6pm. May, Sept & Nov Tue–Sun 10am–5pm. Rest of the year by appointment. $4.* ♿ 🅿 *☎514-787-3623.*

Saint-Jean-sur-Richelieu – *40km/25mi southeast of Montreal by Rtes. 10 and 35.* Known today for its Hot Air Balloon Festival and renowned as a manu-facturing centre for pottery and ceramics, this industrial city once formed part of the chain of fortifications erected by the French along the Richelieu. The **Fort Saint-Jean Museum** contains a collection of weapons, uniforms and other military artifacts *(open late May–mid-Aug Tue–Sun 9:30am–4:30pm; $2;* ♿ 🅿 *☎514-358-6500 ext. 5769 or 514-358-6809 off-season).*

Île aux Noix – *48km/30mi south of Montreal by Rtes. 10 and 35 south, and Rte. 223.* This 85ha/210 acre island was fortified by the French in 1759 and captured by the British the following year. Having at various times served as a shipbuilding centre, a holiday resort and an internment centre, the island is now preserved as a national historic site.

★Fort Lennox National Historic Site (Lieu historique national du Fort-Lennox) – *Open mid-May–Jun 23 Mon–Fri 10am–5pm. Jun 24–Labour Day daily 10am–6pm. Mid-Sept–mid-Oct weekends 10am–6pm. $5 (ferry & visit of fort).* ✗ ♿ *☎514-291-5700.* Erected in the 1820s, this bastion-type fortress occupies a pleasant **site★** overlooking the Richelieu River. A wide moat surrounds the fort, which forms a five-pointed star with corners protected by bastions. The Neoclassical stone buildings have been restored to re-create life on a British army base in the mid-19C.

★★Safari Park – Kids *63km/39mi south of Montreal by Rtes. 15 and 202. Open mid-May–mid-Jun Mon–Fri 10am–4pm, weekends 10am–5pm. Late Jun–mid-Sept daily 10am–5pm. $21.* ✗ ♿ 🅿 *☎514-247-2727.* Situated in an apple-growing region west of the Richelieu, this zoological park is renowned for its animals from all over the world that roam freely in large enclosures. Required to remain in their vehicles, visitors can follow the **Car Safari** *(4km/2.5mi)* along which they can take photographs, touch and feed the animals *(food can be purchased).* Highlights include the **Enchanted Forest**, a jungle walk, a theatre and a circus.

SAGUENAY FJORD REGION★★★

Map pp 192-193

Located at the southern tip of the Saguenay region, the immense, saucer-shaped Lake Saint-Jean empties into the Saguenay River. Measuring 155km/96mi in length, this river flows into the southernmost fjord in the world, the majestic Saguenay Fjord, which discharges its waters into the St. Lawrence.

Historical Notes – Fed by a number of rivers, including the Péribonka, Mistassini and Ashuapmushuan, Lake Saint-Jean is a small remnant of an original lake created over 10,000 years ago by the meltwaters of retreating glaciers. First called Piékouagami ("flat lake") by the Montagnais, Lake Saint-Jean was renamed for **Jean Dequen**, the first Frenchman to visit its shores in 1647. The area remained unsettled until the mid-19C when the first sawmills were built and the rivers were harnessed for electricity. Hydro-electric power plants, pulp mills and aluminum smelters still line the shores of the lake and the Upper Saguenay. *In July 1996, severe floods swept parts of the Saguenay-Lake Saint-Jean region. Several sights were destroyed; others may still be closed temporarily.*

Natural Attractions – Beyond Saint-Fulgence, the deep river channel was gouged in Precambrian rock by glaciers during the last Ice Age. Lined by rocky cliffs plunging into the water, the channel is 1,500m/4,920ft wide in places, having an average depth of 240m/787ft. The stark and untamed beauty of the river's southern section has attracted visitors for many years. Most choose to take a scenic river cruise *(below)*, but the fjord can also be enjoyed by exploring the villages nestled along its shores.

Spectacular, natural **Saguenay Park★★** has been created to preserve part of the shoreline *(open daily year-round; $7.75/car;* ⛺ ✗ ♿ 🅿 *☎418-272-2267 in season or 418-544-7388 off-season; cross-country skiing, ice fishing).* The region is famous for the landlocked salmon known as **ouananiche**, a favourite catch for sports fishermen; the wild **blueberries**, or *bleuets*, found on the north shore of the lake; and the famous nine-day **International Swim Marathon** held in July.

★★★SAGUENAY FJORD

★★**Tadoussac** – *220km/136mi northeast of Quebec City by Rtes. 40 and 138.* Thi tiny community occupies a magnificent **site★★** at the mouth of the Saguenay or the cliffs and dunes lining the St. Lawrence. The resort town is popular as a plac to see migrating whales.
In 1600 Pierre Chauvin built Canada's first trading post here, and Tadoussa became an important centre for the fur trade. Settlers moved into the area in th mid-19C, and the community developed into a lovely vacation spot. Toda Tadoussac's principal attractions are whales that swim up the St. Lawrence to th mouth of the Saguenay for a few months each year.
The village is dominated by the red roofs of the **Hotel Tadoussac**, dating from 1941 Facing the hotel a boardwalk extends along the river, connecting a reconstructio of Chauvin's trading post and a tiny Indian chapel (1747). A short walk to th wharf affords fine views of the area.

★★**Whale-watching Cruises** – *Depart from the municipal wharf May–Oct daily 10am, 1pm 2:30pm & 4:15pm. Round-trip 3hrs. Commentary. Choice of cruise in inflatabl boat or passenger boat. Reservations required. From $32.* ♿ 🅿 *Croisières AML ☎418-237-4274.* At Tadoussac, the St. Lawrence is more than 10km/6mi wide Boats head for the centre of the river where whales surface to breathe and to dive in search of food. Spray erupting from their blowholes makes them easy to see. The most common species sighted on cruises are the **fin**, **minke** and **beluga** (white whales). Occasionally, a fortunate visitor may glimpse a **humpback** or even the huge **blue whale**.

★★**Scenic Cruises** – *Depart from La Grève pier (near the marina) late May–late Oct daily 9am, 1pm & 4:15pm. Round-trip 3hrs. Commentary. Reservations suggested. $30.* ♿ 🅿 *($3) Croisières à la Baleine ☎418-235-4879.* A boat trip is the most spectacular way to discover the Saguenay Fjord. The longer cruises lead to Éternité Bay, a lovely cove dominated by twin cliffs, Cap Éternité and Cap Trinité. Rising some 518m/1,700ft over the fjord, **Cap Trinité★★** is renowned for the impressive statue of the Virgin Mary standing on a ledge 180m/590ft above the water.

Sainte-Rose-du-Nord – *94km/58mi from Tadoussac.* Founded in 1838, this charming village occupies an exceptional **site★★** in a cove nestled between two rocky escarpments. The small **nature museum** contains a fascinating collection of nature's oddities *(open year-round daily 8:30am–9pm; $3;* ♿ 🅿 *☎418-675-2348)*.

★**Chicoutimi** – *200km/124mi north of Quebec City by Rte 175.* Meaning "to the edge of deep waters" in the local Montagnais language, Chicoutimi sits on the banks of the Saguenay, at the point where it becomes a spectacular fjord. Site of an important fur-trading post in the mid-17C, the town is today the cultural and administrative centre of the Saguenay region.

★**Chicoutimi Pulp Mill** (Pulperie de Chicoutimi) – *300 Rue Dubuc. Open Jun 24–Jul daily 9am–8pm. Mid-May–Jun 23 & Aug–mid-Oct daily 9am–6pm. Late Oct–Nov & Apr–early May Mon–Fri noon–4pm. $8.50.* ✂ ♿ 🅿 *☎418-698-3100.* This former pulp and paper mill (1896) was one of the most important industrial complexes in Quebec in the early 20C. The former workshop has been converted into an **interpretation centre** that features a fascinating audio-visual presentation on the mill and the lumber industry in general.

★**Saguenay–Lac-Saint-Jean Museum** (Musée du Saguenay–Lac-Saint-Jean) – *In Building 1921. Scheduled opening summer 1999.* Building 1921 is slated to contain the collections of this museum, formerly housed in a local chapel. Visitors to the museum will gain an insightful introduction to the lifestyle of the Montagnais, the first European settlers and the region's industrial development, among other topics.

★★**Scenic Cruises** – *Depart from dock at bottom of Rue Salaberry Jun–Sept daily at 8:30am & 12:30pm. Commentary. Reservations required. Return to Chicoutimi by bus. $30.* ✂ 🅿 *Croisières Marjolaine Inc. ☎418-543-7630. For a description of cruise sights, see Tadoussac p 223.* On the return trip, the views of Ha! Ha! Bay and of Chicoutimi itself are equally magnificent.

★★LAKE SAINT-JEAN

Péribonka – *270km/167mi north of Quebec City by Rtes. 175 and 169.* After spending a few months in this charming community in 1912, the French author Louis Hémon (1880-1913) wrote his well-known novel, *Maria Chapdelaine, récit du Canada français.* Informative exhibits at the **Louis Hémon Museum★** (Musée Louis-Hémon) trace the life and work of the author *(open Jun–Sept daily 9am–5:30pm; rest of the year Mon–Sat 9am–4pm, Sun 1pm–5pm; $4.50;* ♿ 🅿 *☎418-374-2177)*.

Saint-Félicien – *67km/42mi west of Péribonka by Rte. 169.* Located on the western shore of the lake, this agricultural community is best known for its **zoo★★** Kids *(6km/4mi on Blvd. du Jardin; open Jun–Oct daily 9am–5pm; rest of the year by appointment; $17;* ✗ ♿ P ☎ *418-679-0543).* A specially designed train takes visitors through the park, allowing them to admire a variety of animals roaming in natural surroundings. Of particular interest is the **Nature Trails Park★★**, inhabited by some 950 animals native to Canada.

Roberval – *25km/15mi south by Rte 169.* Located on the southwestern shore of Lake Saint-Jean, this community is today an important service centre for the area. It is also the finish point of the annual International Swim Marathon.

Mashteuiatsh Amerindian Museum (Musée Amérindien de Mashteuiatsh) – *9km/6mi north of Roberval by Blvd. Saint-Joseph. Open mid-May–mid-Oct daily 9am–6:30pm. Rest of the year Mon–Fri 8am–4pm. $3.* ♿ P ☎ *418-275-4842.* Located in Mashteuiatsh, an Indian reserve created in 1856, this museum traces the history of the Montagnais and displays traditional tools and clothing. A small shop offers handicrafts created in the area.

★**Val-Jalbert Historic Village** – *9km/6mi south of Roberval by Rte. 169. Open mid-Jun–Labour Day daily 8am–7pm. Mid-May–mid-Jun & mid-Sept–mid-Oct daily 9am–5pm. $8.50.* △ ✗ ♿ P ☎ *418-275-3132. The village belongs to the Quebec government. It can be visited on foot or by tram. Some older homes have been renovated and are available to visitors as rental units year-round.* Today a ghost town, Val-Jalbert was once the site of a thriving pulp mill. Built in 1902, the mill produced up to 50 tonnes/45 tons of pulp a day at the height of production in 1910. By the late 1920s, stiff competition led to the mill's closing, and the village gradually fell into ruins. Visitors can wander through the old residential sector that once contained over 80 residences and shops. Today many of these houses are in decay, creating an eerie atmosphere. The **Old Mill** (Vieux Moulin), standing on the Ouiatchouan River, now contains an exhibit on the mill's operation; a film *(20min)* shows the pulp-to-paper process. A steep stairway *(400 steps; cable car ascent $3.75)* leads to the top of an impressive waterfall on the Ouiatchouan River. From this vantage point, the **view★★** encompasses Lake Saint-Jean and the surrounding area.

TROIS-RIVIÈRES★★

Population 48,419

Map p 197

Tourist Office ☎819-375-1222

Capital of the Mauricie Region, this industrial centre is located on the north shore of the St. Lawrence River at the mouth of the Saint-Maurice. Just before joining the St. Lawrence, the Saint-Maurice branches around two islands, creating the three "rivers" for which the city is named.

Sent by Champlain, **Sieur de Laviolette** established a fur-trading post here in 1634. Home to many great explorers, including Pierre Radisson, Sieur des Groseilliers and Sieur de la Vérendrye, the city flourished. In the 1850s major logging companies began exploiting the surrounding forests, and a thriving pulp and paper industry took root in the area. By the 1930s Trois-Rivières was the world capital for the production of newsprint, a distinction it still holds to this day. This bustling city is also the location of a University of Quebec campus.

SIGHTS

★**Rue des Ursulines** – This charming street is lined with some of the oldest structures of the city that survived a fire in 1908. Distinguished by a gracious dome and large wall sundial, the **Ursuline Monastery★** (Monastère des Ursulines) is the jewel of Trois-Rivières' old quarter. Inside, the **museum** features fine collections of ceramics, silver, books and furniture *(open Mar–Apr Wed–Sun 1:30pm–5pm; May–Nov Tue–Fri 9am–5pm, weekends 1:30pm–5pm; rest of the year by appointment ☎819-375-7922).* Other buildings of interest on this street include St. James' Church, erected in 1742 by the Récollet Brothers, and the Gannes and Hertel de la Fresnière Houses.

★**Waterfront Park (Parc Portuaire)** – This attractive terrace affords superb **views** of the river and Laviolette Bridge, erected in 1967. At the eastern end of the park, a monument commemorates the Sieur de la Vérendrye, first European to reach the Rockies. At the **Pulp and Paper Industry Exhibition Centre** (Centre d'exposition sur l'industrie des pâtes et papiers) displays provide a fascinating introduction to the dominant industry of Trois-Rivières *(open Jun–Sept daily 9am–6pm; Apr–May & Oct by appointment; $3;* ✗ ♿ P ☎ *819-372-4633).*

★**Scenic Cruise** – *Depart from the harbourfront May–Oct daily 1pm & 8pm. Rounc trip 1hr 30min. Commentary. Reservations required. $11.* ✗ 🅿 *Navire M/V L Draveur Inc.* ☎ *819-375-3000.* This cruise offers an unequalled **view** of the port a Trois-Rivières and the pulp and paper installations. The shrine at Cap-de-la-Made leine *(below)* is also visible.

★**Museum of Quebec Folk Arts and Traditions (Musée des Arts et Traditions populaires d Québec)** – *200 rue Laviolette, at the intersection with Rue Hart. Open late Jun–Labou Day daily 10am–7pm. Rest of the year Tue–Sun 10am–5pm. $6 (includes visit t the Old Prison).* ♿ 🅿 ☎ *819-372-0406.* Opened in 1996, this museum display works from its permanent collection of more than 80,000 tools, furniture, textiles toys and other objects to illustrate provincial customs, folk arts, traditional occu pations and other aspects of domestic life.

Adjoining the museum is the **Old Trois-Rivières Prison** (Vieille Prison), an imposin stone structure completed in 1822. Having ceased operations as a prison in 1986 the building houses an interpretation centre with exhibits about prison life; som 20 cells may be viewed.

EXCURSIONS *Map p 197*

Map p 197

★★**Cap-de-la-Madeleine Shrine** – *5km/3mi east of Trois-Rivières by Rtes. 40 and 75 (Exit 10). Open May–mid-Oct daily 8am–9pm (mid-Aug 10pm). Rest of the yea 8am–5pm.* ♿ 🅿 ☎ *819-374-2441.* This shrine attracts thousands of peopl annually. Two events are credited with its renown as a pilgrimage site.

In the mid-19C Father Luc Désilets decided his growing congregation needed a new church to replace the one built on this site in 1717. When unusually mil weather prevented the St. Lawrence from freezing, Désilets could not transpor stones across the river for the church's construction. The Father vowed to preserve the existing church in exchange for a miracle. In March 1879, ic appeared on the river, remaining just long enough for parishioners to take the stones across. On the night of the new church's consecration in 1888, anothe miracle is said to have occurred when the eyes of a statue of the Virgin reportedl opened before three witnesses. Begun in 1955 to accommodate an even large congregation, the present basilica replaced Désilets' church and was complete in 1964.

The imposing octagonal basilica is adorned with magnificent **stained-glass windows** designed in the medieval style by Dutch Oblate father Jan Tillemans. Set in attractive grounds beside the basilica, the original stone church now serves as a votive chapel. The miraculous statue stands above the altar. Winding their way through the park, the Stations of the Cross end before the replicas of the Crucifixion and the tomb of Jesus in Jerusalem.

★**Mauricie Region** – Surrounding the valley of the Saint-Maurice River, this region ranks among the most industrialized in the province and the nation. Forestry operations began in the 1850s, and hydro-electric plants were erected in the late 19C. Hugging the river, which is still used to transport logs from the forests to the pulp mills, the drive along Route 155 affords fine **views**★ of the Saint-Maurice and the rocky cliffs lining its sides. Located northwest of Grand-Mère, the **Mauricie National Park**★★ offers a glorious landscape of dense forests interspersed with numerous lakes and rivers *(park open year-round; visitor centers at the Saint-Jean-des-Piles and Saint-Mathieu entrances open mid-May–Labour Day daily 7am–10pm; mid-Sept–early Oct daily 9am–4:30pm (Fri 10pm) & offer information, entrance permits, canoe rentals and interpretative displays; $2.50;* △ ✗ ♿ 🅿 ☎ *819-538-3232).*

★★**Saint-Maurice Ironworks National Historic Site** (Lieu historique national des Forges-du-Saint-Maurice) – *13km/8mi from Trois-Rivières by Blvd. des Forges. Open early May–early Sept daily 9:30am–5:30pm. Mid-Sept–mid-Oct daily 9:30am–4:30pm.* ♿ 🅿 ☎ *819-378-5116.* Established in 1729, these ironworks produced a variety of implements, including stoves, guns, ploughshares and dumbbells until 1883, when the iron ore and wood of the region were depleted. Only ruins remain, but the shapes of the original buildings are suggested by metal structures resembling scaffolding. At the **blast furnace** (haut fourneau), displays explain the smelting process. Beside the river a spring known as **Devil's Fountain** (Fontaine du Diable) emits natural gas.

French terms used in the text and on the maps in this guide:

anse	cove, bay
autoroute	highway
baie	bay
belvédère	viewpoint
cap	cape
centrale hydro-électrique	hydro-electric power station
centre d'accueil	welcome centre
centre d'interprétation	interpretation centre
chute	waterfall
côte	shore, coast
croisière	cruise, boat trip
Est	east
écluse	lock
église	church
gare	train station
hôtel de ville	city hall
île	island
jardin	garden
lac	lake
maison	house
manoir	manor
métro	subway
monastère	monastery
mont	mount
montagne	mountain
moulin	mill
musée	museum
Nord	north
Ouest	west
palais de justice	courthouse
parc	park
phare	lighthouse
place	square
plage	beach
pont	bridge
rapides	rapids
réserve faunique	wildlife conservation area
rivière	river
rocher	rock
rue	street
stationnement	parking
Sud	south
téléphérique	gondola
traversier	ferry boat
vallée	valley
ville	city, town

Latin Quarter

Atlantic Provinces

Shag Harbour, Nova Scotia – Malak, Ottawa

Battered by the Atlantic Ocean on one side and washed by the calmer Gulf of St. Lawrence on the other, Canada's four Atlantic seacoast provinces (New Brunswick, Nova Scotia, Prince Edward Island and Newfoundland, including Labrador)—also known as Atlantic Canada—lie on the eastern side of the continent. The so-called Maritime provinces (New Brunswick, Nova Scotia and Prince Edward Island), together with Newfoundland, share the pervasive influence of the sea, which has molded, in great measure, their economic, political and cultural development.

Geographical Notes

Landscape – Parts of the region, notably northern New Brunswick and Cape Breton Island, are hilly, lying near the end of the **Appalachian Mountain** chain. In the western part of Newfoundland, the **Long Range Mountains** (average height 610m/2,000ft) are a continuation of this chain. A harsh, mountainous land, Labrador contrasts to Prince Edward Island with its stretches of flat lowland.

Barren and rocky by the sea while densely forested inland, the landmasses possess some fertile areas, however—the SAINT JOHN RIVER VALLEY, the ANNAPOLIS VALLEY and the whole of Prince Edward Island. Their long, deeply indented coastlines are ruggedly beautiful, studded with bays, inlets, cliffs and coves (Newfoundland alone has 9,660km/6,000mi of shoreline). Remarkable for its rapid tides, the **Bay of Fundy** produces the phenomenal tidal bore *(p 241)*. The highest recorded tide in the world occurred at **Burncoat Head** *(map p 231)* on the Nova Scotia shore: a difference of 16.6m/54ft was measured between high and low tides.

Climate – The sea largely determines the climate of this region. Moving south down the Atlantic coast, the cold **Labrador Current** enters the Gulf of St. Lawrence by the Strait of Belle Isle. Because the region lies on the eastern side of an immense landmass, however, it receives air currents from the interior, since air masses generally move

from west to east at these latitudes. Meeting warmer air currents off the continent, the cold waters of the Labrador Current can cause fogs throughout the year—less so in summer—along Newfoundland's and Nova Scotia's coasts especially.
Winters are stormy along the Atlantic but milder than inland. Coastal cities such as HALIFAX and ST. JOHN'S record a mean daily maximum in January of 0°C/32°F and 1°C/34°F respectively, whereas in northwestern New Brunswick extreme minimum temperatures of –34°C/–30°F are experienced.
Summers are cooler and less humid than in Ontario and Quebec at the same latitude. The coast is cooler than inland (Halifax 23°C/74°F, July mean daily maximum; Saint John 21°C/70°F) whereas extreme maximum temperatures in excess of 38°C/100°F have been recorded in northwestern New Brunswick.
In general, precipitation is evenly distributed throughout the year. Precipitation is greatest annually along the coasts of Newfoundland (St. John's 1,345mm/53in) and Nova Scotia (Halifax 1,372mm/54in) and least in Newfoundland's interior (Gander 1,016mm/40in) and northwestern New Brunswick (1,016mm/40in). The Great Northern Peninsula of Newfoundland is the driest region. Snow falls in all the provinces, but is heaviest in northwestern New Brunswick (254-305cm/8-10ft) and lightest along the coast (Halifax 163cm/5ft). Labrador experiences a more severe climate than other parts of the region with more extreme temperatures but less precipitation. Goose Bay registers a mean maximum of –14°C/7°F in January, and 21°C/70°F in July, with 737mm/29in of precipitation annually. With its sub-Arctic climate, Northern Labrador is colder: winter mean temperatures, recorded at sea level, average –20°C/–4°F.

Population – More than two million people live in the Atlantic provinces, with Nova Scotia the most populous (909,282), followed by New Brunswick (738,133). Prince Edward Island has the lowest population (134,557). The majority of inhabitants claim origins in the British Isles (England, Scotland and Ireland). The most homogeneous of any province, Newfoundland sustains a population of 551,792 with 98 percent declaring English as their mother tongue. Yet there is a noticeable French-speaking minority in the region (largely Acadians), concentrated as follows: 1 percent in Newfoundland in the St. George's/Port au Port region; 4 percent in Nova Scotia; 17 percent in Prince Edward Island; and 34 percent in New Brunswick (mainly in the north and east). Nearly 30 percent of Nova Scotia's population is of Scottish origin, living mainly in Cape Breton Island and on the shores of Northumberland Strait; another 4 percent living on the south coast, west of Halifax, have German origins. The Micmac are the most populous of the Indians in Newfoundland, New Brunswick and Nova Scotia. Inuit and Montagnais-Naskapi Indians are found primarily in Northern Labrador. The black population, which accounts for less than 1 percent of the region's inhabitants, is concentrated primarily in the towns of Nova Scotia and New Brunswick.

Historical Notes

Native Cultures – Before the arrival of Europeans, the Atlantic provinces were inhabited by Indians of the **Eastern Woodlands** culture *(map p 22)*: **Micmac** in New Brunswick, Nova Scotia and Prince Edward Island lived by hunting and fishing; **Maliseets** cultivated the land in southern New Brunswick like their Iroquoian brothers in Ontario *(p 127)*; and the **Beothuk** in Newfoundland also fished and hunted. As their ancestors had done, the latter painted themselves with red-powdered ochre, perhaps the origin of the term "redskins." The Beothuk's belief that all goods were held in common increased hostilities with the early European fishermen who frequently found their supplies missing. Mass murder and European diseases diminished these people greatly. The last known surviving Beothuk died in St. John's in 1829.

The First Europeans – Although he is credited as the first European arrival, **John Cabot** (1450-98)—an Italian navigator on a 1497 voyage of discovery for England's Henry VII—was not the first European to set foot in the region. One school of thought claims the Norse settled in Nova Scotia about AD 1000, but irrefutable evidence is lacking. Archaeological remains prove that the Norse settled on the Newfoundland coast at that time *(p 280)*. There is reason to believe the **Irish** reached the province's shore in the 6C, and it is possible that **Basques** fished the North Atlantic as early as the 14C. At Red Bay in Labrador, archaeologists have discovered the presence of a large 16C Basque whaling port. Cabot's importance lies in his publicizing the region's rich fisheries. The Basques, English, French, Portuguese and Spanish came for the cod, especially abundant off Newfoundland's Grand Banks. Dried on racks on shore, the fish was light, almost indestructible, and easily transportable to a ready market in Europe.
Settlement was generally discouraged by the English West Country merchant owners of the fishing fleets, who feared competition from a resident population. Before the close of the 16C, English fishermen established small communities on Newfoundland's coasts, despite stiff antisettlement laws.
In 1583 Newfoundland—the subject of great rivalry in Europe—was proclaimed the territory of Elizabeth I *(p 282)* at St. John's. Only the French attempted to wrest control of the region from the English. **Jacques Cartier** had claimed Prince Edward Island for France in 1534, renaming it Île-St.-Jean, but serious attempts to colonize it were not forthcoming until the 18C. French efforts at settlement met with success in Nova Scotia, largely with the aid of the Micmac who taught them survival skills, when Sieur de Monts and Samuel de Champlain established **Port Royal** in 1605 *(p 252)*.

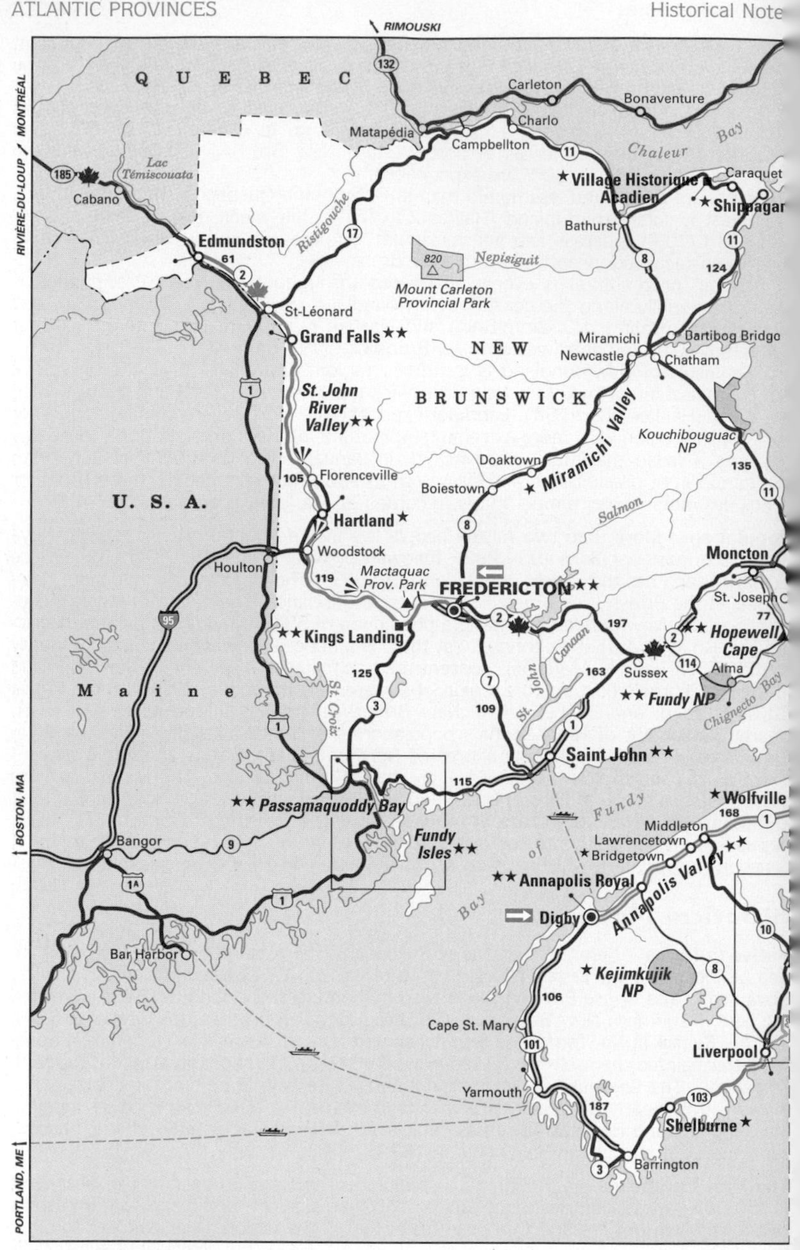

"New Scotland" – Port Royal fell to a force from Virginia in 1613 and, although the French reestablished it later, in the interim it was British. In 1621 James I granted present-day Nova Scotia, Prince Edward Island and New Brunswick to **Sir William Alexander** to establish a "New Scotland" there (both men were Scots)—hence the Latin name *Nova Scotia* used on the original charter. The settlements Alexander founded were short-lived, and in 1632 Charles I, who apparently did not share his father's desire for a New Scotland, returned the region to the French by the Treaty of St.-Germain-en-Laye. The future Nova Scotia had nonetheless been born—the coat of arms granted in 1621 is still the provincial emblem today.

"Acadie" – *Acadie* (Acadia) was what the French called a vague area covering much of Nova Scotia, Prince Edward Island, New Brunswick and Maine. The Acadians are descendants mainly of French colonists who came from western France to La Have and Port Royal between 1632 and 1651. As their numbers grew, settlements spread along the ANNAPOLIS VALLEY to Chignecto Bay *(p 238)*. Repeatedly attacked by expeditions from New England during the Anglo-French wars of the 17C, these settlements changed hands several times.

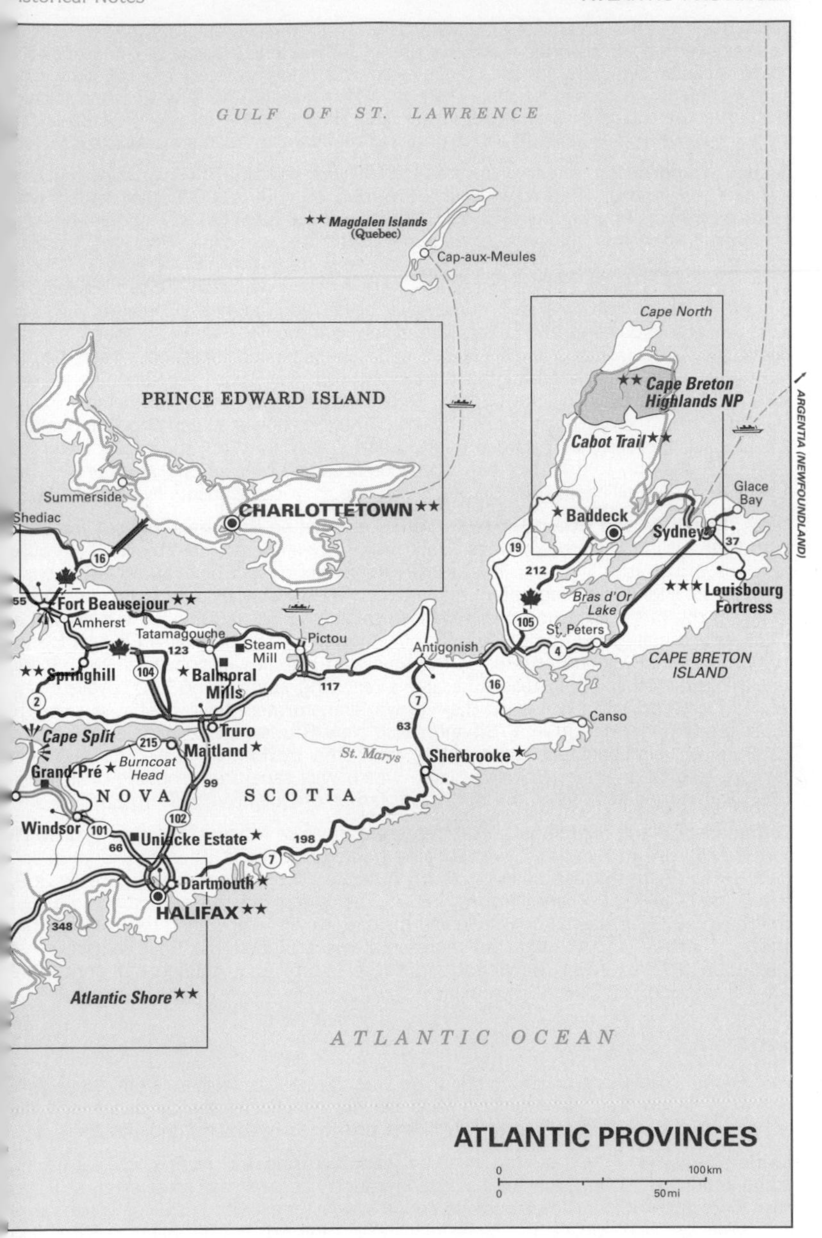

British Regime – The English Crown granted a few charters in the 17C for colonies on Newfoundland, but authority for local law and order, granted in 1634 by Charles I, belonged largely to the **fishing admiral**—master of the first British ship to enter a harbour, regardless if there were residents. Fear of French expansion prompted the British to create permanent settlements in Newfoundland. Only with a strong, stable base could Britain properly defend her Atlantic harbours from the French who attacked from their colony at **Placentia**, established in 1662. French claims to the region ended in 1713 when, by the Treaty of Utrecht, France retained only the small islands of **Saint-Pierre and Miquelon** and ceded all of mainland Nova Scotia to the British. Port Royal, renamed Annapolis Royal, became its capital.

Nova Scotia Again – The Treaty of Utrecht gave Acadians the choice of leaving British territory, or becoming British subjects. Taking an oath of allegiance to Britain would mean possibly having to bear arms against fellow Frenchmen. Leaving the area would deprive them of their rich farmlands. The Acadians maintained they were neutral, stating they would take the oath with exemption from military service. Initially the British governor agreed—his soldiers needed provisions that the Acadians supplied. In peaceful times the agreement may have lasted, but Anglo-French fighting in Europ was renewed and British rule in Nova Scotia was threatened by the building of Louis bourg. Acadian sympathy for the French cause was undeniable, though it seems like most Acadians were truly neutral. Then, in 1747, nearly 100 New England soldier billeted in the village of Grand Pré were killed, as they slept, in a surprise attack b a French force from Quebec. Treachery among the Acadian inhabitants was suspected

Acadian Deportation – Fear of future attacks hardened the British toward the Aca dians, especially after 1749 when Halifax was founded with 2,500 English settlers wh could provision the army. In 1755 **Gov. Charles Lawrence** delivered his ultimatum—tak an unqualified oath of allegiance or be removed from Nova Scotia. When the Acadian refused, Lawrence quickly issued the Deportation Order, with no reference to Britain Over the next 8 years, 14,600 Acadians were forcibly deported. Others escaped to Quebec. Families were separated, some never to be reunited. Unwelcomed in the colo nies, the Acadians were able to establish a new community only in Louisiana and, a **Cajuns**, survive to this day. Some escaped to Saint-Pierre and Miquelon. Others fled to Île-St.-Jean until 1758 when the island was captured by a British expedition under **Lor Rolo**, and later annexed by Nova Scotia. Left untouched was a small settlement in the Malpeque area, the origins of Prince Edward Island's French-speaking population today When peace was restored between England and France in 1763, most exiles returned to Nova Scotia only to find their rich farmlands occupied by new English colonists. The Acadians settled mainly in New Brunswick, where their descendants live to this day.

Scots, Loyalists and Other Settlers – After Deportation the British offered free land to anyone willing to settle in Nova Scotia. New Englanders from the south, groups from the British Isles and from the German states along the Rhine, and the first wave of Scottish Highlanders accepted the offer. Dispossessed by big landowners who sought profit in sheep raising over tenant farming, the first 200 Scots who arrived in 1773 settled mainly in Cape Breton, Pictou, Antigonish and on Prince Edward Island In 1775 when revolution erupted in the American colonies, it appeared Nova Scotia would join the other 13. Instead it became a receiving point for 30,000 Loyalists who fled the new US after the war. Their arrival transformed Nova Scotia. A separate administration was set up in 1784 and called New Brunswick for the German duchy of Braunschweig-Lüneburg, governed at that time by England's George III. Other Loyalists settled in Prince Edward Island, which was separated from Nova Scotia in 1769 and named in 1799 in honour of the father of Queen Victoria *(p 269)*.

Confederation – In September 1864, representatives of Nova Scotia, New Brunswick and Prince Edward Island met with a delegation from Canada (then only Ontario and Quebec) to discuss British union in North America. This historic conference *(p 269)* paved the way for Confederation in 1867. The island refused at first to join, but entered in 1873, pressured by Britain and threatened with impending bankruptcy from railway construction. Although its representatives attended the final conference in Quebec in October 1864, Newfoundland chose not to join, holding out until 1949 when it became Canada's 10th province.

Economy

The Atlantic provinces benefit from their vast forests as well as from other land resources. Magnificent scenery has made tourism a major economic factor, and the sea constitutes a rich resource on which the provinces have long depended.

Fishing Industry – Overtaken in value by manufacturing and mining, coastal fishing is still important to Newfoundland's economy. Cod has been the great catch as it has been since the 15C. (In Newfoundland cod is synonymous with "fish"; all other varieties such as herring, caplin or salmon are referred to by name.) Extending 500km/300mi from the coast, the submerged continental shelf known as the **Grand Banks** has been one of the most extensive fish breeding grounds in the world. However, since the late 1980s there has been a marked decrease in cod stocks there, and in 1992, the Canadian government placed a two-year moratorium on cod fishing off the northeast coast of the island. The ban was subsequently extended to 1997 and widened to cover all waters, not only around Newfoundland, but also around all the Maritime provinces, excepting an area off the coast of southwest Nova Scotia. There are restrictions on redfish, plaice and other groundfish as well. Despite signs that some of the fish stocks are recovering, the ban has been extended indefinitely.

Maritime Fishing – Nova Scotia's commercial fishery ranks second in Canada behind British Columbia, while New Brunswick's share of the east coast fishing industry is 18 percent. Nova Scotia has an offshore fleet that fishes the Banks, but 70 percent of its fishermen are based inshore. The most valuable catch for the three Maritime provinces is **lobster**. Since the season is tightly controlled, saltwater pounds keep the catch year round to be sold fresh on the world market. Most of these pounds are located in New Brunswick, notably on Deer Island *(p 242)*. The province is also known for its sardines and Atlantic salmon; Prince Edward Island is famous for Malpeque **oysters**, and Nova Scotia for Digby **scallops**. Giant **bluefin tuna** are caught off the shores of all hree provinces. In New Brunswick and in Nova Scotia, north of Dartmouth, **aquacul-ure** is a province-supported industry, concentrating on the cultivation of mussels, lams and oysters.

ealing – The catching of seals for their skins and meat is as old as settlement in New-oundland. In early winter adult seals leave their feeding grounds in the Arctic, floating outh on ice floes carried by the Labrador Current to their birthing sites off northeast lewfoundland and in the Gulf of St. Lawrence. Here, mostly young adult harp and ooded seals are hunted by small-boat fishermen principally from Newfoundland and Quebec's MAGDALEN ISLANDS, for whom the harvest is a seasonal supplement to fishery ncome.

n 1987 Canada banned the killing of young seals (up to a year old) and the hunting of seals from large offshore vessels in response to international protests. In recent ears the hunts have become controversial again. In 1996 the Canadian government anctioned expanded harp seal quotas in an attempt to help revive the cod fishery, lthough, until 1996, quotas had never been reached in any year since 1987. Imma-ure Atlantic cod are eaten by harp seals, but scientific opinion is divided as to whether heir harvest will hasten the recovery of cod stocks.

Agriculture – Agriculture is important to the economies of the Maritimes, but it is he backbone of Prince Edward Island. While the island supports a wide range of arming, it is most famous for its **potatoes**. Together with New Brunswick, Prince Edward Island produces 86 percent of Canada's table exports (potatoes destined for consumption) and 80 percent of the country's seed exports.

The Saint John River Valley and the Annapolis Valley are the region's other great agri-cultural areas. Farms do exist in glacier-ravaged Newfoundland on **Avalon Peninsula** and n **Codroy Valley**, but they supply local markets only.

Forestry – Land not under cultivation in New Brunswick (85 percent) and Nova Scotia (77 percent) supports a sizeable forest industry. New Brunswick's **pulp, paper** and **lumber** industries have overtaken agriculture in domestic production. Previously dependent upon the fishing industry, Newfoundland's economy has diversified to include mining, and manufacture based on forest resources.

Mining and Energy – **Iron ore** has been mined in Newfoundland since the turn of the century. The Bell Island works in Conception Bay, now closed, were important enough to be attacked twice by German submarines. Today the mines of the **Labrador Trough** in western Labrador are the source of approximately 55 percent of Canada's iron ore products. Labrador City is the site of one of the world's largest open-pit mining, concentrate and pelletizing operations. Copper and gold are mined in New-foundland.

Mining makes a sizeable contribution to New Brunswick's economy: in 1995 the value of production reached a billion dollars. One of the world's largest base metals (zinc, lead and copper) mines is located near Bathurst; a second mine is operating in the vicinity of Miramichi. Antimony is mined near FREDERICTON and two potash mines are situated near Sussex. **Coal** continues to be extracted at Minto-Chipman, where mining was first undertaken in 1639. In Nova Scotia coal, gypsum and salt are mined. Once a mainstay of the economy, Nova Scotia's coal industry slumped badly after World War II. Today, with renewed interest in coal as a fuel, several mines are operating again, producing some metallurgical coal for the steel industry, but primarily thermal coal for generating electricity.

New Brunswick's electric power resources are significant. The Saint John River has been harnessed in several locations, notably Mactaquac and Beechwood *(p 236)*. The Maritimes' only nuclear power station is located at Point Lepreau on the Bay of Fundy. Labrador's **hydro-electric** potential is enormous. Virtually all the power produced by the huge generating station at **Churchill Falls** goes to the province of Quebec. Technological advances are being applied to exploit the considerable **natural gas** and **oil** reserves off Newfoundland *(p 285)* and Labrador, where drifting icebergs have always posed a threat. Canada's first offshore oil production platform has been in operation since 1992 near Sable Island, 120 miles southeast of HALIFAX. Both New Brunswick and Nova Scotia realize the potential of the mighty Bay of Fundy tides; a pilot project has pro-duced electricity at ANNAPOLIS ROYAL since 1983.

Manufacturing – The food sector dominates Atlantic Canada's manufacturing as a whole, fish processing being the largest industry. More than 300 companies engage in pharmaceutical and medical research, telecommunications and advanced technologies such as satellite remote sensing, environmental survival systems and ocean mapping. Manufacturing within the provinces is also diverse. Three tire-manufacturing facilities, an automobile assembly plant (Halifax), one steel plant (Sydney) and an aircraft engine plant (Halifax) are located in Nova Scotia. Oil refineries and shipbuilding/ship-repair faci-lities have been established at Halifax as well as at SAINT JOHN, New Brunswick. Newfoundland's large-scale manufacturing includes shipbuilding at Marystown, oil refining at Come by Chance and paint manufacture in ST. JOHN'S. An international airport, road and rail links and the deepest ice-free ports in the country aid in trans-porting Atlantic Canada's products to domestic and overseas markets.

Recreation

For specific information on the activities below, contact the appropriate provincia tourism office: New Brunswick p 237, Nova Scotia p 250, Prince Edward Island p 27 and Newfoundland p 275.

Parks – All four provinces have excellent national and provincial parks with camping facilities and activities. Washed by the surprisingly warm waters of the Gulf o St. Lawrence, Prince Edward Island National Park has lovely beaches. Miles of sand dunes are part of New Brunswick's **Kouchibouguac National Park**. Hiking trails abound in the province's Fundy National Park, Mactaquac Provincial Park and Mt. Carleton Provincial Park, as they do in Nova Scotia's National Park in Cape Breton's Highlands and Newfoundland's national parks.

Water Sports – With so much coastline the provinces offer unparalleled opportunities for swimming, boating and sailing. Water temperatures are surprisingly warm of Prince Edward Island's northern shores and New Brunswick's Northumberland Strait in the vicinity of Shediac's Parlee Beach Provincial Park. Those who find Atlantic waters rough for boating may prefer huge Bras d'Or Lake in Cape Breton, or the beautiful Saint John River, where **houseboats** can be rented by the week. Canoeing is gaining popularity in this region: **Kejimkujik National Park** has several routes, and there are sailing and canoeing opportunities in Newfoundland's lakes and rivers. **Sea kayaking** is offered along Nova Scotia's eastern shore, off Cape Breton in particular, and **river rafting** is available on the province's Medway River, or even the Fundy Tidal Bore. **Windsurfing** is practised on the bays and off the north shore beaches of Prince Edward Island, particularly Stanhope Beach, in the Eel River Bar of New Brunswick's Restigouche region and off the Acadian Peninsula.

Fishing – Trout and salmon fishing in Newfoundland and Labrador are probably unequalled elsewhere in eastern North America. A famous place to watch the salmon leap *(August)* is **Squires Memorial Park** near Deer Lake *(map p 276)*. Especially noted for its Atlantic **salmon** are the Margaree Valley in Nova Scotia and the Miramichi and Restigouche Valleys of northern New Brunswick. **Fly fishing** is the only legal method for anglers to catch salmon in Nova Scotia. **Deep-sea fishing** is popular in the Maritimes, where boats can be chartered.

Whale Watching – Whales usually can be seen throughout the summer *(August and September, especially)* off the coasts of Newfoundland, New Brunswick and Nova Scotia. Cruises are available in Newfoundland in the vicinity of St. John's, TERRA NOVA NATIONAL PARK, Trinity and Twillingate. Deer Island, Grand Manan Island and St. Andrews are departure points for whale-watching voyages in New Brunswick. In Nova Scotia cruises depart from northern Cape Breton Island and from Digby Neck. Humpback, finback and minke are just some of the varieties of whales that can be seen. Tour boats attempt to get close to the mammals for a memorable sound and sight experience.

Bird Watching – There are many popular birding areas in the region, especially along the coasts. The bird population of **Grand Manan Island** drew James Audubon to its shores to sketch its many species. In Nova Scotia, south of Liverpool, the **Seaside Adjunct** of Kejimkujik National Park protects a breeding grounds for piping plovers. Yarmouth

Gannets at Cape St. Mary's Ecological Reserve

arbours cormorants and black-backed gulls. The **Bird Islands** attract a variety of sea irds to its protected sanctuaries and McNab's Island in Halifax harbour provides a esting site for osprey. Bald eagles can be seen in the Bras d'Or Lake area as well as ı Cape Breton Highlands National Park.

)f the 520 species found in Canada, 300 have been recorded in Newfoundland (and n Prince Edward Island as well). At its three famous sea bird colonies—**Cape St. Mary's**, **Vitless Bay** and **Funk Island** *(map p 276)*—gannets, murres, kittiwake gulls, razor-billed uks, puffins, guillemots and dovekies can be observed. Bald eagles, and even occasionally a golden eagle, are sighted along the south coast.

)ther Activities – **Adventure tours** on foot, by river boat, dogsled or even **snowmobiles** re offered by outfitters in the wilds of Newfoundland. Operating mainly out of HALIFAX, vilderness expeditions in Nova Scotia can include back-packing, photography and even ross-country skiing.

Helicopter tours depart Prince Edward Island in March for the ice fields of the Gulf of St. Lawrence where thousands of baby harp seals can be seen. Seal-watch excursions also depart Halifax, NS in February/March; contact Natural Habitat Wildlife Adventures, 2945 Center Green Court, Boulder, CO 80301 United States ☎303-449-3711 or 800-543-8917 (Canada/US). Year-round flight-seeing tours of Newfoundland and Labrador, some by **seaplane** or helicopter, are available. Both Prince Edward Island and New Brunswick contain some excellent golf courses.

Winter Sports – Downhill slopes and cross-country skiing trails are located in the northern part of Nova Scotia, notably Cape Breton Island. A number of snowmobile clubs have trails, accessible to the public, in the province's open fields and woods. Charlo bills itself as New Brunswick's cross-country ski capital. The province boasts some alpine ski centres as well. Skating on frozen ponds and lakes, and winter camping are popular in the region.

New Brunswick

Map pp 230-231

Bounded by the US on the west and Quebec to the north, New Brunswick is th Atlantic provinces' connection to the continental mainland. The province is linked t Nova Scotia by the Isthmus of Chignecto. Separated from Prince Edward Island b the Northumberland Strait, New Brunswick has relied on ferry service for access t the island in the past. Recently, however, the two provinces were connected by 13km/8mi-long bridge, completed in 1997 *(p 269)*.

Geographical Notes

Coastline and Interior – An extensive coastline faces Chaleur Bay in the north, th Gulf of St. Lawrence to the east and the Bay of Fundy in the south. Extending int the bay are the three **Fundy islands** of Deer, Campobello and Grand Manan *(p 242)* The 73,436sq km/28,354sq mi interior consists of mountainous uplands reachin 820m/2,690ft in the northwest, central highlands of hills 610m/2,000ft above se level, the nearly L-shaped SAINT JOHN RIVER VALLEY draining at the southern tida shore, and a sloping plain extending east to Chaleur Bay.

The Saint John River – Named by Champlain and de Monts *(p 252)* in honour o Saint John, this largely tranquil, 673km/418mi river flows northeast from norther Maine along the US/New Brunswick border to empty into the Bay of Fundy.
Between Edmundston and Grand Falls, rural villages intersperse the farmed rive valley. Turbulent at Grand Falls gorge, the river cascades over 25m/76ft cataracts an 18m/59ft at Beechwood—both sites of hydro-electric dams. After the provincia capital of **Fredericton**, the river gradually broadens, traversing a picturesque valley o patchwork farmland. Fertile soil in its upper and lower regions sustains extensive cultivation, particularly the north's thriving **potato** industry. At the city of its namesake, the river is thrown back by the mighty Fundy tides in a slim gorge called **Reversing Falls** *(p 245)*. Fredericton and the major port city of **Saint John** are situated on the banks of this important waterway. Today the river carries little except pleasure boaters and sailing enthusiasts who find its wide expanses and deep waters a paradise, especially in the lower sections.

Historical Notes

Era of Wooden Ships – Pre-Loyalists and Loyalists established a great industry—the building of ships of timber cut from the region's forests, especially New Brunswick's. Beginning as mast making for British naval vessels, the industry grew, particularly at Saint John, which became one of the world's great shipbuilding centres by the mid-19C. Two brothers who opened a shipyard in Chatham were to become famous as founders of the **Cunard line**. Skilled craftsmen perfected clipper ships, schooners, brigs and barques for worldwide use as shipyards sprang up along the coasts of Nova Scotia and Prince Edward Island.
By Confederation in 1867, New Brunswick was well established and wealthy. In the latter half of the 19C, the province was the most prosperous in Canada. The prosperity did not last, however. By 1900 steam replaced sail power and steel hulls superseded wooden ones. Lack of foresight doomed the shipbuilding industry; only a few shipyards converted their operations to the newer technology. By World War I, wooden ships were no longer built, and the age of prominence was over.

Cultural Heritage – The social fabric of New Brunswick was woven over two centuries by a diverse population of Micmac and Maliseet Indians, New England Loyalists, Acadians, Scots, Irish, Germans, Danes and Dutch. Each group has left its imprint in the pioneer structures and celebrated traditions of rural communities and coastal villages throughout the province. Historic settlements such as **Kings Landing** *(p 246)*, MacDonald Farm Historic Park *(p 241)* and Acadian Historical Village *(p 248)* preserve the pioneer skills and crafts of the province's founders. The richness of place names, such as Kouchibouguac, Memramcook, Shediac and Richibucto, stems from original Indian designations. The Brayons' custom of flying the flag of their "republic," the Acadians' yearly "Blessing of the Fleet," Canada's largest Irish festival, an annual folk music celebration and a francophone festival featuring performers from France, Belgium and Louisiana illustrate the cultural variety of the province. Traditional feasts of seafood—particularly salmon, clams, oysters and lobster—or of earth's bounty ("corn boils," strawberry fests, "spud" days and even a brussels sprout festival) are staged from May through October. Generations have enjoyed hot Hodge Podge, a mix of new potatoes and vegetables in milk. Acadian potato and clam pie, a Loyalist dish of fish chowder, and buckwheat pancakes topped with maple syrup are old-time favourites.

PRACTICAL INFORMATION

Getting There

By Air – Air Canada and its affiliates provide direct air service to Saint John and Fredericton ☎902-429-7111; Air Nova has daily service from the US to Saint John and Moncton. Air Atlantic (an affiliate of Canadian Airlines International) has scheduled service to cities within the province and flights from the US ☎800-426-7000 (Canada/US).

By Train – **VIA Rail** services Moncton via Montreal, with connecting bus service to Saint John ☎800-561-3949

By Boat – Government-operated ferries *(free)* provide service in the lower Saint John River area and to islands in the Bay of Fundy. Ferries *(toll)* connect the province with Nova Scotia and Quebec. For information, contact New Brunswick Tourism *(below)*.

General Information

Accommodations and Visitor Information – The official tourist office publishes an annual travel guide giving information on history, attractions and scheduled events. Government-inspected hotels and motels, Bed & Breakfast lodgings and country inns, farm vacations and campgrounds are also listed. For a free copy of the guide and a map, contact **New Brunswick Tourism**, PO Box 12345, Woodstock, NB, E0J 2B0 www.gov.nb.ca/tourism ☎800-561-0123 (Canada/US).

Language – New Brunswick is officially bilingual; approximately 35 percent of the population speaks French. All road signs are in English and French.

Road Regulations – *(Driver's license and insurance requirements p 304.)* The province has good paved roads. Speed limits, unless otherwise posted, are 80km/h (50mph) on provincial highways and 50km/h (30mph) in cities. **Seat belt** use is mandatory. **Canadian Automobile Assn. (CAA)** Saint John ☎506-634-1400.

Time Zone – New Brunswick is on Atlantic Standard Time. Daylight Saving Time is observed from the first Sunday in April to the last Sunday in October.

Taxes – In New Brunswick, the national GST has been combined with the provincial sales tax to form a Harmonized Sales Tax (HST). The HST for New Brunswick is levied at a single rate of 15% (some items are exempt). Nonresidents may be entitled to a rebate on certain goods taken out of the country within 60 days of purchase *(rebate information p 308)*.

Liquor Laws – The legal drinking age is 19. Liquor is sold in government stores. Some privately owned stores sell liquor as agencies for the provincial liquor corporation.

Provincial Holiday *(National Holidays p 308)*

New Brunswick Day .... 1st Monday in August

Recreation *p 234*

Principal Festivals

Jul	**Loyalist Days Festival** (p 244)	*Saint John*
	Lobster Festival	*Shediac*
Jul–Aug	**Foire Brayonne**	*Edmundston*
	Bon Ami Festival Get Together	*Dalhousie*
Aug	**Festival Acadien**	*Caraquet*
Sept	**Harvest Jazz and Blues Festival**	*Fredericton*

FORT BEAUSÉJOUR★★

Map p 231

Overlooking the Cumberland Basin—an arm of Chignecto Bay—the Missiguash Rive Valley, and the Tantramar Marshes, this former French fort is exceptional for it impressive **panorama★★** of the surrounding country *(fog or rain may hamper visibility)* The scant remains of the mid-18C outpost testify to its turbulent history during th Anglo-French conflict in the New World.

Historical Notes – The fort stands on the Chignecto Isthmus, a narrow strip of lan joining New Brunswick and Nova Scotia, which once marked the division betweer French and British lands. In 1672 the Acadians first settled in this area, which the called Beaubassin, reclaiming it from the sea by an extensive system of dikes. Afte the Treaty of Utrecht ceded mainland Nova Scotia to Britain in 1713, they found them selves in the middle of a border conflict. The British built Fort Lawrence on their side of the isthmus; the French built Fort Beauséjour on their side. Captured in 1755 by a British force under Col. Robert Monckton, the latter was renamed Fort Cumberland The Acadians were the first to be removed from the land under the Deportation Orde *(p 232)* of that same year. Strengthened by the British, the fort withstood an attack in 1776 by New England settlers sympathetic to the American Revolution. Although manned during the War of 1812, the outpost saw no further military action. In 1926 the fort, rechristened Fort Beauséjour, was designated a National Historic Park.

Access – *At Aulac near Nova Scotia border, just off Trans-Can Hwy., Exit 550A.*

VISIT *1hr*

Open Jun–mid-Oct daily 9am–5pm. $2.50. ♿ ☎506-536-0720 (summer) or 506-876-2443. The **visitor centre** houses displays on the history of the fort, the Acadians and the region. Three restored underground casemates can be visited, and the earthworks are in good repair.

FREDERICTON★★

Population 46,507

Map p 230

Tourist Office ☎506-460-2020

Set on a bend in the placid Saint John River, opposite its junction with the Nashwaak River, this quiet city of elm-lined streets and elegant houses is the capital of New Brunswick. Largely because of the munificence of a locally raised benefactor, **Lord Beaverbrook**, the city is also the cultural centre of the province.

Historical Notes

From Fort to Capital – In 1692 the French governor of Acadie, Joseph Robineau de Villebon, constructed a fort at the mouth of the Nashwaak. Soon abandoned, the fort became an Acadian settlement called St. Anne's Point, which survived until the Seven Years' War. However, Fredericton's true beginning came, like Saint John's, with the arrival of the Loyalists *(p 244)* in 1783. Upon the formation of the province in 1784, the settlement they founded, complete with a college that is now the **University of New Brunswick**, was chosen as the capital. The more obvious choice, Saint John, was considered a less central site, vulnerable to sea attack. Named Fredericton after the second son of George III, the new capital soon became the social centre for the governor and the town's military garrison. Garden parties, gala dinners and visits from royalty were commonplace. In many ways, little has changed in this century. The vast majority of the population works for the provincial government or the university.

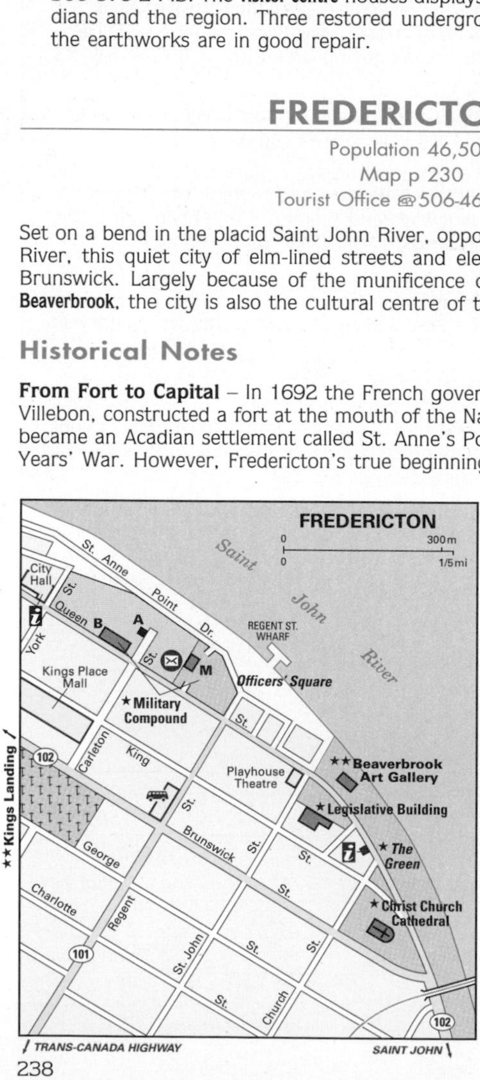

.ord Beaverbrook – Born William Maxwell Aitken in Ontario, and reared in Newcastle, ·lew Brunswick, Lord Beaverbrook (1879-1964) was a successful businessman in :anada before leaving for England in 1910. After entering politics he was elevated to he peerage in 1917, adopting his title from a small New Brunswick town. Having :stablished Beaverbrook Newspapers, he built a vast empire on London's Fleet Street. nfluential in the government of **Winston Churchill**, he held several key cabinet posts luring World War II. Although absent from the province most of his life, Beaverbrook ıever forgot New Brunswick. In addition to gifts to Newcastle, he financed, in whole ›r in part, an art gallery, a theatre and several university buildings in Fredericton.

SIGHTS *3hrs*

Stretching along the southern bank of the Saint John River, the strip of parkland known as **The Green★** is one of Fredericton's most attractive landscapes. This grassy, tree-lined expanse provides a lovely setting for the city's historic buildings.

★★**Beaverbrook Art Gallery** – *Open Jun–Labour Day Mon–Fri 9am–6pm, weekends 10am–5pm. Rest of the year Tue–Fri 9am–5pm, Sat 10am–5pm, Sun noon–5pm. Closed Dec 25. $3. ♿ www.beaverbrookart gallery.org ☎506-458-8545.* Designed and built by Lord Beaverbrook, the original structure was his gift to the people of New Brunswick. Opened in 1959 and expanded in 1983, the gallery is a major art centre of Atlantic Canada, featuring the donor's personally selected collection of British, European and Canadian art. At the gallery's entrance is Salvador Dali's huge surrealistic canvas, **Santiago el Grande**, depicting St. James on horseback being carried to heaven. Particularly strong in portraiture, the collection of **British art** is the most comprehensive in Canada. Paintings by Hogarth, Lawrence, Romney, Gainsborough and Reynolds are juxtaposed with striking works by Turner, Stanley Spencer, Augustus John and Graham Sutherland *(Portrait of Lord Beaverbrook)*. An important collection of 18C and 19C English porcelain complements the artwork. Continental Europe is represented by paintings by Cranach, Botticelli, Delacroix, Tissot, Corneille de Lyon and Ribera. Fine European tapestries and furniture are arranged in period settings. The **Canadian Collection** features works by most of the country's best-known artists including Cornelius Krieghoff, Paul Kane, Emily Carr, David Milne and the Group of Seven.

★**Legislative Building** – *Open Jun–Aug daily 8:30am–7pm. Rest of the year Mon–Fri 9am–4pm. Closed national holidays. ♿ www.gov.nb.ca/legis/index.htm ☎506-453-2527.* Opposite the art gallery stands the stately Georgian seat of provincial government, with its handsome classical dome and double-columned portico. Constructed of sandstone in 1880, this building replaced the old Province Hall, which was destroyed by fire. Visitors are permitted to see the assembly chamber with its tiered balcony and to view **portraits** of Queen Charlotte and George III, replicas of paintings by Joshua Reynolds. The parliamentary library is accessed by a striking wooden spiral staircase.

Malak, Ottawa

Legislative Building

★**Christ Church Cathedral** – *Open mid-Jun–Aug Mon–Fri 9am–6pm, Sat 10am–5pm, Sun 1pm–5pm. Rest of the year Mon–Fri 8am–4pm, Sun 1pm–5pm. ♿ ☎506-450-8500.* This elegant stone church, distinguished by a copper-green spire and pointed arch windows, is surrounded by large, attractive Loyalist-built frame houses and tall shade trees. Completed in 1853 the church, modelled after the parish church of St. Mary in Snettisham, Norfolk, is an example of decorated Gothic Revival architecture. The interior is dominated by a hammer-beam wooden pointed **ceiling**. At the entrance to the south transept stands a cenotaph with a **marble effigy** of the Rt. Rev. John Medley, the first bishop of Fredericton.

★**Military Compound** – *Changing of the guard daily in summer, weather permitting.* The central location of the former British military headquarters shows the importance of the infantry garrison in early Fredericton. (Today the country's major military training area—Canadian Armed Forces Base Gagetown—lies just to the southeast.) In 1869 shortly after Confederation, the British garrison vacated the quarters. Once stretching from Queen Street to the river between York and Regent Streets, the compound retains few of its original buildings.

Now a pleasant park known as **Officers' Square**, the old parade ground is the site of the former **officers' quarters**, a three-storey stone building with white arches, constructed in 1839 with additions in 1851. A few blocks to the west, the **Old Guard House (A)**, built in 1827, stands adjacent to the **soldiers' barracks (B)**, a stone building with red-painted wooden terraces. Both have been restored and furnished *(open mid-Jun–Labour Day daily 10am–6pm; rest of the year by appointment ☎506-460-2129)*.

York-Sunbury Historical Society Museum (M) – *In Officers' Quarters. Open Mar–May Mon Wed & Fri 11am–3pm. Jun–Sept Mon–Sat 10am–6pm, Sun noon–5pm. Oct–Dec Mon–Sat 10am–5pm. Rest of the year by appointment. ☎506-455-6041.* This museum provides a portrait of the Fredericton area from its settlement by the Indian population to the present. Exhibits on the Loyalists and the garrison are included, and a World War I trench has been reconstructed. The mounted Coleman frog, which weighed 19kg/42lbs, is on display.

EXCURSION

★★**Kings Landing Historical Settlement** – *37km/23mi. Description p 246.*

FUNDY NATIONAL PARK★★

Map p 230

Extending 13km/8mi along the Bay of Fundy's steep cliffs, this rolling parkland is interrupted by deep-cut rivers and streams in deep valleys. Created by 9m/29ft or higher tides, the vast tidal flats, explorable at low tide, contain a wealth of marine life.

Access – *77km/48mi south of Moncton by Rte. 114.*

VISIT *1/2 day*

Open year-round. Golf, boat rental, swimming, tennis, mountain biking, hiking. Visitor centre (east entrance) open mid-Jun–Labour Day daily 8am–10pm; rest of Sept–mid-Oct Mon–Fri 8:15am–4:30pm, weekends 10am–6pm; late Oct–early Jun Mon–Fri 8:15am–4:30pm (also open weekends early Jan–late Mar 9am–4pm). $3.50 entry fee. ☎506-887-6000. Note: views described may be obscured by fog.

Eastern Park Entrance – From the park gate there is a fine **view**★ of the tranquil Upper Salmon River, the hills to the north, the small fishing village of Alma, Owl's Head and the bay. To appreciate the contrast, visit at both low and high tides.

Herring Cove – *11km/7mi from entrance.* At the end of the road, there is a good **view**★ of the cove from above and a display on the tides. A path leads down to a cove that has tidal pools brimming with limpets, barnacles, sea anemones and other life at low tide.

★★**Point Wolfe** – *10km/6mi from entrance.* The road crosses Point Wolfe River by a covered wooden bridge, below which is a small gorge forming the river's entry into Wolfe Cove. On this site a mill community once stood. To collect logs floated downstream from the north, a dam was constructed. Schooners loaded the sawn wood at wharves built in the coves. Today only the bridge and dam remain.

At the end of the road, a path leads to the cove, providing good **views**★★ on the descent. At low tide the sand and rock pools are alive with sea creatures.

MIRAMICHI VALLEY★

Map p 230

The name Miramichi has long been associated with fine salmon fishing. A major spawning ground for Atlantic salmon, the river has two branches (the Southwest Miramichi and the Little Southwest Miramichi), which together traverse the province. The area is also lumber country; Newcastle and Chatham, twin towns near the river's mouth, are known for their shipbuilding past. Joseph Cunard, founder of the famous shipping line, was born in Chatham.

SIGHTS

★**Atlantic Salmon Museum** – *94km/58mi from Fredericton by Rte. 8 in Doaktown. Open early Jun–Sept daily 9am–5pm. $4. ☎506-365-7787.* Overlooking a series of pools on the Miramichi River, this pleasant museum is devoted to the area's famed Atlantic salmon. Displays include boats, nets and fishing rods, migration routes and predators. The theatre features an audio-visual show on salmon fishing, and the small aquarium contains specimens of the fish.

Central New Brunswick Woodmen's Museum – *68km/42mi north of Fredericton by Rte. 8 in Boiestown. Open May–Sept daily 9am–5:30pm. $5.* ⚠ ♿ 🅿 *www.angelfire.com/biz/woodmensmuseum ☎506-369-7214.* Set in the geographical centre of the province, this museum presents life in a lumber camp. On display is a sawmill with its original equipment and a range of tools from axes to chain saws. The re-created bunkhouse and cookhouse evoke the flavour of camp life. A small train makes a tour of the site *(runs continuously; $1).*

MacDonald Farm Historic Park – *11km/8mi east of Chatham on Rte. 11 near Bartibog Bridge. Open Jun–Sept daily 9:30am–4:30pm. $2.50. ☎506-778-6085.* Overlooking the Miramichi estuary, this old stone farmhouse (1820) has been restored to the period when Alexander MacDonald and his family lived in it. Beside the river a "net" shed, complete with fishing gear, can be seen.

MONCTON

Population 59,313
Map p 230
Tourist Office ☎506-853-3590

Set on a bend of the Petitcodiac River, Moncton is famous for its tidal bore, which rushes up the river from the Bay of Fundy. Named after **Robert Monckton**, the British commander in the capture of Fort Beauséjour, the city is generally considered the capital of Acadie.
The first settlers in the area were German and Dutch families from Pennsylvania, but they were joined by Acadians when the latter were allowed to return to British territory after Deportation. Today one-third of the population is French-speaking, and the city boasts a French-language university, founded in 1963.

SIGHT

★**Tidal Bore** – In the open ocean, the ebb and flow of the tide is barely noticeable, but in certain V-shaped bays or inlets, the tide enters the broad end and literally piles up as it moves up the bay. This buildup occurs in the Bay of Fundy, 77km/48mi wide at its mouth, narrowing and becoming shallower along its 233km/145mi length. Thus, the tide is squeezed as it travels the bay, a ripple increasing to a wave several feet high as it enters the rivers emptying into the bay. This wave is known as a "bore," a tidal wave of unusual height. At Moncton the bore varies from a few inches to nearly two feet. The highest bores occur when the earth, moon and sun are aligned.

Bore Park – *Off Main St. at the corner of King St. Bore schedules available from city hall; arrive 20min prior to view lowest level and return 2hrs later to see high tide. www.greater.moncton.nb.ca ☎506-853-3590.* The tidal bore and changing levels of the Petitcodiac River are best viewed from the park. A small stream at low tide, the river lies in the centre of a vast bed of red mud. At high tide the river widens to 1.6km/1mi, and the water level increases by 7m/23ft.

EXCURSIONS

★**Monument Lefebvre National Historic Site** – *20km/12.5mi southeast by Rte. 106 in St.-Joseph. Open Jun–mid-Oct daily 9am–5pm. $2.* ♿ *http://parkscanada.pch.gc.ca ☎506-876-2443.* Located in the Lefebvre Building of the **College St.-Joseph**, the first Acadian institution of higher learning, the site chronicles the past struggles and present strength of this French-speaking culture.
Founded by Rev. Camille Lefebvre in 1864, the college trained Acadian leaders for nearly 100 years before its amalgamation with the Université de Moncton. The site of the first National Convention of Acadians in 1881, this small museum today features displays and audio-visual presentations, including those on the Memramcook Valley, one of the few regions in which Acadians maintained continuous settlement despite Deportation.

★★**Hopewell Cape** – *35km/22mi south of Moncton by Rte. 114. Directional signs en route. Morning light is best for photography. Note: Be sure to climb stairs at the posted time to avoid the 10m/32ft tides.* Near this little village overlooking Shepody Bay is an interesting phenomenon known as **The Rocks**★★. Sculpted by tidal action, wind and frost, these red standstone formations, as high as 15m/50ft, stand on the beach, cut off from the cliffs. Tiny tree-covered islands at high tide, these shapes become "giant flowerpots" at low tide, their narrow bases widening to support balsam fir and dwarf black spruce at the top. Visitors can walk around them when the tide is out and look at crevices in the cliffs that, in time, will become new flowerpots.

PASSAMAQUODDY BAY/FUNDY ISLES★★

Map p 230

An inlet of the Bay of Fundy between Maine and New Brunswick, this body of water is dotted with islands and indented with harbours along its irregular shoreline, which includes the estuary of the **St. Croix River**. A popular resort, the area is also famous for its lobster and an edible seaweed known as **dulse**, a regional delicacy that is served in a variety of ways *(p 243)*.
According to Indian legend, one day the Micmac hero-god **Glooscap** saw wolves about to attack a deer and a moose. Using his magical powers, he turned the animals into islands. In 1604 Samuel de Champlain chose the bay as the site of his first settlement and spent the winter with his followers on St. Croix Island (today in Maine) in the estuary of the river of the same name. However, the bleak conditions forced them to move the next year across the Bay of Fundy to Nova Scotia *(p 252)*. Loyalists, arriving in 1783, settled the communities of St. Stephen, St. Andrews and St. George, and of Deer and Campobello Islands. *Fog and cold weather occur even in summer, particularly on the islands.*

SIGHTS

★**St. Andrews** – Situated at the end of a peninsula that juts into the bay, this charming town is lined with tree-covered residential and commercial avenues. A resort centre for summer visitors who like tranquility, and boating in pleasant surroundings, the town supports the **Algonquin Hotel**, one of the foremost hostelries of the province.
Founded by Loyalists, St. Andrews became a prosperous mercantile and fishing town. In 1842 some of its century-old houses were floated intact across the estuary when the Webster-Ashburton Treaty declared the Canadian/US border to be the St. Croix River—and some Loyalists discovered they were on the "wrong" side of it. Among famous Canadians who have owned homes here is **William Van Horne**, president of Canadian Pacific Railway from 1888 to 1899.
The town's quaint main thoroughfare, **Water Street**, mixes boutiques and cafes.

★**HMSC Aquarium-Museum** – Kids *At Brandy Cove. Open mid-May–Jun daily 10am–4:30pm. Jul–Aug daily 10am–6pm. Sept–Oct Mon–Tue noon–4:30pm, Wed–Sun 10am–4:30pm. $4.50. ☎ 506-529-1202.* This interesting little aquarium has fish tanks and displays on the marine ecosystems of the Bay of Fundy and neighbouring Atlantic waters. The star attraction, however, is a family of harbour seals, which perform all kinds of antics for visitors. Films are shown regularly in the theatre.

St. Andrews Blockhouse – *On Joe's Point Rd. Open Jun–early Sept daily 9am–8pm. Early–mid-Sept daily 9am–5pm. $1. http://parkscanada.pch.gc.ca ☎ 506-887-6000.* Constructed during the War of 1812, the square wooden structure stands guard over the harbour. Built to protect New Brunswick's western frontier from American invasion, it is the only blockhouse remaining of the original 14 erected. Inside, there are displays on the settlement of the town and on the blockhouse itself.

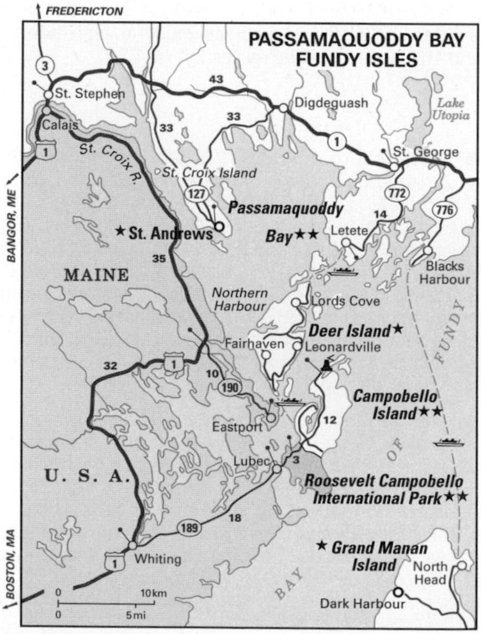

★**Deer Island** – *Toll-free car ferry departs from Letete mid-May–Oct daily 7am–6:30pm every 30 min & 7pm–10pm every hour; rest of the year daily 7am–11am & 6pm–9pm every hour, 11:30am–5:30pm every 30min & at 10:30pm. ☎ 506-466-7340. From Eastport, Maine Jun–Sept daily 9:30am–7:30pm every hour (last departure Jun & Sept 6:30pm); 30min; $10/car & driver, $2/passenger; ☎ 506-747-2159. Ferry from Campobello Island p 243. Note: ferries operate on first-come, first-served basis. Lines form on weekends and at peak times.* Positioned so as to nearly enclose the bay, this Fundy island is a quiet place, inhabited primarily by fishermen. The world's largest lobster pound is located on its western side. A pleasant **trip★** is the ferry ride to the island from Letete, among the smaller islands covered with birds. Swept by the tide in part of the narrow inlet of **Northern Harbour**, a corral where lobsters are kept year-round has been built with nets and fences. At the southern end of the island, a large whirlpool forms when the Fundy tides are running strong. Called "**Old Sow**" for the noise it makes, this vortex is visible from Deer Island Point or from the ferry to Campobello Island.

★★ **Campobello Island** – *Car ferry departs from Deer Island Jun–Sept daily 9:15am–6:15pm (last departure Jun & Sept 4:40pm). 45min. $13/car & driver, $2/passenger. ♿ 🅿 ☎506-747-2159. Accessible by bridge from Lubec, Maine. Non-Americans need valid passport (p 302). See also Michelin Green Guide to New England.* Known as the "beloved island" of US President **Franklin D. Roosevelt** (1882-1945), the site is a summer resort for vacationing Americans. Sandy beaches, picturesque coves, headlands, lighthouses and an international park named in Roosevelt's honour attract numerous visitors annually.

First settled in the 1770s, Campobello was named for **William Campbell**, the governor of Nova Scotia, and for its beauty (*campo bello* means "beautiful pasture" in Italian). By the end of the 19C, it had become a retreat for wealthy Americans. In 1883 one-year-old FDR first visited the island. Thereafter he spent summers on Campobello with his parents and later with his wife, Eleanor. He taught his five children to appreciate nature, and took them fishing, boating and swimming—activities he had done as a child. Then, in 1921, FDR contracted polio and left the island for 12 years. In 1964 the Canadian and American governments jointly established the park to commemorate him.

★★ **Roosevelt Campobello International Park** – *Open late May–mid-Oct daily 10am–6pm. ♿ ☎506-752-2922.* Preserved as a memorial to FDR, the southern part of the island is natural parkland—forests, bogs, lakes, cliffs and beaches—crisscrossed by several lovely **drives★★**. Note the view of Passamaquoddy Bay from Friar's Head *(turn right at picnic area sign just south of visitor centre)*, and of Herring Cove from Con Robinson's Point *(follow Glensevern Rd. East)*. Built in the Dutch colonial style, the red-shingled, green-roofed **cottage★** with 34 rooms belonged to FDR. Simply furnished, the rustic interior contains personal reminders of his childhood and years as president. The west side rooms, especially the living room, have pleasant views of Friar's Bay. Films on the life of Roosevelt are shown in the **visitor centre**. North of the visitor centre, **East Quoddy Head Lighthouse★** *(12km/7mi by Wilson's Beach and gravel road to the Point)* has a picturesque site overlooking Head Harbour Island.

★ **Grand Manan Island** – *Car ferry departs Blacks Harbour Jun 30–Labour Day daily 7:30am, 9:30am, 11:30am, 1:30pm, 3:30pm & 5:30pm (no departure Sun 7:30am). Rest of the year approximately 3 crossings daily. 1hr 30min. $26/car, $8.70/passenger. ✕ ☎506-662-3724.* The largest of the Fundy islands, Grand Manan is noted for its rugged scenery that includes cliffs of 120m/400ft and picturesque harbours. A sizeable bird population inhabits the island; about 230 species have been sighted. On the island's rocky west coast, **Dark Harbour** is a processing centre for **dulse**, which grows on submerged rocks in the Bay of Fundy. Collected at low tide and dried in the sun, dulse has a salty, tangy flavour. Rich in iron and iodine, it can be added to soups and stews or eaten raw or toasted.

SAINT JOHN★★

Population 72,494
Map p 230
Tourist Office ☎506-658-2990

The province's largest city, this industrial centre and major port is fondly called "fog city" because of the dense sea mists that roll in off the Bay of Fundy. Its rocky, hilly site at the mouth of the Saint John River at the junction with the bay has resulted in a city with few straight roads and many culs-de-sac.

Historical Notes

Part of Acadie – In 1604 Samuel de Champlain and the Sieur de Monts landed briefly at the mouth of the river. Another Frenchman, **Charles de La Tour**, built a trading fort in 1630 on the site of present-day Saint John. In 1645 de Menou d'Aulnay *(p 251)*, his compatriot from Port Royal, destroyed the post. The ensuing trade rivalry among the French in Acadia was compounded by the Anglo-French struggles. Although the area was ceded by the 1763 Treaty of Paris to the English, who established their own post, Saint John records 1783 as the year of its inception.

The Loyalists Arrive – On May 18, 1783 some 4,000 Loyalists disembarked at the mouth of the river from their square-rigged ships. Overnight the tiny trading post became a boomtown. Their wealth dissipated by the American Revolution, they possessed few pioneering skills needed to carve new lives out of the wilderness. However, they not only survived, but created a prosperous city of shipyards and social gatherings. Thriving on trade and shipbuilding, Saint John was known as the "Liverpool of America" during the 19C.

Decline and Renewal – From 1860 to 1880, however, Saint John began to decline: demand for wooden ships was decreasing; an international depression had set in by early 1874; and in 1877 more than half the city was destroyed by a great fire. During the 1880s the waterfront was modernized, a railway terminus established and by 1900, grain elevators completed. The port remained active, but not until the 1960s did the economy revive. Huge investment was made in pulp and paper, sugar and oil refining. A container shipping service was established and a deep-water terminal built for tankers.

Every July the city recalls its founding with a celebration known as **Loyalist Days**. Inhabitants dress in 18C costumes and reenact the landing of 1783. Sidewalk breakfasts and a large parade complete the festival.

★★ DOWNTOWN *1/2 day. Map p 245.*

Saint John's downtown has been revitalized, making it a pleasant area for visitors to explore on foot *(contact tourist office for designated walks)*.

★★ **Market Square Area** – Opened in 1983 the square contains an attractive shopping mall with a central atrium and several levels, a hotel, convention centre and the New Brunswick Museum.

Incorporated into the complex, a row of late-19C warehouses fronts a pleasant plaza around the **market slip** where Loyalists landed in 1783. In summer there are outdoor cafes and concerts in the plaza.

On the plaza's south side stands an 1867 clapboard structure with gingerbread decoration, **Barbour's General Store** (**A**), stocked with merchandise of the period *(open mid-May–early Jun daily 9am–6pm; mid-Jun–Labour Day daily 9am–7pm; mid-Sept–mid-Oct daily 9am–6pm; $1; P www.city.saint-john.nb.ca ☎506-658-2939)*.

Over St. Patrick Street a pedestrian bridge links the square with the Canada Games **Aquatic Centre** and **City Hall** (**B**), which has an observation gallery on the top floor *(open year-round Mon-Fri 8:30am–4:30pm)*. **Brunswick Square** (**C**) is a complex of shops, offices and hotel.

★ **New Brunswick Museum** (**M**) – *Open year-round Mon–Fri 9am–9pm, Sat 10am–6pm, Sun & holidays noon–5pm. Closed Good Friday & Dec 25. $6. ♿ ☎506-643-2300.* Devoted to the human, natural and artistic life of the province, this museum has excellent examples of Indian birchbark, quill and beadwork. European settlement is traced from contact with native inhabitants to the lumbering and shipbuilding industries of the 19C.

The gallery of natural science features displays of the province's animal life and geological specimens. There are exhibits of fine and decorative arts from New Brunswick and from other parts of Canada and the world.

Loyalist House (**D**) – *Open Jul–Aug daily 10am–5pm. Mid-May–Jun & early Sept Mon–Fri 10am–5pm. Rest of the year by appointment. $3. ☎506-652-3590.* One of the oldest structures in the city, this house was built in 1817 by David Merritt, a Loyalist who fled New York State in 1783. One of the few buildings to escape

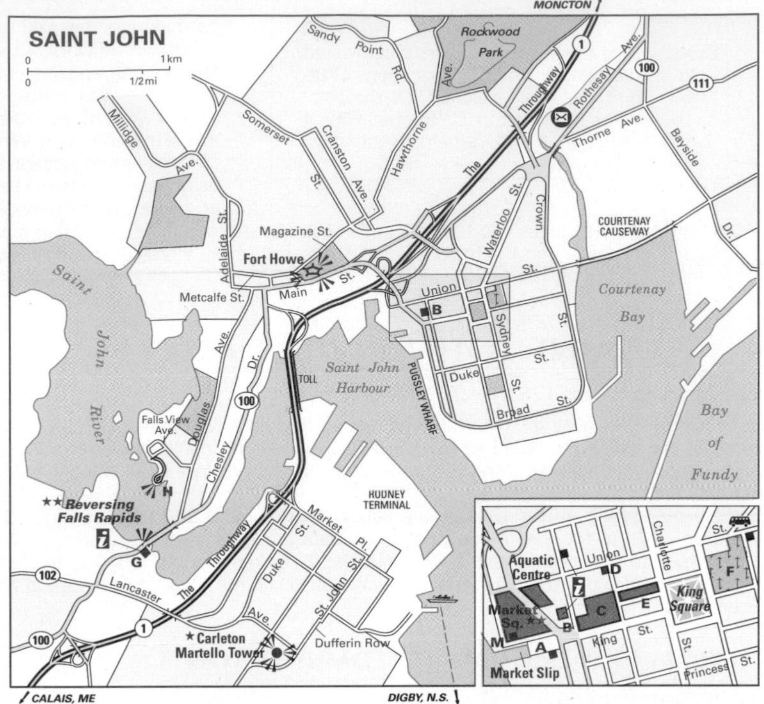

the fire of 1877, the house has a shingled exterior on two sides, and clapboard on the other. An expensive material at the time, clapboard was installed on only the north and east sides as weather protection. The plain exterior belies the elegant and spacious Georgian interior with its fine curved staircase and arches between rooms. Upon departure note the solid rock foundations on the Germain Street side. All of Saint John is built on such rock.

King Square Area – Generally considered the centre of Saint John, this square has trees, flowerbeds arranged in the form of the Union flag *(p 251)* and a two-storey bandstand. In one corner stands the old **city market** (**E**), where a variety of New Brunswick produce can be bought, including dulse *(p 243)*. On the other side of the square, the **Loyalist burial ground** (**F**) can be seen.

ADDITIONAL SIGHTS *1/2 day*

Fort Howe Lookout – *From Main St., take Metcalf St., then sharp right turn onto Magazine St.* From this wooden blockhouse *(not open)* on a rocky cliff above the surrounding hills, there is a **panorama**★ of the docks, harbour, river and city.

★★**Reversing Falls Rapids** – *To fully appreciate the rapids, visit at low tide, slack tide (below) and high tide. Contact tourist office for times of tides.* Where the Saint John River empties into the Bay of Fundy the tides are 8m/28ft high. At high tide when the bay water is more than 4m/14ft above river level, the water flows swiftly upstream. At low tide the bay is more than 4m/14ft below the level of the river, so the river rushes into it. As the tide rises, the rush of river water is gradually halted and the river becomes as calm as a mill pond (slack tide) before gradually being reversed in direction. This reversal of the river current is marked just before the river, narrowing and curving around a bend in a deep gorge, enters the bay. The narrow bend creates rapids and whirlpools whenever the current is great in either direction, a phenomenon known as "reversing falls rapids."

Reversing Falls Bridge Lookout (**G**) – *Parking at west end of bridge. Visitor centre open mid-May–mid-Oct daily 8am–8pm. www.city.saint-john.nb.ca ☎506-658-2937. Take steps to roof.* From this lookout fine **views**★★ of the changing river current are afforded. Visitors unable to stay for the tidal cycle will enjoy the **film** *($1.25)*, which condenses the 24-hour event.

Falls View Park Lookout (**H**) – *Parking at end of Falls View Ave.* The **views**★ of the rapids from the park are not as dramatic as those from the bridge.

★**Carleton Martello Tower** – *Open Jun–Labour Day daily 9am–5pm. Rest of Sept–mid-Oct daily 1pm–5pm. $2.50. http://parkscanada.pch.gc.ca ☎506-887-6000.* Built in 1813 as a defence for the city, this Martello tower *(p 265)* was

■ Not one of the Martello towers constructed in British North America between 1796 and 1848 was ever attacked. Of the total 16 (Halifax 5, Kingston 6, Quebec City 4 and Saint John 1), 11 remain to this day.

used during the 19C and in both world wars. A two-storey steel and concrete structure was added in World War II. to house antiaircraft and fire-control headquarters for Saint John. Inside the tower there are displays on the history of the area. The tower stands above its surroundings, providing a **panorama★★** encompassing the harbour, the docks, rail yards, a breakwater that leads to Partridge Island, the bay, river and city.

SAINT JOHN RIVER VALLEY★★

Map p 230

In the south the valley of this wide and scenic river is rolling and rural, supporting some of the richest farmland in New Brunswick. Heading north, the river traverses hilly, almost mountainous forests, the source of the province's substantial lumber industry.

Settlements sprang up throughout the valley when some 4,000 Loyalists arrived in 1783 *(p 244)*. In the 19C numerous steamboats moved among these communities. Traffic took to the roads in the 1940s, but the valley remains the principal transportation route since the Trans-Canada Highway parallels it for much of its length in New Brunswick.

FROM FREDERICTON TO EDMUNDSTON

Allow 1 day. 285km/177mi.

★★**Fredericton** – *Description p 238.*

Leave Fredericton on the Trans-Can Hwy. (Rte. 2).

After traversing the provincial capital, the highway follows the river upstream to the Mactaquac Dam, New Brunswick's largest power project. The dam has created a reservoir, or headpond, about 105km/65mi long, affecting the valley as far as Woodstock.

On the north bank of the headpond lies **Mactaquac Provincial Park**, a haven for sports enthusiasts. The Trans-Canada Highway travels the south side of the pond with fine **views★** as the country becomes increasingly rural.

★★**Kings Landing Historical Settlement** – Kids *37km/23mi. Open late May–mid-Oct daily 10am–5pm. $9. ✗ www.gov.nb.ca/kingslanding ☎506-363-4999.* This restored village has a beautiful **site★★** on the sloping banks of the Saint John, beside a creek that joins the river via a small cove. Typical of the Loyalist riverbank settlements where lumbering, farming and some shipbuilding were principal occupations, the village provides an authentic glimpse of life in the river valley from 1783 to 1900.

After the Revolutionary War the land on which the village stands was given to veterans of the King's American Dragoons. When the Mactaquac dam project flooded their original sites, the houses and other buildings were moved here.

Apart from the well-restored farms with their fields of crops, the village has a church, school, forge, store and a **theatre** with live entertainment *(ask for details at entrance)*. As they carry out routine chores, about 100 costumed interpreters explain aspects of 19C rural life.

Beside the millstream is an operating water-powered **sawmill**. Activated by the large waterwheel, a saw blade cuts through logs by moving along a wooden carriage. An example of a roadhouse of the period, the **Kings Head Inn** serves traditional refreshments. The commodious Morehouse residence stands near the elegant Ingraham house with its delightful garden overlooking the river.

Moored at the wharf (the "landing"), a half-size replica of a 19C **wood boat★** typifies vessels that transported lumber from sawmills and hay from farms to market.

Between Kings Landing and Woodstock, there are excellent **views★★** from the Trans-Canada Highway of the Saint John River traversing lovely rolling country of farms and forests.

After Woodstock, leave Trans-Can Hwy. and take Rte. 103 to Hartland.

★**Hartland** – Settled by Loyalists, this town in the centre of the potato-growing district is known for the longest **covered bridge★** in the world. Completed in 1901 and rebuilt in 1920, the 391m/1,282ft bridge crosses the Saint John River in seven spans. Until 1960 the Trans-Canada Highway was routed over it, but today it links Routes 103 and 105.

As in other provinces the first bridges built in New Brunswick were of wood, covered to protect the large timbers from weathering. These coverings could lengthen the lifespan of a bridge by 50 or 60 years.
Upon descending the hill on Route 103, note the good **view★** of the bridge, which resembles a barnlike tunnel. The woodwork construction can be appreciated only from the interior *(cars can be driven through; no trucks)*.

Take Rte. 105 on the east bank to Florenceville and Trans-Can Hwy. to Grand Falls.

There are fine **views★** from the highway of the river and farms of the agricultural area north of Florenceville. The Saint John gradually approaches the Maine border and enters the more mountainous country of the north.

Leave Trans-Can Hwy. and enter Grand Falls.

★★**Grand Falls** – Built on a plateau above the river, this town is the centre of the potato belt. Here the Saint John changes suddenly and dramatically. The previous wide and tranquil river with gently sloping banks plunges over falls and, for about 1.6km/1mi, churns through a deep and narrow gorge. A power plant has diverted much of the water of the falls, but there are two good vantage points for the gorge.

Falls Park – *Accessible from Malabeam reception centre on Madawaska Rd. Open Jun–early Aug daily 9am–9pm. Mid-May–late May & mid-Aug–mid-Oct daily 9am–6pm. ✗ ♿ ☎506-475-7788.* This park offers a good **view★** of the gorge and the falls below the power plant.

★**La Rochelle Centre** – *In Centennial Park. Accessible from Malabeam reception centre on Madawaska Rd. Open daily mid-May–Labour Day. $2. ♿ ☎506-475-7766.* Stairs descend into the gorge, which has walls as high as 70m/230ft in places. At the bottom, there are some deep holes in the rock called wells, but it is the **gorge★★** that is impressive.

Return to Trans-Can Hwy.

After Grand Falls the Saint John becomes wide and placid again, marking the Canadian/US border. The towns and villages seen across it are in Maine.

Edmundston – Situated at the junction of the Madawaska and Saint John Rivers, this industrial city, dominated by the twin-spired **Cathedral of the Immaculate Conception**, contrasts sharply with the rural landscape of the surrounding valley. Once called *Petit-Sault* ("little falls") to distinguish the rapids at the mouth of the Madawaska from those of Grand Falls, Edmundston was renamed in 1856 in honour of **Sir Edmund Head**, Lieutenant-Governor of New Brunswick (1848-54). The city's inhabitants are mainly French-speaking, although they claim Acadian, Quebecer, Indian, American, English and Irish origins.

Republic of Madawaska – Long contested among Ontario, Quebec, New Brunswick and the US, the land south of Lake Témiscouata in Quebec and New Brunswick, and the area north of the Aroostook River in Maine were once collectively called Madawaska. When boundaries were finally fixed, New Brunswick was left with the city of Edmundston and a thumb-shaped stretch of land *(map p 230)*. The long-standing dispute forged a spirited independence among the Madawaskans, who created for themselves a legend, rather than a political entity—the Republic of Madawaska. Known as the Brayons because they crushed flax with a tool called a "brake," the Madawaskans have their own flag with an eagle and six stars (representing their different origins) and their own president, the mayor of Edmundston. The **Madawaska Museum** *(165 Herbert Blvd. at Trans-Can Hwy.; open late Jun–Labour Day daily 9am–8pm; rest of the year Wed 7pm–10pm & Sun 1pm–5pm; ♿ P ☎506-737-5282)* presents the history of this region.

■ Harvested from the riverbanks of the Saint John in spring, edible fiddlehead ferns, boiled and topped with butter and lemon, are a New Brunswick delicacy.

SHIPPAGAN★

Population 2,862
Map p 230

This town on the Acadian peninsula has an important commercial fishing industry and peat-moss processing plants. A bridge leads to Lameque Island with its peat moss bogs. From there a ferry *(toll free)* crosses to Miscou Island, which has fine beaches on the Gulf of St. Lawrence.

SIGHT

★**Aquarium and Marine Centre** – Kids *Open mid-May–Labour Day daily 10am–6pm. $6.* ✗ ♿ *http://acm.cus.ca ☏506-336-3013.* Devoted to the marine life of the gulf, this pleasant museum features exhibits on the St. Lawrence River and New Brunswick's lakes and rivers. An audio-visual presentation *(20min)* explains the history of the fishing industry. In a series of aquariums and an outdoor seal pool, fish native to these waters are on view. Visitors can enter the cabin of a modern-day reconstructed trawler to see the mass of electronic devices used to find and catch fish.

VILLAGE HISTORIQUE ACADIEN★

Map p 230

This reconstructed village depicts the life of the Acadians from 1780 to 1890, a time of great hardship after Deportation.
Most of the gulf shore along New Brunswick is inhabited by Acadians still living traditional lives as farmers and fishermen. Each August nearby **Caraquet** hosts an annual Acadian festival that is opened by a **blessing of the fleet**, symbolic of Christ's benediction to the fishermen of Galilee. As many as 60 fishing boats, decked with bunting, arrive from all over the province to be blessed by the bishop of Bathurst.

Access – *11km/7mi west of Caraquet by Rte. 11.*

VISIT *3hrs*

Kids *Open Jun–early Sept daily 9:45am–6pm. Mid-Sept–mid-Oct daily 10am–5pm. $9.* ✗ *www.gov.nb.ca/vha ☏506-727-2600.*
The village is entered through the **visitor centre** *(centre d'accueil)*, where a **slide show** *(18min)* covering the history of the Acadians provides a good introduction.
"Inhabited" by Acadians wearing traditional costumes, the village extends along a road nearly 1.6km/1mi long *(transport by horse and oxen-drawn carts provided)*. Houses moved from various parts of the province have been furnished to represent the period. Only the wooden church is a copy of an original building.
Over the village flies the **flag of Acadie**, the French red, white and blue tricolour with a star symbolizing the Virgin Mary at the top left corner. The flag is often seen in Acadian regions of Nova Scotia and Prince Edward Island.

Acadian Flag

Nova Scotia

Map pp 230-231

Extending north to south, Nova Scotia consists of Cape Breton Island, and a 565km/350mi long, fairly narrow peninsula, 130km/81mi at its widest. Linked to New Brunswick by the Isthmus of Chignecto, the province is surrounded by the Gulf of St. Lawrence, Atlantic Ocean, Northumberland Strait and Bay of Fundy, with 7,460km/4,625mi of serrated coastline. Proximity to the sea and natural harbours have defined its historical role as largely strategic. The provincial capital, HALIFAX, has long served as a military stronghold.

Geographical Notes

The Peninsula – The mainland is largely flat terrain, except for a rocky, indented eastern shore, and a forested interior (maximum elevation of 210m/689ft). **South Mountain** forms the northern border of this upland interior. Stretching from Cape Blomidon to the tip of Digby Neck, the **North Mountain** range parallels South Mountain for 190km/118mi along the Bay of Fundy shore. Sheltered between them is the heart of the province's apple industry, the fertile Annapolis and Cornwallis River Valleys. The cropped 300m/984ft **Cobequid Mountain** extends 120km/74mi over Cumberland County, which borders the Isthmus of Chignecto.

The Island – Northern Cape Breton Island is mostly a wooded plateau rising to 532m/1,745ft above sea level, a height that permits expansive views of the wildly beautiful, often mist-enshrouded, coastline. At the northern end is **Cape Breton Highlands National Park** with its celebrated route, the Cabot Trail. Culminating in the Strait of Canso, the south is predominantly lowland. A vast inland sea 930sq km/359sq mi wide, **Bras d'Or Lake** nearly bisects the island.

Historical Notes

Seafaring Nation – Peopled with fishermen, sea merchants, privateers and boat-builders, Nova Scotia's colourful past is interwoven with the sea. One great industry established by the Loyalists was **shipbuilding**. Blanketed by virgin forest, little of which remains today, the province used its rich timber resources to bring prosperity to its inhabitants, especially during the Napoleonic Wars (1803-15) when Britain's need for wooden ships and ship parts was great. Along the south coast, Nova Scotia's schooners became legend, as did the sailors who manned them—universally called **Bluenoses**, an American term of derision for people who could survive the region's cold climate.
More than a few fortunes were made from privateering: the east coast's plentiful coves and inlets, particularly around Liverpool, once concealed many an anchored pirate ship. Piracy diminished under threat of prosecution, and by 1900, the prominence of shipbuilding waned. Steam replaced sail power; steel hulls superseded wooden ones. Today wooden vessels are still crafted on a limited basis in the Lunenburg area.

Preserving the Past – Nova Scotia boasts more historic sites than any province in Canada except Quebec. In recent years the federal and provincial governments have played active roles in heritage preservation, as have countless local organizations and historical societies. Administered by the provincial museum system, the Nova Scotia Museum Complex, more than 20 historic sites, from heritage houses to restored mills, are open to the public.
Genealogy is popular here: local museums, schools and universities, genealogical societies, and churches have archival facilities for tracing one's roots. The migration of Nova Scotia's black population is chronicled in Dartmouth, New England's planter immigrants in Kentville. Descendants of Dutch, English, French, German, Greek, Hungarian, Irish, Italian, Lebanese and Polish settlers diversify the population today.
Traditional dishes—Acadia's rappie pie, Cape Breton lamb, Scottish oat cakes and the "truly Nova Scotian" blueberry grunt—tempt visitors to partake of a **regional cookery** harking back to Samuel de Champlain's gourmandise. The gastronomy of his Order of Good Cheer *(p 252)* endures in the province's formalized food promotion entitled "Taste of Nova Scotia," offered by over 45 member dining establishments.
Various cultural events and festivals preserve ancestral traditions, one of the largest being the International **Gathering of the Clans**, a tribute to the province's Scottish beginnings as *New Scotland (p 230)*. The province encourages local arts and crafts through its design centre and crafts council as well as a college of art in Halifax. Rug hooking guilds, craft cooperatives and quilting groups are common across Nova Scotia. Acadian crafts and demonstrations of handiwork skills are featured in local shops and museums, particularly along the west coast of Cape Breton Island, while Gaelic wares abound along the east coast and on the mainland.

PRACTICAL INFORMATION

Getting There

By Air – Air Canada offers daily flights from the US and from Montreal and St. John's, Newfoundland to Halifax ☎902-429-7111, or 800-776-3000 (US). Its affiliate Air Nova provides connections within Atlantic Canada as does Air Atlantic, an affiliate of Canadian Airlines International (CAI). CAI provides daily service to Nova Scotia from the US and many Canadian cities ☎800-426-7000 (Canada/US).

By Bus and Train – Bus travel is offered by Acadian Lines ☎902-454-9321 or 902-454-9326. **VIA Rail** connects Nova Scotia through its transcontinental train service ☎800-561-3949.

By Boat – Passenger & car ferry service connects Bar Harbor, Maine with Yarmouth *(departs mid-Jun–early Oct daily 8am; limited service in off-season; no service Nov–Apr; one-way 3hrs 45min; reservations required; US$55/car, $44.95/passenger)* and Saint John, NB with Digby *(departs daily year-round; one-way 2hrs 45min; reservations required; US$50/car, $24.50/passenger)*. For ferry schedules & reservations contact Marine Atlantic ☎ 800-341-7981 *(Canada/US)*. Yarmouth can also be reached by car ferry from Portland, Maine *(departs early May–late Oct on days scheduled 9pm; no service Nov–Apr; one-way 11hrs; reservations strongly suggested; US $80/car, $98 mid-Jun–mid-Sept, $60/passenger, $80 mid-Jun–mid-Sept; cabin extra $20–95; discount rates for some midweek days)*. For schedules & reservations, contact Prince of Fundy Cruises ☎ 800-341-7540 (Canada/US).

General Information

Accommodations and Visitor Information – The official tourist office publishes a travel guide annually giving information on history, attractions and outdoor activities, scheduled events, accommodations, farm and country vacations as well as campgrounds. For a free copy of the guide and a map, contact **Tourism Nova Scotia**, PO Box 519, Halifax, NS, B3J 2R7. For information or hotel reservations contact ☎800-565-0000 (Canada/US).

Road Regulations – *(Driver's license and insurance requirements p 304.)* Nova Scotia has good paved roads; some interior roads are loose-surface. Speed limits, unless otherwise posted, are 110km/h (65mph) on the Trans-Canada Highway, 80km/h (50mph) on highways and 50km/h (30mph) in cities and towns. **Seat belt** use is mandatory. **Canadian Automobile Assn. (CAA)**, Halifax ☎902-443-5530.

Time Zone – Nova Scotia is on Atlantic Standard Time. Daylight Saving Time is observed from the first Sunday in April to the last Sunday in October.

Taxes – In Nova Scotia, the national GST has been combined with the provincial sales tax to form the Harmonized Sales Tax (HST). The HST for Nova Scotia is levied at a single rate of 15% (some items are exempt). Foreign visitors may be entitled to a rebate on certain goods taken out of the country within 60 days of purchase *(rebate information p 308)*.

Liquor Laws – The legal drinking age is 19. Liquor is sold in government stores.

Recreation *p 234*

Principal Festivals

May–Jun	**Apple Blossom Festival**	*Annapolis Valley*
Jul	**Nova Scotia International Tattoo**	*Halifax*
	Metropolitan Scottish Festival and Highland Games	*Halifax*
	Antigonish Highland Games	*Antigonish*
	Gathering of the Clans and Fishermen's Regatta	*Pugwash*
	Acadian Days	*Grand-Pré*
Aug	**Natal Day**	*Province-wide*
	Nova Scotia Gaelic Mod	*St. Ann's*
	International Buskerfest	*Halifax*
Sept	**Nova Scotia Fisheries Exhibition & Fishermen's Reunion (p 256)**	*Lunenburg*
	Kentville Pumpkin People	*Kentville*
Oct	**Octoberfest**	*Lunenburg*

ANNAPOLIS ROYAL★★

Population 583
Map p 230
Tourist Office ☎902-532-5769

One of Canada's oldest settlements, Annapolis Royal has a pleasant **site**★ overlooking the great basin of the Annapolis where it narrows into the river of the same name. Acadians reclaimed the marshland by building a dam across the river with floodgates to control the water level. Twice a day the Bay of Fundy tides rush in, reversing the river's flow. The quiet charm of this gracious town belies its turbulent past as site of French-English battles and Acadian struggles.

Historical Notes – The earliest settlement was a French colony at **Port Royal** *(p 252)* under nobleman, **Pierre du Gua, Sieur de Monts**, destroyed in 1613 by a force from Virginia. By 1635 the French governor, **Charles de Menou d'Aulnay**, had built a new Port Royal on the site of Annapolis Royal. Over the next century French settlement grew, forming the region called Acadia *(p 230)*. Port Royal suffered many raids by the New England colonies to the south. The predecessor of the present Fort Anne *(below)* was constructed by the French, but funds were insufficient to maintain it. In 1710 it fell to a New England expedition under Col. Francis Nicholson.

Renamed Annapolis Royal after England's **Queen Anne**, the fortified settlement became the provincial capital when the mainland was ceded to the British by the Treaty of Utrecht in 1713. Constantly threatened by surrounding Acadian settlements sympathetic to soldiers from Quebec or Louisbourg, it frequently withstood French attack. In 1749 the capital was relocated to Halifax where British military force was being strengthened. Annapolis Royal was relegated to an outpost, eventually losing detachments to Halifax. In 1854 the few troops remaining were removed to New Brunswick. Annapolis Royal had lost its importance.

Much of the area's history is evident today: de Monts' habitation has been reconstructed near Port Royal, Fort Anne has been partially re-created, and the older buildings along **Lower Saint George Street** have been renovated.

SIGHTS *1/2 day*

★**Fort Anne National Historic Site** – *Grounds open all year. Visitor centre open mid-May–mid-Oct daily 9am–6pm. $2.50. ♿ P www.parkscanada.pch.gc.ca ☎902-532-2397.* A peaceful expanse of green in the centre of town, this fort was once the most fought-over place in Canada, suffering 14 sieges during the Anglo-French wars. In 1917 Fort Anne became the first National Historic Park in Canada.

Existing earthworks were built by the French from 1702 to 1708 with later alterations by the British. In one of the bastions stands a stone **powder magazine** of the French period. From the earthworks there is a **view**★ of the Annapolis Basin.

★**Officers' Quarters** – A distinctive building with high chimneys and dormer windows stands in the centre of the fort. Built in 1797 by order of Prince Edward *(p 262)*, the quarters, now restored, house a **museum**★, which includes a display on the fort's military history.

Outside flies the flag of the Grand Union, a combination of the English cross of St. George, and the Scottish cross of St. Andrew. The Union Jack as we know it today did not come into existence until the union with Ireland in 1801, when the cross of St. Patrick was added.

★**Historic Gardens** – *On Upper Saint George St. (Rte. 8) just south of Fort Anne. Open late-May–mid-Oct daily dawn–dusk. $4. ♿ ☎902-532-7018.* Situated on a 4ha/10 acre site overlooking Allain's River, a tributary of the Annapolis, this series of theme gardens exemplifies the horticultural diversity of the region's past as well as recent gardening technology.

The Acadian Garden has a traditional cottage and a replica of the dike system *(p 254)*. Formal in style, the Governor's Garden is characteristic of early-18C landscape architecture when the English governor was based in Annapolis Royal. The Victorian Garden reveals a more natural setting, a trend that became fashionable in the 19C. The Rose Garden traces the development of this ever-popular species.

★**Annapolis Tidal Generating Station** – *On the Causeway (Rte. 1). Visitor centre open daily mid-Jun–late Aug 8am–8pm. Mid-May–early Jun & Sept–mid-Oct daily 10am–5pm. ♿ P ☎902-532-5454.* North America's first tidal power project, this station uses a low-head, straight-flow turbine generator to harness the enormous energy of the Bay of Fundy tides to produce electricity.

The exhibit area upstairs in the visitor centre explains the project and its construction through models, photographs and a video presentation *(10min)*. A causeway over the dam affords views of tidal activity and of the generating station.

EXCURSIONS

★**North Hills Museum** – *In Granville Ferry on road to Port Royal. Open Jun–mid-Oct Mon–Sat 9:30am–5:30pm, Sun 1pm–5:30pm. Contribution requested.* ♿ *www.ednet.ns.ca/educ/museum/* ☎*902-532-2168.* Despite a series of modifications, this small wood-framed 18C house has retained a pioneer look. It provides a fitting setting for the predominantly 18C antique collection of a retired Toronto banker. Bequeathed to the province upon his death in 1974, the collection includes English furniture, ceramics, silver and Georgian glass.

★★**Port Royal Habitation** – *10km/6mi from Annapolis Royal Causeway.* The *habitation* (French word for "dwelling") is a replica of Canada's first European settlement of any permanence. This collection of dark, weathered, fortified buildings joined around a central courtyard was designed in a style reminiscent of 16C French farms by **Samuel de Champlain** (1567-1635), captain and navigator of the expedition of Sieur de Monts.

Granted permission by Henry IV of France to set up a colony and develop the fur trade, de Monts began his expedition to the New World in 1604. The first winter in Canada was spent on an island in the St. Croix River *(map p 242)*—a poor choice, as it was cut off from the fresh food of the mainland by the Bay of Fundy's storms and ice. The next year, the company moved to the Annapolis Basin where the habitation was reconstructed. Boredom and sickness prompted Champlain to form a social club wherein members alternated as grand master and organizers of gourmet feasts. In 1606 member Marc Lescarbot wrote the first play performed in Canada, the **Theatre of Neptune**. The **Order of Good Cheer**, as the club was called proved successful. Crops were grown, and trade with the Indians was established. Just as the settlement seemed rooted, de Monts' trading rights were revoked in 1607, and the expedition returned to France. Destroyed in 1613 by English forces the buildings were reconstructed in 1938 by the Canadian government, using Champlain's sketch and writings as guides.

Visit – *Open mid-May–mid-Oct daily 9am–6pm. $2.75.* ♿ *www.parkscanada.pch.gc.ca* ☎*902-532-2898.* Over the gateway entry hangs the **coat of arms** of France and Navarre, ruled by King Henry IV (French kings held the additional title of King of Navarre from 1589 until the French Revolution). A **well** with a shingled roof stands in the middle of the courtyard. Around it are the residences of the governor, priest and artisans. The kitchen, blacksmith's shop, community room where the Order met, and the chapel can be visited as can the storerooms, wine cellar and trading room where Indians brought their furs. All furnishings are meticulous reproductions of early-17C styles.

Each structure has a steeply pitched roof and, except for the storeroom, a fieldstone chimney. A building technique known as **colombage**, the term used in France for log-filled wooden frame construction, was employed to form the walls. This construction can be appreciated only from the interior, since the exterior of the buildings is covered with lapped boarding. No nails or spikes join the timbers: they are mortised and tenoned and pinned together.

★**Kejimkujik National Park** – *Rte. 8. From Annapolis Royal 48km/30mi to park entrance, near Maitland Bridge. Open mid-Jun–Labour Day daily 8:30am–9pm. Rest of the year daily 8:30am–4:30pm. $3. Visitor centre open same hours as park. Hiking, cycling, swimming, canoeing, cross-country skiing. Canoe & bicycle rental at Jakes Landing.* △♿ *http: //parkscanada.pch.gc.ca* ☎*902-682-2772.* Recreation and beauty await visitors to this 381sq km/147sq mi forest with its accessible lakes and plentiful wildlife. For centuries the park's waterways served the Micmac Indians as canoe routes and still afford peaceful passage through largely untouched wilderness.

The **Mill Falls** hiking trail leads through fern-filled woods along the amber **Mersey River** to its foamy rapids. The viewing tower *(on main park road, 10km/6mi from park entrance)* permits an elevated **view**★ of lovely Kejimkujik Lake.

ANNAPOLIS VALLEY★★

Maps pp 230-231

Flowing 112km/70mi southwest to the sea, the Annapolis River widens into the **Annapolis Basin**, a tidal lake connected to the Bay of Fundy by a narrow outlet known as Digby Gut. The area commonly referred to as the Annapolis Valley includes other rivers and extends approximately 160km/100mi from Digby to Windsor on the Minas Basin. Some of the earliest French colonists settled in this region, only to be deported by the British in 1755 *(p 232)*. The Acadians built dikes to reclaim the marshland for agricultural production. In addition, the valley is sheltered on both sides from heavy wind and fog by the North and South Mountains, a feature that has nurtured the valley's famed **apple orchards**. Today other fruits and crops are also grown in the fertile soil, while dairy cattle graze the meadows bordering the river.

FROM DIGBY TO WINDSOR *2 days. 168km/104mi.*

Digby – From this waterfront town, home of the famous scallop, ferries cross to New Brunswick. The harbour is often busy with fishing fleets. Local restaurants feature **Digby scallops** prepared in a variety of ways.

Take Hwy. 101 and then Rte. 1.

Highway 101 follows the shore of the Annapolis Basin with pleasant views until it turns inland at Deep Brook, where Route 1 continues along the shoreline.

★**Annapolis Royal** – *1/2 day. Description* *p 251.*

Remains of the old French dike system can be seen from the road. Route 1 crosses the river and continues through country that becomes more rural. Wide meadows line the riverbanks. At **Bridgetown**★ elm-shaded streets contain fine houses, many built by Loyalists. **Lawrencetown** and **Middleton** are similarly graced with trees. Apple orchards line the hills, particularly between Kingston and Waterville, where fruit-selling stands and "U-pick" farms are common. This drive is especially lovely in apple blossom time *(late May or early June).*

Continue 14km/9mi on Rte. 1 to junction with Rte. 358.

★★**Excursion to Cape Split** – *28km/17mi north by Rte. 358.*

★**Prescott House Museum** – *In Starr's Point, off Rte. 358, about 5km/3mi north of Rte. 1. Open Jun–mid-Oct Mon–Sat 9:30am–5:30pm, Sun 1pm–5:30pm. Contribution requested. ♿ www.ednet.ns.ca/educ/museum/ ☎902-542-3984.* This attractive whitewashed-brick house, set in lovely grounds, was built in the early 19C by **Charles Prescott**, legislator, successful merchant and acclaimed horticulturalist. On this estate Prescott experimented with new strains of wheat, planted nut trees, grapes and pear trees and introduced many varieties of cherries and apples. He gave away cuttings to valley farmers and is partly responsible for the development of the apple industry in this area.

The interior is attractively furnished with some original pieces. A pleasant **sun room** was added by Prescott's great-granddaughter. The **garden** is also worth visiting.

Return to Rte. 358 and continue north.

★★**The Lookoff** – *Approximately 14km/9mi north of Starr's Point. Follow the signs on Rte. 358. Watch for paved pull-off with steel barricade.* Although there is no official marker for this site, one cannot pass by without stopping. The **view**★★ of Annapolis Valley is magnificent: a 180-degree sweep of patterned farmlands reaching toward the vast Minas Basin, interrupted only by the South Mountain in the distance. At least four counties are visible from this popular vantage point.

About 8km/5mi north of The Lookoff, as Route 358 descends into the tiny community of Scots Bay, there is a lovely **view**★ of this bay, the Minas Channel and the Parrsboro Shore of Nova Scotia. At Little Cove boats can be seen resting on the channel bottom at low tide.

Cape Split – *Rte. 358 ends. Hiking trail 13km/8mi through woods to tip of cape.* This hook of forested land juts into the Bay of Fundy, edged by magnificent cliffs. Since the tides constantly ebb and flow, the bay's waters in the Minas Channel are muddied. From road's end there are **views** of the wide bay, the shoreline of the cape and the Parrsboro Shore.

Return via Rte. 358. After about 9km/6mi take the unpaved road on the left (Stewart Mountain Rd.). At junction turn left. Road terminates at provincial park. Follow signs. Hiking trails for Cape Blomidon are shown on the panel in the visitor parking lot.

★**Blomidon** – As the road leaves the woods and descends into flatlands, the first **view**★ of the Minas Basin is grand. The patchwork farmlands of this rural coastland stretch to the cliffs of the basin. Bright red barns and two-storey farmhouses dot the landscape, dominated by the reddish cliffs of Cape Blomidon. From the end of the picnic area, the **views**★★ in both directions of the wide red beach (at low tide), and the stratified pinkish red cliffs, contrasted with the blue waters of the basin, are breathtaking.

At Blomidon junction, continue south via Pereau and Delhaven to Rte. 221.

About 2km/1.2mi south of the junction, there is a **view**★ from Pereaux Small Crafts Harbour of the hole in a rock formation known locally as **Paddys Island**, fully visible at low tide.

At the junction with Rte. 221, turn right to Canning for Rte. 358 back to Rte. 1.

★**Wolfville** – This charming town with shaded streets and heritage properties is home to Acadia University, founded 1838. Several mansions have been converted into wayside inns. Boutiques and eateries line the main thoroughfare, and during college sessions, the community is alive with scurrying students.

★**Grand-Pré National Historic Site** – *Just north of Rte. 1, 4km/2.5mi east of Wolfville.* Inhabited between 1680 and 1755, the former Acadian village of Grand-Pré (French for "great meadow") has been transformed into a spacious park overlooking the flat dikelands the early settlers reclaimed. The well-maintaine expanse of hedged lawns, flowerbeds and large shade trees serves as a permaner memorial to the Acadians.

Before Deportation, Grand-Pré was the most important Acadian settlement in Nov Scotia, with about 200 farms along the edge of the Minas Basin. Residents wh had moved here from Port Royal *(p 252)* realized the richness of the soil covere by the sea at high tide. They constructed a system of **dikes** to keep the sea ou while marsh water was allowed to escape through floodgates. The cultivated lan soon supported crops, livestock and orchards. After Deportation, the farmland were given to planters from New England, and later to Loyalists.

The American poet **Henry Wadsworth Longfellow** chose Grand-Pré as the setting for hi poem *Evangeline.* Published in 1847, the work describes a young couple's sepa ration during Deportation and Evangeline's subsequent search throughout th eastern US for her lover Gabriel—only to find him dying. Symbolic of the traged of Deportation, the poem has become part of popular Acadian culture.

Visit – *Open mid-May–mid-Oct daily 9am–6pm. $2.50.* ♿ P *☎902-542-3631.* O the site of the first church of Grand-Pré stands a small **chapel** in a setting of maple horse chestnut and willow trees. Completed in 1930, the chapel is constructed o local stone in a style reminiscent of churches in France. Inside, there are **display** illustrating Acadian settlement, the British takeover, and the final Deportation. A bronze **statue** of Evangeline by **Louis-Philippe Hébert** stands on the grounds.

Windsor – Famous as the home of Thomas Haliburton, one of the foremost Nov Scotians of his day, the town is set at the confluence of the Avon and St. Croi Rivers. The Avon is sealed off from the Bay of Fundy by a causeway. A shippin point for lumber and gypsum mined nearby, the community was once the site o the 18C Acadian settlement of Piziquid, which was taken over by New Englander after Deportation and renamed Windsor.

★ **Haliburton House** – *On Clifton Ave. Follow signs from causeway. Open Jun–mid-Oc Mon–Sat 9:30am–5:30pm, Sun 1pm–5:30pm. Contribution requested. ☎902 798-2915.* At the end of a long, impressive drive stands this house, built in 183 on the tree-covered estate of **Thomas Chandler Haliburton** (1796-1865), famous as th creator of **Sam Slick**, a fictitious Yankee peddler.

Judge, legislator, author and humorist of international renown, Haliburton starte publishing stories in 1836 under the title, *The Clockmaker; or, The Sayings an Doings of Samuel Slick of Slickville.* Slick travelled all over Nova Scotia, making fu of its unenterprising inhabitants. Many of the epigrams he coined are still in us today: "six of one and half a dozen of the other," "an ounce of prevention is wort a pound of cure," "facts are stranger than fiction," "the early bird gets the worm," "as quick as a wink," and "jack of all trades and master of none" are among th most familiar.

The interior of the house with its spacious entry hall, elegant dining room an sitting room reflects the man.

Shand House Museum – *Avon St. Street parking prohibited. Upon entrance to Windsor, watch for signs to separate parking area. Uphill walk to house. Open Jun–mid-Oc Mon–Sat 9:30am–5:30pm, Sun 1pm–5:30pm. Contribution requested. www.ednet.ns.ca/educ/museum/ ☎902-798-8213.* The most imposing of the houses atop Ferry Hill overlooking the Avon River, this Victorian dwelling was completed in 1891. The staircase is of cherry, and several rooms have oak interiors. Furnishings are those of the original and only owners. Visitors can ascend the square tower.

Fort Edward – *Off King St. near causeway. Grounds open year-round. Fort open Jul–Aug daily 10am–4pm. Sept 11am–3pm.* P *www.parkscanada.pch.gc.ca ☎902-532-2321.* Possessing the oldest blockhouse in Canada, this fort is situated on a hillock at the edge of town. Built in 1750 as a British stronghold in Acadian territory, it was later a point of departure for Acadians assembled for deportation. From the grassy fortification, there are **views** of the tidal river, the causeway and Lake Pesaquid in the distance. Made of squared timbers, the dark wooden **blockhouse** is the only remaining building of the fort. The walls of its two storeys—the upper storey overhanging the lower—are pierced by square portholes for cannon and loopholes for musket fire. Inside, there are displays on the blockhouse defence system and the fort's history.

Teahouses are common in many Canadian towns and cities. "Afternoon tea" can consist of cake and a cup of hot tea or the traditional repast of Britain's "high tea," complete with scones, finger sandwiches and crumpets.

ATLANTIC SHORE★★

Map pp 230-231

ova Scotia's eastern shore is known for its rugged coastline, granite coves, sandy eaches, pretty fishing villages and attractive tree-lined towns with elegant houses uilt from shipbuilding or privateering fortunes. The entire coast from Canso to Yarnouth can be followed by road, but a greater concentration of quaint seaside ommunities is found south of Halifax.

FROM HALIFAX TO LIVERPOOL *3 days. 348km/216mi. Map p 256.*

★★ **Halifax** – *2 days. Description p 262.*

Leave Halifax by Rte. 3. Turn left on Rte. 333.

As the coast is approached, the landscape becomes wild, almost desolate. Huge boulders left by retreating glaciers, and stunted vegetation give the area a lunar appearance. *Fog is least common mid-July to October, but can occur any time.*

★★ **Peggy's Cove** – Immortalized by artists and photographers across Canada, this tiny village is unique among coastal communities, set as it is on a treeless outcropping of massive, deeply lined boulders. Its tranquil harbour, with colourful boats and fishing shacks built on stilts over the water, is indeed picturesque. Housing an operating post office *(seasonal)*, the **lighthouse** stands alone on a huge granite slab pounded by the Atlantic Ocean. *Sudden high waves and slippery boulders have resulted in personal tragedy. Use extreme caution when walking in this area.*

Upon departing, be sure to note the **carvings** of village residents sculpted in the granite rock by William deGarthe (1907-83).

The road follows the coast with views of the villages on **St. Margarets Bay**.

© Dick Dietrich

Peggy's Cove

Rte. 333 joins Rte. 3 at Upper Tantallon; follow Rte. 3 until Rte. 329 turns off after Hubbards. Tour the peninsula and rejoin Rte. 3 just before Chester.

★ **Chester** – Perched on cliffs rising out of Mahone Bay, this charming town has beautiful elm and oak trees and traditional New England frame houses. Founded by New Englanders in 1759, the community is a popular summer residence of Americans and a favourite retirement spot for Canadians.

Take Rte. 12 north, 7km/4mi after Chester.

★ **Ross Farm** – Kids *24km/15mi one way. Open Jun–mid-Oct daily 9:30am–5:30pm. Early Jan–mid-Mar weekends only 9:30am–4:30pm. $5. ☎ 902-689-2210.* Cleared from wilderness in 1816 by William Ross, this farm belonged to five generations of his family before acquisition by the Nova Scotia Museum Complex. Maintained as a living museum of 19C agrarian life, the farm features coopering, candle making, forging, sheep shearing and other demonstrations that vary with the season. There are displays of plows and harrows, buggies and other transport, including a well-stocked peddler's wagon. Horse-drawn wagon rides are available.

Return to Rte. 3.

★ **Mahone Bay** – Founded in 1754 by Capt. Ephraim Cook, the community was once a centre of piracy and privateering. Today this placid town is distinguished by three neighbouring churches lining the bay of the same name. Between 1756 and 1815 hundreds of small ships sailed from Nova Scotia ports to harass French, Spanish, Dutch and American vessels, from New England to the Caribbean. These acts of piracy were carried out with royal blessing. After obtaining a license, a privateer owner could attack only enemy ships. All prizes had to be taken to Halifax where the Court of Vice Admiralty decided their legality. Despite these restrictions, profits were enormous and coastal communities prospered.

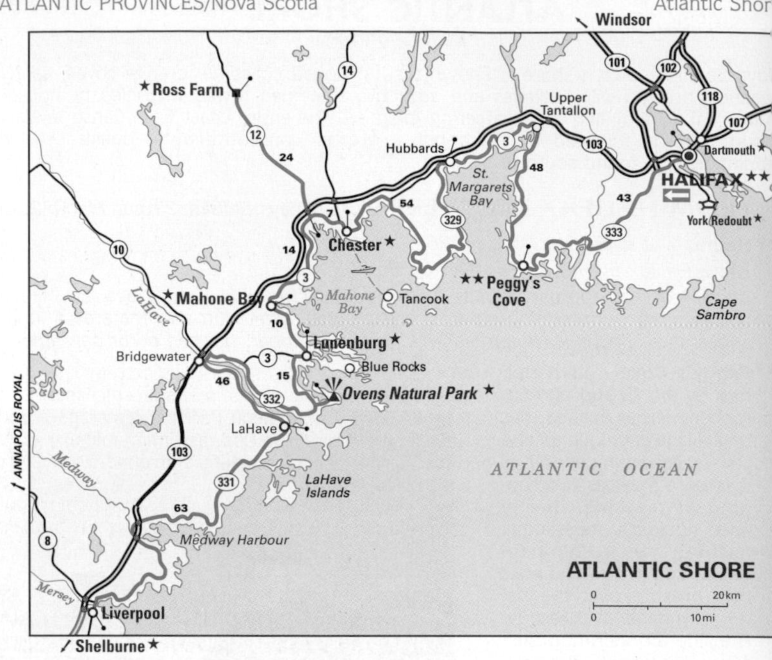

Upon approaching the town, there is a lovely **view★** of the churches reflected in the water. Shops and restaurants, elegant frame houses and churches are set along tree-lined streets close to the bay.

Follow Rte. 3 south 10km/6mi.

★**Lunenburg** – Situated on a hilly peninsula with "front" and "back" harbours, picturesque Lunenburg is named for the northern German hometown (Lüneburg) of the first settlers who arrived in 1753. Colourful historic houses grace the grid-patterned streets rising from the waterfront.

Once a pirates' haven, the town was sacked by American privateers in 1782. Known for its former shipbuilding industry, Lunenburg was the construction site of many schooners that fished the "banks" *(p 274)*, including the **Bluenose**, undefeated champion of the North American fishing fleet and winner of four international schooner races from 1921 to 1938. The **Bluenose II**, a replica of the original *(p 264)*, was also constructed here in 1963 and offers seasonal **cruises** when in port *(departs from Fisheries Museum Jun–Sept daily 9:30am & 1pm; round-trip 2hrs; $20; ♿ Bluenose II Preservation Trust ☎ 902-634-1963 or 800-763-1963, Canada/US)*.

Every August the popular **Fisheries Exhibition and Fishermen's Reunion** is celebrated in Lunenburg. Dory, yacht and schooner races, fish-filleting and scallop-shucking contests, parades and displays are featured.

★★**Fisheries Museum of the Atlantic** – Kids *Lunenburg harbour. Open Jun–mid-Oct daily 9:30am–5:30pm. Rest of the year Mon–Fri 8:30am–4:30pm. $7.* ✕ ♿ *www.ednet.ns.ca/educ/museum/fma ☎ 902-634-4794.* Housed in a former fish-processing plant on the waterfront, this three-storey centre features a wide array of maritime displays. Exhibits range from the history of the Bluenose, and the illicit "rum-running" trade during Prohibition to the development of the banks fishery. A sailmaker's workshop and a 1920s fish company office have been re-created, and ship models, tools and navigational equipment are on display. A theatre *(regularly scheduled films)*, working dory shop and aquarium complete the museum.

Moored at the wharf, the **Theresa E. Connor**, one of the last saltbank schooners to fish the Grand Banks, can be boarded. Built in 1938, the vessel has been refurbished to illustrate the era of dory fishing when small, two-manned boats (dories) would haul in fish using trawl lines. The fish were salted on board a schooner, aptly called a "saltbanker," which served as a supply and delivery base. Characteristic of craft that replaced dory schooners, the steel-hulled side trawler, **Cape Sable**, can also be boarded. Built in Holland in 1962, this boat hauled trawl nets off Lunenburg until 1982. A replica of a shucking house shelters equipment and mounted scallop shells.

Follow Rte. 3 and turn left on Rte. 332 for 15km/9mi. Turn left at Feltzen South and right on Ovens Rd.

★**Ovens Natural Park** – *Open mid-May–mid-Oct daily 8:30am–dusk. $5.* ⛺ ✕ ♿ *www.ovenspark.com ☎ 902-766-4621.* The park has a lovely site, which offers **views★** across Lunenburg Bay to Blue Rocks. A path along the cliff top leads to several sets of stairs by which visitors can descend to see the oven-like caves, cut into the cliffs by the action of the sea.

Continue on Rte. 332 and then left on Rte. 3.

The road follows the wide and tranquil estuary of LaHave River. Boats can be seen along this stretch of water lined with frame houses and trees. The river is crossed at **Bridgewater**, a large, industrial town.

Turn left on Rte. 331.

The road passes the town of **LaHave** itself, one of the earliest settlements in the province. Isaac de Razilly, Lieutenant-Governor of Acadie, built a fort here in 1632. The road continues along the coast with many pleasant views of the sea and fishing villages, especially in the vicinity of **Medway Harbour**.

Liverpool – Founded in 1760 by New Englanders, Liverpool, like its great English namesake, is on the Mersey River. The privateering, fishing and ship repairing of the past have largely been supplanted by the modern industries of papermaking, fish processing and machine building.

★**Perkins House Museum** – *On Main St. Open Jun–mid-Oct Mon–Sat 9:30am–5:30pm, Sun 1pm–5pm. Contribution requested. www.ednet.ns.ca/educ/museum/ ☎902-354-4058.* This low-lying New England frame house, with odd-shaped corners and winding hidden stairs, was built in 1767 for Col. Simeon Perkins. A merchant and ship owner, Perkins moved to Nova Scotia from Cape Cod, assuming military, judicial and legislative roles beyond his business and family life. Surrounded by other elegant residences, the house is set in fine gardens among tall trees.

On display next door in the Queens County Museum is a copy of the colonel's diary, which captures life in a colonial town from 1766 to 1812.

EXCURSION TO SHELBURNE

★**Shelburne** – *64km/38mi south by Hwy. 103. Exit 25. Tourist bureau on Dock St. ☎902-875-4547.* Founded by Loyalists in 1783, this small waterfront town was once one of the largest 18C cities in North America. The community's population swelled to an estimated 10,000 when additional British sympathizers sought sanctuary in Nova Scotia from the American Revolution. The expansion was short-lived, however, since many settlers moved elsewhere.
Historic homes and commercial buildings line Dock Street, former hub of the town's bustling mercantile activity. Work continues at the barrel factory and in the **Dory Shop Museum**, a museum spotlighting the dory's historical importance and method of construction *(open Jun–Sept daily 9:30am–5:30pm; $2. www.ednet.ns.ca/educ/museum/ ☎902-875-3219).*

★**Ross-Thomson House and Store Museum** – *Charlotte Lane. Open Jun–mid-Oct daily 9:30am–5:30pm. $2. www.ednet.ns.ca/educ/museum/ ☎902-875-3141.* This two-storey structure was in use by 1785 as a combination house, store and warehouse for items of international trade. Note the two roof shapes: gambrel and gable. Visitors can tour the well-stocked interior of the old store as well as the residence. Seasonal flower and herb gardens grace the front entrance.

BALMORAL MILLS★

Map p 231

Standing beside a stream in a pleasant valley, this fully operational **gristmill** was built in 1874. Although commercial use ceased in 1954, the mill has been completely restored.

VISIT *1hr*

10km/6mi southeast of Tatamagouche by Rte. 311. Grounds open year-round. Gristmill museum open Jun–mid-Oct Mon–Sat 9:30am–5:30pm, Sun 1pm–5:30pm. Contribution requested. ♿ www.ednet.ns.ca/educ/museum/ ☎902-657-3016. When in operation *(a few hours daily)*, the mill is a hive of activity. Weighing over a tonne, the original millstones grind barley, oats, wheat and buckwheat into flour and meal *(for sale)*. The grain is moved from storey to storey by means of a series of buckets mounted on leather belts. Various milling processes are explained. Below the mill the revolving waterwheel can be seen.

EXCURSION

Sutherland Steam Mill Museum – *In Denmark, 10km/6mi northeast by Rte. 311, minor road and Rte. 326. Open Jun–mid-Oct Mon–Sat 9:30–5:30pm, Sun 1pm–5:30pm. Contribution requested. www.ednet.ns.ca/educ/museum/ ☎902-657-3365.* When Alexander Sutherland built this sawmill in 1894, steam was replacing water power as the most efficient means of cutting wood. He made sleighs, carriages and sleds; his brother and partner produced doors and windows for local houses. All machinery is in working order, and the mill "steams up" once a month *(phone ahead for schedule).*

CABOT TRAIL★★

Map p 260

Named for explorer John Cabot, who is reputed to have landed at the northern tip c
Cape Breton Island in 1497, this route is one of the most beautiful drives in easter
North America. Opened in 1936 the paved, two-lane highway makes a circle tour c
the northern part of the island.
Initially traversing tranquil farmland, the trail then hugs the coast and winds up an
down, providing scenic views of the immense Atlantic Ocean, craggy mountains, rock
inlets, magnificent headlands and dense forests. Some areas are reminiscent of th
Scottish Highlands, ancestral home of many of the island's inhabitants. The east coas
is especially rich in Gaelic culture. Derived from the language of the Celts in Irelan
and the Scottish Highlands, Gaelic was the third most common European languag
spoken in Canada in the early 19C, and can still be heard here today.

Cabot Trail, Cape Breton Island

DRIVING TOUR *Allow 2 days*

Round-trip of 301km/187mi from Baddeck. The trail can be driven in either direction, but visitors may prefer clockwise travel for the security of hugging the mountainside during steep, curvy stretches.

★Baddeck

Overlooking Baddeck Bay, this charming village is the starting point of the Cabot Trail. The popular resort town has a lovely **site★★** on the north shore of **Bras d'Or Lake**. This immense inland sea nearly cuts Cape Breton in two and is fed in the north by the Atlantic via two channels, the Great Bras d'Or and the Little Bras d'Or on either side of Boularderie Island. Bras d'Or Lake's resemblance to a Scottish loch has attracted many settlers of Scottish origin to its shores. Among them was **Alexander Graham Bell** (1847-1922), humanitarian, researcher and prolific inventor.

★★ **Alexander Graham Bell National Historic Site** – *On Hwy. 205 in Baddeck.* Bell's favourite shape, the tetrahedron, is used extensively in the design of this fascinating museum. Exhibits illustrate the genius of this remarkable man. A number of films and videos are shown during peak season.
In 1885 Bell first visited Baddeck, where he was to conduct much of his aeronautical work. Eventually he chose the location for his summer residence, naming his home *Beinn Bhreagh*, "beautiful mountain" in Gaelic. His work as a teacher of the deaf led to the invention of the telephone, conceived in Brantford, Ontario, in 1874, and tested in Boston the following year. The discovery brought him fame and the capital to continue other research. In Baddeck he built kites and heavier-than-air craft, using combinations of the tetrahedron shape—an almost perfect form because it is lightweight but strong. In 1907, with other pioneer aviators, he founded the Aerial Experiment Assn. and sponsored the first manned flight in Canada when the **Silver Dart** flew across Baddeck Bay in 1909. Before his death, he witnessed his hydrofoil craft reach the incredible speed (for 1919) of 114km/70mph on Bras d'Or Lake.

Visit – *Open Jun daily 9am–6pm. Jul–Aug daily 8:30am–7:30pm. Sept–mid-Oct daily 8:30am–6pm. Rest of the year daily 9am–5pm. $3.75. www.cbisland.com ☎902-295-2069.* There are models of the telephone, the vacuum jacket (a forerunner of the iron lung), the surgical probe (a device used prior to the invention of the X ray) and Bell's kites. His project to prevent stranded sailors from dying of thirst at sea is on view—a model for converting fog to drinking water, using breath and salt water. A highlight is the superb **photograph collection**, oversized black-and-white prints of Bell's life and work. One wing of the museum is devoted to his hydrofoil, the HD-4. Both the original hull and a reconstruction of the entire craft are on exhibit. From the museum's rooftop garden, there is a **view** of the wooded headland across Baddeck Bay. *Beinn Bhreagh (not open to the public)*, Bell's Canadian estate, can be seen among the trees.

★From Baddeck to Chéticamp *88km/55mi*

The Cabot Trail follows the valley of the Middle River, passes the Lakes O'Law and joins the Margaree River's lush green **valley★** of meadows and abundant salmon pools, reputed to offer some of Canada's finest salmon fishing.

North East Margaree – Located in the heart of salmon-fishing country, the tiny rural community has a museum of note.

★**Margaree Salmon Museum** – *Open mid-Jun–mid-Oct daily 9am–5pm. $1. ☎902-248-2848.* This pleasant little museum features a large collection of colourful fishing flies and rods—one actually 5.5m/18ft long, made in Scotland in 1880. Fishing tackle on display includes a sampling of illegal spears used by poachers. The life cycle of the Atlantic salmon is illustrated from birth to a full-grown adult's return trip upriver to reproduce. Unlike its Pacific cousin, the Atlantic salmon can make several such trips.

The Cabot Trail parallels the Margaree River northward, affording pastoral **views★** of the wide river valley and the town of East Margaree on the opposite side. The sudden vista of the wide expanse of the sea, after the road ascends out of farmland, is dramatic. Upon descent the **view★** of Margaree Harbour is lovely. The trail crosses the estuary of the Margaree River and heads north along the Acadian coast, with views of the Gulf of St. Lawrence.

Chéticamp – An enclave of Acadian culture, this fishing community sprawls along the coast opposite Chéticamp Island. A protected harbour and a large stone church dedicated to St. Peter distinguish the town. The Acadian tricolour flag *(p 248)* can be seen atop flagpoles scattered throughout the town. Locally made hand-hooked rugs are Chéticamp's claim to fame.

Acadian Museum – *Open May–Oct daily 7am–10pm. Rest of the year Tue & Fri 1pm–3pm. ☎902-224-2170.* Operated by a cooperative of Acadian women, the museum and gift shop feature a large array of hooked mats, rugs and other crafted items. There are demonstrations of hooking, spinning, carding and weaving. The on-site dining room specializes in Acadian cooking.

From Chéticamp to Cape Smokey *124km/77mi*

★★**Cape Breton Highlands National Park** – Spanning coast to coast across northern Cape Breton, this 950sq km/367sq mi wilderness park combines seashore and mountains. Hills ascend directly from the ocean to form a tableland more than 500m/1700ft high.

The west coast borders the relatively calm waters of the Gulf of St. Lawrence. On the eastern side, the Atlantic Ocean pounds the bare rocks with great force, yet there are several fine beaches throughout this preserve. Whales, and even bald eagles, can be found on either shore.

Inland, the park is heavily forested and boggy—the realm of moose, lynx and snowshoe hare. Several trails reach the interior *(details from the park office)*, but the main attraction is the beautiful coastline.

Visit – *Open year-round. $3.50 entry fee. Hiking, picknicking, swimming. Information office (open mid-May–Jun daily 9am–5pm; Jul–Labour Day daily 8am–6pm; mid-Sept–mid-Oct daily 9am–5pm) at park entrances north of Chéticamp ☎902-224-2306 and at Ingonish Beach ☎902-285-2691 (year-round). There are many designated lookouts within the park along Cabot Trail.* From the park entrance at the Chéticamp River, Cabot Trail winds up Chéticamp Canyon to emerge on the coast and parallel the sea. Fine **views★★** of the ocean and the road weaving up and down in the distance are afforded. From **Cap Rouge** lookout, there is an especially lovely **view★★**. The road gradually climbs French Mountain and heads inland across the plateau, the highest point on the highway.

After crossing several deep stream-lined valleys, the road descends to Mackenzie Mountain. Then, by a series of switchbacks, it reaches Pleasant Bay with outstanding **views★★** on the descent. The **Lone Shieling**, a tiny hut of stone with rounded corners and a thatched roof *(about 6.5km/4mi from Pleasant Bay, then short*

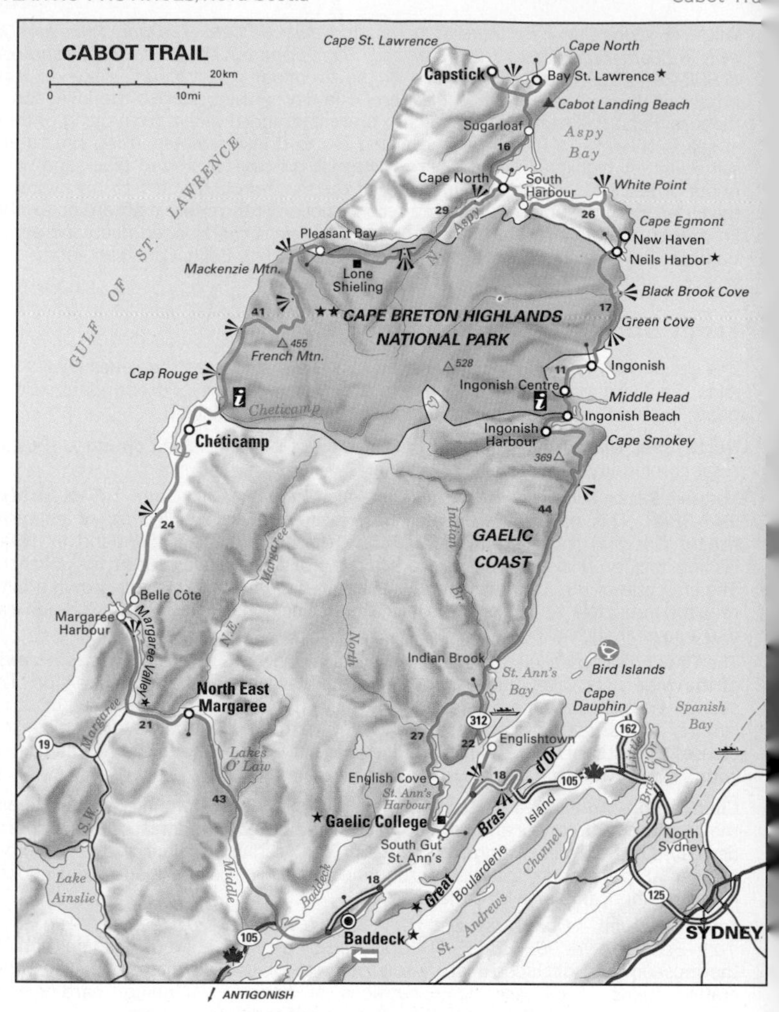

walk), is a replica of a Scottish crofter's cottage, common in the Highlands and islands of Scotland. It was built to form a visible link between the adopted home of the Highland Scots who settled Cape Breton and their ancestral land.

Along its course Cabot Trail first climbs over North Mountain, descends steeply, allowing pretty **views★**, and then enters the valley of the North Aspy River, which it follows to the village of **Cape North**.

★★ **Bay St. Lawrence** – *Excursion: 38km/24mi round-trip from Cape North.* This scenic drive rounds Aspy Bay with views of its long sandbar, and then heads inland across grassy hills spotted with pink rock to St. Lawrence Bay at the north end of Cape Breton Island. Before leaving the bay, the road passes Cabot Landing Beach, supposedly the first North American landfall of John Cabot. Whether visited by Cabot or not, it is a refreshing scene of a long beach backed by Sugarloaf Mountain.

At the end of the road is the tiny fishing village of **Bay St. Lawrence★** built around a small lake with a narrow exit to the sea. Upon the approach to the village, a large white clapboard church (St. Margaret's) is prominent. From its grounds the **view★** of the bay community is picturesque. The church's fine wooden interior has a ceiling shaped like the hull of a ship.

Upon leaving Bay St. Lawrence, turn right and continue 3km/1.8mi to Capstick.

Capstick – Less populous than Bay St. Lawrence, this hillside settlement consists of a few isolated houses on the grassy slopes above the seacliffs. The dramatic **views★** of the inlets through the scraggy pines are enhanced by the beauty of the water's colour.

Return to Cabot Trail. After South Harbour, take coast road.

Revealing fine **views★** of Aspy Bay, its sand bar and the long Cape North peninsula, this coastal route is a pretty drive. The road turns south after White Point through the charming fishing villages of **New Haven** and **Neils Harbour★**, the latter with an artificial harbour beside a sandy bay.

Rejoin Cabot Trail.

This section of the trail is an especially splendid drive along the coast, particularly after **Black Brook Cove**. Worn, pink boulders stretch into the sea, while green forests cover the inlands. There are many little bays and coves, **Green Cove** being one of the loveliest. From Lakie's Head lookout the narrow peninsula of **Middle Head** and towering Cape Smokey can be identified, sometimes rising from a mist reminiscent of the Scottish Highlands.

The Ingonishs – The relative solitude of the trail is left behind in the resort area of Ingonish Centre, Ingonish Beach, Ingonish Harbour and other Ingonish designations, popular for various forms of recreation *(fishing, boating, swimming, golf, tennis and winter skiing)*. Many cruise ships stop over at the harbour.
The bay itself is cut into two parts—north and south—by Middle Head, the dramatic setting of the **Keltic Lodge**, one of Canada's best known resort hotels. To the south **Cape Smokey** rises 369m/1,210ft out of the sea. This headland is at times partially obscured by cloud, hence its name.

The Gaelic Coast

From Cape Smokey to Baddeck – *89km/55mi.* The trail climbs over Cape Smokey and then drops again, permitting several good **views★**. Descending the coast farther inland, the road passes through several fishing villages.
Offshore are the **Bird Islands**, a sanctuary where vast numbers of sea birds nest in summer. The trail rounds St. Ann's Harbour, offering lovely views after Goose Cove, but especially at South Gut St. Ann's.

★**Gaelic College** – *In St. Ann's.* Founded in 1938 by Rev. A.W.R. MacKenzie, this school is the only one on the continent to teach the Gaelic language and Highland arts and crafts. Attracting youth from all over North America, the college offers courses in bagpipe music, clan law, Gaelic singing, Highland dancing and hand weaving of family and clan tartans. Students can often be seen performing Highland flings, sword dances and step dancing.
In August, a week-long **Gaelic Mod** is held when prizes are awarded to the best performers in each field *(for details, contact the college).*

Great Hall of the Clans – *On campus. Open Jun–Oct daily 8:30am–5pm. $2. ♿ www.gaeliccollege.edu ☎902-295-3411.* At the rear of the entrance is a room displaying Highlands pioneer crafts and memorabilia. Inside the large meeting hall, wall **exhibits** illustrate clan history and life. A variety of tartans and costumes are also on display. At one end of the hall stands a statue of Angus MacAskill (1825-63), the 236cm/7ft 9in tall,193kg/425lb "Cape Breton giant" who toured the US with the midget Tom Thumb.

★**Alternative Route** – *22km/14mi by Rte. 312 and Trans-Can Hwy.* This road enters St. Ann's Bay via a narrow spit of land that divides the bay from St. Ann's harbour. At the end of the spit, there is a ferry across the 270m/300yd outlet *(24hrs daily, every 5min; Feb–Apr no crossing if ice; $1.75/car; ☎902-929-2404).*

EXCURSIONS

★**Great Bras d'Or** – *Map p 260. 18km/11mi northeast along Trans-Can Hwy. from South Gut St. Ann's.* The road ascends Kelly's Mountain with a fine **view★** from the lookout of the harbour, spit of land and the ferry. Crossing Cape Dauphin peninsula, it descends to the Great Bras d'Or. There are good **views★** of this stretch of water, of the bridge that spans it, and, in the distance, of **Sydney**, Cape Breton's principal city and the site of eastern Canada's richest coalfields, which have fostered a sizeable steel industry.

★★**Miners' Museum** – *Map p 260. In Glace Bay, 19km/12mi northeast of Sydney. Follow museum signs from town to Quarry Point.* Overlooking the vast Atlantic Ocean from its 6ha/15 acre site, this low-lying, geometric museum stands as a monument to Cape Breton's coal-mining history.
Sprawling Glace Bay—home of the museum—has been a mining town since 1720 when French soldiers from Louisbourg found coal in the cliffs at Port Morien to the southeast. The region is underlain with bituminous coal seams that dip seaward under the Atlantic. By the late 19C numerous coal mines were operating. When iron ore deposits were found in nearby Newfoundland *(p 233)*, a steel industry mushroomed in the vicinity of Sydney, using coal as coke in the refining process. Immigrants poured into the area in the 20C for mining jobs. By the early 1950s, use of oil and gas had reduced the demand for coal. Economic depression hit as the mines began to close. The federal government created the Cape Breton Development Corp., which operated the Glace Bay colliery until 1984, when coal mining in the area ceased.

Visit – *Open Jun–Sept daily 10am–6pm (Tue 7pm). Rest of the year Mon–Fri 9am–4pm. $3.50 (guided mine tour an additional $3). Protective clothing provided. ✗ ♿ ☎902-849-4522.* The museum has well-presented, colourful exhibits

on coal formation and mining methods. Coal samples, equipment and transport ar also on display. Films *(20-30min)* about Cape Breton's mining industry and labou history are shown in the theatre.
Retired miners conduct **mine tours** *(30min)*, interspersing commentary with tale from personal experience. Visitors walk down a sloping tunnel under the Atlanti Ocean to see the machinery and coal face of the Ocean Deep Colliery. *Coal sample can be collected as souvenirs. Note: low mine ceilings may necessitate stooping fo periods of time.*
Beside the museum building, a **miners' village** has been reconstructed. The minin company supplied employee housing and owned the only store. Transactions wer based on credit secured against a miner's wages. After a week of work, a mine sometimes drew no pay, finding he owed for food, clothing and other necessities In addition to a store, a miner's house of the period 1850-1900 has been re created. The restaurant *(Jun–Labour Day)* serves home-cooked specialties such a "coal dust pie."

HALIFAX★★

Population 113,910
Map p 231
Tourist Office ☎902-421-8736

Situated on the east coast at about the mainland's midpoint, the capital of Nova Scotia overlooks one of the finest harbours in the world. The deep outer inlet of the Atlantic Ocean narrows into a protected inner harbour called the **Bedford Basin**. The foot-shaped peninsula upon which the city was built is dominated by a hill, topped with a star-shaped citadel. These two factors—a natural harbour and a man-made fortress—were the basis of the city's founding.

Historical Notes

Early History – Halifax came into being because of the existence of Louisbourg. New Englanders had successfully captured the French fortress in 1745, only to see it later returned to France. Their anger prodded the British government to build a fortress as a counterweight to Louisbourg. In July 1749 the appointed governor of Nova Scotia, Col. **Edward Cornwallis**, and about 2,500 English settlers constructed a fortified settlement on the site of the present-day city.
From its inception Halifax was a military stronghold filled with soldiers from the fort and sailors from numerous naval vessels docked in the harbour. From the social gatherings of the nobility (officers in both services) to the presence of brothels along the wharves, the military shaped the town. Indeed, even law was martial; citizens were deprived of control over their affairs for nearly 100 years, until Halifax achieved city status.

The Royal Princes – Forbidden by their father to remain in England, two scapegrace sons of **George III** made Halifax their home. The future **William IV** spent his 21st birthday in wild revels off the port. His brother **Edward**, Duke of Kent, and later the father of Queen Victoria, served as commander-in-chief in Halifax from 1794 to 1800. Spending a fortune on defences, he made Halifax a member of the famous quadrilateral of British defences, which included Gibraltar and Bermuda. A rigid disciplinarian, he had his men flogged or hanged for misdemeanours. He installed the first telegraph system in North America by which he could relay orders to his men from Annapolis Royal or from his love nest on the Bedford Basin, where his mistress lived.

The Halifax Explosion – The city's history has not always been so colourful, but its prosperity has coincided with times of war, whereas peace has often brought economic depression. The Napoleonic Wars, the American Civil War, World Wars I and II saw great military activity in Halifax, great wealth—and great tragedy.
During both world wars, the Bedford Basin was used as a convoy assembly point so ships could cross the Atlantic in the safety of numbers when German submarines were encountered. In December 1917 a Belgian relief ship, the **Imo**, had a fatal collision in the harbour with the **Mont Blanc**, a French munitions ship. The *Mont Blanc* was carrying a lethal combination of picric acid, guncotton, TNT and benzol. The explosion was the world's largest, until the atom bomb was dropped on Hiroshima in 1945. The entire north end of the city was wiped out; rail yards and docks were destroyed. Windows were shattered as far as Truro 100km/60mi away; the explosion was heard over 160km/100mi. Only the *Mont Blanc's* cannon (found in Albro Lake behind Dartmouth) and an anchor shaft (which landed more than 3km/2mi away) were left. Miraculously, the crew survived, having abandoned ship in time. However, 1,400 people were killed outright, an estimated 600 died later, 199 were blinded and another 9,000 were injured. There are people in Halifax today who, injured for life as children, are still receiving compensation.

he City Today – Halifax is the largest city in the Atlantic provinces and the region's ommercial and financial centre. Nova Scotia's administrative hub and an important entre for scientific research, Halifax is also a major commercial seaport and serves s the Atlantic base of the **Canadian Navy**. The 6.5km/4mi long outer habour inlet is ned with docks and piers where it narrows into the 5km/3mi long, 2.5km/1.5mi wide edford Basin. The port has two container terminals, a grain elevator, an automobile-andling facility and oil refineries for arriving tankers.

SIGHTS *2 days*

★★ Halifax Citadel – Situated on a hill overlooking the city's commercial district, the citadel is the fourth of forts dating to 1749 to occupy this site, with its commanding views of the area. The present star-shaped masonry structure is a repository of Halifax's military history and tradition.

Begun in 1828 at the order of the Duke of Wellington, the bastioned fort was not completed until 1856. Although never attacked, the fortification served the British Army until 1906 and the Canadian military until after World War II.

Easily approached from downtown, or driven around via Citadel Road, the citadel's site offers **views★** of the city, harbour, Dartmouth, George's Island and the Angus McDonald suspension bridge. Note the attractive **clock tower★**, the symbol of Halifax. Completed in 1803, the original was ordered by Prince Edward with four faces and bells to ring out the hours. Restored in 1962, it remains a memento to the punctilious prince.

Surrounded by a dry defensive ditch, the fortification contains a large central parade ground where soldiers attired in 19C uniforms perform military drills *(mid-Jun–Labour Day daily)*.

Visit – *Grounds open year-round. Citadel open mid-Jun–Aug daily 9am–6pm. Mid-May–early Jun & Sept–mid-Oct daily 9am–5pm. Admission fee.* ✗ P ☎ *902-426-5080.* This sprawling complex houses an orientation centre, barracks, powder magazines, a small museum and numerous other exhibits. Visitors can walk on the ramparts, look at guns that served as the citadel's main defence and visit the outer ditches and ravelins. An audio-visual presentation *(50min)*, **Tides of History★**, covers the history of Halifax and its defences.

★ Historic Properties and the Harbour – Off Upper Water Street, the pedestrian area between Duke Street and the Cogswell interchange is commonly known as Historic Properties. Completely renovated, several 19C stone warehouses and wooden buildings house interesting shops, studios, restaurants and pubs, with outdoor seating overlooking the harbour.

From Historic Properties visitors can walk west through a series of restored buildings to the Granville Street Mall and Scotia Square. A **boardwalk** follows the harbourfront north around the Sheraton Hotel and south past the Law Courts and

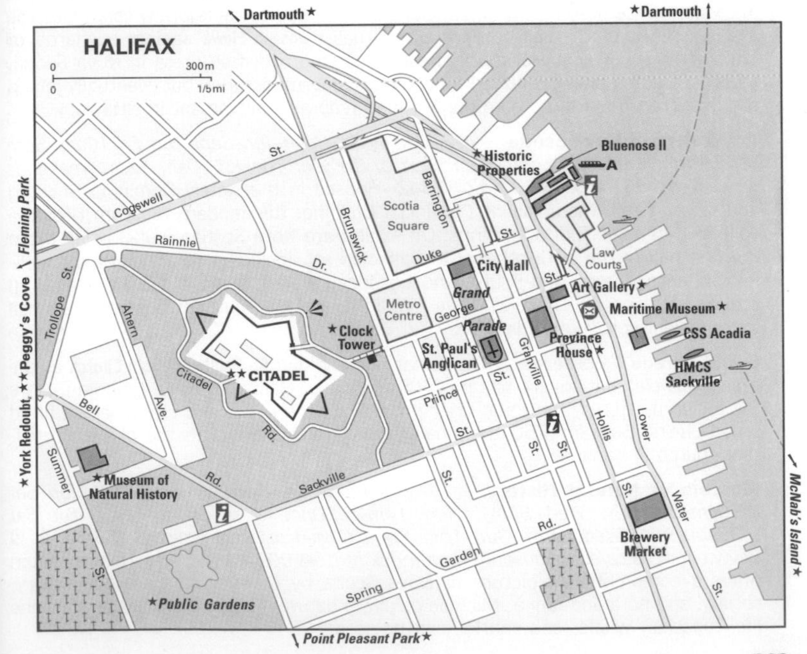

the terminus of the passenger ferry to Dartmouth to the **brewery market**. A forme brewery, the complex now houses several restaurants, shops and a farmers' marke *(Sat 7am–1pm)* within its restored interior courtyards.

★★ **Harbour Cruise** (**A**) – *Departs from Cable Wharf May–Oct daily from 9am. Round trip 2hrs. Commentary. $16.95 Murphy's on the Water Tour www.murphysonthewater.com 902-420-1015.* The *Haligonian III* cruise provide interesting commentary on the Halifax shipyards where 7,000 vessels were repaired during World War II; the naval dockyards with destroyers, preservers, submarines and other ships; the National Harbours Board terminal with its huge grain elevator; the container terminal where giant gantry cranes load odd-shaped ships specially constructed to carry containers; and other points of interest seen on the tour.

The cruise rounds Point Pleasant and enters the **North West Arm**★, a lovely stretch of water extending along the peninsula's west side and bordered by expensive homes and yacht clubs.

★ **Maritime Museum of the Atlantic** – *1675 Lower Water St. Open Jun–mid-Oct Mon–Sat 9:30am–5:30pm (Tue 8pm), Sun 1pm–5:30pm. Rest of the year Tue–Sat 9:30am–5pm (Tue 8pm), Sun 1pm–5pm. Closed Jan 1, Dec 25. $4.50. www.ednet.ns.ca/educ/museum/mma/ 902-424-7490.* Located on the waterfront with a view of Halifax Harbour, this interesting museum presents a variety of small craft, ship models, photographs and displays on maritime history. Note the restored ship's **chandlery**, housed in an old warehouse where a range of mariner's equipment is exhibited. Sections are also devoted to the days of sail, the age of steam and naval history.

Outside the museum are two authentic vessels. Moored at the museum's wharf is the **CSS Acadia**, a steamship built in 1913 for the Canadian Hydrographic Service *(can be boarded Jun–mid-Oct)*. Berthed at Sackville Landing, adjacent to the museum, is the restored **HMCS Sackville**, a World War II corvette that served in the Battle of the Atlantic *(can be boarded Jun–late Sept; 902-429-2132)*.

Berthed here seasonally is the **Bluenose II**, a replica of the schooner that held the International Fishermen's trophy for 17 years, after capturing it in 1921. Constructed in 1963 as a goodwill ambassador for Nova Scotia, the *Bluenose II* offers **cruises** in Halifax Harbour, when not visiting other ports *(departs from museum's wharf Jun–Sept daily 9:30am & 1pm; round-trip 2hrs; $20; Bluenose II Preservation Trust 902-634-1963 or 800-763-1963 Canada/US)*.

★ **Province House** – *Main entrance on Hollis St. Open Jul–Aug Mon–Fri 9am–5pm, weekends & holidays 10am–4pm. Rest of the year Mon–Fri 9am–4pm. 902-424-4661.* Completed in 1819 this Georgian sandstone structure houses the Legislative Assembly of Nova Scotia, an institution that has existed since 1758.

The **Red Chamber**, where the Legislative Council used to meet, can be visited. Note the portraits of King George III and Queen Charlotte at the head of the room. In the **assembly chamber** visitors might witness some spirited debates when the body is in session. Once housing the provincial Supreme Court, the **legislative library** was the site, in 1835, of the self-defence of journalist **Joseph Howe** against a charge of criminal libel. His acquittal marked the beginning of a free press in Nova Scotia. Later he entered politics and led a fight against Confederation but eventually joined the Dominion (now more commonly called federal) government in Ottawa.

★ **Art Gallery of Nova Scotia** – *1723 Hollis St. Open Jun–Sept Tue–Fri 10am–5pm (Thu 9pm), weekends noon–5pm. Rest of the year Tue–Fri 10am–5pm, weekends noon–5pm. $5. 902-424-7542.* Housed in the stately Dominion Building and, as of 1998, the adjacent Provincial Building, this modern museum boasts a collection of some 6,000 holdings. On exhibit are Nova Scotian works of art from the first half of the 20C; other 20C Canadian art, including paintings of the well-known **Group of Seven**; and British and European works. Regional **folk art**—painting, sculptures, paper and textiles—is a highlight, and the museum possesses a small but excellent collection of **Inuit art**.

Grand Parade – Bordered by **City Hall** at one end and **St. Paul's Anglican Church** at the other, this pleasant square has been the centre of Halifax since its founding. Here the militia mustered, the town crier proclaimed the news, and city dwellers hired sedan chairs. Built in 1750 the small timber-framed church is the oldest Protestant church in Canada.

★ **Museum of Natural History** – *1747 Summer St. Open Jun–mid-Oct Mon–Sat 9:30am–5:30pm (Wed 8pm), Sun 1pm–5:30pm. Rest of the year Tue–Sat 9:30am–5pm (Wed 8pm), Sun 1pm–5pm. Closed national holidays. $3.50. www.ednet.ns.ca/educ/museum/mnh/index.htm 902-424-7375.* This museum offers a comprehensive picture of Nova Scotia by covering its geology, history, society, and flora and fauna. Micmac displays, natural-history dioramas and marine life, especially whales and sharks, can be seen.

★**Public Gardens** – *Main entrance at corner of Spring Garden Rd. and South Park St. Open mid-Apr–mid-Nov daily 8am–dusk. ♿ ☎902-490-4894.* Opened to the public in 1867, this 7ha/17acre park is a fine example of an immense Victorian garden, complete with weeping trees, ponds, fountains, statues, formal plantings and an ornate bandstand. Note the massive wrought-iron entrance gate.

★**Point Pleasant Park** – *Closed to traffic; parking on Point Pleasant Dr. at Tower Rd. and near container terminal. Open year-round daily 6am–midnight. ☎902-490-4894.* Situated at the southernmost point of the peninsula, this lovely 75ha/185 acre park has excellent **views**★★ of the harbour and the North West Arm. For many years the park was dominated by the military, who filled it with batteries and forts, the remains of which can still be seen.

Prince of Wales Tower – *Open Jul–Labour Day daily 10am–6pm. Grounds open year-round. ☎902-426-5080.* The prototype of what came to be called a **Martello tower**, this circular stone structure was the first of its kind in North America. Prince Edward ordered its construction in 1797, naming the tower for his brother—the future George IV. Its design was adapted from a tower on Mortella Point in Corsica that had proved almost impregnable. Such towers were built later in Canada and England to counter invasion by Napoleon's troops.
Exhibits portray the tower's history, architectural features and importance as a defensive structure.

EXCURSIONS

★**McNab's Island** – *Access by ferry from Halifax Harbourfront. For schedules contact tourist office, Halifax ☎902-490-5946.* Located in Halifax Harbour, east of Point Pleasant Park, the island has beaches, walking trails, good views and the remains of military fortifications.

Sir Sandford Fleming Park – *5.5km/3mi by Cogswell St., Quinpool Rd. and Purcell's Cove Rd. (Rte. 253). Open year-round daily 8am–dusk. Walking trails, swimming, boating, picnic area. ♿ 🅿 ☎902-490-4894.* A peaceful haven in a residential suburb of Halifax, this park is a tribute to **Sir Sandford Fleming** (1827-1915), a prominent engineer from Scotland. Instrumental in the construction of Canada's first continental railway system, he also designed the nation's first postage stamp and urged the adoption of international standard time.
The long stretch of North West Arm can be seen from **Dingle Tower** *(open May–Oct daily 8am–5pm)*.

★**York Redoubt** – *11km/7mi by Cogswell St., Quinpool Rd. and Purcell's Cove Rd. (Rte. 253). Open Jun–late Oct daily 9am–dusk. Rest of the year grounds only, daily 9am–5pm. 🅿 ☎902-426-5080.* Located on the bluffs above Halifax Harbour, this coastal fort played an integral role in the city's defensive and warning systems. First constructed in 1793, the defences were strengthened by Prince Edward, who named the redoubt for his brother, the Duke of York. The Martello tower Edward erected in 1798 was part of his signal communication system. During World War II, the redoubt became the centre for coordinating defence of the harbour and city against German attack.

At the north end, the remains of the stone tower can be seen. Aligned along the top of the bluff, a series of gun emplacements face the harbour approach. At the south end, the **command post** contains displays on the defences, and from it *(weather permitting)* there are good **views**★ of the harbour.

★**Dartmouth** – *Map p 231.* Site of a large naval dockyard and research centre, Halifax's twin city on the other side of the inlet has a pleasant waterfront with several shop-lined streets descending to it. Connected to Halifax by two bridges, Dartmouth is serviced by **ferry**, from which the views of both cities are expansive *(departs from Lower Water St. in Halifax Jun–Sept Mon–Sat 6:45am–11:45pm, Sun 12:15pm–5:45pm; rest of the year Mon–Sat 6:45am–11:45pm; holidays 7:45am–11:45pm; no service Jan 1, Good Friday, Easter Sunday & Dec 25. $1.50; ♿ ☎902-421-6600)*.

William Ray House – *59 Ochterloney St. Open Jun–Aug Sun–Thu 10am–1:30pm & 2:30pm–7pm. Rest of the year by appointment. ☎902-464-2300.* This house is the sole survivor of 22 dwellings built for a group of Quaker whalers who moved to the province from New England in 1785. Its shingled exterior with paned windows is typical of the houses constructed along the coast from Massachusetts to Nova Scotia in the 18C. Note the framed walls, off-centre front door, exposed beams and narrow winding staircase.

Black Cultural Centre for Nova Scotia – *In Westphal. Rte 7 at Cherrybrook Road. Open Jun–Aug Mon–Fri 9am–5pm, Sat 10am–4pm. Rest of the year Mon–Fri 9am–5pm. $3. ♿ 🅿 //home.istar.ca/~bccns ☎902-434-6223.* This sizeable museum, library and meeting hall opened in 1983 to foster the province's black history and culture. Exhibits cover early migration and settlement, military service, religion and community. There is a memorial to naval hero **William Hall** (1827-1904), the first Nova Scotian and first black to be awarded the Victoria Cross, the Commonwealth's military medal for exceptional courage.

★**Uniacke Estate Museum Park** – *Map p 231. In Mt. Uniacke, 40km/25mi northwest by Rtes. 7 and 1. Grounds open year-round daily dawn–dusk. House open Jun–mid-Oct Mon–Sat 9:30am–5:30pm, Sun 11am–5:30pm. Contribution requested. www.ednet.ns.ca/educ/museum/ ☎ 902-866-0032.* This fine example of plantation-style colonial architecture, with its wide portico rising the two storeys of the house, stands on a peaceful lakeshore estate. Completed in 1815, it was the country home of Richard Uniacke, Attorney General of Nova Scotia from 1797 to 1830.

The interior looks today as it did in 1815 with the original furnishings of the Uniacke family, including several mahogany pieces crafted by George Adams of London.

★★**Peggy's Cove** – *43km/27mi. Description p 255.*

The beaver symbol indicates that the point of interest described has been designated a national park or national historic site.

LOUISBOURG FORTRESS★★★

Map p 231

Guarding the entrance of the St. Lawrence River, the approach to Quebec, Louisbourg was once the great 18C fortress of New France, manned by the largest garrison in North America. The $25 million restoration project is the most expensive preservation ever undertaken by the Canadian government.

Historical Notes

A Bleak Beginning – The French had long planned a fortress in Nova Scotia, even considering Halifax as a possible site. When they lost the mainland in 1713 *(p 231)*, they chose the eastern peninsula of Île Royale (now Cape Breton) and commenced construction of a fortified town in 1719.

Following fortification designs elaborated by French military engineers, the plan called for a citadel, six bastions and detached batteries. The considerable expense was still less than the cost of a French warship's six-month patrol of the Atlantic waters to guard the lucrative French fishery. Nonetheless, this massive undertaking was riddled with problems: a harsh climate, a boggy site where the mortar sometimes crumbled, scarce building materials and a few corrupt French officials who lined their pockets at royal expense. Difficult living conditions and lack of discipline among the common soldiers contributed to a mutiny in 1744.

A Not-So-Impregnable Fortress – In 1745, prior to completion, 4,000 New Englanders attacked the "impregnable" fortress. Less than two months later the French surrendered. In 1748 the British agreed to return the fort to the island colony of King **Louis XV**. The following year the French reoccupied the stronghold, while the British founded Halifax as a counter-fortress *(p 262)*. Ten years later Louisbourg was under siege again, this time by British regulars. **James Wolfe**, the second in command, managed to land his forces, and the fortress had to be surrendered a second time. Wolfe went on to capture Quebec City in 1759. To prevent further threat to British interests, Louisbourg was destroyed in 1760.

Since 1961 one-quarter of the fortress has been rebuilt according to the original plans and historical records. Furnishings are either original or reproductions.

Access – *37km/23mi south of Sydney by Rte. 22, southwest of town of Louisbourg.*

VISIT *Allow minimum 1/2 day*

Open Jul–Aug daily 9am–7pm. May–Jun & Sept–Oct daily 9:30am–5pm. $11 (May & Oct $4.50). //fortress.uccb.ns.ca ☎ 902-733-2280. Note: Be prepared for cool temperatures, rain and fog. Comfortable walking shoes recommended.
Models of the fortress and displays on the history of Louisbourg provide orientation in the **visitor centre** *(departure point for bus to fortress; onboard commentary serves as preview of visit)*. Visitors cross a drawbridge to enter the walled town through the elaborate **Dauphine Gate**, manned by a sentry. Over 50 buildings *(most open to the public)* are constructed of wood or roughcast masonry, some furnished to their 1740s appearance, others housing themed exhibits. In the summer season, costumed staff portray 18C French society's leisure, propertied and working classes. Popular attractions include a **bakery**, where visitors can buy bread similar to the kind King Louis' troops lined up for in 1744. Three **period restaurants** serve 18C meals on earthenware and pewter. Along the quay stands the high wooden **Frédéric Gate**, the entrance through which important visitors to this once-bustling port were ushered from the harbour. The rich furnishings on the ground floor of the **ordonnateur's residence** include a harpsichord of the period. Archaeological artifacts recovered during reconstruction are on display at various locations.

★★**King's Bastion** – Once one of the largest in North America, this military stronghold has become the symbol of reconstructed Louisbourg. Quarters for the garrison provide insight into the lives of the privileged and impoverished in Old World society. The **governor's apartments** consist of 10 elegant rooms, lavishly furnished. Not as comfortable but well accommodated are the **officers' quarters**. Drafty and spartan, the **soldiers' barracks** are not at all conducive to a long stay. The **prison**, and a **chapel** that once served as the town's parish church, can also be visited.

MAITLAND★

Map p 231

Overlooking Cobequid Bay in the Minas Basin, Maitland was once an important shipbuilding centre. The town is best known as the site of the construction of the largest wooden ship built in Canada, the **William D. Lawrence**. Today Maitland's fine houses attest to the wealth created by the former industry.

SIGHT

★**Lawrence House Museum** – *On Hwy. 15. Open Jun–mid-Oct Mon–Sat 9:30am–5:30pm, Sun 1pm–5:30pm. Contribution requested. www.ednet.ns.ca/educ/museum/ ☎ 902-261-2628.* Surrounded by elm trees, this two-and-a-half-storey house is a splendid example of the grand residences of Nova Scotia's shipbuilders and sea captains. The entrance portico with its double, curved staircase is reminiscent of a ship's bridge.

William Dawson Lawrence built this house (c.1870) to overlook his shipyard on the Shubenacadie River at the point where it joins Cobequid Bay. Believing he could double a ship's size without doubling its operating costs, Lawrence constructed an 80m/262ft ship, which weighed 2,459 tons and had three masts, the highest being over 60m/200ft. To complete the vessel, he had to mortgage his house, but the investment proved to be profitable. Launched in 1874, the ship sailed all over the world with many varied cargoes.

The house contains most of its original furnishings, including shipbuilding artifacts, pictures of 19C ships and a 2m/7ft model of the *William D. Lawrence*.

A lookout area across the road from the house affords visitors a good **view**★ of the tidal flats.

SHERBROOKE★

Map p 231

This village occupies a pretty **site** on the St. Mary's River, once the location of a French fort (1655). After capture by the English in 1669, the settlement was abandoned until people were attracted by the rich timberlands in 1800. During the early 19C, sawmills sprang up and wooden ships were built. Gold was discovered in 1861, and for about 20 years, the town flourished. The gold did not last, but Sherbrooke survived as a lumber town. Today it is a peaceful rural community and a centre for sports fishing and tourism.

SIGHT

★★**Sherbrooke Village** – Restored beginning in 1969, this historic village is actually an extension of the town of Sherbrooke. Streets have been closed to traffic, and only a few houses within the village are private residences.

Visit – Kids *Open Jun–mid-Oct daily 9:30am–5:30pm. $6.* ✗ ♿ *☎ 902-522-2400 or 888-743-7845.* Renovated to reflect the period, the buildings were constructed between 1860 and 1870. A church, schoolhouse, post office, blacksmith shop and several homes can be visited. Built in 1862 with separate downstairs and upstairs cells for men and women, the **jail** occupied half the jailer's house. Of particular interest is the **boatbuilding shop** where wooden boats are still constructed. Above Cumminger Brothers' general store, visitors can don 19C costumes and be photographed in the **ambrotype photography studio**. The process of producing a picture from a negative on dark surfaced glass was used until c.1900. Furnished to the period, **Greenwood Cottage** is an example of a spacious house of the well-to-do, while **McMillan House** reflects the humble status of a village weaver *(spinning demonstrations)*. The hotel serves 1880s fare such as cottage pudding and gingerbread *(copies of recipes upon request)*. The telephone exchange is still operable, and the courthouse is in use today.

Removed from the village is **McDonald Brothers' Mill**★ *(.4km/.3mi)*, an operational water-powered sawmill capable of full production. A short walk away *(3min)* through woodlands, a reconstructed **lumber camp** of the 19C shows the living conditions of loggers.

SPRINGHILL★★

Population 4,193
Map p 231
Tourist Office ☎902-597-3135

Located inland on the "arm" of the peninsula, east of the Isthmus of Chignecto, this town is famous as a coal-mining centre that has suffered more disasters than any other place of its size in Canada.

In 1891 an enormous blast in one of the mines tore out a vast area. When a subsequent flame swept through the mine workings, 125 men died. Then, in 1916, a subterranean fire filled the galleries. No one was killed, but much damage was done. An explosion and fire in 1956 caused 39 deaths. The next year a fire wiped out most of the business district of the town. Finally, in 1958, an underground upheaval or "bump" caused the deaths of 76 men. All the mines closed after this final disaster, the death knell of an industry already doomed by conversion to oil and gas as heating fuels.

SIGHT

★★**Miners' Museum** – *On Black River Rd. Follow signs along Rte. 2 (Parrsboro direction). Open mid-May–mid-Oct daily 9am–5pm. $4.50. ☎902-597-3449.* This museum commemorates the tragedy of the disasters and the bravery of the rescuers through displays such as newspaper clippings and mining equipment. The interesting **mine tour** is conducted by retired miners. Equipped with hard hats, rubber coats and boots, visitors descend about 270m/900ft into the old Syndicate Mine via a tunnel of regular height, rather than those the miners had to crawl along. Both old and new mining methods are demonstrated *(coal souvenirs can be removed by pick-ax)*.

TRURO

Population 11,983
Map p 231
Tourist Office ☎902-893-2922

Set on the Salmon River near its mouth, this city experiences the high tides of the Bay of Fundy and the tidal bore *(p 241)*. Site of a thriving Acadian community called Cobequid before the Deportation, Truro was later settled by people from Northern Ireland and New Hampshire. Today this manufacturing centre is home to the Nova Scotia Agricultural College.

SIGHT

★**Tidal Bore** – *Viewpoint: leave Hwy. 102 at Exit 14 and take Tidal Bore Rd. (left on Robie and left again on Tidal Bore Rd., if coming from Halifax). Parking area beside Palliser restaurant; contact tourist office for time of next bore ☎902-893-2922 (summer season); arrive 15min prior and if possible, stay 1hr to see high tide.* Twice a day the tide rushes up the Salmon River from the Bay of Fundy, causing a wave that may vary from a ripple to several feet in height. What is more interesting than this tidal wave is the tremendous inrush of water and the rapid rise in water level immediately following it. In fact, high tide is reached just over an hour after the arrival of the bore.

Addresses, telephone numbers, opening hours and prices published in this guide are accurate at press time. We apologize for any inconvenience resulting from outdated information. Please send us your comments:

Michelin Travel Publications
Editorial Department
P.O. Box 19001
Greenville, SC 29602-9001

Prince Edward Island

Map p 231

The birthplace of Canadian Confederation, and Canada's smallest province, this crescent-shaped island is only 225km/140mi long; a deeply indented coastline varies its width. Separated from Newfoundland by the Gulf of St. Lawrence, the island is just 14km/9mi from New Brunswick and 22km/14mi from Nova Scotia across the **Northumberland Strait**. Iron oxides give the soil its characteristic brick red colour, and on fine summer days, the rolling landscape presents a stunning kaleidoscope of green fields, blue sea and sky, red soil and puffy white clouds.

Historical Notes

Île-St.-Jean and the Acadian Deportation – Jacques Cartier claimed the island for France in 1534, naming it Île-St.-Jean. Concerted efforts at colonization did not occur until the early 18C when French settlers founded **Port la Joye**, near the present site of Charlottetown, as a dependency of Île Royale, today Cape Breton Island in Nova Scotia. France's plan to strengthen its claims in the New World brought Acadian farmers to Île-St.-Jean in 1720. In 1755 the British demanded an oath of fealty from Acadians on British territory. Several thousand Acadians chose instead to resettle on Île-St.-Jean. In 1758 England captured Île-St.-Jean, removing the Acadians under the Deportation Order *(p 232)*. About 30 families went into hiding—the ancestors of many of today's island Acadians.

St. John's Island and the British Regime – Renamed St. John's Island under British rule, the island was annexed to Nova Scotia. The land was granted to wealthy Englishmen and military officers, who petitioned the British government to recognize the territory as a separate colony. In 1769 a new administration was established; and in 1799 the colony was renamed Prince Edward Island in honour of the son of King George III of England. The island was the site of the historic **Charlottetown Conference** in September 1864, the first of several meetings that led to Canadian Confederation in 1867.

The Island Today – Principal industries today are agriculture, tourism and fishing. Agricultural and aquacultural processing form the backbone of manufacturing on the island, renowned for its dairy products, lobsters and shellfish, and more than 50 varieties of **potatoes**. Annually over 700,000 visitors are drawn to the unhurried pace of life; **farm vacations** are popular, and **lobster suppers**, held during the summer in church and community halls, provide a sampling of fresh regional seafood and abundant garden produce. A 13km/8mi-long **bridge** *(toll)* over Northumberland Strait, completed in 1997, links Borden, PEI with Jourimain Island, New Brunswick, replacing the existing Borden-Cape Tormentine ferry service.

Visiting the Island

Three scenic drives established by the provincial government are a good approach to touring the island. Organized as circuits of the three counties (Prince, Queens and Kings), the routes provide a leisurely, in-depth means of experiencing splendid scenery, charming community life, historical attractions and recreational activities. The main **tourist office** for the island is located at 178 Water Street in Charlottetown *(open May–early Jun daily 8:30am–6pm; mid-Jun–Aug daily 8am–10pm; Sept–mid-Oct Mon–Fri 8am–6pm; rest of the year Mon–Fri 9am–5pm; ☎902-368-5540)*.

PRACTICAL INFORMATION

Getting There

By Air – Service from Halifax, NS is provided by Air Canada affiliates ☎902-429-7111, or 800-776-3000 (US) to the Charlottetown airport (less than 5km/3mi from downtown) ☎902-566-7997. Taxis and major car rental agencies at the airport.

By Car – Opened in 1997, the 13km/8mi two-lane Confederation Bridge links Borden/Carleton, Prince Edward Island (PEI) with Cape Jourimain, NB *(open year-round 24hrs/day)* and takes approximately 10min to cross. The normal speed limit is 80km/h (50mph). Call boxes are located at regular intervals. No passing or stopping is permitted, except for emergencies. A toll *($35.50/car)* is collected at Borden/Carleton upon exiting the island *(cash, debit card or major credit cards accepted)*. www.confederationbridge.com *☎902-437-7300 or 888-437-6565.*

By Boat – Northumberland Ferries connects the eastern part of the island at Wood Islands with Caribou, NS *(departs mid-Jun–Labour Day daily 6:30am–7:30pm; rest of Sept–mid-Nov daily 7am–6:30pm; late Nov–mid-Dec 7am–5pm; phone for May–early Jun hours; no service late Dec–Apr; one-way 1hr 15min; $46/car round-trip; ☎902-566-3838 or 800-565-0201, in Canada)*. From Souris a ferry crosses to the Magdalen Islands, Quebec *(p 202)*.

General Information

Accommodations and Visitor Information – The official tourist office publishes the annual *Visitors Guide* giving information on history, attractions, festivals, sports, vacation packages and accommodations. A highway map is included. For a free copy contact **Tourism Prince Edward Island**, PO Box 940, Charlottetown, PE, C1A 7M5 ☎800-463-4734 (Canada/US).

Road Regulations – *(Driver's license and insurance requirements p 304.)* Main roads are paved, particularly along the coasts; some roads are either dirt or gravel surface. Speed limits, unless otherwise posted, are 90km/h (55mph) or 80km/h (50mph) on highways and 50km/h (30mph) in urban districts. **Seat belt** use is mandatory. **Canadian Automobile Assn. (CAA)**, Charlottetown ☎902-892-1612.

Time Zone – PEI is on Atlantic Standard Time. Daylight Saving Time is observed from the first Sunday in April to the last Sunday in October.

Taxes – The national GST of 7% *(rebate information p 308)* and a provincial sales tax of 10% are levied.

Liquor Laws – The legal drinking age is 19. Liquor is sold in government stores.

Recreation *p 234*

Principal Festivals

Jun–Sept	**Charlottetown Festival**	*Charlottetown*
Jun	**Highland Gathering and Military Tattoo**	*Summerside*
Jul	**Bluegrass and Oldtime Music Festival**	*Rollo Bay*
Aug	**Lucy Maud Montgomery Festival**	*Cavendish*
	New Old Home Week Provincial Exhibition	*Charlottetown*
Sept	**Storytelling Festival**	*Province-wide*
	Shellfish Festival	*Charlottetown*

CHARLOTTETOWN★★

Population 32,531
Map p 271
Tourist Office ☎902-368-4444

Located near the confluence of the West, North and Hillsborough Rivers at Northumberland Strait, this gracious provincial capital is also a thriving commercial centre, its port serving as a funnel for the region's agricultural bounty. Named for the wife of King George III, the city was founded in 1768.

SIGHTS *1/2 day*

Attractively situated along the water's edge, **Victoria Park** is home to the regal, white Neoclassical **Government House**, designed by Isaac Smith as the lieutenant-governor's official residence *(not open to the public)*. From the shore, expansive **views**★ extend across the harbour to the site of Fort Amherst.

★★**Province House National Historic Site** – *At the top of Great George St. Open Jul–Aug daily 9am–6pm. Jun & Sept–mid-Oct daily 9am–5pm. Rest of the year Mon–Fri 9am–5pm. Closed national holidays.* ♿ *☎902-566-7050.* A native of Yorkshire, England, Isaac Smith designed this three-storey sandstone building (1847) in the Georgian style with Neoclassical details. The **Confederation Chamber**, site of the Charlottetown Conference *(p 269)*, is restored to its 19C appearance with many of the original furnishings. The provincial legislature still meets in the legislative chamber.

★**Confederation Centre of the Arts** – *Grafton St., adjacent to Province House. Open Jun–Sept Mon–Sat 9am–9pm. Rest of the year Mon–Sat noon–5pm.* ✗ ♿ *☎902-566-1267.* Commemorating the centennial of the 1864 Charlottetown Conference, this national memorial arts centre (1964) houses theatres, the provincial archives, display areas and a restaurant. Temporary exhibits in the **art gallery** feature selections from a large collection of works by Canadian artists, and the main theatre hosts the annual **Charlottetown Festival** musical production, *Anne of Green Gables.*

St. Dunstan's Basilica – *Great George St. Open Jun–Sept daily 8am–9pm. Rest of the year daily 8am–4pm.* ♿ *☎902-894-3486.* The twin 61m/200ft spires of this Gothic edifice (1917) gracefully punctuate Charlottetown's skyline. Interior features include fan vaulting, streaked marble, and a stunning rose window from Munich, Germany. The contemporary stained-glass windows in the facade were designed by island native Henry Purdy.

BLUE HERON DRIVE★★

Map below

Encircling most of Queens County and central Prince Edward Island, this scenic drive encompasses the stunning white beaches of the north coast; charming Acadian fishing villages; sights related to *Anne of Green Gables*; and the red cliffs of the southern coast, bordered by Northumberland Strait.

DRIVING TOUR *1 day*

190km/118mi circuit indicated by blue and white signs depicting a blue heron. Visitor centre in Charlottetown.

★**Prince Edward Island National Park** – *In Cavendish, 24km/15mi northwest of Charlottetown. Open year-round. $3. ⚠. Visitor centre at intersection of Rtes. 6 and 13; open Jun daily 9am–5pm, Jul–Aug daily 9am–9pm, Sept–mid-Oct daily 9am–5pm. ☎902-672-6350.* One of Canada's smallest but most popular national parks stretches for about 40km/25mi along the north shore of the island, fringing the Gulf of St. Lawrence. Interspersed with boardwalks and paths to the water's edge, the **Gulf Shore Parkway** offers displays on shoreline ecology and views of some of eastern Canada's loveliest **beaches**, sand dunes, sandstone cliffs, salt marshes and freshwater ponds. Picnic sites are scattered throughout seaside and woodland areas, and a variety of interpretation programs are available.

Near the park's eastern entrance, a glance to the south reveals **Dalvay-by-the-Sea**, an elegant Victorian structure (1896), formerly the summer home of Standard Oil magnate, Alexander MacDonald, and now a hotel. The lobby features beautiful woodwork and an enormous fireplace with a hearth of local sandstone.

★**Green Gables House** – Kids *In Cavendish. Rte. 6 west of Rte. 13, in PEI National Park. Open early May–mid-Jun daily 9am–5pm. Late Jun–Aug 30 daily 9am–8pm. Aug 31–Oct daily 9am–5pm. $5. ✗ ♿ ☎902-672-6350.* This small green and white farmhouse belonged to relatives of **Lucy Maud Montgomery**, author of *Anne of Green Gables*. During her childhood years in Cavendish, she visited here frequently and used the house as a setting for the novel, which tells the story of an irrepressible orphan girl adopted by a strict but kindly brother and sister living at "Green Gables" farm. Once described by Mark Twain as the "sweetest creation of child life ever written," this story has become popular in 18 languages, and draws summer visitors to the island from as far away as Japan.

Today the refurbished house *(damaged by a fire in 1997)* re-creates scenes from the novel, including Anne's gable bedroom. In the downstairs hallway, Montgomery's typewriter and several family photographs are displayed.

Anne of Green Gables Museum at Silverbush – *In Park Corner, Rte. 20. Open Jun–Sept daily 9am–6pm. Early–end May & Oct daily 9am–5pm. $2.75. ✗ ♿ ☎902-886-2884.* Throughout her life, author L.M. Montgomery visited relatives at this spacious house; her 1911 wedding was held in the drawing room. The dwelling and its surroundings appear as settings in the *Anne of Green Gables* series. First editions of the author's books, personal correspondence and family heirlooms are displayed throughout the house.

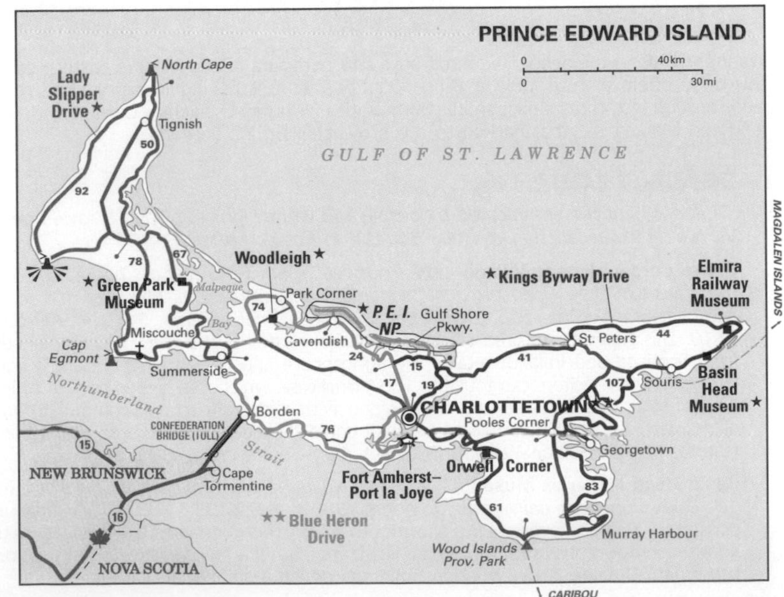

Prince Edward Island Coastline

★**Woodleigh** – Kids *In Burlington, Rte. 234 northeast of Kensington. Open Jul–Aug daily 9am–7pm. Jun & Sept–mid-Oct daily 9am–5pm. $6.80. ✗ ♿ ☎902-836-3401.* Scattered about a pleasant, tree-shaded site are some 17 large-scale replicas of historic British structures. Highlights include an 8m/26ft replica of York Minster Cathedral, complete with 145 glass windows; St. Paul's Cathedral in London; and Scotland's Dunvegan Castle. *Video presentation available on request in the theatre adjacent to the gift shop.*

Fort Amherst/Port la Joye – *In Rocky Point, on Blockhouse Point Rd. off Rte. 19. Open late Jun–Labour Day daily 10am–6pm. Early–mid Jun Wed–Fri 10am–4pm. Grounds open May–Nov. $2.25. ✗ ☎902-675-2220.* The first permanent European settlement on the island was established here by the French in 1720. The British, who captured the area in 1758, erected Fort Amherst, a series of defenses on the site of the original French garrison, and occupied the post until 1768. Today only the earthworks remain—rolling, grass-covered mounds from which sweeping **views**★★ of Charlottetown harbour extend. In the **visitor centre**, displays and a video presentation *(15min)* offer an introduction to the site's history.

KINGS BYWAY DRIVE★

Map p 271

Wandering along the deeply indented bays and harbours of the island's eastern coast, this drive offers a close look at Kings County's vibrant fishing industry. Side roads lead through lush forests past small communities with names such as Cardigan, Greenfield and Glenmartin, that harken to the province's British heritage.

DRIVING TOUR *1 day*

375km/233mi circuit indicated by purple and white signs depicting a royal crown. Visitor centre at junction of Rtes. 3 and 4 in Pooles Corner.

Orwell Corner Historic Village – Kids *In Orwell, 30km/19mi east of Charlottetown on the Trans-Can Hwy. Open late Jun–Labour Day daily 9am–5pm. Mid-May–mid-Jun & mid-Sept–late Oct Tue–Sun 10am–3pm. Closed national holidays. $4. ✗ ☎902-651-8510.* This superbly restored crossroads village, settled in the early 19C by pioneers from Scotland and Ireland, retains the atmosphere and flavour of the island's agricultural origins. Visitors can tour the 1864 **farmhouse**, which also served as post office, general store and dressmaker's shop, along with a church, school, community hall, blacksmith's shop, shingle mill and animal barns. Fiddle music and step dancing are features of the traditional *ceilidh* (KAY-lee) *(Jun–Sept every Wed 8pm).*

★**Basin Head Fisheries Museum** – *In Basin Head, 10 km/6mi east of Souris on Rte. 16. Open Jun–Sept daily, call for hours. $3. ✗ ☎902-357-7233.* This museum occupies a fine site overlooking the mouth of Northumberland Strait. Boats, nets, hooks, photographs and dioramas illustrate the life and work of an inshore fisherman. Outside, small wooden buildings house a small craft exhibit.

Elmira Railway Museum – *In Elmira, 16km/10mi east of Souris on Rte. 16A. Open mid-Jun–Labour Day daily 10am–6pm. $2. ♿ ☎ 902-357-7234.* Formerly the eastern terminus of a railway system linking the island with the continent, this charming station has been transformed into a museum that recounts the railway's 19C–early-20C development. Features include a photographic display highlighting architectural differences among island rail stations, a 1911 station log and still-operational telegraph equipment.

LADY SLIPPER DRIVE★

Map p 271

The picturesque landscape of western Prince Edward Island is fringed with capes and beaches. Named for the province's official flower, this scenic circuit introduces the visitor to shipbuilding at Green Park; the Malpeque Bay, famed for its fine oysters; and fox farming, a major island industry from 1890 to 1939.

DRIVING TOUR *1 day*

288km/179mi circuit indicated by red and white signs depicting a Lady Slipper blossom. Visitor centre on Rte 1A in Wilmot, 2km east of Summerside.

Acadian Museum of Prince Edward Island – *In Miscouche, 8km/5mi west of Summerside, on Rte. 2. Open late Jun–Labour Day Mon–Sat 9:30am–5pm, Sun 1pm–5pm. Rest of the year Mon–Fri 9:30am–5pm. $3. ♿ ☎ 902-436-6237.* Erected in 1991, this modern facility for the preservation of Acadian heritage combines an historical museum with a documentation centre for genealogical research. Main gallery dioramas and texts present Acadian history after 1720, incorporating objects from an extensive collection of artifacts, photographs, textiles and journals donated by area families. Audio-visual presentations in the theatre introduce topics such as religion, education and economy. An adjacent gallery presents temporary thematic exhibits of Acadian culture and heritage.

★**Green Park Shipbuilding Museum** – *In Port Hill, 34km/21mi northwest of Summerside on Rte. 12. Open Jun–Sept daily 10am–5:30pm. $3. ♿ ☎ 902-831-2206.* Formerly the grounds of an active shipyard, Green Park is today a provincial heritage site commemorating the shipbuilding industry, the island's principal economic activity during the 19C.
Erected by the shipyard's owner, **Yeo House** (1865) is a large, steeply gabled Victorian structure restored to reflect the lifestyle of a prominent family of the period. Maps, photographs and tools on display in the **visitor centre** present the art and science of shipbuilding during the industry's 19C heyday.

West Point Lighthouse – *In Cedar Dunes Provincial Park, Rte. 14. Open Jul–Aug daily 8am–9:30pm. Jun & Sept daily 8am–8pm. $2.50. ✕ ♿ www.peisland.com/westpoint/light.htm ☎ 902-859-3605 or 800-764-6854.* This distinctive 30m/85ft striped lighthouse (1875) was automated by electricity in 1963. A narrow stairway rises past photographs and displays documenting the history of island lighthouses. The tower itself contains numerous examples of lighthouse lenses and lanterns. From the observation platform at the summit, **views** stretch across the shoreline's dark red dunes.

Our Lady of Mont-Carmel Acadian Church – *In Mont-Carmel, on Rte. 11, east of Rte. 124. Open mid-May–mid-Sept daily 8am–9pm. Rest of the year daily 9am–5pm. ♿ ☎ 902-854-2789.* Overlooking Northumberland Strait just east of Cap-Egmont, this twin-steepled brick church (1896) replaces two earlier wooden structures, the first of which was built in 1820 as a mission church for the Acadian community of Mont-Carmel. The church's symmetrical facade and rounded interior vaults are reminiscent of religious architecture in France's Poitou region, original home of most of the island's first Acadian settlers.

We welcome corrections and suggestions that may assist us in preparing the next edition. Please send us your comments:

Michelin Travel Publications
Editorial Department
P. O. Box 19001
Greenville, SC 29602-9001

Newfoundland

Map p 276

The largest of the Atlantic provinces, Newfoundland consists of a rocky island of the same name and the mountainous mainland of Labrador, with a combined landmass of 405,720sq km/156,648sq mi. The remote shores and wilderness interior of Canada's easternmost province appeal particularly to nature lovers in search of adventure.

Geographical Notes

The Island – Called "The Rock" for its craggy profile, the island of the province has a 9,650km/6,000mi beautiful, deeply indented coastline, studded with bays, coves and islands. In the north and west, the coast is grandiose with towering cliffs and deep fjords *(pp 278 and 279)*. From the heights of the **Long Range Mountains** in the west, a continuation of the Appalachians, the land slopes east and northeast. Parts of the interior are heavily forested; others are expanses of rocky barrens and boggy peat-lands, a legacy of glaciers, as are the multitude of lakes and rivers.

Labrador – A rugged land of high mountains (Cirque Mountain, in the **Torngats** of the north, reaches 1,676m/5,500ft), Labrador also possesses coastal settlements nestling under high cliffs, and inland, a barren, largely treeless terrain. Unlike the island, it forms part of the Canadian Shield. Labrador's 29,100 people reside primarily along the coast and around the mines in its rich iron-ore belt.

The Banks – In Newfoundland "banks" are not money-lending institutions but vast areas of shallow water in the Atlantic to the south and east of the province—usually less than 100m/328ft deep extensions of the continental shelf. For 500 years these waters have attracted fishermen to the fish-breeding grounds. The largest and richest of the grounds is the **Grand Banks**, an area of approximately 282,500sq km/109,073sq mi where the cold Labrador Current meets the warmer Gulf Stream. Sinking below the warmer one, the cold current stirs up plankton on the sea bed. The plankton rises to the surface, attracting great schools of fish.

Newfoundland Today

Fishing Industry – Though herring is also found, **cod** is the traditional catch in the Grand Banks. In recent years, because of depleted stocks, the Canadian government ordered a ban on cod fishing *(p 232)*. Newfoundlanders have always talked about "fishing the banks" however, and the boats they used were called "bankers."

Inshore Fishing – In early summer, the **caplin** "run": these small fish swim ashore to spawn, bringing with them their main predator, the cod. Using large square traps made of netting, a fisherman traditionally earned most of his livelihood during the few weeks of the run. **Cod jigging**, slow and inefficient, is used to a limited extent at other times during the year: shiny lead "jiggers" or baited hooks on small lines attached to a trawl line attract the cod. The use of trawl lines payed out from a boat is known as **longlining**. The method of weighting nets and keeping them vertical with floats is called **gill netting**, a more recent practice. Larger boats called **longliners**, which can stay at sea several days to pursue schools of fish, use either method. Squid, lobster, salmon and caplin (once used only as bait) are taken in as well.

Offshore Fishing – Traditionally, large schooners left the province's ports to fish the banks for months at a time. When schools of fish were located, actual fishing was done from **dories**, small flat-bottomed open craft carried on deck. The catch was either salted on the schooner's deck and stored in the hold ("wet" fishery) or taken ashore and dried on land on wooden racks known as **flakes** ("dry" fishery). The trend since 1945 has been to use draggers, trawlers and longliners instead of schooners and dories because fish can be caught en masse. Filleting plants have replaced flakes, and refrigeration has supplanted salting.

Offshore Oil – Completed in 1997, the **Hibernia oil platform** constructed at Bull Arm is said to be the heaviest offshore oil rig manufactured to date. Secured to its drill site some 315km/200mi out in the Grand Banks, the platform weighs over 1.2 million tonnes/1.3 million tons, heavy enough, it is projected, to withstand collision with the giant icebergs common in these waters. The controversial project, funded both privately and publicly, is estimated to cost nearly $6 billion. Anticipated output when at full production is 135,000 barrels of oil a day—about six percent of the country's total oil production over the next 20 years.

Lifestyle and Customs – Functional rather than fancy characterizes the lives of many Newfoundlanders. About one-quarter of the island's population of 551,792 resides in the capital city of ST. JOHN'S; the remainder live mainly in coastal fishing villages known as **outports**. Traditionally, an outport was any community outside St. John's, but today, with the rise of industrial centres such as Corner Brook, the term is applied to tiny coastal settlements with moored dories and trap skiffs, weather-beaten fishing **stages** (wooden platforms perched on poles above the water for drying fish) and colourful

PRACTICAL INFORMATION

Getting There

By Air – Newfoundland and Labrador are serviced by major domestic and international air carriers such as Air Canada and Canadian Airlines International through Toronto, Montreal and other hubs. Air Canada (☎800-4-CANADA, ☎800-776-3000 US), Canadian Airlines (☎800-426-7000, Canada/US) and Air Labrador (☎709-753-5593) provide regular connections within the province.

By Boat – Passenger & car ferry service is available from North Sydney, NS to Channel-Port aux Basques *(departs year-round daily; 6hrs 30min, 5hrs in summer; connecting bus service to inland destinations DRL Coachlines ☎ 709-738-8088)* and to Argentia *(Jul–Aug Mon, Wed & Fri 3:30pm; early–mid-Sept twice weekly; 14hrs)*. For schedules & reservations contact Marine Atlantic, North Sydney, NS ☎800-341-7981 (Canada/US).
From Lewisporte, NF to Goose Bay, Labrador *(departs mid-Jun–Sept twice weekly; 35hrs)*. Passenger service from St. Anthony, NF to Nain, Labrador *(departs every 12 days)*. For information & reservations contact Tourism Newfoundland ☎800-563-6353 (Canada/US).
The southern coast of Labrador is accessible by ferry from St. Barbe, NF via Blanc-Sablon, PQ *(departs Jul–Aug twice daily; May–Jun & Sept–Dec 1-2 departures daily; no crossing Dec 25; 1hr 45min; $18.50/car, $9/passenger; Northern Cruiser Ltd., St. John's, NF ☎ 709-931-2309)*.

Note: Advance reservations are suggested for all ferry services. Fuel tanks must be no more than three-quarters full. For ferry service to **Saint-Pierre and Miquelon** *see p 286*.

General Information

Accommodations and Visitor Information – The government tourist office publishes an annually updated travel guide giving detailed information about attractions and activities, calendar of events, boat and adventure tours, and a listing of accommodations including hospitality homes (private homes that accept paying guests). A copy of this guide, a road map and other useful information are available free of charge from **Tourism Newfoundland and Labrador**, PO Box 8700, St. John's, NF, A1B 4J6 ☎709-729-2830 or 800 563 6353 (Canada/US).

Road Regulations – *(Driver's license and insurance requirements p 304.)* The Trans-Canada Highway Rte. 1 *(910km/565mi)*, which traverses Newfoundland from Channel-Port aux Basques to St. John's, and most secondary highways are paved. The condition of gravel roads varies according to traffic and weather. Main roads are passable during winter, but it is advisable to check with local authorities before departure *(☎ 709-729-2381, Dec–Mar)*. **Seat belt** use is compulsory. Speed limits, unless otherwise posted, are: 100km/h (60mph) on four-lane divided highways, 80km/h (50mph) on secondary and 50km/h (30mph) on gravel roads.

Time Zones – Most of Labrador observes Atlantic Standard Time. Newfoundland Standard Time is 30min ahead of Atlantic Standard Time and 1hr 30min ahead of Eastern Standard Time. Daylight Saving Time is observed from the first Sunday in April to the last Sunday in October.

Taxes – In Newfoundland and Labrador a Harmonized Sales Tax (HST) is levied at a single rate of 15%. Nonresidents may be entitled to a rebate on certain goods taken out of the country within 60 days of purchase and may request a rebate by contacting: Tax Administration Branch, Department of Finance, PO Box 8720, St. John's, NF, A1B 4K1 ☎709-729-3831.

Liquor Laws – Liquor and wine are available only from government stores except in remote areas where local stores are licensed. Beer is available in most convenience stores. The legal drinking age is 19.

Provincial Holiday *(National Holidays p 308)*

The Queen's Birthday (Victoria Day) .... Monday nearest May 24

Recreation *p 234*

Principal Festivals

mid-Feb	**Corner Brook Winter Carnival**	*Corner Brook*
Jul–early-Aug	**Stephenville Festival**	*Stephenville*
Aug	**Royal St. John's Regatta (p 282)**	*St. John's*
	Annual Newfoundland and Labrador Folk Festival	*St. John's*
mid-Aug	**Labrador Straits Bakeapple Folk Festival**	*Point Amour*

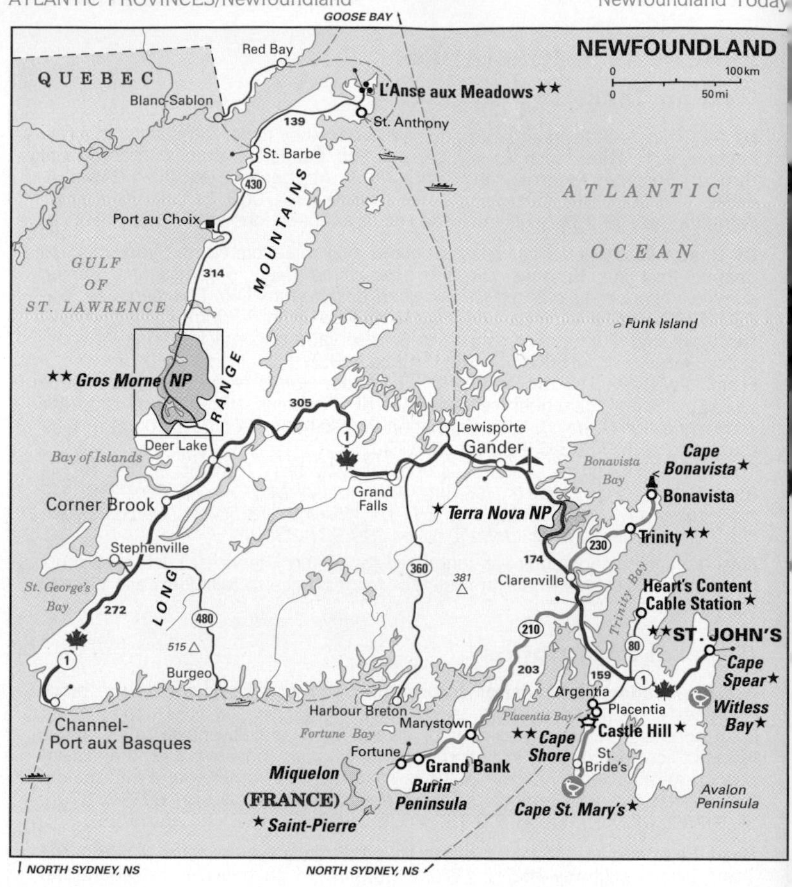

two-storey "box" houses. In some outports a small "museum" preserves each community's past. Housed in historic homes or commercial buildings (often with a craft shop annexed), these collections of donated artifacts are primarily of local interest. Short on flamboyance, the articles are largely practical, reflective of the modest, hardy lives of the outport inhabitants.

Oral Traditions – Hard times have repeated themselves over the generations of these sea-dependent people, ebbing and flowing with the size of each catch. There's rarely a depression of the human spirit, however. Reserved exuberance abounds. Visitors to Newfoundland are captivated by the wealth of unusual idioms and wonderful accents of its inhabitants. Centuries of isolation have chiselled a character that is independent, individualistic and humourous. Where else are there settlements named Stinking Cove, Useless Bay, Jerry's Nose, Cuckold Cove, Come by Chance and Happy Adventure, or local terms like *tickle* (a narrow waterway)?

English is the first language of 98 percent of the islanders, but remarkably varied dialects enrich the provincial tongue. Some have definite Irish overtones; others are reminiscent of England's West Country (Dorset, Devon, Cornwall). Local expressions such as "to have a noggin to scrape" (a very hard task), "to be all mops and brooms" (to have untidy hair) and "long may your big jib draw" (good luck for the future) add colour and humour to every-day conversations.

Rich in tradition, Newfoundlanders possess a wealth of legend, weather lore, folk dances and songs, which attest to their wry perspective on life. Often parodies of British creations, sea shanties such as *Squid-Jiggin' Ground, Let Me Fish off Cape St. Mary's, Jack Was Every Inch a Sailor* record island character and yearnings with relish, melancholy or humour.

Seafood Specialities – Not surprisingly, cod—eaten fresh, dried or salted—has traditionally been the staple of the provincial diet. **Fish and brewis**, a mixture of boiled salt cod and hardtack (a hard, dry biscuit) soaked overnight, is a traditional dish. Of greater fame is **fried cod tongues**, a dish that should be prepared only with fish caught the same day. Arctic char, salmon, shrimp and halibut are other favourites.

"If some countries have too much history, we have too much geography."
William Lyon Mackenzie King, 1936

BURIN PENINSULA

Map p 276

The doorstep to a vast offshore fishing industry in the **Grand Banks**, this barren peninsula of isolated mountain plateaus juts down like a boot into the Atlantic Ocean from the southern coast of Newfoundland between Placentia and Fortune bays. Just off the "toe" are the island remnants of France's once-great empire in North America: SAINT-PIERRE AND MIQUELON.

DRIVING TOUR

Allow 3 hrs. 203km/126mi south of Trans-Can Hwy. by Hwy. 210 to Fortune.

The drive on Highway 210 is long and deserted until **Marystown**, situated on Little Bay. Its huge shipyard (inaccessible to the public), where the trawlers used off Newfoundland's shores are built, is the largest in the province. South of Marystown, Route 210 crosses the peninsula and descends to Fortune Bay, providing views of the southern coast of Newfoundland. Just before entering Grand Bank, there is a view of the south coast and Brunette Island. To the west the coast of the French island of Miquelon is just visible, weather permitting.

Grand Bank – *199km/123mi south of Trans-Can Hwy. by Hwy. 210.* An important fishing centre, this community was once the home of the famous "bankers" *(p 274)*. Some of the houses from that era are examples of the Queen Anne style with their widow's walks or small open rooftop galleries from which women could watch for the return of their men from the sea.

★**Southern Newfoundland Seamen's Museum** – Kids *Marine Dr. Open May–Oct Mon–Fri 9am–5pm, weekends 10am–6pm.* ♿ ☎ *709-832-1484.* Housed in the former Yugoslavian Pavilion of Montreal's Expo '67, this branch of the Newfoundland Museum network features displays on the history of the Banks fishing industry. Of particular interest are the photographs of ships and fishing, and **models** of the types of ships used. A large glass-encased relief model of Newfoundland shows the banks and the depths of the Atlantic.

Highway 210 continues to **Fortune**, another fishing community with an artificial harbour, and the departure point for ferries to the French islands of Saint-Pierre and Miquelon.

THE CAPE SHORE★★

Map p 276

Perhaps Newfoundland's most dramatic coastline, the southwest arm of the Avalon Peninsula from Placentia to St. Bride's delights visitors with its natural wonders and historic sites. Magnificent ocean views and remnants of Europe's territorial struggles await those who travel this isolated shore.

SIGHTS

★**Castle Hill** – *In Placentia, 44km/27mi south of Trans-Can Hwy. by Rte. 100. About 8km/5 mi from Argentia ferry. Open mid-May–mid-Oct daily 8:30am–8pm. Apr–early May & rest of Oct daily 8:30am–4:30pm. $2.50. ☎ 709-227-2401.* This park contains the remains of Fort Royal, built by the French at the turn of the 17C, and rebuilt and renamed Castle Hill by the British. Renowned for its commanding position overlooking the small town of **Placentia**, the site affords a **panorama**★★ of the city itself, Placentia Bay and **The Gut**—a small channel that separates the bay from two long, deep inlets.

As early as 1500, Placentia's harbour, plentiful fresh water and beaches (where cod could be dried) attracted European fishermen, especially the Basques. To protect their interests in the Newfoundland fishery, the French established a small colony called Plaisance in 1662, building fortifications at sea level and in the hills. After the **Treaty of Utrecht** in 1713 confirmed Newfoundland as British territory, the British kept a small garrison at Placentia until 1811, when it was moved to ST. JOHN'S. Placentia settled down to a prosperous life of fishing and shipbuilding. When the era of wooden ships ended, the shipbuilding industry died, but fishing remains important today. During World War II, construction of a large American base at nearby **Argentia** brought major changes to Placentia. The centre of anti-submarine patrol during the war, Argentia was the site of the famous 1941 offshore meeting between Churchill and Roosevelt that produced the **Atlantic Charter**, a statement of peace goals adopted in 1942 by the United Nations.

Visit – An interesting **visitor centre** with dioramas, models and panels describes the French and English presence in the area *(same hours as the park; ♿).* Visitors walk uphill to the cannons and scant remains of the fort. A pleasant pathway through evergreen forests *(10min walk)* past drystone walls leads to **Le Gaillardin**, a redoubt built by the French in 1692.

★★**Cape Shore Drive** – *46km/29mi from Placentia to St. Bride's on Rte. 100. Fuel and food available infrequently. Fog may hamper visibility.* Traversing a straggly, hilly coast, Route 100 is a spectacular ocean drive, providing numerous **views** of beautiful coves, crashing surf and windswept pines. Sparsely populated communities such as picturesque **Gooseberry Cove** *(25km/16mi south of Placentia)* dot the wide inlets of this curving coastline. Colourful flat-topped houses, wool-laden sheep by the roadside and an occasional fishing boat anchored offshore are common scenes until the road turns inland at St. Bride's. The landscape then changes to isolated flatlands and pale green hillocks, extending to the horizon.

★**Cape St. Mary's Ecological Reserve** – *Approximately 14km/9mi east of St. Bride's. Leave St. Bride's via Rte 100. Turn right on unpaved road (turnoff for reserve is clearly marked) and continue 8km/5mi. Open year-round. Mid-Jun to mid-Aug is best season to view birds.* Located at the southwest end of the cape, this site has been an official sanctuary for sea birds since 1964 and is one of the largest nesting grounds in North America for **gannets**, relatives of the pelican family *(illustration p 234)*. Atop a dramatic shoreline alive with the sights and sounds of an active bird population, its pastoral **setting**★★ is unique.

What is especially thrilling about this preserve is that visitors can get within a few feet of the birds. Providing spectacular **views**★ of the rugged coast, a trail *(25min)* from the lighthouse and visitor centre over short-grass hills reminiscent of moors and often covered with grazing sheep and goats, leads to **Bird Rock**, the precarious domain of hundreds of gannets. Surrounding cliffs attract throngs of noisy black-legged kittiwakes, common murres and razorbills.

GROS MORNE NATIONAL PARK★★

Map p 276

Covering 1,805sq km/697sq mi along the west coast of the province's **Great Northern Peninsula**, this vast, pristine park includes some of the most spectacular scenery in eastern Canada. Designated a UNESCO World Heritage Site in 1987, the park contains geological features that have become a magnet for international scientific research. Consisting of rock 1,250 million years old, the flat-topped **Long Range Mountains** are the northernmost part of the Appalachians. Between them and the coast lies a poorly drained plain, sometimes high above the sea, with a variety of cliffs, sandy shores and little fishing communities.

Access – *44km/27mi northwest of Deer Lake. Take Rte. 430 from Deer Lake to Wiltondale, then Rte. 431 to park, 13km/8mi.*

VISIT *2 days. Map below*

Open year-round. $3.25 entry fee (mid-May–mid-Oct). Hiking, cross-country skiing. △. Contact visitor centre near Rocky Harbour for guided boat tours and trail information (open mid-May–mid-Jun daily 10am–6pm; late Jun–Labour Day daily 9am–10pm; mid-Sept–mid-Oct daily 9am–5pm; closed national holidays; ♿ ☎ 709-458-2417). Accommodations available throughout local communities.

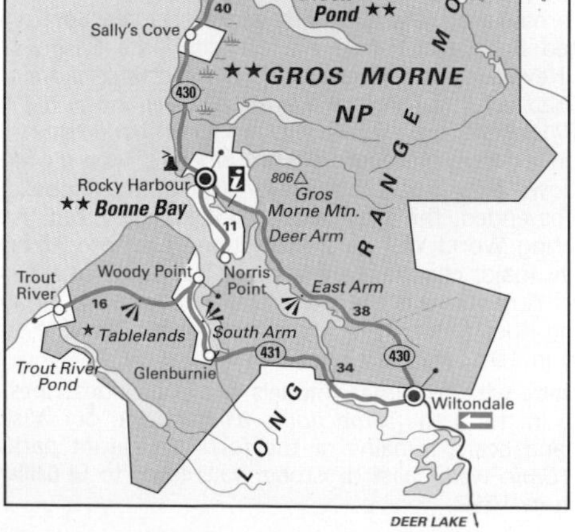

★★**Bonne Bay Area** – *Take Rte. 431 from Wiltondale 50km/31mi to Trout River (food, fuel).* This is a beautiful drive along a deep fjord—a glacial trough whose several arms are surrounded by the squat peaks of the Long Range Mountains. The road travels westward along the **South Arm** from Glenburnie, offering gorgeous **views**★★ of the bay. Fishing boats and small houses are set against the dark blue waters of the arm with the flat-topped mountains rising all around.

From Woody Point, as Route 431 ascends to the west, the red-brown rubble of a desertlike area known as the **Tablelands★** is abruptly visible, a jarring contrast to the lush green vegetation of the rest of the park. These mountains consist of rock that was once part of the earth's mantle—a magnesium and iron layer surrounding the planet's core—and are evidence of **plate tectonics**, the shifting of the plates within the earth's crust. For a closer look at the Tablelands, stop at the turnoff *(4.5km/2.8 mi from Woody Point)* where a **panel display** describes the geological history of this unique natural feature. This vantage point offers a striking **view** of the barren expanse. A foot path leads from the parking area into the heart of the Tablelands *(for information on guided hikes, contact the visitor centre)*. Beyond the little fishing village of Trout River is the long finger lake called **Trout River Pond** *(tour boats depart mid-Jun–mid-Sept daily 10am–4pm; round-trip 2hrs 30min; commentary; reservations required; $25; ♿ Tableland Boat Tours ☎ 709-451-2101)*. Dominating the return drive to Woody Point is the vast bulk of **Gros Morne Mountain** (806m/2,644ft) to the north, the highest point in the park and the park's namesake. *Ferry service from Woody Point to Norris Point may be available; otherwise, visitors must retrace the route to Wiltondale.* From Wiltondale Route 430 travels northeast along **East Arm**, a vantage point for lovely **views★★** of Bonne Bay, and along Deer Arm. For an in-depth preview of the park's unique geology, stop at the **visitor centre** near Rocky Harbour. There videos, talks, literature, photographs and rock displays are provided as well as a telescope for eyeing nearby Gros Morne Mountain *(to reach the summit, take the James Callaghan Trail, 3km/1.8mi south of visitor centre; 6-8hrs round-trip)*.

★**From Rocky Harbour to St. Pauls** – *40km/25mi by Rte. 430. Fuel and food available in settlements along the way.* Overlooking a wide inlet of Bonne Bay, the small coastal community of **Rocky Harbour** functions as a service and accommodation centre for park visitors.

On a promontory just north of Rocky Harbour, **Lobster Cove Head lighthouse** *(open daily in summer)* provides expansive **views★★** of the town, Gros Morne Mountain, the mouth of the bay and the Gulf of St. Lawrence.

Built on a narrow plain between the sea and the Long Range Mountains, the road affords a pretty drive up the coast past Sally's Cove, one of several little fishing communities along this coastal route. Sometimes the road is at sea level, sometimes higher above a rocky coast, but all along, the Long Range Mountains, just inland, appear like a gigantic step up from the sea because of their cropped tops. Before the turnoff to Western Brook Pond's trailhead, the rusty remains of the **SS Ethie** shipwreck can be seen on the beach. A small panel describes the fate of the ship's 1919 voyage.

★★**Western Brook Pond** – *29km/18mi from Rocky Harbour.* Western Brook runs through a spectacular gorge (which, in typical Newfoundland understatement, is called a "pond") in the Long Range Mountains before it crosses the narrow coastal plain and reaches the sea. The pond is flanked by almost vertical cliffs that rise to a desolate boulder-strewn alpine plateau where snow remains in crevices, even in August. Resembling a fjord because of these towering cliffs, this gorge is not a true fjord because it does not extend to the sea; the pond is fresh water. Bonne Bay, St. Paul's Inlet, Parson's Pond (just north of the park) and the large Bay of Islands *(map p 276)* are fjords. Whether "pond" or "fjord," all of these bodies of water are the result of glacial gouging in the last Ice Age.

Gros Morne National Park

Western Brook Pond

A trail leads across the boggy coastal plain *(boardwalks over marshy areas)* to the edge of the pond *(4km/2.5mi walk to boat dock; allow 40min one way)*. Gradually the deep gorge and truncated mountains become clearly visible, weather permitting. The only way to see the interior of Western Brook Pond is to take the **boat trip** *(departs Jun 1–Jun 19 daily 1pm; Jun 20–Labour Day daily 10am, 1pm & 4pm; rest of Sept–mid-Oct daily 1pm; round-trip 2hrs 15min; commentary; reservations required; $27; Norock Assn. www.oceanviewmotel.com ☎ 709-458-2730 or 800-563-9887; jacket recommended entire season)*. By viewing the varied shapes and exposed surfaces of the cliffs from the vantage point of the boat, at pond level, visitors can sense the geological uniqueness of this ancient glacial valley. The sheer granite cliffs (600m/2,000ft) and the depth of the water (approaching 200m/600ft) can be appreciated. Impressive waterfalls spill over the towering peaks to the cliff bases below.

After Western Brook Pond, the road follows along the coast with views of the mountains, spotted with seasonal snow caught in crevices, and of the shore covered with rocks, boulders and driftwood. The road continues to **St. Pauls**, a small fishing settlement clustered at the mouth of a deep fjord against a backdrop of mountains.

Designated "The Viking Trail," Route 430 exits the park above Shallow Bay and continues north along the coast for another 300km/200mi to L'Anse aux Meadows, with similar sea views but less dramatic mountain views, since the Long Range peaks are smaller and farther inland. Several native burial grounds are located at the archaeological site in **Port au Choix National Historic Site** *(135km/84mi north of St. Pauls)*.

HEART'S CONTENT Cable Station★

Map p 276

A little town founded about 1650 on Trinity Bay, Heart's Content is the site of the first successful landing, in 1866, of the **transatlantic telegraph cable**. North America's major relay site for nearly 100 years, the now obsolete station has been converted into a museum by the provincial government.

The landing was the result of years of work by the New York, Newfoundland and London Telegraph Co., led by American financier Cyrus W. Field. The first attempt to lay a cable in 1858 failed after inaugural messages were sent between Queen Victoria and US President James Buchanan. A second attempt in 1865 also failed. Finally in the following year, Field successfully used the ocean liner *Great Eastern* to lay the cable between Valencia, Ireland and Heart's Content, where it joined a cable to New York. Messages initially cost $5 a word, and the station handled 3,000 messages a day. Improved communications technology led to the station's eventual closing in 1965.

VISIT *1.5hrs*

Kids *58km/36mi north of Trans-Can Hwy. by Rte. 80, Avalon Peninsula. Open mid-Jun–early-Oct daily 10am–5:30pm. Rest of the year open by appointment only. ☎ 709-729-0592 or 709-583-2160.*

Displays tell the story of communications with special emphasis on the cable's impact on communications. There is a **film** *(20min)* and special section on the laying of the transatlantic cables, the part played by the *Great Eastern* and the importance of Heart's Content. Costumed guides are on site for tours of the replica of the first cable office (1866) and operating room. The original equipment can be compared to the complex equipment in use at the station's closing in 1965.

L'ANSE AUX MEADOWS★★

Map p 276

On a grassy ledge facing Epaves Bay at the northernmost tip of Newfoundland's Great Northern Peninsula, the remains of what is the oldest European settlement in North America authenticated to date are preserved for posterity. This remote site has been included on UNESCO's World Heritage List as a property of universal value.

Historical Notes

The Vikings Explore – By AD 900 the Vikings (also known as the Norse) from present-day Scandinavia had settled in Iceland, and from there explored Greenland, Baffin Island and beyond. The account of a land sighting by a Greenland-destined ship blown off course inspired **Leif Ericsson**, then residing in Greenland, to go exploring. About AD 1000 Ericsson landed at a fertile spot and built a settlement for the winter. He named the location "Vinland" for the wild grapes his crew is said to have found there. This story is preserved in two Norse tales: the *Saga of the Greenlanders* and the *Saga of Eric the Red*, which were communicated by word of mouth for hundreds of years before being recorded.

n Search of Vinland – Though many scholars have tried to find Vinland, its location ; unknown. Generally thought to be on the southeastern coast of the US because of he grapes, this location was, however, too far for ships to have sailed in the time uggested by the sagas. Then in 1960, **Helge Ingstad**, a Norwegian explorer and writer, nd his archaeologist wife, **Anne Stine**, began a systematic search of the coast from lew England northward. Led to a group of overgrown mounds near L'Anse aux Aeadows by a local resident, they excavated them from 1961 to 1968. Foundations f eight sod buildings of the type the Norse built in Iceland were uncovered and several rtifacts undeniably Norse in origin were found. Evidence of iron working—an art nknown to the North American Indian—was unearthed. Samples of bone, turf and harcoal were carbon dated to around AD 1000.

'hough impossible to prove it is the elusive Vinland (no one can envisage grapes rowing in Newfoundland), L'Anse aux Meadows is certainly a Norse settlement, and he only one ever discovered to date in North America. Experts believe the settlement vas a base of encampment for further exploration, especially trips south in search of imber and trading goods. Occupied by about 100 men and women, the camp was robably deserted after five or ten years. Newfoundland's harsh conditions, coupled vith the growing accessibility to southern European markets, most likely led to its bandonment.

ccess – *453km/281mi north of Trans-Can Hwy. by Rtes. 430 and 436.*

VISIT *3hrs*

Open mid-Jun–Labour Day daily 9am–8pm. Rest of Sept daily 9:30am–4:30pm. $5. ♿ *http://parkscanada.pch.gc.ca/parks/newfoundland/l'anse_meadows/l'anse_meadowse.htm ☎ 709-623-2608.*

In the **visitor centre** displays depict the Norse way of life and what a settlement might have looked like, but the highlight is the collection of artifacts found on-site. A stirring **film** *(28min)* on the Ingstads' search provides an enlightening introduction to the visit.

Completely excavated, the site has been preserved as grassy borders that outline the foundations of the original structures. The layout of the dwellings, work buildings and a smithy (the location of the earliest-known iron smelting in North America) can be clearly distinguished. Nearby, three **sod buildings**—a long house, a building and a workshed—have been faithfully reconstructed.

Inside, wooden platforms that served as beds line the walls. Firepits are placed at intervals in the middle of the earthen floors. A few animals skins and iron cooking utensils suggest the spartan existence of the inhabitants.

At the end of "The Viking Trail," **St. Anthony**, a large service centre, is the nearest city (*food, accommodations and air service)* to L'Anse aux Meadows. At the turn of the century, a British doctor, **Sir Wilfred Grenfell** (1865-1940), began his medical missionary work in the area, including Labrador. He became world renowned in his time, and today St. Anthony preserves his memory through the hospital he established, a cooperative craft shop and the house local residents built for him. Now called the **Grenfell House Museum** *(open late Jun–Labour Day daily 9am–8pm; late May–mid-Jun & rest of Sept daily 9am–5pm; rest of the year by appointment; $4; ☎ 709-454-4010)*, the home contains displays about his social involvement in the province, his medical practice and his personal life.

Len Klingen

L'Anse aux Meadows

ST. JOHN'S★★

Population 101,936
Map p 276
Tourist Office ☎709-729-2830

One of the oldest cities in North America, the capital of Newfoundland sits on the northeast arm of the Avalon Peninsula, facing the expansive Atlantic Ocean. This historic sea port owes its founding to a fine natural harbour that now services an international shipping trade.

Historical Notes

Early Years – According to tradition **John Cabot** entered the harbour on Saint John's day in 1497. Whether this claim is true or not, it has been established that, by the turn of the century, ships from several European countries were using the harbour as a fishing base. Under charter from Elizabeth I of England, **Sir Humphrey Gilbert** (c.1537-83) sailed to North America, arriving in St. John's harbour in 1583. Finding the crews of several countries assembled in one place, he seized the opportunity to declare Her Majesty's sovereignty, and thus is credited with giving England its first possession in the New World. Before his death at sea, Gilbert reputedly joined in the customary celebrations in St. John's of "fishing admiral" elections. Determined to maintain their fishing monopolies, England's West Country merchants *(p 229)* opposed settlement of Newfoundland, aided by the captains of their ships—the fishing admirals whose often harsh and abusive rule discouraged prospective settlers. From 1675 to 1677 a formal ban on settlement was in effect. But gradually people associated with the growing fishing industry began to take up year-round residence.

The Anglo-French Wars – Fear of French expansion changed the attitude of the British government toward permanent settlement. The French had established fortifications at Placentia in 1662 and proceeded to mount attacks on British harbours, especially St. John's. When a French force from Placentia destroyed St. John's in 1696, the British realized they must have more settlers—permanent residents—to defend their territory. St. John's fell twice again to the French, with the final battle in 1762 at the end of the Seven Years' War, though the city was recaptured soon afterwards. These attacks prompted the British to fortify the harbour entrance and Signal Hill *(p 284)*, a strategic promontory between the sea and the city, but St. John's was never again threatened.

Devastating Fires – In the 19C the capital suffered five fires that virtually wiped out the entire community each time. The first in 1816 was followed by others in 1817, 1819, 1846, and the most extensive of all in 1892. A photo taken by Sir Wilfred Grenfell at the time shows the twin towers of the Basilica of St. John the Baptist, one of the few structures still partially standing amid the devastation. Each time, the city was rebuilt, primarily in prevailing architectural styles such as Gothic Revival and, after the 1892 fire, Second Empire, styles still evident in the historic structures of the city today. The rapid expansion of St. John's as a commercial centre during the 19C was reversed each time by the fires.

Confederation and the 20C – St. John's was a wealthy city in the early 20C and during World War II when it served as a base for North American convoys. After the war the Dominion of Newfoundland's decision to enter Confederation resulted in a decline in the city's economy, despite a substantial infusion of federal funds. Its industries collapsed as cheaper Canadian manufactured goods entered Newfoundland. Port activity suffered and St. John's importance as a fish-exporting centre was reduced as major firms abandoned the salt-fish trade for growing wholesale consumer markets. Today the city's harbour serves as a supply and repair depot for international and local shipping. Over 1,000 commercial vessels of approximately 22 nationalities annually visit this major refueling station. Further resurgence is anticipated as a result of the discovery of offshore oil reserves in recent years.

Regatta Day – Each year **Quidi Vidi** (KID-dy VID-dy) **Lake** is the site of St. John's Regatta, the oldest continuing sporting event in North America (since 1826). Held on the first Wednesday in August (or the first fine day thereafter), the regatta is probably the only civic holiday decided that morning. The local population waits for the cry, "The races are on!" and then crowds the lakeshore to watch competitors row the 2.6km/1.6mi course, the major event of the all-day carnival.

★★HARBOUR AND OLD CITY *1 day. Map p 283.*

The city's **site**★ borders a harbour almost landlocked except for a slim passage to the ocean known as **The Narrows**. Only about 207m/680ft wide, this channel is flanked by 150m/500ft cliffs rising on the north side to form Signal Hill. For about 1.6km/1mi, the harbour widens to nearly 800m/.5mi, surrounded by the steep slopes on which the city is built. Parallel to the water, **Harbour Drive** skirts the busy dock where ships from Portugal, Spain, Poland, Russia and Japan as well as Cana-

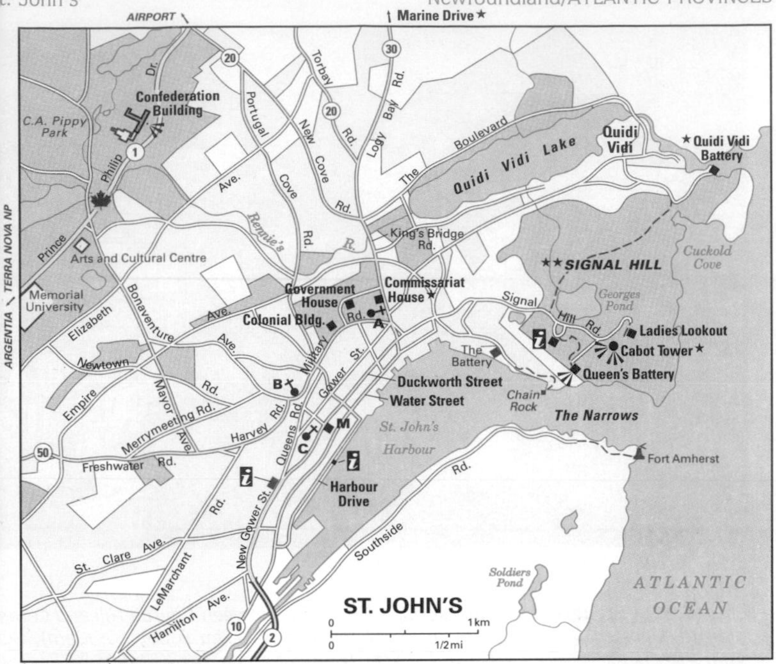

dian ships are often berthed. Narrow streets lined with brightly painted wooden houses, topped with flat or mansard roofs, ascend the hills. Perpendicular to them, the main thoroughfares of the old city, **Water** and **Duckworth Streets**, contain restaurants, shops and banks. Especially colourful, **George Street** is home to several pubs and eateries.

★ **Newfoundland Museum** (**M**) – *Duckworth St. Open Jul–Aug daily 10am–6pm (Thu 9pm). Rest of the year Tue–Fri 9am–5pm (Thu 9pm), weekends 10am–6pm. Closed national holidays. www.delweb.com/nfmuseum ☎ 709-729-2329.* Offering an insightful introduction to the province, this small museum is devoted to Newfoundland's history and prehistory. The ground-floor gallery permits a behind-the-scene's view of the museum through its natural history collection. The second floor features displays on native cultures, notably those of the Beothuk Indians and Labrador Inuit. On the third floor re-created rooms and reconstructions such as a fishing "stage" with its flakes, ropes and nets depict the life of European settlers from the 18C onward. Replicas of a schoolroom and grocery store of the late 19C are particularly noteworthy.

★ **Commissariat House** – *King's Bridge Rd. Open mid-Jun–early Oct daily 10am–5:30pm. ☎ 709-729-6730.* Dating from 1821 this large clapboard house with its tall chimneys was one of the few buildings to escape the 19C fires. Used for many years by the Commissariat—the department responsible for supplying the military post of St. John's with nonmilitary provisions—the house also served as the local government pay office. After 1871 it became the rectory for adjacent **Church of St. Thomas** (**A**), an elegantly simple edifice (1836) of painted wood. Restored to reflect the 1830 period, the house contains the commissariat offices and kitchen *(ground floor)*, entertaining rooms and bedrooms *(second floor)*. Reconstructed on the grounds, a **coach house** lodges an exhibit on the restoration process.

Within walking distance *(Military Rd.)* stand two other historic structures: the residence of the lieutenant-governor called **Government House**, a Georgian stone building (1830) surrounded by pleasant grounds *(only the grounds can be visited without appointment; for house tour, ☎ 709-729-4494)* and the former seat of the provincial assembly, the **Colonial Building** *(open year-round Mon–Fri 9am–4:15pm & Wed 6:30pm–9:45pm; closed first week Dec; 🅿 ☎ 709-729-3065)*, a limestone structure with a Neoclassical portico (1850), which now houses the provincial archives *(access weekdays only; no guided tours)*.

Basilica of St. John the Baptist (**B**) – *Corner Harvey Rd., Military Rd. and Bonaventure Ave. Open year-round Mon–Fri 8am–4:30pm (Wed 8pm), Sat 8am–6:30pm, Sun 8:30am–12:30pm. Closed national holidays except for mass. 🅿 ♿ ☎ 709-754-2170.* Situated on the highest point of the ridge above the city, this twin-towered Roman Catholic church has become a landmark, clearly distinguishable from the harbour, Signal Hill and other vantage points. Opened for worship in 1850, the basilica has an ornate interior with statuary and altar carving.

St. John's

Cathedral of St. John the Baptist (**C**) – *Gower St. between Church Hill and Cathedral Rd. Open mid-Jun–Sept Mon–Sat 10am–4:30pm (Thu & Sat 10:30am), Sun 1pm–4pm & for services. Rest of the year by appointment. ☎ 709-726-5677.* This imposing stone structure was originally designed in 1843 by noted British architect **Sir George Gilbert Scott** (1811–78). Destroyed by fire in 1892, the Anglican church was reconstructed only in this century, a good example of Gothic Revival architecture with a finely sculpted interior, wooden vaulted ceilings and **reredos**, an ornamental stone or wooden partition behind an altar.

★★**Signal Hill** – Topped by Cabot Tower, Signal Hill is formed of cliffs rising steeply at the mouth of the harbour. A natural lookout commanding the sea approach, the hill permits splendid views of the city and environs by day and night.

Despite its obvious strategic value, Signal Hill was not strongly fortified until the Napoleonic Wars (1803–15). Traditionally used as a signal station to warn of enemy ships, the hill acted in later years as a means to alert merchants to the arrival of their fleets. In 1901 **Guglielmo Marconi** chose the site for an experiment to prove that radio signals could be transmitted long distances by electromagnetic waves. When he received the letter "S" in Morse code from Poldhu in Cornwall, England—a distance of 2,700km/1,700mi—he made history.

Visit – *Open mid-Jun–Labour Day daily 8:30am–8pm. Rest of the year daily 8:30am–4:30pm. $2.50. ♿ P ☎ 709-772-5367.* The **visitor centre** contains artifacts, dioramas, audiovisuals and panels on the history of Newfoundland, emphasizing the development of St. John's.

Completed in 1898 to memorialize the quadcentenary of John Cabot's visit to Newfoundland, **Cabot Tower**★ also commemorates the diamond jubilee of Queen Victoria's accession. Inside, displays on Signal Hill are complemented by information on communications, including a section about Marconi. The summit of the tower affords a **panorama**★★★ of the city, the harbour and the coastline as far as Cape Spear, the most easterly point in North America *(p 285)*.

A path leads to **Ladies Lookout**, the crown of the hill (160m/525ft) and a vantage point offering views of the surroundings. From **Queen's Battery**—the fortification (1833) that dominates the Narrows—there is a good **view**★ of the harbour. Below is Chain Rock—a white pillar in the Narrows from which a chain was stretched across the harbour entrance in the 18C to keep enemy vessels out. On the other side of the Narrows stand the remains of Fort Amherst (1763) now housing a lighthouse.

From mid-July through August, students in the 19C uniforms of the Royal Newfoundland Regiment perform a **military tattoo** *(Wed, Thu, Sat, Sun 3pm & 7pm, weather permitting)* consisting of fife and drum corps and military drill near the Queen's Battery. Derived from a Dutch word, *tattoo* is a bugle or drum signal to call soldiers to quarters at night.

Additional Sights *Map p 283*

★**Quidi Vidi Battery** – *Take King's Bridge Rd. Turn right on Forest Rd. When road becomes Quidi Vidi Village Rd., drive 2km/1.2mi to Cuckhold's Cove Rd. Turn right. May be closed for the season; phone for hours ☎ 709-729-2977.* Built by the French during their occupation of St. John's in 1762, this emplacement, with a colonial-style wooden house at its centre, stands above the community. In the early

19C the British tried to move fishermen away from the inlet and block the channel since it provided a means of attacking St. John's from the rear. The fishermen refused to budge, so the plan was abandoned and the battery strengthened. Restored to the early-19C period, the house re-creates the living quarters of soldiers stationed there.

Below is the tiny fishing community of **Quidi Vidi**, which has a narrow channel connecting to the larger Quidi Vidi Lake, site of the annual St. John's Regatta *(p 282)*.

Confederation Building – *Prince Philip Dr. Open year-round Mon–Fri 8:30am–4:30pm. Closed national holidays. Information office on ground floor.* ✗ ♿ 🅿 ☎ *709-729-2300.* Newfoundland's Parliament and some provincial government offices are housed in this imposing building. Constructed in 1960 and expanded in 1985, the edifice stands high above the city, providing a good **view** from its front entrance of the harbour and Signal Hill. When in session the **legislative assembly** can be observed *(sessions Feb–May Mon–Fri, third floor Visitors' Gallery)*. Note that the government benches are to the left of the Speaker's chair. Accepted practice elsewhere is for the government to sit on the right. When the Newfoundland Assembly met in the Colonial Building *(p 283)*, there was only one fireplace—to the left of the Speaker. The governing body exercised their prerogative and sat by the fire. The tradition remains.

EXCURSIONS

★**Cape Spear** – ◉ *Map p 276. About 11km/7mi south; follow Water St. to Leslie St. Turn left at Leslie St. Go over bridge, continue straight after stop sign, following the road (Hwy. 11). Grounds open year-round. Visitor centre open mid-May–mid-Oct daily 10am–6pm.* ☎ *709-722-4444.* At longitude 52°37'24", Cape Spear is North America's most easterly point. On clear days there are marvelous **views★** of the coast and of the entrance to St. John's harbour. Whales can usually be seen in the waters off the cape seasonally *(Jun–Sept)*.

Walkways from the parking lot lead to the actual point, the visitor centre, an operational lighthouse *(not open to the public)* and the World War II battery where gun emplacements and bunkers remain. The visitor centre features a small display on the function and evolution of lighthouses. Restored to evoke the life of a lighthouse keeper in the 1840s, the domed, square **1835 lighthouse★** *(visit by 30min guided tour only, mid-May–mid-Oct daily 10am–6pm; $2.50)* is the province's oldest lighthouse.

The return trip to St. John's *(30km/19mi)* can be made via the villages of Maddox Cove and **Petty Harbour**, the latter a pleasant fishing village with fishing shacks and flakes—wooden racks used to dry the fish.

★**Witless Bay Ecological Reserve** – *Map p 276. Disembarkation on the islands is not permitted. They can be viewed only by boat. Embarkation from town of Bay Bulls, 30km/19mi south of St. John's via Rte. 10. Then watch for directional signs of your chosen boat tour company to the dock. (Shuttle service to Bay Bulls available from major hotels in St. John's.) Departs Apr–Sept daily 9:30am–5pm; round-trip 2hrs 30min; commentary; reservations required; $28-$32;* ✗ ♿ *O'Brien's Whale & Bird Tours, Inc.* ☎ *709-753-4850. Departs mid-Apr–Oct daily 10am–6:30pm; round-trip 2hr 30min; commentary; $28;* ♿ *Gatherall's* ☎ *709-334-2887.* As feeding and nesting sites, the fish-filled waters and shore islands of Witless Bay attract thousands of sea birds annually. Three barren islets house the bird population: Great, Green and Gull Islands. In summer common murres, greater black-backed gulls, black guillemots and blacked-legged kittiwakes are plentiful. The **Atlantic puffin** colony here is reputedly the largest on the east coast of North America. Tour boats get as close as possible to two of the rocky isles where hundreds of sea birds skim the water, dive, circle overhead or light in the crevices and crannies of the rocks.

An additional highlight of the cruise is **whale watching★★** (late spring and summer). The reserve is a seasonal feeding area for humpback, minke, pothead and fin whales, particularly in summer. Good opportunities to view icebergs at close range may also occur (late spring and early summer).

★**Marine Drive** – *12km/8mi north on Hwys. 30 and 20. Leave St. John's on Logy Bay Rd. (Rte. 30). After 5.5 km/3mi, turn right to Marine Dr.* A pleasant drive up the coast through residential areas north of St. John's, the road ascends and descends, affording endless views of the sea, headlands, cliffs, beaches, boats and fields. The **view★** from **Outer Cove** is especially lovely. At **Middle Cove** there is an accessible beach, good for strolling along the shore.

Admission prices and hours published in this guide are accurate at press time. We apologize for any inconvenience resulting from outdated information.

SAINT-PIERRE AND MIQUELON★

(France)
Population 6,392
Map p 276
Tourist Office ☎508-41-22-22

Few people realize that part of France lies off the coast of North America on tin[y] islands 48km/30mi by boat from Newfoundland. The two principal islands—Saint Pierre, and the larger Miquelon, connected by a long sand bar to what was once [a] third island, Langlade—are home to a French-speaking population. A decidedly Continental flavour pervades these rocky and remote shores.

Historical Notes – Cod fishing is the reason for settlement on these islands. From th[e] early 16C, the archipelago was used as a base for Basque and Breton fishermen working the Grand Banks. By the Treaty of Paris in 1763, it became official French territory, but ownership changed repeatedly as France and England fought for hegemony on the continent. Although France was the loser in this battle, she retained these islands as a *pied à terre* for her fishing fleets.

During US prohibition (1920-33), the islands experienced brief prosperity as a "rum running" centre. Today only tourism adds to income from the fishing industry. Until 1976 the islands were an overseas French territory. Now they are a *collectivité territoriale* of France, sending a *deputé* to the French Parliament and a member to the Senate.

VISIT *2 days*

Passenger ferry from Fortune to Saint-Pierre island: departs from Fortune May–Sept daily 2:45pm. Next day departs 1pm from Saint-Pierre. 1hr. Commentary. Reservations required. Round-trip $64.95. ✕ ♿ Lake's Travel Ltd. in Fortune ☎709-832-2006. Warning: the sea crossing can be rough.

Air service from Sydney and Halifax, NS and Montreal, PQ provided by Air Saint Pierre. For information & reservations Air Saint-Pierre ☎508-41-47-18 in Saint-Pierre, or Canadian Airlines International ☎800-665-1177 (Canada), ☎800-426-7000 (US).

English is not commonly spoken on the islands. Telephone operators and tourist office staffs are bilingual, however. For accommodations, contact the **Regional Tourist Agency Saint-Pierre**, *B.P. 4274, 97500 Saint-Pierre et Miquelon, Amérique du Nord ☎011-508-41-22-22.*

★**Saint-Pierre** – From the sea Saint-Pierre appears to be a desolate island of stunted trees and low plants. Upon arrival in the harbour of the island's capital and administrative centre, also named Saint-Pierre, visitors can sense a striking cultural difference from the rest of North America. Lining the waterfront, tall stone buildings house pastry shops, fine restaurants and boutiques stocked with imported goods; the streets are narrow and full of French cars.

At the entrance to the harbour sits the picturesque islet of **Ile-aux-Marins**★ *(accessible from Saint-Pierre, in front of the tourist office, by 10min ferry ride)*, once a community of over 800 inhabitants, many of whom were active in cod fishing. Villagers progressively abandoned the site for Saint-Pierre whose fishing industry continued to modernize.

Today the few remaining houses on Ile-aux-Marins are primarily vacation homes for Saint-Pierre residents. Centered in the old schoolhouse, the **museum** contains a highly poetic presentation of isle history through artifacts and memorabilia *(open Jul-Aug daily 1:30pm–5:30pm; May–Jun & Sept–Oct by appointment only; 10FF; ☎508-41-22-22)*. The treeless terrain permits good **views** of Saint-Pierre and the remains of one of the more than 600 shipwrecks that have occurred in the archipelago.

Miquelon and Langlade – *Boat departures to Miquelon and Langlade available from Saint-Pierre. In summer, daily ferry to Langlade. Transportation by shuttle van to the village of Miquelon may be arranged (contact Tourist Agency Saint-Pierre above).* Except for the small working town of the same name, the northern island of Miquelon is untouched moorland of soft hills and long beaches. Along the unpaved road from Miquelon to Langlade (25km/16mi), herds of shaggy wild horses may be spotted roaming the deserted meadows. At low tide seals can be seen lying on the rocks of **Grand Barachois** and a variety of sea birds frequenting the shores. The road crosses the isthmus known as the Dune of Langlade, a sand bar formed in part by debris from the numerous shipwrecks that have occurred since 1800. Situated at the southern end is the "island" of Langlade, largely uninhabited except for a tiny settlement in the hills above the ferry landing. Along the east side of the dune, a wide beach stretches out in the vicinity of Anse du Gouvernement.

TERRA NOVA NATIONAL PARK★

Map p 276

Scarred by glaciers of the past, this 396sq km/153sq mi area on the shores of Bonavista Bay is a combination of rolling country and indented coastline. Deep fjords or "sounds" reach inland, and in early summer these coastal waters are dotted with icebergs that float down with the Labrador Current. The Trans-Canada Highway bisects the park with some good views of the sounds, but visitors must leave the highway to truly appreciate its natural beauty.

Access – *On Trans-Can Hwy. 58km/36mi from Gander, or 210km/130mi from St. John's.*

VISIT *1 day*

Open year-round. $3.25/day use fee (mid-May–mid-Oct). Visitor centre open mid-Jun–Labour Day daily 9am–9pm; mid-May–early Jun & mid-Sept–mid-Oct daily 9am–5pm. △ ✗ ♿ *http://parkscanada.pch.gc.ca ☎ 709-533-2801.*

★★ **Bluehill Pond Lookout** – *7km/5mi from park's north entrance. Turn onto gravel road and continue approximately 2km/1mi to the observatory platform.* From the lookout platform there is a **panorama**★★ of the whole park—deep inlets, cliffs, rocks, lakes, forest, bog and hills. To the south Newman Sound and the ocean, scattered with icebergs *(in season)*, can clearly be seen in good weather.

★ **Newman Sound** – *12km/8mi from park's north entrance, take road to the visitor centre and Newman Sound. About 1.5km/1mi to the trail.* The beauty of this sound—a deep inlet with a sandy beach—can be appreciated by taking the walking trail along its wooded shore. Seasonal wildflowers and tiny seashells complement the setting.

Ochre Lookout – *18km/11mi from park's north entrance; take gravel road to the tower, about 3km/2mi. Observation deck.* From this lookout tower, another **panorama**★ allows visitors to comprehend the vastness of the park. At this height, Clode and Newman Sounds are clearly visible, weather permitting.

TRINITY★★

Population 277

Map p 276

Situated on a hilly peninsula jutting into Trinity Bay, this charming seaside community has a lovely **setting**★ with **views** of the sea, rocks, fields and the small protected harbour. One of the oldest settlements in Newfoundland, the village evokes a feeling of a bygone era with its narrow streets, tiny gardens and colourful "box" houses. Sufficiently established in 1615, the town became the site of the first Admiralty Court in Canada's history. Sir Richard Whitbourne was sent from Britain to settle disputes between the resident fishermen and those who crossed the Atlantic just for the season. In time, Trinity rivaled St. John's in socio-economic standing, but receded in importance when the latter became the provincial capital. Today a small fishing industry and tourism are its mainstays. It is a popular area for **whale watching** *(departures*

W. Sturge/Government of Newfoundland

Cape Bonavista Lighthouse

Jun–Labour Day daily 6am–6pm, weather permitting; minimum 6 people; rounc trip 3hrs; commentary; reservations required; $44; Ocean Contact Ltc www.oceancontact.com ☎ 709-464-3269).

Access – *74km/46mi northeast of Trans-Can Hwy. by Rte. 230. Turn off Rte. 230 fc 5km/3mi.*

VISIT *1 day*

Located in a restored house overlooking the harbour, the **visitor centre** *(open mic Jun–mid-Oct daily 10am–6pm; ♿ ☎ 709-464-2042)* has displays presenting th community's history. They chronicle Trinity's rise to prominence from the mid-18(to the early 19C as a center of commerce and society, only to be eclipsed b St. John's in the 1850s. Housed in a seven-room "salt box" dating to the 1880s the **Trinity Museum and Archives** *(open mid-Jun–mid-Sept daily 10am–6pm; $2 ☎ 709-464-2244)* contains local artifacts and historical documents.

The **Hiscock House** *(open mid-Jun–mid-Oct daily 10am–6pm; ☎ 709-464-2042)* ha been restored to its early-1900s appearance and contains some original furnishing of the Hiscock family for whom the home was built in 1881.

In a pastoral setting with the sea in the background, **St. Paul's Anglican Church** (1892 stands as a distinctive village landmark. The 31m/102ft clock spire of this larg wooden house of worship towers above the town, visible from all vantage points A small graveyard adjoins the property.

In use for over 150 years, the **Holy Trinity Roman Catholic Church** is distinguished b its detached belfry as well as the clean simplicity of its elegant tower.

EXCURSION TO CAPE BONAVISTA

From Trinity, Route 230 northbound continues inland and returns to the sea a Port Union and Catalina, two fishing communities set along the shore. At Catalin Route 237 crosses the peninsula, ending at Amherst Cove, where Route 23 continues northward to the cape town of Bonavista *(52km/31mi north of Trinity)*

Bonavista – This large seaside town is another fishing community with houses se around an outer harbour protected by a breakwater and a sheltered inner harbou for small boats.

Throughout the 16C, European fishing fleets used the harbour. By about 1600 the area had become a British settlement and remained so, despite several attempts by the French to capture it in the 18C.

Situated by the sea toward the capeside of town, the .6ha/1.5 acre **Mockbeggar Property** *(open mid-Jun–early Oct daily 10am–5:30pm; ☎ 709-468-7300)* features a barn, a storage building and the Bradley House. Restored to the 1930s period, the house contains the personal belongings of prosperous local businessman anc senator Frederick Gordon Bradley.

From the town drive about 5km/3mi on Rte. 235, which becomes Church St. Continue past town hall over bridge and bear right at fork.

★**Cape Bonavista** – Supposedly named Bonavista ("good view") by explorer John Cabot in 1497, the cape is a superb setting with pounding waves, a clear blue sea and interesting rock formations.

A drive through fields with **views** of the sea leads to the remote tip of the cape. A **statue** of Cabot commemorates his first North American landing, though recent research has cast doubt on the authenticity of this claim. Although he sailed under British colours, Cabot was Italian by birth. Completed in 1843 the **lighthouse**★ *(open mid-Jun–early Oct daily 10am–5:30pm; ☎ 709-468-7444)* has been restored by the provincial government to portray a lightkeeper's living quarters in the 1870s. Exhibits include the construction and restoration of the lighthouse, the operation of the lamps and the lightkeeper's duties. There are sweeping **views** of the rocky coast from the lighthouse itself.

Times given in this guide are approximate. When given with the distance, times allow the visitor to enjoy the scenery; when given for sightseeing, times are intended to provide an idea of the possible length of a visit.

Northwest Territories

Dan Heringa/ED&T – GNWT

Contrary to the misconception that the Canadian North is a frozen wilderness, this spectacular continental rooftop abounds in varied landscape: Arctic coastline, myriad lakes, meandering rivers, massive glaciers and polar expanses, all transformed by the light of the midnight sun. A vast region encompassing over a third of Canada, the Territories sustain less than one percent of the country's population. Except for the capital city of YELLOWKNIFE, few large settlements exist in this otherwise frontier wilderness, best suited for lovers of adventure, nature and indigenous cultures. Its planned partitioning before the turn of the century will result in native administration of ancestral lands *(Nunavut p 291)*.

Geographical Notes

Landscape – Comprising lands above the 60th parallel (except parts of Quebec and Labrador), the Territories stretch from Hudson Bay to the Yukon. They include the Arctic archipelago between the mainland and the North Pole, and the Hudson and James Bay islands south of the parallel. Even larger prior to 1905, the Territories also encompassed most of Alberta, Saskatchewan, Manitoba, northern Ontario and Quebec.

Mountains border this immense northland on two sides. In the east stand the glacier-strewn peaks of Baffin, Bylot, Devon and Ellesmere Islands. In the west rise the Mackenzie, Selwyn and Richardson Ranges—part of the rugged western backbone of North America. East of the Mackenzie Mountains is a tongue of lowlands, an extension of the plains of central Canada. Down this tongue runs the great Mackenzie River. East of the lowlands lies the scarred face of the Canadian Shield, pitted with lakes. Glaciers that retreated from this region 10,000 years ago scoured and gouged the ancient rocks, leaving behind an intricate pattern of lakes and deep coastal fjords that still exists today. Glacial debris—huge boulders, piles of moraine, **eskers** (narrow ridges of sand and gravel) and **drumlins** (elliptical-shaped hills inclining in the direction of the glacier's retreat)—bear witness to the region's geological history.

Permafrost – After the last Ice Age, a layer of permanently frozen earth developed in all regions where the ground remains at or below 0°C/32°F for two or more years (at least 40 percent of Canada). Permafrost, as it is known, generally starts about 0.3m/1ft or more below the surface and can be very shallow or as much as 370m/1,200ft deep, as at Resolute on Cornwallis Island.

Vegetation – The tree line crosses the Territories diagonally northwest to southea from the MACKENZIE DELTA to Hudson Bay at the Manitoba border. South and west this line extends the **boreal forest** of spruce, poplar, tamarack and jack pine. To th north and east is the **tundra**, sometimes called "the barren lands" for its bleak look winter and lack of trees. In summer dwarf shrubs, tiny flowers of all hues ar lichens—flat, rootless growths, part fungus, part algae that survive where no oth plant could possibly grow—thrive in the surface ground above the permafrost. Th latter prevents moisture from draining away. Known as **muskeg**, this surface ground sometimes very boggy because it cannot drain.

Climate – Annual precipitation over much of the Territories is so low (Yellowkni 254mm/10in, Inuvik 276mm/11in, Baker Lake 208mm/8in, Iqaluit 409mm/16in) th a great part of the region would be desert if the permafrost did not cradle wh moisture there is on the surface. Generally the winters are long, cold and dark and th summers surprisingly war and sunny, with long hours o daylight. The southern pa has 20 hours of daylight, whi north, in the Arctic Circle, never gets dark. The mea daily maximum temperature for July are 21°C/70°F in Ye lowknife, 19°C/66°F in Inuvik 15°C/59°F in Baker Lake an 12°C/53°F in Iqaluit. Th highest recorded temperatur in July was 36°C/97°F in Fo Simpson; the lowest wa –3°C/26°F in Holman, Victori Island.

Aurora Borealis

©Pekka Paviainen/Dembinsky Photo Assoc.

Aurora Borealis – Also know as the Northern Lights, thi amazing phenomenon ca usually be viewed in fall an winter. The sky "dissolves" int folded curtains of elusive, danc ing lights, sometimes many col oured, other times black an white. They seem to occu when electrically charged par ticles, emitted by the sun, col lide with atoms and molecule in the earth's outer atmo sphere, causing the latter to emit radiation, sometimes in th form of visible light. Researc on these displays is conducte at CHURCHILL, Manitoba.

Historical Notes

Earliest Settlement – The first inhabitants of North America came from Asia some 15,000–20,000 years ago, across the land bridge that is now the Bering Strait. They settled south of the ice cap that covered the continent. As it retreated, some moved north. Today these people form two distinct groups.

The Inuit – The life of the aboriginal people of the Arctic Coast revolved largely around hunting sea mammals—especially seal and whale—as a source of food; blubber for heat and light; skins for clothing, shelter and boats; and bone or ivory for the blades of their harpoons or other tools. The smaller sea mammals were hunted from **kayaks** (one-person canoes); whales were hunted from **umiaks**, which held up to 12 men. In winter animals were sought at openings in the ice. The occasional excursion south was made by **dogsled** to hunt caribou, the skins of which were used for clothing or bedding. The Inuit were nomadic—several families living and moving together. In winter they constructed **igloos**, dome-shaped snow houses made of blocks of ice, and entered by a tunnel. For insulation, the interior was lined with skins. In summer they lived in tents made of skins. Time not spent hunting or making clothes—especially their famous parkas—was devoted to carving bone and soapstone, a craft for which they are famous today.

Since the arrival of Europeans their lifestyle has changed drastically: a nomadic way of life is practically nonexistent, and igloos and dogsleds are no longer commonplace. Many still live by hunting, however, supplemented by income from arts and crafts. On the whole they retain more of their traditional lifestyle than North America's other ative cultures. A sizeable number of Inuit inhabit their Quebec homeland of Nunavik see *Michelin Green Guide to Quebec)*, a socio-cultural region established through rass-roots referendum in 1986 and officially recognized by the provincial governent. The creation of a homeland in the Northwest Territories *(Nunavut p 291)* should esult in greater autonomy in the 21C for the Inuit of northern Canada.

he Dene – The Athapaskan-speaking peoples of the sub-Arctic lived a difficult life in meagre environment. Travelling by canoe in summer and toboggan in winter, they unted caribou and fished, constantly on the move to find food. Home was a conicalhaped lodge similar to the teepees of the Plains Indians *(p 22)*. Today some of these eople have preserved a fairly traditional lifestyle based on hunting and fishing, but nany live on the fringe of contemporary society.

he Northwest Passage – A sea route between the Atlantic and Pacific Oceans around ne north of the American continent was the quest of explorers for centuries after it ecame obvious that America was a continent and not an adjunct of Asia. The first uropeans to visit this vast region came in search of a trade route to the Orient around ne north of the continent. British sailor **Martin Frobisher** made the first attempt in 1576. lis voyages were followed by those of **John Davis**, **Henry Hudson** and **William Baffin**, all of vhom have left their names on the map, and Sir John Franklin's in 1845. Their reports f ice-filled seas somewhat dampened enthusiasm for the passage. Except for exploation at the western end, no more attempts were made until the early 19C.

ur Traders – At the same time, other explorers were penetrating the interior of the erritories for skins of abundant fur-bearing animals. **Samuel Hearne** of the Hudson's Bay Company traversed much of the region, especially during his famous 1770-72 rip from CHURCHILL to Great Slave Lake, and later down the Coppermine River to the Beaufort Sea. Not long afterwards in 1789, **Alexander Mackenzie** of the rival North West Company travelled the river that bears his name. He named it the "river of disappointment": it led to the Arctic, not the Pacific Ocean, as he had hoped. After the two ur companies joined in 1821, several trading posts were established in the Territoies, some of which remain to this day.

Naval Explorers – Mackenzie's voyage sparked new interest in a northwest passage. The first half of the 19C saw the British Navy equipping expeditions to find a navigable oute. **John Franklin** made two overland trips to the western end, sailing a third time, in 1845, to locate the connecting channel from the east. Years passed with no word from im. Eventually a series of expeditions, 38 in all, were sent to discover his fate. It was established that he and his entire crew had perished after years of being marooned in he frozen waters. One effect of this tragedy was the exploration by his would-be escuers of a large part of the Territories. Finally a passable route of the passage was ound between the Canadian mainland and the Arctic islands, but not successfully navigated until Norwegian **Roald Amundsen** did so between 1903 and 1906. Since then many ships have followed the hazardous route, among them the schooner *St. Roch (p 76)*.

20C Development – In the late 19C and early 20C, the Geological Survey of Canada mounted expeditions under such men as Joseph Burr Tyrrell, Sir William Logan (after whom Mt. Logan is named), George Mercer Dawson (of Dawson City fame) and Vilhjalmar Stefansson to explore and map the Territories. By this time both Anglican and Roman Catholic missionaries were established in the region. In the 1930s a new breed of explorer arrived—the prospector. Several major mineral finds *(below)* encouraged more outsiders to come to the Territories. Mineral as well as oil exploration has continued to attract investment.

Goods are transported to and from the Territories by the Mackenzie and Dempster Highways. Huge strings of barges float up and down the Mackenzie River all summer. Between November and April, winter roads crisscross the frozen land, giving heavy transport access to places reachable only by air the rest of the year.

Partitioning of the Territories – In 1992 the residents of the Northwest Territories voted to divide their land by creating a new territory in the eastern portion. Stretching 2,000,156sq km/772,260sq mi nearly to Greenland from the Manitoba/Saskatchewan border, this homeland has been designated **Nunavut** meaning "our land" in the native language, Inuktitut. After a seven-year transition period, Nunavut is to be administered by its Inuit inhabitants.

Population – Of the 64,402 inhabitants in the Northwest Territories, over half claim aboriginal origin. Of these, the majority are Inuit. (The well-known name *eskimo*, meaning "eaters of raw meat," was given to the Inuit by the Indians of the south. *Inuit* means "the people" in Inuktitut.) The Dene or Athapaskan-speaking Indians comprise a sizeable portion of the population. The rest are Métis and nonnative residents.

Resources and Industries

Mining – Since the 1930s the basis of the economy has been mining. Fur trapping, forestry, fishing, tourism and the sale of native arts and crafts also contribute, but to a much lesser extent. Deposits of pitchblende—a source of uranium—and silver were discovered on the shores of the Great Bear Lake in 1930, arousing interest in the mineral possibilities of other regions, and leading to the great gold discoveries a YELLOWKNIFE. Today gold is still mined at Yellowknife, and at Indin Lake and a Contwoyto Lake farther north.

In 1964 the vast zinc and lead deposits at Pine Point on Great Slave Lake were founc These minerals are being mined at Nanisivik near Arctic Bay in the north of Baffin Islan and on Little Cornwallis Island. The search for diamonds has become the principal focu of mineral exploration since their discovery in 1991 in the Lac de Gras area.

Oil and Gas – Near Fort Liard, there is a small natural gas extraction and processin plant, and producing oil wells and a refinery at Norman Wells on the Mackenzie. Th 1968 discovery of major oil and gas fields in northern Alaska spurred the search fo such resources in northern Canada. Two potentially rich areas were identified: th Mackenzie Delta–Beaufort Sea region, and the high Arctic islands. Most oil explora tion has been confined to the MACKENZIE DELTA. Limited production and seasona shipping continue from Bent Horn, the northernmost oil field in the high Arctic islands Since 1985 lower oil prices have curtailed exploration and development. Recently however, interest in oil and gas exploration north of the 60th parallel has revived sinc the lifting of a 25-year moratorium on issuing rights in the Mackenzie Valley.

Handicrafts – The arts and crafts of the native inhabitants as well as the natura beauty and abundant wildlife of the Territories are mainstays of its growing tourism Largely because of their expressiveness and depiction of a disappearing lifestyle, th distinctive works produced by the aboriginal peoples have long been popular amon collectors and connoisseurs. Most famous are the **sculptures** of the Inuit. The grey o green soapstone can easily be worked with chisels and files before being polished t give it a distinctive finish.

Delicate carvings are fashioned from walrus tusks, caribou antlers or whalebone. Wal hangings and prints are also produced. Cape Dorset on Baffin Island is especiall famous for the latter. Clothing suited to this climate, particularly Inuit *parkas* an Indian *mukluks* decorated with beautiful beadwork, has become popular farther south

PRACTICAL INFORMATION

Getting There

By Air – Regular service to Yellowknife is provided by Canadian Airlines International and its affiliates from major Canadian gateway cities ☎800-426-7000 (Canada/US). Scheduled and chartered service in the Northwest Territories is offered by First Air ☎613-738-0200, or 800-267-1247 (US), and NWT Air ☎867-920-2500.

General Information

Accommodations and Visitor Information – Every year the government of the Northwest Territories publishes the *Explorers' Guide*, which lists hotels, motels, lodges, camps and outfitters. For a free copy and road map, contact **NWT Arctic Tourism**, Box 610, Yellowknife, NT, X1A 2N5 www.nwttravel.nt.ca ☎867-873-5007 or 800-661-0788 (Canada/US). Information is available for the new territory of Nunavut; contact **Nunavut Tourism**, PO Box 1450, Iqaluit, NT, X0A 0H0 www.nunatour.nt.ca ☎867-979-6551 or 800-491-7910 (Canada/US).

Driving in the North – *(Driver's license and insurance requirements p 304.)* Roads have all-weather gravel surfaces and are well maintained. Motorists are cautioned to pass other vehicles slowly to prevent flying rocks or skidding. Unless otherwise posted, the speed limit is 90km/h (55mph). **Seat belt** use is mandatory. Distances between gasoline stations can be great; it is advisable to fill up frequently. It is recommended that motorists carry at least one spare tire, water, insect repellant, first-aid kit, emergency flares and, in winter, snow shovel, parka, warm clothes, and a sleeping bag for each person in the vehicle. For highway conditions ☎800-661-0750 (Canada) or 800-661-0752 (Canada). Government **ferry** service (free) is provided along the Mackenzie, Dempster and Liard Highways; for information ☎800-661-0751 (Canada). To access Yellowknife, the **Mackenzie Highway** crosses the river at Fort Providence. The **Dempster Highway** crosses the Mackenzie River at Arctic Red River and the Peel River to reach Fort McPherson. Near Fort Simpson the **Liard Highway**, which connects with the Alaska Highway, crosses the Liard River. There are ice bridges across these rivers in winter. During the three- to six-week freeze-up and thaw periods *(Nov & May)*, the rivers cannot be crossed.

Time Zones – The Northwest Territories is in the Mountain Standard time zone. (The new territory of Nunavut will span Central and Eastern Standard time zones). Daylight Saving Time is observed from the first Sunday in April to the last Sunday in October.

Taxes – There is no provincial sales tax, but the 7% GST *(rebate information p 308)* applies.

Liquor Laws – The legal drinking age is 19. Liquor, wine and beer are sold in government liquor stores in the larger communities. Some communities have voted for restrictions on liquor including prohibition of possession.

Provincial Holiday *(National Holidays p 308)*

Civic Holiday ....1st Monday in August

Recreation

Outdoor Activities – The Northwest Territories are a wonderland for outdoor enthusiasts. Charter planes transport hikers, fishermen and **canoeists** (with their canoes) to remote regions. The northern summer with its long, sunny days (20 hours of daylight) makes a visit to this area a unique experience. Outfitters organize and equip wilderness travel year-round. One of the world's great canoe trips is down the **South Nahanni River** *(p 296)*, but other routes of varying degrees of difficulty are available. There are also opportunities for hiking, although this activity is less popular than canoeing in this land of rivers and lakes, with the exception of **Auyuittuq National Park Reserve**. All wilderness travellers (including boaters, canoeists and hikers) are asked to register with the Royal Canadian Mounted Police detachment nearest their point of departure, and to notify the police when their trip is completed. Warm clothing, a sleeping bag and, beyond the tree line, a stove and fuel should be carried.

Wood Buffalo National Park *(map p 3)* harbours a large free-roaming herd of bison and is the last natural breeding habitat for the rare whooping crane. Owing to four North American flyways that pass through the park, the Peace-Athabasca Delta is well known for its abundance of geese, duck and other waterfowl. The park is open year-round; camping is available at Pine Lake. For details contact the Superintendent, Box 750, Fort Smith, NT, X0E 0P0 ☎867-872-7900.

Lodges are scattered on remote lakes and coasts from the Mackenzie Mountains to the Arctic coast, where **fishing** is superb (Arctic char, Arctic grayling, great northern pike among others). All nonresident hunters of big game (wolf, moose, caribou, Dall sheep, grizzly, black and polar bears) must be accompanied by a licensed outfitter. Details regarding seasons, package tours, accommodations, outfitters, wilderness excursions as well as hunting and fishing regulations can be obtained by contacting Northwest Territories Arctic Tourism *(p 292)*.

Special Excursions – Located 48km/30mi north of the Arctic Circle, **Bathurst Inlet Lodge** offers rafting and canoeing on Arctic rivers, fishing, guided hikes and outdoor natural-history interpretations mid-May–mid-Aug. Seven-day packages include air transportation from Yellowknife, accommodations, meals and guided excursions. For more information, schedules & reservations contact Bathurst Inlet Lodge, PO Box 820, Yellowknife, NT, X1A 2N6 ☎867-873-2595.

In 1986 a national park reserve was created in the northern corner of **Ellesmere Island**, accessible from Resolute Bay. Covering nearly 40,000sq km/15,000sq mi of mountains, glaciers, valleys and fjords, this reserve is the world's northernmost park (latitude 82°N). For information contact the Superintendent, Eastern Arctic District National Parks, PO Box 353, Pangnirtung, NT X0A 0R0 ☎867-473-8828.

Principal Festivals

Mar	**Caribou Carnival**	*Yellowknife*
Jun	**Canadian North Yellowknife Midnight Classic**	*Yellowknife*
Jun/Jul	**Biannual Midnight Sun Seaplane Fly-In**	*Yellowknife*
Jul	**Folk on the Rocks**	*Yellowknife*
	Annual Great Northern Arts Festival	*Inuvik*
	Festival of the Midnight Sun	*Yellowknife*

Provincial abbreviations used in this guide, such as AB (Alberta), NS (Nova Scotia), PQ (Province of Quebec) and NT (Northwest Territories) are the official Canadian postal designations. A complete listing may be found on p 313.

BAFFIN ISLAND★★★

Population 13,218
Map of Principal Sights p 4

Named for British sailor **William Baffin**, who explored coastal waters between 1615 an 1616, the island is the largest, most inhabited and scenically spectacular in the Arcti archipelago. Its mountains rise more than 2,100m/7,000ft with numerous glaciers; it coasts are deeply indente with fjords. About two-third of the island lies north of th Arctic Circle (66.5°N) and i the continuous daylight o summer, the tundra bloom with an infinite variety of tiny colourful flowers.

Dan Heringa/ED&T/GNWT

Inukshuk

Most inhabitants are Inuit li ving in small settlement along the coasts. In some res pects their lifestyle remain traditional *(p 290)*, althoug they have adopted certai 20C ways (dress, housing etc.). Their soapstone car vings, prints and lithograph are internationally renowned especially those from **Cape Dor set**, a settlement on the wes coast. The administrative centre and largest communit is **Iqaluit** (eh-CALL-oo-it)—for merly called Frobisher Bay— where most nonnatives live.

Access – *Daily scheduled flight between Ottawa or Montrea and Iqaluit by First Air ☎ 800 267-1247 (Canada, US) an Air Inuit ☎ 514-636-9445; between Toronto and Iqaluit by Air Canada ☎ 800-661-078 (Canada), 800-776-3000 (US); regular service between Iqaluit and other communities Accommodations in Cape Dorset, Iqaluit, Pangnirtung and Pond Inlet.*

SIGHTS

★★ **Pangnirtung** – Dominated by the snow-capped mountains surrounding the Penny Ice Cap in Auyuittuq National Park Reserve, this little village occupies a spectacular **site★★** on the fjord of the same name. Situated just south of the Arctic Circle, Pangnirtung is an ideal spot for viewing the midnight "light" in summer (there is no sun at midnight, but it never gets dark). It is also a good place to study the tundra landscape and wildlife (small mammals, and some large sea mammals in Cumberland Sound) and to purchase locally woven goods, soapstone carvings and other specialities at the Inuit cooperative.

Even if a visit to the park itself is not planned, the **trip★** down the fjord to the park entrance by boat when the ice has melted *(Jul–Sept; round-trip 1hr 30min; $75, if same-day return; warm clothing essential)* or by snowmobile the rest of the year is impressive. *Outfitters' services offered year-round; for information & reservations contact Angmarlik Interpretive Centre in Pangnirtung ☎ 867-473-8737.*

★★ **Auyuittuq National Park Reserve** – *Park headquarters are located in Pangnirtung. Park open year-round. Visitor centre open mid-May–Labour Day Mon–Fri 8:30am–5pm (Mon, Wed & Fri 9pm), weekends 1pm–5pm. Rest of the year daily 8:30am–5pm. $15/day use fee. ☎ 867-473-8828.* A stark landscape of perpetual ice, jagged peaks of 2,000m/7,000ft and glacier-scarred valleys that become deep fjords along a coast of sheer cliffs (up to 900m/3,000ft high). *Auyuittuq* (ow-you-EE-took) means "land that never melts" in Inuktitut—an appropriate name for Canada's first national park north of the Arctic Circle. Fully one quarter of its 21,470sq km/8,290sq mi is covered by the **Penny Ice Cap**. Only lichens grow on rocks bared by the ice, but in the valleys, moss heath and a few dwarf shrubs thrive during the long hours of the Arctic summer.

Since its creation in 1972, the park has drawn climbers from all over the world to scale its rugged peaks. Backpackers and campers also come for the challenge of surviving this remote, yet breathtakingly grand landscape. The most visited region is **Pangnirtung Pass**, a huge U-shaped trench that stretches 96km/60mi across the peninsula and rises to 390m/1,280ft. By early July the pass is usually free of ice at the south entrance of Pangnirtung Fjord, and by late July, at North

Malak, Ottawa

Auyuittuq National Park Reserve

Pangnirtung Fjord, although some years the ice never melts. It can be crossed by properly equipped hikers accustomed to rough mountain terrain and prepared to ford frequent streams of glacial meltwater. There is constant wind, little shelter, and most of the route is on glacial moraine *(on average, 3km/2mi an hour maximum can be covered per day)*. However, this is a spectacular trip for those willing to make the effort.

Pond Inlet – Situated in the northern part of the island, this community overlooks the mountains of Bylot Island—summer home of thousands of snow geese—across the inlet of the same name. Soapstone and whalebone carvings as well as Inuit parkas and footwear can be purchased in the community.

MACKENZIE DELTA★★

Map of Principal Sights p 2

labyrinth of channels among thousands of lakes 160km/100mi from the mouth of he Beaufort Sea, the 100km/70mi wide delta—one of the world's largest—fractures he northwest edge of the Territories' mainland. It is the estuary of the vast and fast-noving Mackenzie River, and the terminus of its 1,800km/1,100mi journey from the nterior's Great Slave Lake.

)ne of the most prolific areas for wildlife in Canada's Arctic, the delta supports innu-nerable muskrats, beaver, mink, marten, fox, bear, moose, caribou and smaller nammals. Its channels and lakes abound with fish. Beluga whales calve in the warm vaters, and migratory birds congregate here in the spring.

'he livelihood of many of the inhabitants of the delta communities—Arctic Red River, nuvik, Aklavik, Fort McPherson and Tuktoyaktuk—depends on trapping, hunting and ishing. However huge reserves of oil and gas discovered under the Beaufort Sea have mpacted the area's economy in more recent times.

ccess – *Dempster Highway from the Yukon (Dawson City to Inuvik 798km/496mi) open all year except during freeze-up and thaw periods, p 292). Few services on road. Motorists should be outfitted for emergencies (p 292). Also accessible by air from Edmonton via Yellowknife, and from Whitehorse, Yukon. The best way to appreciate the delta is to fly over it; charters can be arranged in Inuvik.*

VISIT

The Delta – Viewed from the air, this delta is an amazing place. The tangle of muddy arteries belonging to the Mackenzie and the Peel Rivers, which join at this point, can be distinguished from the lakes by their colour. The western edge is clearly marked by the frequently snow-capped **Richardson Mountains**, the eastern edge by the low, humped **Caribou Hills**. Heading north, the land seemingly gives way as the areas of water become greater, until the vast Beaufort Sea is reached and the land disappears completely from view.

Except for areas of tundra along the coast, the land is covered with low scrubs (dwarf willow and juniper) that turn bright yellow with the first frost (usually late August), a most attractive array. The tundra itself is full of lakes, and many colourful, multihued mosses, lichens and flowers bloom in the short but light (24 hours of daylight) Arctic summer.

Inuvik – *On Dempster Hwy.; airport; accommodations.* Meaning "place of mar in Inuktitut, this outpost lies on a large stretch of flat land beside the east chann of the Mackenzie. A thriving community, Inuvik is an administrative centre of th territorial government.

In 1954 the government moved their administrative facilities here from Aklavi which was frequently flooded. A model northern community was built and opene in 1959. Over the entire delta, the permafrost is only a few inches from the surfac causing problems for house building. The heat from a dwelling soon melts the ic and residents find themselves living in a swamp. As a result, the houses wer constructed on pilings, steamed into the permafrost before construction. Wate sewage and heating ducts are housed together in above-ground **utilidors**, or covere corridors, to keep them from freezing.

The **Roman Catholic Church** is built in the shape of an igloo. It features a marvellous expressive **interior★** with paintings of the Stations of the Cross done in 1960 b Mona Thrasher, then a young Inuit girl.

★Tuktoyaktuk – *Daily flights from Inuvik; ice road in winter; accommodations.* former centre for oil and gas exploration in the region, this pleasant little com munity on the shores of the Beaufort Sea is known simply as "Tuk" to northerners It is best known for one of nature's most curious phenomena: **pingos**, or huge moss and turf-covered mounds of solid ice pushed out of the otherwise flat tundra b permafrost action. From the air, they resemble giant boils. Of the thousands in th Canadian North, the vast majority are located on the Tuktoyaktuk peninsula. At th **Fur Garment Shop**, visitors can observe Inuit women making parkas and other items c clothing.

"If some countries have too much history, we have too much geography."
William Lyon Mackenzie King, 1936

NAHANNI NATIONAL PARK RESERVE★★★

Map of Principal Sights p 2

A wild, remote and staggeringly beautiful place in the southwest corner of the Terri tories, this park, extending over 4,700sq km/1,815sq mi, covers a large section o the South Nahanni River, which flows through the Selwyn, Mackenzie and Frankli Mountains before ultimately adding its waters to the Liard River, a tributary of th mighty Mackenzie. In 1978 UNESCO recognized the universal value of this reserve b designating it a World Heritage Site.

Historical Notes – Early in the 20C, tales of placer gold lured prospectors to th valley of the South Nahanni. In 1908 the headless bodies of two adventurers wer found. Other men disappeared without trace. Stories of fierce native inhabitants an of mythical mountain men were spread abroad, and the South Nahanni became know as a place to avoid. The mystery remains and the legends are recalled by names i the park such as Deadmen Valley, Headless Range, Broken Skull River and Funera Range. The park's very inaccessibility is part of its beauty. Unlike other national parks it will probably never have roads and tourist facilities. But for those willing to mak the effort, one of the world's great natural glories awaits.

Access by Road and Air – *From British Columbia: take Alaska Highway to Fort Nelso (p 38), Liard Highway to Fort Liard. From the Yukon: take Alaska Highway to Watso Lake (p 38). In the Northwest Territories: take Mackenzie Highway to Fort Simpson or Liard Highway to Fort Liard. Air transportation available from Yellowknife with Firs Air ☎ 867-669-6600.*

Access by Water – *Various outfitters offer trips descending the river by rubber raft o canoe (equipment is flown in first). Intermediate white-water specialists can descen the river in their own canoe; permission must be obtained from the park first. Fo details contact the park (below) or NWT Arctic Tourism, Yellowknife, NT (p 292).*

VISIT

Open year-round. Day use fee (higher fees for overnight). Advance reservations required. For reservations and for details about fees, activities & outfitters contact Park Superintendent, Nahanni National Park Reserve, Postal Bag 300, Fort Simpson, NT, X0E 0N0 ☎ 867-695-2713.

★★★South Nahanni River – For more than 320km/198mi, this serpentine waterway coils through the park, entering majestic canyons, cascading over a precipice twice the height of Niagara and passing a series of hot mineral springs that create surrounding vegetation unusual at this latitute (61°–62°N). Each year, this magnificent river attracts countless canoeists and raft-riders to its adventurous waters and wilderness beauty.

Nahanni National Park Reserve

Virginia Falls

The following describes highlights of a descent of the river. The 200km/125mi excursion downriver from Virginia Falls to Nahanni Butte is one of the world's great wilderness trips. Over this distance the river drops more than 120m/400ft (which is why canoeists generally prefer to descend it).

The jewel of the park and one of the North's most spectacular sights is **Virginia Falls★★★**. Parted by a central pointed rock at the precipice, volumes of water plunge 90m/294ft to the gorge below. The Albert Faille Portage can be followed around the falls *(1.6km/1mi)*. From it, a trail leads to the brink of the cataract where the river can be seen in spectacular rapids, just before it cascades over the rocks. Fourth Canyon is the first of four awesome canyons with immense cliffs and depths as great as 1,200m/3,900ft. Then come the surging waves of Figure of Eight Rapids. The river makes a 90-degree turn known as The Gate, guarded by mighty Pulpit Rock. Third Canyon is followed by the 34km/21mi stretch of Second Canyon. **Deadman Valley**, where headless bodies were found, separates Second Canyon from First Canyon, a twisting 27km/17mi channel. The river passes close to a hot spring where pools of water, at nearly 37°C/98°F, have caused ferns, chokecherries, rose bushes and flowering parsnip plants to proliferate. Before reaching Nahanni Butte, the river divides into a series of channels known as the **Splits**.

"I don't even know what street Canada is on."
Al Capone, 1931

YELLOWKNIFE★

Population 17,275
Map of Principal Sights p 2
Tourist Office ☎867-873-4262

The administrative capital of the Northwest Territories lies beside Yellowknife Bay on the northern shore of the Great Slave Lake. Almost completely surrounded by water, the city has a pretty site, set on pink granite, glacier-scarred rocks topped by small trees. A pleasant "old town" (c.1934) coexists with a modern "new town," where most of the population lives, shops and works.

Historical Notes

Foundation of Gold – Named not for the colour of metal underlying it, but for the copper knives traded by local Indians, Yellowknife is a recent settlement. Its site was visited by Samuel Hearne in 1771, Alexander Mackenzie on his epic journey to the mouth of the river that bears his name, and John Franklin, all of whom were too preoccupied with their travels to notice the gold. Prospectors en route for the Klondike at the end of the 19C did record some sightings, but without pursuit. Not until the discovery of pitchblende in 1930 on the shores of the Great Bear Lake was there interest in the rest of the region. In 1934 exposed gold was found beside the bay and a boom town sprang up overnight.

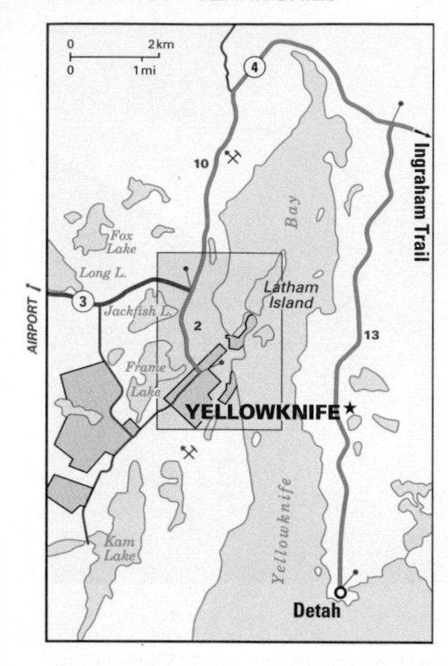

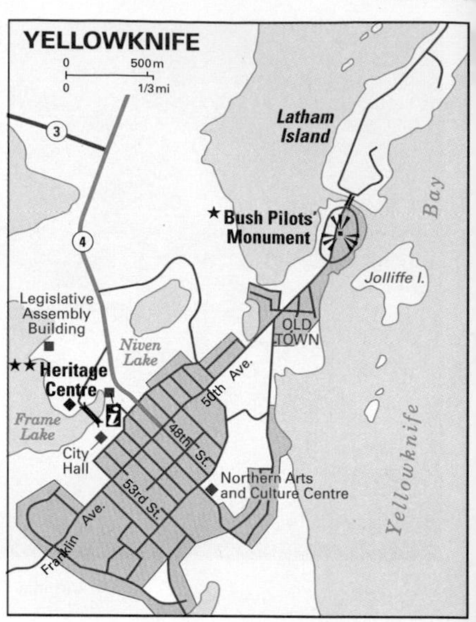

The boom did not last, however, and the place was almost a ghost town in 1945 when new discoveries were made. The city is still thriving from this second boom. The mining and separating process is very expensive at the two operating mines, but the price of the yellow metal makes them economically viable. When the city became the territorial capital in 1967, Yellowknife's importance was finally acknowledged.

Midnight Twilight – The city lies just north of latitude 62° and thus in summer, experiences nearly 24 hours of daylight. Every year a golf tournament is held on the weekend closest to June 21. The tee-off commences at midnight. Among other hazards on a golf course that is largely sand are the enormous black ravens (depicted on the city's emblem) that delight in making off with the balls.
Yellowknife is also a good centre for boating, canoeing, fishing and camping. Its stores carry a fine selection of Dene and Inuit art and handicrafts.

Access – *By Rte. 3 and Mackenzie River ferry (free) in summer; "ice road" in winter. No road access during freeze-up and thaw periods (p 292). Also accessible by air from Edmonton, Winnipeg, Ottawa and Iqaluit.*

SIGHTS *1 day*

★★ **Prince of Wales Northern Heritage Centre** – *Entrance off Ingraham Trail. Open Jun–Aug daily 10:30am–5:30pm, weekends noon–5pm. Rest of the year Tue–Fri 10:30am–5pm, weekends noon–5pm. Closed Jan 1 & Dec 25. ✗ ♿ ☎867-873-7551.* Overlooking Frame Lake, this attractive museum is an important archaeological and ethnological research centre. It houses displays on the history of settlement of the Territories and a fine collection of Inuit sculpture. The ways of life of Dene and Inuit peoples are described, as are the reasons European settlers came to the North.

★ **Bush Pilots' Monument** – *Steps from Ingraham Dr. in Old Town.* Set on a rock that is the highest point in Yellowknife, this memorial honours the men who opened up the North. From this spot there is a splendid **panorama**★ of the city, the surrounding waters and rocky site. The red-topped tower of the Cominco gold mine dominates the skyline.
A hive of activity, the bay ripples with numerous small float planes arriving from the mining camps or departing with supplies for oil and gas exploration teams. Large black ravens can frequently be seen on the rocks.

From the old town, a causeway crosses to **Latham Island**, where houses perch on rocks and stilts. Here, a Dogrib Indian settlement and views of the Giant and Con gold mines can be seen.

Boat Trips – *Dinner cruises on Yellowknife Bay depart from Government Dock in Old Town first 3 weeks in Jun; round-trip 4 hrs; reservations required; $50. Also cruises (5-12 days) on the Mackenzie River (Jul) and Great Slave Lake (Aug); reservations required; ✗ Norweta Cruises ☎867-873-2180. For other excursions contact Northern Frontier Visitors Assn. ☎867-873-4262.* These cruises enable visitors to see portions of this enormous lake (28,930sq km/ 11,170sq mi), which is part of the Mackenzie River system and an important fishing area.

EXCURSIONS

Detah and the Ingraham Trail – These excursions by vehicle in the vicinity of the capital allow the visitor to see the landscape in this transitional area between boreal forest and tundra. The drive to Detah provides views of Yellowknife and its bay.

Detah – *25km/16mi.* This Dogrib Indian settlement has a fine **site★** on flat rocks overlooking the Great Slave Lake.

Ingraham Trail – *64km/40mi to Reid Lake.* This all-weather road northwest of Yellowknife skirts five lakes—a paradise for campers and canoeists.

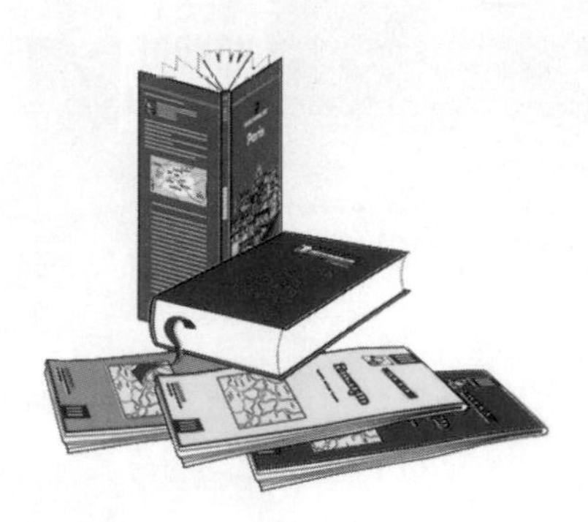

DONALDA
Canada's Lamp Capital
EDENWOLD
MARGARET "GRABBERT" WOODSTOCK ILL. AUGUST 1981
WERNER HARRY KOMMEL ULM HARTMUT SEITZ GERMANY JUNE 1977
Welcome to LA VERNE
POP 15,600 ELEV 1,050
ENTERING NORTH COWICHAN
WILLIAMSVILLE
TOWN OF PLEASANT VALLEY
The Pinkleys Troy, Mich.
1240 miles DRUMHELLER DINOSAUR Capital of Canada
BLUFF SPRINGS ILLINOIS
STOP
BRITT
RESTON MAN
VRENI + ERNST SCHULTHESS JULY 1985 SWITZERLAND
NORTH BATTLEFORD
THE BIGGEST CITY IN NORTHWEST SASKATCHEWAN
GROVELAND FLORIDA
WEST MONROE LOUISIANA
BOR-EY315
WI-ND 422
AMBERG WISCONSIN
BRIDGEPORT
LEAHY
ETTE WYO
KUEFLER'S
APSLEY
MICHIGAN
GREENBUSH
NORTH BEND OREGON
Wenholthausen Sauerland Germany
INTERSTATE PENNSYLVANIA 81
JEREMY-JASON
NAPA CITY LIMIT
BEAR, DE. 4916 MI.
ROWLATT HAVRE, MONTANA
449-AXL
TAHLEQUAH OKLA. 3,000 MI.
BELL 734-2525
Dortmund 11103 km
VREDEN
SHAUNAVON SASK.
JAMESTOWN N.D.
LEWISTON IDAHO
KREIDER MARTINSBURG, PA. 3395 MI.
PAULSEN'S ISLE, MN.
7483
SKIPPERS MICH-TEX
CanAm 1988

Watson Lake Signposts/Earl L. Brown

Practical Information

The contents of this section pertain to the country as a whole.

Practical information specific to Canada's **provinces** may be found in the regional introductions.

Consult the pages shown for detailed information about:

Queen Charlotte Islands *(p 50)*, **Rocky Mountain Parks** *(p 54)*, and the cities of **Montreal** *(p 203)*, **Toronto** *(p 167)*, **Vancouver** *(p 70)*.

Planning Your Trip

Tourist Offices – Official government tourist offices operated by provincial, municipal and regional agencies distribute road maps and brochures that give information on attractions, seasonal events, accommodations, adventure travel, sports and recreational activities. All publications are available free of charge *(see regional introductions for addresses)*. Information centres are indicated on the maps by the symbol **ℹ**.

Outside Canada – If unable to obtain tourist information from the above offices, foreign visitors can request tourist information from the Canadian embassy or consulate in their country of residence. For locations in the US and in other countries, contact the Tourist Department at the nearest Canadian embassy, high commission or consulate or at those shown below.

Embassies of other countries are located in Canada's capital, Ottawa. Most foreign countries maintain consulates in Canada's regional capitals. For further information on all Canadian embassies and consulates abroad, contact the website of the Canadian Department of Foreign Affairs and International Trade: www.dfait-maeci.gc.ca.

Selected Canadian Consulates and Embassies

US	**1175 Peachtree St., NE, 100 Colony Square, Suite 1700 Atlanta, GA 30361-6205**	☎404-532-2000
	1251 Avenue of the Americas, New York, NY 10020-1175	☎212-596-1600
	550 South Hope St., 9th floor, Los Angeles, CA 90071	☎213-346-2700
Australia	**Quay West Bldg., 111 Harrington St., Sydney NSW 2000**	☎9-364-3000
Germany	**Godesberger Allee 119, Bonn 53175**	☎228-968-3459
United Kingdom	**One Grosvenor Square, Macdonald House, London W1X 0AA**	☎1-71-258-6600

Foreign Visitors – Citizens of the US visiting Canada need proof of citizenship (a valid **passport**, *or* a driver's license together with a birth certificate or a voter's registration card). Naturalized US citizens should carry their US naturalization certificate. Permanent residents of the US are advised to carry their Alien Registration. Persons under 18 who are not accompanied by an adult should carry a letter from a parent or guardian stating name and duration of travel in Canada. Students should carry their student identification.

All other visitors to Canada must have a valid passport and, in some cases, a **visa**. No vaccinations are necessary. For **entry into Canada via the US**, all persons other than US citizens or legal residents are required to present a valid passport. It is advisable to ask the Canadian embassy or consulate in your home country about entry regulations and proper travel documents. Visitors who wish to return to the US after staying in Canada should check with the US Immigration and Naturalization Service.

Health Insurance – Before travelling, visitors should check with their health care insurance to determine if doctor's visits, medication and hospitalization in Canada are covered; otherwise supplementary insurance may be necessary. Liberty Health offers reimbursement for expenses as a result of emergencies under their *Visitors to Canada Plan*. The plan must be purchased before arrival, or within five days of arrival, in Canada. For details contact Liberty Health, 3500 Steeles Ave. East, Markham, ON, L3R 0X4 ☎800-268-3763 (Canada/US).

Canada Customs – Nonresidents may import personal baggage temporarily without payment of duties. Persons of legal age as prescribed by the province or territory *(see regional introductions)* may bring into Canada duty-free 200 cigarettes, 50 cigars and some other forms of **tobacco** (contact Revenue Canada at address below). **Alcohol** is limited to 1.14 litres (40 imperial ounces) of wine or spirits, or 24 bottles (355ml or 12 ounces) of beer or ale. All **prescription drugs** should be clearly labelled and for personal use only; it is recommended that visitors carry a copy of the prescription.

Canada has stringent legislation on **firearms**. A firearm cannot be brought into the country for personal protection while travelling. Only long guns (no permit required) may be imported by visitors 18 years or older for hunting or sporting purposes. Certain firearms are prohibited entry; restricted firearms, which include handguns, may only be imported with a permit by a person attending an approved shooting competition. For more information telephone the Automated Customs Information Service ☎416-973-8022 (Toronto) or 604-666-0545 (Vancouver) or write Revenue Canada, Customs and Excise, Ottawa, ON, K1A 0L5.

Most animals, except domesticated dogs and cats, must be issued a Canadian import permit prior to entry into Canada. **Pets** must be accompanied by an official certificate of vaccination against rabies from the country of origin. Payment of an inspection fee may be necessary. For details, contact Canadian Food Inspection Agency, Nepean, ON, K1A 0Y9 ☎613-225-2342.

Disabled Travellers – *Wheelchair access is indicated in this guide by ♿ symbol.* Most public buildings and many attractions, restaurants and hotels provide wheelchair access. Disabled parking is provided and the law is strictly enforced. For details contact the provincial tourist office *(see regional introductions)*.
To obtain a guide for travel planning entitled *Handi-Travel,* write to Easter Seals/March of Dimes, Suite 511, 90 Eglinton Ave. East, Toronto, ON, M4P 2Y3 ☎416-932-8382. Prepayment of $12.95 plus $3 postage is required for all orders.

Currency Exchange – *See "Money" p 308.*

When to Go

Climate – Climatic conditions vary greatly throughout Canada *(for climate information see regional introductions)*. Daily weather reports by Environment Canada are available through television, radio and newspapers.

Seasons – From mid-March to mid-May, visitors can enjoy comfortable daytime temperatures but chilly nights in the **spring**; in some areas, spring skiing is still possible. Ontario, Quebec and New Brunswick celebrate the harvest of maple syrup with sugaring-off parties.
Most visitors go to Canada during the **summer** season, extending from the last weekend in May (Victoria Day) to the first weekend in September (Labour Day). July and August are considered peak season and are ideal for outdoor activities such as sailing, kayaking, canoeing or hiking. Hot and often humid days with temperatures ranging from 22°-32°C/70°-90°F can be enjoyed in most provinces. May and September are pleasant months with warm days but cool evenings. However, many tourist attractions have curtailed visiting hours, and it is advisable to phone ahead. The southern regions along the Canada/US border offer spectacular displays of **fall** colours from mid-September until early October.
For the sports enthusiast, the Canadian **winter**, generally from mid-November to mid-March, offers excellent opportunities to enjoy numerous winter activities such as downhill skiing, cross-country skiing and snowmobiling. Most provinces experience heavy snowfall. Main highways are snowploughed, but vehicles should be winterized and snow tires are recommended.

Note: The extreme northern regions of Canada are most accessible during July and August since the temperature rises above 0°C/32°F for only a few months each year.

Malak, Ottawa

Wakefield Steam Train, Gatineau Park

Getting There

From the US – American carriers offer **air** service to Canada's major airports. Air Canada ☎800-776-3000 (US) and Canadian Airlines International ☎800-426-7000 (Canada/US) fly from larger US cities. Amtrak offers daily **rail** service to Montreal from Washington DC and New York City, as well as from New York City to Toronto. Aside from these direct routes, connections are offered from many major US cities. For schedules in the US ☎800-872-7245. **Bus** travel from the US is offered by Greyhound. For information and schedules call the local US bus terminal. It is advisable to book well in advance when travelling during peak season.

From Overseas – Major airports in Canada serviced by international airlines are: Calgary, Edmonton, Halifax, Montreal, Ottawa, St. John's, Toronto, Vancouver and Winnipeg. Air Canada and Canadian Airlines International offer service to all major European cities, Latin America and the Middle East. Vancouver is the gateway city offering connections to Australia, New Zealand and the Far East.

Getting Around

Given Canada's enormous size, it is impossible to cover all of the country during one visit. *See regional driving tours (pp 6-12) for several two- to three-week itineraries.*

By Air – Domestic air service is offered by Canada's two national airlines: **Air Canada** (consult the local telephone directory in Canada; the US ☎800-776-3000) and **Canadian Airlines International** (☎800-426-7000 Canada/US) as well as affiliated regional airlines. Air service to remote areas is provided by many charter companies. Contact the provincial tourist office *(see regional introductions)*.

By Train – **VIA Rail**, Canada's extensive rail network, traverses the country with 18 major routes from coast to coast. First-class, coach and sleeping accommodations are available on transcontinental, regional and intercity trains. Amenities offered are dome cars, dining cars and lounges, baggage handling (including bicycles), reservation of medical equipment, wheelchairs and preboarding aid with 24hr minimum notice. Unlimited train travel for 12 to 15 days within a 30-day period is available systemwide through **CANRAILPASS** *(Jun to mid-Oct, 12 days $569, 15 days $716; off-season, 12 days $369, 15 days $462)*. Special rates are offered for students with an ISIC card, youth and senior citizens.
Reservations should be made well in advance, especially during summer months and on popular routes like Edmonton to Vancouver. Canada's legendary cross-country train, *The Canadian*, travels the almost 4,424km/2,700mi from Toronto to Vancouver in four days *(one-way from $311, advance purchase, plus sleeping accommodation surcharge)*. For information and schedules in Canada contact the nearest VIA Rail office. In the US call VIA Rail www.viarail.ca ☎800-561-3949.

VIA Rail general sales agents abroad are:		☎
Australia	Walshes World, 92 Pitt St., Sydney	2-232-7499
Germany	Canada Reisedienst, Rathausplatz 2, Ahrensburg	4102-51167
United Kingdom	Long-Haul Leisurail, Peterborough	1733-335599

By Bus – Long-distance buses reach almost every corner of Canada. Greyhound Canada Transportation Corp., 877 Greyhound Way SW, Calgary, AB, T3C 3V8 operates the only trans-Canadian service and offers **Canada Travel Passes**, which are sold internationally. Unlimited travel from 7 days up to 30 days is available. Peak season rates range from $230 to $627 *(reduced rates available in off-season and for senior citizens)*. For fares and schedules call Greyhound ☎800-661-8747 *(Canada only)*; in the US, call the local bus terminal. A 14-day **Rout-Pass** for travel from Feb–Nov *($225)* is available for most of Quebec and Ontario ☎416-393-7911 or 514-842-2281. Other regional companies supplement Canada's extensive motorcoach service *(see the yellow pages of local telephone directories)*.

By Car – Canada has an extensive system of well-maintained major roads. In the northern regions and off main arteries, however, many roads are gravel or even dirt. Extreme caution should be taken when travelling these roads.
Foreign **driver's licenses** are valid for varying time periods depending on the province. Drivers must carry vehicle **registration** information and/or rental contract at all times. Vehicle **insurance** is compulsory in all provinces (minimum liability is $200,000, except $50,000 in Quebec). US visitors should obtain a Canadian Non-Resident Inter-Province Motor Vehicle Insurance Liability Card (**yellow card**), available from US insurance companies. For additional information contact the Insurance Bureau of Canada, 151 Yonge St. 18th Floor, Toronto, ON, M5C 2W7 ☎416-362-9528.

Gasoline is sold by the litre (1 gallon = 3.78 litres); prices vary from province to province. All distances and speed limits are posted in kilometres (1 mile =1.6 kilometre). During winter it is advisable to check road conditions before setting out. **Snow tires** and an **emergency kit** are imperative. Studded tires are allowed in winter in some provinces; for seasonal limitations, contact the regional Ministry of Transportation *(check the blue pages in the local telephone directories)*.

Road Regulations – The **speed limit** on divised highways, unless otherwise posted, is 100km/h (60mph). The speed limit on rural highways is 80km/h (50mph) and in urban areas 50km/h (30mph). Service stations that are open 24 hours can be found in large cities and along major highways. The use of **seat belts** is mandatory for all drivers and passengers. On Yukon highways, driving with headlights on at all times is required by law. Most provinces prohibit **radar detection devices** in vehicles. Traffic in both directions must stop (except on divided roads) for a yellow school bus when signals are flashing. In all provinces except Quebec, **right turns on red** are allowed after coming to a complete stop. Information on highway conditions in each province can be obtained by contacting the regional Ministry of Transportation *(check the blue pages in the local telephone directories)*.

In Case of Accident – If you are involved in an accident resulting in property damage and/or personal injury, you must notify the local police and remain at the scene until dismissed by investigating officers. For assistance contact the local Government Insurance Corporation. First aid stations are clearly designated along highways.

Canadian Automobile Association (CAA) – This national member-based organization *(1145 Hunt Club Rd., Ottawa, ON, K1V 0Y3 www.caa.ca* ☎613-247-0117) offers, through its offices across Canada, services such as travel information, maps and tour books, accommodation reservations, insurance, technical and legal advice, and emergency roadside assistance. These benefits are extended to members of the American Automobile Association (AAA), Alliance Internationale de Tourisme (AIT), Fédération Internationale de l'Automobile (FIA), the Federation of Interamerican Touring and Automobile Clubs (FITAC) and other affiliated clubs. Proof of membership is required. The CAA maintains for its members a 24hr emergency road service ☎800-222-HELP *(see regional introductions for CAA listings)*.

Rental Cars – Most major rental car agencies have offices at airports and in large cities in Canada. Minimum age for rental is usually 25. To avoid a large cash deposit, payment by credit card is recommended. More favourable rates can sometimes be obtained by making a reservation before arriving in Canada, but be aware of drop-off charges.

Avis	☎800-331-1212	**Hertz**	☎800-654-3131
Budget	☎800-527-0700	**Tilden/National**	☎800-227-7368

By Ferry – Canada maintains an extensive ferry-boat system. Contact the regional tourist offices for information and schedules *(see regional introductions for details)*.

Precautions

- ▲ Although Canada experiences severe winters, many regions are afflicted by hordes of biting insects in the summer. Late May to June is black-fly season and in July the mosquitoes arrive. For outdoor activities, insect repellent is a must.
- ▲ Sturdy footwear with nonslip soles is recommended for hiking.
- ▲ To protect against surprise storms or cool mountain evenings, carry raingear and warm clothing.

Accommodations

Canada offers accommodation suited to every taste and pocketbook from luxury hotels in major cities, roadside motels, quaint B&Bs in the countryside, hunting and fishing lodges in remote wilderness areas, farm and country vacation houses to campsites and resorts. Many resorts operate year-round offering tennis, golf and water-sports facilities; winter activities include downhill skiing, cross-country skiing and snowmobiling. Government tourist offices supply listings *(free)* that give locations, phone numbers, types of service, amenities, prices and other details *(see regional introductions for addresses)*. Canada is a vast country, and in less populated regions it may be difficult to find accommodations at the end of a long day's drive. Advance reservations are recommended especially during the tourist season *(Victoria Day to Labour Day)*.
During the off-season, establishments outside urban centers may be closed; it is therefore advisable to telephone ahead. Guaranteeing reservations with a credit card is recommended. However, in remote areas, credit cards may not be accepted.

Hotels – Major hotel chains with locations throughout Canada are:

	☎ in Canada	☎ in the US
Canadian Pacific Hotels & Resorts	800-441-1414	800-828-7447
Delta Hotels	800-268-1133	800-268-1133
Four Seasons Hotels	800-268-6282	800-332-3442
Hilton	800-445-8667	800-445-8667
Holiday Inn	800-465-4329	800-465-4329
Radisson International	800-333-3333	800-333-3333
Sheraton Hotels	800-325-3535	800-325-3535
Ramada International	800-228-2828	800-228-2828
Hotel Novotel	800-221-4542	800-221-4542
Best Western International	800-528-1234	800-528-1234
Westin Hotels	800-228-3000	800-228-3000

The above-listed hotels, mostly located in large urban areas, offer a full range of facilities and amenities designed for business people as well as for vacationers. Prices are higher during the summer months. In resort areas, the ski season is also considered high season. Expect to pay more in large cities and resorts. However, many hotels offer packages and weekend specials that are worth investigating.

Motels – Along major highways or close to urban areas motels such as Comfort Inn (☎800-221-2222), Travelodge (☎800-667-3529), Days Inn (☎800-325-2525) and Choice Hotels (☎800-668-4200) offer accommodations at moderate prices *($54-$115)*, depending upon the location. Amenities include television, restaurants and swimming pools. Family-owned establishments and small, independent guest houses that offer basic comfort can be found all across Canada.

Bed and Breakfasts and Country Inns – B&Bs and country inns can be found in cities as well as in the countryside. Most are privately owned and can be housed in an an elegant Georgian mansion, a Victorian homestead, an old mill, a restored farmhouse, a country estate or a cozy cottage by the sea. A continental breakfast is usually included in the room rate. A private bath is not always offered. Some have restaurants. Room rates vary according to the location and amenities offered *($35-$150)*. Some accept major credit cards, but it is advisable to check at the time the reservation is placed *(see regional introductions for reservation services)*.

Hostels – Hostelling International-Canada, affiliated with the International Youth Hostel Federation, offers a network of budget accommodations from coast to coast. Hostels provide basic accommodations such as separate dormitory-style rooms (blankets and pillows are provided), shared bath, social areas, laundry facilities and self-service kitchens for $9-$25/night per person. Many hostels provide private room facilities as well. In some resort areas outdoor saunas, swimming pools, interpretive programs, theatre workshops and other amenities are offered.
Advance booking is advisable during peak travel times; walk-ins are welcome. Membership is $25/year, but nonmembers are also admitted. To obtain an application or further information, contact Hostelling International-Canada, 205 Catherine St. Suite 400, Ottawa, ON K2P 1C3 www.hostellingintl.ca ☎613-237-7884.

Universities and Colleges – Most universities make their dormitory space available to travellers during summer vacation *(May–August)*. Rates average $20-$35/day per person. Reservations are accepted. For more information contact the local tourist office or the university directly.

Farm Vacations/Guest Ranches – Farm and ranch lodgings are rustic and especially suited for families with children. The visitor is a paying guest on a working farm, and participation in daily activities depends on the host's preference. Meals are included and are taken with the host family. Guest ranches may be located in rugged country but holiday packages usually include comfortable accommodations and hearty meals. A variety of activities such as hiking, trail riding and campfire gatherings can be enjoyed by the whole family.

Camping – Canada has excellent campgrounds that are operated privately or by the federal and provincial governments. Government sites are located in the many national and provincial parks. Fees are nominal. These campgrounds are well equipped and fill up quickly *(for description of national park campgrounds see p 310)*. Commercially operated campgrounds, often located adjacent to national parks and provincial parks, are more costly but offer amenities such as electrical and water hookups, bathrooms with showers, restaurants, recreational facilities, grocery stores and gas stations. For a list of campgrounds contact the provincial tourist office *(see regional introductions for addresses)*.

Fishing Camps, Fly-in Lodges and Wilderness Camps – Canada offers the experienced angler or the outdoor enthusiast a variety of fishing lodges and camps, some of which are so remote, they can only be reached by private boat or plane. Outfitters offer packages that include transportation, accommodations, meals, supplies, equipment and expeditions led by experienced guides.
Wilderness camps located in Canada's northern regions offer all-inclusive hunting packages. Nonresidents must be accompanied by licensed guides. Permits can be obtained through the outfitter, who can also assist with game registration (required by law). These packages are costly and the number of spaces is usually limited. It is advisable to make reservations well in advance. For information on fishing and hunting regulations and license fees, as well as listings of outfitters, contact the provincial tourist office *(see regional introductions)*.

© Tourisme Québec/Marcel Gignac

General Information

Business Hours – Business hours are Monday to Friday 9am–5pm. In general, retail stores are open Monday to Friday 9am–6pm (until 9pm Thursday and Friday), and Saturday 9am–5pm. In Canada's largest cities, shops are usually open on Sunday afternoon. Depending upon local laws, many neighbourhood stores that sell groceries, small personal items and newspapers remain open in the evenings and on Sunday.

Electricity – 120 volts, 60 cycles. Most small American appliances can be used. European appliances require an electrical transformer, available at electric supply stores.

Language – Canada practises institutional bilingualism: English and French are the official languages for all federal and judicial bodies, federally mandated administrative agencies and crown corporations. The practice has spread to provincial governments and some parts of the private sector. However, in the province of Quebec the official language is French.

Liquor Laws – Each province abides by different liquor laws, which are strictly enforced *(see regional introductions)*. The legal blood alcohol limit is 0.08%.

Mail – Post offices across Canada are generally open Monday to Friday 8am–5:30pm; extended hours are available in some locations. Sample rates for first-class mail are: letter (up to 30 grams) or postcard within Canada 45 cents, to the US (up to 30 grams) 52 cents; international mail (up to 20 grams) 90 cents. Visitors can receive mail c/o "General Delivery" addressed to Main Post Office, City, Province and Postal Code. Mail will be held for 15 days and has to be picked up by the addressee. Some post offices have fax services and all post offices offer international courier service.

Metric System – Canada has partially adopted the International System of weights and measures. Weather temperatures are given in Celsius (C°), milk and wine are sold by millilitres and litres, and grocery items are measured in grams. All distances and speed limits are posted in kilometres (to obtain the equivalent in miles, multiply by .6). Some examples of metric conversions are:

1 kilometre (km)	=	0.6 miles
1 metre (m)	=	3.3 feet
1 kilogram (kg)	=	2.2 pounds
1 litre (L)	=	33.8 fluid ounces = 0.26 gallons (1 US quart=32 fluid ounces)

Money – Canadian currency is based on the decimal system (100 cents to the dollar). Bills are issued in $5, $10, $20, $50, $100, $500 and $1,000 denominations; coins are minted in 1 cent, 5 cents, 10 cents, 25 cents, 50 cents, $1 and $2. It is recommended that visitors exchange money at banking institutions to receive the most favourable exchange rate.

Banks – Banking institutions are generally open Monday to Friday 9am–5pm. Some banks are open on Saturday morning. Banks at large airports have foreign exchange counters and extended hours. Traveller's cheques in Canadian or American currency are accepted universally. Some institutions may charge a small fee for cashing traveller's cheques. Most principal bank cards are honored at affiliated Canadian banks.

Credit Cards – The following major credit cards are accepted in Canada: American Express, Carte Blanche, Discover, Diners Club, MasterCard/Eurocard and Visa.

Currency Exchange – Although US dollars are usually accepted in Canada, visitors should exchange their money for Canadian currency. The most favourable exchange rate can usually be obtained at branch offices of a national bank or other financial institution. Some banks charge a small fee for this transaction. Private exchange companies generally charge higher fees. Airports and visitor centres in large cities may have exchange outlets as do some hotels; however, it is advisable to first check the prevailing rate at local banks. The Canadian dollar fluctuates with the international money market. At press time, $1.45 Canadian equalled US $1.
Exchange facilities tend to be limited in rural and remote areas. If arriving in Canada late in the day or on a weekend, visitors may wish to exchange some funds prior to arrival (a few banks are open on Saturday mornings in major cities, however).

Taxes and Tips – Canada levies a 7% Goods and Services Tax (GST) on most goods and services. Foreign visitors can request a cash **rebate** of up to $500 for short-term accommodations and, for most consumer goods taken out of Canada within 60 days of purchase, by submitting original receipts and identification to any participating Canadian Duty Free Shop or by mail. Rebate claims above $500 must be mailed with an application and original receipts. Provincial sales taxes vary, and are refundable in some provinces *(see regional introductions)*. For additional information and rebate forms contact: Revenue Canada, Visitor Rebate Program, 275 Pope Rd., Summerside, PEI C1N 6C6, www.rc.gc.ca ☎800-668-4748 (in Canada) or 902-432-5608.
Tips or service charges are not normally added to a bill in Canada. However, it is customary to give 10-15% of the total amount.

National Holidays – *For provincial holidays see regional introductions.* The following holidays are observed throughout Canada. Most banks, government offices and schools are closed:

New Year's Day	January 1
Good Friday	Friday before Easter Sunday
Easter Monday	Monday after Easter Sunday
Victoria Day	closest Monday to May 24
Canada Day	July 1
Labour Day	1st Monday in September
Thanksgiving	2nd Monday in October
Remembrance Day	2nd Wednesday in November
Christmas Day	December 25
Boxing Day	December 26

Telephones – To call long distance within Canada and to the US, dial 1+ Area Code + number. For overseas calls, dial "0" for operator assistance. All operators speak English and French. Collect calls and credit card calls can be made from public pay phones. For local directory assistance, check the white pages of the phone directory or dial 411; outside the local area code dial 1+ Area Code + 555-1212. Most 800 numbers are toll-free. A local call costs 25 cents. Visitors should be aware that many hotels place a surcharge on all calls.

Note: A new area code has been introduced into the current 514 area code region in Quebec: **450** is effective for Laval, the North and South Shores, the Laurentians and Richelieu.

Emergency Numbers – **911** service is operative in major cities; otherwise dial "0" for the operator and ask for the police. In most provinces a Tourist Alert Program is operated by the Royal Canadian Mounted Police from June until September. If you see your name in the newspaper or hear it on the radio, contact the nearest RCMP office immediately.

Time Zones – Canada spans six time zones, but the coast-to-coast time difference is only 4hrs 30min because Newfoundland time is 30min in advance of the Maritime provinces, which are on Atlantic Time. Daylight Saving Time (clocks are advanced 1 hour) is in effect from the first Sunday in April to the last Sunday in October *(see regional introductions for details)*.

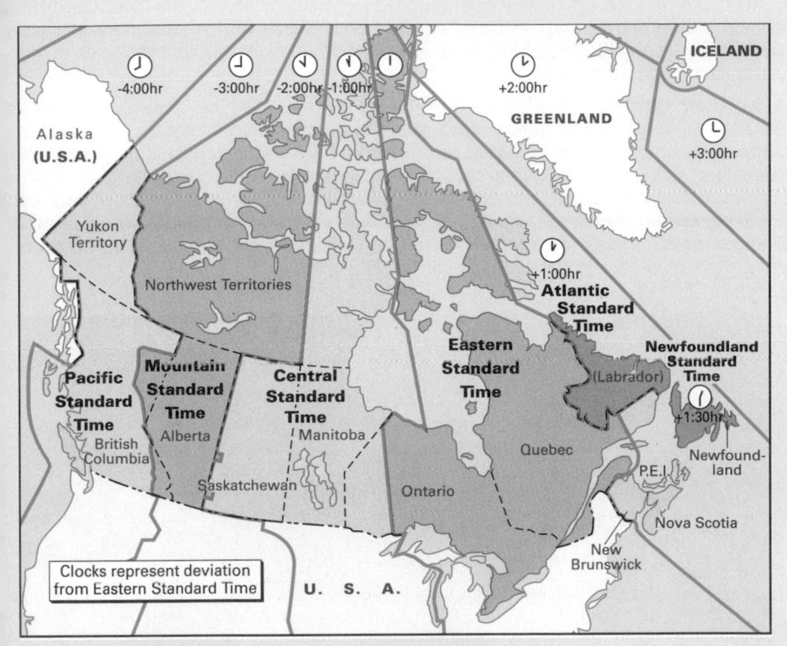

National Parks and Reserves

Since the creation of the first national park in Banff in 1885, the amount of protected land managed by Parks Canada has grown to 244,466sq km/86,666sq mi. Canada's 32 national parks (including two marine parks) and 8 national park reserves offer the visitor spectacular scenery, a wealth of wildlife and fauna, as well as unlimited recreational opportunities.

Some 14 million people visit the parks each year. Most points of interest are in the southern national parks, accessible by car. Well-marked hiking trails permit outdoor enthusiasts and novices alike to enjoy the backcountry. Parks are open year-round; however, some roads may be closed during the winter. Daily **entry fees** range from $2.50-$5 per adult. Discounts are offered at some parks to senior citizens (25%) and children (50%). Fees are charged for camping, fishing and guided programs.

Visitor centres *(open daily late May–Labour Day; reduced hours the rest of the year)* are usually located at park entrances. Staff are available to help visitors plan activities. Trail maps and literature on park facilities, hiking trails, nature programs, camping and in-park accommodations are available on-site free of charge. Interpretation programs, guided hikes, exhibits and self-guided trails introduce the visitor to each park's history, geology and habitats. *For a listing of in-park activities, see the a description of specific parks within each province.*

Activities and Facilities – All **hikers** in backcountry areas are required to register at the park office before setting out and to deregister upon completion of the trip. It is a good idea to ask park officials about trail conditions, weather forecasts and safety precautions. Trail distances are given from trailhead to destination, not round-trip, unless otherwise posted. Topographic maps and a compass are indispensable for backcountry hiking. To obtain information about ordering topographic maps, contact Canada Map Office, 615 Booth St., Ottawa, ON, K1A 0E9 ☎800-465-6277 (Canada/US).

Licenses are required for **fishing** and can be obtained from the park office, designated sporting goods stores or other retail businesses. Some parks offer boat and canoe rentals. Hunting is not permitted within the national parks.
Most park **campgrounds** are open mid-May through Labour Day, and usually operate on a first-come, first-served basis. Dates are subject to change, and it is recommended that visitors check with the park superintendent for rates and maximum length of stay. Some parks offer reservation services and some offer winter camping. Usually campsites include a level tent pad, picnic table, fireplace or fire grill with firewood, and parking space close to a water source. Most have toilet buildings and kitchen shelters. Some campgrounds are for tents only, while others allow recreational vehicles. Most campgrounds do not have trailer hookups, but many have sewage disposal stations. Many accommodate persons with disabilities. In some locations, certain equipment restrictions apply. Primitive campgrounds, located near hiking trails in the backcountry, can be reached only on foot.
Contact the national office of Parks Canada, Department of Canadian Heritage, Hull, PQ, K1A 0M5 www.parkscanada.pch.gc.ca ☎819-997-0055 or the individual park *(see listing below)* to obtain additional information and descriptive brochures on services, including outfitters and activities.

A word of caution – Bears and other large animals may be present in many of Canada's national parks. Human encounters with them may result in serious injury. Visitors are asked to respect **wildlife** and observe park rules: don't hike alone; do not take along a dog; stay in open areas wherever possible; never go near a bear or bear cub; keep campsites clean; and store food away from tent or in the trunk of your car. Avoid **hypothermia**. Beware of wind, dampness and exhaustion in regions where weather changes rapidly; carry weatherproof clothing, plastic sheeting and nylon twine for emergency shelter; and eat high-calorie foods.

Travel Alberta

Black Bear

National Parks and Reserves ☎

Pacific and Yukon Office
300 West Georgia St., Suite 300, Vancouver, BC V6B 6C6 — 604-666-0176

Glacier
Box 350, Revelstoke, BC, V0E 2S0 — 250-837-7500

Gwaii Haanas
Box 37, Queen Charlotte, BC, V0T 1S0 — 250-559-8818

Ivvavik
Box 1840, Inuvik, NT, X0E 0T0 — 867-777-3248

Kluane
Box 5495, Haines Junction, YT, Y0B 1L0 — 867-634-7250

Kootenay
Box 220, Radium Hot Springs, BC, V0A 1M0 — 250-347-9615

Mount Revelstoke
Box 350, Revelstoke, BC, V0E 2S0 — 250-837-7500

Pacific Rim
Box 280, Ucluelet, BC, V0R 3A0 — 250-726-7721

untut
205-300 Main St., Whitehorse, YT Y1A 2B5 — 867-667-3910

oho
Box 99, Field, BC, V0A 1G0 — 250-343-6324

lberta Office
Box 2989, 220 Fourth Ave. SE, Calgary, AB, T2G 4X3 — 403-292-4401

anff
Box 900, Banff, AB, T0L 0C0 — 403-762-1500

lk Island
Site 4, RR 1, Fort Saskatchewan, AB, T8L 2N7 — 403-992-2950

asper
Box 10, Jasper, AB, T0E 1E0 — 403-852-6176

Vaterton Lakes
Waterton, AB, T0K 2M0 — 403-859-2224

rairies and Northwest Territories Office
457 Main St. 8th Floor, Winnipeg, MB, R3B 3E8 — 204-983-2122

ulavik (Banks Island)
General Delivery, Sachs Harbour, NT, X0E 0T0 — 867-690-3904

uyuittuq
PO Box 353, Pangnirtung, NT, X0A 0R0 — 67-473-8828

llesmere Island
PO Box 353, Pangnirtung, NT, X0A 0R0 — 867-473-8828

rasslands
PO Box 150, Val Marie, SK, S0N 2T0 — 306-298-2257

ahanni
Postal Bag 300, Fort Simpson, NT, X0E 0N0 — 867-695-2713

rince Albert
PO Box 100, Waskeslu Lake, SK, S0J 2Y0 — 306-663-4500

iding Mountain
Wasagaming, MB, R0J 2H0 — 204-848-7275

uktut Nogait
Box 1840, Inuvik, NT, X0E 0T0 — 867-777-3248

Vapusk
PO Box 127, Churchill, MB R0B 0E0 — 204-848-7275

Wood Buffalo
PO Box 750, Fort Smith, NT, X0E 0P0 — 867-872-7900

Ontario Office
5160 Yonge St., Suite 500, North York, ON, M2N 6L9 — 800-839-8221

Bruce Peninsula
PO Box 189, Tobermory, ON, N0H 2R0 — 519-596-2233

Fathom Five National Marine Park
PO Box 189, Tobermory, ON N0H 2R0 — 519-596-2233

Georgian Bay Islands
PO Box 28, Honey Harbour, ON, P0E 1E0 — 705-756-2415

Point Pelee
RR No. 1, Leamington, ON, N8H 3V4 — 519-322-2365

Pukaskwa
Heron Bay, ON, P0T 1R0 — 807-229-0801

St. Lawrence Islands
2 Country Rd. #5, RR No. 3,
Mallorytown Landing, ON, K0E 1R0 — 613-923-5261

Quebec Office
3 Passage du Chien-d'Or, CP6060, Quebec, PQ, G1R 4V7 — 418-648-4177

Forillon
CP 1220, Gaspé, PQ, G0C 1R0 — 418-368-5505

La Mauricie
Box 758, Shawinigan, PQ, G9N 6V9 — 819-538-3232

Mingan Archipelago
CP 1180, Havre-Saint-Pierre, PQ, G0G 1P0 — 418-538-3285

Saguenay–St. Lawrence Marine Park
Box 220, Tadoussac, PQ, G0T 2A0 — 418-235-4703

Atlantic Office
Upper Water St., Halifax, NS, B3J 1S9 — 902-426-3436

Cape Breton Highlands
Ingonish Beach, NS, B0C 1L0 — 902-285-2270

Fundy
PO Box 40, Alma, NB, E0A 1B0 — 506-887-6000

Gros Morne
PO Box 130, Rocky Harbour, NF, A0K 4N0 — 709-458-241

Kejimkujik
PO Box 236, Maitland Bridge, NS, B0T 1B0 — 902-682-277

Kouchibouguac
Kouchibouguac, Kent County, NB, E0A 2A0 — 506-876-244

Prince Edward Island
2 Palmers Lane, Charlottetown, PE, C1A 5V6 — 902-566-705

Terra Nova
Glovertown, NF, A0G 2L0 — 709-533-280

Good references for planning a visit to Canada's national parks are: **Canada's Nationa Parks: A Visitor's Guide** by Marylee Stephenson *(Prentice Hall, 1997)* and **Canada' National Parks** *(National Geographic Society, 1998)*.

In addition to the national parks, there are over 600 **provincial parks** to explore. More than 100 **national historic sites**, such as the French fortress of Louisbourg *(p 266)*, the site of one of the oldest European settlements in Canada *(p 252)* and homes of severa Canadian prime ministers, can be found from coast to coast. Designed for daytime visit only, most sites are open from Victoria Day to Labour Day, with reduced hours in the early spring and fall. Some charge a nominal admission fee. At many of these sites interpretation centres and costumed guides provide insight into Canada's history and cultural heritage. For more information contact the appropriate regional office of the Parks Canada.

© Lynn M. Stone

Barren-Ground Caribou

Index

Winnipeg .... City, town, region or other point of interest
Mackenzie, Alexander .... Person, historic event or term
Whale watching .... Practical Information
98, **107** .... Page reference, **principal reference**

The principal sights in **Montreal, Toronto** and **Vancouver** are listed separately as are **National Parks** and Provincial Parks. Place names appear with the following abbreviations: AB Alberta, BC British Columbia, MB Manitoba, NB New Brunswick, NF Newfoundland, NS Nova Scotia, NT Northwest Territories, ON Ontario, PE Prince Edward Island, PQ Quebec, QCI Queen Charlotte Islands, SK Saskatchewan, YT Yukon Territory. **Maps** are listed on page 13.

A

B

C – D

E – F

G – H

I – J – K

L – M

N – O

P

Q–R

S

T

U – V

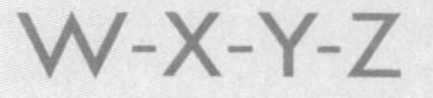

MANUFACTURE FRANÇAISE DES PNEUMATIQUES MICHELIN
Société en commandite par actions au capital de 2 000 000 000 de francs
Place des Carmes-Déchaux – 63 Clermont-Ferrand (France)
R.C.S. Clermont-Fd B 855 200 507

Dépôt légal janvier 99 – ISBN 2-06-159407-2 – ISSN 0763-1383

Printed in the EU 12-98/1